Stanley Gibbons
Commonwealth Stamp

Canada & Provinces
4th edition 2011

STANLEY GIBBONS LTD
London and Ringwood

By Appointment to Her Majesty The Queen
Stanley Gibbons Ltd, London
Philatelists

Published by Stanley Gibbons Ltd
Editorial, Publications Sales Offices
and Distribution Centre:
7 Parkside, Christchurch Road, Ringwood,
Hants BH24 3SH

© Stanley Gibbons Ltd 2011

Copyright Notice

The contents of this Catalogue, including the numbering system and illustrations, are fully protected by copyright. No part of this publication may be reproduced, stored in a retrieval system, or transmitted in any form or by any means, electronic, mechanical, photocopying, recording or otherwise, without the prior permission of Stanley Gibbons Limited. Requests for such permission should be addressed to the Catalogue Editor. This Catalogue is sold on condition that it is not, by way of trade or otherwise, lent, re-sold, hired out, circulated or otherwise disposed of other than in its complete, original and unaltered form and without a similar condition including this condition being imposed on the subsequent purchaser.

British Library Cataloguing in
Publication Data.
A catalogue record for this book is available from the British Library.

Errors and omissions excepted
the colour reproduction of stamps is only as accurate as the printing process will allow.

ISBN-10: 0-85259-828-9
ISBN-13: 978-0-85259-828-3

Item No. R 2871-11

Printed by
Stephens & George, Wales

Contents

Stanley Gibbons Publications	
Overseas Representation	iv
Complete lists of parts	v
General Philatelic Information	vi
Prices	vi
Guarantee	vii
Condition Guide	ix
Acknowledgements	ix
The Catalogue in General	x
Contacting the editor	x
Technical matters	xi
Abbreviations	xxi
Features Listing	xxii
International Philatelic Glossary	xxv
Guide to Entries	xxx
Canada	**1**
British Columbia & Vancouver Island	1
Vancouver Island	1
British Columbia	1
Colony of Canada	1
New Brunswick	5
Newfoundland	5
Stamp Booklets	17
Postage Due Stamps	18
Nova Scotia	18
Prince Edward Island	19
Dominion of Canada	20
Design Index	121
Stamp Booklets	127
Registration Stamps	162
Special Delivery Stamps	162
Postage Due Stamps	163
Official Stamps	164
Official Special Delivery Stamps	166
Index	**167**

Stanley Gibbons Holdings Plc

Stanley Gibbons Limited, Stanley Gibbons Auctions
399 Strand, London WC2R OLX
Tel: +44 (0)207 836 8444
Fax: +44 (0)207 836 7342
E-mail: help@stanleygibbons.com
Website: www.stanleygibbons.com
for all departments, Auction and Specialist Stamp Departments.
Open Monday–Friday 9.30 a.m. to 5 p.m.
Shop. Open Monday–Friday 9 a.m. to 5.30 p.m. and Saturday 9.30 a.m. to 5.30 p.m.

Stanley Gibbons Publications Gibbons Stamp Monthly and Philatelic Exporter
7 Parkside, Christchurch Road, Ringwood, Hampshire BH24 3SH.
Tel: +44 (0)1425 472363
Fax: +44 (0)1425 470247
E-mail: help@stanleygibbons.com
Publications Mail Order.
FREEPHONE 0800 611622
Monday–Friday 8.30 a.m. to 5 p.m.

Stanley Gibbons (Guernsey) Limited
18–20 Le Bordage, St Peter Port, Guernsey GY1 1DE.
Tel: +44 (0)1481 708270
Fax: +44 (0)1481 708279
E-mail: investment@stanleygibbons.com

Stanley Gibbons (Jersey) Limited
18 Hill Street, St Helier, Jersey, Channel Islands JE2 4UA.
Tel: +44 (0)1534 766711
Fax: +44 (0)1534 766177
E-mail: investment@stanleygibbons.com

Benham Collectibles Limited
Unit K, Concept Court, Shearway Business Park
Folkestone Kent CT19 4RG
E-mail: benham@benham.com

Fraser's
(a division of Stanley Gibbons Ltd)
399 Strand, London WC2R OLX
Autographs, photographs, letters and documents
Tel: +44 (0)207 836 8444
Fax: +44 (0)207 836 7342
E-mail: sales@frasersautographs.com
Website: www.frasersautographs.com
Monday–Friday 9 a.m. to 5.30 p.m. and Saturday 10 a.m. to 4 p.m.

Stanley Gibbons Publications Overseas Representation
Stanley Gibbons Publications are represented overseas by the following

Australia *Renniks Publications PTY LTD*
Unit 3 37-39 Green Street,
Banksmeadow, NSW 2019, Australia
Tel: +612 9695 7055
Website: www.renniks.com

Canada *Unitrade Associates*
99 Floral Parkway, Toronto,
Ontario M6L 2C4, Canada
Tel: +1 416 242 5900
Website: www.unitradeassoc.com

Germany *Schaubek Verlag Leipzig*
Am Glaeschen 23, D-04420
Markranstaedt, Germany
Tel: +49 34 205 67823
Website: www.schaubek.de

India *Trustin Philatelic*
96 Richmond Road,
Bangalore 560 025, India
Tel: +9180 222 11 555/ 22 97 516
Tel: +9180500 49500
Email: trustin@vsnl.net

Italy *Ernesto Marini S.R.L.*
V. Struppa, 300, Genova, 16165, Italy
Tel: +3901 0247-3530
Website: www.ernestomarini.it

Japan *Japan Philatelic*
PO Box 2, Suginami-Minami,
Tokyo 168-8081, Japan
Tel: +81 3330 41641
Website: www.yushu.co.jp

Netherlands also covers Belgium Denmark, Finland & France
Uitgeverij Davo BV
PO Box 411, Ak Deventer, 7400
Netherlands
Tel: +315 7050 2700
Website: www.davo.nl

New Zealand *House of Stamps*
PO Box 12, Paraparaumu,
New Zealand
Tel: +61 6364 8270
Website: www.houseofstamps.co.nz

New Zealand *Philatelic Distributors*
PO Box 863
15 Mount Edgecumbe Street
New Plymouth 4615, New Zealand
Tel: +6 46 758 65 68
Website: www.stampcollecta.com

Norway *SKANFIL A/S*
SPANAV. 52 / BOKS 2030
N-5504 HAUGESUND, Norway
Tel: +47-52703940
E-mail: magne@skanfil.no

Singapore *C S Philatelic Agency*
Peninsula Shopping Centre #04-29
3 Coleman Street, 179804, Singapore
Tel: +65 6337-1859
Website: www.cs.com.sg

South Africa *Peter Bale Philatelics*
P O Box 3719, Honeydew,
2040, South Africa
Tel: +27 11 462 2463
Tel: +27 82 330 3925
E-mail: balep@iafrica.com

Sweden *Chr Winther Sorensen AB*
Box 43, S-310 20 Knaered, Sweden
Tel: +46 43050743
Website: www.ifsda.org/i/dealer.php?mid=2100&asscd=SE

USA *Regency Superior Ltd*
229 North Euclid Avenue
Saint Louis, Missouri 63108, USA
PO Box 8277, St Louis,
MO 63156-8277, USA
Toll Free Tel: (800) 782-0066
Tel: (314) 361-5699
Website: www.RegencySuperior.com
Email: info@regencysuperior.com

We have catalogues to suit every aspect of stamp collecting

Our catalogues cover stamps issued from across the globe - from the Penny Black to the latest issues. Whether you're a specialist in a certain reign or a thematic collector, we should have something to suit your needs. All catalogues include the famous SG numbering system, making it as easy as possible to find the stamp you're looking for.

Catalogues published by Stanley Gibbons include:

1 Commonwealth & British Empire Stamps 1840–1970 (114th edition, 2012)

Stamps of the World 2012
Volume 1 A–Char
Volume 2 Chil–Geo
Volume 3 Ger–Ja
Volume 4 Je–New R
Volume 5 New S–Sin
Volume 6 Sir–Z

Commonwealth Country Catalogues
Australia and Dependencies (6th edition, 2010)
Bangladesh, Pakistan & Sri Lanka (2nd edition, 2011)
Belize, Guyana, Trinidad & Tobago (1st edition, 2009)
Brunei, Malaysia & Singapore (3rd edition, 2009)
Canada (4th edition, 2011)
Central Africa (2nd edition, 2008)
Cyprus, Gibraltar & Malta (3rd edition, 2011)
East Africa with Egypt and Sudan (2nd edition, 2010)
Eastern Pacific (2nd edition, 2011)
Falkland Islands (4th edition, 2010)
Hong Kong (3rd edition, 2010)
India (including Convention and Feudatory States) (3rd edition, 2009)
Indian Ocean (1st edition, 2006)
Ireland (4th edition, 2008)
Leeward Islands (1st edition, 2007)
New Zealand (4th edition, 2010)
Northern Caribbean, Bahamas & Bermuda (2nd edition, 2009)
St. Helena & Dependencies (4th edition, 2011)
Southern Africa (2nd edition, 2007)
West Africa (1st edition, 2009)
Western Pacific (2nd edition, 2009)
Windward Islands and Barbados (1st edition, 2007)

Foreign Countries
2 **Austria & Hungary** (7th edition, 2009)
3 **Balkans** (5th edition, 2009)
4 **Benelux** (6th edition, 2010)
5 **Czechoslovakia & Poland** (6th edition, 2002)
6 **France** (7th edition, 2010)
7 **Germany** (9th edition, 2011)
8 **Italy & Switzerland** (7th edition, 2010)
9 **Portugal & Spain** (6th edition, 2011)
10 **Russia** (6th edition, 2008)
11 **Scandinavia** (6th edition, 2008)
12 **Africa since Independence A-E** (2nd edition, 1983)
13 **Africa since Independence F-M** (1st edition, 1981)
14 **Africa since Independence N-Z** (1st edition, 1981)
15 **Central America** (3rd edition, 2007)
16 **Central Asia** (4th edition, 2006)
17 **China** (8th edition, 2011)
18 **Japan & Korea** (5th edition, 2008)
19 **Middle East** (7th edition, 2009)
20 **South America** (4th edition, 2008)
21 **South-East Asia** (4th edition, 2004)
22 **United States of America** (7th edition, 2010)

Thematic Catalogues
Stanley Gibbons Catalogues for use with *Stamps of the World*.
Collect Aircraft on Stamps (2nd edition, 2009)
Collect Birds on Stamps (5th edition, 2003)
Collect Chess on Stamps (2nd edition, 1999)
Collect Fish on Stamps (1st edition, 1999)
Collect Motor Vehicles on Stamps (1st edition, 2004)

Great Britain Catalogues
Collect British Stamps (62nd edition, 2011)
Great Britain Concise Stamp Catalogue (26th edition, 2011)
Volume 1 **Queen Victoria** (15th edition, 2008)
Volume 2 **King Edward VII to King George VI** (13th edition, 2009)
Volume 3 **Queen Elizabeth II Pre-decimal issues** (12th edition, 2011)
Volume 4 **Queen Elizabeth II Decimal Definitive Issues – Part 1** (10th edition, 2008)
Queen Elizabeth II Decimal Definitive Issues – Part 2 (10th edition, 2010)
Volume 5 **Queen Elizabeth II Decimal Special Issues** (3rd edition, 1998 with 1998-99 and 2000/1 Supplements)

Other publications
Africa Simplified Volume 1 (1st edition, 2011)
Asia Simplified Volume 1 (1st edition, 2010)
Antarctica (including Australian and British Antarctic Territories, French Southern and Antarctic Territories and Ross Dependency) (1st edition, 2010)
Collect Channel Islands and Isle of Man Stamps (26th edition, 2010)
Commonwealth Simplified (4th edition, 2010)
Enjoy Stamp Collecting (7th edition, 2006)
Great Britain Numbers Issued (3rd edition, 2008)
How to Identify Stamps (4th edition, 2007)
North America Combined (1st edition, 2010)
Philatelic Terms Illustrated (4th edition, 2003)
United Nations (also including International Organizations based in Switzerland and UNESCO) (1st edition, 2010)
Western Europe Simplified (2005)

Visit stanleygibbons.com to find out more about our full range of philatelic literature

STANLEY GIBBONS Est 1856

Stanley Gibbons Publications
7 Parkside, Christchurch Road, Ringwood, Hampshire BH24 3SH
UK: 0800 611 622 Int: +44 1425 363 | orders@stanleygibbons.co.uk

www.stanleygibbons.com

General Philatelic Information and Guidelines to the Scope of Stanley Gibbons Commonwealth Catalogues

These notes reflect current practice in compiling the Stanley Gibbons Commonwealth Catalogues.

The Stanley Gibbons Stamp Catalogue has a very long history and the vast quantity of information it contains has been carefully built up by successive generations through the work of countless individuals. Philately is never static and the Catalogue has evolved and developed over the years. These notes relate to the current criteria upon which a stamp may be listed or priced. These criteria have developed over time and may have differed somewhat in the early years of this catalogue. These notes are not intended to suggest that we plan to make wholesale changes to the listing of classic issues in order to bring them into line with today's listing policy, they are designed to inform catalogue users as to the policies currently in operation.

PRICES

The prices quoted in this Catalogue are the estimated selling prices of Stanley Gibbons Ltd at the time of publication. They are, unless it is specifically stated otherwise, for examples in fine condition for the issue concerned. Superb examples are worth more; those of a lower quality considerably less.

All prices are subject to change without prior notice and Stanley Gibbons Ltd may from time to time offer stamps below catalogue price. Individual low value stamps sold at 399 Strand are liable to an additional handling charge. Purchasers of new issues should note the prices charged for them contain an element for the service rendered and so may exceed the prices shown when the stamps are subsequently catalogued. Postage and handling charges are extra.

No guarantee is given to supply all stamps priced, since it is not possible to keep every catalogued item in stock. Commemorative issues may, at times, only be available in complete sets and not as individual values.

Quotation of prices. The prices in the left-hand column are for unused stamps and those in the right-hand column are for used.

A dagger (†) denotes that the item listed does not exist in that condition and a blank, or dash, that it exists, or may exist, but we are unable to quote a price.

Prices are expressed in pounds and pence sterling. One pound comprises 100 pence (£1 = 100p).

The method of notation is as follows: pence in numerals (e.g. 10 denotes ten pence); pounds and pence, up to £100, in numerals (e.g. 4.25 denotes four pounds and twenty-five pence); prices above £100 are expressed in whole pounds with the '£' sign shown.

Unused stamps. Great Britain and Commonwealth: the prices for unused stamps of Queen Victoria to King George V are for lightly hinged examples. Unused prices for King Edward VIII, King George VI and Queen Elizabeth issues are for unmounted mint.

Some stamps from the King George VI period are often difficult to find in unmounted mint condition. In such instances we would expect that collectors would need to pay a high proportion of the price quoted to obtain mounted mint examples. Generally speaking lightly mounted mint stamps from this reign, issued before 1945, are in considerable demand.

Used stamps. The used prices are normally for stamps postally used but may be for stamps cancelled-to-order where this practice exists.

A pen-cancellation on early issues can sometimes correctly denote postal use. Instances are individually noted in the Catalogue in explanation of the used price given.

Prices quoted for bisects on cover or large piece are for those dated during the period officially authorised.

Stamps not sold unused to the public (e.g. some official stamps) are priced used only.

The use of 'unified' designs, that is stamps inscribed for both postal and fiscal purposes, results in a number of stamps of very high face value. In some instances these may not have been primarily intended for postal purposes, but if they are so inscribed we include them. We only price such items used, however, where there is evidence of normal postal usage.

Cover prices. To assist collectors, cover prices are quoted for issues up to 1945 at the beginning of each country.

The system gives a general guide in the form of a factor by which the corresponding used price of the basic loose stamp should be multiplied when found in fine average condition on cover.

Care is needed in applying the factors and they relate to a cover which bears a single of the denomination listed; if more than one denomination is present the most highly priced attracts the multiplier and the remainder are priced at the simple figure for used singles in arriving at a total.

The cover should be of non-philatelic origin; bearing the correct postal rate for the period and distance involved and cancelled with the markings normal to the offices concerned. Purely philatelic items have a cover value only slightly greater than the catalogue value for the corresponding used stamps. This applies generally to those high-value stamps used philatelically rather than in the normal course of commerce. Low-value stamps, e.g. ¼d. and ½d., are desirable when used as a single rate on cover and merit an increase in 'multiplier' value.

First day covers in the period up to 1945 are not within the scope of the system and the multiplier should not be used. As a special category of philatelic usage, with wide variations in valuation according to scarcity, they require separate treatment.

Oversized covers, difficult to accommodate on an album page, should be reckoned as worth little more than the corresponding value of the used stamps. The condition of a cover also affects its value. Except for 'wreck covers', serious damage or soiling reduce the value where the postal markings and stamps are ordinary ones. Conversely, visual appeal adds to the value and this can include freshness of appearance,

Information and Guidelines

important addresses, old-fashioned but legible handwriting, historic town-names, etc.

The multipliers are a base on which further value would be added to take account of the cover's postal historical importance in demonstrating such things as unusual, scarce or emergency cancels, interesting routes, significant postal markings, combination usage, the development of postal rates, and so on.

Minimum price. The minimum catalogue price quoted is 10p. For individual stamps prices between 10p. and 95p. are provided as a guide for catalogue users. The lowest price charged for individual stamps or sets purchased from Stanley Gibbons Ltd is £1

Set prices. Set prices are generally for one of each value, excluding shades and varieties, but including major colour changes. Where there are alternative shades, etc., the cheapest is usually included. The number of stamps in the set is always stated for clarity. The prices for sets containing *se-tenant* pieces are based on the prices quoted for such combinations, and not on those for the individual stamps.

Varieties. Where plate or cylinder varieties are priced in used condition the price quoted is for a fine used example with the cancellation well clear of the listed flaw.

Specimen stamps. The pricing of these items is explained under that heading.

Stamp booklets. Prices are for complete assembled booklets in fine condition with those issued before 1945 showing normal wear and tear. Incomplete booklets and those which have been 'exploded' will, in general, be worth less than the figure quoted.

Repricing. Collectors will be aware that the market factors of supply and demand directly influence the prices quoted in this Catalogue. Whatever the scarcity of a particular stamp, if there is no one in the market who wishes to buy it cannot be expected to achieve a high price. Conversely, the same item actively sought by numerous potential buyers may cause the price to rise.

All the prices in this Catalogue are examined during the preparation of each new edition by the expert staff of Stanley Gibbons and repriced as necessary. They take many factors into account, including supply and demand, and are in close touch with the international stamp market and the auction world.

Commonwealth cover prices and advice on postal history material originally provided by Edward B Proud.

GUARANTEE

All stamps are guaranteed originals in the following terms:

If not as described, and returned by the purchaser, we undertake to refund the price paid to us in the original transaction. If any stamp is certified as genuine by the Expert Committee of the Royal Philatelic Society, London, or by BPA Expertising Ltd, the purchaser shall not be entitled to make any claim against us for any error, omission or mistake in such certificate.

Consumers' statutory rights are not affected by the above guarantee.

The recognised Expert Committees in this country are those of the Royal Philatelic Society, 41 Devonshire Place, London W1G, 6JY, and BPA Expertising Ltd, PO Box 1141, Guildford, Surrey GU5 0WR. They do not undertake valuations under any circumstances and fees are payable for their services.

Information and Guidelines

MARGINS ON IMPERFORATE STAMPS

| Superb | Very fine | Fine | Average | Poor |

GUM

| Unmounted | Very lightly mounted | Lightly mounted | Mounted/ large part original gum (o.g.). | Heavily mounted small part o.g. |

CENTRING

| Superb | Very fine | Fine | Average | Poor |

CANCELLATIONS

| Superb | Very fine | Fine | Average | Poor |

| Superb | Very fine |

| Fine | Average | Poor |

viii

Information and Guidelines

CONDITION GUIDE

To assist collectors in assessing the true value of items they are considering buying or in reviewing stamps already in their collections, we now offer a more detailed guide to the condition of stamps on which this catalogue's prices are based.

For a stamp to be described as 'Fine', it should be sound in all respects, without creases, bends, wrinkles, pin holes, thins or tears. If perforated, all perforation 'teeth' should be intact, it should not suffer from fading, rubbing or toning and it should be of clean, fresh appearance.

Margins on imperforate stamps: These should be even on all sides and should be at least as wide as half the distance between that stamp and the next. To have one or more margins of less than this width, would normally preclude a stamp from being described as 'Fine'. Some early stamps were positioned very close together on the printing plate and in such cases 'Fine' margins would necessarily be narrow. On the other hand, some plates were laid down to give a substantial gap between individual stamps and in such cases margins would be expected to be much wider.

An 'average' four-margin example would have a narrower margin on one or more sides and should be priced accordingly, while a stamp with wider, yet even, margins than 'Fine' would merit the description 'Very Fine' or 'Superb' and, if available, would command a price in excess of that quoted in the catalogue.

Gum: Since the prices for stamps of King Edward VIII, King George VI and Queen Elizabeth are for 'unmounted' or 'never hinged' mint, even stamps from these reigns which have been very lightly mounted should be available at a discount from catalogue price, the more obvious the hinge marks, the greater the discount.

Catalogue prices for stamps issued prior to King Edward VIII's reign are for mounted mint, so unmounted examples would be worth a premium. Hinge marks on 20th century stamps should not be too obtrusive, and should be at least in the lightly mounted category. For 19th century stamps more obvious hinging would be acceptable, but stamps should still carry a large part of their original gum—'Large part o.g.'—in order to be described as 'Fine'.

Centring: Ideally, the stamp's image should appear in the exact centre of the perforated area, giving equal margins on all sides. 'Fine' centring would be close to this ideal with any deviation having an effect on the value of the stamp. As in the case of the margins on imperforate stamps, it should be borne in mind that the space between some early stamps was very narrow, so it was very difficult to achieve accurate perforation, especially when the technology was in its infancy. Thus, poor centring would have a less damaging effect on the value of a 19th century stamp than on a 20th century example, but the premium put on a perfectly centred specimen would be greater.

Cancellations: Early cancellation devices were designed to 'obliterate' the stamp in order to prevent it being reused and this is still an important objective for today's postal administrations. Stamp collectors, on the other hand, prefer postmarks to be lightly applied, clear, and to leave as much as possible of the design visible. Dated, circular cancellations have long been 'the postmark of choice', but the definition of a 'Fine' cancellation will depend upon the types of cancellation in use at the time a stamp was current—it is clearly illogical to seek a circular datestamp on a Penny Black.

'Fine', by definition, will be superior to 'Average', so, in terms of cancellation quality, if one begins by identifying what 'Average' looks like, then one will be half way to identifying 'Fine'. The illustrations will give some guidance on mid-19th century and mid-20th century cancellations of Great Britain, but types of cancellation in general use in each country and in each period will determine the appearance of 'Fine'.

As for the factors discussed above, anything less than 'Fine' will result in a downgrading of the stamp concerned, while a very fine or superb cancellation will be worth a premium.

Combining the factors: To merit the description 'Fine', a stamp should be fine in every respect, but a small deficiency in one area might be made up for in another by a factor meriting an 'Extremely Fine' description.

Some early issues are so seldom found in what would normally be considered to be 'Fine' condition, the catalogue prices are for a slightly lower grade, with 'Fine' examples being worth a premium. In such cases a note to this effect is given in the catalogue, while elsewhere premiums are given for well-centred, lightly cancelled examples.

Stamps graded at less than fine remain collectable and, in the case of more highly priced stamps, will continue to hold a value. Nevertheless, buyers should always bear condition in mind.

ACKNOWLEDGEMENTS

We are grateful to individual collectors, members of the philatelic trade and specialist societies and study circles for their assistance in improving and extending the Stanley Gibbons range of catalogues. The addresses of societies and study circles relevant to this volume are:

Canadian Philatelic Society of Great Britain
Secretary — Mr. J. M. Wright
12 Milchester House, Staveley Road,
Meads, Eastbourne, East Sussex BN20 7JX

British North America Philatelic Society
Secretary — Mr. P. Jacobi
6, 2168-150A Street,
Surrey, BC Canada, V4A 9WA

Information and Guidelines

The Catalogue in General

Contents. The Catalogue is confined to adhesive postage stamps, including miniature sheets. For particular categories the rules are:
(a) Revenue (fiscal) stamps or telegraph stamps are listed only where they have been expressly authorised for postal duty.
(b) Stamps issued only precancelled are included, but normally issued stamps available additionally with precancel have no separate precancel listing unless the face value is changed.
(c) Stamps prepared for use but not issued, hitherto accorded full listing, are nowadays foot-noted with a price (where possible).
(d) Bisects (trisects, etc.) are only listed where such usage was officially authorised.
(e) Stamps issued only on first day covers or in presentation packs and not available separately are not listed but may be priced in a footnote.
(f) New printings are only included in this Catalogue where they show a major philatelic variety, such as a change in shade, watermark or paper. Stamps which exist with or without imprint dates are listed separately; changes in imprint dates are mentioned in footnotes.
(g) Official and unofficial reprints are dealt with by footnote.
(h) Stamps from imperforate printings of modern issues which occur perforated are covered by footnotes, but are listed where widely available for postal use.

Exclusions. The following are excluded:
(a) non-postal revenue or fiscal stamps;
(b) postage stamps used fiscally (although prices are now given for some fiscally used high values);
(c) local carriage labels and private local issues;
(d) bogus or phantom stamps;
(e) railway or airline letter fee stamps, bus or road transport company labels or the stamps of private postal companies operating under licence from the national authority;
(f) cut-outs;
(g) all types of non-postal labels and souvenirs;
(h) documentary labels for the postal service, e.g. registration, recorded delivery, air-mail etiquettes, etc.;
(i) privately applied embellishments to official issues and privately commissioned items generally;
(j) stamps for training postal officers.
(k) Telegraph stamps

Full listing. 'Full listing' confers our recognition and implies allotting a catalogue number and (wherever possible) a price quotation.

In judging status for inclusion in the catalogue broad considerations are applied to stamps. They must be issued by a legitimate postal authority, recognised by the government concerned, and must be adhesives valid for proper postal use in the class of service for which they are inscribed. Stamps, with the exception of such categories as postage dues and officials, must be available to the general public, at face value, in reasonable quantities without any artificial restrictions being imposed on their distribution.

For errors and varieties the criterion is legitimate (albeit inadvertent) sale through a postal administration in the normal course of business. Details of provenance are always important; printers' waste and deliberately manufactured material are excluded.

Certificates. In assessing unlisted items due weight is given to Certificates from recognised Expert Committees and, where appropriate, we will usually ask to see them.

Date of issue. Where local issue dates differ from dates of release by agencies, 'date of issue' is the local date. Fortuitous stray usage before the officially intended date is disregarded in listing.

Catalogue numbers. Stamps of each country are catalogued chronologically by date of issue. Subsidiary classes are placed at the end of the country, as separate lists, with a distinguishing letter prefix to the catalogue number, e.g. D for postage due, O for official and E for express delivery stamps.

The catalogue number appears in the extreme left-column. The boldface Type numbers in the next column are merely cross-references to illustrations.

Once published in the Catalogue, numbers are changed as little as possible; really serious renumbering is reserved for the occasions when a complete country or an entire issue is being rewritten. The edition first affected includes cross-reference tables of old and new numbers.

Our catalogue numbers are universally recognised in specifying stamps and as a hallmark of status.

Illustrations. Stamps are illustrated at three-quarters linear size. Stamps not illustrated are the same size and format as the value shown, unless otherwise indicated. Stamps issued only as miniature sheets have the stamp alone illustrated but sheet size is also quoted. Overprints, surcharges, watermarks and postmarks are normally actual size. Illustrations of varieties are often enlarged to show the detail. Stamp booklet covers are illustrated half-size, unless otherwise indicated.

Designers. Designers' names are quoted where known, though space precludes naming every individual concerned in the production of a set. In particular, photographers supplying material are usually named only where they also make an active contribution in the design stage; posed photographs of reigning monarchs are, however, an exception to this rule.

CONTACTING THE CATALOGUE EDITOR

The editor is always interested in hearing from people who have new information which will improve or correct the Catalogue. As a general rule he must see and examine the actual stamps before they can be considered for listing; photographs or photocopies are insufficient evidence.

Submissions should be made in writing to the Catalogue Editor, Stanley Gibbons Publications at the Ringwood office. The cost of return postage for items submitted is appreciated, and this should include the registration fee if required.

Where information is solicited purely for the benefit of the enquirer, the editor cannot undertake to reply if the answer is already contained in these published notes or if return postage is omitted. Written communications are greatly preferred to enquiries by telephone or e-mail and the editor regrets that he or his staff cannot see personal callers without a prior appointment being made. Correspondence may be subject to delay during the production period of each new edition.

The editor welcomes close contact with study circles and is interested, too, in finding reliable local correspondents who will verify and supplement official information in countries where this is deficient.

We regret we do not give opinions as to the genuineness of stamps, nor do we identify stamps or number them by our Catalogue.

TECHNICAL MATTERS

The meanings of the technical terms used in the catalogue will be found in our *Philatelic Terms Illustrated*.

References below to (more specialised) listings are to be taken to indicate, as appropriate, the Stanley Gibbons *Great Britain Specialised Catalogue* in five volumes or the *Great Britain Concise Catalogue*.

1. Printing

Printing errors. Errors in printing are of major interest to the Catalogue. Authenticated items meriting consideration would include: background, centre or frame inverted or omitted; centre or subject transposed; error of colour; error or omission of value; double prints and impressions; printed both sides; and so on. Designs *tête-bêche*, whether intentionally or by accident, are listable. *Se-tenant* arrangements of stamps are recognised in the listings or footnotes. Gutter pairs (a pair of stamps separated by blank margin) are not included in this volume. Colours only partially omitted are not listed. Stamps with embossing omitted are reserved for our more specialised listings.

Printing varieties. Listing is accorded to major changes in the printing base which lead to completely new types. In recess-printing this could be a design re-engraved; in photogravure or photolithography a screen altered in whole or in part. It can also encompass flat-bed and rotary printing if the results are readily distinguishable.

To be considered at all, varieties must be constant.

Early stamps, produced by primitive methods, were prone to numerous imperfections; the lists reflect this, recognising re-entries, retouches, broken frames, misshapen letters, and so on. Printing technology has, however, radically improved over the years, during which time photogravure and lithography have become predominant. Varieties nowadays are more in the nature of flaws and these, being too specialised for this general catalogue, are almost always outside the scope.

In no catalogue, however, do we list such items as: dry prints, kiss prints, doctor-blade flaws, colour shifts or registration flaws (unless they lead to the complete omission of a colour from an individual stamp), lithographic ring flaws, and so on. Neither do we recognise fortuitous happenings like paper creases or confetti flaws.

Overprints (and surcharges). Overprints of different types qualify for separate listing. These include overprints in different colours; overprints from different printing processes such as litho and typo; overprints in totally different typefaces, etc. Major errors in machine-printed overprints are important and listable. They include: overprint inverted or omitted; overprint double (treble, etc.); overprint diagonal; overprint double, one inverted; pairs with one overprint omitted, e.g. from a radical shift to an adjoining stamp; error of colour; error of type fount; letters inverted or omitted, etc. If the overprint is handstamped, few of these would qualify and a distinction is drawn. We continue, however, to list pairs of stamps where one has a handstamped overprint and the other has not.

Varieties occurring in overprints will often take the form of broken letters, slight differences in spacing, rising spaces, etc. Only the most important would be considered for listing or footnote mention.

Sheet positions. If space permits we quote sheet positions of listed varieties and authenticated data is solicited for this purpose.

De La Rue plates. The Catalogue classifies the general plates used by De La Rue for printing British Colonial stamps as follows:

VICTORIAN KEY TYPE

Die I

1. The ball of decoration on the second point of the crown appears as a dark mass of lines.
2. Dark vertical shading separates the front hair from the bun.
3. The vertical line of colour outlining the front of the throat stops at the sixth line of shading on the neck.
4. The white space in the coil of the hair above the curl is roughly the shape of a pin's head.

Die II

1. There are very few lines of colour in the ball and it appears almost white.
2. A white vertical strand of hair appears in place of the dark shading.

Information and Guidelines

3. The line stops at the eighth line of shading.
4. The white space is oblong, with a line of colour partially dividing it at the left end.

Plates numbered 1 and 2 are both Die I. Plates 3 and 4 are Die II.

GEORGIAN KEY TYPE

Die I

A. The second (thick) line below the name of the country is cut slanting, conforming roughly to the shape of the crown on each side.
B. The labels of solid colour bearing the words "POSTAGE" and "& REVENUE" are square at the inner top corners.
C. There is a projecting "bud" on the outer spiral of the ornament in each of the lower corners.

Die I

A. The second line is cut vertically on each side of the crown.
B. The labels curve inwards at the top.
C. There is no "bud" in this position.

Unless otherwise stated in the lists, all stamps with watermark Multiple Crown CA (w **8**) are Die I while those with watermark Multiple Crown Script CA (w **9**) are Die II. The Georgian Die II was introduced in April 1921 and was used for Plates 10 to 22 and 26 to 28. Plates 23 to 25 were made from Die I by mistake.

2. Paper
All stamps listed are deemed to be on (ordinary) paper of the wove type and white in colour; only departures from this are normally mentioned.
Types. Where classification so requires we distinguish such other types of paper as, for example, vertically and horizontally laid; wove and laid bâtonné; card(board); carton; cartridge; glazed; granite; native; pelure; porous; quadrillé; ribbed; rice; and silk thread.

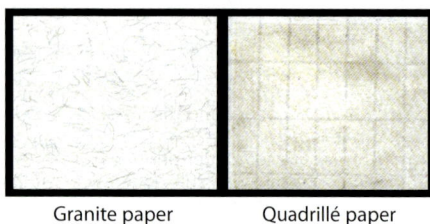

Wove paper   Laid paper

Granite paper   Quadrillé paper

Burelé band

The various makeshifts for normal paper are listed as appropriate. The varieties of double paper and joined paper are recognised. The security device of a printed burelé band on the back of a stamp, as in early Queensland, qualifies for listing.
Descriptive terms. The fact that a paper is handmade (and thus probably of uneven thickness) is mentioned where necessary. Such descriptive terms as "hard" and "soft"; "smooth" and "rough"; "thick", "medium" and "thin" are applied where there is philatelic merit in classifying papers.
Coloured, very white and toned papers. A coloured paper is one that is coloured right through (front and back of the stamp). In the Catalogue the colour of the paper is given in italics, thus:
black/*rose* = black design on rose paper.
   Papers have been made specially white in recent years by, for example, a very heavy coating of chalk. We do not classify shades of whiteness of paper as distinct varieties. There does exist, however, a type of paper from early days called toned. This is off-white, often brownish or buffish, but it cannot be assigned any definite colour. A toning effect brought on by climate, incorrect storage or gum staining is disregarded here, as this was not the state of the paper when issued.
"Ordinary" and "Chalk-surfaced" papers. The availability of many postage stamps for revenue purposes made necessary some safeguard against the illegitimate re-use of stamps with removable cancellations. This was at first secured by using fugitive inks and later by printing on paper surfaced by coatings containing either chalk or china clay, both of which made it difficult to remove any form of obliteration without damaging the stamp design.
   This catalogue lists these chalk-surfaced paper varieties from their introduction in 1905. Where no indication is given, the paper is "ordinary".

The "traditional" method of indentifying chalk-surfaced papers has been that, when touched with a silver wire, a black mark is left on the paper, and the listings in this catalogue are based on that test. However, the test itself is now largely discredited, for, although the mark can be removed by a soft rubber, some damage to the stamp will result from its use.

The difference between chalk-surfaced and pre-war ordinary papers is fairly clear: chalk-surfaced papers being smoother to the touch and showing a characteristic sheen when light is reflected off their surface. Under good magnification tiny bubbles or pock marks can be seen on the surface of the stamp and at the tips of the perforations the surfacing appears "broken". Traces of paper fibres are evident on the surface of ordinary paper and the ink shows a degree of absorption into it.

Initial chalk-surfaced paper printings by De La Rue had a thinner coating than subsequently became the norm. The characteristics described above are less pronounced in these printings.

During and after the Second World War, substitute papers replaced the chalk-surfaced papers, these do not react to the silver test and are therefore classed as "ordinary", although differentiating them without recourse to it is more difficult, for, although the characteristics of the chalk-surfaced paper remained the same, some of the ordinary papers appear much smoother than earlier papers and many do not show the watermark clearly. Experience is the only solution to identifying these, and comparison with stamps whose paper type is without question will be of great help.

Another type of paper, known as "thin striated" was used only for the Bahamas 1s. and 5s. (Nos. 155a, 156a, 171 and 174) and for several stamps of the Malayan states. Hitherto these have been described as "chalk-surfaced" since they gave some reaction to the silver test, but they are much thinner than usual chalk-surfaced papers, with the watermark showing clearly. Stamps on this paper show a slightly 'ribbed' effect when the stamp is held up to the light. Again, comparison with a known striated paper stamp, such as the 1941 Straits Settlements Die II 2c. orange (No. 294) will prove invaluable in separating these papers.

Glazed paper. In 1969 the Crown Agents introduced a new general-purpose paper for use in conjunction with all current printing processes. It generally has a marked glossy surface but the degree varies according to the process used, being more marked in recess-printing stamps. As it does not respond to the silver test this presents a further test where previous printings were on chalky paper. A change of paper to the glazed variety merits separate listing.

Green and yellow papers. Issues of the First World War and immediate postwar period occur on green and yellow papers and these are given separate Catalogue listing. The original coloured papers (coloured throughout) gave way to surface-coloured papers, the stamps having "white backs"; other stamps show one colour on the front and a different one at the back. Because of the numerous variations a grouping of colours is adopted as follows:

Yellow papers
(1) The original *yellow* paper (throughout), usually bright in colour. The gum is often sparse, of harsh consistency and dull-looking. Used 1912–1920.
(2) The *white-backs*. Used 1913–1914.
(3) A bright lemon paper. The colour must have a pronounced greenish tinge, different from the "yellow" in (1). As a rule, the gum on stamps using this lemon paper is plentiful, smooth and shiny, and the watermark shows distinctly. Care is needed with stamps printed in green on yellow paper (1) as it may appear that the paper is this lemon. Used 1914–1916.
(4) An experimental *orange-buff* paper. The colour must have a distinct brownish tinge. It is not to be confused with a muddy yellow (1) nor the misleading appearance (on the surface) of stamps printed in red on yellow paper where an engraved plate has been insufficiently wiped. Used 1918–1921.
(5) An experimental *buff* paper. This lacks the brownish tinge of (4) and the brightness of the yellow shades. The gum is shiny when compared with the matt type used on (4). Used 1919–1920.
(6) A *pale yellow* paper that has a creamy tone to the yellow. Used from 1920 onwards.

Green papers
(7) The original "green" paper, varying considerably through shades of blue-green and yellow-green, the front and back sometimes differing. Used 1912–1916.
(8) The *white backs*. Used 1913–1914.
(9) A paper blue-green on the surface with *pale olive* back. The back must be markedly paler than the front and this and the pronounced olive tinge to the back distinguish it from (7). Used 1916–1920.
(10) Paper with a vivid green surface, commonly called *emerald-green*; it has the olive back of (9). Used 1920.
(11) Paper with *emerald-green* both back and front. Used from 1920 onwards.

3. Perforation and Rouletting

Perforation gauge. The gauge of a perforation is the number of holes in a length of 2 cm. For correct classification the size of the holes (large or small) may need to be distinguished; in a few cases the actual number of holes on each edge of the stamp needs to be quoted.

Measurement. The Gibbons *Instanta* gauge is the standard for measuring perforations. The stamp is viewed against a dark background with the transparent gauge put on top of it. Though the gauge measures to decimal accuracy, perforations read from it are generally quoted in the Catalogue to the nearest half. For example:

Just over perf 12¾ to just under 13¼ = perf 13
Perf 13¼ exactly, rounded up = perf 13½
Just over perf 13¼ to just under 13¾ = perf 13½
Perf 13¾ exactly, rounded up = perf 14

However, where classification depends on it, actual quarter-perforations are quoted.

Notation. Where no perforation is quoted for an issue it is imperforate. Perforations are usually abbreviated (and spoken) as follows, though sometimes they may be spelled out for clarity. This notation for rectangular stamps (the majority) applies to diamond shapes if "top" is read as the edge to the top right.

P 14: perforated alike on all sides (read: "perf 14").
P 14×15: the first figure refers to top and bottom, the second to left and right sides (read: "perf 14 by 15"). This is a compound perforation. For an upright triangular stamp the first figure refers to the two sloping sides and second to the base. In inverted

Information and Guidelines

triangulars the base is first and the second figure to the sloping sides.

P 14–15: perforation measuring anything between 14 and 15: the holes are irregularly spaced, thus the gauge may vary along a single line or even along a single edge of the stamp (read: "perf 14 to 15").

P 14 *irregular*: perforated 14 from a worn perforator, giving badly aligned holes irregularly spaced (read: "irregular perf 14").

P *comp(ound)* 14×15: two gauges in use but not necessarily on opposite sides of the stamp. It could be one side in one gauge and three in the other; or two adjacent sides with the same gauge. (Read: "perf compound of 14 and 15".) For three gauges or more, abbreviated as "P 12, 14½, 15 *or compound*" for example.

P 14, 14½: perforated approximately 14¼ (read: "perf 14 or 14½"). It does *not* mean two stamps, one perf 14 and the other perf 14½. This obsolescent notation is gradually being replaced in the Catalogue.

Imperf: imperforate (not perforated)

Imperf×P 14: imperforate at top ad bottom and perf 14 at sides.

P 14×*imperf*: perf 14 at top and bottom and imperforate at sides.

Such headings as "P 13×14 (*vert*) and P 14×13 (*horiz*)" indicate which perforations apply to which stamp format—vertical or horizontal.

Some stamps are additionally perforated so that a label or tab is detachable; others have been perforated for use as two halves. Listings are normally for whole stamps, unless stated otherwise.

Imperf×perf

Other terms. Perforation almost always gives circular holes; where other shapes have been used they are specified, e.g. square holes; lozenge perf. Interrupted perfs are brought about by the omission of pins at regular intervals. Perforations merely simulated by being printed as part of the design are of course ignored. With few exceptions, privately applied perforations are not listed.

In the 19th century perforations are often described as clean cut (clean, sharply incised holes), intermediate or rough (rough holes, imperfectly cut, often the result of blunt pins).

Perforation errors and varieties. Authenticated errors, where a stamp normally perforated is accidentally issued imperforate, are listed provided no traces of perforation (blind holes or indentations) remain. They must be provided as pairs, both stamps wholly imperforate, and are only priced in that form.

Stamps imperforate between stamp and sheet margin are not listed in this catalogue, but such errors on Great Britain stamps will be found in the *Great Britain Specialised Catalogue*.

Pairs described as "imperforate between" have the line of perforations between the two stamps omitted.

Imperf between (horiz pair): a horizontal pair of stamps with perfs all around the edges but none between the stamps.

Imperf between (vert pair): a vertical pair of stamps with perfs all around the edges but none between the stamps.

Imperf between (vertical pair) Imperf horizontally (vertical pair)

Where several of the rows have escaped perforation the resulting varieties are listable. Thus:

Imperf vert (horiz pair): a horizontal pair of stamps perforated top and bottom; all three vertical directions are imperf—the two outer edges and between the stamps.

Imperf horiz (vert pair): a vertical pair perforated at left and right edges; all three horizontal directions are imperf—the top, bottom and between the stamps.

Straight edges. Large sheets cut up before issue to post offices can cause stamps with straight edges, i.e. imperf on one side or on two sides at right angles. They are not usually listable in this condition and are worth less than corresponding stamps properly perforated all round. This does not, however, apply to certain stamps, mainly from coils and booklets, where straight edges on various sides are the manufacturing norm affecting every stamp. The listings and notes make clear which sides are correctly imperf.

Malfunction. Varieties of double, misplaced or partial perforation caused by error or machine malfunction are not listable, neither are freaks, such as perforations placed diagonally from paper folds, nor missing holes caused by broken pins.

Types of perforating. Where necessary for classification, perforation types are distinguished.
These include:

Line perforation from one line of pins punching single rows of holes at a time.

Comb perforation from pins disposed across the sheet in comb formation, punching out holes at three sides of the stamp a row at a time.

Harrow perforation applied to a whole pane or sheet at one stroke.

Rotary perforation from toothed wheels operating across a sheet, then crosswise.

Sewing machine perforation. The resultant condition,

xiv

clean-cut or rough, is distinguished where required.

Pin-perforation is the commonly applied term for pin-roulette in which, instead of being punched out, round holes are pricked by sharp-pointed pins and no paper is removed.

Mixed perforation occurs when stamps with defective perforations are re-perforated in a different gauge.

Punctured stamps. Perforation holes can be punched into the face of the stamp. Patterns of small holes, often in the shape of initial letters, are privately applied devices against pilferage. These (perfins) are outside the scope except for Australia, Canada, Cape of Good Hope, Papua and Sudan where they were used as official stamps by the national administration. Identification devices, when officially inspired, are listed or noted; they can be shapes, or letters or words formed from holes, sometimes converting one class of stamp into another.

Rouletting. In rouletting the paper is cut, for ease of separation, but none is removed. The gauge is measured, when needed, as for perforations. Traditional French terms descriptive of the type of cut are often used and types include:

Arc roulette (percé en arc). Cuts are minute, spaced arcs, each roughly a semicircle.

Cross roulette (percé en croix). Cuts are tiny diagonal crosses.

Line roulette (percé en ligne or en ligne droite). Short straight cuts parallel to the frame of the stamp. The commonest basic roulette. Where not further described, "roulette" means this type.

Rouletted in colour or coloured roulette (percé en lignes colorées or en lignes de coleur). Cuts with coloured edges, arising from notched rule inked simultaneously with the printing plate.

Saw-tooth roulette (percé en scie). Cuts applied zigzag fashion to resemble the teeth of a saw.

Serpentine roulette (percé en serpentin). Cuts as sharply wavy lines.

Zigzag roulette (percé en zigzags). Short straight cuts at angles in alternate directions, producing sharp points on separation. US usage favours "serrate(d) roulette" for this type.

Pin-roulette (originally *percé en points* and now *perforés trous d'epingle*) is commonly called pin-perforation in English.

4. Gum

All stamps listed are assumed to have gum of some kind; if they were issued without gum this is stated. Original gum (o.g.) means that which was present on the stamp as issued to the public. Deleterious climates and the presence of certain chemicals can cause gum to crack and, with early stamps, even make the paper deteriorate. Unscrupulous fakers are adept in removing it and regumming the stamp to meet the unreasoning demand often made for "full o.g." in cases where such a thing is virtually impossible.

The gum normally used on stamps has been gum ararbic until the late 1960s when synthetic adhesives were introduced. Harrison and Sons Ltd for instance use *polyvinyl alcohol*, known to philatelists as PVA. This is almost invisible except for a slight yellowish tinge which was incorporated to make it possible to see that the stamps have been gummed. It has advantages in hot countries, as stamps do not curl and sheets are less likely to stick together. Gum arabic and PVA are not distinguished in the lists except that where a stamp exists with both forms this is indicated in footnotes. Our more specialised catalogues provide separate listing of gums for Great Britain.

Self-adhesive stamps are issued on backing paper, from which they are peeled before affixing to mail. Unused examples are priced as for backing paper intact, in which condition they are recommended to be kept. Used examples are best collected on cover or on piece.

5. Watermarks

Stamps are on unwatermarked paper except where the heading to the set says otherwise.

Detection. Watermarks are detected for Catalogue description by one of four methods: (1) holding stamps to the light; (2) laying stamps face down on a dark background; (3) adding a few drops of petroleum ether 40/60 to the stamp laid face down in a watermark tray; (4) by use of the Stanley Gibbons Detectamark, or other equipment, which work by revealing the thinning of the paper at the watermark. (Note that petroleum ether is highly inflammable in use and can damage photogravure stamps.)

Listable types. Stamps occurring on both watermarked and unwatermarked papers are different types and both receive full listing.

Single watermarks (devices occurring once on every stamp) can be modified in size and shape as between different issues; the types are noted but not usually separately listed. Fortuitous absence of watermark from a single stamp or its gross displacement would not be listable.

To overcome registration difficulties the device may be repeated at close intervals *(a multiple watermark)*, single stamps thus showing parts of several devices. Similarly, a *large sheet watermark* (or *all-over watermark*) covering numerous stamps can be used. We give informative notes and illustrations for them. The designs may be such that numbers of stamps in the sheet automatically lack watermark: this is not a listable variety. Multiple and all-over watermarks sometimes undergo modifications, but if the various types are difficult to distinguish from single stamps notes are given but not separate listings.

Papermakers' watermarks are noted where known but not listed separately, since most stamps in the sheet will lack them. Sheet watermarks which are nothing more than officially adopted papermakers' watermarks are, however, given normal listing.

Marginal watermarks, falling outside the pane of stamps, are ignored except where misplacement caused the adjoining row to be affected, in which case they may be footnoted.

Watermark errors and varieties. Watermark errors are recognised as of major importance. They comprise stamps intended to be on unwatermarked paper but issued watermarked by mistake, or stamps printed on paper with the wrong watermark. Varieties showing letters omitted from the watermark are also included, but broken or deformed bits on the dandy roll are not listed unless they represent repairs.

Watermark positions. The diagram shows how watermark position is described in the Catalogue. Paper has a side intended for printing and watermarks are usually impressed so that they read normally when looked through from that printed side. However, since philatelists customarily detect watermarks by looking at the back of the stamp the watermark diagram also makes clear what is actually seen.

Information and Guidelines

Illustrations in the Catalogue are of watermarks in normal positions (from the front of the stamps) and are actual size where possible.

Differences in watermark position are collectable varieties. This Catalogue now lists inverted, sideways inverted and reversed watermark varieties on Commonwealth stamps from the 1860s onwards except where the watermark position is completely haphazard.

Great Britain inverted and sideways inverted watermarks can be found in the *Great Britain Specialised Catalogue* and the *Great Britain Concise Catalogue*.

Where a watermark comes indiscriminately in various positions our policy is to cover this by a general note: we do not give separate listings because the watermark position in these circumstances has no particular philatelic importance.

AS DESCRIBED (Read through front of stamp)		AS SEEN DURING WATERMARK DETECTION (Stamp face down and back examined)
GvR	Normal	ЯvᎮ
ᎮvЯ	Inverted	ᎮʌЯ
ЯvᎮ	Reversed	GvR
ᎮʌЯ	Reversed and Inverted	ЯʌᎮ
GvR (rotated)	Sideways	ЯvᎮ (rotated)
GvR (rotated)	Sideways Inverted	ЯvᎮ (rotated)

Standard types of watermark. Some watermarks have been used generally for various British possessions rather than exclusively for a single colony. To avoid repetition the Catalogue classifies 11 general types, as under, with references in the headings throughout the listings being given either in words or in the form ("W w **9**") (meaning "watermark type w **9**"). In those cases where watermark illustrations appear in the listings themselves, the respective reference reads, for example, W **153**, thus indicating that the watermark will be found in the normal sequence of illustrations as (type) **153**.

The general types are as follows, with an example of each quoted.

W	Description	Example
w **1**	Large Star	St. Helena No. 1
w **2**	Small Star	Turks Is. No. 4
w **3**	Broad (pointed) Star	Grenada No. 24
w **4**	Crown (over) CC, small stamp	Antigua No. 13
w **5**	Crown (over) CC, large stamp	Antigua No. 31
w **6**	Crown (over) CA, small stamp	Antigua No. 21
w **7**	Crown CA (CA over Crown), large stamp	Sierra Leone No. 54
w **8**	Multiple Crown CA	Antigua No. 41
w **9**	Multiple Script CA	Seychelles No. 158
w **9***a*	do. Error	Seychelles No. 158a
w **9***b*	do. Error	Seychelles No. 158b
w **10**	V over Crown	N.S.W. No. 327
w **11**	Crown over A	N.S.W. No. 347

CC in these watermarks is an abbreviation for "Crown Colonies" and CA for "Crown Agents". Watermarks w **1**, w **2** and w **3** are on stamps printed by Perkins, Bacon; w **4** onwards on stamps from De La Rue and other printers.

w **1**
Large Star

w **2**
Small Star

w **3**
Broad-pointed Star

Watermark w **1**, *Large Star*, measures 15 to 16 mm across the star from point to point and about 27 mm from centre to centre vertically between stars in the sheet. It was made for long stamps like Ceylon 1857 and St. Helena 1856.

Watermark w **2**, *Small Star* is of similar design but measures 12 to 13½ mm from point to point and 24 mm from centre to centre vertically. It was for use with ordinary-size stamps such as Grenada 1863–71.

When the Large Star watermark was used with the smaller stamps it only occasionally comes in the centre of the paper. It is frequently so misplaced as to show portions of two stars above and below and this eccentricity will very often help in determining the watermark.

Watermark w **3**, *Broad-pointed Star*, resembles w **1** but the points are broader.

Information and Guidelines

w 4 Crown (over) CC

w 5 Crown (over) CC

Two *Crown (over) CC* watermarks were used: w **4** was for stamps of ordinary size and w **5** for those of larger size.

w 6 Crown (over) CA

w 7 CA over Crown

Two watermarks of *Crown CA* type were used, w **6** being for stamps of ordinary size. The other, w **7**, is properly described as *CA over Crown*. It was specially made for paper on which it was intended to print long fiscal stamps: that some were used postally accounts for the appearance of w **7** in the Catalogue. The watermark occupies twice the space of the ordinary Crown CA watermark, w **6**. Stamps of normal size printed on paper with w **7** watermark show it *sideways*; it takes a horizontal pair of stamps to show the entire watermark.

w 8 Multiple Crown CA

w 9 Multiple Script CA

Multiple watermarks began in 1904 with w **8**, *Multiple Crown CA,* changed from 1921 to w **9**, *Multiple Script CA.* On stamps of ordinary size portions of two or three watermarks appear and on the large-sized stamps a greater number can be observed. The change to letters in script character with w **9** was accompanied by a Crown of distinctly different shape.

It seems likely that there were at least two dandy rolls for each Crown Agents watermark in use at any one time with a reserve roll being employed when the normal one was withdrawn for maintenance or repair.

Both the Mult Crown CA and the Mult Script CA types exist with one or other of the letters omitted from individual impressions. It is possible that most of these occur from the reserve rolls as they have only been found on certain issues. The MCA watermark experienced such problems during the early 1920s and the Script over a longer period from the early 1940s until 1951.

During the 1920s damage must also have occurred on one of the Crowns as a substituted Crown has been found on certain issues. This is smaller than the normal and consists of an oval base joined to two upright ovals with a circle positioned between their upper ends. The upper line of the Crown's base is omitted, as are the left and right-hand circles at the top and also the cross over the centre circle.

Substituted Crown

The *Multiple Script CA* watermark, w **9**, is known with two errors, recurring among the 1950–52 printings of several territories. In the first a crown has fallen away from the dandy-roll that impresses the watermark into the paper pulp. It gives w **9a**, *Crown missing*, but this omission has been found in both "Crown only" (*illustrated*) and "Crown CA" rows. The resulting faulty paper was used for Bahamas, Johore, Seychelles and the postage due stamps of nine colonies

w **9a**: Error, Crown missing

w **9b**: Error, St. Edward's Crown

When the omission was noticed a second mishap occurred, which was to insert a wrong crown in the space, giving w **9b**, St. Edward's Crown. This produced varieties in Bahamas, Perlis, St. Kitts-Nevis and Singapore and the incorrect crown likewise occurs in (Crown only) and (Crown CA) rows.

Information and Guidelines

w 10
V over Crown

w 11
Crown over A

Resuming the general types, two watermarks found in issues of several Australian States are: w **10**, *V over Crown*, and w **11**, *Crown over A*.

w 12
Multiple St. Edward's Crown Block CA

w 13
Multiple PTM

The *Multiple St. Edward's Crown Block CA* watermark, w **12**, was introduced in 1957 and besides the change in the Crown (from that used in Multiple Crown Script CA, w **9**) the letters reverted to block capitals. The new watermark began to appear sideways in 1966 and these stamps are generally listed as separate sets.

The watermark w **13**, *Multiple PTM*, was introduced for new Malaysian issues in November 1961.

w 14
Multiple Crown CA Diagonal

By 1974 the two dandy-rolls (the "upright" and the "sideways") for w **12** were wearing out; the Crown Agents therefore discontinued using the sideways watermark one and retained the other only as a stand-by. A new dandy-roll with the pattern of w **14**, *Multiple Crown CA Diagonal*, was introduced and first saw use with some Churchill Centenary issues.

The new watermark had the design arranged in gradually spiralling rows. It is improved in design to allow smooth passage over the paper (the gaps between letters and rows had caused jolts in previous dandy-rolls) and the sharp corners and angles, where fibres used to accumulate, have been eliminated by rounding.

This watermark had no "normal" sideways position amongst the different printers using it. To avoid confusion our more specialised listings do not rely on such terms as "sideways inverted" but describe the direction in which the watermark points.

w 15
Multiple POST OFFICE

During 1981 w **15**. *Multiple POST OFFICE* was introduced for certain issues prepared by Philatelists Ltd, acting for various countries in the Indian Ocean, Pacific and West Indies.

w 16
Multiple Crown Script CA Diagonal

A new Crown Agents watermark was introduced during 1985, w **16**, *Multiple Crown Script CA Diagonal*. This was very similar to the previous w **14**, but showed "CA" in script rather than block letters. It was first used on the omnibus series of stamps commemorating the Life and Times of Queen Elizabeth the Queen Mother.

6. Colours

Stamps in two or three colours have these named in order of appearance, from the centre moving outwards. Four colours or more are usually listed as multicoloured.

In compound colour names the second is the predominant one, thus:

orange-red = a red tending towards orange;
red-orange = an orange containing more red than usual.

Standard colours used. The 200 colours most used for stamp identification are given in the Stanley Gibbons Stamp Colour Key. The Catalogue has used the Stamp Colour Key as standard for describing new issues for some years. The names are also introduced as lists

xviii

are rewritten, though exceptions are made for those early issues where traditional names have become universally established.

Determining colours. When comparing actual stamps with colour samples in the Stamp Colour Key, view in a good north daylight (or its best substitute; fluorescent "colour matching" light). Sunshine is not recommended. Choose a solid portion of the stamp design; if available, marginal markings such as solid bars of colour or colour check dots are helpful. Shading lines in the design can be misleading as they appear lighter than solid colour. Postmarked portions of a stamp appear darker than normal. If more than one colour is present, mask off the extraneous ones as the eye tends to mix them.

Errors of colour. Major colour errors in stamps or overprints which qualify for listing are: wrong colours; one colour inverted in relation to the rest; albinos (colourless impressions), where these have Expert Committee certificates; colours completely omitted, but only on unused stamps (if found on used stamps the information is footnoted) and with good credentials, missing colours being frequently faked.

Colours only partially omitted are not recognised, Colour shifts, however spectacular, are not listed.

Shades. Shades in philately refer to variations in the intensity of a colour or the presence of differing amounts of other colours. They are particularly significant when they can be linked to specific printings. In general, shades need to be quite marked to fall within the scope of this Catalogue; it does not favour nowadays listing the often numerous shades of a stamp, but chooses a single applicable colour name which will indicate particular groups of outstanding shades. Furthermore, the listings refer to colours as issued; they may deteriorate into something different through the passage of time.

Modern colour printing by lithography is prone to marked differences of shade, even within a single run, and variations can occur within the same sheet. Such shades are not listed.

Aniline colours. An aniline colour meant originally one derived from coal-tar; it now refers more widely to colour of a particular brightness suffused on the surface of a stamp and showing through clearly on the back.

Colours of overprints and surcharges. All overprints and surcharges are in black unless stated otherwise in the heading or after the description of the stamp.

7. Specimen Stamps
Originally, stamps overprinted SPECIMEN were circulated to postmasters or kept in official records, but after the establishment of the Universal Postal Union supplies were sent to Berne for distribution to the postal administrations of member countries.

During the period 1884 to 1928 most of the stamps of British Crown Colonies required for this purpose were overprinted SPECIMEN in various shapes and sizes by their printers from typeset formes. Some locally produced provisionals were handstamped locally, as were sets prepared for presentation. From 1928 stamps were punched with holes forming the word SPECIMEN, each firm of printers using a different machine or machines. From 1948 the stamps supplied for UPU distribution were no longer punctured.

Stamps of some other Commonwealth territories were overprinted or handstamped locally, while stamps of Great Britain and those overprinted for use in overseas postal agencies (mostly of the higher denominations) bore SPECIMEN overprints and handstamps applied by the Inland Revenue or the Post Office.

SPECIMEN   SPECIMEN
De La Rue & Co. Ltd.

SPECIMEN.   SPECIMEN.
Bradbury, Wilkinson & Co. Ltd.

SPECIMEN   SPECIMEN
Waterlow & Sons Ltd.

SPECIMEN   SPECIMEN   SPECIMEN
Great Britain overprints

Some of the commoner types of overprints or punctures are illustrated here. Collectors are warned that dangerous forgeries of the punctured type exist.

The *Stanley Gibbons Commonwealth Catalogues* record those Specimen overprints or perforations intended for distribution by the UPU to member countries. In addition the Specimen overprints of Australia and its dependent territories, which were sold to collectors by the Post Office, are also included.

Various Perkins Bacon issues exist obliterated with a "CANCELLED" within an oval of bars handstamp.

(CANCELLED)

Perkins Bacon "CANCELLED" Handstamp

This was applied to six examples of those issues available in 1861 which were then given to members of Sir Rowland Hill's family. 75 different stamps (including four from Chile) are recorded with this handstamp although others may possibly exist. The unauthorised gift of these "CANCELLED" stamps to the Hill family was a major factor in the loss of the Agent General for the Crown Colonies (the forerunner of the Crown Agents) contracts by Perkins Bacon in the following year. Where examples of these scarce items are known to be in private hands the catalogue provides a price.

For full details of these stamps see *CANCELLED by Perkins Bacon* by Peter Jaffé (published by Spink in 1998).

All other Specimens are outside the scope of this volume.

Specimens are not quoted in Great Britain as they are fully listed in the Stanley Gibbons *Great Britain Specialised Catalogue*.

Information and Guidelines

In specifying type of specimen for individual high-value stamps, "H/S" means handstamped, "Optd" is overprinted and "Perf" is punctured. Some sets occur mixed, e.g. "Optd/Perf". If unspecified, the type is apparent from the date or it is the same as for the lower values quoted as a set.

Prices. Prices for stamps up to £1 are quoted in sets; higher values are priced singly. Where specimens exist in more than one type the price quoted is for the cheapest. Specimen stamps have rarely survived even as pairs; these and strips of three, four or five are worth considerably more than singles.

8. Luminescence

Machines which sort mail electronically have been introduced in recent years. In consequence some countries have issued stamps on flourescent or phosphorescent papers, while others have marked their stamps with phosphor bands.

The various papers can only be distinguished by ultraviolet lamps emitting particular wavelengths. They are separately listed only when the stamps have some other means of distinguishing them, visible without the use of these lamps. Where this is not so, the papers are recorded in footnotes or headings.

For this catalogue we do not consider it appropriate that collectors be compelled to have the use of an ultraviolet lamp before being able to identify stamps by our listings. Some experience will also be found necessary in interpreting the results given by ultraviolet. Collectors using the lamps, nevertheless, should exercise great care in their use as exposure to their light is potentially dangerous to the eyes.

Phosphor bands are listable, since they are visible to the naked eye (by holding stamps at an angle to the light and looking along them, the bands appear dark). Stamps existing with or without phosphor bands or with differing numbers of bands are given separate listings. Varieties such as double bands, bands omitted, misplaced or printed on the back are not listed.

Detailed descriptions appear at appropriate places in the listings in explanation of luminescent papers; see, for example, Australia above No.363, Canada above Nos. 472 and 611, Cook Is. above 249, etc.

For Great Britain, where since 1959 phosphors have played a prominent and intricate part in stamp issues, the main notes above Nos. 599 and 723 should be studied, as well as the footnotes to individual listings where appropriate. In general the classification is as follows.

Stamps with phosphor bands are those where a separate cylinder applies the phosphor after the stamps are printed. Issues with "all-over" phosphor have the "band" covering the entire stamp. Parts of the stamp covered by phosphor bands, or the entire surface for "all-over" phosphor versions, appear matt. Stamps on phosphorised paper have the phosphor added to the paper coating before the stamps are printed. Issues on this paper have a completely shiny surface.

Further particularisation of phosphor – their methods of printing and the colours they exhibit under ultraviolet – is outside the scope. The more specialised listings should be consulted for this information.

9. Coil Stamps

Stamps issued only in coil form are given full listing. If stamps are issued in both sheets and coils the coil stamps are listed separately only where there is some feature (e.g. perforation or watermark sideways) by which singles can be distinguished. Coil stamps containing different stamps *se-tenant* are also listed.

Coil join pairs are too random and too easily faked to permit of listing; similarly ignored are coil stamps which have accidentally suffered an extra row of perforations from the claw mechanism in a malfunctioning vending machine.

10. Stamp Booklets

Stamp booklets are now listed in this catalogue.

Single stamps from booklets are listed if they are distinguishable in some way (such as watermark or perforation) from similar sheet stamps.

Booklet panes are listed where they contain stamps of different denominations *se-tenant*, where stamp-size labels are included, or where such panes are otherwise identifiable. Booklet panes are placed in the listing under the lowest denomination present.

Particular perforations (straight edges) are covered by appropriate notes.

11. Miniature Sheets and Sheetlets

We distinguish between "miniature sheets" and "sheetlets" and this affects the catalogue numbering. An item in sheet form that is postally valid, containing a single stamp, pair, block or set of stamps, with wide, inscribed and/or decorative margins, is a miniature sheet if it is sold at post offices as an indivisible entity. As such the Catalogue allots a single MS number and describes what stamps make it up. The sheetlet or small sheet differs in that the individual stamps are intended to be purchased separately for postal purposes. For sheetlets, all the component postage stamps are numbered individually and the composition explained in a footnote. Note that the definitions refer to post office sale—not how items may be subsequently offered by stamp dealers.

12. Forgeries and Fakes

Forgeries. Where space permits, notes are considered if they can give a concise description that will permit unequivocal detection of a forgery. Generalised warnings, lacking detail, are not nowadays inserted, since their value to the collector is problematic.

Forged cancellations have also been applied to genuine stamps. This catalogue includes notes regarding those manufactured by "Madame Joseph", together with the cancellation dates known to exist. It should be remembered that these dates also exist as genuine cancellations.

For full details of these see *Madame Joseph Forged Postmarks* by Derek Worboys (published by the Royal Philatelic Society London and the British Philatelic Trust in 1994) or *Madame Joseph Revisited* by Brian Cartwright (published by the Royal Philatelic Society London in 2005).

Fakes. Unwitting fakes are numerous, particularly "new shades" which are colour changelings brought about by exposure to sunlight, soaking in water contaminated with dyes from adherent paper, contact with oil and dirt from a pocketbook, and so on. Fraudulent operators, in addition, can offer to arrange: removal of hinge marks; repairs of thins on white or coloured papers; replacement of missing margins or perforations; reperforating in true or false gauges; removal of fiscal cancellations; rejoining of severed pairs, strips and blocks; and (a major hazard) regumming. Collectors can only be urged to purchase from reputable sources and to insist upon Expert Committee certification where there is any kind of doubt.

The Catalogue can consider footnotes about fakes where these are specific enough to assist in detection.

Abbreviations

Printers
A.B.N. Co.	American Bank Note Co, New York.
B.A.B.N.	British American Bank Note Co. Ottawa
B.D.T.	B.D.T. International Security Printing Ltd, Dublin, Ireland
B.W.	Bradbury Wilkinson & Co, Ltd.
Cartor	Cartor S.A., La Loupe, France
C.B.N.	Canadian Bank Note Co, Ottawa.
Continental	Continental Bank Note Co. B.N. Co.
Courvoisier	Imprimerie Courvoisier S.A., La-Chaux-de-Fonds, Switzerland.
D.L.R.	De La Rue & Co, Ltd, London.
Enschedé	Joh. Enschedé en Zonen, Haarlem, Netherlands.
Format	Format International Security Printers Ltd., London
Harrison	Harrison & Sons, Ltd. London
J.W.	John Waddington Security Print Ltd., Leeds
P.B.	Perkins Bacon Ltd, London.
Questa	Questa Colour Security Printers Ltd, London
Walsall	Walsall Security Printers Ltd
Waterlow	Waterlow & Sons, Ltd, London.

General Abbreviations
Alph	Alphabet
Anniv	Anniversary
Comp	Compound (perforation)
Des	Designer; designed
Diag	Diagonal; diagonally
Eng	Engraver; engraved
F.C.	Fiscal Cancellation
H/S	Handstamped
Horiz	Horizontal; horizontally
Imp, Imperf	Imperforate
Inscr	Inscribed
L	Left
Litho	Lithographed
mm	Millimetres
MS	Miniature sheet
N.Y.	New York
Opt(d)	Overprint(ed)
P or P-c	Pen-cancelled
P, Pf or Perf	Perforated
Photo	Photogravure
Pl	Plate
Pr	Pair
Ptd	Printed
Ptg	Printing
R	Right
R.	Row
Recess	Recess-printed
Roto	Rotogravure
Roul	Rouletted
S	Specimen (overprint)
Surch	Surcharge(d)
T.C.	Telegraph Cancellation
T	Type
Typo	Typographed
Un	Unused
Us	Used
Vert	Vertical; vertically
W or wmk	Watermark
Wmk s	Watermark sideways

(†) = Does not exist
(–) (or blank price column) = Exists, or may exist, but no market price is known.
/ between colours means "on" and the colour following is that of the paper on which the stamp is printed.

Colours of Stamps
Bl (blue); blk (black); brn (brown); car, carm (carmine); choc (chocolate); clar (claret); emer (emerald); grn (green); ind (indigo); mag (magenta); mar (maroon); mult (multicoloured); mve (mauve); ol (olive); orge (orange); pk (pink); pur (purple); scar (scarlet); sep (sepia); turq (turquoise); ultram (ultramarine); verm (vermilion); vio (violet); yell (yellow).

Colour of Overprints and Surcharges
(B.) = blue, (Blk.) = black, (Br.) = brown, (C.) = carmine, (G.) = green, (Mag.) = magenta, (Mve.) = mauve, (Ol.) = olive, (O.) = orange, (P.) = purple, (Pk.) = pink, (R.) = red, (Sil.) = silver, (V.) = violet, (Vm.) or (Verm.) = vermilion, (W.) = white, (Y.) = yellow.

Arabic Numerals
As in the case of European figures, the details of the Arabic numerals vary in different stamp designs, but they should be readily recognised with the aid of this illustration.

٠ ١ ٢ ٣ ٤ ٥ ٦ ٧ ٨ ٩
0 1 2 3 4 5 6 7 8 9

Features Listing

An at-a-glance guide to what's in the Stanley Gibbons catalogues

Area	Feature	Collect British Stamps	Stamps of the World	Thematic Catalogues	Stamps and country catalogues) and British Empire Commonwealth	Comprehensive Catalogue, Parts 1-22 (including	Great Britain Concise	Specialised catalogues
General	SG number	√	√	√		√	√	√
General	Specialised Catalogue number							√
General	Year of issue of first stamp in design	√	√	√		√	√	√
General	Exact date of issue of each design					√	√	√
General	Face value information	√	√	√		√	√	√
General	Historical and geographical information	√	√	√		√	√	√
General	General currency information, including dates used	√	√	√		√	√	√
General	Country name	√	√	√		√	√	√
General	Booklet panes					√	√	√
General	Coil stamps					√		√
General	First Day Covers	√					√	√
General	Brief footnotes on key areas of note	√	√	√		√	√	√
General	Detailed footnotes on key areas of note					√	√	√
General	Extra background information					√	√	√
General	Miniature sheet information (including size in mm)	√	√	√		√	√	√
General	Sheetlets					√		
General	Stamp booklets					√	√	√
General	Perkins Bacon "Cancelled"					√		
General	PHQ Cards	√					√	√
General	Post Office Label Sheets						√	
General	Post Office Yearbooks	√					√	√
General	Presentation and Souvenir Packs	√					√	√
General	*Se-tenant* pairs	√				√	√	√
General	Watermark details - errors, varieties, positions					√	√	√
General	Watermark illustrations	√				√	√	√
General	Watermark types	√				√	√	√
General	Forgeries noted					√		√
General	Surcharges and overprint information	√	√	√		√	√	√
Design and Description	Colour description, simplified		√	√				
Design and Description	Colour description, extended	√				√	√	√
Design and Description	Set design summary information	√	√	√		√	√	√
Design and Description	Designer name						√	√	√
Design and Description	Short design description	√	√	√		√	√	√

Features Listing

Area	Feature	Collect British Stamps	Stamps of the World	Thematic Catalogues	Comprehensive Catalogue, Parts 1-22 (including Commonwealth and British Empire Stamps and country catalogues)	Great Britain Concise	Specialised catalogues
Design and Description	Shade varieties				√	√	√
Design and Description	Type number	√	√		√	√	√
Illustrations	Multiple stamps from set illustrated	√			√	√	√
Illustrations	A Stamp from each set illustrated in full colour (where possible, otherwise mono)	√	√	√	√	√	√
Price	Catalogue used price	√	√	√	√	√	√
Price	Catalogue unused price	√	√	√	√	√	√
Price	Price - booklet panes				√	√	√
Price	Price - shade varieties				√	√	√
Price	On cover and on piece price				√	√	√
Price	Detailed GB pricing breakdown	√			√	√	√
Print and Paper	Basic printing process information	√	√	√	√	√	√
Print and Paper	Detailed printing process information, e.g. Mill sheets				√		√
Print and Paper	Paper information				√		√
Print and Paper	Detailed perforation information	√			√	√	√
Print and Paper	Details of research findings relating to printing processes and history						√
Print and Paper	Paper colour	√	√		√	√	√
Print and Paper	Paper description to aid identification				√	√	√
Print and Paper	Paper type				√	√	√
Print and Paper	Ordinary or chalk-surfaced paper				√	√	√
Print and Paper	Embossing omitted note						√
Print and Paper	Essays, Die Proofs, Plate Descriptions and Proofs, Colour Trials information						√
Print and Paper	Glazed paper				√	√	√
Print and Paper	Gum details				√		√
Print and Paper	Luminescence/Phosphor bands - general coverage	√			√	√	√
Print and Paper	Luminescence/Phosphor bands - specialised coverage						√
Print and Paper	Overprints and surcharges - including colour information	√	√	√	√	√	√
Print and Paper	Perforation/Imperforate information	√	√		√	√	√
Print and Paper	Perforation errors and varieties				√	√	√
Print and Paper	Print quantities				√		
Print and Paper	Printing errors				√	√	√
Print and Paper	Printing flaws						√
Print and Paper	Printing varieties				√	√	√
Print and Paper	Punctured stamps - where official				√		
Print and Paper	Sheet positions				√	√	√
Print and Paper	Specialised plate number information						√
Print and Paper	Specimen overprints (only for Commonwealth & GB)				√	√	√
Print and Paper	Underprints					√	√
Print and Paper	Visible Plate numbers	√			√	√	√
Print and Paper	Yellow and Green paper listings				√		√
Index	Design index	√			√	√	

xxiii

Thinking of selling all or part of your collection?

Contact us today in order to make the most of strong auction realisations in the current market

- Reach over 200,000 potential buyers
- The largest philatelic audience in the UK
- Unrivalled expertise in the field of philately
- 100% exceptional clearance rate
- Download each catalogue for FREE
- We can offer featured write-ups about any auction in GSM
- Confidence and trust make Stanley Gibbons Auctions the first port of call for people selling their collections
- Auctions hosted on www.stanleygibbons.com, offering massive worldwide exposure

Consignments are always considered for auction
Contact us today to get the best price for your collection

All World, specialised and one vendor sales

Postal auction lots from £5 - £5,000

Mixed lots, boxes and One Country Albums

Est 1856
STANLEY GIBBONS

Stanley Gibbons Auction Department
399 Strand, London WC2R 0LX
Contact Ryan Epps or Steve Matthews on Tel: +44 (0)20 7836 8444
Fax: +44 (0)20 7836 7742 | Email: auctions@stanleygibbons.co.uk
www.stanleygibbons.com/auctions

International Philatelic Glossary

English	French	German	Spanish	Italian
Agate	Agate	Achat	Agata	Agata
Air stamp	Timbre de la poste aérienne	Flugpostmarke	Sello de correo aéreo	Francobollo per posta aerea
Apple Green	Vert-pomme	Apfelgrün	Verde manzana	Verde mela
Barred	Annulé par barres	Balkenentwertung	Anulado con barras	Sbarrato
Bisected	Timbre coupé	Halbiert	Partido en dos	Frazionato
Bistre	Bistre	Bister	Bistre	Bistro
Bistre-brown	Brun-bistre	Bisterbraun	Castaño bistre	Bruno-bistro
Black	Noir	Schwarz	Negro	Nero
Blackish Brown	Brun-noir	Schwärzlichbraun	Castaño negruzco	Bruno nerastro
Blackish Green	Vert foncé	Schwärzlichgrün	Verde negruzco	Verde nerastro
Blackish Olive	Olive foncé	Schwärzlicholiv	Oliva negruzco	Oliva nerastro
Block of four	Bloc de quatre	Viererblock	Bloque de cuatro	Bloco di quattro
Blue	Bleu	Blau	Azul	Azzurro
Blue-green	Vert-bleu	Blaugrün	Verde azul	Verde azzuro
Bluish Violet	Violet bleuâtre	Bläulichviolett	Violeta azulado	Vioitto azzurrastro
Booklet	Carnet	Heft	Cuadernillo	Libretto
Bright Blue	Bleu vif	Lebhaftblau	Azul vivo	Azzurro vivo
Bright Green	Vert vif	Lebhaftgrün	Verde vivo	Verde vivo
Bright Purple	Mauve vif	Lebhaftpurpur	Púrpura vivo	Porpora vivo
Bronze Green	Vert-bronze	Bronzegrün	Verde bronce	Verde bronzo
Brown	Brun	Braun	Castaño	Bruno
Brown-lake	Carmin-brun	Braunlack	Laca castaño	Lacca bruno
Brown-purple	Pourpre-brun	Braunpurpur	Púrpura castaño	Porpora bruno
Brown-red	Rouge-brun	Braunrot	Rojo castaño	Rosso bruno
Buff	Chamois	Sämisch	Anteado	Camoscio
Cancellation	Oblitération	Entwertung	Cancelación	Annullamento
Cancelled	Annulé	Gestempelt	Cancelado	Annullato
Carmine	Carmin	Karmin	Carmín	Carminio
Carmine-red	Rouge-carmin	Karminrot	Rojo carmín	Rosso carminio
Centred	Centré	Zentriert	Centrado	Centrato
Cerise	Rouge-cerise	Kirschrot	Color de ceresa	Color Ciliegia
Chalk-surfaced paper	Papier couché	Kreidepapier	Papel estucado	Carta gessata
Chalky Blue	Bleu terne	Kreideblau	Azul turbio	Azzurro smorto
Charity stamp	Timbre de bienfaisance	Wohltätigkeitsmarke	Sello de beneficenza	Francobollo di beneficenza
Chestnut	Marron	Kastanienbraun	Castaño rojo	Marrone
Chocolate	Chocolat	Schokolade	Chocolate	Cioccolato
Cinnamon	Cannelle	Zimtbraun	Canela	Cannella
Claret	Grenat	Weinrot	Rojo vinoso	Vinaccia
Cobalt	Cobalt	Kobalt	Cobalto	Cobalto
Colour	Couleur	Farbe	Color	Colore
Comb-perforation	Dentelure en peigne	Kammzähnung, Reihenzähnung	Dentado de peine	Dentellatura e pettine
Commemorative stamp	Timbre commémoratif	Gedenkmarke	Sello conmemorativo	Francobollo commemorativo
Crimson	Cramoisi	Karmesin	Carmesí	Cremisi
Deep Blue	Blue foncé	Dunkelblau	Azul oscuro	Azzurro scuro
Deep bluish Green	Vert-bleu foncé	Dunkelbläulichgrün	Verde azulado oscuro	Verde azzurro scuro

xxv

International Philatelic Glossary

English	French	German	Spanish	Italian
Design	Dessin	Markenbild	Diseño	Disegno
Die	Matrice	Urstempel. Type, Platte	Cuño	Conio, Matrice
Double	Double	Doppelt	Doble	Doppio
Drab	Olive terne	Trüboliv	Oliva turbio	Oliva smorto
Dull Green	Vert terne	Trübgrün	Verde turbio	Verde smorto
Dull purple	Mauve terne	Trübpurpur	Púrpura turbio	Porpora smorto
Embossing	Impression en relief	Prägedruck	Impresión en relieve	Impressione a relievo
Emerald	Vert-eméraude	Smaragdgrün	Esmeralda	Smeraldo
Engraved	Gravé	Graviert	Grabado	Inciso
Error	Erreur	Fehler, Fehldruck	Error	Errore
Essay	Essai	Probedruck	Ensayo	Saggio
Express letter stamp	Timbre pour lettres par exprès	Eilmarke	Sello de urgencia	Francobollo per espresso
Fiscal stamp	Timbre fiscal	Stempelmarke	Sello fiscal	Francobollo fiscale
Flesh	Chair	Fleischfarben	Carne	Carnicino
Forgery	Faux, Falsification	Fälschung	Falsificación	Falso, Falsificazione
Frame	Cadre	Rahmen	Marco	Cornice
Granite paper	Papier avec fragments de fils de soie	Faserpapier	Papel con filamentos	Carto con fili di seta
Green	Vert	Grün	Verde	Verde
Greenish Blue	Bleu verdâtre	Grünlichblau	Azul verdoso	Azzurro verdastro
Greenish Yellow	Jaune-vert	Grünlichgelb	Amarillo verdoso	Giallo verdastro
Grey	Gris	Grau	Gris	Grigio
Grey-blue	Bleu-gris	Graublau	Azul gris	Azzurro grigio
Grey-green	Vert gris	Graugrün	Verde gris	Verde grigio
Gum	Gomme	Gummi	Goma	Gomma
Gutter	Interpanneau	Zwischensteg	Espacio blanco entre dos grupos	Ponte
Imperforate	Non-dentelé	Geschnitten	Sin dentar	Non dentellato
Indigo	Indigo	Indigo	Azul indigo	Indaco
Inscription	Inscription	Inschrift	Inscripción	Dicitura
Inverted	Renversé	Kopfstehend	Invertido	Capovolto
Issue	Émission	Ausgabe	Emisión	Emissione
Laid	Vergé	Gestreift	Listado	Vergato
Lake	Lie de vin	Lackfarbe	Laca	Lacca
Lake-brown	Brun-carmin	Lackbraun	Castaño laca	Bruno lacca
Lavender	Bleu-lavande	Lavendel	Color de alhucema	Lavanda
Lemon	Jaune-citron	Zitrongelb	Limón	Limone
Light Blue	Bleu clair	Hellblau	Azul claro	Azzurro chiaro
Lilac	Lilas	Lila	Lila	Lilla
Line perforation	Dentelure en lignes	Linienzähnung	Dentado en linea	Dentellatura lineare
Lithography	Lithographie	Steindruck	Litografía	Litografia
Local	Timbre de poste locale	Lokalpostmarke	Emisión local	Emissione locale
Lozenge roulette	Percé en losanges	Rautenförmiger Durchstich	Picadura en rombos	Perforazione a losanghe
Magenta	Magenta	Magentarot	Magenta	Magenta
Margin	Marge	Rand	Borde	Margine
Maroon	Marron pourpré	Dunkelrotpurpur	Púrpura rojo oscuro	Marrone rossastro
Mauve	Mauve	Malvenfarbe	Malva	Malva
Multicoloured	Polychrome	Mehrfarbig	Multicolores	Policromo
Myrtle Green	Vert myrte	Myrtengrün	Verde mirto	Verde mirto
New Blue	Bleu ciel vif	Neublau	Azul nuevo	Azzurro nuovo
Newspaper stamp	Timbre pour journaux	Zeitungsmarke	Sello para periódicos	Francobollo per giornali

International Philatelic Glossary

English	French	German	Spanish	Italian
Obliteration	Oblitération	Abstempelung	Matasello	Annullamento
Obsolete	Hors (de) cours	Ausser Kurs	Fuera de curso	Fuori corso
Ochre	Ocre	Ocker	Ocre	Ocra
Official stamp	Timbre de service	Dienstmarke	Sello de servicio	Francobollo di
Olive-brown	Brun-olive	Olivbraun	Castaño oliva	Bruno oliva
Olive-green	Vert-olive	Olivgrün	Verde oliva	Verde oliva
Olive-grey	Gris-olive	Olivgrau	Gris oliva	Grigio oliva
Olive-yellow	Jaune-olive	Olivgelb	Amarillo oliva	Giallo oliva
Orange	Orange	Orange	Naranja	Arancio
Orange-brown	Brun-orange	Orangebraun	Castaño naranja	Bruno arancio
Orange-red	Rouge-orange	Orangerot	Rojo naranja	Rosso arancio
Orange-yellow	Jaune-orange	Orangegelb	Amarillo naranja	Giallo arancio
Overprint	Surcharge	Aufdruck	Sobrecarga	Soprastampa
Pair	Paire	Paar	Pareja	Coppia
Pale	Pâle	Blass	Pálido	Pallido
Pane	Panneau	Gruppe	Grupo	Gruppo
Paper	Papier	Papier	Papel	Carta
Parcel post stamp	Timbre pour colis postaux	Paketmarke	Sello para paquete postal	Francobollo per pacchi postali
Pen-cancelled	Oblitéré à plume	Federzugentwertung	Cancelado a pluma	Annullato a penna
Percé en arc	Percé en arc	Bogenförmiger Durchstich	Picadura en forma de arco	Perforazione ad arco
Percé en scie	Percé en scie	Bogenförmiger Durchstich	Picado en sierra	Foratura a sega
Perforated	Dentelé	Gezähnt	Dentado	Dentellato
Perforation	Dentelure	Zähnung	Dentar	Dentellatura
Photogravure	Photogravure, Heliogravure	Rastertiefdruck	Fotograbado	Rotocalco
Pin perforation	Percé en points	In Punkten durchstochen	Horadado con alfileres	Perforato a punti
Plate	Planche	Platte	Plancha	Lastra, Tavola
Plum	Prune	Pflaumenfarbe	Color de ciruela	Prugna
Postage Due stamp	Timbre-taxe	Portomarke	Sello de tasa	Segnatasse
Postage stamp	Timbre-poste	Briefmarke, Freimarke, Postmarke	Sello de correos	Francobollo postale
Postal fiscal stamp	Timbre fiscal-postal	Stempelmarke als Postmarke verwendet	Sello fiscal-postal	Fiscale postale
Postmark	Oblitération postale	Poststempel	Matasello	Bollo
Printing	Impression, Tirage	Druck	Impresión	Stampa, Tiratura
Proof	Épreuve	Druckprobe	Prueba de impresión	Prova
Provisionals	Timbres provisoires	Provisorische Marken. Provisorien	Provisionales	Provvisori
Prussian Blue	Bleu de Prusse	Preussischblau	Azul de Prusia	Azzurro di Prussia
Purple	Pourpre	Purpur	Púrpura	Porpora
Purple-brown	Brun-pourpre	Purpurbraun	Castaño púrpura	Bruno porpora
Recess-printing	Impression en taille douce	Tiefdruck	Grabado	Incisione
Red	Rouge	Rot	Rojo	Rosso
Red-brown	Brun-rouge	Rotbraun	Castaño rojizo	Bruno rosso
Reddish Lilac	Lilas rougeâtre	Rötlichlila	Lila rojizo	Lilla rossastro
Reddish Purple	Poupre-rouge	Rötlichpurpur	Púrpura rojizo	Porpora rossastro
Reddish Violet	Violet rougeâtre	Rötlichviolett	Violeta rojizo	Violetto rossastro
Red-orange	Orange rougeâtre	Rotorange	Naranja rojizo	Arancio rosso
Registration stamp	Timbre pour lettre chargée (recommandée)	Einschreibemarke	Sello de certificado lettere	Francobollo per raccomandate
Reprint	Réimpression	Neudruck	Reimpresión	Ristampa
Reversed	Retourné	Umgekehrt	Invertido	Rovesciato

xxvii

International Philatelic Glossary

English	French	German	Spanish	Italian
Rose	Rose	Rosa	Rosa	Rosa
Rose-red	Rouge rosé	Rosarot	Rojo rosado	Rosso rosa
Rosine	Rose vif	Lebhaftrosa	Rosa vivo	Rosa vivo
Roulette	Percage	Durchstich	Picadura	Foratura
Rouletted	Percé	Durchstochen	Picado	Forato
Royal Blue	Bleu-roi	Königblau	Azul real	Azzurro reale
Sage green	Vert-sauge	Salbeigrün	Verde salvia	Verde salvia
Salmon	Saumon	Lachs	Salmón	Salmone
Scarlet	Écarlate	Scharlach	Escarlata	Scarlatto
Sepia	Sépia	Sepia	Sepia	Seppia
Serpentine roulette	Percé en serpentin	Schlangenliniger Durchstich	Picado a serpentina	Perforazione a serpentina
Shade	Nuance	Tönung	Tono	Gradazione de colore
Sheet	Feuille	Bogen	Hoja	Foglio
Slate	Ardoise	Schiefer	Pizarra	Ardesia
Slate-blue	Bleu-ardoise	Schieferblau	Azul pizarra	Azzurro ardesia
Slate-green	Vert-ardoise	Schiefergrün	Verde pizarra	Verde ardesia
Slate-lilac	Lilas-gris	Schierferlila	Lila pizarra	Lilla ardesia
Slate-purple	Mauve-gris	Schieferpurpur	Púrpura pizarra	Porpora ardesia
Slate-violet	Violet-gris	Schieferviolett	Violeta pizarra	Violetto ardesia
Special delivery stamp	Timbre pour exprès	Eilmarke	Sello de urgencia	Francobollo per espressi
Specimen	Spécimen	Muster	Muestra	Saggio
Steel Blue	Bleu acier	Stahlblau	Azul acero	Azzurro acciaio
Strip	Bande	Streifen	Tira	Striscia
Surcharge	Surcharge	Aufdruck	Sobrecarga	Soprastampa
Tête-bêche	Tête-bêche	Kehrdruck	Tête-bêche	Tête-bêche
Tinted paper	Papier teinté	Getöntes Papier	Papel coloreado	Carta tinta
Too-late stamp	Timbre pour lettres en retard	Verspätungsmarke	Sello para cartas retardadas	Francobollo per le lettere in ritardo
Turquoise-blue	Bleu-turquoise	Türkisblau	Azul turquesa	Azzurro turchese
Turquoise-green	Vert-turquoise	Türkisgrün	Verde turquesa	Verde turchese
Typography	Typographie	Buchdruck	Tipografia	Tipografia
Ultramarine	Outremer	Ultramarin	Ultramar	Oltremare
Unused	Neuf	Ungebraucht	Nuevo	Nuovo
Used	Oblitéré, Usé	Gebraucht	Usado	Usato
Venetian Red	Rouge-brun terne	Venezianischrot	Rojo veneciano	Rosso veneziano
Vermilion	Vermillon	Zinnober	Cinabrio	Vermiglione
Violet	Violet	Violett	Violeta	Violetto
Violet-blue	Bleu-violet	Violettblau	Azul violeta	Azzurro violetto
Watermark	Filigrane	Wasserzeichen	Filigrana	Filigrana
Watermark sideways	Filigrane couché liegend	Wasserzeichen	Filigrana acostado	Filigrana coricata
Wove paper	Papier ordinaire, Papier uni	Einfaches Papier	Papel avitelado	Carta unita
Yellow	Jaune	Gelb	Amarillo	Giallo
Yellow-brown	Brun-jaune	Gelbbraun	Castaño amarillo	Bruno giallo
Yellow-green	Vert-jaune	Gelbgrün	Verde amarillo	Verde giallo
Yellow-olive	Olive-jaunâtre	Gelboliv	Oliva amarillo	Oliva giallastro
Yellow-orange	Orange jaunâtre	Gelborange	Naranja amarillo	Arancio giallastro
Zig-zag roulette	Percé en zigzag	Sägezahnartiger Durchstich	Picado en zigzag	Perforazione a zigzag

STANLEY GIBBONS
Est 1856

About Us

Our History
Edward Stanley Gibbons started trading postage stamps in his father's chemist shop in 1856. Since then we have been at the forefront of stamp collecting for over 150 years. We hold the Royal Warrant, offer unsurpassed expertise and quality and provide collectors with the peace of mind of a certificate of authenticity on all of our stamps. If you think of stamp collecting, you think of Stanley Gibbons and we are proud to uphold that tradition for you.

399 Strand
Our world famous stamp shop is a collector's paradise, with all of our latest catalogues, albums and accessories and, of course, our unrivalled stockholding of postage stamps.

www.stanleygibbons.com   shop@stanleygibbons.co.uk   +44 (0)20 7836 8444

Specialist Stamp Sales
For the collector that appreciates the value of collecting the highest quality examples, Stanley Gibbons is the only choice. Our extensive range is unrivalled in terms of quality and quantity, with specialist stamps available from all over the world.

www.stanleygibbons.com/stamps   shop@stanleygibbons.co.uk   +44 (0)20 7836 8444

Stanley Gibbons Auctions and Valuations
Sell your collection or individual rare items through our prestigious public auctions or our regular postal auctions and benefit from the excellent prices being realised at auction currently. We also provide an unparalleled valuation service.

www.stanleygibbons.com/auctions   auctions@stanleygibbons.co.uk   +44 (0)20 7836 8444

Stanley Gibbons Publications
The world's first stamp catalogue was printed by Stanley Gibbons in 1865 and we haven't looked back since! Our catalogues are trusted worldwide as the industry standard and we print countless titles each year. We also publish consumer and trade magazines, Gibbons Stamp Monthly and Philatelic Exporter to bring you news, views and insights into all things philatelic. Never miss an issue by subscribing today and benefit from exclusive subscriber offers each month.

www.stanleygibbons.com/shop   orders@stanleygibbons.co.uk   +44 (0)1425 472 363

Stanley Gibbons Investments
The Stanley Gibbons Investment Department offers a unique range of investment propositions that have consistently outperformed more traditional forms of investment, from capital protected products with unlimited upside to portfolios made up of the world's rarest stamps and autographs.

www.stanleygibbons.com/investment   investment@stanleygibbons.co.uk   +44 (0)1481 708 270

Fraser's Autographs
Autographs, manuscripts and memorabilia from Henry VIII to current day. We have over 60,000 items in stock, including movie stars, musicians, sport stars, historical figures and royalty. Fraser's is the UK's market leading autograph dealer and has been dealing in high quality autographed material since 1978.

www.frasersautographs.com   sales@frasersautographs.co.uk   +44 (0)20 7557 4404

stanleygibbons.com
Our website offers the complete philatelic service. Whether you are looking to buy stamps, invest, read news articles, browse our online stamp catalogue or find new issues, you are just one click away from anything you desire in the world of stamp collecting at stanleygibbons.com. Happy browsing!

www.stanleygibbons.com

Guide to Entries

(A) Country of Issue – When a country changes its name, the catalogue listing changes to reflect the name change, for example Namibia was formerly known as South West Africa, the stamps in Southern Africa are all listed under Namibia, but split into South West Africa and then Namibia.

(B) Country Information – Brief geographical and historical details for the issuing country.

(C) Currency – Details of the currency, and dates of earliest use where applicable, on the face value of the stamps.

(D) Illustration – Generally, the first stamp in the set. Stamp illustrations are reduced to 75%, with overprints and surcharges shown actual size.

(E) Illustration or Type Number – These numbers are used to help identify stamps, either in the listing, type column, design line or footnote, usually the first value in a set. These type numbers are in a bold type face – **123**; when bracketed (**123**) an overprint or a surcharge is indicated. Some type numbers include a lower-case letter – **123a**, this indicates they have been added to an existing set.

(F) Date of issue – This is the date that the stamp/set of stamps was issued by the post office and was available for purchase. When a set of definitive stamps has been issued over several years the Year Date given is for the earliest issue. Commemorative sets are listed in chronological order. Stamps of the same design, or issue are usually grouped together, for example some of the New Zealand landscapes definitive series were first issued in 2003 but the set includes stamps issued to May 2007.

(G) Number Prefix – Stamps other than definitives and commemoratives have a prefix letter before the catalogue number.
Their use is explained in the text: some examples are A for airmail, D for postage due and O for official stamps.

(H) Footnote – Further information on background or key facts on issues.

(I) Stanley Gibbons Catalogue number – This is a unique number for each stamp to help the collector identify stamps in the listing. The Stanley Gibbons numbering system is universally recognized as definitive.
Where insufficient numbers have been left to provide for additional stamps to a listing, some stamps will have a suffix letter after the catalogue number (for example 214a). If numbers have been left for additions to a set and not used they will be left vacant.
The separate type numbers (in bold) refer to illustrations (see **E**).

(J) Colour – If a stamp is printed in three or fewer colours then the colours are listed, working from the centre of the stamp outwards (see **R**).

(K) Design line – Further details on design variations

(L) Key Type – Indicates a design type on which the stamp is based. These are the bold figures found below each illustration, for example listed in Cameroon, in the West Africa catalogue, is the Key type A and B showing the ex-Kaiser's yacht *Hohenzollern*. The type numbers are also given in bold in the second column of figures alongside the stamp description to indicate the design of each stamp. Where an issue comprises stamps of similar design, the corresponding type number should be taken as indicating the general design. Where there are blanks in the type number column it means that the type of the corresponding stamp is that shown by the number in the type column of the same issue. A dash (–) in the type column means that the stamp is not illustrated. Where type numbers refer to stamps of another country, e.g. where stamps of one country are overprinted for use in another, this is always made clear in the text.

(M) Coloured Papers – Stamps printed on coloured paper are shown – e.g. "brown/*yellow*" indicates brown printed on yellow paper.

(N) Surcharges and Overprints – Usually described in the headings. Any actual wordings are shown in bold type. Descriptions clarify words and figures used in the overprint. Stamps with the same overprints in different colours are not listed separately. Numbers in brackets after the descriptions are the catalogue numbers of the non-overprinted stamps. The words "inscribed" or "inscription" refer to the wording incorporated in the design of a stamp and not surcharges or overprints.

(O) Face value – This refers to the value of each stamp and is the price it was sold for at the Post Office when issued. Some modern stamps do not have their values in figures but instead it is shown as a letter, for example Great Britain use 1st or 2nd on their stamps as opposed to the actual value.

(P) Catalogue Value – Mint/Unused. Prices quoted for Queen Victoria to King George V stamps are for lightly hinged examples.

(Q) Catalogue Value – Used. Prices generally refer to fine postally used examples. For certain issues they are for cancelled-to-order.

Prices
Prices are given in pence and pounds. Stamps worth £100 and over are shown in whole pounds:

Shown in Catalogue as	Explanation
10	10 pence
1.75	£1.75
15.00	£15
£150	£150
£2300	£2300

Prices assume stamps are in 'fine condition'; we may ask more for superb and less for those of lower quality. The minimum catalogue price quoted is 10p and is intended as a guide for catalogue users. The lowest price for individual stamps purchased from Stanley Gibbons is £1.
Prices quoted are for the cheapest variety of that particular stamp. Differences of watermark, perforation, or other details, often increase the value. Prices quoted for mint issues are for single examples, unless otherwise stated. Those in *se-tenant* pairs, strips, blocks or sheets may be worth more. Where no prices are listed it is either because the stamps are not known to exist (usually shown by a †) in that particular condition, or, more usually, because there is no reliable information on which to base their value.
All prices are subject to change without prior notice and we cannot guarantee to supply all stamps as priced. Prices quoted in advertisements are also subject to change without prior notice.

(R) Multicoloured – Nearly all modern stamps are multicoloured (more than three colours); this is indicated in the heading, with a description of the stamp given in the listing.

(S) Perforations – Please see page xi for a detailed explanation of perforations.

Bangladesh

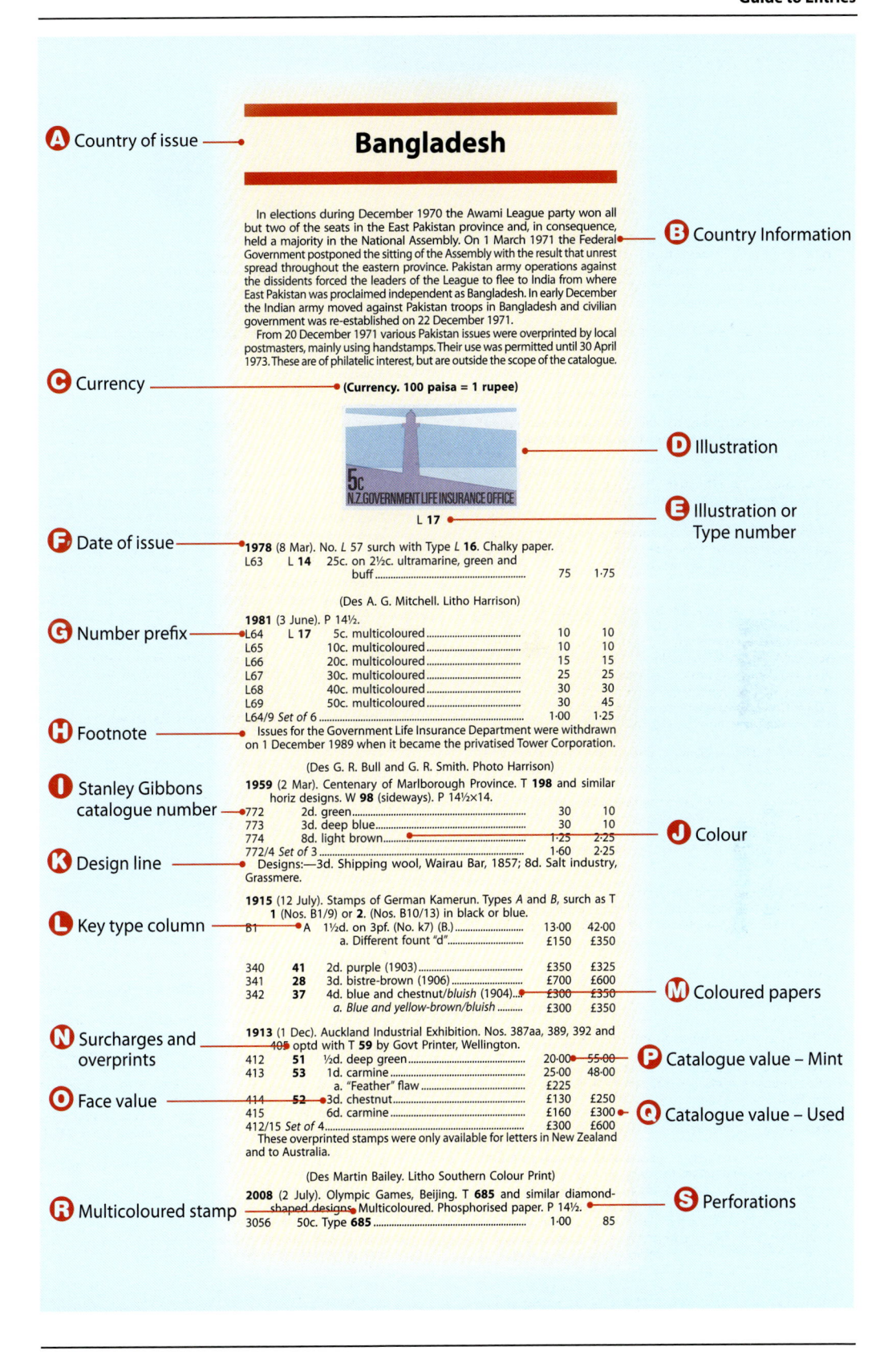

(A) Country of issue

(B) Country Information

In elections during December 1970 the Awami League party won all but two of the seats in the East Pakistan province and, in consequence, held a majority in the National Assembly. On 1 March 1971 the Federal Government postponed the sitting of the Assembly with the result that unrest spread throughout the eastern province. Pakistan army operations against the dissidents forced the leaders of the League to flee to India from where East Pakistan was proclaimed independent as Bangladesh. In early December the Indian army moved against Pakistan troops in Bangladesh and civilian government was re-established on 22 December 1971.

From 20 December 1971 various Pakistan issues were overprinted by local postmasters, mainly using handstamps. Their use was permitted until 30 April 1973. These are of philatelic interest, but are outside the scope of the catalogue.

(C) Currency — (Currency. 100 paisa = 1 rupee)

(D) Illustration

5c N.Z. GOVERNMENT LIFE INSURANCE OFFICE

L 17

(E) Illustration or Type number

(F) Date of issue

1978 (8 Mar). No. L 57 surch with Type L **16**. Chalky paper.
L63 L **14** 25c. on 2½c. ultramarine, green and
              buff 75   1·75

(Des A. G. Mitchell. Litho Harrison)

1981 (3 June). P 14½.
(G) Number prefix
L64 L **17** 5c. multicoloured 10   10
L65   10c. multicoloured 10   10
L66   20c. multicoloured 15   15
L67   30c. multicoloured 25   25
L68   40c. multicoloured 30   30
L69   50c. multicoloured 30   45
L64/9 Set of 6 .... 1·00 1·25

(H) Footnote — Issues for the Government Life Insurance Department were withdrawn on 1 December 1989 when it became the privatised Tower Corporation.

(Des G. R. Bull and G. R. Smith. Photo Harrison)

1959 (2 Mar). Centenary of Marlborough Province. T **198** and similar horiz designs. W **98** (sideways). P 14½×14.

(I) Stanley Gibbons catalogue number
772   2d. green 30   10
773   3d. deep blue 30   10
774   8d. light brown .... 1·25 2·25   **(J) Colour**
772/4 Set of 3 .... 1·60 2·25

(K) Design line — Designs:—3d. Shipping wool, Wairau Bar, 1857; 8d. Salt industry, Grassmere.

1915 (12 July). Stamps of German Kamerun. Types A and B, surch as T **1** (Nos. B1/9) or **2**. (Nos. B10/13) in black or blue.

(L) Key type column
B1   A   1½d. on 3pf. (No. k7) (B.) .... 13·00 42·00
          a. Different fount "d" £150   £350

340 **41** 2d. purple (1903) £350   £325
341 **28** 3d. bistre-brown (1906) £700   £600
342 **37** 4d. blue and chestnut/*bluish* (1904).. £300   £350   **(M) Coloured papers**
          a. Blue and yellow-brown/*bluish* £300   £350

1913 (1 Dec). Auckland Industrial Exhibition. Nos. 387aa, 389, 392 and 405 optd with T **59** by Govt Printer, Wellington.

(N) Surcharges and overprints
412 **51** ½d. deep green .... 20·00 55·00   **(P) Catalogue value – Mint**
413 **53** 1d. carmine .... 25·00 48·00
          a. "Feather" flaw £225
414 **52** 3d. chestnut £130   £250
415   6d. carmine .... £160   £300   **(Q) Catalogue value – Used**
412/15 Set of 4 .... £300   £600

(O) Face value

These overprinted stamps were only available for letters in New Zealand and to Australia.

(Des Martin Bailey. Litho Southern Colour Print)

2008 (2 July). Olympic Games, Beijing. T **685** and similar diamond-shaped designs. Multicoloured. Phosphorised paper. P 14½.
3056 50c. Type **685** .... 1·00   85

(R) Multicoloured stamp   **(S) Perforations**

xxxi

THE WORLD OF STAMP COLLECTING IN YOUR HANDS

- The UK's biggest selling stamp magazine • Consistently over 150 pages per issue
- Written by stamp collectors for stamp collectors • Monthly colour catalogue supplement
- Philatelic news from around the world • Dedicated GB stamp section
- Regular offers exclusively for subscribers

FREE SAMPLE

For your **FREE** sample, contact us by:

Telephone: +44(0)1425 472 363
Email: orders@stanleygibbons.co.uk
Post: Stanley Gibbons Limited, 7 Parkside, Christchurch Road, Ringwood, Hampshire, BH24 3SH

Gibbons Stamp Monthly
The Ultimate Stamp Magazine

For more information please visit
www.gibbonsstampmonthly.com

Our buying roadshow could be coming to a town near you

We hold regular roadshows throughout the year, covering the whole of the United Kingdom.

- Free verbal appraisals
- Put forward material for future auctions
- Excellent prices paid for selected Great Britain and Commonwealth
- Our team will be happy to examine anything remotely philatelic

So, if you were thinking of selling that single rare stamp, a part of your collection or the whole thing, then speak to our expert team first at Stanley Gibbons Ltd on +44(0)20 7836 8444 or auctions@stanleygibbons.com

For a list of our forthcoming roadshows, visit **www.stanleygibbons.com/auctions**

Est 1856

STANLEY GIBBONS

Stanley Gibbons Auction Department
399 Strand, London, WC2R 0LX
Contact Steve Matthews or Ryan Epps on Tel: +44 (0)20 7836 8444
Fax: +44 (0)20 7836 7342 | Email: auctions@stanleygibbons.com

www.stanleygibbons.com/auctions

SOMETHING MISSING FROM YOUR COLLECTION?

We are sure to have a few things that you have been looking for. Our auction sales always contain a nice selection of classics to modern varieties. Contact us for a free catalogue or view our sales, including colour photos, on line.

INTERESTED IN SELLING? Contact us today to take advantage of the strong Canadian dollar, as well as our philatelic expertise and marketing. We will maximize your results.

Since 1924. Canada's Premier auction house

r. maresch & son

5TH FLOOR 6075 YONGE ST TORONTO ON M2M 3W2 CANADA
☎ 416-363-7777   www.maresch.com   FAX 416-363-6511

Gibbons Stamp Monthly
The Ultimate Stamp Magazine

- Monthly colour catalogue supplement
- Written by stamp collectors for stamp collectors
- Philatelic news from around the world

- The UK's biggest selling stamp magazine
- Consistently 150 pages per issue

FREE SAMPLE
For your FREE sample, contact us by:

Telephone: 01425 472 363
Email: subscriptions@stanleygibbons.co.uk
Post: Stanley Gibbons Limited, 7 Parkside, Christchurch Road, Ringwood, Hampshire, BH24 3SH

For more information, please visit **www.gibbonsstampmonthly.com**

CANADA / British Columbia & Vancouver Island / Vancouver Island / British Columbia / Colony of Canada

Canada

Separate stamp issues appeared for British Columbia and Vancouver Island, Canada, New Brunswick, Newfoundland, Nova Scotia and Prince Edward Island before these colonies joined the Dominion of Canada.

BRITISH COLUMBIA & VANCOUVER ISLAND

Vancouver Island was organised as a Crown Colony in 1849 and the mainland territory was proclaimed a separate colony as British Columbia in 1858. The two colonies combined, as British Columbia, on 19 November 1866.

PRICES FOR STAMPS ON COVER	
Nos. 2/3	from × 6
Nos. 11/12	from × 2
Nos. 13/14	from × 6
Nos. 21/2	from × 10
Nos. 23/7	from × 6
Nos. 28/9	from × 10
No. 30	—
No. 31	from × 10
Nos. 32/3	—

1

(Typo D.L.R.)

1860. No wmk. P 14.
| 2 | 1 | 2½d. deep reddish rose | £425 | £200 |
| 3 | | 2½d. pale reddish rose | £425 | £200 |

When Vancouver Island adopted the dollar currency in 1862 the 2½d. was sold at 5c. From 18 May until 1 November 1865 examples of Nos. 2/3 were used to prepay mail from Vancouver Island to British Columbia at the price of 15 cents a pair.

From 20 June 1864 to 1 November 1865, the 2½d. was sold in British Columbia for 3d. and was subsequently used for the same purpose during a shortage of 3d. stamps in 1867.

Imperforate plate proofs exist in pale dull red (*Price* £10,000 *un*).

VANCOUVER ISLAND

(New Currency. 100 cents = 1 dollar)

2    **3**

(Typo D.L.R.)

1865 (19 Sept). Wmk Crown CC.

(a) Imperf (1866)
| 11 | 2 | 5c. rose | £30000 | £9000 |
| 12 | 3 | 10c. blue | £1900 | £850 |

(b) P 14
13	2	5c. rose	£350	£190
		w. Wmk inverted	£1700	£850
		x. Wmk reversed	†	£900
14	3	10c. blue	£250	£160
		w. Wmk inverted	£800	£600

Medium or poor examples of Nos. 11 and 12 can be supplied at much lower prices, when in stock.

After the two colonies combined Nos. 13/14 were also used in British Columbia.

BRITISH COLUMBIA

4

(Typo D.L.R.)

1865 (1 Nov)–**67**. Wmk Crown CC. P 14.
21	4	3d. deep blue	£110	80·00
22		3d. pale blue (19.7.67)	£100	80·00
		w. Wmk inverted	£425	£275
		y. Wmk inverted and reversed	†	£475

British Columbia changed to the dollar currency on 1 January 1866. Remaining stocks of No. 21 and the supply of No. 22, when it finally arrived, were sold at 12½c. a pair.

(New Currency. 100 cents = 1 dollar)

TWO CENTS   **5. CENTS. 5**
(5)   (6)

1868–71. T **4** in various colours. Surch as T **5** or **6**. Wmk Crown CC.

(a) P 12½ (3.69)
23	5c. red (Bk.)	£1500	£1200
24	10c. lake (B.)	£900	£700
25	25c. yellow (V.)	£600	£600
26	50c. mauve (R.)	£800	£700
27	$1 green (G.)	£1300	£1400

(b) P 14
28	2c. brown (Bk.) (1.68)	£170	£140
29	5c. pale red (Bk.) (5.69)	£225	£160
30	10c. lake (B.)	£1300	
31	25c. yellow (V.) (21.7.69)	£250	£160
32	50c. mauve (R.) (23.2.71)	£650	£1100
	w. Wmk inverted	£1100	
33	$1 green (G.)	£1000	

Nos. 30 and 33 were not issued.

British Columbia joined the Dominion of Canada on 20 July 1871.

COLONY OF CANADA

The first British post offices in what was to become the Colony of Canada were opened at Quebec, Montreal and Trois Rivières during, 1763. These, and subsequent, offices remained part of the British G.P.O. system until 6 April 1851.

The two provinces of Upper Canada (Ontario) and Lower Canada (Quebec) were united in 1840.

QUEBEC

CROWNED-CIRCLE HANDSTAMPS

CC **1**   CC **1** QUEBEC L.C. (R.) (13.1.1842).......... *Price on cover*   £150

PRICES FOR STAMPS ON COVER	
Nos. 1/23	from × 2
Nos. 25/8	from × 3
Nos. 29/43a	from × 3
Nos. 44/5	from × 8

1 American Beaver (Designed by Sir Sandford Fleming)    **2** Prince Albert    **3**

Major re-entry: Line through "EE PEN" (Upper pane R. 5/7)

1

CANADA / Colony of Canada

(T **1/6**. Eng and recess Rawdon, Wright, Hatch and Edson, New York)

1851. Laid paper. Imperf.
1	1	3d. red (23 April)	£28000	£950
1a		3d. orange-vermilion	£28000	£950
		b. Major re-entry	—	£2750
2	2	6d. slate-violet (15 May)	£40000	£1200
3		6d. brown-purple	£42000	£1400
		a. Bisected (3d.) on cover	†	£35000
4	3	12d. black (14 June)	£170000	£95000

There are several re-entries on the plate of the 3d. in addition to the major re-entry listed. All re-entries occur in this stamp on all papers.

Forgeries of the 3d. are known without the full stop after "PENCE". They also omit the foliage in the corners, as do similar forgeries of the 6d.

4   **5**   **6** Jacques Cartier

Re-entry (R. 10/12)

1852–57. Imperf.
A. Handmade wove paper, varying in thickness (1852–56)
5	1	3d. red	£2000	£200
		a. Bisected (1½d.) on cover (1856)	†	£35000
6		3d. deep red	£2250	£250
7		3d. scarlet-vermilion	£2750	£250
8		3d. brown-red	£2250	£250
		a. Bisected (1½d.) on cover (1856)	†	£35000
		b. Major re-entry *(all shades)* from	£5500	£800
9	2	6d. slate-violet	£35000	£1000
		a. Bisected (3d.) on cover	†	£18000
10		6d. greenish grey	£35000	£1100
11		6d. brown grey	£38000	£1300
12	5	7½d. yellow-green *(shades)* (2.6.57)	£10000	£2250
13	6	10d. bright blue (1.55)	£11000	£1600
14		10d. dull blue	£10000	£1500
15		10d. blue *to* deep blue	£11000	£1600
		a. Major re-entry *(all shades)* from	—	£2750
16	3	12d. black	†	£120000

B. Machine-made medium to thick wove paper of a more even hard texture with more visible mesh. Clearer impressions (1857)
17	4	½d. deep rose (1.8.57)	£900	£550
		a. Re-entry	£2750	£1300
18	1	3d. red	£2750	£450
		a. Bisected (1½d.) on cover	†	£35000
		b. Major re-entry	—	£1500
19	2	6d. grey-lilac	£40000	£2250
20	6	10d. blue *to* deep blue	£13000	£2250
		a. Major re-entry	£22000	£3000

C. Thin soft horizontally ribbed paper (1857)
21	4	½d. deep rose	£8500	£2000
		a. Vertically ribbed paper	£9000	£3000
22	1	3d. red	£4000	£450
		a. Major re-entry	—	£1500

D. Very thick soft wove paper (1857)
23	2	6d. reddish purple	£40000	£3500
		a. Bisected (3d.) on cover	†	£28000

Bisected examples of the 3d. value were used to make up the 7½d. Canadian Packet rate to England from May 1856 until the introduction of the 7½d. value on 2 June 1857.

The 7½d. and 10d. values can be found in wide and narrow versions. These differences are due to shrinkage of the paper, which was wetted before printing and then contracted unevenly during drying. The width of these stamps varies between 17 and 18 mm.

The listed major re-entry on the 10d. occurs on R. 3/5 and shows strong doubling of the top frame line and the left-hand "8d. stg." with a line through the lower parts of "ANAD" and "ENCE". Smaller re-entries occur on all values.

Examples of the 12d. on wove paper come from a proof sheet used for postal purposes by the postal authorities.

The 3d. is known perforated 14 and also *percé en scie* 13. Both are contemporary, but were unofficial.

1858–59. P 11¾.
A. Machine-made medium to thick wove paper with a more even hard texture
25	4	½d. deep rose (12.58)	£4000	£900
		a. Lilac-rose	£4000	£950
		b. Re-entry (R. 10/10)	£7000	£2000
26	1	3d. red (1.59)	£9500	£350
		a. Major re-entry	—	£1300
27	2	6d. brownish grey (1.59)	£15000	£3750
		a. Slate-violet	£15000	£3500

B. Thin soft horizontally ribbed paper
27b	4	½d. deep rose-red	—	£4500
28	1	3d. red	—	£1800
		a. Major re-entry		

The re-entry on the imperforate and perforated ½d sheets was the same, but occurred on R. 10/10 of the perforated sheets because the two left-hand vertical rows were removed prior to perforation.

(New Currency. 100 cents = 1 dollar)

7   **8** American Beaver

9 Prince Albert   **10**   **11** Jacques Cartier

(On 1 May 1858, Messrs. Rawdon, Wright, Hatch and Edson joined with eight other firms to form "The American Bank Note Co" and the "imprint" on sheets of the following stamps has the new title of the firm with "New York" added.)

(Recess A.B.N. Co)

1859 (1 July). P 12.
29	7	1c. pale rose (to rose-red)	£400	45·00
30		1c. deep rose (to carmine-rose)	£475	65·00
		a. Imperf (pair)	£4250	
		b. Imperf×perf		
31	8	5c. pale red	£425	17·00
32		5c. deep red	£425	17·00
		a. Re-entry* (R.3/8)	£3250	£450
		b. Imperf (pair)	£15000	
		c. Bisected (2½c.) with 10c. on cover.	†	£6000
33	9	10c. black-brown	£13000	£2000
		a. Bisected (5c.), on cover	†	£9000
33b		10c. deep red-purple	£3750	£650
		ba. Bisected (5c.), on cover	†	£6000
34		10c. purple *(shades)*	£1300	75·00
		a. Bisected (5c.), on cover	†	£5500
35		10c. brownish purple	£1200	75·00
36		10c. brown (to pale)	£1200	75·00
		a. Bisected (5c.), on cover	†	£6500
37		10c. dull violet	£1300	80·00
38		10c. bright red-purple	£1300	75·00
		a. Imperf (pair)	£12000	
39	10	12½c. deep yellow-green	£1100	70·00
40		12½c. pale yellow-green	£1000	70·00
41		12½c. blue-green	£1300	85·00
		a. Imperf (pair)	£5000	
		b. Imperf between (vert pair)		
42	11	17c. deep blue	£1400	90·00
		a. Imperf (pair)	£5500	
43		17c. slate-blue	£1700	£130
43a		17c. indigo	£1600	95·00

*The price of No. 32a is for the very marked re-entry showing oval frame line doubled above "CANADA". Slighter re-entries are worth from £30 upwards in used condition.

As there were numerous P.O. Dept. orders for the 10c., 12½c. and 17c. and some of these were executed by more than one separate printing, with no special care to ensure uniformity of colour, there is a wide range of shade, especially in the 10c., and some shades recur at intervals after periods during which other shades predominated. The colour-names given in the above list therefore represent groups only.

It has been proved by leading Canadian specialists that the perforations may be an aid to the approximate dating of a particular stamp, the gauge used measuring 11¾×11¾ from mid-July 1859 to mid-1863, 12×11¾ from March 1863 to mid-1865 and 12×12 from April 1865 to 1868. Exceptionally, in the 5c. value many sheets were perforated 12×12 between May and October, 1862, whilst the last printings of the 12½c. and 17c. perf 11¾×11¾ were in July 1863, the perf 12×11¾ starting towards the end of 1863.

2

STANLEY GIBBONS

Commonwealth Department

Recently offered from our ever changing stock

SG 4

1851 12d black unused

If you would like to receive our bi-monthly illustrated list, contact
Pauline MacBroom on 020 7557 4450 or by email at pmacbroom@stanleygibbons.com
or Brian Lucas on 020 7557 4418 or by email at blucas@stanleygibbons.com

Stanley Gibbons Limited, 399 Strand, London WC2R 0LX
Tel: 020 7836 8444   Fax: 020 7557 4499

To view all of our stock 24 hours a day visit **www.stanleygibbons.com**

STANLEY GIBBONS

Commonwealth Department

Recently offered from our ever changing stock

SG6a
1858 Beautiful 1s bisect with a splendid pedigree.
Ex Argenti, Cartier, 'Foxbridge', Wood and Koh

If you would like to receive our bi-monthly illustrated list, contact
Pauline MacBroom on 020 7557 4450 or by email at pmacbroom@stanleygibbons.com
or Brian Lucas on 020 7557 4418 or by email at blucas@stanleygibbons.com

Stanley Gibbons Limited, 399 Strand, London WC2R 0LX
Tel: 020 7836 8444   Fax: 020 7557 4499

To view all of our stock 24 hours a day visit **www.stanleygibbons.com**

CANADA / Colony of Canada / New Brunswick / Newfoundland

12

(Recess A.B.N. Co)

1864 (1 Aug). P 12.
44	12	2c. rose-red	£600	£170
45		2c. bright rose	£600	£170
		a. Imperf (pair)	£3000	

The Colony of Canada became part of the Dominion of Canada on 1 July 1867.

NEW BRUNSWICK

New Brunswick, previously part of Nova Scotia, became a separate colony in June 1784. The colony became responsible for its postal service on 6 July 1851.

PRICES FOR STAMPS ON COVER	
Nos. 1/4	from × 2
Nos. 5/6	from × 3
Nos. 7/9	from × 10
Nos. 10/12	from × 30
No. 13	—
Nos. 14/17	from × 2
No. 18	from × 5
No. 19	from × 100

1 Royal Crown and Heraldic Flowers of the United Kingdom

(Recess P.B.)

1851 (5 Sept)–60. Blue paper. Imperf.
1	1	3d. bright red	£2750	£350
2		3d. dull red	£2500	£325
		a. Bisected (1½d.) (1854) (on cover)	†	£3000
2b		6d. mustard-yellow	£7500	£1500
3		6d. yellow	£4500	£800
4		6d. olive-yellow	£4500	£700
		a. Bisected (3d.) (1854) (on cover)	†	£3000
		b. Quartered (1½d.) (1860) (on cover)	†	£42000
5		1s. reddish mauve	£17000	£4500
6		1s. dull mauve	£20000	£5000
		a. Bisected (6d.) (1855) (on cover)	†	£24000
		b. Quartered (3d.) (1860) (on cover)	†	£38000

Reprints of all three values were made in 1890 on thin, hard, white paper. The 3d. is bright orange, the 6d. and 1s. violet-black.

Nos. 2a and 4b were to make up the 7½d. rate to Great Britain, introduced on 1 August 1854.

(New Currency. 100 cents = 1 dollar)

2 Locomotive  **3**  **3a** Charles Connell

4  **5**  **6** Paddle-steamer *Washington*

7 King Edward VII when Prince of Wales

(Recess A.B.N. Co)

1860 (15 May)–63. No wmk. P 12.
7	2	1c. brown-purple	70·00	50·00
8		1c. purple	60·00	48·00
9		1c. dull claret	60·00	48·00
		a. Imperf vert (horiz pair)	£600	
10	3	2c. orange (1863)	29·00	27·00
11		2c. orange-yellow	35·00	27·00
12		2c. deep orange	38·00	27·00
		a. Imperf horiz (vert pair)	£450	
13	3a	5c. brown	£7500	
14	4	5c. yellow-green	27·00	18·00
15		5c. deep green	27·00	18·00
16		5c. sap-green (deep yellowish green)	£300	40·00
17	5	10c. red	60·00	65·00
		a. Bisected (5c.) (on cover) (1860)	†	£600
18	6	12½c. indigo	70·00	42·00
19	7	17c. black	42·00	70·00

Beware of forged cancellations.

No. 13 was not issued due to objections to the design showing Charles Connell, the Postmaster-General. Most of the printing was destroyed.

New Brunswick joined the Dominion of Canada on 1 July 1867 and its stamps were withdrawn in March of the following year.

NEWFOUNDLAND

Newfoundland became a self-governing colony in 1855 and a Dominion in 1917. In 1934 the adverse financial situation led to the suspension of the constitution.

The first local postmaster, at St. John's, was appointed in 1805, the overseas mails being routed via Halifax, Nova Scotia. A regular packet service was established between these two ports in 1840, the British G.P.O. assuming control of the overseas mails at the same time.

The responsibility for the overseas postal service reverted to the colonial administration on 1 July 1851.

ST. JOHN'S

CROWNED-CIRCLE HANDSTAMPS

CC 1a

CC1 CC **1a** ST. JOHN'S NEWFOUNDLAND (R.)
(27.6.1846) .... *Price on cover* £950

PRICES FOR STAMPS ON COVER TO 1945	
No. 1	from × 30
Nos. 2/4	from × 3
No. 5	from × 20
No. 6	from × 10
No. 7	from × 3
No. 8	from × 30
No. 9	from × 8
No. 10	—
No. 11	from × 8
No. 12	from × 3
Nos. 13/14	from × 20
Nos. 15/17	—
Nos. 18/20	from × 20
No. 21	from × 15
Nos. 22/3	—
No. 25	from × 30
No. 26	from × 5
No. 27	from × 8
No. 28	from × 3
Nos. 29/30	from × 10

CANADA / Newfoundland

PRICES FOR STAMPS ON COVER TO 1945

No. 31	from × 30
No. 32	from × 8
No. 33	from × 5
No. 33a	—
Nos. 34/9	from × 8
Nos. 40/1	from × 5
Nos. 42/3	from × 30
Nos. 44/8	from × 8
No. 49	from × 50
Nos. 50/3	from × 10
No. 54	from × 4
Nos. 55/8b	from × 10
No. 59	from × 100
No. 59a	from × 10
Nos. 60/1	from × 4
Nos. 62/5	from × 8
Nos. 65a/79	from × 3
Nos. 83/90	from × 10
Nos. 91/3	from × 2
No. 94	from × 50
Nos. 95/141	from × 3
Nos. 142/a	from × 1½
No. 143	from × 8
Nos. 144/8f	from × 2
Nos. 149/62	from × 3
No. 163	—
Nos. 164/78	from × 2
Nos. 179/90	from × 3
No. 191	—
Nos. 192/220	from × 2
No. 221	—
Nos. 222/9	from × 3
Nos. 230/4	from × 2
No. 235	—
Nos. 236/91	from × 2
Nos. D1/6	from × 10

1 **2**

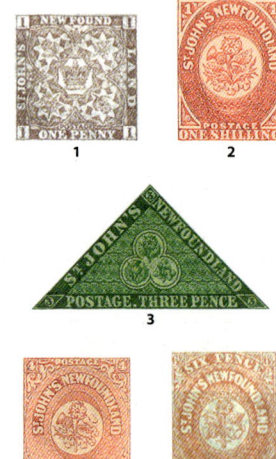

3

4 **5**

Royal Crown and Heraldic flowers of the United Kingdom

(Recess P.B.)

1857 (1 Jan)–**64**. Thick, machine-made paper with a distinct mesh. No wmk. Imperf.

1	1	1d. brown-purple	£160	£250
		a. Bisected (½d.) (1864) (on cover)	†	£38000
2	2	2d. scarlet-vermilion (15 Feb)	£20000	£6000
3	3	3d. yellowish green (H/S "CANCELLED" in oval £12000)	£1600	£425
4	4	4d. scarlet-vermilion	£12000	£3000
5	1	5d. brown-purple	£325	£475
6	4	6d. scarlet-vermilion	£24000	£4000
7	5	6½d. scarlet-vermilion	£3750	£4000
8	4	8d. scarlet-vermilion	£375	£700
		a. Bisected (4d.) (1859) (on cover)	†	£4250
9	2	1s. scarlet-vermilion	£23000	£8500
		a. Bisected (6d.) (1860) (on cover)	†	£16000

The 6d. and 8d. differ from the 4d. in many details, as does also the 1s. from the 2d.

PERKINS BACON "CANCELLED". For notes on these handstamps, showing "CANCELLED" between horizontal bars forming an oval, see Catalogue Introduction.

1860 (15 Aug–Dec). Medium, hand-made paper without mesh. Imperf.

10	2	2d. orange-vermilion	£475	£600
11	3	3d. grn *to* dp grn* (H/S "CANCELLED" in oval £11000)	£100	£180
12	4	4d. orange-verm (H/S "CANCELLED" in oval £14000)	£3500	£950
		a. Bisected (2d.) (12.60) (on cover)	†	£20000
13	1	5d. Venetian red (H/S "CANCELLED" in oval £13000)	£130	£400
14	4	6d. orange-vermilion	£4250	£700
15	2	1s. orange-verm (H/S "CANCELLED" in oval £17000)	£32000	£10000
		a. Bisected (6d.) (12.60) (on cover)	†	£42000

*No. 11 includes stamps from the July and November 1861 printings which are very difficult to distinguish.

The 1s. on horizontally or vertically *laid* paper is now considered to be a proof (*Price* £20000).

Stamps of this and the following issue may be found with part of the paper-maker's watermark "STACEY WISE 1858".

BISECTS. Collectors are warned against buying bisected stamps of these issues without a reliable guarantee.

1861–64. New colours. Hand-made paper without mesh. Imperf.

16	1	1d. chocolate-brown	£325	£425
		a. Red-brown		£8000
17	2	2d. rose-lake	£275	£500
18	4	4d. rose-lake (H/S "CANCELLED" in oval £13000)	50·00	£110
		a. Bisected (2d.) (1864) (on cover)	†	£35000
19	1	5d. chocolate-brown (*shades*)	£100	£325
		a. Red-brown (shades)	85·00	£200
20	4	6d. rose-lake (H/S "CANCELLED" in oval £11000)	30·00	£100
		a. Bisected (3d.) (1863) (on cover)	†	£9000
21	5	6½d. rose-lake (H/S "CANCELLED" in oval £11000)	95·00	£450
22	4	8d. rose-lake	£120	£650
23	2	1s. rose-lake (H/S "CANCELLED" in oval £12000)	50·00	£300
		a. Bisected (6d.) (1863) (on cover)	†	£22000

Nos. 16/23 come from printings made in July (2d., 4d., 6d., 6½d., and 1s. only) or November 1861 (all values). The paper used was from the same manufacturer as that for Nos. 10/15, but was of more variable thickness and texture, ranging from a relatively soft medium paper, which can be quite opaque, to a thin hard transparent paper. The rose-lake stamps also show a considerable variation in shade ranging from pale to deep. The extensive remainders of this issue were predominantly in pale shades on thin hard paper, but it is not possible to distinguish between stamps from the two printings with any certainty. Deep shades of the 2d., 4d., 6d., 6½d. and 1s. on soft opaque paper do, however, command a considerable premium.

Beware of buying used examples of the stamps which are worth much less in unused condition, as many unused stamps have been provided with faked postmarks. A guarantee should be obtained.

(New Currency. 100 cents = 1 dollar)

6 Atlantic Cod    **7** Common Seal on Ice-floe

8 Prince Consort    **9** Queen Victoria

10 Schooner    **11** Queen Victoria

CANADA / Newfoundland

(Recess A.B.N. Co, New York)
1865 (15 Nov)–**71**. P 12.

		(a) Thin yellowish paper		
25	6	2c. yellowish green	£150	85·00
		a. Bisected (1c.) (on cover) (1870)	†	£8000
26	7	5c. brown	£550	£180
		a. Bisected (2½c.) (on cover)	†	£9500
27	8	10c. black	£375	£110
		a. Bisected (5c.) (on cover) (1869)	†	£6500
28	9	12c. red-brown	£550	£150
		a. Bisected (6c.) (on cover)	†	£4250
29	10	13c. orange-yellow	£120	£120
30	11	24c. blue	45·00	38·00
		(b) Medium white paper		
31	6	2c. bluish green (*to* deep) (1870)	95·00	50·00
32	8	10c. black (1871)	£275	48·00
33	9	12c. chestnut (1870)	60·00	48·00

The inland postage rate was reduced to 3c. on 8 May, 1870. Until the 3c. value became available examples of No. 25 were bisected to provide 1c. stamps.

For the 12c. value in deep brown, see No. 61.

12 King Edward VII when Prince of Wales 
14 Queen Victoria

I

II

In Type II the white oval frame line is unbroken by the scroll containing the words "ONE CENT", the letters "N.F." are smaller and closer to the scroll, and there are other minor differences.

(Recess National Bank Note Co, New York)
1868 (Nov). P 12.

34	12	1c. dull purple (I)	75·00	60·00

(Recess A.B.N. Co)
1868 (Nov)–**73**. P 12.

35	12	1c. brown-purple (II) (5.71)	£130	70·00
36	14	3c. vermilion (7.70)	£300	£100
37		3c. blue (1.4.73)	£275	27·00
38	7	5c. black	£275	£110
39	14	6c. rose (7.70)	12·00	26·00

1876–**79**. Rouletted.

40	12	1c. lake-purple (II) (1877)	£120	55·00
41	6	2c. bluish green (1879)	£150	48·00
42	14	3c. blue (1877)	£325	5·00
43	7	5c. blue	£180	3·50
		a. Imperf (pair)		

15 King Edward VII when Prince of Wales 
16 Atlantic Cod

17
18 Common Seal on Ice-floe 

(Recess British American Bank Note Co, Montreal)
1880–**82**. P 12.

44	15	1c. dull grey-brown	40·00	15·00
		a. Dull brown	40·00	15·00
		b. Red-brown	42·00	19·00
46	16	2c. yellow-green (1882)	55·00	32·00
47	17	3c. pale dull blue	£120	9·50
		a. Bright blue	80·00	6·50
48	18	5c. pale dull blue	£300	10·00

19 Newfoundland Dog
20 Atlantic Brigantine 
21 Queen Victoria 

(Recess British American Bank Note Co, Montreal)
1887 (15 Feb)–**88**. New colours and values. P 12.

49	19	½c. rose-red	15·00	9·50
50	15	1c. blue-green (1.88)	15·00	10·00
		a. Green	6·00	3·75
		b. Yellow-green	11·00	11·00
51	16	2c. orange-vermilion (1.88)	23·00	7·50
		a. Imperf (pair)	£350	
52	17	3c. deep brown (1.88)	70·00	2·75
53	18	5c. deep blue (1.88)	£110	5·50
54	20	10c. black (1.88)	70·00	65·00
49/54 *Set* of 6			£250	85·00

For reissues in similar colours, see Nos. 62/5a.

(Recess B.A.B.N.)
1890 (Nov). P 12.

55	21	3c. deep slate	45·00	3·25
		a. Imperf (pair)		
56		3c. slate-grey (*to* grey)	42·00	3·25
		a. Imperf horiz (vert pair)	£550	
57		3c. slate-violet	60·00	6·50
58		3c. grey-lilac	60·00	3·25
58a		3c. brown-grey	65·00	7·50
58b		3c. purple-grey	65·00	7·50

There is a very wide range of shades in this stamp, and those given only cover the main groups.

Stamps on pink paper are from a consignment recovered from the sea and which were affected by the salt water.

(Recess British American Bank Note Co, Montreal)
1894 (Aug–Dec). Changes of colour. P 12.

59	19	½c. black (11.94)	10·00	7·50
59a	18	5c. bright blue (12.94)	70·00	4·75
60	14	6c. crimson-lake (12.94)	27·00	22·00
61	9	12c. deep brown	80·00	75·00

The 6c. is printed from the old American Bank Note Company's plates.

1896 (Jan)–**98**. Reissues. P 12.

62	19	½c. orange-vermilion	60·00	55·00
63	15	1c. deep brown	85·00	55·00
63a		1c. deep green (1898)	26·00	18·00
64	16	2c. green	£110	65·00
65	17	3c. deep blue	80·00	26·00
65a		3c. chocolate-brown	£110	90·00
62/65a *Set* of 6			£425	£275

The above were *reissued* for postal purposes. The colours were generally brighter than those of the original stamps.

22 Queen Victoria
23 John Cabot 
24 Cape Bonavista 

7

CANADA / Newfoundland

25 Caribou hunting
26 Mining 
27 Logging 
28 Fishing 
29 *Matthew* (Cabot) 
30 Willow Grouse 
31 Group of Grey Seals 
32 Salmon-fishing 
33 Seal of the Colony 
34 Iceberg off St. John's 
35 Henry VII 

(Des R. O. Smith. Recess A.B.N. Co)

1897 (24 June). 400th Anniv of Discovery of Newfoundland and 60th year of Queen Victoria's reign. P 12.

66	22	1c. green	6·00	9·50
67	23	2c. bright rose	2·75	2·75
		a. Bisected (1c.) on cover	†	£325
68	24	3c. bright blue	3·50	1·00
		a. Bisected (1½c.) on cover	†	£325
69	25	4c. olive-green	11·00	7·00
70	26	5c. violet	14·00	3·25
71	27	6c. red-brown	9·50	3·25
		a. Bisected (3c.) on cover	†	£350
72	28	8c. orange	21·00	9·00
73	29	10c. sepia	42·00	11·00
74	30	12c. deep blue	38·00	9·50
75	31	15c. bright scarlet	23·00	18·00
76	32	24c. dull violet-blue	27·00	28·00
77	33	30c. slate-blue	50·00	90·00
78	34	35c. red	65·00	80·00
79	35	60c. black	24·00	18·00
66/79		Set of 14	£300	£250

The 60c. surcharged "TWO—2—CENTS" in three lines is an essay made in December 1918 (*Price* £400).

(36)
(37) 
(38) 

1897 (19 Oct). T **21** surch with T **36/8** by Royal Gazette, St. John's, on stamps of various shades.

80	36	1c. on 3c. grey-purple	70·00	30·00
		a. Surch double, one diagonal	£1300	
		d. Vert pair, one without lower bar and "ONE CENT"	£4000	
81	37	1c. on 3c. grey-purple	£150	£110
82	38	1c. on 3c. grey-purple	£550	£475

Nos. 80/2 occur in the same setting of 50 (10×5) applied twice to each sheet. Type **36** appeared in the first four horizontal rows, Type **37** on R. 5/1–8 and Type **38** on R. 5/9 and 10.

Trial surcharges in red or red and black were not issued. (*Price*: Type **36** *in red* £900, *in red and black* £900: Type **37** *in red* £3000, *in red and black* £3000: Type **38** *in red* £7500, *in red and black* £8000).

These surcharges exist on stamps of various shades, but those on brown-grey are clandestine forgeries, having been produced by one of the printers at the *Royal Gazette*.

39 Prince Edward later Duke of Windsor
40 Queen Victoria 
41 King Edward VII when Prince of Wales 
42 Queen Alexandra when Princess of Wales 
43 Queen Mary when Duchess of York 
44 King George V when Duke of York 

(Recess A.B.N. Co)

1897 (4 Dec)–**1918**. P 12.

83	39	½c. olive (8.98)	2·25	1·50
		a. Imperf (pair)	£600	
84	40	1c. carmine	4·75	5·00
85		1c. blue-green (6.98)	16·00	20
		a. Yellow-green	16·00	20
		b. Imperf horiz (vert pair)	£275	
86	41	2c. orange	8·00	7·00
		a. Imperf (pair)	—	£500
87		2c. scarlet (6.98)	21·00	40
		a. Imperf (pair)	£375	£375
		b. Imperf between (pair)	£550	
88	42	3c. orange (6.98)	26·00	30
		a. Imperf horiz (vert pair)	£450	
		b. Imperf (pair)	£375	£375
		c. Red-orange/*bluish* (6.18)	45·00	3·50
89	43	4c. violet (21.10.01)	30·00	7·00
		a. Imperf (pair)	£600	90
	44	5c. blue (6.99)	48·00	3·00
83/90		Set of 8	£140	22·00

No. 88c was an emergency war-time printing made by the American Bank Note Co from the old plate, pending receipt of the then current 3c. from England.

The imperforate errors of this issue are found used, but only as philatelic "by favour" items. It is possible that No. 86a only exists in this condition.

Nos. 91/3 are vacant.

45 Map of Newfoundland

(Recess A.B.N. Co)

1908 (31 Aug). P 12.

94	45	2c. lake	27·00	1·00

CANADA / Newfoundland

46 King James I
47 Arms of Colonisation Co 
48 John Guy 
49 Endeavour (immigrant ship), 1610 
50 Cupids 
51 Sir Francis Bacon 
52 View of Mosquito 
53 Logging Camp, Red Indian Lake 
54 Paper Mills, Grand Falls 
55 King Edward VII 
56 King George V 

1c. "NFWFOUNDLAND" (Right pane, R. 5/1)
1c. "JAMRS" (Right pane, R. 5/2) 

6c. (A) "Z" in "COLONIZATION" reversed. (B) "Z" correct.

(Litho Whitehead, Morris & Co Ltd)

1910 (15 Aug).

(a) P 12

95	46	1c. green	16·00	2·50
		a. "NFWFOUNDLAND"	75·00	£100
		b. "JAMRS"	75·00	£100
		c. Imperf between (horiz pair)	£350	£375
96	47	2c. rose-carmine	24·00	2·00
97	48	3c. olive	12·00	22·00
98	49	4c. violet	23·00	21·00
99	50	5c. bright blue	45·00	14·00
100	51	6c. claret (A)	50·00	£160
100a		6c. claret (B)	28·00	£100
101	52	8c. bistre-brown	65·00	£120
102	53	9c. olive-green	65·00	£100
103	54	10c. purple-slate	65·00	£130
104	55	12c. pale red-brown	65·00	95·00
		a. Imperf (pair)	£325	
105	56	15c. black	65·00	£130
95/105		Set of 11	£425	£650

(b) P 12×14

106	46	1c. green	7·00	13·00
		a. "NFWFOUNDLAND"	60·00	£150
		b. "JAMRS"	60·00	£150
		c. Imperf between (horiz pair)	£650	£700
107	47	2c. rose-carmine	7·50	40
		a. Imperf between (horiz pair)	£700	
108	50	5c. bright blue (P 14×12)	8·50	3·00

(c) P 12×11

109	46	1c. green	3·00	30
		a. Imperf between (horiz pair)	£325	
		b. Imperf between (vert pair)	£375	
		c. "NFWFOUNDLAND"	40·00	55·00
		e. "JAMRS"	40·00	55·00

(d) P 12×11½

110	47	2c. rose-carmine	£400	£275

(Dies eng Macdonald & Sons. Recess A. Alexander & Sons, Ltd)

1911 (7 Feb). As T **51** to **56**, but recess printed. P 14.

111		6c. claret (B)	18·00	50·00
112		8c. yellow-brown	50·00	75·00
		a. Imperf between (horiz pair)	£1000	
113		9c. sage-green	50·00	£140
		a. Imperf between (horiz pair)	£1000	
114		10c. purple-black	90·00	£140
		a. Imperf between (horiz pair)	£1000	
115		12c. red-brown	70·00	70·00
116		15c. slate-green	65·00	£130
111/116		Set of 6	£300	£550

The 9c. and 15c. exist with papermaker's watermark "E. TOWGOOD FINE".
Nos. 111/16 exist imperforate. (Price £250, unused, for each pair).

57 Queen Mary
58 King George V 
59 Duke of Windsor when Prince of Wales 
60 King George VI when Prince Albert 
61 Princess Mary, the Princess Royal 
62 Prince Henry, Duke of Gloucester 
63 Prince George, Duke of Kent 
64 Prince John 
65 Queen Alexandra 
66 Duke of Connaught 
67 Seal of Newfoundland 

(1c. to 5c., 10c. eng and recess D.L.R.; others eng Macdonald & Co, recess A. Alexander & Sons)

1911 (19 June)–**16**. Coronation. P 13½×14 (comb) (1c. to 5c., 10c.) or 14 (line) (others).

117	57	1c. yellow-green	10·00	30
		a. Blue-green (1915)	22·00	30
118	58	2c. carmine	10·00	20
		a. Rose-red (blurred impression). Perf 14 (1916)	14·00	1·00
119	59	3c. red-brown	22·00	48·00
120	60	4c. purple	21·00	35·00
121	61	5c. ultramarine	7·00	1·50
122	62	6c. slate-grey	13·00	25·00
123	63	8c. aniline blue	60·00	85·00
		a. Greenish blue	90·00	£120

9

CANADA / Newfoundland

124	64	9c. violet-blue	28·00	55·00
125	65	10c. deep green	42·00	50·00
126	66	12c. plum	29·00	50·00
127	67	15c. lake	27·00	50·00
117/127		Set of 11	£225	£350

The 2c. rose-red, No. 118a is a poor war-time printing by Alexander & Sons.

Although No. 123 has a typical aniline appearance it is believed that the shade results from the thinning of non-aniline ink.

Nos. 117/18, 121 and 126/7 exist imperforate, without gum. (*Prices for 1c., 2c., 5c., 12c., £250, for 15c. £75, unused, per pair*).

Nos. 128/9 are vacant.

FIRST TRANS-ATLANTIC AIR POST
April, 1919.

68 Caribou   (69)

(Des J. H. Noonan. Recess D.L.R.)

1919 (2 Jan). Newfoundland Contingent, 1914–1918. P 14.

130	68	1c. green (*a*) (*b*)	3·75	20
131		2c. scarlet (*a*) (*b*)	3·75	85
		a. Carmine-red (*b*)	22·00	80
132		3c. brown (*a*) (*b*)	8·00	20
		a. Red-brown (*b*)	15·00	60
133		4c. mauve (*a*)	12·00	80
		a. Purple (*b*)	22·00	80
134		5c. ultramarine (*a*) (*b*)	14·00	1·25
135		6c. slate-grey (*a*)	16·00	65·00
136		8c. bright magenta (*a*)	16·00	65·00
137		10c. deep grey-green (*a*)	7·50	6·00
138		12c. orange (*a*)	19·00	75·00
139		15c. indigo (*a*)	16·00	85·00
		a. Prussian blue (*a*)	£110	£150
140		24c. bistre-brown (*a*)	30·00	40·00
141		36c. sage-green (*a*)	20·00	45·00
130/141		Set of 12	£150	£350

Each value bears with "Trail of the Caribou" the name of a different action: 1c. Suvla Bay; 3c. Gueudecourt; 4c. Beaumont Hamel; 6c. Monchy; 10c. Steenbeck; 15c. Langemarck; 24c. Cambrai; 36c. Combles; 2c., 5c., 8c., and 12c. inscribed "Royal Naval Reserve-Ubique".

Perforations. Two perforating heads were used: (*a*) comb 14×13.9; (*b*) line 14.1×14.1.

Nos. 130/41 exist imperforate, without gum. (*Price £275 unused, for each pair*).

1919 (12 Apr). Air. No. 132 optd with T **69**, by Robinson & Co Ltd, at the offices of the "Daily News".

142	68	3c. brown	£20000	£10000

These stamps franked correspondence carried by Lieut. H. Hawker on his Atlantic flight. 18 were damaged and destroyed, 95 used on letters, 11 given as presentation copies, and the remaining 76 were sold in aid of the Marine Disasters Fund.

1919 (19 April). Nos. 132 inscribed in MS. "Aerial Atlantic Mail. J.A.R.".

142*a*	68	3c. brown	£70000	£20000

This provisional was made by W. C. Campbell, the Secretary of the Postal Department, and the initials are those of the Postmaster, J. A. Robinson, for use on correspondence intended to be carried on the abortive Morgan-Raynham Trans-Atlantic flight. The mail was eventually delivered by sea.

In addition to the 25 to 30 used examples, one unused, no gum, example of No. 142*a* is known.

Single examples of a similar overprint on the 2c., (No. 131) and 5c. (No. 134) are known used on cover, the former with an unoverprinted example of the same value.

Trans-Atlantic AIR POST, 1919. ONE DOLLAR.
(70)

THREE CENTS
(71)

1919 (9 June). Air. No. 75 surch with T **70** by Royal Gazette, St. John's.

143	31	$1 on 15c. bright scarlet	£120	£120
		a. No comma after "AIR POST"	£150	£160
		b. As var a and no stop after "1919"	£350	£400
		c. As var a and "A" under "a" of "Trans"	£350	£400

These stamps were issued for use on the mail carried on the first successful flight across the Atlantic by Capt. J. Alcock and Lieut. A. Brown, and on other projected Trans-Atlantic flights (Alcock flown cover, *Price £3000*).

The surcharge was applied in a setting of which 16 were normal, 7 as No. 143*a*, 1 as No. 143*b* and 1 as No. 143*c*.

1920 (Sept). Nos. 75 and 77/8 surch as T **71**, by Royal Gazette (2c. with only one bar, at top of stamp).

A. Bars of surch 10½ mm apart
B. Bars 13½ mm apart

144	33	2c. on 30c. slate-blue (24 Sept)	5·00	26·00
		a. Surch inverted	£1100	£1300
145	31	3c. on 15c. bright scarlet (A) (13 Sept)	£250	£250
		a. Surch inverted	£2500	
146		3c. on 15c. bright scarlet (B) (13 Sept)	32·00	29·00
147	34	3c. on 35c. red (15 Sept)	16·00	23·00
		a. Surch inverted	£2000	
		b. Lower bar omitted	£180	£225
		c. "THREE" omitted	£1200	

Our prices for Nos. 147*b* and 147*c* are for stamps with lower bar or "THREE" entirely missing. The bar may be found in all stages of incompleteness and stamps showing broken bar are not of much value.

On the other hand, stamps showing either only the top or bottom of the letters "THREE" are scarce, though not as rare as No. 147*c*.

The 6c. T **27** surcharged "THREE CENTS", in red or black, is an essay (*Price £700*). The 2c. on 30c. with red surcharge is a colour trial (*Price £950*).

AIR MAIL to Halifax, N.S. 1921.
(72)

1921 (16 Nov). Air. No. 78 optd with T **72** by Royal Gazette.

I. 2¾ mm between "AIR" and "MAIL"

148	34	35c. red	£140	90·00
		a. No stop after "1921"	£120	80·00
		b. No stop and first "1" of "1921" below "f" of "Halifax"	£325	£225
		c. As No. 148, inverted	£6000	
		d. As No. 148*a*, inverted	£4750	
		e. As No. 148*b*, inverted	£22000	

II. 1½ mm between "AIR" and "MAIL"

148*f*	34	35c. red	£160	£100
		g. No stop after "1921"	£190	£130
		h. No stop and first "1" of "1921" below "f" of "Halifax"	£325	£225
		i. As No. 148*f*, inverted	£7500	
		k. As No. 148*g*, inverted	£13000	
		l. As No. 148*h*, inverted	£22000	

Type **72** was applied as a setting of 25 which contained ten stamps as No. 148*a*, seven as No. 148, four as No. 148*f*, two as No. 148*g*, one as No. 148*b* and one as No. 148*h*.

73 Twin Hills, Tor's Cove

74 South-West Arm, Trinity

75 Statue of the Fighting Newfoundlander St. John's

76 Humber River

77 Coast at Trinity

78 Upper Steadies, Humber River

79 Quidi Vidi, near St. John's

80 Caribou crossing lake

81 Humber River Canyon

82 Shell Bird Island

83 Mount Moriah, Bay of Islands

84 Humber River nr. Little Rapids

CANADA / Newfoundland

85 Placentia
86 Topsail Falls 
96 War Memorial, St. John's
97 G.P.O., St. John's

(Recess D.L.R.)

1923 (9 July)–**24**. T **73**/**86**. P 14 (comb or line).

149	73	1c. green	2·25	20
150	74	2c. carmine	1·00	10
		a. Imperf (pair)	£170	
151	75	3c. brown	3·00	10
152	76	4c. deep purple	1·00	30
153	77	5c. ultramarine	4·00	1·75
154	78	6c. slate	9·50	14·00
155	79	8c. purple	12·00	3·50
156	80	9c. slate-green	18·00	32·00
157	81	10c. violet	11·00	6·50
		a. Purple	17·00	3·00
158	82	11c. sage-green	4·25	26·00
159	83	12c. lake	5·50	15·00
160	84	15c. Prussian blue	5·50	30·00
161	85	20c. chestnut (28.4.24)	22·00	18·00
162	86	24c. sepia (22.4.24)	55·00	85·00
149/162		Set of 14	£140	£200

Perforations. Three perforating heads were used: comb 13.8×14 (all values); line 13.7 and 14, and combinations of these two (for all except 6, 8, 9 and 11c.).

Nos. 149 and 151/60 also exist imperforate, but these are usually without gum. (*Price per pair from £180, unused*)

Air Mail
DE PINEDO
1927
(**87**)

1927 (18 May). Air. No. 79 optd with T **87**, by Robinson & Co, Ltd.

163	35	60c. black (R.)	£35000	£11000

For the mail carried by De Pinedo to Europe 300 stamps were overprinted, 230 used on correspondence, 66 presented to De Pinedo, Government Officials, etc., and 4 damaged and destroyed. Stamps without overprint were also used.

88 Newfoundland and Labrador
89 S.S. *Caribou* 
90 King George V and Queen Mary 
91 Duke of Windsor when Prince of Wales 
92 Express Train 
93 Newfoundland Hotel, St. John's 
94 Heart's Content 
95 Cabot Tower, St. John's 
98 Vickers "Vimy" Aircraft
99 Parliament House, St. John's 
100 Grand Falls, Labrador 

(Recess D.L.R.)

1928 (3 Jan)–**29**. Publicity issue. P 14 (1c.) 13½×13 (2, 3, 5, 6, 10, 14, 20c.), 13½×13 (4c.) (all comb), or 14–13½* (line) (others).

164	88	1c. deep green	3·50	1·25
165	89	2c. carmine	3·50	50
166	90	3c. brown	9·00	1·25
		a. Perf 14–13½ (line)	2·75	1·25
167	91	4c. mauve	7·50	4·00
		a. Rose-purple (1929)	11·00	10·00
168	92	5c. slate-grey	13·00	12·00
		a. Perf 14–13½ (line)	35·00	11·00
169	93	6c. ultramarine	11·00	45·00
		a. Perf 14–13½ (line)	24·00	38·00
170	94	8c. red-brown	7·00	45·00
171	95	9c. deep green	2·00	23·00
172	96	10c. deep violet	20·00	26·00
		a. Perf 14–13½ (line)	6·00	27·00
173	97	12c. carmine-lake	2·00	26·00
174	95	14c. brown-purple (8.28)	26·00	12·00
		a. Perf 14–13½ (line)	15·00	9·00
175	98	15c. deep blue	9·00	42·00
176	99	20c. grey-black	24·00	18·00
		a. Perf 14–13½ (line)	6·00	9·00
177	97	28c. deep green (11.28)	28·00	65·00
178	100	30c. sepia	6·00	20·00
164/178		(*cheapest*) Set of 15	£110	£300

*Exact gauges for the various perforations are: 14 comb = 14×13.9; 13½×13 comb = 13.5×12.75; 14–13½ line = 14–13.75.

See also Nos. 179/87 and 198/208.

1c. D
1c. P 
2c. D 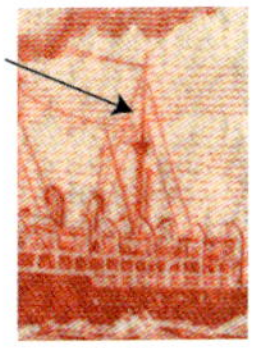
2c. P

CANADA / Newfoundland

3c. D    3c. P

4c. D    4c. P

5c. D    5c. P

6c. D    6c. P    10c. D    10c. P

15c. D    15c. P

20c. D    20c. P

D. De La Rue printing

P. Perkins, Bacon printing

1929 (10 Aug)–**31**. Perkins, Bacon printing. Former types re-engraved. No wmk. P 14 (comb) (1c.), 13½ (comb) (2, 6c.), 14–13½ (line) (20c.) or 13½×14 (comb) (others)*.

179	88	1c. green (26.9.29)	4·50	1·25
		a. Perf 14–13½ (line)	4·25	30
		b. Imperf between (vert pair)	£225	
		c. Imperf (pair)	£160	
180	89	2c. scarlet	1·75	40
		a. Imperf (pair)	£170	
		b. Perf 14–13½ (line)	4·50	1·25
181	90	3c. red-brown	1·00	20
		a. Imperf (pair)	£160	
182	91	4c. reddish purple (26.8.29)	2·75	80
		a. Imperf (pair)	£180	
183	92	5c. deep grey-green (14.9.29)	7·00	5·00
184	93	6c. ultramarine (8.11.29)	12·00	21·00
		a. Perf 14–13½ (line)	2·25	26·00
185	96	10c. violet (5.10.29)	6·50	5·00
186	98	15c. blue (1.30)	17·00	95·00
187	99	20c. black (1.1.31)	60·00	60·00
179/187		Set of 9	90·00	£170

*Exact gauges for the various perforations are: 14 comb = 14×13.9; 13½ comb = 13.6×13.5; 14–13½ line = 14–13.75; 13½ ×14 comb = 13.6×13.8.

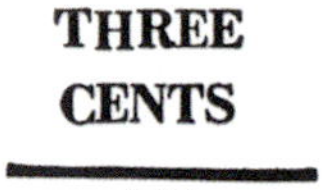

Trans-Atlantic AIR MAIL By B. M. "Columbia" September 1930 Fifty Cents

THREE CENTS (101)    (102)

(Surch by Messrs D. R. Thistle, St. John's)

1929 (23 Aug). No. 154 surch with T **101**.

188		3c. on 6c. slate (R.)	2·25	8·50
		a. Surch inverted	£850	£1300
		b. Surch in black	£950	

The issued surcharge shows 3 mm. space between "CENTS" and the bar. The black surcharge also exists with 5 mm. space, from a trial setting (*Price*, £900).

Nos. 189/90 are vacant.

1930 (25 Sept). Air. No. 141 surch with T **102** by Messrs D. R. Thistle.

191	68	50c. on 36c. sage-green	£6000	£5000

103 Aeroplane and Dog-team

104 Vickers-Vimy Biplane and early Sailing Packet

105 Routes of historic Transatlantic Flights

106

(Des A. B. Perlin. Recess P.B.)

1931. Air. P 14.

(a) Without wmk (2.1.31)

192	103	15c. chocolate	9·00	17·00
		a. Imperf between (horiz pair)	£950	
		b. Imperf between (vert pair)	£1000	
		c. Imperf (pair)	£550	
193	104	50c. green	38·00	55·00
		a. Imperf between (horiz pair)	£1200	£1200
		b. Imperf between (vert pair)	£1500	
		c. Imperf (pair)	£800	
194	105	$1 deep blue	50·00	95·00
		a. Imperf between (horiz pair)	£1100	
		b. Imperf between (vert pair)	£1200	
		c. Imperf (pair)	£800	
192/194		Set of 3	85·00	£150

(b) Wmk W **106**, *(sideways*)* (13.3.31)

195	103	15c. chocolate	11·00	27·00
		a. Pair, with and without wmk	40·00	
		b. Imperf between (horiz pair)	£900	
		c. Imperf between (vert pair)	£1000	
		ca. Ditto, one without wmk (vert pair)	£1500	
		d. Imperf (pair)	£550	
		e. Wmk Cross (pair)	£150	

CANADA / Newfoundland

196	**104**	50c. green	35·00	75·00
		a. Imperf between (horiz pair)	£1000	
		b. Imperf between (vert pair)	£1400	
		c. Imperf (pair)	£475	
		d. Pair, with and without wmk	£475	
		w. Wmk top of shield to right	90·00	
197	**105**	$1 deep blue	80·00	£150
		a. Imperf between (horiz pair)	£1200	
		b. Imperf between (vert pair)	£1000	
		c. Imperf horiz	£800	
		d. Pair, with and without wmk	£800	
		e. Imperf (pair)	£700	
195/197 *Set of 3*			£110	£225

The normal sideways wmk on this issue shows the top of the shield to right on the 15c., but top of the shield to left on the 50c. and $1.

> **"WITH AND WITHOUT WMK" PAIRS** listed in the issues from No. 195a onwards must have one stamp *completely* without any trace of watermark.

1931 (25 March–July). Perkins, Bacon printing (re-engraved types). W **106** (sideways on 1c, 4c, 30c). P 13½ (1c.) or 13½×14 (others), both comb*.

198	**88**	1c. green (7.31)	12·00	3·00
		a. Imperf between (horiz pair)	£650	
199	**89**	2c. scarlet (7.31)	7·00	6·00
		w. Wmk inverted	65·00	
200	**90**	3c. red-brown (7.31)	3·00	3·50
		w. Wmk inverted	65·00	
201	**91**	4c. reddish purple (7.31)	3·25	1·25
202	**92**	5c. deep grey-green (7.31)	7·00	17·00
203	**93**	6c. ultramarine	7·00	30·00
		w. Wmk inverted	75·00	
204	**94**	8c. chestnut (1.4.31)	38·00	48·00
		w. Wmk inverted	80·00	
205	**96**	10c. violet (1.4.31)	23·00	27·00
206	**98**	15c. blue (1.7.31)	21·00	80·00
207	**99**	20c. black (1.7.31)	60·00	26·00
208	**100**	30c. sepia (1.7.31)	29·00	55·00
198/208 *Set of 11*			£190	£275

*Exact gauges for the two perforations are: 13½ = 13.6×13.5; 13½×14 = 13.6×13.8.

(Recess P.B.)

1932 (2 Jan). W **106** (sideways* on vert designs). P 13½ (comb).

209	**107**	1c. green	3·50	30
		a. Imperf (pair)	£170	
		b. Perf 13 (line)	22·00	42·00
		ba. Imperf between (vert pair)	£130	
		w. Wmk top of shield to right	65·00	
210	**108**	2c. carmine	1·50	20
		a. Imperf (pair)	£180	
		c. Perf 13 (line)	18·00	30·00
		w. Wmk top of shield to right	65·00	
211	**109**	3c. orange-brown	1·50	20
		a. Imperf (pair)	£100	
		c. Perf 13 (line)	27·00	42·00
		ca. Imperf between (vert pair)	£250	
		d. Perf 14 (line). Small holes	30·00	40·00
		w. Wmk top of shield to right	65·00	
212	**110**	4c. bright violet	8·50	2·25
		w. Wmk top of shield to right	65·00	
213	**111**	5c. maroon	8·00	4·75
		a. Imperf (pair)	£170	
		w. Wmk top of shield to right	65·00	
214	**112**	6c. light blue	4·00	14·00
215	**113**	10c. black-brown	70	65
		a. Imperf (pair)	70·00	
		w. Wmk inverted	10·00	
216	**114**	14c. black	4·25	5·50
		a. Imperf (pair)	£160	
217	**115**	15c. claret	1·25	2·00
		a. Imperf (pair)	£180	
		b. Perf 14 (line)	8·00	10·00
218	**116**	20c. green	1·00	1·00
		a. Imperf (pair)	£180	
		b. Perf 14 (line)	£130	£130
		w. Wmk inverted	40·00	
219	**117**	25c. slate	2·00	2·25
		a. Imperf (pair)	£180	
		b. Perf 14 (line)	65·00	80·00
		ba. Imperf between (vert pair)	£475	
220	**118**	30c. ultramarine	40·00	38·00
		a. Imperf (pair)	£550	
		b. Imperf between (vert pair)	£1300	
		c. Perf 14 (line)	£425	
209/220 *Set of 12*			65·00	65·00

The Caribou shown on T **111** is taken from the monument to the Royal Newfoundland Regiment, near Beaumont Hamel, France.

*The normal sideways watermark shows the top of the shield to left, *as seen from the back of the stamp*.

Nos. 209b, 210c and 211c were only issued in stamp booklets.

For similar stamps in different perforations see Nos. 222/8c and 276/89.

107 Atlantic Cod
108 King George V
109 Queen Mary
110 Duke of Windsor when Prince of Wales
111 Caribou
112 Queen Elizabeth II when Princess
113 Atlantic Salmon
114 Newfoundland Dog
115 Harp Seal
116 Cape Race
117 Sealing Fleet
118 Fishing Fleet

TRANS-ATLANTIC WEST TO EAST
Per Dornier DO-X
May, 1932.
One Dollar and Fifty Cents

(**119**)

1932 (19 May). Air. No. 197 surch as T **119**, by Messrs. D. R. Thistle. P 14.

221	**105**	$1.50 on $1 deep blue (R.)	£250	£225
		a. Surch inverted	£20000	

120 Queen Mother, when Duchess of York
121 Corner Brook Paper Mills 
122 Loading Iron Ore, Bell Island 

13

CANADA / Newfoundland

(Recess P.B.)

1932 (15 Aug)–**38**. W **106** (sideways* on vert designs). P 13½ (comb.)

222	**107**	1c. grey	3·25	10
		a. Imperf (pair)	48·00	
		c. Perf 14 (line)	8·00	18·00
		d. Perf 14 (line). Small holes	20·00	40·00
		e. Pair, with and without wmk	80·00	
		w. Wmk top of shield to right	65·00	
223	**108**	2c. green	2·50	10
		a. Imperf (pair)	40·00	
		c. Perf 14 (line)	8·00	18·00
		ca. Imperf between (horiz pair)	£275	
		d. Perf 14 (line). Small holes	20·00	42·00
		e. Pair, with and without wmk	80·00	
		w. Wmk top of shield to right	50·00	
224	**110**	4c. carmine (21.7.34)	5·50	40
		a. Imperf (pair)	60·00	
		b. Perf 14 (line)	7·50	11·00
		ba. Imperf between (horiz pair)	£275	
		bb. Imperf between (vert pair)	£140	
		c. Pair, with and without wmk	85·00	
		w. Wmk top of shield to right	70·00	
225	**111**	5c. violet (Die I)	4·00	1·75
		a. Imperf (pair)	75·00	
		b. Perf 14 (line). Small holes	27·00	40·00
		c. Die II	1·00	30
		ca. Imperf (pair)	70·00	
		cb. Perf 14 (line)	24·00	38·00
		cbw. Wmk top of shield to right	70·00	
		cc. Imperf between (horiz pair)	£250	
		cd. Pair, with and without wmk	£180	
226	**120**	7c. red-brown	3·00	3·75
		b. Perf 14 (line)	£200	
		ba. Imperf between (horiz pair)	£600	
		c. Imperf (pair)	£190	
		w. Wmk top of shield to right		
227	**121**	8c. brownish red	3·75	2·00
		a. Imperf (pair)	£110	
		w. Wmk inverted		
228	**122**	24c. bright blue	1·00	3·25
		a. Imperf (pair)	£325	
		b. Doubly printed	£1400	
		w. Wmk inverted	55·00	
228c	**118**	48c. red-brown (1.1.38)	13·00	10·00
		a. Imperf (pair)	£120	
222/228c Set of 8			30·00	18·00

*The normal sideways watermark shows the top of the shield to left, as seen from the back of the stamp.

No. 223. Two dies exist of the 2c., Die I was used for No. 210 and both dies for No. 213. The differences, though numerous, are very slight.

No. 225. There are also two dies of the 5c., Die I only being used for No. 213 and both dies for the violet stamp. In Die II the antler pointing to the "T" of "POSTAGE" is taller than the one pointing to the "S" and the individual hairs on the underside of the caribou's tail are distinct.

For similar stamps in a slightly larger size and perforated 12½ or 13½ (5c.) see Nos. 276/89.

(**123**) "L.&S."—Land and Sea

1933 (9 Feb). No. 195 optd with T **123** for ordinary postal use, by Messrs D. R. Thistle. W **106** (sideways top of shield to right from back). P 14.

229	**103**	15c. chocolate	4·75	18·00
		a. Pair, one without wmk	26·00	
		b. Opt reading up	£4250	
		c. Vertical pair, one without opt	£6500	

124 Put to Flight

125 Land of Heart's Delight

126 Spotting the Herd

127 News from Home

128 Labrador

(Des J. Scott. Recess P.B.)

1933 (9 June). Air. T **124/8** and similar horiz designs. W **106** (sideways*). P 14 (5c., 30c., 75c.) or 11½ (10c., 60c.).

230		5c. red-brown	22·00	22·00
		a. Imperf (pair)	£190	
		b. Imperf between (horiz pair)	£1000	
		c. Imperf between (vert pair)	£1100	
231		10c. orange-yellow	18·00	35·00
		a. Imperf (pair)	£160	
232		30c. light blue	32·00	48·00
		a. Imperf (pair)	£500	
233		60c. green	50·00	£120
		a. Imperf (pair)	£550	
234		75c. yellow-brown	50·00	£120
		a. Imperf (pair)	£500	
		b. Imperf between (horiz or vert pair)	£5000	
		w. Wmk top of shield to left	£150	
230/234 Set of 5			£150	£300

*The normal sideways watermark shows the top of the shield to right, as seen from the back of the stamp.

1933
GEN. BALBO FLIGHT.
$4.50

(**129**)

(Surch by Robinson & Co, St. John's)

1933 (24 July). Air. Balbo Transatlantic Mass Formation Flight. No. 234 surch with T **129**. W **106**. P 14.

235		$4.50 on 75c. yellow-brown	£275	£325
		a. Surch inverted	£80000	
		b. Surch on 10c. (No. 231)	£70000	
		w. Wmk top of shield to left		

No. 235a. When this error was discovered the stamps were ordered to be officially destroyed but four copies which had been torn were recovered and skilfully repaired. In addition, four undamaged examples exist and the price quoted is for one of these (*Price for repaired example, £20000, unused*).

130 Sir Humphrey Gilbert

131 Compton Castle, Devon

132 Gilbert Coat of Arms

133 Eton College

134 Anchor token

135 Gilbert commissioned by Elizabeth I

136 Fleet leaving Plymouth, 1583

137 Arrival at St. John's

14

CANADA / Newfoundland

138 Annexation, 5th August, 1583
139 Royal Arms 
140 Gilbert in the *Squirrel* 
141 Map of Newfoundland, 1626 
142 Queen Elizabeth 
143 Gilbert's statue at Truro 

(Recess P.B.)

1933 (3 Aug). 350th Anniv of the Annexation by Sir Humphrey Gilbert. T **130/43**. W **106** (sideways* on vert designs). P 13½ (comb†).

236	130	1c. slate	1·00	1·50
		a. Imperf (pair)	55·00	
237	131	2c. green	2·00	70
		a. Imperf (pair)	50·00	
		b. Doubly printed	£425	
238	132	3c. chestnut	2·50	1·25
239	133	4c. carmine	1·00	50
		a. Imperf (pair)	55·00	
240	134	5c. violet	2·00	1·00
241	135	7c. greenish blue	15·00	17·00
		a. Perf 14 (line)	18·00	55·00
242	136	8c. vermilion	9·50	20·00
		a. Brownish red	£475	
		b. Bisected (4c.) (on cover)	†	£425
243	137	9c. ultramarine	7·00	21·00
		a. Imperf (pair)	£300	
		b. Perf 14 (line)	80·00	95·00
244	138	10c. brown-lake	6·00	15·00
		a. Imperf (pair)	£300	
		b. Perf 14 (line)	£110	£130
245	139	14c. grey-black	21·00	40·00
		a. Perf 14 (line)	24·00	60·00
246	140	15c. claret	22·00	42·00
		w. Wmk top of shield to right	7·50	29·00
247	141	20c. grey-green	18·00	20·00
		a. Perf 14 (line)	27·00	55·00
		w. Wmk inverted	75·00	
248	142	24c. maroon	20·00	28·00
		a. Imperf (pair)	£130	
		b. Perf 14 (line)	40·00	55·00
		w. Wmk top of shield to right	42·00	
249	143	32c. olive-black	11·00	60·00
		a. Perf 14 (line)	22·00	85·00
		w. Wmk top of shield to right	18·00	70·00
236/249 Set of 14			£110	£225

*The normal sideways watermark shows the top of the shield to left, as seen from the back of the stamp.
†Exact gauges for the two perforations are: 13½ comb = 13.4; 14 line = 13.8.

143a Windsor Castle
143b King George VI and Queen Elizabeth 

(Des H. Fleury. Recess D.L.R.)

1935 (6 May). Silver Jubilee. Wmk Mult Script CA. P 11×12.

250	143a	4c. rosine	1·00	1·75
251		5c. bright violet	1·25	4·25
252		7c. blue	3·75	7·00
253		24c. olive-green	5·00	25·00
250/253 Set of 4			10·00	35·00
250s/253s Perf "SPECIMEN" Set of 4			£190	

(Des D.L.R. Recess B.W.)

1937 (12 May). Coronation Issue. Wmk Mult Script CA. P 11×11½.

254	143b	2c. green	1·00	3·00
255		4c. carmine	1·60	4·00
256		5c. purple	3·00	4·00
254/256 Set of 3			5·00	10·00
254s/256s Perf "SPECIMEN" Set of 3			£140	

144 Atlantic Cod 
145 Map of Newfoundland 
146 Caribou 
147 Corner Brook Paper Mills 
148 Atlantic Salmon 
149 Newfoundland Dog 
150 Harp Seal 
151 Cape Race 
152 Bell Island 
153 Sealing Fleet 
154 The Banks Fishing Fleet

Die I
Die II 

No. 258. In Die II the shading of the King's face is heavier and dots have been added down the ridge of the nose. The top frame line is thicker and more uniform.

15

CANADA / Newfoundland

1c. Fish-hook flaw (R. 1/7 or 3/3)
7c. Re-entry to right of design (inscr oval, tree and value) (R. 4/8) 
20c. Extra chimney (R. 6/5) 

(Recess P.B.)

1937 (12 May). Additional Coronation Issue. T **144/54**. W **106**. P 14 (line)*.

257	144	1c. grey	3·50	30
		a. Pair, with and without wmk	30·00	
		b. Fish-hook flaw	32·00	
		cw. Wmk inverted	65·00	
		d. Perf 13½ (line)	5·00	75
		da. Pair, with and without wmk	40·00	
		db. Fish-hook flaw	45·00	
		e. Perf 13 (comb)	35·00	70·00
		ea. Pair, with and without wmk		
		eb. Fish-hook flaw	£180	
258	145	3c. orange-brown (I)	23·00	6·00
		a. Pair, with and without wmk	£130	
		b. Imperf between (horiz pair)	£475	
		c. Perf 13½ (line)	23·00	8·50
		ca. Pair, with and without wmk	£130	
		cb. Imperf between (vert pair)	£600	
		d. Perf 13 (comb)	12·00	4·00
		e. Die II (P 14, *line*)	13·00	7·50
		ea. Pair, with and without wmk	£180	
		ec. Perf 13½ (line)	12·00	8·00
		eca. Pair, with and without wmk	£190	
		ecb. Imperf between (vert pair)	£700	
		ed. Perf 13 (comb)	9·50	4·75
		eda. Pair, with and without wmk	£170	
259	146	7c. bright ultramarine	3·75	1·25
		a. Pair, with and without wmk	£120	
		b. Re-entry at right	80·00	80·00
		c. Perf 13½ (line)	4·00	1·75
		ca. Pair, with and without wmk	£130	
		cb. Re-entry at right	80·00	
		d. Perf 13 (comb)	£550	£650
		db. Re-entry at right	£2500	
260	147	8c. scarlet	4·00	4·00
		a. Pair, with and without wmk	£100	
		b. Imperf between (horiz pair)	£1100	
		c. Imperf between (vert pair)	£1200	
		d. Imperf (pair)	£425	
		e. Perf 13½ (line)	5·00	6·50
		ea. Pair, with and without wmk	£120	
		eb. Imperf between (vert pair)		
		f. Perf 13 (comb)	12·00	20·00
261	148	10c. blackish brown	7·00	9·00
		a. Pair, with and without wmk	£140	
		b. Perf 13½ (line)	8·00	13·00
		ba. Pair, with and without wmk	£130	
		c. Perf 13 (comb)	3·25	20·00
		cw. Wmk inverted	90·00	
262	149	14c. black	2·25	4·00
		a. Pair, with and without wmk	£120	
		b. Perf 13½ (line)	2·50	6·00
		ba. Pair, with and without wmk	£120	
		c. Perf 13 (comb)	£20000	£12000
263	150	15c. claret	19·00	9·00
		a. Pair, with and without wmk	£140	
		bw. Wmk inverted	£120	
		c. Perf 13½ (line)	20·00	11·00
		ca. Pair, with and without wmk	£140	
		cb. Imperf between (vert pair)	£1100	
		d. Perf 13 (comb)	32·00	50·00
		da. Pair, with and without wmk	£225	
264	151	20c. green	6·50	16·00
		a. Pair, with and without wmk	£130	
		c. Extra chimney	95·00	
		dw. Wmk inverted	£140	
		e. Perf 13½ (line)	6·50	18·00
		ea. Pair, with and without wmk	£200	
		eb. Imperf between (vert pair)	£1500	
		ec. Extra chimney	90·00	£140
		f. Perf 13 (comb)	4·50	9·50
		fc. Extra chimney	85·00	
265	152	24c. light blue	2·75	3·00
		a. Pair, with and without wmk	£250	
		c. Perf 13½ (line)	2·75	3·00
		ca. Pair, with and without wmk	£250	
		cb. Imperf between (vert pair)	£2250	
		d. Perf 13 (comb)	40·00	45·00
266	153	25c. slate	4·50	4·50
		a. Pair, with and without wmk	£200	
		b. Perf 13½ (line)	6·00	5·00
		ba. Pair, with and without wmk	£200	
		c. Perf 13 (comb)	42·00	95·00
267	154	48c. slate-purple	11·00	6·50
		a. Pair, with and without wmk	£325	
		c. Perf 13½ (line)	13·00	13·00
		ca. Pair, with and without wmk	£325	
		cb. Imperf between (vert pair)	£2250	
		cw. Wmk inverted	£275	
		d. Perf 13 (comb)	55·00	£120
257/267 *Set of 11*			60·00	50·00

The line perforations measure 14.1 (14) or 13.7 (13½). The comb perforation measures 13.3×13.2. One example of the 7c. has been reported perforated 13½×14.

The paper used had the watermarks spaced for smaller format stamps. In consequence, the individual watermarks are out of alignment so that stamps from the second vertical row were sometimes without watermark.

155 King George VI 
156 Queen Mother

157 Queen Elizabeth II as princess
158 Queen Mary 

(Recess P.B.)

1938 (12 May). T **155/8**. W **106** (sideways*). P 13½ (comb).

268	155	2c. green	4·25	1·25
		a. Pair, with and without wmk	£225	
		b. Imperf (pair)	£130	
		w. Wmk top of shield to right	£100	
269	156	3c. carmine	1·00	1·00
		a. Perf 14 (line)	£700	£450
		b. Pair, with and without wmk	£350	
		c. Imperf (pair)	£130	
270	157	4c. light blue	3·25	1·00
		a. Pair, with and without wmk	£140	
		b. Imperf (pair)	£120	
		w. Wmk top of shield to right	95·00	
271	158	7c. deep ultramarine	1·00	11·00
		a. Pair, with and without wmk	£225	
		b. Imperf (pair)	£190	
268/271 *Set of 4*			8·50	13·00

* The normal sideways watermark shows the top of the shield to left, *as seen from the back of the stamp*.
For similar designs, perf 12½, see Nos. 277/81.

159 King George VI and Queen Elizabeth

(Recess B.W.)

1939 (17 June). Royal Visit. No wmk. P 13½.

272	159	5c. deep ultramarine	3·25	1·00

2 CENTS
(160)

"CENTL" (R. 5/3)

1939 (20 Nov). No. 272 surch as T **160**, at St. John's.
273	**159**	2c. on 5c. deep ultramarine (Br.)	2·50	50
274		4c. on 5c. deep ultramarine (C.)	2·00	1·00
		a. "CENTL"	42·00	

161 Grenfell on the *Strathcona* (after painting by Gribble)
162 Memorial University College

(Recess C.B.N.)
1941 (1 Dec). 50th Anniv of Sir Wilfred Grenfell's Labrador Mission. P 12.
| 275 | **161** | 5c. blue | 30 | 1·00 |

Damaged "A" (R. 5/9)

(Recess Waterlow)
1941–44. W **106** (sideways* on vert designs). P 12½ (line).
276	**107**	1c. grey	20	2·75
277	**155**	2c. green	40	75
		w. Wmk top of shield to right	50·00	
278	**156**	3c. carmine	40	30
		a. Pair, with and without wmk	£130	
		b. Damaged "A"	80·00	40·00
		w. Wmk top of shield to right	50·00	
279	**157**	4c. blue (As No. 270)	2·50	40
		a. Pair, with and without wmk	£225	
		w. Wmk top of shield to right	60·00	
280	**111**	5c. violet (Die I) (P 13½ *comb*)	£170	
		a. Perf 12½ (line) (6.42)	2·75	85
		ab. Pair, with and without wmk	£200	
		ac. Printed double	£700	
		ad. Imperf vert (horiz pair)	£600	
		b. Imperf (pair)	£225	
281	**158**	7c. deep ultramarine (As No. 271)	10·00	27·00
		a. Pair, with and without wmk	£250	
282	**121**	8c. rose-red	2·25	4·50
		a. Pair, with and without wmk	£200	
283	**113**	10c. black-brown	1·75	2·25
284	**114**	14c. black	7·50	12·00
285	**115**	15c. claret	6·00	8·50
286	**116**	20c. green	6·00	8·50
287	**122**	24c. blue	3·25	25·00
		w. Wmk inverted	85·00	
288	**117**	25c. slate	11·00	20·00
289	**118**	48c. red-brown (1944)	5·00	9·50
276/289 Set of 14			55·00	£110

*The normal sideways watermark shows the top of the shield to left, as seen from the back of the stamp.

Nos. 276/89 are redrawn versions of previous designs with slightly larger dimensions; the 5c. for example, measures 21 mm in width as opposed to the 20.4 mm of the Perkins Bacon printings.

No. 280. For Die I see note relating to No. 225.

(Recess C.B.N.)
1943 (1 Jan). P 12.
| 290 | **162** | 30c. carmine | 1·75 | 4·75 |

TWO CENTS
(164)

163 St. John's

(Recess C.B.N.)
1943 (1 June). Air. P 12.
| 291 | **163** | 7c. ultramarine | 50 | 1·25 |

1946 (21 Mar). No. 290 surch locally with T **164**.
| 292 | **162** | 2c. on 30c. carmine | 30 | 2·00 |

165 Queen Elizabeth II when Princess
166 Cabot off Cape Bonavista

(Recess Waterlow)
1947 (21 Apr). Princess Elizabeth's 21st Birthday. W **106** (sideways). P 12½.
| 293 | **165** | 4c. light blue | 40 | 1·00 |
| | | a. Imperf vert (horiz pair) | £475 | |

(Recess Waterlow)
1947 (24 June). 450th Anniv of Cabot's Discovery of Newfoundland. W **106** (sideways). P 12½.
| 294 | **166** | 5c. mauve | 50 | 1·00 |

STAMP BOOKLETS

1926. Black on pink cover with Ayre and Sons advertisement on front. Stapled.
SB1   40c. booklet containing eight 1c. and sixteen 2c. (Nos. 149/50) in blocks of 8 .... £1700

B **1**

1932 (2 Jan). Black on buff cover as Type B **1**. Stapled.
SB2   40c. booklet containing four 1c., twelve 2c. and four 3c. (Nos. 209b, 210c, 211c) in blocks of 4 .... £450
    a. Contents as No. SB2, but containing Nos. 209b, 210 and 211c £550
    b. Contents as No. SB2, but containing Nos. 222d, 223d and 211c £500

B **2**

1932. Black on cream cover as Type B **2**. Stapled.
SB3   40c. booklet containing four 1c., twelve 2c. and four 3c. (Nos. 222, 223, 211) in blocks of 4 .... £500

CANADA / Newfoundland / Nova Scotia

POSTAGE DUE STAMPS

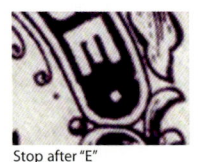

D 1

"POSTAGE LUE"
(R. 3/3 and 3/8)

Stop after "E"
(R. 10/1 and 10/6)

(Litho John Dickinson & Co, Ltd)
1939 (1 May)–**49**. P 10.

D1	D **1**	1c. green	2·25	19·00
		a. Perf 11 (1949)	3·25	22·00
D2		2c. vermilion	14·00	8·50
		a. Perf 11×9 (1946)	14·00	25·00
D3		3c. ultramarine	5·00	32·00
		a. Perf 11×9 (1949)	13·00	60·00
		b. Perf 9	£1600	
D4		4c. orange	9·00	27·00
		a. Perf 11×9 (May 1948)	12·00	65·00
D5		5c. brown	6·50	38·00
D6		10c. violet	9·00	26·00
		a. Perf 11 (W **106**) (1949)	18·00	£100
		ab. Ditto. Imperf between (vert pair)	£1200	
		ac. "POSTAGE LUE"	£150	£425
		ad. Stop after "E"	£120	£350
D1/6 Set of 6			42·00	£140

Newfoundland joined the Dominion of Canada on 31 March 1949.

NOVA SCOTIA

Organised postal services in Nova Scotia date from April 1754 when the first of a series of Deputy Postmasters was appointed, under the authority of the British G.P.O. This arrangement continued until 6 July 1851 when the colony assumed responsibility for its postal affairs.

AMHERST

CROWNED-CIRCLE HANDSTAMPS

| CC1 | CC **1** AMHERST. N.S.(R) (25.2.1845)............ *Price on cover* | £1000 |

ST. MARGARETS BAY

CROWNED-CIRCLE HANDSTAMPS

| CC2 | CC **1** ST. MARGARETS BAY. N.S. (R) (30.6.1845) .... *Price on cover* | £9500 |

Nos. CC1/2 were later used during temporary shortages of stamps, struck in red or black.

PRICES FOR STAMPS ON COVER	
No. 1	from × 5
Nos. 2/4	from × 2
Nos. 5/8	from × 4
Nos. 9/10	from × 10
Nos. 11/13	from × 2
Nos. 14/15	—
No. 16	from × 4
Nos. 17/19	from × 10
Nos. 20/5	from × 2
No. 26	from × 50
Nos. 27/8	from × 4
No. 29	from × 10

1   2

Crown and Heraldic Flowers of United Kingdom and Mayflower of Nova Scotia.

(Recess P.B.)
1851 (1 Sept)–**60**. Bluish paper. Imperf.

1	**1**	1d. red-brown (12.5.53)	£2500	£425
		a. Bisected (½d.) (on cover) (1857)	†	£50000
2	**2**	3d. deep blue	£1200	£160
		a. Bisected (1½d.) (on cover)	†	£2500
3		3d. bright blue	£1000	£140
		a. Bisected (1½d.) (on cover)	†	£2500
4		3d. pale blue (1857)	£900	£140
		a. Bisected (1½d.) (on cover)	†	£2500
5		6d. yellow-green	£4750	£500
		a. Bisected (3d.) (on cover)	†	£3250
		b. Quartered (1½d.) (on cover) (1860)	†	£60000
6		6d. deep green (1857)	£10000	£850
		a. Bisected (3d.) (on cover)	†	£5000
7		1s. cold violet	£25000	£5500
7c		1s. deep purple (1851)	£18000	£4000
		d. Watermarked	£22000	£6000
8		1s. purple (1857)	£18000	£3250
		a. Bisected (6d.) (on cover) (1860)	†	£38000
		b. Quartered (3d.) (on cover) (1858)	†	£90000

The watermark on No. 7d consists of the whole or part of a letter from the name "T. H. SAUNDERS" (the papermakers).

The stamps formerly catalogued on almost white paper are probably some from which the bluish paper has been discharged.

Reprints of all four values were made in 1890 on thin, hard, white paper. The 1d. is brown, the 3d. blue, the 6d. deep green, and the 1s. violet-black.

The 3d. bisects, which were authorised on 19 October 1854, are usually found used to make up the 7½d. rate.

(New Currency. 100 cents = 1 dollar)

3   4   5

(Recess American Bank Note Co, New York)
1860–63. P 12.

(a) Yellowish paper

9	**3**	1c. jet black	4·25	18·00
		a. Bisected (½c.) (on cover)	†	£8000
10		1c. grey-black	4·25	18·00
11		2c. grey-purple	11·00	16·00
11a		2c. purple	17·00	15·00
12		5c. blue	£475	24·00
13		5c. deep blue	£475	24·00
14	**4**	8½c. deep green	4·50	50·00
15		8½c. yellow-green	3·75	50·00
16		10c. scarlet	23·00	35·00
17	**5**	12½c. black	35·00	30·00
17a		12½c. greyish black	—	30·00

(b) White paper

18	**3**	1c. black	4·25	21·00
		a. Imperf vert (horiz pair)	£170	
19		1c. grey	4·25	21·00
20		2c. dull purple	4·75	14·00
21		2c. purple	4·75	14·00
22		2c. grey-purple	4·75	14·00
		a. Bisected (1c.) (on cover)	†	£3500
23		2c. slate-purple	4·75	13·00
24		5c. blue	£550	28·00
25		5c. deep blue	£550	28·00
26	**4**	8½c. deep green	22·00	50·00
27		10c. scarlet	8·50	35·00
28		10c. vermilion	5·00	35·00
		a. Bisected (5c.) (on cover)	†	£750
29	**5**	12½c. black	55·00	32·00

Nova Scotia joined the Dominion of Canada on 1 July 1867.

PRINCE EDWARD ISLAND

Prince Edward Island, previously administered as part of Nova Scotia, became a separate colony in 1769.

PRICES FOR STAMPS ON COVER	
Nos. 1/4	from × 4
No. 5	—
No. 6	from × 5
Nos. 7/8	from × 10
Nos. 9/11	from × 8
Nos. 12/18	from × 6
Nos. 19/20	from × 10
Nos. 21/6	from × 4
Nos. 27/31	from × 8
Nos. 32/3	from × 40
Nos. 34/7	from × 8
No. 38	from × 30
Nos. 39/41	from × 20
No. 42	from × 50
Nos. 43/7	from × 8

Two Dies of 2d.:
Die I. Left-hand frame and circle merge at centre left (all stamps in the sheet of 60 (10×6) except R. 2/5)
Die II. Left-hand frame and circle separate at centre left (R. 2/5). There is also a break in the top frame line.

(Typo Charles Whiting, London)
1861 (1 Jan). Yellowish toned paper.

(a) P 9

1	1	2d. rose (I)	£475	£190
		a. Imperf between (horiz pair)	£9000	
		b. Imperf horiz (vert pair)		
		c. Bisected (1d.) (on cover)	†	£4750
		d. Die II		
2		2d. rose-carmine (I)	£500	£200
		a. Die II		
3	2	3d. blue	£1000	£450
		a. Bisected (1½d.) (on cover)	†	£4250
		b. Double print	£3250	
4	3	6d. yellow-green	£1600	£750

(b) Rouletted

5	1	2d. rose (I)	†	£12000

The 2d. and 3d., perf 9, were authorised to be bisected and used for half their normal value.

1862–69. Yellowish toned paper.

(a) P 11 (1862) or 11¼ (1869)

6	4	1d. brown-orange	70·00	90·00
6a		2d. rose (I) (1869)	†	£500
7	6	9d. bluish lilac (29.3.62)	£130	90·00
8		9d. dull mauve	£130	90·00

(b) P 11½–12 (1863-69)

9	4	1d. yellow-orange (1863)	48·00	65·00
		a. Bisected (½d.) (on cover)	†	£3250
		b. Imperf between (horiz pair)	£550	
10		1d. orange-buff	50·00	65·00
11		1d. yellow	60·00	65·00
12	1	2d. rose (I) (1863)	24·00	18·00
		a. Imperf vert (horiz pair)		
		b. Bisected (1d.) (on cover)	†	£2250
		c. Die II	£100	£100
13		2d. deep rose (I)	25·00	21·00
		a. Die II	£110	£110
14	2	3d. blue (1863)	30·00	30·00
		a. Imperf horiz (vert pair)		
		b. Bisected (1½d.) (on cover)		
15		3d. deep blue	30·00	30·00
16	5	4d. black (1869)	30·00	45·00
		a. Imperf vert (horiz pair)	£350	
		b. Bisected (2d.) (on cover)	†	£2000
		c. Imperf between (horiz strip of 3)	£550	
17	3	6d. yellow-green (15.12.66)	£150	£120
		a. Bisected (3d.) (on cover)	†	£4250
18		6d. blue-green (1868)	£140	£120
19	6	9d. lilac (1863)	£100	95·00
20		9d. reddish mauve (1863)	£100	95·00
		a. Imperf vert (horiz pair)	£850	
		b. Bisected (4½d.) (on cover)	†	£4000

A new perforator, gauging exactly 11¼, was introduced in 1869. Apart from No. 6a, it was used in compound with the perf 11½–12 machine.

(c) Perf compound of 11 or 11¼ (1869) and 11½–12

21	4	1d. yellow-orange	£200	85·00
22	1	2d. rose (I)	£180	70·00
		a. Die II		
23	2	3d. blue	£225	70·00
24	5	4d. black	£325	£250
25	3	6d. yellow-green	£300	£300
26	6	9d. reddish mauve	£350	£300

1870. Coarse, wove bluish white paper. P 11½–12.

27	1	2d. rose (I)	16·00	17·00
		a. Die II	90·00	£100
28		2d. rose-pink (I)	9·00	15·00
		a. Die II	70·00	80·00
		b. "TWC" (R. 6/4)	80·00	90·00
		c. Imperf between (horiz pair)	£250	
		d. Imperf horiz (vert pair)	£250	
29	2	3d. pale blue	14·00	19·00
30		3d. blue	11·00	19·00
		a. Imperf between (horiz pair)	£375	
31	5	4d. black	5·50	35·00
		a. Imperf between (horiz pair)	£225	
		b. Bisected (2d.) (on cover)	†	£2000

(New Currency. 100 cents = 1 dollar)

(Recess British-American Bank Note Co., Montreal and Ottawa)
1870 (1 June). P 12.

32	7	4½d. (3d. stg), yellow-brown	65·00	75·00
33		4½d. (3d. stg), deep brown	65·00	80·00

(Typo Charles Whiting, London)
1872 (1 Jan).

(a) P 11½–12

34	8	1c. orange	9·50	26·00
35		1c. yellow-orange	10·00	23·00
36		1c. brown-orange	8·50	26·00
37	10	3c. rose	27·00	38·00
		a. Stop between "PRINCE. EDWARD" (R. 2/7)	80·00	£100
		b. Bisected (1½c.) (on cover)		
		c. Imperf horiz (vert pair)	£550	

(b) Perf 12 to 12¼ large holes

38	9	2c. blue	26·00	60·00
		a. Bisected (1c.) (on cover)	†	£3500
39	11	4c. yellow-green	9·50	28·00
40		4c. deep green	10·00	26·00
		a. Bisected (2c.) (on cover)	†	£3250

CANADA / Prince Edward Island / Canada

41	**12**	6c. black	6·50	27·00
		a. Bisected (3c.) (on cover)	†	£1800
		b. Imperf between (horiz pair)	£300	
		c. Imperf vert (horiz pair)		
42	**13**	12c. reddish mauve	8·00	55·00
		(c) P 12½–13, smaller holes		
43	**8**	1c. orange		22·00
44		1c. brown-orange	9·00	27·00
45	**10**	3c. rose	24·00	45·00
		a. Stop between "PRINCE. EDWARD" (R. 2/2)	80·00	£120
45*b*	**12**	6c. black	—	£250
		(d) Perf compound of (a) and (c) 11½–12×12½–13		
46	**8**	1c. orange	50·00	55·00
47	**10**	3c. rose	55·00	60·00
		a. Stop between "PRINCE. EDWARD" (R. 2/2)	£250	£275

Prince Edward Island joined the Dominion of Canada on 1 July 1873.

DOMINION OF CANADA

On 1 July 1867, Canada, Nova Scotia and New Brunswick were united to form the Dominion of Canada.

The provinces of Manitoba (1870), British Columbia (1871), Prince Edward Island (1873), Alberta (1905), Saskatchewan (1905), and Newfoundland (1949) were subsequently added, as were the Northwest Territories (1870) and Yukon Territory (1898).

PRICES FOR STAMPS ON COVER TO 1945		
Nos.	46/67	from × 2
Nos.	68/71	from × 10
Nos.	72/89	from × 3
Nos.	90/100	from × 2
Nos.	101/2	from × 5
Nos.	103/11	from × 3
Nos.	115/20	from × 6
Nos.	121/49	from × 3
Nos.	150/65	from × 2
Nos.	166/72	from × 3
Nos.	173/87	from × 5
Nos.	188/95	from × 2
Nos.	196/215	from × 3
Nos.	219/224*b*	from × 4
Nos.	225/45	from × 2
Nos.	246/55	from × 8
Nos.	256/310	from × 2
No.	312	from × 20
No.	313	from × 10
Nos.	315/18	from × 2
Nos.	319/28	from × 3
Nos.	329/40	from × 2
Nos.	341/400	from × 1
Nos.	R1/7*a*	from × 5
Nos.	R8/9	from × 50
Nos.	R10/11	from × 20
Nos.	S1/3	from × 8
No.	S4	from × 6
No.	S5	from × 5
Nos.	S6/11	from × 3
Nos.	S12/14	from × 5
Nos.	D1/8	from × 4
Nos.	D9/13	from × 5
Nos.	D14/24	from × 4

13  **14**  **15**

Large types

PRINTERS. Nos. 46/120 were recess-printed by the British American Bank Note Co at Ottawa or Montreal.

1868 (1 Apr)–**90**. As T **13/15** (various frames).
I. Ottawa printings. P 12
(a) Thin rather transparent crisp paper

46	**13**	½c. black (1.4.68)	95·00	75·00
47	**14**	1c. red-brown (1.4.68)	£600	75·00
48		2c. grass-green (1.4.68)	£650	60·00
49		3c. red-brown (1.4.68)	£1300	32·00
50		6c. blackish brown (1.4.68)	£1600	£170
51		12½c. bright blue (1.4.68)	£1000	£130
52		15c. deep reddish purple	£1200	£180

In these first printings the impression is generally blurred and the lines of the background are less clearly defined than in later printings.

(b) Medium to stout wove paper (1868–71)

53	**13**	½c. black	75·00	60·00
54		½c. grey-black	75·00	60·00
		a. Imperf between (pair)		
		b. Watermarked	£17000	£9000
55	**14**	1c. red-brown	£450	55·00
		a. Laid paper	£17000	£3750
		b. Watermarked (1868)	£2750	£300
56		1c. deep orange (Jan, 1869)	£1400	£120
56*a*		1c. orange-yellow (May (?), 1869)	£1000	90·00
56*b*		1c. pale orange-yellow	£1100	£100
		ba. Imperf		
57		2c. deep green	£600	45·00
57*a*		2c. pale emerald-green (1871)	£750	70·00
		ab. Bisected (1c. with 2c. to make 3c. rate) on cover	†	£4750
		ac. Laid paper	†	£110000
57*d*		2c. bluish green	£650	45·00
		da. Watermarked (1868)	£2750	£250
58		3c. brown-red	£1100	21·00
		a. Laid paper	£13000	£600
		b. Watermarked (1868)	£3500	£225
59		6c. blackish brown (*to chocolate*)	£1200	65·00
		a. Watermarked (1868)	£6000	£1100
59*b*		6c. yellow-brown (1870)	£1100	55·00
		ba. Bisected (3c.), on cover	†	£3000
60		12½c. bright blue	£850	60·00
		a. Imperf horiz (vert pair)	†	£22000
		b. Watermarked (1868)	£3250	£300
60*c*		12½c. pale dull blue (milky)	£900	75·00
61		15c. deep reddish purple	£750	65·00
61*a*		15c. pale reddish purple	£650	65·00
		ab. Watermarked (1868)	—	£1400
61*b*		15c. dull violet-grey	£250	32·00
		ba. Watermarked (1868)	£4250	£800
61*c*		15c. dull grey-purple	£325	32·00

The official date of issue was 1 April 1868. Scattered examples of most values can be found used in the second half of March.

The watermark on the stout paper stamps consists of the words "E & G BOTHWELL CLUTHA MILLS," in large double-lined capitals which can be found upright, inverted or reversed. Portions of one or two letters only may be found on these stamps, which occur in the early printings of 1868.

The paper may, in most cases, be easily divided if the stamps are laid face downwards and carefully compared. The thin hard paper is more or less transparent and shows the design through the stamp; the thicker paper is softer to the feel and more opaque.

Of the 2c. laid paper No. 57*ac* two examples only are known.

No. 60*a* is only known as a vertical strip of five.

II. Montreal printings. Medium to stout wove paper
(a) P 11½×12 or 11¾×12

62	**13**	½c. black (1873)	95·00	75·00
63	**15**	5c. olive-green (28.9.75)	£850	85·00
		a. Perf 12	£3500	£800
64	**14**	15c. dull grey-purple (1874)	£1000	£200
65		15c. lilac-grey (3.77)	£1100	£200
		a. Script watermark	£23000	£3250
		b. "BOTHWELL" watermark	†	£800
66		15c. slate	£1100	£300

(b) P 12

67	**14**	15c. clear deep violet (1879)	£3500	£600
68		15c. deep slate (1881)	£160	32·00
69		15c. slaty blue (1887)	£170	32·00
70		15c. slate-purple (*shades*) (7.88–92)	70·00	19·00

No. 63*a* gauges 12 or above on all four sides.

The watermark on No. 65*a* is part of "Alex.Pirie & Sons" which appeared as script letters once per sheet in a small batch of the paper used for the 1877 printing. For a description of the sheet watermark on No. 65*b*, see note after No. 61*c*.

Several used examples of the 12½c. have been reported perforated 11½×12 or 11¾×12.

The last printing of the 15c. slate-purple, No. 70, took place at Ottawa.

III. Ottawa printings. Thinnish paper of poor quality, often toned grey or yellowish. P 12

71	**14**	15c. slate-violet (*shades*) (5.90)	70·00	21·00
		a. Imperf (pair). Brown-purple	£1400	

Examples of No. 71 are generally found with yellowish streaky gum.

21 *Small type*

CANADA

Strand of hair

Straw in hair

1870–88. As T **21** (various frames). Ottawa (1870–73) and Montreal printings. P 12 (or slightly under).

Papers	(a)	1870–80. Medium to stout wove.
	(b)	1870–72. Thin, soft, very white.
	(c)	1878–97. Thinner and poorer quality.

72	**21**	1c. bright orange (a, b) (2.1870–73)......	£200	35·00
		a. Thick soft paper (1871)	£550	£140
73		1c. orange-yellow (a) (1876–79)............	80·00	4·25
74		1c. pale dull yellow (a) (1877–79)..........	55·00	3·50
75		1c. bright yellow (a, c) (1878–97)..........	38·00	2·00
		a. Imperf (pair) (c)	£550	
		b. Bisected (½c.) (on *Railway News*).....	†	£4250
		c. Printed both sides.............................	£1800	
		d. Strand of hair	£900	£325
76		1c. lemon-yellow (c) (1880)	£100	18·00
77		2c. deep green (a, b) (1872–73 and 1876–78)..	90·00	4·00
78		2c. grass-green (c) (1878–88)................	55·00	2·25
		a. Imperf (pair)	£650	
		b. Bisected on cover.............................	†	£2500
		c. Stamp doubly printed.......................	†	£5000
79		3c. Indian red (a) (1.70)	£1100	50·00
		a. Perf 12½ (2.70)	£7500	£700
80		3c. pale rose-red (a) (9.70)	£350	13·00
81		3c. deep rose-red (a, b) (1870–73).........	£375	13·00
		a. Thick soft paper (1.71)......................	—	£150
82		3c. dull red (a, c) (1876–88)	95·00	3·25
83		3c. orange-red (*shades*) (a, c) (1876–88)	70·00	2·75
84		3c. rose-carm (c) (10.88.–4.89)	£375	15·00
85		5c. olive-green (a, c) (2.76–88)	£400	14·00
		a. Straw in hair	£1900	£650
86		6c. yellowish brown (a, b, c) (1872–73 and 1876–90).........................	£325	18·00
		a. Bisected (3c.) on cover	†	£1200
		b. Perf 12×11½ (1873)............................	†	—
		c. Perf 12×12½.....................................	†	£2500
87		10c. pale lilac-magenta (1876–?)	£700	55·00
88		10c. deep lilac-magenta (a, c) (3.76–88)	£800	65·00
89		10c. lilac-pink (3.88)	£350	45·00

Nos. 75 and 78 were printed in the same shades during the second Ottawa period. Nos. 75a and 78a date from *circa* 1894–95.

There are four variants of the Strand of Hair, with the strand in the same position but varying in length. R. 2/13 and R. 3/16 have been identified. The illustration shows the "Long Strand".

Examples of paper (a) can often be found showing traces of ribbing, especially on the 2c. value.

No. 79a was issued in New Brunswick and Nova Scotia.
One used copy of the 10c. perf 12½ has been reported.

1873–79. Montreal printings. Medium to stout wove paper. P 11½×12 or 11¾×12.

90	**21**	1c. bright orange............................	£300	50·00
91		1c. orange-yellow (1873–79)	£250	17·00
92		1c. pale dull yellow (1877–79)	£250	21·00
93		1c. lemon-yellow (1879)	£300	21·00
94		2c. deep green (1873–78)	£400	24·00
95		3c. dull red (1875–79)..........................	£300	24·00
96		3c. orange-red (1873–79)......................	£300	24·00
97		5c. olive-green (1.2.76–79)	£650	35·00
98		6c. yellowish brown (1873–79)	£550	50·00
99		10c. very pale lilac magenta (1874).........	£1500	£350
100		10c. deep lilac-magenta (1876–79)	£1100	£200

27

5c. on 6c. re-entry (R. 3/5)

1882–97. Montreal (to March 1889) and Ottawa printings. Thinnish paper of poor quality. P 12.

101	**27**	½c. black (7.82–97)	18·00	11·00
102		½c. grey-black.....................................	18·00	11·00
		ab. Imperf (pair) (1891–93?)..................	£650	
		ac. Imperf between (horiz pair).............	£900	

1889–97. Ottawa printings. Thinnish paper of poor quality, often toned grey or yellowish. P 12.

103	**21**	2c. dull sea-green................................	65·00	2·25
104		2c. blue-green (7.89–91)	50·00	3·25
105		3c. bright vermilion (4.89–97)..............	45·00	1·25
		a. Imperf (pair) (1891–93?)...................	£500	
106		5c. brownish grey (5.89)	90·00	1·75
		a. Imperf (pair) (1891–93)	£650	
107		6c. deep chestnut (10.90)....................	45·00	14·00
		a. "5c." re-entry*..................................	£3250	£1500
		b. Imperf (pair) (1891–93?)...................	£700	
108		6c. pale chestnut.................................	55·00	14·00
109		10c. salmon-pink.................................	£325	£110
110		10c. carmine-pink (4.90)	£275	35·00
		a. Imperf (pair) (1891–93?)...................	£800	
111		10c. brownish red (1894?)....................	£250	32·00
		a. Imperf (pair)	£700	

On No. 107a the top portion of the 5c. design cuts across "CANADA POSTAGE", the white circle surrounding the head, and can be seen on the top of the head itself. Lesser re-entries are visible on R. 2/10 and R. 3/1 from another plate.

The 1c. showed no change in the Ottawa printings, so is not included. The 2c. reverted to its previous grass-green shade in 1891.

Nos. 112/4 are vacant.

28    29

(Recess B.A.B.N.)

1893 (17 Feb). P 12.

115	**28**	20c. vermilion....................................	£225	60·00
		a. Imperf (pair)	£1600	
116		50c. blue...	£250	45·00
		a. Imperf (*Prussian blue*) (pair).............	£1700	

1893 (1 Aug). P 12.

117	**29**	8c. pale bluish grey	£160	8·00
		a. Imperf (pair)	£900	
118		8c. bluish slate.....................................	£150	8·00
119		8c. slate-purple....................................	£130	8·00
120		8c. blackish purple...............................	£110	8·00
		a. Imperf (pair)	£900	

PRINTERS. The following stamps to No. 287 were recess-printed by the American Bank Note Co, Ottawa, which in 1923 became the Canadian Bank Note Co.

30

CANADA

(Des L. Pereira and F. Brownell)
1897 (19 June). Jubilee issue. P 12.

121	**30**	½c. black	65·00	65·00
122		1c. orange	11·00	5·50
123		1c. orange-yellow	11·00	5·50
		a. Bisected (½c.) (on *Railway News*)	†	£5500
124		2c. green	21·00	9·00
125		2c. deep green	21·00	9·00
126		3c. carmine	12·00	2·25
127		5c. slate-blue	45·00	14·00
128		5c. deep blue	45·00	14·00
129		6c. brown	£110	£100
130		8c. slate-violet	42·00	32·00
131		10c. purple	70·00	60·00
132		15c. slate	£120	£100
133		20c. vermilion	£130	£100
134		50c. pale ultramarine	£170	£110
135		50c. bright ultramarine	£180	£120
136		$1 lake	£500	£475
137		$2 deep violet	£900	£400
138		$3 bistre	£1200	£750
139		$4 violet	£1100	£650
140		$5 olive-green	£1100	£650
121/140 Set of 16			£5000	£3000
133s/140s Handstamped "SPECIMEN" Set of 7				£2250

No. 123a was used on issues of the *Railway News* of 5, 6 and 8 November 1897 and must be on a large part of the original newspaper with New Glasgow postmark.

31 **32**
(From photograph by W. & D. Downey, London)

1897–98. P 12.

141	**31**	½c. grey-black (9.11.97)	12·00	6·50
142		½c. black	11·00	5·00
		a. Imperf (pair)	£400	
143		1c. blue-green (12.97)	23·00	90
		a. Imperf (pair)	£400	
144		2c. violet (12.97)	21·00	1·50
		a. Imperf (pair)	£400	
145		3c. carmine (1.98)	40·00	2·25
		a. Imperf (pair)	£750	
146		5c. deep blue/*bluish* (12.97)	70·00	2·75
		a. Imperf (pair)	£400	
147		6c. brown (12.97)	60·00	29·00
		a. Imperf (pair)	£750	
148		8c. orange (12.97)	85·00	7·50
		a. Imperf (pair)	£450	
149		10c. brownish purple (1.98)	£140	55·00
		a. Imperf (pair)	£475	
141/149 Set of 8			£400	95·00

BOOKLET PANES. Most definitive booklets issued from 1900 onwards had either the two horizontal sides or all three outer edges imperforate. Stamps from the panes show one side or two adjacent sides imperforate.

Two types of the 2c.
Die Ia. Frame consists of four fine lines.
Die Ib. Frame has one thick line between two fine lines.

The die was retouched in 1900 for Plates 11 and 12, producing weak vertical frame lines and then retouched again in 1902 for Plates 15 to 20 resulting in much thicker frame lines. No. 155b covers both states of the retouching.

1898–1902. P 12.

150	**32**	½c. black (9.98)	6·50	1·10
		a. Imperf (pair)	£425	
151		1c. blue-green (6.98)	27·00	60
152		1c. deep green/*toned paper*	32·00	2·50
		a. Imperf (pair)	£900	
153		2c. dull purple (Die Ia) (9.98)	38·00	30
		a. Thick paper (6.99)	£110	10·00
154		2c. violet (Die Ia)	26·00	30
154a		2c. reddish purple (Die Ia)	55·00	1·75
155		2c. rose-carmine (Die Ib) (20.8.99)	38·00	30
		a. Imperf (pair)	£375	
155b		2c. rose-carmine (Die Ib) (1900)	70·00	1·50
		ba. Booklet pane of 6 (11.6.00)	£750	
156		3c. rose-carmine (6.98)	70·00	1·00
157		5c. slate-blue/*bluish*	£110	3·75
		a. Imperf (pair)	£950	
158		5c. Prussian blue/*bluish*	£120	3·75
159		6c. brown (9.98)	£100	65·00
		a. Imperf (pair)	£850	
160		7c. greenish yellow (23.12.02)	70·00	22·00

161		8c. orange-yellow (10.98)	£130	40·00
162		8c. brownish orange	£120	40·00
		a. Imperf (pair)	£850	
163		10c. pale brownish purple (11.98)	£170	14·00
164		10c. deep brownish purple	£170	14·00
		a. Imperf (pair)	£900	
165		20c. olive-green (29.12.00)	£300	50·00
150/165 Set of 11			£950	£180

The 7c. and 20c. also exist imperforate, but unlike the values listed in this condition, they have no gum. (*Price*, 7c. £425, 20c. £2750 *pair, un*).

33

(Des R. Weir Crouch, G. Hahn, A. H. Howard and R. Holmes. Eng C. Skinner. Design recess, colours added by typo)

1898 (7 Dec). Imperial Penny Postage. Design in black. British possessions in red. Oceans in colours given. P 12.

166	**33**	2c. lavender	29·00	6·50
		a. Imperf (pair)	£375	
167		2c. greenish blue	32·00	7·00
		a. Imperf (pair)	£425	
168		2c. blue	35·00	7·00
		a. Imperf (pair)	£450	

Forgeries of Type **33** are without horizontal lines across the continents and have a forged Montreal postmark of 24.12.98.

1899 (4 Jan). Provisionals used at Port Hood, Nova Scotia. No. 156 divided vertically and handstamped.

169	**32**	"1" in blue, on 13 of 3c.	—	£3500
170		"2" in violet, on 23 of 3c.	—	£3000

Nos. 169/70 were prepared by the local postmaster during a shortage of 2c. stamps caused by a change in postage rates.

2 CENTS
(**34**)

35 King Edward VII

1899. Surch with T **34**, by Public Printing Office.

171	**31**	2c. on 3c. carmine (8 Aug)	20·00	8·00
		a. Surch inverted	£350	
172	**32**	2c. on 3c. rose-carmine (28 July)	19·00	4·25
		a. Surch inverted	£350	

(Des King George V when Prince of Wales and J. A. Tilleard)

1903 (1 July)–**12**. P 12.

173	**35**	1c. pale green	32·00	50
174		1c. deep green	28·00	50
175		1c. green	28·00	50
176		2c. rose-carmine	20·00	50
		a. Booklet pane of 6	£800	£950
177		2c. pale rose-carmine	20·00	50
		a. Imperf (pair) (18.7.09)	29·00	42·00
178		5c. blue/*bluish*	85·00	2·50
179		5c. indigo/*bluish*	85·00	2·75
180		7c. yellow-olive	70·00	2·75
181		7c. greenish bistre	85·00	2·75
181a		7c. straw (1.12)	£120	50·00
182		10c. brown-lilac	£150	20·00
183		10c. pale dull purple	£150	20·00
184		10c. dull purple	£150	20·00
185		20c. pale olive-green (27.9.04)	£275	28·00
186		20c. deep olive-green	£300	28·00
		s. Handstamped "SPECIMEN"	90·00	
187		50c. deep violet (19.11.08)	£425	£100
173/187 Set of 7			£950	£140

The 1c., 5c., 7c. and 10c. exist imperforate but are believed to be proofs. (*Prices per pair*, 1c. £500, 5c. £950. 7c. £600, 10c. £950).

IMPERFORATE AND PART-PERFORATED SHEETS. Prior to 1946 many Canadian issues exist imperforate, or with other perforation varieties, in the colours of the issued stamps and, usually, with gum. In the years before 1927 such examples are believed to come from imprimatur sheets, removed from the Canadian Post Office archives. From 1927 until 1946 it is known that the printers involved in the production of the various issues submitted several imperforate plate proof sheets of each stamp to the Post Office authorities for approval. Some of these sheets or part sheets were retained for record purposes, but the remainder found their way on to the philatelic market.

Part-perforated sheets also occur from 1927–29 issues.
From 1908 until 1946 we now only list and price such varieties of this type which are known to be genuine errors, sold from post offices. Where other imperforate or similar varieties are known they are recorded in footnotes.

It is possible, and in some cases probable, that some imperforate varieties listed before 1908 may have also been removed from the archives as mentioned above, but it is far harder to be explicit over the status of this earlier material.

36 King George V and Queen Mary when Prince and Princess of Wales

37 Jacques Cartier and Samuel Champlain

Re-entry (R. 5/4)

38 King Edward VII and Queen Alexandra

39 Champlain's house in Quebec

40 Generals Montcalm and Wolfe

41 Quebec in 1700

42 Champlain's departure for the West

43 Cartier's arrival before Quebec

1908 (16 July). Quebec Tercentenary. T **36/43**. P. 12.

188	36	½c. sepia	4·50	3·50
		a. Re-entry	60·00	60·00
189	37	1c. blue-green	23·00	2·75
190	38	2c. carmine	23·00	1·00
191	39	5c. indigo	60·00	30·00
192	40	7c. olive-green	85·00	65·00
193	41	10c. violet	95·00	80·00
194	42	15c. brown-orange	£110	80·00
195	43	20c. dull brown	£150	£120
188/195 Set of 8			£500	£350

Some values exist on both toned and white papers.
Nos. 188/95 exist imperforate. (*Price £550, un, for each pair*).

WET AND DRY PRINTINGS. Until the end of December 1922 all Canadian stamps were produced by the "wet" method of recess-printing in which the paper was dampened before printing, dried and then gummed.

In late December 1922 the Canadian Bank Note Co. began to use the "dry" process in which the paper was gummed before printing. Late printings of the 3c. brown were the first stamps to be produced by this method, but the changeover was not completed until January 1926.

"Dry" printings have a sharper appearance and can often be found with a degree of embossing showing on the reverse. Stamps from "wet" printings shrink during drying and are narrower than "dry" examples. In many cases the difference can be as great as 0.5 mm. On some early booklet panes the difference is in the vertical, rather than the horizontal, measurement.

On Nos. 196/215 all values only exist from "wet" printings, except the 3c., 20c. and 50c. which come from both types of printing.

44

1911–22. P. 12.

196	44	1c. yellow-green (22.12.11)	8·50	50
		a. With fine horiz lines across stamp..	45·00	9·00
197		1c. bluish green	5·50	50
		a. Booklet pane of 6 (1.5.13)	50·00	
198		1c. deep bluish green	6·00	50
199		1c. deep yellow-green	7·00	80
		a. Booklet pane of 6	18·00	
200		2c. rose-red (15.12.11)	7·50	50
201		2c. deep rose-red	6·00	50
		a. Booklet pane of 6 (1.12)	32·00	
202		2c. pale rose-red	6·50	50
		a. With fine horiz lines across stamp..	25·00	15·00
203		2c. carmine	7·50	50
204		3c. brown (6.8.18)	6·00	50
205		3c. deep brown	5·50	50
		a. Booklet pane of 4+2 labels (2.22)..	55·00	
205*b*		5c. deep blue (17.1.12)	60·00	75
206		5c. indigo	90·00	6·50
206*a*		5c. grey-blue	£100	4·00
206*b*		7c. straw (12.1.12)	85·00	18·00
207		7c. pale sage-green (1914)	£250	45·00
208		7c. olive-yellow (1915)	22·00	3·00
209		7c. yellow-ochre (1916)	22·00	3·00
210		10c. brownish purple (12.1.12)	90·00	2·75
211		10c. reddish purple	£120	5·50
212		20c. olive-green (23.1.12)	40·00	1·50
213		20c. olive	40·00	1·75
214		50c. grey-black (26.1.12)	£120	10·00
215		50c. sepia	50·00	3·75
196/215 Set of 8			£250	12·00

The 20c. and 50c. values exist imperforate (*Price £2750 un, for each pair*).

1912 (1 Nov)–**21**. For use in coil-machines.

(a) P 12×imperf

216	44	1c. yellow-green (1914)	3·50	14·00
217		1c. blue-green	23·00	25·00
		a. Two large holes at top and bottom (vert pair) (7.18)	80·00	90·00
218		2c. deep rose-red (1914)	32·00	24·00
218*a*		3c. brown (1921)	3·75	7·50

No. 217a has two large holes about 3½ mm in diameter in the top and bottom margins. They were for experimental use in a vending machine at Toronto in July 1918 and were only in use for two days.

The 1c. and 2c. also exist with two small "V" shaped holes about 9.5 mm apart at top which are gripper marks due to modifications made in vending machines in 1917.

(b) Imperf×perf 8

219	44	1c. yellow-green (9.12)	18·00	6·00
220		1c. blue-green	24·00	5·50
		a. With fine horiz lines across stamp..	65·00	
221		2c. carmine (9.12)	15·00	1·50
222		2c. rose-red	16·00	2·25
223		2c. scarlet	42·00	6·50
224		3c. brown (8.18)	5·00	2·00

(c) P 8×imperf

224*a*	44	1c. blue-green (15.2.13)	65·00	50·00
224*b*		2c. carmine (15.2.13)	65·00	50·00

The stamps imperf×perf 8 were sold in coils over the counter; those perf 8×imperf were on sale in automatic machines. Varieties showing perf 12 on 2 or 3 adjacent sides and 1 or 2 sides imperf are from booklets, or the margins of sheets.

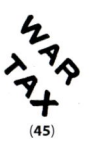

(**45**) **46** **47**

1915 (12 Feb). Optd with T **45**.

225	44	5c. blue	£120	£200
226		20c. olive-green	60·00	£100
227		50c. sepia (R.)	£120	£160
225/227 Set of 3			£275	£425

These stamps were intended for tax purposes, but owing to ambiguity in an official circular dated 16 April 1915, it was for a time believed that their use for postal purposes was authorised. The position was clarified by a further circular on 20 May 1916 which made clear that Nos. 225/7 were for fiscal use only.

1915. P 12.

228	46	1c. green (15.4.15)	8·00	50
229		2c. carmine-red (16.4.15)	24·00	2·50
230		2c. rose-carmine	26·00	4·25

Die I   Die II

In Die I there is a long horizontal coloured line under the foot of the "T", and a solid bar of colour runs upwards from the "1" to the "T".

In Die II this solid bar of colour is absent, and there is a short horizontal line under the left side of the "T", with two short vertical dashes and a number of dots under the right-hand side.

1916 (1 Jan). P 12.

231	47	2c. +1c. rose-red (Die I)	50·00	1·25
232		2c. +1c. bright carmine (Die I)	40·00	1·25
233		2c. +1c. scarlet (Die I)	45·00	2·00

1916 (Feb). Imperf×perf 8 (coils).

234	47	2c. +1c. rose-red (Die I)	70·00	12·00

1916 (July). P 12×8.

235	47	2c. +1c. carmine-red (Die I)	30·00	60·00
236		2c. +1c. bright rose-red (Die I)	35·00	60·00

1916 (Aug). P 12.

237	47	2c. +1c. carmine (Die II)	£140	25·00

1916 (Aug). Colour changed.

(a) P 12

238	47	2c. + 1c. brown (Die I)	£275	23·00
239		2c. + 1c. yellow-brown (Die II)	5·00	50
		a. Imperf (pair)	£1200	
240		2c. + 1c. deep brown (Die II)	16·00	50

(b) Imperf×perf 8

241	47	2c. + 1c. brown (Die I)	£110	9·50
		a. Pair, 241 and 243	£350	
243		2c. + 1c. deep brown (Die II)	55·00	3·75

No. 239a, which is a genuine error, should not be confused with ungummed proofs of the Die I stamp, No. 238 (*Price per pair, £140*).

This value also exists p 12×imperf or imperf×p 12, but was not issued with these perforations (*Price, in either instance, £350, un, per pair*).

No. 242 is vacant.

48 Quebec Conference, 1864, from painting "The Fathers of Confederation", by Robert Harris

1917 (15 Sept). 50th Anniv of Confederation. P 12.

244	48	3c. bistre-brown	21·00	3·25
245		3c. deep brown	23·00	4·00

No. 244 exists imperforate, without gum (*Price per pair, £475 un*).

Die I (top). Space between top of "N" and oval frame line and space between "CENT" and lower frame line.

Die II (bottom). "ONE CENT" appears larger so that "N" touches oval and "CENT" almost touches frame line. There are other differences but this is the most obvious one.

Die I (top). The lowest of the three horizontal lines of shading below the medals does not touch the three heavy diagonal lines; three complete white spaces over both "E's" of "THREE"; long centre bar to figures "3". Vertical spandrel lines fine.

Die II (bottom). The lowest horizontal line of shading touches the first of the three diagonal lines; two and a half spaces over first "E" and spaces over second "E" partly filled by stem of maple leaf; short centre bar to figures "3". Vertical spandrel lines thick. There are numerous other minor differences.

WET AND DRY PRINTINGS. See notes above No. 196.

On Nos. 246/63 all listed items occur from both "wet" and "dry" printings except Nos. 246aa/ab, 248aa, 256, 259, 260 and 262 which come "wet" only, and Nos. 246a, 248/a, 252/4a, 256b and 263 which are "dry" only.

1922–31. As T **44**.

(a) P 12

246	44	1c. chrome-yellow (Die I) (7.6.22)	2·75	60
		aa. Booklet pane of 4+2 labels (7.22)	60·00	
		ab. Booklet pane of 6 (12.22)	40·00	
		a. Die II (1925)	6·00	30
247		2c. deep green (6.6.22)	2·25	10
		aa. Booklet pane of 4+2 labels (7.22)	55·00	
		ab. Booklet pane of 6 (12.22)	£325	
		b. Thin paper (9.24)	3·00	4·75
248		3c. carmine (Die I) (18.12.23)	3·75	10
		aa. Booklet pane of 4+2 labels (12.23)	50·00	
		a. Die II (11.24)	32·00	80
249		4c. olive-yellow (7.7.22)	8·00	3·50
		a. Yellow-ochre	8·00	3·50
250		5c. violet (2.2.22)	5·00	1·75
		a. Thin paper (9.24)	5·00	9·00
		b. *Reddish violet* (1925)	8·00	2·00
251		7c. red-brown (12.12.24)	12·00	9·00
		a. Thin paper	£160	45·00
252		8c. blue (1.9.25)	21·00	11·00
253		10c. blue (20.2.22)	15·00	3·25
254		10c. bistre-brown (1.8.25)	23·00	4·00
		a. Yellow-brown	18·00	4·00
255		$1 brown-orange (22.7.23)	55·00	9·50
246/255 Set of 10			£130	38·00

The $1 differs from T **44** in that the value tablets are oval.

Nos. 249/52 and 254/5 exist imperforate (*Prices per un pair* 4c. to 8c. £2000 *each*, 10c. £2250, $1 £2750).

(b) Imperf×perf 8

256	44	1c. chrome-yellow (Die I) (1922)	4·00	7·50
		a. Imperf horiz (vert pair) (1924)	£180	
		b. Die II (1925)	4·50	7·00
		c. Do. Imperf horiz (vert pair) (1927)	8·00	27·00
257		2c. deep green (26.7.22)	7·00	2·25
		b. Imperf horiz (vert pair) (1927)	9·00	27·00
258		3c. carmine (Die I) (9.4.24)	80·00	14·00
		a. Imperf horiz (vert pair) (1924)	£250	
		b. Die II (1925)	£100	30·00
256/258 Set of 3			85·00	21·00

Nos. 256a, 256c, 257b and 258a come from coil printings sold in sheet form. Those issued in 1924 were from "wet" printings and those in 1927 from "dry". A "wet" printing of No. 257b, issued in 1924, also exists (*Price £180 mint*), but cannot be identified from that issued in 1927 except by the differences between "wet" and "dry" stamps.

(c) Imperf (pairs)

259	44	1c. chrome-yellow (Die I) (6.10.24)	50·00	70·00
260		2c. deep green (6.10.24)	50·00	70·00
261		3c. carmine (Die I) (31.12.23)†	32·00	55·00

(d) P 12×imperf

262	44	2c. deep green (9.24)	65·00	65·00

(e) P 12×8

263	44	3c. carmine (Die II) (24.6.31)	4·00	3·25

†Earliest known postmark.

Nos. 259 to 261 were on sale only at the Philatelic Branch, P.O. Dept, Ottawa.

No. 263 was produced by adding horizontal perforations to unused sheet stock of No. 258b. The stamps were then issued in 1931 pending the delivery of No. 293.

2 CENTS (49)   **2 CENTS** (50)

CANADA

1926. No. 248 surch.

*(a) With T **49**, by the Govt Printing Bureau*

264	**44**	2c. on 3c. carmine (12.10.26)	50·00	60·00
		a. Pair, one without surch	£450	
		b. On Die II	£400	

*(b) With T **50**, by the Canadian Bank Note Co*

265	**44**	2c. on 3c. carmine (4.11.26)	16·00	26·00
		a. Surch double (partly treble)	£200	

51 Sir J. A. Macdonald
52 "The Fathers of Confederation" 
53 Parliament Buildings, Ottawa 
54 Sir W. Laurier 
55 Canada, Map 1867–1927 

1927 (29 June). 60th Anniv of Confederation. P 12.

I. Commemorative Issue. Inscr "1867–1927 CANADA CONFEDERATION"

266	**51**	1c. orange	2·50	1·50
267	**52**	2c. green	2·25	30
268	**53**	3c. carmine	8·50	5·00
269	**54**	5c. violet	5·50	4·25
270	**55**	12c. blue	27·00	7·00
266/270	Set of 5		42·00	16·00

Nos. 266/70 exist imperforate, imperf×perf or perf×imperf (*Prices from £100, un, per pair*).

56 Darcy McGee
57 Sir W. Laurier and Sir J. A. Macdonald 
58 R. Baldwin and L. H. Lafontaine 

II. Historical Issue.

271	**56**	5c. violet	3·00	2·50
272	**57**	12c. green	17·00	4·50
273	**58**	20c. carmine	17·00	13·00
271/273	Set of 3		32·00	18·00

Nos. 271/3 exist imperforate, imperf×perf or perf×imperf (*Prices from £100, un, per pair*).

59

(Des H. Schwartz)

1928 (21 Sept). Air. P 12.

274	**59**	5c. olive-brown	7·50	5·00

No. 274 exists imperforate, imperf×perf or perf×imperf (*Price per pair, £200, un*).

60 King George V
61 Mt. Hurd and Indian Totem Poles 
62 Quebec Bridge 
63 Harvesting with Horses 
64 *Bluenose* (fishing schooner) 
65 Parliament Buildings, Ottawa 

1928–29.

(a) P 12

275	**60**	1c. orange (25.10.28)	2·75	2·25
		a. Booklet pane of 6	18·00	
276		2c. green (16.10.28)	1·25	20
		a. Booklet pane of 6	18·00	
277		3c. lake (12.12.28)	19·00	21·00
278		4c. olive-bistre (16.8.29)	13·00	9·50
279		5c. violet (12.12.28)	6·50	5·50
		a. Booklet pane of 6 (6.1.29)	£130	
280		8c. blue (21.12.28)	7·50	7·50
281	**61**	10c. green (5.12.28)	8·50	2·25
282	**62**	12c. grey-black (8.1.29)	26·00	16·00
283	**63**	20c. lake (8.1.29)	32·00	16·00
284	**64**	50c. blue (8.1.29)	£150	50·00
285	**65**	$1 olive-green (8.1.29)	£140	80·00
		a. Brown-olive	£225	£100
275/285	Set of 11		£375	£190

(b) Imperf×perf 8 (5.11.28)

286	**60**	1c. orange	14·00	25·00
287		2c. green	18·00	8·00

Slight differences in the size of many Canadian stamps, due to paper shrinkage, are to be found.

Nos. 275/85 exist imperforate, imperf×perf or perf×imperf (*Prices per unused pair, 1c. to 8c., from £95, 10c. to 20c., from £170, 50c. and $1, from £500*). *Tête-bêche* horizontal pairs of the 1c., 2c. and 5c. are also known from uncut booklet sheets (*Prices per pair, £300, un*).

PRINTERS. The following stamps to No. 334 were recess-printed by the British American Bank Note Co, Ottawa.

66
67 Parliamentary Library, Ottawa 
68 The Old Citadel, Quebec 
69 Harvesting with Tractor 

25

CANADA

70 Acadian Memorial Church and Statue of "Evangeline", Grand Pre, Nova Scotia

71 Mt. Edith Cavell, Canadian Rockies

72 Mercury and Western Hemisphere

73 Sir Georges Etienne Cartier

Die I 1c. Die II Die I 2c. Die II

1c. Die I. Three thick coloured lines and one thin between "P" and ornament, at right. Curved line in ball-ornament short.
Die II. Four thick lines. Curved line longer.

2c. Die I. Three thick coloured lines between "P" and ornament, at left. Short line in ball.
Die II. Four thick lines. Curved line longer.

2c. "Cockeyed King"

1930–31.

		(a) P 11		
288	66	1c. orange (I) (17.7.30)	1·75	1·25
289		1c. green (I) (6.12.30)	2·00	10
		b. Booklet pane of 6 (21.7.31)	32·00	
		d. Die II (8.31)	2·00	10
		da. Imperf (pair)	£2000	
		db. Booklet pane of 4+2 labels (13.11.31)	£100	
290		2c. green (I) (6.6.30)	1·75	10
		a. Booklet pane of 6 (17.6.30)	42·00	
291		2c. scarlet (I) (17.11.30)	2·25	3·00
		a. Booklet pane of 6 (17.11.30)	27·00	
		b. Die II	1·00	10
292		2c. deep brown (I) (4.7.31)	1·50	4·75
		a. Booklet pane of 6 (23.7.31)	50·00	
		b. Die II (4.7.31)	1·50	10
		ba. Booklet pane of 4+2 labels (13.11.31)	£140	
293		3c. scarlet (13.7.31)	1·50	10
		a. Booklet pane of 4+2 labels	48·00	
294		4c. yellow-bistre (5.11.30)	9·00	4·50
295		5c. violet (18.6.30)	2·75	6·50
296		5c. deep slate-blue (13.11.30)	5·50	20
		a. Dull blue	22·00	1·00
297		8c. blue (13.8.30)	11·00	16·00
298		8c. red-orange (5.11.30)	7·50	5·50
299	67	10c. olive-green (15.9.30)	20·00	1·25
		a. Imperf (pair)	£1700	
300	68	12c. grey-black (4.12.30)	14·00	5·50
301	69	20c. red (4.12.30)	22·00	1·75
302	70	50c. blue (4.12.30)	90·00	17·00
303	71	$1 olive-green (4.12.30)	£120	30·00
288/303		Set of 16	£275	80·00
		(b) Imperf×perf 8½		
304	66	1c. orange (14.7.30)	11·00	19·00
305		1c. green (I) (4.2.31)	6·00	7·00
306		2c. green (I) (27.6.30)	4·00	9·00
		a. Cockeyed King	60·00	75·00
307		2c. scarlet (I) (19.11.30)	4·50	9·50
		a. Cockeyed King	65·00	80·00
308		2c. deep brown (I) (4.7.31)	9·00	1·50
		a. Cockeyed King	65·00	60·00
309		3c. scarlet (13.7.31)	14·00	1·50
304/309		Set of 6	42·00	42·00

Nos. 300/3 exist imperforate (Prices per unused pair, 12c. £850, 20c. £850, 50c. £900, $1 £950).

Some low values in the above and subsequent issues have been printed by both Rotary and "Flat plate" processes. The former can be distinguished by the gum, which has a striped appearance.

For 13c. bright violet, T **68**, see No. 325.

(Des H. Schwartz)

1930 (4 Dec). Air. P 11.
310   **72**   5c. deep brown .... 23·00   23·00

No. 311 is vacant.

1931 (30 Sept). P 11.
312   **73**   10c. olive-green .... 12·00   20
No. 312 exists imperforate (Price per pair, £450, un).

(74) (75)

1932 (22 Feb). Air. No. 274 surch with T **74**.
313   59   6c. on 5c. olive-brown .... 3·00   2·50
Examples of this stamp with surcharge inverted, surcharge double, surcharge triple or surcharge omitted in pair with normal are not now believed to have been regularly issued. Such "errors" have also been forged and collectors are warned against forged examples, some of which bear unauthorized markings which purport to be the guarantee of Stanley Gibbons Ltd.

1932 (21 June). Nos. 291/b surch with T **75**.
314   66   3c. on 2c. scarlet (I) .... 4·25   3·75
           a. Die II .... 1·00   60

76 King George V

77 Duke of Windsor when Prince of Wales

78 Allegory of British Empire

OTTAWA CONFERENCE 1932

(79)

1932 (12 July). Ottawa Conference. P 11.
(a) Postage stamps
315   **76**   3c. scarlet 70   80
316   **77**   5c. blue .... 12·00   5·00
317   **78**   13c. green .... 12·00   6·00
(b) Air. No. 310 surch with T **79**
318   **72**   6c. on 5c. deep brown (B.) .... 12·00   20·00
315/318   Set of 4 .... 32·00   29·00

80 King George V

"3" level Die I  "3" raised Die II

CANADA

1932 (1 Dec)–**33**.

(a) P 11

319	**80**	1c. green	60	10
		a. Booklet pane of 6 (28.12.33)	16·00	
		b. Booklet pane of 4+2 labels (19.9.33)	85·00	
320		2c. sepia	70	10
		a. Booklet pane of 6 (7.9.33)	22·00	
		b. Booklet pane of 4+2 labels (19.9.33)	95·00	
321		3c. scarlet (Die I)	1·50	10
		a. Booklet pane of 4+2 labels (22.8.33)	60·00	
		b. Die II (29.11.32)	85	10
		ba. Booklet pane of 4+2 labels (19.9.33)	42·00	
322		4c. yellow-brown	42·00	11·00
323		5c. blue	11·00	10
		a. Imperf vert (horiz pair)	£1700	
324		8c. red-orange	32·00	4·25
325	**68**	13c. bright violet	65·00	2·25
319/325		*Set of 7*	£140	16·00

Nos. 319/25 exist imperforate (*Prices per unused pair*, 1c. to 8c. £225, 13c. £750).

(b) Imperf×perf 8½ (1933)

326	**80**	1c. green (3.11.33)	20·00	4·75
327		2c. sepia (15.8.33)	23·00	4·75
328		3c. scarlet (Die II) (16.8.33)	12·00	2·75
326/328		*Set of 3*	50·00	11·00

81 Parliament Buildings, Ottawa

1933 (18 May). U.P.U. Congress Preliminary Meeting. P 11.
329   **81**   5c. blue .... 9·50   3·00
No. 329 exists imperforate (*Price per pair* £750, *un*).

WORLD'S GRAIN EXHIBITION & CONFERENCE

REGINA 1933
(**82**)

1933 (24 July). World's Grain Exhibition and Conference, Regina. No. 301 optd with T **82** in blue.
330   **69**   20c. red .... 19·00   8·50
No. 330 exists imperforate (*Price per pair* £750, *un*).

83 S.S. *Royal William* (after S. Skillett)

84 Jacques Cartier approaching Land

1933 (17 Aug). Centenary of First Trans-Atlantic Steamboat Crossing. P 11.
331   **83**   5c. blue .... 19·00   3·75
No. 331 exists imperforate (*Price per pair* £750, *un*).

1934 (1 July). Fourth Centenary of Discovery of Canada. P 11.
332   **84**   3c. blue .... 5·50   1·50
No. 332 exists imperforate (*Price per pair* £700, *un*).

85 U.E.L. Statue, Hamilton

86 Seal of New Brunswick

1934 (1 July). 150th Anniv of Arrival of United Empire Loyalists. P 11.
333   **85**   10c. olive-green .... 10·00   7·50
No. 333 exists imperforate (*Price per pair* £1500, *un*).

1934 (16 Aug). 150th Anniv of Province of New Brunswick. P 11.
334   **86**   2c. red-brown .... 1·50   3·25
No. 334 exists imperforate (*Price per pair* £700, *un*).

> **PRINTERS.** The following stamps were recess-printed (except where otherwise stated) by the Canadian Bank Note Co, Ottawa, until No. 616.

87 Queen Elizabeth II when Princess

88 King George VI when Duke of York

89 King George V and Queen Mary

90 King Edward VIII when Prince of Wales

91 Windsor Castle

92 Royal Yacht *Britannia*

"Weeping Princess" (Pl 1 upper right pane R. 3/1)

"Shilling mark" (Pl 1 upper right pane R. 8/8)

1935 (4 May). Silver Jubilee. T **87/92**. P 12.

335	**87**	1c. green	70	80
		a. Weeping Princess	£120	90·00
336	**88**	2c. brown	70	80
337	**89**	3c. carmine-red	3·00	1·25
338	**90**	5c. blue	5·50	7·50
339	**91**	10c. green	9·00	9·50
340	**92**	13c. blue	9·50	9·50
		a. Shilling mark	£450	£400
335/340		*Set of 6*	25·00	26·00

Nos. 335/40 exist imperforate (*Price* £275, *un*, for each pair).

93 King George V

94 Royal Canadian Mounted Policeman

95 Confederation Conference, Charlottetown, 1864

96 Niagara Falls

27

CANADA

97 Parliament Buildings, Victoria, British Columbia
98 Champlain Monument, Quebec  
105 Entrance, Vancouver Harbour
106 Chateau de Ramezay, Montreal
99 Daedalus
107 Fairchild 45-80 Sekani Seaplane over *Distributor* on River Mackenzie
Crease on collar (Pl 2 upper right pane R. 9/5)

1935 (1 June–5 Nov). T **93**/**99**.

(a) Postage
(i) P 12

341	**93**	1c. green	1·75	10
		a. Booklet pane of 6 (19.8.35)	28·00	
		b. Booklet pane of 4+2 labels (22.7.35)	65·00	
342		2c. brown	1·75	10
		a. Booklet pane of 6 (16.11.35)	29·00	
		b. Booklet pane of 4+2 labels (22.7.35)	65·00	
343		3c. scarlet	1·75	10
		a. Booklet pane of 4+2 labels	42·00	
		b. Printed on the gummed side	£300	
344		4c. yellow	3·50	2·75
345		5c. blue	3·50	10
		a. Imperf vert (horiz pair)	£225	
346		8c. orange	4·25	5·00
347	**94**	10c. carmine	6·50	50
348	**95**	13c. purple	7·50	65
349	**96**	20c. olive-green	25·00	1·50
350	**97**	50c. deep violet	25·00	7·00
351	**98**	$1 bright blue	40·00	11·00
341/351 Set of 11			£110	25·00

(ii) Coil stamps. Imperf×perf 8

352	**93**	1c. green (5.11.35)	18·00	12·00
353		2c. brown (14.10.35)	11·00	5·00
354		3c. scarlet (20.7.35)	9·00	1·75
352/354 Set of 3			35·00	17·00

(b) Air. P 12

355	**99**	6c. red-brown	3·25	1·00
		a. Imperf vert (horiz pair)	£7500	

Nos. 341/51 (*Prices per pair*, 1c. to 8c. each £150, 10c. to 50c. each £275, $1 £325, *un*) and 355 (*Price per pair £650, un*) exist imperforate.

100 King George VI and Queen Elizabeth

1937 (10 May). Coronation. P 12.

356	**100**	3c. carmine	1·75	1·50

No. 356 exists imperforate (*Price per pair £800, un*).

101 King George VI 
102 Memorial Chamber, Parliament Buildings, Ottawa 
103 Entrance to Halifax Harbour 
104 Fort Garry Gate, Winnipeg

(T **101**. Photograph by Bertram Park)

1937–38. T **101**/**107**.

(a) Postage
(i) P 12

357	**101**	1c. green (1.4.37)	2·00	10
		a. Booklet pane of 4+2 labels (14.4.37)	28·00	
		b. Booklet pane of 6 (18.5.37)	7·00	
358		2c. brown (1.4.37)	2·50	10
		a. Booklet pane of 4+2 labels (14.4.37)	60·00	
		b. Booklet pane of 6 (3.5.38)	11·00	
359		3c. scarlet (1.4.37)	1·75	10
		a. Booklet pane of 4+2 labels (14.4.37)	4·25	
		b. Crease on collar	70·00	35·00
360		4c. yellow (10.5.37)	5·50	1·75
361		5c. blue (10.5.37)	6·50	10
362		8c. orange (10.5.37)	6·50	3·75
363	**102**	10c. rose-carmine (15.6.38)	5·00	60
		a. Red	5·00	10
364	**103**	13c. blue (15.11.38)	28·00	2·75
365	**104**	20c. red-brown (15.6.38)	24·00	2·75
366	**105**	50c. green (15.6.38)	48·00	16·00
367	**106**	$1 violet (15.6.38)	60·00	16·00
		a. Imperf horiz (vert pair)	£5500	
357/367 Set of 11			£170	40·00

Nos. 357/67 exist imperforate (*Prices per pair* 1c. to 8c. each £300, 10c. to 50c. each £550, $1 £750 *un*).

(ii) Coil stamps. Imperf×perf 8

368	**101**	1c. green (15.6.37)	4·50	5·50
369		2c. brown (18.6.37)	3·75	5·50
370		3c. scarlet (15.4.37)	28·00	2·00
368/370 Set of 3			32·00	11·50

(b) Air. P 12

371	**107**	6c. blue (15.6.38)	17·00	2·25

No. 371 exists imperforate (*Price per pair £700, un*).

108 Queen Elizabeth II when Princess and Princess Margaret
109 National War Memorial 
110 King George VI and Queen Elizabeth 

28

CANADA

1939 (15 May). Royal Visit. P 12.
372	**108**	1c. black and green	2·50	25
373	**109**	2c. black and brown	2·75	2·00
374	**110**	3c. black and carmine	2·00	25
372/374 Set of 3			6·50	2·25

Nos. 372/4 exist imperforate (*Price £650, un, for each pair*).

111 King George VI in Naval uniform
112 King George VI in Military uniform 
113 King George VI in Air Force uniform 
114 Grain Elevator 
115 Farm Scene 
116 Parliament Buildings 
117 Ram Tank 
118 Launching of Corvette H.M.C.S. *La Malbaie*, Sorel 
119 Munitions Factory 
120 H.M.S. *Cossack* (destroyer) 
121 Air Training Camp 

1942 (1 July)–**48**. War Effort. T **111/121** and similar designs.

(a) Postage
(i) P 12

375	**111**	1c. green	1·50	10
		a. Booklet pane of 4+2 labels (12.9.42)	29·00	
		b. Booklet pane of 6 (24.11.42)	2·50	
376	**112**	2c. brown	1·75	10
		a. Booklet pane of 4+2 labels (12.9.42)	35·00	
		b. Booklet pane of 6 (6.10.42)	24·00	
377	**113**	3c. carmine-lake	1·25	60
		a. Booklet pane of 4+2 labels (20.8.42)	4·25	
378		3c. purple (30.6.43)	1·25	10
		a. Booklet pane of 4+2 labels (28.8.43)	6·00	
		b. Booklet pane of 6 (24.11.47)	16·00	
379	**114**	4c. slate	5·50	2·50
380	**112**	4c. carmine-lake (9.4.43)	70	10
		a. Booklet pane of 6 (3.5.43)	3·50	
381	**111**	5c. blue	3·00	10
382	**115**	8c. red-brown	5·50	1·00
383	**116**	10c. brown	12·00	10
384	**117**	13c. dull green	9·00	9·50
385		14c. dull green (16.4.43)	26·00	1·00
386	**118**	20c. chocolate	21·00	45
387	**119**	50c. violet	26·00	7·00
388	**120**	$1 blue	45·00	9·50
375/388 Set of 14			£140	29·00

Nos. 375/88 exist imperforate (*Prices per pair* 1c. to 8c. *each* £325, 10c. to 20c. *each* £550, 50c. and $1 *each* £650, *un*).

(ii) Coil stamps. Imperf×perf 8

389	**111**	1c. green (9.2.43)	1·00	1·50
390	**112**	2c. brown (24.11.42)	2·25	2·50
391	**113**	3c. carmine-lake (23.9.42)	2·00	9·00
392		3c. purple (19.8.43)	12·00	9·00
393	**112**	4c. carmine-lake (13.5.43)	12·00	2·25
389/393 Set of 5			26·00	22·00

(iii) Booklet stamps. Imperf×perf 12 (1.9.43)

394	**111**	1c. green	4·00	1·25
		a. Booklet pane of 3	11·00	
395	**113**	3c. purple	4·00	1·75
		a. Booklet pane of 3	11·00	
396	**112**	4c. carmine-lake	4·00	2·25
		a. Booklet pane of 3	11·00	
394/396 Set of 3			11·00	4·75

Nos. 394/6 are from booklets in which the stamps are in strips of three, imperforate at top and bottom and right-hand end.

(iv) Coil stamps. Imperf×perf 9½

397	**111**	1c. green (13.7.48)	3·50	4·00
397a	**112**	2c. brown (1.10.48)	8·50	19·00
398	**113**	3c. purple (2.7.48)	4·75	6·00
398a	**112**	4c. carmine-lake (22.7.48)	8·50	4·75
397/398a Set of 4			23·00	30·00

(b) Air. P 12

399	**121**	6c. blue (1.7.42)	30·00	13·00
400		7c. blue (16.4.43)	4·50	50

Nos. 399/400 exist imperforate (*Price £800, un, for each pair*).

122 Ontario Farm Scene
123 Great Bear Lake 
124 St. Maurice River Power Station 
125 Combine Harvester 
126 Lumbering in British Columbia 
127 *Abegweit* (train ferry), Prince Edward Is. 
128 Canada Geese in Flight 
129 Alexander Graham Bell and "Fame" 

1946 (16 Sept)–**47**. Peace Re-conversion. T **122/128**. P 12.

(a) Postage

401	**122**	8c. brown	1·75	2·75
402	**123**	10c. olive-green	2·75	10
403	**124**	14c. sepia	5·00	3·25
404	**125**	20c. slate	3·25	10
405	**126**	50c. green	16·00	6·50
406	**127**	$1 purple	26·00	6·50

(b) Air

407	**128**	7c. blue	5·50	40
		a. Booklet pane of 4 (24.11.47)	9·00	
401/407 Set of 7			55·00	17·00

1947 (3 Mar). Birth Centenary of Bell (inventor of telephone). P 12.
408	**129**	4c. blue	15	50

29

CANADA

130 "Canadian Citizenship"
131 Queen Elizabeth II when Princess 

1947 (1 July). Advent of Canadian Citizenship and Eightieth Anniv of Confederation. P 12.
| 409 | 130 | 4c. blue | 10 | 40 |

(From photograph by Dorothy Wilding)
1948 (16 Feb). Princess Elizabeth's Marriage. P 12.
| 410 | 131 | 4c. blue | 10 | 15 |

132 Queen Victoria, Parliament Building, Ottawa, and King George VI
133 Cabot's Ship *Matthew* 

1948 (1 Oct). One Hundred Years of Responsible Government. P 12.
| 411 | 132 | 4c. grey | 10 | 10 |

1949 (1 Apr). Entry of Newfoundland into Canadian Confederation. P 12.
| 412 | 133 | 4c. green | 30 | 10 |

134 "Founding of Halifax, 1749" (C. W. Jefferys)

1949 (21 June). Bicentenary of Halifax, Nova Scotia. P 12.
| 413 | 134 | 4c. violet | 45 | 10 |

135    **136**    **137**

138 King George VI
139 King George VI 

(From photographs by Dorothy Wilding)
1949 (15 Nov)–**51**.
(i) P 12
414	135	1c. green	50	10
415	136	2c. sepia	2·25	45
415a		2c. olive-green (25.7.51)	2·25	10
416	137	3c. purple	30	10
		a. Booklet pane of 4+2 labels (12.4.50)	2·25	
417	138	4c. carmine-lake	20	10
		a. Booklet pane of 6 (5.5.50)	22·00	
417b		4c. vermilion (2.6.51)	60	10
		ba. Booklet pane of 6	6·00	
418	139	5c. blue	2·50	60
414/418 Set of 7			7·75	1·00

(ii) Imperf×perf 9½ (coil stamps)
419	135	1c. green (18.5.50)	2·75	2·00
420	136	2c. sepia (18.5.50)	9·00	6·00
420a		2c. olive-green (9.10.51)	1·75	5·00
421	137	3c. purple (18.5.50)	2·25	3·75
422	138	4c. carmine-lake (20.4.50)	14·00	11·00
422a		4c. vermilion (27.11.51)	3·00	2·75
419/422a Set of 6			29·00	27·00

(iii) Imperf×perf 12 (booklets)
422b	135	1c. green (18.5.50)	50	2·25
		ba. Booklet pane of 3	1·50	
423	137	3c. purple (18.5.50)	1·25	1·00
		a. Booklet pane of 3	3·75	
423b	138	4c. carmine-lake (18.5.50)	18·00	10·00
		ba. Booklet pane of 3	50·00	
423c		4c. vermilion (25.10.51)	9·50	9·00
		ca. Booklet pane of 3	26·00	
422b/423c Set of 4			26·00	20·00

These booklet panes are imperforate at top, bottom and right-hand end.

140 King George VI
141 Oil Wells in Alberta 

(From photograph by Dorothy Wilding)
1950 (19 Jan). As T **135**/9 but without "POSTES POSTAGE", as T **140**.
(i) P 12
424		1c. green	70	1·00
425		2c. sepia	70	4·25
426		3c. purple	70	65
427		4c. carmine-lake	70	20
428		5c. blue	70	2·25
424/428 Set of 5			3·25	7·50

(ii) Imperf×perf 9½ (coil stamps)
| 429 | | 1c. green | 30 | 1·25 |
| 430 | | 3c. purple | 80 | 2·25 |

1950 (1 Mar). P 12.
| 431 | 141 | 50c. green | 6·00 | 1·00 |

142 Drying Furs
143 Fisherman 

1950 (2 Oct). P 12.
| 432 | 142 | 10c. brown-purple | 4·50 | 10 |

1951 (1 Feb). P 12.
| 433 | 143 | $1 ultramarine | 42·00 | 5·50 |

144 Sir R. L. Borden
145 W. L. Mackenzie King 

1951 (25 June). Prime Ministers (1st issue). P 12.
| 434 | 144 | 3c. blue-green | 20 | 1·50 |
| 435 | 145 | 4c. rose-carmine | 60 | 15 |

See also Nos. 444/5, 475/6 and 483/4.

146 Mail Trains, 1851 and 1951
147 SS. *City of Toronto* and SS. *Prince George*

CANADA

148 Mail Coach and DC-4M North Star
149 Reproduction of 3d., 1851 

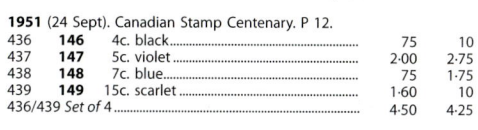

1951 (24 Sept). Canadian Stamp Centenary. P 12.
436	**146**	4c. black	75	10
437	**147**	5c. violet	2·00	2·75
438	**148**	7c. blue	75	1·75
439	**149**	15c. scarlet	1·60	10
436/439 Set of 4			4·50	4·25

150 Queen Elizabeth II when Princess and Duke of Edinburgh
151 Forestery Products 

1951 (26 Oct). Royal Visit. P 12.
440	**150**	4c. violet	20	20

(Des A. L. Pollock)

1952 (1 Apr). P 12.
441	**151**	20c. grey	2·25	10

152 Red Cross Emblem

1952 (26 July). 18th International Red Cross Conference, Toronto. Design recess; cross litho. P 12.
442	**152**	4c. scarlet and blue	15	10

153 Canada Goose
154 Pacific Coast Indian House and Totem Pole 

(Des E. Hahn)

1952 (3 Nov). P 12.
443	**153**	7c. blue	1·25	10

1952 (3 Nov). Prime Ministers (2nd issue). Various portraits as T **144**. P 12.
444		3c. reddish purple	35	75
445		4c. orange-red	25	35

Portraits:—3c. Sir John J. C. Abbott; 4c. A. Mackenzie.

(Des E. Hahn)

1953 (2 Feb). P 12.
446	**154**	$1 black	3·25	20

155 Polar Bear
156 Elk 
157 American Bighorn 

(Des J. Crosby (2c), E. Hahn (others))

1953 (1 Apr). National Wild Life Week. P 12.
447	**155**	2c. blue	10	10
448	**156**	3c. sepia	10	70
449	**157**	4c. slate	15	10
447/449 Set of 3			30	70

158 Queen Elizabeth II
159 Queen Elizabeth II 

(From photograph by Karsh, Ottawa)

1953 (1 May–3 Sept).

(a) Sheet stamps. P 12
450	**158**	1c. purple-brown	10	10
451		2c. green	15	10
452		3c. carmine	15	15
		a. Booklet pane of 4+2 labels (17.7)	1·90	
453		4c. violet	20	10
		a. Booklet pane of 6 (6.7)	4·50	
454		5c. ultramarine	25	10
450/454 Set of 5			75	30

(b) Coil stamps. Imperf×perf 9½
455	**158**	2c. green (30.7)	2·00	1·25
456		3c. carmine (27.7)	2·00	1·00
457		4c. violet (3.9)	2·00	1·25
455/457 Set of 3			5·50	3·25

(c) Booklet stamps. Imperf×perf 12
458	**158**	1c. purple-brown (12.8)	2·00	1·50
		a. Booklet pane of 3	5·50	
459		3c. carmine (17.7)	2·00	1·50
		a. Booklet pane of 3	5·50	
460		4c. violet (6.7)	2·00	1·50
		a. Booklet pane of 3	5·50	
458/460 Set of 3			5·50	4·00

These booklet stamps have top and bottom or top, bottom and right-hand sides imperforate.

(Des E. Hahn)

1953 (1 June). Coronation. P 12.
461	**159**	4c. violet	10	10

160 Textile Industry
161 Queen Elizabeth II 

(Des A. L. Pollock)

1953 (2 Nov). P 12.
462	**160**	50c. deep bluish green	1·75	10

(From photograph by Dorothy Wilding)

1954–62.

(i) P 12
463	**161**	1c. purple-brown (10.6.54)	10	10
		a. Booklet pane. Five stamps plus printed label (1.6.56)	1·50	
		p. Two phosphor bands (13.1.62)	1·00	3·50
464		2c. green (10.6.54)	20	10
		a. Pack. Two blocks of 25 (12.61)	7·00	
		p. Two phosphor bands (13.1.62)	1·00	3·75
465		3c. carmine (10.6.54)	1·00	10
		a. Imperf vert (horiz pair)	£1800	
		p. Two phosphor bands (13.1.62)	1·50	3·50
466		4c. violet (10.6.54)	30	10
		a. Booklet pane of 6 (7.7.55)	4·75	
		b. Booklet pane. Five stamps plus printed label (1.6.56)	1·50	
		p. One phosphor band (13.1.62)	2·25	10·00
467		5c. bright blue (1.4.54)	30	10
		a. Booklet pane. Five stamps plus printed label (14.7.54)	2·00	
		b. Pack. One block of 20 (12.61)	5·50	
		c. Imperf vert (horiz pair)	£5000	
		p. Two phosphor bands (13.1.62)	3·50	8·00
468		6c. red-orange (10.6.54)	1·75	55
463/468 Set of 6			3·25	70
463p/467p Set of 5			8·25	26·00

31

CANADA

(ii) Imperf×perf 9½ (coil stamps)

469	161	2c. green (9.9.54)	1·00	75
470		4c. violet (23.8.54)	55	1·60
471		5c. bright blue (6.7.54)	1·75	45
469/471 *Set of 3*			3·00	2·50

No. 467c is from the left side of a sheet and shows perforations between the stamps and the sheet margin.

Nos. 464a and 467b are blocks with the outer edges imperf. These come from "One Dollar Plastic Packages" sold at post offices.

WINNIPEG PHOSPHOR BANDS. In 1962 facer-cancelling machines were introduced in Winnipeg which were activated by phosphor bands on the stamps. Under long or short wave ultra-violet light the phosphor glows and there is also a short after-glow when the lamp is turned off. This should not be confused with the fluorescent bands introduced in Ottawa in 1971.

162 Walrus
163 American Beaver 
164 Northern Gannet 

(Des E. Hahn)

1954 (1 Apr). National Wild Life Week. P 12.

472	162	4c. slate-black	35	20
473	163	5c. ultramarine	35	10
		a. Booklet pane. Five stamps plus one printed label	2·00	

(Des L. Hyde)

1954 (1 Apr). P 12.

474	164	15c. black	1·25	10

1954 (1 Nov). Prime Ministers (3rd issue). Various portraits as T **144**. P 12.

475		4c. violet	15	75
476		5c. bright blue	15	40

Portraits:—4c. Sir John Thompson; 5c. Sir Mackenzie Bowell.

165 Eskimo Hunter

(Des H. Beament)

1955 (21 Feb). P 12.

477	165	10c. purple-brown	1·25	10

166 Musk Ox
167 Whooping Cranes 

(Des E. Hahn (4c.), Dr. W. Rowan (5c.))

1955 (4 Apr). National Wild Life Week. P 12.

478	166	4c. violet	30	10
479	167	5c. ultramarine	1·00	20

168 Dove and Torch
169 Pioneer Settlers 

(Des W. Lohse)

1955 (1 June). Tenth Anniv of International Civil Aviation Organisation. P 12.

480	168	5c. ultramarine	30	20

(Des L. Hyde)

1955 (30 June). 50th Anniv of Alberta and Saskatchewan Provinces. P 12.

481	169	5c. ultramarine	20	25

170 Scout Badge and Globe
173 Ice-hockey Players 

(Des L. Hyde)

1955 (20 Aug). Eighth World Scout Jamboree, Niagara-on-the-Lake. P 12.

482	170	5c. orange-brown and green	30	10

1955 (8 Nov). Prime Ministers (4th issue). Various portraits as T **144**. P 12.

483		4c. violet	20	60
484		5c. bright blue	20	10

Portraits:—4c. R. B. Bennett; 5c. Sir Charles Tupper.

(Des J. Simpkins)

1956 (23 Jan). Ice-hockey Commemoration. P 12.

485	173	5c. ultramarine	20	20

174 Reindeer
175 Mountain Goat 

(Des E. Hahn)

1956 (12 Apr). National Wild Life Week. P 12.

486	174	4c. violet	20	15
487	175	5c. bright blue	20	10

176 Pulp and Paper Industry
177 Chemical Industry 

(Des A. J. Casson (20c.), A. L. Pollock (25c.))

1956 (7 June). P 12.

488	176	20c. green	60	10
489	177	25c. red	70	10

178

(Des A. Price)

1956 (9 Oct). Fire Prevention Week. P 12.

490	178	5c. red and black	30	10

179 Fishing
180 Swimming

CANADA

(Des L. Hyde)
1957 (7 Mar). Outdoor Recreation. T **179/180** and similar horiz designs. P 12.
491	179	5c. ultramarine	25	10
		a. Block of 4. Nos. 491/4	1·25	1·50
492	180	5c. ultramarine	25	10
493	–	5c. ultramarine	25	10
494	–	5c. ultramarine	25	10
491/494		Set of 4	1·25	35

Designs:—No. 493, Hunting. No. 494, Skiing.

Nos. 491/4 are printed together in sheets of 50 (5×10). In the first, second, fourth and fifth vertical rows the four different designs are arranged in *se-tenant* blocks, whilst the central row is made up as follows (reading downwards):—Nos. 491/4, 491/2 (or 493/4), 491/4.

183 White-billed Diver
184 Thompson with Sextant, and North American Map 

(Des L. Hyde)
1957 (10 Apr). National Wild Life Week. P 12.
495	183	5c. black	50	20

(Des G. A. Gundersen)
1957 (5 June). Death Centenary of David Thompson (explorer). P 12.
496	184	5c. ultramarine	45	30

185 Parliament Buildings, Ottawa
186 Globe within Posthorn 

(Des Carl Mangold)
1957 (14 Aug). 14th U.P.U. Congress, Ottawa. P 12.
497	185	5c. grey-blue	15	10
498	186	15c. blackish blue	55	1·75

187 Miner
188 Queen Elizabeth II and Duke of Edinburgh 

(Des A. J. Casson)
1957 (5 Sept). Mining Industry. P 12.
499	187	5c. black	35	20

(From photographs by Karsh, Ottawa)
1957 (10 Oct). Royal Visit. P 12.
500	188	5c. black	30	10

189 "A Free Press"
190 Microscope 

(Des A. L. Pollock)
1958 (22 Jan). The Canadian Press. P 12.
501	189	5c. black	15	70

(Des A. L. Pollock)
1958 (5 Mar). International Geophysical Year. P 12.
502	190	5c. blue	20	10

191 Miner panning for Gold
192 La Verendrye (statue) 

(Des J. Harman)
1958 (8 May). Centenary of British Columbia. P 12.
503	191	5c. deep turquoise-green	20	10

(Des G. Trottier)
1958 (4 June). La Verendrye (explorer) Commemoration. P 12.
504	192	5c. ultramarine	15	10

193 Samuel de Champlain and the Heights of Quebec
194 Nurse 

(Des G. Trottier)
1958 (26 June). 350th Anniv of Founding of Quebec. P 12.
505	193	5c. brown-ochre and deep green	30	10

(Des G. Trottier)
1958 (30 July). National Health. P 12.
506	194	5c. reddish purple	30	10

195 "Petroleum 1858–1958"
196 Speaker's Chair and Mace 

(Des A. L. Pollock)
1958 (10 Sept). Centenary of Canadian Oil Industry. P 12.
507	195	5c. scarlet and olive	30	10

(Des G. Trottier and C. Dair)
1958 (2 Oct). Bicentenary of First Elected Assembly. P 12.
508	196	5c. deep slate	30	10

197 John McCurdy's *Silver Dart* Biplane
198 Globe showing N.A.T.O. Countries 

1959 (23 Feb). 50th Anniv of First Flight of the Silver Dart in Canada. P 12.
509	197	5c. black and ultramarine	30	10

(Des P. Weiss)
1959 (2 Apr). Tenth Anniv of North Atlantic Treaty Organisation. P 12.
510	198	5c. ultramarine	40	10

199
200 Queen Elizabeth II

CANADA

(Des Helen Fitzgerald)
1959 (13 May). "Associated Country Women of the World" Commemoration. P 12.
511 **199** 5c. black and yellow-olive 15 10

(Des after painting by Annigoni)
1959 (18 June). Royal Visit. P 12.
512 **200** 5c. lake-red 30 10

201 Maple Leaf linked with American Eagle
202 Maple Leaves

(Des A. L. Pollock, G. Trottier (of Canada); W. H. Buckley, A. J. Copeland, E. Metzl (of the United States))
1959 (26 June). Opening of St. Lawrence Seaway. P 12.
513 **201** 5c. ultramarine and red 20 10
          a. Centre inverted £9000 £6000
It is believed that No. 513a occurred on two printer's sheets, each of 200 stamps. About 230 examples have been discovered.

(Des P. Weiss)
1959 (10 Sept). Bicentenary of Battle of Plains of Abraham (Quebec). P 12.
514 **202** 5c. deep green and red 30 10

203
204 Dollard des Ormeaux

(Des Helen Fitzgerald)
1960 (20 Apr). Golden Jubilee of Canadian Girl Guides Movement. P 12.
515 **203** 5c. ultramarine and orange-brown...... 20 10

(Des P. Weiss)
1960 (19 May). Tercentenary of Battle of the Long Sault. P 12.
516 **204** 5c. ultramarine and light brown 20 10

205 Surveyor, Bulldozer and Compass Rose
206 E. Pauline Johnson

(Des B. J. Reddie)
1961 (8 Feb). Northern Development. P 12.
517 **205** 5c. emerald and red 15 10

(Des B. J. Reddie)
1961 (10 Mar). Birth Centenary of E. Pauline Johnson (Mohawk poetess). P 12.
518 **206** 5c. green and red 15 10

207 Arthur Meighen (statesman)
208 Engineers and Dam

1961 (19 Apr). Arthur Meighen Commemoration. P 12.
519 **207** 5c. ultramarine 15 10

(Des B. J. Reddie)
1961 (28 June). Tenth Anniv of Colombo Plan. P 12.
520 **208** 5c. blue and brown 30 10

209 "Resources for Tomorrow"
210 "Education"

(Des A. L. Pollock)
1961 (12 Oct). Natural Resources. P 12.
521 **209** 5c. blue-green and brown................... 15 10

(Des Helen Fitzgerald)
1962 (28 Feb). Education Year. P 12.
522 **210** 5c. black and orange-brown............... 15 10

211 Lord Selkirk and Farmer
212 Talon bestowing Gifts on Married Couple

(Des Phillips-Gutkin Ltd)
1962 (3 May). 150th Anniv of Red River Settlement. P 12.
523 **211** 5c. chocolate and green...................... 20 10

(Des P. Weiss)
1962 (13 June). Jean Talon Commemoration. P 12.
524 **212** 5c. blue.. 20 10

213 Br. Columbia & Vancouver Is. 2½d. stamp of 1860, and Parliament Buildings, B.C.
214 Highway (map version) and Provincial Arms

(Des Helen Bacon)
1962 (22 Aug). Centenary of Victoria, B.C. P 12.
525 **213** 5c. red and black................................. 30 10

(Des A. L. Pollock)
1962 (31 Aug). Opening of Trans-Canada Highway. P 12.
526 **214** 5c. black and orange-brown............... 15 20

215 Queen Elizabeth II and Wheat (agriculture) Symbol
216 Sir Casimir Gzowski

CANADA

(From drawing by Ernst Roch)
1962–64. Horiz designs as T **215** showing Queen Elizabeth II and industry symbols.

(i) P 12

527	1c. chocolate (4.2.63)		10	10
	a. Booklet pane. Five stamps plus one printed label (15.5.63)		4·00	
	p. Two phosphor bands (15.5.63)		15	55
528	2c. green (2.5.63)		15	10
	a. Pack. Two blocks of 25		9·50	
	p. Two phosphor bands (15.5.63)		40	1·00
529	3c. reddish violet† (2.5.63)		15	10
	p. Two phosphor bands (15.5.63)		40	1·00
530	4c. carmine-red (4.2.63)		20	10
	a. Booklet pane. Five stamps plus one printed label (15.5.63)		4·00	
	b. Pack. One block of 25		6·50	
	p. One centre phosphor band (*narrow*)* (2.63)		50	3·00
	pa. One centre phosphor band (*wide*) (8.64)		4·75	8·00
	pb. One side phosphor band (12.64)		60	3·50
531	5c. ultramarine (3.10.62)		50	10
	a. Booklet pane. Five stamps plus one printed label (5.63)		4·25	
	b. Pack. One block of 20		8·00	
	c. Imperf horiz (vert pair)		£3250	£750
	p. Two phosphor bands (31.1.63?)		50	1·50
	pa. Pack. One block of 20		15·00	
	pb. Imperf (pair)		£2750	
527/531 *Set of 5*			1·00	15
527p/531p *Set of 5*			1·75	6·25

(ii) P 9½×imperf (coil stamps)

532	2c. green (1963)		7·50	8·50
532a	3c. reddish violet (1964)		4·75	3·50
533	4c. carmine-red (15.5.63)		3·00	3·50
	a. Imperf (vert pair)		£3250	
534	5c. ultramarine (15.5.63)		4·50	1·50
532/534 *Set of 4*			18·00	15·00

Symbols:—1c. Crystals (Mining); 2c. Tree (Forestry); 3c. Fish (Fisheries); 4c. Electricity pylon (Industrial power).

Nos. 528a, 530b, 531b and 531pa are blocks with the outer edges imperf. These come from "One Dollar Plastic Packages" sold at post offices.

†This is a fugitive colour which tends to become reddish on drying. In successive printings the violet colour became more and more reddish as the printer tried to match the shade of each previous printing instead of referring back to the original shade. A deep reddish violet is also known from Plate 3. As there is such a range of shades it is not practical to list them.

*On No. 530p the band is 4 mm wide as against 8 mm on No. 530pa. No. 530pb exists with the band at either left or right side of the stamp, the bands being applied across alternate vertical perforations.

Postal forgeries are known of the 4c. showing a coarser background and lack of shading on the Queen's face.

(Des P. Weiss)
1963 (5 Mar). 150th Birth Anniv of Sir Casimir Gzowski (engineer). P 12.

535	**216**	5c. reddish purple	10	10

217 "Export Trade"

218 Frobisher and barque *Gabriel*

(Des A. L. Pollock)
1963 (14 June). P 12.

536	**217**	$1 carmine	4·75	2·00

(Des P. Weiss)
1963 (21 Aug). Sir Martin Frobisher Commemoration. P 12.

537	**218**	5c. ultramarine	20	10

219 Horseman and Map

220 Canada Geese

(Des B. J. Reddie)
1963 (25 Sept). Bicentenary of Quebec–Trois-Rivieres–Montreal Postal Service. P 12.

538	**219**	5c. red-brown and deep green	15	25

(Des A. Short and P. Arthur)
1963 (30 Oct). P 12.

539	**220**	15c. blue	1·00	10

221 Douglas DC-9 Airliner and Uplands Airport, Ottawa

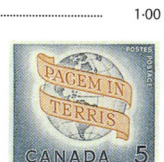

222 "Peace on Earth"

1964. P 12.

540	**221**	7c. blue (11 Mar)	35	70
540a		8c. blue (18 Nov)	50	50

1964 (8 Apr). "Peace". Litho and recess. P 12.

541	**222**	5c. ochre, blue and turquoise-blue	15	10

223 Maple Leaves

1964 (14 May). "Canadian Unity". P 12.

542	**223**	5c. lake-red and light blue	10	10

224 White Trillium and Arms of Ontario

236 Maple Leaf and Arms of Canada

1964–66. Provincial Emblems. T **224**, **236** and similar horiz designs. Recess (No. 555) or litho and recess (others). P 12.

543		5c. green, brown and orange (30.6.64)	40	20
544		5c. green, orange-brown and yellow (30.6.64)	40	20
545		5c. carmine-red, green and bluish violet (3.2.65)	30	20
546		5c. blue, red and green (3.2.65)	30	20
547		5c. purple, green and yellow-brown (28.4.65)	30	20
548		5c. red-brown, deep bluish green and mauve (28.4.65)	30	20
549		5c. slate-lilac, green and light reddish purple (21.7.65)	50	20
550		5c. green, yellow and rose-red (19.1.66)	30	20
551		5c. sepia, orange and green (19.1.66)	30	20
552		5c. black, green and red (23.2.66)	30	20
553		5c. drab, green and yellow (23.3.66)	30	20
554		5c. blue, green and rose-red (23.3.66)	30	20
555		5c. red and blue (30.6.66)	30	20
543/555 *Set of 13*			4·00	2·40

Designs:—No. 543, Type **224**; No. 544, Madonna Lily and Arms of Quebec; No. 545, Purple Violet and Arms of New Brunswick; No. 546, Mayflower and Arms of Nova Scotia; No. 547, Dogwood and Arms of British Columbia; No. 548, Prairie Crocus and Arms of Manitoba; No. 549, Lady's Slipper and Arms of Prince Edward Island; No. 550, Wild Rose and Arms of Alberta; No. 551, Prairie Lily and Arms of Saskatchewan; No. 552, Pitcher Plant and Arms of Newfoundland; No. 553, Mountain Avens and Arms of Northwest Territories; No. 554, Fireweed and Arms of Yukon Territory; No. 555, Type **236**.

8
═
(237)

238 Fathers of the Confederation Memorial, Charlottetown

35

CANADA

1964 (15 July). No. 540 surch with T **237**.
556   221   8c. on 7c. blue 15   15
            a. Surch omitted (left-hand stamp of
               horiz pair) £10000

(Des P. Weiss)

1964 (29 July). Centenary of Charlottetown Conference. P 12.
557   238   5c. black 10   10

239 Maple Leaf and Hand with Quill Pen

240 Queen Elizabeth II

(Des P. Weiss)

1964 (9 Sept). Centenary of Quebec Conference. P 12.
558   239   5c. light red and chocolate 15   10

(Portrait by Anthony Buckley)

1964 (5 Oct). Royal Visit. P 12.
559   240   5c. reddish purple 15   10

241 "Canadian Family"

242 "Co-operation"

1964 (14 Oct). Christmas. P 12.
560   241   3c. scarlet 10   10
            a. Pack. Two blocks of 25 .... 7·00
            p. Two phosphor bands 60   2·50
            pa. Pack. Two blocks of 25 .... 13·00
561   5c. ultramarine 10   10
            p. Two phosphor bands 90   4·00
   Nos. 560a and 560pa are blocks with the outer edges imperf. These come from "$1.50 Plastic Packages" sold at post offices.

1965 (3 Mar). International Co-operation Year. P 12.
562   242   5c. grey-green 35   10

243 Sir W. Grenfell

244 National Flag

1965 (9 June). Birth Centenary of Sir Wilfred Grenfell (missionary). P 12.
563   243   5c. deep bluish green 20   10

1965 (30 June). Inauguration of National Flag. P 12.
564   244   5c. red and blue 15   10

245 Sir Winston Churchill

246 Peace Tower, Parliament Buildings, Ottawa

(Des P. Weiss from photo by Karsh. Litho)

1965 (12 Aug). Churchill Commemoration. P 12.
565   245   5c. purple-brown 15   10

(Des Philips-Gutkin)

1965 (8 Sept). Inter-Parliamentary Union Conference, Ottawa. P 12.
566   246   5c. deep green 10   10

247 Parliament Buildings, Ottawa, 1865

248 "Gold, Frankincense and Myrrh"

(Des G. Trottier)

1965 (8 Sept). Centenary of Proclamation of Ottawa as Capital. P 12.
567   247   5c. brown 10   10

(Des Helen Fitzgerald)

1965 (13 Oct). Christmas. P 12.
568   248   3c. olive-green 10   10
            a. Pack. Two blocks of 25 .... 5·00
            p. Two phosphor bands 10   1·75
            pa. Pack. Two blocks of 25 .... 5·50
569   5c. ultramarine 10   10
            p. Two phosphor bands 30   50
   Nos. 568a and 568pa are blocks with the outer edges imperf. These come from "$1.50 Plastic Packages" sold at post offices.

249 "Alouette 2" over Canada

250 La Salle

1966 (5 Jan). Launching of Canadian Satellite, "Alouette 2". P 12.
570   249   5c. ultramarine 15   10

(Des Brigdens Ltd., Toronto)

1966 (13 Apr). 300th Anniv of La Salle's Arrival in Canada. P 12.
571   250   5c. deep bluish green 15   10

251 Road Signs

252 Canadian Delegation and Houses of Parliament

(Des Helen Fitzgerald)

1966 (2 May). Highway Safety. Invisible gum. P 12.
572   251   5c. yellow, blue and black 15   10

(Des P. Pederson (Brigdens Ltd.))

1966 (26 May). London Conference Centenary. P 12.
573   252   5c. red-brown 10   10

253 Douglas Point Nuclear Power Station

254 Parliamentary Library, Ottawa

(Des A. L. Pollock)

1966 (27 July). Peaceful Uses of Atomic Energy. P 12.
574   253   5c. ultramarine 10   10

(Des Brigdens Ltd)

1966 (8 Sept). Commonwealth Parliamentary Association Conference, Ottawa. P 12.
575   254   5c. purple 10   10

36

CANADA

255 "Praying Hands", after Dürer
256 Flag and Canada on Globe 

(Des G. Holloway)

1966 (12 Oct). Christmas. P 12.
576	**255**	3c. carmine	10	10
		a. Pack. Two blocks of 25	4·50	
		p. Two phosphor bands	1·25	1·00
		pa. Pack. Two blocks of 25	7·50	
577		5c. orange	10	10
		p. Two phosphor bands	1·25	1·00

Nos. 576a and 576pa are blocks with the outer edges imperf. These come from "$1.50 Plastic Packages" sold at post offices.

(Des Brigdens Ltd.)

1967 (11 Jan). Canadian Centennial. Invisible gum. P 12.
578	**256**	5c. scarlet and blue	10	10
		p. Two phosphor bands	30	1·75

257 Northern Lights and Dog-team 
258 Totem pole 
259 Combine-harvester and oil derrick

260 Ship in lock 
261 Harbour scene 
261a "Transport"

262 "Alaska Highway" (A.Y. Jackson) 
263 The Jack Pine (T. Thomson)

264 "Bylot Island" (L. Harris) 
265 "Quebec Ferry" (J. W. Morrice)

266 "The Solemn Land" (J. E. H. MacDonald) 
267 "Summer's Stores" (grain elevators) (J. Ensor)

268 "Oilfield" (near Edmonton) (H. G. Glyde)
268a Library of Parliament 

1967 (8 Feb)–73. T 257/268a.

A. Recess C.B.N.
(i) P 12

579		1c. brown	10	10
		a. Booklet pane. Five stamps plus one printed label (2.67)	75	
		b. Printed on the gummed side	£800	
		c. White paper (6.71)	10	
		ca. White fluorescent paper	1·00	
		p. Two phosphor bands	40	1·00
		pa. Centre phosphor band (12.68)	30	2·00
		pac. Centre phosphor band, white paper (9.71)	30	
		paca. Centre phosphor band, white fluorescent paper	3·00	
		q. Two fluorescent bands (11.71)	30	30
580		2c. green	10	10
		a. Glazed fluorescent paper (booklets) (26.10.70)	25	
		b. Booklet pane. No. 580a×4 se-tenant with No. 581a×4 with gutter margin between	1·75	
		c. White paper (3.72)	10	
		p. Two phosphor bands	65	1·75
		pa. Centre phosphor band (12.68)	30	1·00
		pac. Centre phosphor band, white paper (3.72)	40	
		q. Two fluorescent bands (12.72)	55	30
581		3c. slate-purple	30	40
		a. Glazed fluorescent paper (booklets) (26.10.70)	25	
		p. Two phosphor bands	30	2·50
		q. Two fluorescent bands (1972?)	1·75	2·00
582		4c. red	20	10
		a. Booklet pane. Five stamps plus one printed label (2.67)	1·75	
		b. Pack. One block of 25 (8.2.67)	10·00	
		c. White paper (5.72)	20	
		p. One side phosphor band	1·25	3·00
		pa. Centre phosphor band (3.69)	30	1·00
		pac. Centre phosphor band, white paper (5.72)	35	
		paca. Centre phosphor band, white fluorescent paper	—	
		q. Two fluorescent bands (4.73)	40	30
583		5c. blue	20	10
		a. Booklet pane. Five stamps plus one printed label (3.67)	5·50	
		b. Pack. One block of 20 (2.67)	17·00	
		c. White paper (12.71?)	15	
		ca. White fluorescent paper	80	
		p. Two phosphor bands	50	2·25
		pa. Pack. One block of 20 (8.2.67)	35·00	
		pb. Centre phosphor band (12.68)	30	2·25
		pbc. Centre phosphor band, white paper (12.71?)	80	
		pbca. Centre phosphor band, white fluorescent paper	80	
583c		6c. black (*white paper*) (2.72)	1·25	30
		ca. Printed on the gummed side	10·00	
		cp. Centre phosphor band	3·75	4·00
		cq. Two fluorescent bands	50	60
584		8c. purple-brown	25	1·00
		c. White paper (7.71)	12·00	
585		10c. olive-green	25	10
		c. White paper (12.71)	80	
		ca. White fluorescent paper	70	
		p. Two phosphor bands (9.12.69)	1·50	3·00
		pc. Two phosphor bands, white paper (1.72)	75	
		pca. Two phosphor bands, white fluorescent paper	4·50	
		q. Two fluorescent bands (1.72)	75	50
		qa. Two fluorescent bands, white fluorescent paper	4·50	
586		15c. dull purple	30	10
		c. White paper (3.71)	65	
		ca. White fluorescent paper	2·00	
		p. Two phosphor bands (9.12.69)	1·50	2·75
		pc. Two phosphor bands, white paper (3.72)	1·25	
		q. Two fluorescent bands (2.72)	80	1·50

37

587	20c. deep blue		1·60	10
	c. White paper (8.71)		1·40	
	ca. White fluorescent paper		2·00	
	p. Two phosphor bands (9.12.69)		2·50	4·25
	pc. Two phosphor bands, white paper		1·25	
588	25c. myrtle-green		1·50	10
	ca. White fluorescent paper (10.71)		2·25	
	p. Two phosphor bands (9.12.69)		4·25	7·00
	pca. Two phosphor bands, white fluorescent paper (9.71)		16·00	
589	50c. cinnamon		1·50	10
	c. White paper (3.71)		2·50	
	ca. White fluorescent paper		2·50	
590	$1 scarlet		1·50	1·00
	c. White paper (3.71)		3·00	
	ca. White fluorescent paper		3·00	
579/590 Set of 13			7·50	2·75
579pa/588p Set of 10			13·50	26·00

(ii) Perf 9½×imperf (coil stamps)

591	3c. slate-purple (3.67)	2·00	4·00
592	4c. red (3.67)	2·00	2·50
593	5c. blue (2.67)	2·00	3·25

(iii) Perf 10×imperf (coil stamps)

594	6c. orange-red (1.69)	90	35
	a. Imperf (vert pair)	£225	
	c. White fluorescent paper (12.69)	9·00	
	ca. Imperf (vert pair)	—	
595	6c. black (*white fluorescent paper*) (8.70)	35	2·25
	a. Imperf (vert pair)	£2000	
596	7c. green (*white fluorescent paper*) (30.6.71)	40	2·50
	a. Imperf (vert pair)	£850	
597	8c. black (*white paper*) (30.12.71)	1·00	1·50
	a. Imperf (vert pair)	£425	
	q. Two fluorescent bands	30	30
	qa. Two fluorescent bands, white fluorescent paper	1·00	
	qb. Imperf (vert pair)	£800	

B. Recess B.A.B.N.

(i) P 10 (sheets (601/p) or booklets)

598	1c. brown (9.68)	30	2·50
	a. Booklet pane. No. 598×5 *se-tenant* with No. 599×5 (9.68)	1·75	
	b. Booklet pane. No. 601×4 *se-tenant* with No. 598 plus one printed label (10.68)	2·00	
	c. White fluorescent paper (11.69)	7·50	
	cb. Booklet pane. No. 601c×4 *se-tenant* with No. 598c plus one printed label (11.69)	16·00	
599	4c. red (9.68)	20	2·50
	a. Booklet pane. 25 stamps plus two printed labels	6·50	
600	5c. blue (9.68)	30	2·50
	a. Booklet pane of 20	4·50	
601	6c. orange-red (10.68)	45	10
	a. Booklet pane. 25 stamps plus two printed labels (1.69)	9·00	
	c. White fluorescent paper (11.69)	2·00	
	p. Two phosphor bands (1.11.68)	75	1·00
602	6c. black (1.70)	75	1·40
	a. Booklet pane. 25 stamps plus two printed labels	14·00	
	c. White fluorescent paper (11.69)	—	
	ca. Booklet pane. 25 stamps plus two printed labels	—	
603	6c. black (*re-engraved die*) (8.70)	3·00	3·50
	a. Booklet pane of 4	11·00	

(ii) P 12½×12 (sheets (606/10) or booklets)

604	1c. brown (30.6.71)	50	2·50
	a. Booklet pane. Nos. 604×4, 605×4 and 609×12 *se-tenant*	13·00	
	b. Booklet pane. Nos. 604/5 and 609×3 *se-tenant* plus one printed label	4·00	
	c. Booklet pane. Nos. 604×3, 608 and 610×2 *se-tenant* (30.12.71)	1·50	
	d. Booklet pane. Nos. 604×6, 608 and 610×11 *se-tenant* (30.12.71)	6·50	
	e. Booklet pane. Nos. 604×4, 608 and 610×5 *se-tenant* (8.72)	4·50	
	f. White fluorescent paper (30.12.71)	10	10
	fa. Booklet pane. No. 604f×4, 608 and 610×5 *se-tenant* (30.12.71)	1·75	
	q. Two fluorescent bands (30.12.71)	40	2·25
	qc. Booklet pane. Nos. 604q×3, 608q and 610q×2 *se-tenant*	2·00	
	qd. Booklet pane. Nos. 604q×6, 608q and 610q×11 *se-tenant*	5·00	
	qe. Booklet pane. Nos. 604q×4, 608q and 610q×5 *se-tenant* (8.72)	4·50	
	qf. Two fluorescent bands, white fluorescent paper (30.12.71)	10	
	qfa. Booklet pane. No. 604qfa×4, 608 and 610×5 *se-tenant* (30.12.71)	2·50	
605	3c. slate-purple (30.6.71)	3·50	5·50
606	6c. orange-red (3.69)	60	25
	f. White fluorescent paper (12.69)	17·00	
	p. Two phosphor bands	1·25	1·50
	pf. Two phosphor bands, white fluorescent paper (12.69)	—	
607	6c. black (7.1.70)	30	10
	a. Booklet pane. 25 stamps plus two printed labels (8.70)	16·00	
	f. White fluorescent paper	14·00	
	p. Two phosphor bands	1·50	2·75
608	6c. black (*re-engraved die*) (9.70)	1·00	10
	a. Booklet pane of 4 (11.70)	4·00	
	f. White fluorescent paper	50	
	p. One centre phosphor band (9.71)	2·50	3·50
	q. Two fluorescent bands (30.12.71)	1·50	45
	qf. Two fluorescent bands, white fluorescent paper	35	
609	7c. myrtle-green (30.6.71)	30	60
	p. Two phosphor bands	1·00	3·25
610	8c. slate-black (30.12.71)	30	10
	c. White paper	25	
	cf. White fluorescent paper	2·75	
	p. Two phosphor bands	60	1·00
	pf. Two phosphor bands, white paper (1972)	50	
	pfa. Two phosphor bands, white fluorescent paper	4·00	
	q. Two fluorescent bands (30.12.71)	45	15
	qf. Two fluorescent bands, white paper	35	
	qfa. Two fluorescent bands, white fluorescent paper	1·00	

No. 581q only exists as a pre-cancel.

Nos. 582b, 583b, 583pa are blocks with the outer edges imperf. These come from "One Dollar Plastic Packages" sold at post offices.

No. 582p comes with the band to the left or right of the stamp, the phosphor having been applied across alternate vertical perforations.

Postal forgeries exist of the 6c. orange printed in lithography and perforated 12½.

Normal

Re-engraved

When the basic postal rate was changed to 6c. the C.B.N. lent their die to B.A.B.N. who made a duplicate die from it by transfer. Parts of this proved to be weak, but it was used for Nos. 601/2 and 606/7. B.A.B.N. later re-engraved their die to make fresh plates which were used for Nos. 603 and 608. No. 608 first appeared on sheets from Plate 4.

There are no records of dates of issue of the booklets, packs and coils, but supplies of these were distributed to depots in the months indicated.

IMPERF BETWEEN PAIRS FROM COIL STAMPS. Nos. 594/7 are known in blocks or horizontal pairs imperf between vertically. Coils are supplied to post offices in batches of ten coils held together by roulettes between every fourth stamp so that they can easily be split apart. If two or more unsplit coils are purchased it is possible to obtain blocks or pairs imperf between vertically.

Vertical coil stamps are also known imperf between horizontally or with some stamps apparently completely imperf. These can result from blind perforations identifiable by slight indentations.

WHITE PAPERS. Original printings of the sheet and coil stamps were made on toned paper. From the later part of 1969 experimental printings were made on white fluorescent paper, as referred to in the note below No. 620; this paper is distinct from the glazed type used for the "Opal" booklet (see Nos. 580a and 581a).

During 1971 a further type of paper, white but non-fluorescent, was introduced. The two white papers cannot be distinguished from each other without the use of a U.V. lamp.

CANADA

FLUORESCENT BANDS. During the second half of 1971 new sorting machines were installed in the Ottawa area which were activated by stamps bearing fluorescent bands. These differ from the Winnipeg phosphor bands in that they react green and have no after-glow. To the naked eye the fluorescent bands appear shiny when compared with the remainder of the stamp when looking along its surface. Winnipeg phosphor bands appear matt.

The experiments were successful and what was at first called "Ottawa tagging" has since come into more general use and the Winnipeg phosphor was phased out. However, the substance at first used (known as OP-4) was found to migrate to envelopes, documents, album pages, etc. as well as to adjoining stamps. Late in 1972 this fault was cured by using another substance (called OP-2). The migrating bands were used on early printings of Nos. 604q, 608q and 610q as well as certain stamps referred to in a footnote after No. 692. It is most advisable to use plastic mounts for housing stamps with migrating bands or else clear acetate should be affixed to the album leaves.

Several stamps exist with fluorescent bands omitted in error. We do not list these varieties.

269 Canadian Pavilion

270 Allegory of "Womanhood" on Ballot-box

(Des C.B.N.)
1967 (28 Apr). World Fair, Montreal. P 12.
611   **269**   5c. blue and red 10   10

(Des Helen Fitzgerald. Litho)
1967 (24 May). 50th Anniv of Women's Franchise. P 12.
612   **270**   5c. reddish purple and black 10   10

271 Queen Elizabeth II and Centennial Emblem

272 Athlete

(Portrait from photo by Anthony Buckley)
1967 (30 June). Royal Visit. P 12.
613   **271**   5c. plum and orange-brown 15   10

(Des Brigdens Ltd.)
1967 (19 July). Fifth Pan-American Games, Winnipeg. P 12.
614   **272**   5c. rose-red 10   10

273 "World News"

274 Governor-General Vanier

(Des W. McLauchlan)
1967 (31 Aug). 50th Anniv of the Canadian Press. P 12.
615   **273**   5c. blue 10   10

(Des from photo by Karsh)
1967 (15 Sept). Vanier Commemoration. P 12.
616   **274**   5c. black 10   10

PRINTERS. The following were printed either by the Canadian Bank Note Co, Ottawa (C.B.N.) or the British American Bank Note Co, Ottawa (B.A.B.N.), except where otherwise stated.

275 People of 1867 and Toronto, 1867

276 Carol Singers

(Des and recess C.B.N.)
1967 (28 Sept). Centenary of Toronto as Capital City of Ontario. P 12.
617   **275**   5c. myrtle-green and vermilion 10   10

(Des and recess B.A.B.N.)
1967 (11 Oct). Christmas. P 12.
618   **276**   3c. scarlet 10   10
          a. Pack. Two blocks of 25 .... 3·25
          p. Two phosphor bands 20   1·00
          pa. Pack. Two blocks of 25 .... 3·25
619   5c. emerald-green 10   10
          p. Two phosphor bands 70   1·00

Nos. 618a and 618pa are blocks with the outer edges imperf. These come from "$1.50 Plastic Packs" sold at post offices.

277 Grey Jays

278 Weather Map and Instruments

(Des M. G. Loates. Litho C.B.N.)
1968 (15 Feb). Wild Life. P 12.
620   **277**   5c. multicoloured 30   10
See also Nos. 638/40.

WHITE FLUORESCENT PAPER. Different papers with varying degrees of whiteness have been used for Canadian stamps and it is understood that much of the paper contained a high percentage of recycled pulp. The fluorescent content of this paper varies, but during 1968–70 a distinctive very white and highly fluorescent paper was used known by the tradename "hybrite"; this fluoresces on the back and front. Some issues were wholly printed on this paper, and these can be used for distinguishing those which appeared on ordinary paper as well, both being listed.

See also notes following No. 610qa.

(Des and litho B.A.B.N.)
1968 (13 Mar). Bicentenary of First Meteorological Readings. White fluorescent paper. P 11.
621   **278**   5c. multicoloured 15   10
          a. Ordinary paper 70

279 Narwhal

280 Globe, Maple Leaf and Rain Gauge

(Des J. A. Crosby. Litho B.A.B.N.)
1968 (10 Apr). Wildlife. White fluorescent paper. P 11.
622   **279**   5c. multicoloured 15   10
          a. Ordinary paper .... 2·00

No. 622 has a background of yellow-green and pale blue but copies are known with the yellow-green apparently missing. This "yellow-green" is produced by an overlay of yellow on the blue but we have not come across any examples where the yellow is completely missing and the wide range of colour variation is due to technical difficulties in maintaining an exact blend of the two colours.

(Des I. von Mosdossy. Litho B.A.B.N.)
1968 (8 May). International Hydrological Decade. White fluorescent paper. P 11.
623   **280**   5c. multicoloured 15   10
          a. Ordinary paper 40

IMPERF EDGES. On Nos. 624/54, 657 and 659 (stamps printed by the B.A.B.N. Co.) the outer edges of the sheets were guillotined to remove the imprints for P.O. stock so that single stamps may, therefore, be found with either one, or two adjacent sides imperforate.

39

CANADA

281 Nonsuch
282 Lacrosse Players 

(Recess and photo B.A.B.N.)
1968 (5 June). 300th Anniv of Voyage of the "Nonsuch". P 10.
624 281 5c. multicoloured 20 10

(Des J. E. Aldridge. Recess and photo B.A.B.N.)
1968 (3 July). Lacrosse. P 10.
625 282 5c. black, red and lemon 15 10

283 Front Page of *The Globe*, George Brown and Legislative Building
284 H. Bourassa 

(Des N. Sabolotny. Recess and photo B.A.B.N.)
1968 (21 Aug). 150th Birth Anniv of George Brown (politician and journalist). P 10.
626 283 5c. multicoloured 10 10

(Des, recess and litho C.B.N.)
1968 (4 Sept). Birth Centenary of Henri Bourassa (journalist and politician). White fluorescent paper. P 12.
627 284 5c. black, red and pale cream 10 10

285 John McCrae, Battlefield and First Lines of "In Flanders Fields"
286 Armistice Monument, Vimy 

(Des I. von Mosdossy. Litho C.B.N.)
1968 (15 Oct). 50th Death Anniv of John McCrae (soldier and poet). White fluorescent paper. P 12.
628 285 5c. multicoloured 10 10

(Des and recess C.B.N.)
1968 (15 Oct). 50th Anniversary of 1918 Armistice. P 12.
629 286 15c. slate-black 30 40

287 Eskimo Family (carving)
288 "Mother and Child" (carving) 

(Designs from Eskimo carvings by Munamee (6c.) and unknown carver (5c.). Photo C.B.N.)
1968. Christmas. White fluorescent paper. P 12.
630 287 5c. black and new blue (1.11.68) 10 10
           a. Booklet pane of 10 (15.11.68) ...... 2·25
           p. One centre phosphor band .... 10 1·50
           pa. Booklet pane of 10 (15.11.68) ..... 3·00
631 288 6c. black and ochre (15.11.68) 10 10
           p. Two phosphor bands .... 20 1·50

289 Curling
290 Vincent Massey 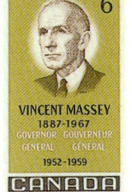

(Des D. Eales. Recess and photo B.A.B.N.)
1969 (15 Jan). Curling. P 10.
632 289 6c. black, new blue and scarlet 15 15

(Des I. von Mosdossy. Recess and litho C.B.N.)
1969 (20 Feb). Vincent Massey, First Canadian-born Governor-General. White fluorescent paper. P 12.
633 290 6c. sepia and yellow-ochre 10 10

291 "Return from the Harvest Field" (Suzor-Côté)
292 Globe and Tools 

(Photo C.B.N.)
1969 (14 Mar). Birth Centenary of Marc Aurèle de Foy Suzor-Côté (painter). White fluorescent paper. P 12.
634 291 50c. multicoloured .... 1·50 2·75

(Des J. Hébert. Recess B.A.B.N.)
1969 (21 May). 50th Anniv of International Labour Organisation. White fluorescent paper. P 12½×12.
635 292 6c. bronze-green 10 10
           a. Ordinary paper .... 1·00

293 Vickers FB-27 Vimy Aircraft over Atlantic Ocean
294 "Sir William Osler" (J. S. Sargent) 

(Des R. W. Bradford. Recess and photo B.A.B.N.)
1969 (13 June). 50th Anniv of First Non-stop Transatlantic Flight. White fluorescent paper. P 12×12½.
636 293 15c. chocolate, bright green and pale blue 40 55

(Des, recess and photo B.A.B.N.)
1969 (23 June). 50th Death Anniv of Sir William Osler (physician). P 12½×12.
637 294 6c. deep blue, light blue and chestnut 20 10
           a. White fluorescent paper 80

295 White-throated Sparrows
298 Flags of Winter and Summer Games 

40

CANADA

(Des M. G. Loates. Litho C.B.N.)

1969 (23 July). Birds. T **295** and similar multicoloured designs. White fluorescent paper. P 12.
638		6c. Type **295**...........................	25	10
639		10c. Savannah Sparrow ("Ipswich Sparrow") (horiz)..............................	35	1·10
640		25c. Hermit Thrush (horiz)............	1·10	3·75
638/640 Set of 3..			1·50	4·50

(Des C. McDiarmid. Recess and litho C.B.N.)

1969 (15 Aug). Canadian Games. White fluorescent paper. P 12.
641	**298**	6c. emerald, scarlet and blue.................	10	10

299 Outline of Prince Edward Island showing Charlottetown

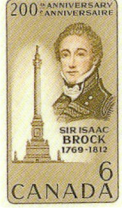

300 Sir Isaac Brock and Memorial Column

(Des L. Fitzgerald. Recess and photo B.A.B.N.)

1969 (15 Aug). Bicentenary of Charlottetown as Capital of Prince Edward Island. White fluorescent paper. P 12×12½.
642	**299**	6c. yellow-brown, black and blue.........	20	20
		a. Ordinary paper.........................	80	

(Des I. von Mosdossy. Recess and litho C.B.N.)

1969 (12 Sept). Birth Bicentenary of Sir Isaac Brock. P 12.
643	**300**	6c. orange, bistre and bistre-brown.....	10	10

301 Children of the World in Prayer

302 Stephen Butler Leacock, Mask and "Mariposa"

(Des Rapid Grip and Batten Ltd. Litho C.B.N.)

1969 (8 Oct). Christmas. White fluorescent paper. P 12.
644	**301**	5c. multicoloured................................	10	10
		a. Booklet pane of 10.....................	1·50	
		p. One centre phosphor band...........	10	1·50
		pa. Booklet pane of 10.....................	2·50	
645		6c. multicoloured...............................	10	10
		a. Black (inscr, value and frame omitted)..................................	£1700	£1300
		p. Two phosphor bands.....................	20	1·50

(Des, recess and photo B.A.B.N.)

1969 (12 Nov). Birth Centenary of Stephen Butler Leacock (humorist). P 12×12½.
646	**302**	6c. multicoloured................................	10	10

303 Symbolic Cross-roads

304 "Enchanted Owl" (Kenojuak)

(Des K. C. Lochhead. Litho C.B.N.)

1970 (27 Jan). Centenary of Manitoba. P 12.
647	**303**	6c. ultramarine, lemon and vermilion..	15	10
		p. Two phosphor bands.....................	15	1·50

(Des N. E. Hallendy and Miss S. Van Raalte. Recess C.B.N.)

1970 (27 Jan). Centenary of Northwest Territories. White fluorescent paper. P 12.
648	**304**	6c. carmine, red and black....................	10	10

305 Microscopic View of Inside of Leaf

306 Expo 67 Emblem and Stylized Cherry Blossom

(Des I. Charney. Recess and photo B.A.B.N.)

1970 (18 Feb). International Biological Programme. P 12×12½.
649	**305**	6c. emerald, orange-yellow and ultramarine.............................	15	10

(Des E. R. C. Bethune. Litho C.B.N.)

1970 (18 Mar). World Fair, Osaka. T **306** and similar horiz designs. Multicoloured; colour of Cherry Blossom given. P 12.
650		25c. red..	1·50	2·25
		a. Block of 4. Nos. 650/3.................	5·50	8·00
		p. Two phosphor bands.....................	1·50	2·50
		pa. Block of 4. Nos. 650p/3p.............	5·50	9·00
651		25c. violet...	1·50	2·25
		p. Two phosphor bands.....................	1·50	2·50
652		25c. green..	1·50	2·25
		p. Two phosphor bands.....................	1·50	2·50
653		25c. blue...	1·50	2·25
		p. Two phosphor bands.....................	1·50	2·50
650/653 Set of 4...			5·50	8·00
650p/653p Set of 4...			5·50	9·00

Designs:—No. 650, Type **306**; No. 651, Dogwood and stylized cherry blossom; No. 652, White Trillium and stylized cherry blossom; No. 653, White Garden Lily and stylized cherry blossom.

Nos. 650/3 and 650p/3p are printed together in sheets of 50 (5×10). In the first, second, fourth and fifth vertical rows the four different designs are arranged in se-tenant blocks, whilst the centre row is composed as follows (reading downwards):—650(p)/3(p), 650(p) ×2, 653(p), 651(p), 652(p) and 650(p).

310 Henry Kelsey

311 "Towards Unification"

(Des D. Burton. Recess and photo B.A.B.N.)

1970 (15 Apr). 300th Birth Anniv of Henry Kelsey (explorer). P 12×12½.
654	**310**	6c. multicoloured................................	10	10

(Des B. Fisher. Litho B.A.B.N.)

1970 (13 May). 25th Anniv of United Nations. P 11.
655	**311**	10c. blue...	75	1·50
		p. Two phosphor bands.....................	1·00	2·50
656		15c. magenta and bluish lilac.................	75	50
		p. Two phosphor bands.....................	1·00	2·50

312 Louis Riel (Métis leader)

313 Mackenzie's Inscription, Dean Channel

(Des R. Derreth. Photo B.A.B.N.)

1970 (19 June). Louis Riel Commemoration. P 12½×12.
657	**312**	6c. greenish blue and vermilion.............	10	10

(Design from Government Archives photo. Recess C.B.N.)

1970 (25 June). Sir Alexander Mackenzie (explorer). White fluorescent paper. P 12×11½.
658	**313**	6c. bistre-brown.................................	15	10

41

CANADA

314 Sir Oliver Mowat (statesman)
315 "Isles of Spruce" (A. Lismer) 

(Des E. Roch. Recess and photo B.A.B.N.)
1970 (12 Aug). Sir Oliver Mowat Commemoration. P 12×12½.
659 314 6c. vermilion and black............................. 10 10

(Litho Ashton-Potter)
1970 (18 Sept). 50th Anniv of "Group of Seven" (artists). P 11.
660 315 6c. multicoloured.. 10 10

316 "Horse-drawn Sleigh" (D. Niskala)
317 "Christ in Manger" (C. Fortier) 

(Des from children's drawings. Litho C.B.N.)
1970 (7 Oct). Christmas. Horiz designs as T **316/17**, showing children's drawings. Multicoloured. White fluorescent paper. P 12.
661	5c. Type **316**...	40 20
	a. Strip of 5. Nos. 661/5	1·75 2·50
	p. One centre phosphor band..............	70 1·25
	pa. Strip of 5. Nos. 661p/5p.................	3·25 5·00
662	5c. "Stable and Star of Bethlehem" (L. Wilson) (26×21 *mm*)...............	40 20
	p. One centre phosphor band..............	70 1·25
663	5c. "Snowmen" (M. Lecompte) (26×21 *mm*)	40 20
	p. One centre phosphor band..............	70 1·25
664	5c. "Skiing" (D. Durham) (26×21 *mm*)....	40 20
	p. One centre phosphor band..............	70 1·25
665	5c. "Santa Claus" (A. Martin) (26×21 *mm*).....	40 20
	p. One centre phosphor band..............	70 1·25
666	6c. "Santa Claus" (E. Bhattacharya) (26×21 *mm*)..	40 20
	a. Strip of 5. Nos. 666/70.....................	1·75 2·50
	p. Two phosphor bands.........................	70 1·25
	pa. Strip of 5. Nos. 666p/70p................	3·25 5·00
667	6c. "Christ in Manger" (J. McKinney) (26×21 *mm*)..	40 20
	p. Two phosphor bands.........................	70 1·25
668	6c. "Toy Shop" (N. Whateley) (26×21 *mm*)....	40 20
	p. Two phosphor bands.........................	70 1·25
669	6c. "Christmas Tree" (J. Pomperleau) (26×21 *mm*)..	40 20
	p. Two phosphor bands.........................	70 1·25
670	6c. "Church" (J. McMillan) (26×21 *mm*).....	40 20
	p. Two phosphor bands.........................	70 1·25
671	10c. Type **317**..	25 30
	p. Two phosphor bands.........................	45 1·25
672	15c. "Trees and Sledge" (J. Dojcak) (35×21 *mm*)..	35 60
	p. Two phosphor bands.........................	55 1·75
661/672 *Set of* 12		4·25 2·50
661p/672p *Set of* 12		7·25 12·50

The designs of the 5c. and 6c. were each issued with the various designs *se-tenant* in a diamond shaped arrangement within the sheet. This generally results in *se-tenant* pairs both vert and horiz, but due to the sheet arrangement vert and horiz pairs of the same design exist from the two centre vert and horiz rows.

328 Sir Donald A. Smith
329 "Big Raven" (E. Carr) 

(Des Dora de Pédery-Hunt. Litho C.B.N.)
1970 (4 Nov). 150th Birth Anniv of Sir Donald Alexander Smith. P 12.
673 328 6c. yellow, brown and bronze-green..... 15 10

(Litho C.B.N.)
1971 (12 Feb). Birth Centenary of Emily Carr (painter). P 12.
674 329 6c. multicoloured.. 20 30

330 Laboratory Equipment
331 "The Atom" 

(Des R. Webber. Litho B.A.B.N.)
1971 (3 Mar). 50th Anniv of Discovery of Insulin. P 10½.
675 330 6c. multicoloured.. 30 30

(Des R. Webber. Litho B.A.B.N.)
1971 (24 Mar). Birth Centenary of Lord Rutherford (scientist). P 11.
676 331 6c. yellow, red deep chocolate and black... 20 20
         a. Black omitted.. £6000

332 Maple "Keys"
333 Louis Papineau 

(Des Alma Duncan. Litho Ashton-Potter)
1971. "The Maple Leaf in Four Seasons". T **332** and similar vert designs. Multicoloured. P 11.
677	6c. Type **332** (Spring) (14.4)	20 20
	a. Imperf (pair)	£700
678	6c. Green leaves (Summer) (16.6)	20 20
679	7c. Autumn leaves (3.9)	20 20
	a. Grey (inscr and value) omitted	£2250
680	7c. Withered leaves and snow (Winter) (19.11)...	20 20
677/680 *Set of* 4		70 70

(Des L. Marquart. Recess and photo B.A.B.N.)
1971 (7 May). Death Centenary of Louis-Joseph Papineau (politician). Ordinary paper. P 12½×12.
681 333 6c. multicoloured.. 15 25

334 Chart of Coppermine River
335 "People" and Computer Tapes 

(Des L. Marquart. Recess and photo B.A.B.N.)
1971 (7 May). Bicentenary of Samuel Hearne's Expedition to Coppermine River. Ordinary paper. P 12½×12½.
682 334 6c. red, sepia and pale buff....................... 40 40

(Des H. Kleefeld. Litho C.B.N.)
1971 (1 June). Centenary of First Canadian Census. P 11½.
683 335 6c. blue, red and black.............................. 30 20

336 Maple Leaves

42

CANADA

(Des B. Kramer. Litho C.B.N.)
1971 (1 June). Radio Canada International. P 12.
684　336　15c. red, yellow and black............................ 50　1·50
　　　　　　p. Two phosphor bands......................... 1·75　3·50

337 "BC"

(Des E. R. C. Bethune. Litho C.B.N.)
1971 (20 July). Centenary of British Columbia's Entry into the Confederation. P 12.
685　337　7c. multicoloured............................ 15　10

338 "Indian Encampment on Lake Huron" (Kane)

339 "Snowflake"

(Des and litho B.A.B.N.)
1971 (11 Aug). Death Centenary of Paul Kane (painter). P 12½.
686　338　7c. multicoloured............................ 20　10

(Des Lisl Levinsohn. Recess (6c., 7c.) or recess and litho (others) C.B.N.)
1971 (6 Oct). Christmas. T **339** and similar design. P 12.
687　339　6c. deep blue .... 10　10
　　　　　　o. Ordinary paper......................... 1·00
　　　　　　p. One centre phosphor band,
　　　　　　　ordinary paper .... 1·25　60
　　　　　　po. One centre phosphor band................ 30　60
688　　　　7c. deep emerald .... 15　10
　　　　　　p. Two phosphor bands.................... 40　65
689　—　10c. silver and cerise .... 50　1·25
　　　　　　p. Two phosphor bands.................... 1·00　2·25
690　—　15c. silver, brown-purple and lavender . 65　2·00
　　　　　　p. Two phosphor bands.................... 1·00　2·75
687/690 *Set of* 4 .... 1·25　3·00
687p/690p *Set of* 4 .... 2·40　5·50
　Design:—10c., 15c. "Snowflake" design similar to Type **339**, but square (26×26 mm).

340 Pierre Laporte (Quebec Cabinet Minister)

341 Skaters

(Des G. Gundersen. Recess and litho B.A.B.N.)
1971 (20 Oct). First Anniv of the Assassination of Pierre Laporte. Ordinary paper. P 12½×12.
691　340　7c. black/*pale buff*............................ 15　10

(Des Design Workshop, Toronto. Litho C.B.N.)
1972 (1 Mar). World Figure Skating Championships, Calgary. P 12.
692　341　8c. purple .... 15　20

MIGRATING FLUORESCENT BANDS. These are referred to in the notes after No. 610. In the following issues they exist on Nos. 719q/22q, 731q/2q and on early printings only of Nos. 702/6.

342 J. A. Mac Donald

343 Forest, Central Canada

344 Vancouver

Type I

Type II

Two types of 10c. (No. 702):
　Type I. Light impression of green recess colour. Crosshatching around "Canada" clearly visible (plate 1).
　Type II. Green recess colour much more deeply etched. Cross-hatching around "Canada" entirely obscured (plates 2 and 3).

Type I

Type II

Two types of 15c.:
　Type I. Trees on hillside, shown in blue, clearly detailed (plate 1).
　Type II. Trees shown in solid colour (plate 2).

Two types of 25c.:
　Type I. Bears' shadows evenly shaded.
　Type II. Shadows have a solid central area.

(Des D. Annesley (1 to 10c. (701)), R. Derreth (others))
1972–77. Various designs as T **342**/4.
(*a*) T **342** and similar vert portraits. Recess C.B.N. (1 to 6c.) and last ptgs of 7 and 8c. (No. 700), B.A.B.N (7, 8, 10c. and booklet panes). Two fluorescent bands. P 12×12½ (1 to 8c.) or 13 (10c.). (17.10.73)
693　　　1c. orange .... 10　30
　　　a. Booklet pane. Nos. 693×3, 698 and
　　　　700×2 (10.4.74) 75
　　　b. Booklet pane. Nos. 693×6, 698 and
　　　　700×11 (17.1.75)............................... 2·25
　　　c. Booklet pane. Nos. 693×2, 694×4 and
　　　　701a×4 (1.9.76)................................ 1·50
　　　d. Printed on the gummed side £475

43

CANADA

694	2c. deep green		10	10
695	3c. agate		10	50
696	4c. black		10	50
697	5c. deep magenta		10	10
698	6c. Indian red		10	50
	a. Printed on the gummed side		£100	
699	7c. reddish brown (8.4.74)		40	50
700	8c. dull ultramarine		15	10
	a. Perf 13 (12.76)		1·25	1·00
701	10c. brown-lake (1.9.76)		75	10
	a. Perf 12×12½ (booklets)		75	1·00

(b) T 343 and similar vert designs. Recess and photo B.A.B.N. Two fluorescent bands. P 12½×12 (8.9.72)

702	10c. deep green, blue-green and yellow-orange (I)		60	10
	a. Type II (7.74)		40	15
	b. Perf 13½ (2.76)		75	10
	p. Two phosphor bands		1·00	2·00
703	15c. dull ultramarine and orange-brown (I)		10	15
	a. Type II (1975)		4·00	2·25
	b. Perf 13½ (2.76)		1·25	10
	p. Two phosphor bands		2·25	2·75
704	20c. pale orange, reddish violet and ultramarine		1·00	10
	a. Perf 13½ (30.1.76)		1·50	10
	p. Two phosphor bands		2·50	3·50
705	25c. deep ultramarine and pale blue (I)		1·50	10
	a. Type II (1975)		8·00	3·50
	b. Perf 13½ (2.76)		1·00	10
	p. Two phosphor bands		3·50	4·25
706	50c. blue-green, royal blue and buff		1·00	30
	a. Blue-green, ultramarine and buff (8.74)		80	20
	b. Perf 13½ (2.76)		1·75	10

(c) T 344 and similar horiz design. Recess B.A.B.N. and litho Ashton-Potter. No fluorescent bands. P 11 (17.3.72)

707	$1 multicoloured		4·50	5·00
708	$2 multicoloured		1·50	2·00
	a. Brown (value and inscr) ptd albino		£2500	

(d) T 344. Recess and photo B.A.B.N. Two fluorescent bands. P 12½×12 (24.10.73)

709	$1 multicoloured		3·00	1·25
	a. Perf 13½ (4.77)		85	70
	b. White fluorescent paper (8.74)		2·75	

(e) As Nos. 700/1. Recess C.B.N. Imperf×perf 10 (coil stamps)

710	8c. dull ultramarine (10.4.74)		1·00	20
	a. Imperf (horiz pair)		85·00	
711	10c. brown-lake (1.9.76)		30	20
	a. Imperf (horiz pair)		£110	

Designs (1 to 7c. show Canadian Prime Ministers):—2c. W, Laurier; 3c. R. Borden; 4c. W. L. Mackenzie King; 5c. R. B. Bennett; 6c. L. B. Pearson; 7c. Louis St. Laurent; 8 and 10 c, (Nos. 701/a, 711), Queen Elizabeth II; 15c. American Bighorn sheep; 20c. Prairie landscape from the air; 25c. Polar Bears: 50c. Seashore, Eastern Canada; $2 Quebec.

Stamps from booklets (Nos. SB80/2) exist with one or two adjacent sides imperforate.

Nos. 712/8 are vacant.

PAPER. Various papers were used for the low value stamps. Nos 693/701, most of which show some degree of fluorescence under U.V. light. The 1 c., 2 c., 6 c., 7 c. and 8 c. also exist on paper which does not react. In addition all the low values, except the 3 c., 5 c., 7 c. and 10c., occur on paper showing a ribbing effect.

The medium values were printed on fluorescent paper, although the amount of fluorescence visible under U.V. light varies greatly between printings.

A small part of the printing of the $1 (No. 707) was on a paper with a distinct textured effect. This paper was used for stamp production in error.

345 Heart

346 Frontenac and Fort Saint-Louis, Quebec

(Des Joyce Wieland. Recess B.A.B.N.)

1972 (7 Apr). Heart Disease (World Health Day). P 12×12½.

719	**345**	8c. carmine	30	10
		o. Ordinary soft toned paper	60	
		q. Two fluorescent bands	75	25
		qo. Two fluorescent bands, ordinary paper	70	

The chemical used on No. 719q migrates.

(Des L. Marquart. Recess and photo B.A.B.N.)

1972 (17 May). 300th Anniv of Governor Frontenac's Appointment to New France. Ordinary paper. P 12×12½.

720	**346**	8c. brown-red, orange-brown and deep ultram	15	15
		q. Two fluorescent bands	15	15

The chemical used on No. 720q migrates.

347 Plains Indians' Artefacts

347a Buffalo Chase

(Des G. Beaupré. Litho Ashton-Potter (721/2, 725/6 and 729/30), B.A.B.N. (723/4), C.B.N. (727/8))

1972–76. Canadian Indians. Two fluorescent bands (Nos. 723/30 and 733/40). P 12×12½ (721/2, 725/6), 12 (723/4), 13 (727/30), 12½×12 (731/6) or 12½ (737/40).

(a) Horiz designs issued in se-tenant pairs the first showing Artefacts as T 347, the second showing Scenes from Indian Life as T 347a

721	8c. multicoloured (6.7.72)		40	10
	a. Pair. Nos. 721/2		85	1·00
	q. Two fluorescent bands		40	15
	qa. Pair. Nos. 721q/2q		85	1·00
722	8c. deep brown, yellow and grey-black (6.7.72)		40	10
	q. Two fluorescent bands		40	15
723	8c. multicoloured (21.2.73)		40	10
	a. Pair. Nos. 723/4		85	1·00
724	8c. multicoloured (21.2.73)		40	10
725	8c. multicoloured (16.1.74)		40	10
	a. Pair. Nos. 725/6		85	1·25
726	8c. deep brown, yellow and grey-black (16.1.74)		40	10
727	8c. multicoloured (4.4.75)		40	10
	a. Pair. Nos. 727/8		85	1·25
	b. Imperf between (horiz pair)		£700	
728	8c. multicoloured (4.4.75)		40	10
729	10c. multicoloured (17.9.76)		40	20
	a. Pair. Nos. 729/30		85	1·00
730	10c. light stone and black (17.9.76)		40	20

Designs show the following tribes: Nos. 721/2 (T **347***a*), Plains Indians; 723/4, Algonkians; 725/6, Pacific Coast Indians; 727/8, Subarctic Indians; 729/30, Iroquoians.

348 Thunderbird and Tribal Pattern

348a Dancer in Ceremonial Costume

(Des G. Beaupré. Recess and photo B.A.B.N. (731/6). Litho and embossed Ashton-Potter (737, 739). Litho Ashton-Potter (738, 740))

*(b) Vert designs issued in se-tenant pairs, the first showing Thunderbird and pattern as T **348**, the second Costumes as T **348a***

731	8c. light yellow-orange, rose-red and black (4.10.72)		40	15
	a. Pair. Nos. 731/2		85	1·00
	q. Two fluorescent bands		40	15
	qa. Pair. Nos. 731q/2q		85	1·00
732	8c. multicoloured (4.10.72)		40	15
	q. Two fluorescent bands		40	15
733	8c. light rose-red, violet and black (28.11.73)		40	10
	a. Pair. Nos. 733/4		85	1·00
734	8c. turquoise-green, lake-brown and black (28.11.73)		40	10
735	8c. rose-red and black (22.2.74)		40	10
	a. Pair. Nos. 735/6		85	1·00
	c. White fluorescent paper		1·25	
	ca. Pair. Nos. 735c/6c		2·50	
736	8c. multicoloured (22.2.74)		40	10
	c. White fluorescent paper		1·25	
737	8c. myrtle-green, grey-brown and black (4.4.75)		40	10
	a. Pair. Nos. 737/8		85	1·25

738		8c. multicoloured (4.4.75)	40	10
739		10c. olive-bistre, reddish orange and black (17.9.76)	40	20
		a. Pair. Nos. 739/40	85	1·00
740		10c. multicoloured (17.9.76)	40	20
721/740 *Set of 20*			7·50	2·10

Designs show the following tribes: Nos. 731/2 (T **348/a**), Plains Indians; 733/4, Algonkians; 735/6, Pacific Coast Indians; 737/8, Subarctic Indians; 739/40, Iroquoians.

The paper and gum of Nos. 735/6 are yellowish; on Nos 735c/6c they are white. Fluorescent paper printings of Nos. 733/4, but there is no apparent difference to the naked eye, except that the fluorescent paper is slightly more transparent.

The fluorescent bands on Nos. 721q/2q and 731q/2q migrate.

349 Earth's Crust

350 Candles

(Des Gottschalk and Ash Ltd. Litho Ashton-Potter)

1972 (2 Aug). Earth Sciences. T **349** and similar square designs. P 12.

741		15c. multicoloured	1·10	1·90
		a. Block of 4. Nos. 741/4	4·00	7·00
		q. Two fluorescent bands	1·75	2·25
		qa. Block of 4. Nos. 741q/4q	6·00	7·50
742		15c. pale grey, dull ultramarine and black	1·10	1·90
		q. Two fluorescent bands	1·75	2·25
743		15c. multicoloured	1·10	1·90
		q. Two fluorescent bands	1·75	2·25
744		15c. light emerald, red-orange and black	1·10	1·90
		q. Two fluorescent bands	1·75	2·25
741/744 *Set of 4*			4·00	7·00
741q/744q *Set of 4*			6·00	8·00

Designs and Events:—No. 741, Photogrammetric surveying (12th Congress of International Society of Photogrammetry); No. 742, "Siegfried" lines (6th Conference of International Cartographic Association); No. 743, Type **349** (24th International Geological Congress; No. 744, Diagram of village at road-intersection (22nd International Geographical Congress).

Nos. 741/4 were issued in sheets of 64, made up of 4 panes of 16, each pane having a marginal commemorative inscription. Within a pane are 4 copies of each design, arranged in *se-tenant* blocks of 4.

(Des R. Webber. Litho Ashton-Potter)

1972 (1 Nov). Christmas. T **350** and similar designs. P 12½×12 (6 and 8c.) or 11×10½ (others).

745	**350**	6c. multicoloured	15	10
		p. One centre phosphor band	35	60
		q. Two fluorescent bands	20	15
746		8c. multicoloured	15	10
		p. Two phosphor bands	40	70
		q. Two fluorescent bands	25	15
747	–	10c. multicoloured	50	1·25
		p. Two phosphor bands	1·40	1·75
		q. Two fluorescent bands	60	90
748	–	15c. multicoloured	60	2·00
		p. Two phosphor bands	1·75	2·50
		q. Two fluorescent bands	90	1·50
745/748 *Set of 4*			1·25	3·00
745p/748p *Set of 4*			3·50	5·00
745q/748q *Set of 4*			1·75	2·40

Designs: *Horiz* (36×20 *mm*)—10c. Candles with fruits and pine boughs; 15c. Candles with prayer-book, caskets and vase.

WHITE FLUORESCENT PAPER. All issues are on white fluorescent paper, *unless otherwise stated*. From November 1972 stamps printed by lithography were produced on two types of this paper, one fluorescing on both sides, the other on one side only. Some issues exist on both papers. Those on the single-sided coating can be found with the fluorescence on the front or back of the stamp.

351 "The Blacksmith's Shop" (Krieghoff)

352 François de Montmorency-Laval

(Des and litho B.A.B.N. and Saults & Pollard Ltd., Winnipeg)

1972 (29 Nov). Death Centenary of Cornelius Krieghoff (painter). P 12½.

749	**351**	8c. multicoloured	30	15
		q. Two fluorescent bands	30	40

FLUORESCENT BANDS. Stamps from No. 750 onwards were issued only with two fluorescent bands, *unless otherwise stated*. Examples are known with the bands omitted in error, but such varieties are outside the scope of the catalogue.

(Des M. Fog and G. Lorange. Litho Ashton-Potter)

1973 (31 Jan). 350th Birth Anniv of Monsignor de Laval (First Bishop of Quebec). P 11.

750	**352**	8c. ultramarine, gold and silver	20	40

353 Commissioner French and Route of the March West

354 Jeanne Mance

(Des Dallaire Morin DeVito Inc. Litho Ashton-Potter)

1973 (9 Mar). Centenary of Royal Canadian Mounted Police. T **353** and similar horiz designs. Multicoloured (except 8c.). P 11.

751		8c. Type **353** (deep reddish brown, dull orange and orange-vermilion)	35	20
752		10c. Spectrograph	1·00	1·25
753		15c. Mounted policeman	2·25	2·00
751/753 *Set of 3*			3·25	3·00

(Des R. Bellemare. Litho Ashton-Potter)

1973 (18 Apr). 300th Death Anniv of Jeanne Mance (nurse). P 11.

754	**354**	8c. multicoloured	20	40

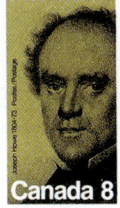

355 Joseph Howe

356 "Mist Fantasy" (MacDonald)

(Des A. Fleming. Litho Ashton-Potter)

1973 (16 May). Death Centenary of Joseph Howe (Nova Scotian politician). P 11.

755	**355**	8c. gold and black	20	40

(Des and litho Ashton-Potter)

1973 (8 June). Birth Centenary of J. E. H. MacDonald (artist). P 12½.

756	**356**	15c. multicoloured	30	55

357 Oaks and Harbour

358 Scottish Settlers

(Des A. Mann. Recess and photo B.A.B.N.)

1973 (22 June). Centenary of Prince Edward Island's Entry into the Confederation. P 12.

757	**357**	8c. pale orange and brown-red	20	30

(Des P. Swan. Litho Ashton-Potter)

1973 (20 July). Bicentennial of Arrival of Scottish Settlers at Pictou, Nova Scotia. P 12×12½.

758	**358**	8c. multicoloured	25	20

CANADA

359 Queen Elizabeth II
360 Nellie McClung 

(Des A. Fleming from photograph by Anthony Buckley, Eng G. A. Gundersen. Recess and photo B.A.B.N.)

1973 (2 Aug). Royal Visit and Commonwealth Heads of Government Meeting, Ottawa. Ordinary paper. P 12×12½.

759	359	8c. multicoloured	25	20
		a. White fluorescent paper	2·75	
760		15c. red, black and bright gold	80	1·50
		a. Red, black and pale dull gold	1·25	1·90

(Des S. Mennie. Litho Ashton-Potter)

1973 (29 Aug). Birth Centenary of Nellie McClung (feminist). P 10½×11.

761	360	8c. multicoloured	20	50

361 Emblem of 1976 Olympics
362 Ice-skate 

(Des Wallis and Matanovic. Litho Ashton-Potter)

1973 (20 Sept). Olympic Games, Montreal (1976) (1st issue). P 12×12½.

762	361	8c. multicoloured	25	15
763		15c. multicoloured	45	1·25

See also Nos. 768/71, 772/4, 786/9, 798/802, 809/11, 814/16, 829/31, 833/7 and 842/4.

(Des A. Maggs. Litho Ashton-Potter)

1973 (7 Nov). Christmas. T **362** and similar vert designs. Multicoloured. P 12½×12 (6, 8c.) or 11 (others).

764		6c. Type **362**	15	10
765		8c. Bird decoration	15	10
766		10c. Santa Claus (20×36 *mm*)	50	1·10
767		15c. Shepherd (20×36 *mm*)	60	1·50
764/767 Set of 4			1·25	2·50

363 Diving
364 Winnipeg Signpost, 1872 

(Des Hunter, Straker, Templeton Ltd. Recess C.B.N.)

1974 (22 Mar). Olympic Games, Montreal (1976) (2nd issue). "Summer Activities". T **363** and similar vert designs. Each deep blue. P 12.

768		8c. Type **363**	30	50
		a. Block of 4. Nos. 768/71	1·10	1·75
769		8c. "Jogging"	30	50
770		8c. Cycling	30	50
771		8c. Hiking	30	50
768/771 Set of 4			1·10	1·75

Nos. 768/71 were printed in *se-tenant* blocks of four throughout the sheet. Each design has a second (latent) image—the Canadian Olympic Games symbol—which appears when the stamp is viewed obliquely to the light.

See also Nos. 786/9.

(Des Wallis and Matanovic. Litho Ashton-Potter)

1974 (17 Apr). Olympic Games, Montreal (1976) (3rd issue). As T **361** but smaller (20×36½ mm). P 12½.

772	361	8c.+2c. multicoloured	25	45
773		10c.+5c. multicoloured	40	1·00
774		15c.+5c. multicoloured	45	1·40
772/774 Set of 3			1·00	2·50

(Des J. R. MacDonald. Litho and embossed Ashton-Potter)

1974 (3 May). Winnipeg Centennial. P 12½×12.

775	364	8c. multicoloured	20	15

365 Postmaster and Customer
366 "Canada's Contribution to Agriculture" 

(Des S. Mennie. Litho Ashton-Potter)

1974 (11 June). Centenary of Canadian Letter Carrier Delivery Service. T **365** and similar horiz designs. Multicoloured. P 13½.

776		8c. Type **365**	50	80
		a. Block of 6. Nos. 776/81	2·75	4·25
777		8c. Postman collecting mail	50	80
778		8c. Mail handler	50	80
779		8c. Mail sorters	50	80
780		8c. Postman making delivery	50	80
781		8c. Rural delivery by car	50	80
776/781 Set of 6			2·75	4·25

Nos. 776/81 were printed in *se-tenant* combinations throughout a sheet of 50, giving 6 blocks of 6 and 14 single stamps.

(Des M. Brett, P. Cowley-Brown, and A. McAllister. Litho Ashton-Potter)

1974 (12 July). "Agricultural Education". Centenary of Ontario Agricultural College. P 12½×12.

782	366	8c. multicoloured	20	20

367 Telephone Development
368 Bicycle Wheel 

(Des R. Webber. Litho Ashton-Potter)

1974 (26 July). Centenary of Invention of Telephone by Alexander Graham Bell. P 12½.

783	367	8c. multicoloured	20	20

(Des Burns and Cooper. Recess and photo B.A.B.N.)

1974 (7 Aug). World Cycling Championships, Montreal. P 12×12½.

784	368	8c. black, rosine and silver	20	30

369 Mennonite Settlers
370 Mercury, Winged Horses and U.P.U. Emblem 

(Des W. Davies. Litho Ashton-Potter)

1974 (28 Aug). Centenary of Arrival of Mennonites in Manitoba. P 12½.

785	369	8c. multicoloured	20	20

CANADA

(Des Hunter, Straker, Templeton Ltd. Recess C.B.N.)

1974 (23 Sept). Olympic Games, Montreal (1976) (4th issue). "Winter Activities". Horiz designs as T **363**, each rosine. P 13½×13.

786	8c. Snow-shoeing	55	60
	a. Block of 4. Nos. 786/9	2·00	2·25
	ab. Printed on the gummed side (block of four)	£950	
787	8c. Skiing	55	60
788	8c. Skating	55	60
789	8c. Curling	55	60
786/789 Set of 4		2·00	2·25

(Des G. Gundersen. Recess and photo B.A.B.N.)

1974 (9 Oct). Centenary of Universal Postal Union. Ordinary paper. P 12×12½.

790	**370**	8c. violet, red-orange and cobalt	15	15
791		15c. red-orange, violet and cobalt	50	1·50
		a. White fluorescent paper	2·50	2·50

371 "The Nativity" (J. P. Lemieux)

372 Marconi and St. John's Harbour, Newfoundland

(Des Wallis and Matanovic. Litho Ashton-Potter)

1974 (1 Nov). Christmas. T **371** and similar horiz designs showing paintings. Multicoloured. P 13½.

792	6c. Type **371**	10	10
	a. Creamy ordinary paper		
793	8c. "Skaters in Hull" (H. Masson) (34×31 *mm*)	10	10
794	10c. "The Ice Cone, Montmorency Falls" (R. C. Todd)	30	75
795	15c. "Village in the Laurentian Mountains" (C. A. Gagnon)	35	1·10
792/795 Set of 4		75	1·75

(Des J. Boyle. Litho Ashton-Potter)

1974 (15 Nov). Birth Centenary of Guglielmo Marconi (radio pioneer). P 13.

| 796 | **372** | 8c. multicoloured | 20 | 20 |

373 Merritt and Welland Canal

374 Swimming

(Des W. Rueter. Recess (B.A.B.N.) and litho (C.B.N.))

1974 (29 Nov). William Merritt Commemoration. P 13×13½.

| 797 | **373** | 8c. multicoloured | 20 | 30 |

(Des Wallis and Matanovic. Litho C.B.N.)

1975 (5 Feb). Olympic Games, Montreal (1976) (5th issue). T **374** and similar horiz designs. Multicoloured. P 13.

798	8c.+2c. Type **374**	45	65
799	10c.+5c. Rowing	60	1·25
800	15c.+5c. Sailing	70	1·40
798/800 Set of 3		1·60	3·00

375 "The Sprinter"

376 "Anne of Green Gables" (Lucy Maud Montgomery)

(Des A. R. Fleming. Litho and embossed Ashton-Potter)

1975 (14 Mar). Olympic Games, Montreal (1976) (6th issue). T **375** and similar multicoloured design showing sculpture by R. T. McKenzie. P 12½×12 ($1) or 12×12½ ($2).

801	$1 Type **375**	1·25	2·00
802	$2 "The Diver" (*vert*)	1·75	3·50

(Des P. Swan (No. 803), C. Gagnon (No. 804). Litho Ashton-Potter)

1975 (15 May). Canadian Writers (1st series). T **376** and similar vert design. Multicoloured. P 13½.

803	8c. Type **376**	30	10
	a. Pair. Nos. 803/4	60	1·00
804	8c. "Maria Chapdelaine" (Louis Hémon)	30	10

Nos. 803/4 were printed horizontally and vertically *se-tenant* throughout the sheet.

See also Nos. 846/7, 940/1 and 1085/6.

377 Marguerite Bourgeoys (founder of the Order of Notre Dame)

378 S. D. Chown (founder of United Church of Canada)

(Des Design and Communication, Montreal. Litho Ashton-Potter (Nos. 805/6). Des W. Southern. Eng G. Gundersen. Recess and photo B.A.B.N. (Nos. 807/8))

1975 (30 May). Canadian Celebrities. T **377/8** and similar vert designs.

(a) As T **377**. P 12½×12

805	8c. multicoloured	60	40
806	8c. multicoloured	60	40

(b) As T **378**. P 12×12½

807	8c. sepia, flesh and light yellow	30	75
	a. Pair. Nos. 807/8	60	2·25
808	8c. sepia, flesh and light yellow	30	75
805/808 Set of 4		1·60	2·10

Designs:—No. 805, Type **377**; No. 806, Alphonse Desjardins (leader of Credit Union movement); No. 807, Type **378**; No. 808, Dr. J. Cook (first moderator of Presbyterian Church in Canada).

Nos. 807/8 were printed together in the sheet horizontally and vertically *se-tenant*.

379 Pole-vaulting

380 "Untamed" (photo by Walt Petrigo)

(Des P. Swan. Litho Ashton-Potter)

1975 (11 June). Olympic Games, Montreal (1976) (7th issue). T **379** and similar vert designs. Multicoloured. P 12×12½.

809	20c. Type **379**	40	50
810	25c. Marathon-running	55	80
811	50c. Hurdling	70	1·25
	o. Creamy ordinary paper	7·00	
809/811 Set of 3		1·50	2·25

(Des B. Reilander. Litho C.B.N.)

1975 (3 July). Centenary of Calgary. P 12×12½.

| 812 | **380** | 8c. multicoloured | 30 | 30 |

47

CANADA

381 I.W.Y. Symbol
382 Fencing

(Des Susan McPhee. Recess and photo B.A.B.N.)

1975 (14 July). International Women's Year. P 13.
| 813 | **381** | 8c. light grey-brown, bistre-yellow and black | 30 | 30 |

(Des J. Hill. Litho C.B.N.)

1975 (6 Aug). Olympic Games, Montreal (1976) (8th issue). T **382** and similar vert designs showing combat sports. Multicoloured. P 13.
814	8c.+2c. Type **382**	35	75
815	10c.+5c. Boxing	45	1·50
816	15c.+5c. Judo	55	1·75
814/816	Set of 3	1·25	3·50

383 "Justitia–Justitia" (statue by W. S. Allward)
384 William D. Lawrence (full-rigged ship)

(Des A. Fleming. Litho Ashton-Potter)

1975 (2 Sept). Centenary of Canadian Supreme Court. P 12½.
| 817 | **383** | 8c. multicoloured | 20 | 30 |

(Des T. Bjarnason. Recess and photo B.A.B.N.)

1975 (24 Sept). Canadian Ships (1st series). T **384** and similar horiz designs showing coastal ships. P 13.
818	8c. yellow-brown and black	70	75
	a. Block of 4. Nos. 818/21	2·50	2·75
819	8c. blue-green and black	70	75
820	8c. yellow-green and black	70	75
821	8c. yellow-brown and black	70	75
818/821	Set of 4	2·50	2·75

Designs:—No. 819, *Neptune* (steamer). No. 820, *Beaver* (paddle-steamer). No. 821, *Quadra* (steamer).

Nos. 818/21 were printed together, *se-tenant*, in different combinations throughout the sheet, giving ten blocks of 4 and ten single stamps.
See also Nos. 851/4, 902/5 and 931/4.

385 "Santa Claus" (G. Kelly)
386 Text, Badge and Bugle

(Des B. Reilander from children's paintings. Litho Ashton-Potter)

1975 (22 Oct). Christmas. T **385** and similar multicoloured designs. P 13.
822	6c. Type **385**	15	10
	a. Pair. Nos. 822/3	30	40
823	6c. "Skater" (Bill Cawsey)	15	10
824	8c. "Child" (D. Hébert)	15	10
	a. Pair. Nos. 824/5	30	45
825	8c. "Family" (L. Caldwell)	15	10
826	10c. "Gift" (D. Lovely)	30	50
827	15c. "Trees" (R. Kowalski) (*horiz*)	40	75
822/827	Set of 6	1·10	1·90

Nos. 822/3 and 824/5 were respectively issued together *se-tenant* in an alternate arrangement within the sheet.

(Des R. Kavach. Recess and photo B.A.B.N.)

1975 (10 Nov). 50th Anniv of Royal Canadian Legion. P 12½×13.
| 828 | **386** | 8c. multicoloured | 20 | 20 |

387 Basketball

(Des J. Hill. Litho Ashton-Potter)

1976 (7 Jan). Olympic Games, Montreal (9th issue). T **387** and similar vert designs. Multicoloured. P 13.
829	8c.+2c. Type **387**	1·50	1·00
830	10c.+5c. Gymnastics	60	1·40
831	20c.+5c. Soccer	70	1·60
829/831	Set of 3	2·50	3·50

388 Games Symbol and Snow Crystal
389 "Communications Arts"

(Des R. Harder. Litho Ashton-Potter)

1976 (6 Feb). 12th Winter Olympic Games, Innsbruck. P 12½.
| 832 | **388** | 20c. multicoloured | 20 | 40 |

(Des R. Webber. Litho C.B.N.)

1976 (6 Feb). Olympic Games, Montreal (10th issue). T **389** and similar vert designs. Multicoloured. P 12×12½.
833	20c. Type **389**	40	25
834	25c. "Handicrafts"	65	75
835	50c. "Performing Arts"	95	1·60
833/835	Set of 3	1·75	2·40

390 Place Ville Marie and Notre-Dame Church

(Des J. and P. Mercier. Recess and photo B.A.B.N.)

1976 (12 Mar). Olympic Games, Montreal (11th issue). T **390** and similar horiz design. Multicoloured. P 13.
| 836 | $1 Type **390** | 2·25 | 4·50 |
| 837 | $2 Olympic Stadium and flags | 2·75 | 5·50 |

391 Flower and Urban Sprawl
392 Benjamin Franklin and Map

(Des I. McLeod. Litho Ashton-Potter)

1976 (12 May). U.N. Conference on Human Settlements (HABITAT), Vancouver. P 12×12½.
| 838 | **391** | 20c. multicoloured | 20 | 30 |

48

CANADA

(Des B. Reilander. Recess and photo B.A.B.N.)

1976 (1 June). Bicentenary of American Revolution. P 13.
839	**392**	10c. multicoloured	20	35

393 Wing Parade before Mackenzie Building

394 Transfer of Olympic Flame by Satellite

(Des W. Davies. Litho C.B.N.)

1976 (1 June). Royal Military College Centenary. T **393** and similar vert design. Multicoloured. P 12×12½.
840		8c. Colour party and Memorial Arch	25	30
		a. Pair. Nos. 840/1	50	1·00
		aa. Imperf (pair)	£1200	
		ab. Printed double (pair)	£2000	
841		8c. Type **393**	25	30

Nos. 840/1 were printed horizontally and vertically *se-tenant* throughout the sheet.

(Des P. Swan. Litho Ashton-Potter)

1976 (18 June). Olympic Games, Montreal (12th issue). T **394** and similar horiz designs. Multicoloured. P 13½.
842		8c. Type **394**	20	10
843		20c. Carrying the Olympic flag	45	60
844		25c. Athletes with medals	45	85
842/844	Set of 3		1·00	1·40

395 Archer

(Des T. Bjarnason. Litho C.B.N.)

1976 (3 Aug). Olympiad for the Physically Disabled. P 12×12½.
845	**395**	20c. multicoloured	20	30

396 "Sam McGee" (Robert W. Service)

397 "Nativity" (F. Mayer)

(Des D. Bierk (No. 846), A. Dumas (No. 847). Litho Ashton-Potter)

1976 (17 Aug). Canadian Writers (2nd series). T **396** and similar vert design. Multicoloured. P 13.
846		8c. Type **396**	15	40
		a. Pair. Nos. 846/7	30	1·00
847		8c. "Le Survenant" (Germaine Guèvremont)	15	40

Nos. 846/7 were printed horizontally and vertically *se-tenant* throughout the sheet.

(Des B. Reilander. Litho Ashton-Potter)

1976 (3 Nov). Christmas. T **397** and similar vert designs showing stained-glass windows. Multicoloured. P 13½.
848		8c. Type **397**	10	10
849		10c. "Nativity" (G. Maile & Son)	10	10
850		20c. "Nativity" (Yvonne Williams)	20	60
848/850	Set of 3		30	60

398 *Northcote* (paddle-steamer)

399 Queen Elizabeth II

(Des T. Bjarnason. Recess and litho C.B.N.)

1976 (19 Nov). Canadian Ships (2nd series). T **398** and similar horiz designs showing inland vessels. P 12×12½.
851		10c. ochre, chestnut and black	45	60
		a. Block of 4. Nos. 851/4	1·60	2·25
852		10c. violet-blue and black	45	60
853		10c. bright blue and black	45	60
854		10c. apple-green, olive-green and black	45	60
851/854	Set of 4		1·60	2·25

Designs:—No. 851, Type **398**; No. 852, *Passport* (paddle-steamer); No. 853, *Chicora* (paddle-steamer); No. 854, *Athabasca* (steamer).

Nos. 851/4 were printed together, *se-tenant*, in different combinations throughout the sheet, giving ten blocks of 4 and ten single stamps.

(Des K. Rodmell from photograph by P. Grugeon. Litho ("25" die-stamped) Ashton-Potter)

1977 (4 Feb). Silver Jubilee. P 12½×12.
855	**399**	25c. multicoloured	30	50
		a. Silver (die-stamped "25") omitted	£750	£425

400 Bottle Gentian

401 Queen Elizabeth II (bas-relief by J. Huta)

402 Houses of Parliament

403 Trembling Aspen

404 Prairie Town Main Street

405 Fundy National Park

(Des R. Derreth (Nos. 870/4), T. Bjarnason (880/3*a*), R. Bolt (884), B. Laycock and W. Tibbles (884*b*), B. Laycock (884*c*), A. Collier (885), W. Tibbles and G. Weber (No. 885*a*), W. Terry and W. Tibbles (885*b*), L. Marois and W. Tibbles (885*c*), Heather Cooper (others). Eng Y. Baril (880/3*a*))

1977 (1 Mar)–**86**.

(a) Vert designs as T **400** showing flowers. Multicoloured

(i) Recess and litho C.B.N. Sheet stamps. P 12×12½
856		1c. Type **400** (22.4.77)	10	20
		a. Printed on the gummed side (pre-cancelled only)	£500	
857		2c. Red Columbine (22.4.77)	10	10
		a. Printed on the gummed side	£350	
858		3c. Canada Lily (22.4.77)	10	10
859		4c. Hepatica (22.4.77)	10	10
		a. Printed on the gummed side	£160	
860		5c. Shooting Star (22.4.77)	10	10
861		10c. Franklin's Lady's Slipper Orchid (22.4.77)	15	10
		a. Perf 13×13½ (5.10.78)	70	40

49

CANADA

	(ii) Recess and photo B.A.B.N. Booklet stamps (1, 2c.) or sheet stamps (others). Chalk-surfaced paper. P 12×12½ (1, 2c.) or 13×13½ (others)		
862	1c. Type **400** (1.11.77)	85	2·50
	a. Booklet pane. Nos. 862×2 and 867a×4....	3·00	
	b. Perf 13×13½ (from sheets) (16.6.79)........	20	30
863	2c. Red Columbine (1.4.78)	65	1·00
	a. Booklet pane. Nos. 863×4 and 868a×3 plus one printed label	2·75	
	b. Perf 13×13½ (from sheets) (2.8.79)	30	—
864	3c. Canada Lily (11.4.79)	20	—
864*a*	4c. Hepatica (3.7.79)	50	10
865	5c. Shooting Star (24.1.79)	40	10
865*a*	10c. Franklin's Lady's Slipper Orchid (4.10.79)	60	10
866	12c. Jewelweed (6.7.78)	15	60
866*a*	15c. Canada Violet (16.8.79)	15	15
	(b) T **401**. *Recess and photo B.A.B.N. Chalk-surfaced paper. P 13×13½*		
867	12c. black, grey and cobalt (1.3.77)	15	10
	a. Perf 12×12½ (from booklets) (1.11.77) ...	40	1·00
868	14c. black, grey and rose-red (7.3.78).............	20	10
	a. Rose-red (background) omitted	£1000	
	b. Perf 12×12½ (from booklets) (1.4.78).....	35	1·00
	ba. Booklet pane. No. 868b×25, plus two printed labels (13.11.78)	7·50	
869	17c. black, grey and yellowish green (8.3.79)	50	10
	a. Perf 12×12½ (from booklets) (28.3.79) ...	35	35
	ab. Booklet pane. No. 869a×25, plus two printed labels (3.7.79)	8·00	
869*b*	30c. maroon, grey and reddish purple (11.5.82)	70	1·25
	ba. Maroon, grey and bright mauve (9.83)	2·50	1·40
869*c*	32c. black, grey and light blue (24.5.83)	50	1·25
	ca. Grey printed double	†	—
	(c) T **402**		
	(i) Recess C.B.N. (Nos. 872a, 873/4) or B.A.B.N. (others). Booklet stamps (Nos. 870/1) or sheet stamps (others). Chalk-surfaced paper (1, 5, 12c.). P 12×12½ (1, 5c.) or 13×13½ (others)		
870	1c. indigo (28.3.79)	1·25	3·25
	a. Booklet pane. Nos. 869a×2, 870 and 871×3	2·50	
871	5c. deep rose-lilac (28.3.79)	50	1·25
872	12c. blue (chalk-surfaced paper) (3.5.77)	70	30
	a. New blue (ordinary paper) (4.78)	70	10
	ab. Printed on the gummed side	£130	
873	14c. scarlet (7.3.78)	15	10
	a. Printed on the gummed side	18·00	
874	17c. deep green (8.3.79)	30	10
	a. Printed on the gummed side	19·00	
	(ii) Recess C.B.N. Coil stamps. Imperf×perf 10		
874*b*	12c. new blue (3.5.77)	75	30
	ba. Imperf (horiz pair)	90·00	
874*c*	14c. scarlet (7.3.78)	60	50
	ca. Imperf (horiz pair)	90·00	
874*d*	17c. deep green (8.3.79)	50	20
	da. Imperf (horiz pair)	£100	
	(d) Vert designs as T **403** *showing leaves. Multicoloured. Recess and photo B.A.B.N. Chalk-surfaced paper. P 13½*		
875	15c. Type **403** (8.8.77)	15	10
876	20c. Douglas Fir (8.8.77)	15	10
877	25c. Sugar Maple (8.8.77)	15	10
878	30c. Red Oak (7.3.78)	20	10
879	35c. White Pine (8.3.79)	25	10
	(e) Horiz designs at T **404** *showing city streets. Multicoloured. P 13½*		
	(i) Recess and photo B.A.B.N. Chalk-surfaced paper. No fluorescent bands (75, 80c.) (6.7.78)		
880	50c. Type **404**	1·00	1·25
881	75c. Eastern city street.....................................	1·00	1·50
882	80c. Maritimes street..	85	1·25
	(ii) Recess and litho C.B.N.		
883	50c. Type **404** (13.12.78)	85	1·00
	a. Brown (recess value and inscr) omitted .	£1500	
883*b*	60c. Ontario city street (11.5.82)	65	80
	(f) Horiz designs as T **405** *showing national parks. Multicoloured. Recess and litho C.B.N. or B.A.B.N. (ptgs of Nos. 884ba, 885c and 885e from 26 Sept 1986). No. 884 with or without fluorescent bands, others only exist without. P 13½*		
884	$1 Type **405** (fluorescent bands) (24.1.79) ...	70	50
	a. No fluorescent bands (4.3.81)	1·10	55
	ab. Black (inscr and value) ptd albino	£450	
884*b*	$1 Glacier (*chalk-surfaced paper*) (15.8.84) ..	85	45
	ba. Blue (inscr and value) omitted	£700	
	bb. Ordinary paper (12.7.85)	2·00	1·25
884*c*	$1.50 Waterton Lakes (18.6.82)	1·75	2·75
885	$2 Kluane (27.4.79)	1·00	45
	a. Silver (inscr and value) omitted	£300	
	b. Chalk-surfaced paper (14.12.84)...............	4·25	2·75
885*c*	$2 Banff (21.6.85)...	4·75	2·00
	ca. Bottle-green (inscr and value) omitted ..	£700	
885*d*	$5 Point Pelee (10.1.83).................................	3·00	3·00
	da. Chalk-surfaced paper (14.12.84)...............	7·00	4·00
885*e*	$5 La Mauricie (14.3.86)	8·00	4·50
	ea. Black (inscr and value) omitted	£1700	

Used examples of No. 857 are known with the purple (inscription and face value) omitted.

The main differences between No. 861a and No. 865*a* are in the background. On No. 865*a* this is toned and has the blurred edges typical of photogravure. No. 861a has a background of solid appearance with the edges clean. The B.A.B.N. version also has stronger lines on the recess part of the design.

No. 883 can be identified from 880 in that the brown printing from the recess plate of the former is deeper and the detail more defined; the registration plate of the car in the foreground can clearly be seen under a glass as "1978". The "hidden date" (1977) occurs alongside the grain elevator door on No. 880. Also the colours from the lithographic plates of No. 883 are much bolder than those from the photogravure cylinders of 880. In addition the paper of No. 883 has a shiny appearance.

No. 884ab shows an uninked impression of the recess-printed part of the design.

Stamps with one or two adjacent sides imperforate come from booklets Nos. SB83/8.

406 Puma

407 "April in Algonquin Park"

(Des R. Bateman. Litho Ashton-Potter)

1977 (30 Mar). Endangered Wildlife (1st series). P 12½.
886 **406** 12c. multicoloured 20 20
See also Nos. 906, 936/7, 976/7 and 1006/7.

(Litho Ashton-Potter)

1977 (26 May). Birth Centenary of Tom Thomson (painter). T **407** and similar square design. Multicoloured. P 12.
887 12c. Type **407**... 15 20
 a. Pair. Nos. 887/8.. 30 1·25
888 12c. "Autumn Birches"...................................... 15 20
Nos. 887/8 were printed horizontally and vertically *se-tenant* throughout the sheet.

408 Crown and Lion

409 Peace Bridge, Niagara River

(Des A. Hobbs. Litho (No. 890 also embossed) Ashton-Potter)

1977 (30 June). Anniversaries. T **408** and similar horiz design. Multicoloured. P 12½.
889 12c. Type **408**... 15 25
890 12c. Order of Canada.. 15 25
Events:—No. 889, 25th Anniv of first Canadian-born Governor-General; No. 890, Tenth Anniv of Order of Canada.

(Des R. Harder. Litho Ashton-Potter)

1977 (4 Aug). 50th Anniv of Opening of Peace Bridge. P 12½.
891 **409** 12c. multicoloured 15 15

410 Sir Sandford Fleming (engineer)

(Des W. Davies. Recess B.A.B.N.)

1977 (16 Sept). Famous Canadians. T **410** and similar horiz design. P 13.
892 12c. grey-blue 30 30
 a. Pair. Nos. 892/3.. 60 1·25
893 12c. reddish brown.. 30 30
Design:—No. 892, Joseph E. Bernier (explorer) and *Arctic* (survey ship).
The above were printed together, horizontally and vertically *se-tenant* throughout the sheet.

411 Peace Tower, Parliament Buildings, Ottawa
412 Hunter Braves following Star 

(Des S. Ash. Litho Ashton-Potter)

1977 (19 Sept). 23rd Commonwealth Parliamentary Conference. P 12½.
| 894 | **411** | 25c. multicoloured | 20 | 30 |

(Des R. G. White. Litho C.B.N.)

1977 (26 Oct). Christmas. T **412** and similar horiz designs depicting Canada's first Christmas carol "Jesous Ahatonhia". Multicoloured. P 13½×13.
895		10c. Type **412**	10	10
	a.	Printed on the gummed side	£375	
	b.	Imperf between (horiz pair)	£750	
896		12c. Angelic choir and Northern Lights	10	10
	a.	Imperf (vert pair)	£1100	
897		25c. Christ Child and chiefs	20	45
895/897 Set of 3			35	45

No. 895b also shows both stamps partly imperforate at top and bottom.

413 Seal Hunter (soapstone sculpture)
414 Pinky (fishing boat) 

(Des R. Derreth. Litho Ashton-Potter)

1977 (18 Nov). Canadian Eskimos ("Inuits") (1st series). Hunting. T **413** and similar horiz designs. Multicoloured. P 12×12½.
898		12c. Type **413**	35	35
	a.	Pair. Nos. 898/9	70	70
899		12c. Fishing with spear	35	35
	a.	Grey (value and inscr) omitted	£2000	
900		12c. Disguised archer	35	35
	a.	Pair. Nos. 900/1	70	70
901		12c. Walrus hunting	35	35
898/901 Set of 4			1·40	1·40

Nos. 898/9 and 900/1 were each printed together, *se-tenant*, in horizontal and vertical pairs throughout the sheet.
See also Nos. 924/7, 958/61 and 989/92.

(Des T. Bjarnason. Recess and litho C.B.N.)

1977 (18 Nov). Canadian Ships (3rd series). T **414** and similar horiz designs, showing sailing craft. Multicoloured. P 12×12½.
902		12c. Type **414**	20	35
	a.	Block of 4. Nos. 902/5	70	1·25
	ab.	Imperf (block of 4)		
903		12c. *Malahat* (schooner)	20	35
904		12c. Tern schooner	20	35
905		12c. Mackinaw boat	20	35
902/905 Set of 4			70	1·25

Nos. 902/5 were printed together, *se-tenant*, in different combinations throughout the sheet, giving ten blocks of 4 and ten single stamps.

415 Peregrine Falcon
416 Pair of 1851 12d. Black Stamps 

(Des R. Bateman. Litho Ashton-Potter)

1978 (18 Jan). Endangered Wildlife (2nd series). P 12½.
| 906 | **415** | 12c. multicoloured | 30 | 20 |

(Des C. Brett. Recess and photo B.A.B.N.)

1978 (18 Jan). "CAPEX 78" International Stamp Exhibition, Toronto (1st issue). P 13.
| 907 | **416** | 12c. black and brownish grey | 10 | 10 |

See also Nos. 914/17.

417 Games Emblem
418 "Captain Cook" (Nathaniel Dance) 

(Des S. Ash. Litho Ashton-Potter)

1978 (31 Mar). Commonwealth Games. Edmonton (1st issue). T **417** and similar horiz design. Multicoloured. P 12½.
| 908 | | 14c. Type **417** | 10 | 10 |
| 909 | | 30c. Badminton | 20 | 60 |

See also Nos. 918/21.

(Des W. Rueter. Litho Ashton-Potter)

1978 (26 Apr). Bicentenary of Cook's Third Voyage. T **418** and similar vert design. Multicoloured. P 13½.
910		14c. Type **418**	20	20
	a.	Pair. Nos. 910/11	40	80
911		14c. "Nootka Sound" (J. Webber)	20	20

Nos. 910/11 were printed together, *se-tenant*, in horizontal and vertical pairs throughout the sheet.

419 Hardrock Silver Mine, Cobalt, Ontario
420 Princes' Gate (Exhibition entrance) 

(Des W. Davies. Litho Ashton-Potter)

1978 (19 May). Resource Development. T **419** and similar horiz design. Multicoloured. P 12½.
912		14c. Type **419**	15	20
	a.	Pair. Nos. 912/13	30	1·25
913		14c. Giant excavators, Athabasca Tar Sands	15	20

Nos. 912/13 were printed together, *se-tenant*, in horizontal and vertical pairs throughout the sheet.

(Des C. Brett. Eng R. Couture. Recess and photo B.A.B.N.)

1978 (10 June). "CAPEX 78" International Stamp Exhibition, Toronto (2nd issue). Horiz designs as T **416**. Two fluorescent bands (none on $1.25 from miniature sheet). P 13.
914		14c. Prussian blue, pale grey and brownish grey	15	10
915		30c. deep rose, pale grey and brownish grey	25	40
916		$1.25 slate-violet, pale grey and brownish grey	70	1·50
914/916 Set of 3			1·00	1·75
MS917 101×76 mm. Nos. 914/16			1·25	2·50

Designs:—14c. Pair of 1855 10d. Cartier stamps; 30c. Pair of 1857 ½d. deep rose stamps; $1.25, Pair of 1851 6d. Prince Albert stamps.

(Des S. Ash. Litho Ashton-Potter)

1978 (3 Aug). Commonwealth Games, Edmonton (2nd issue). Horiz designs as T **417**. Multicoloured. P 12½.
918		14c. Games stadium	20	20
	a.	Pair. Nos. 918/19	40	80
919		14c. Running	20	20
920		30c. Alberta Legislature building	50	50
	a.	Pair. Nos. 920/1	1·00	1·60
921		30c. Bowls	50	50
918/921 Set of 4			1·25	1·10

Nos. 918/19 and 920/1 were each printed together, *se-tenant*, in horizontal and vertical pairs throughout the sheet.

(Des T. Dimson, Litho Ashton-Potter)

1978 (16 Aug). Centenary of National Exhibition. P 12½.
| 922 | **420** | 14c. multicoloured | 15 | 30 |

CANADA

421 Marguerite d'Youville

422 "Madonna of the Flowering Pea" (Cologne School)

(Des A. Dumas. Litho C.B.N.)

1978 (21 Sept). Marguerite d'Youville (founder of Grey Nuns) Commemoration. P 13.
| 923 | **421** | 14c. multicoloured | 15 | 30 |

(Des R. Derreth. Litho Ashton-Potter)

1978 (27 Sept). Canadian Eskimos ("Inuits") (2nd series). Travel. Horiz designs as T **413**. Multicoloured. P 13½.
924	14c. Woman on foot (painting by Pitseolak)..	30	40
	a. Pair. Nos. 924/5	60	1·25
925	14c. "Migration" (soapstone sculpture of sailing umiak by Joe Talurinili)	30	40
926	14c. Aeroplane (stonecut and stencil print by Pudlo)	30	40
	a. Pair. Nos. 926/7	60	1·25
927	14c. Dogteam and dogsled (ivory sculpture by Abraham Kingmeatook)	30	40
924/927 Set of 4		1·10	1·40

Nos. 924/5 and 926/7 were each printed together, *se-tenant*, in horizontal and vertical pairs throughout the sheet.

(Des J. Morin. Litho Ashton-Potter)

1978 (20 Oct). Christmas. Paintings. T **422** and similar vert designs. Multicoloured. P 12½.
928	12c. Type **422**	10	10
929	14c. "The Virgin and Child with St. Anthony and Donor" (detail, Hans Memling)	10	10
	a. Black omitted	£750	
930	30c. "The Virgin and Child" (Jacopo di Cione)	25	90
928/930 Set of 3		35	1·00

423 *Chief Justice Robinson* (paddle-steamer)

424 Carnival Revellers

(Des T. Bjarnason. Recess and litho C.B.N.)

1978 (15 Nov). Canadian Ships (4th series). T **423** and similar horiz designs showing ice vessels. Multicoloured. P 13.
931	14c. Type **423**	45	65
	a. Block of 4. Nos. 931/4	1·60	2·40
932	14c. *St. Roch* (steamer)	45	65
933	14c. *Northern Light* (steamer)	45	65
934	14c. *Labrador* (steamer)	45	65
931/934 Set of 4		1·60	2·40

Nos. 931/4 were printed together, *se-tenant*, in different combinations throughout the sheet, giving ten blocks of 4 and ten single stamps.

(Des A. Dumas. Litho Ashton-Potter)

1979 (1 Feb). Quebec Carnival. P 13.
| 935 | **424** | 14c. multicoloured | 20 | 20 |

425 Eastern Spiny Soft-shelled Turtle (*Trionyx spinifera*)

426 Knotted Ribbon round Woman's Finger

(Des G. Lowe (17c.), R. Bateman (35c.) Litho Ashton-Potter)

1979 (10 Apr). Endangered Wildlife (3rd series). T **425** and similar horiz design. Multicoloured. P 12½.
| 936 | 17c. Type **425** | 20 | 10 |
| 937 | 35c. Bowhead Whale (*Balaena mysticetus*) | 90 | 90 |

(Des D. Haws. Litho Ashton-Potter)

1979 (27 Apr). Postal Code Publicity. T **426** and similar vert design. Multicoloured. P 13.
938	17c. Type **426**	20	15
	a. Pair. Nos. 938/9	40	1·00
939	17c. Knotted string round man's finger	20	15

Nos. 938/9 were printed together, *se-tenant*, in horizontal and vertical pairs throughout the sheet.

427 Scene from "Fruits of the Earth" by Frederick Philip Grove

428 Charles-Michel de Salaberry (military hero)

(Des Rosemary Kilbourne (No. 940), Monique Charbonneau (941). Litho C.B.N.)

1979 (3 May). Canadian Writers (3rd series). T **427** and similar horiz design. Multicoloured. P 13.
940	17c. Type **427**	15	15
	a. Pair. Nos. 940/1	30	1·25
	ab. Imperf (vert pair)		
941	17c. Scene from "Le Vaisseau d'Or" by Emile Nelligan	15	15

Nos. 940/1 were printed together, *se-tenant*, in horizontal and vertical pairs throughout the sheet.

(Des T. Dimson. Litho and embossed Ashton-Potter)

1979 (11 May). Famous Canadians. T **428** and similar vert design. Multicoloured. P 13.
942	17c. Type **428**	25	15
	a. Pair. Nos. 942/3	50	1·25
943	17c. John By (engineer)	25	15

Nos. 942/3 were printed together, *se-tenant*, in horizontal and vertical pairs throughout the sheet.

429 Ontario

430 Paddling Kayak

(Des R. Bellemare. Litho Ashton-Potter)

1979 (15 June). Canada Day. Flags. T **429** and similar horiz designs. Multicoloured. P 13.
944a	17c. Type **429**	25	40
	ab. Sheetlet. Nos. 944a/l	2·75	4·50
944b	17c. Quebec	25	40
944c	17c. Nova Scotia	25	40
944d	17c. New Brunswick	25	40
944e	17c. Manitoba	25	40
944f	17c. British Columbia	25	40
944g	17c. Prince Edward Island	25	40
944h	17c. Saskatchewan	25	40
944i	17c. Alberta	25	40
944j	17c. Newfoundland	25	40
944k	17c. Northwest Territories	25	40
944l	17c. Yukon Territory	25	40
944a/944l		2·75	4·50

Nos. 944a/l were printed together, *se-tenant*, in sheetlets of 12.

Nos. 945/55 are vacant.

(Des J. Eby. Litho Ashton-Potter)

1979 (3 July). Canoe-Kayak Championships. P 12½.
| 956 | **430** | 17c. multicoloured | 15 | 30 |

431 Hockey Players  **432** Toy Train

(Des J. Eby. Litho Ashton-Potter)
1979 (16 Aug). Women's Field Hockey Championships, Vancouver. P 12½.
957 **431** 17c. black, yellow and emerald................. 15 30

(Des R. Derreth. Litho Ashton-Potter)
1979 (13 Sept). Canadian Eskimos ("Inuits") (3rd series). "Shelter" (Nos. 958/9) and "Community" (Nos. 960/1). Horiz designs as T **413**. Multicoloured. P 13.
958 17c. "Summer Tent" (print by Kiakshuk)........... 15 40
 a. Pair. Nos. 958/9...................... 30 1·25
959 17c. "Five Eskimos building an Igloo" (soapstone sculpture by Abraham)......... 15 40
960 17c. "The Dance" (print by Kalvak).................. 15 40
 a. Pair. Nos. 960/1...................... 30 1·25
961 17c. "Inuit drum dance" (soapstone sculptures by Madeleine Isserkut and Jean Mapsalak)........................... 15 40
958/961 Set of 4 .... 60 1·40
Nos. 958/9 and 960/1 were each printed together, *se-tenant*, in horizontal and vertical pairs throughout the sheet.

(Des A. Maggs. Litho C.B.N.)
1979 (17 Oct). Christmas. T **432** and similar multicoloured designs showing toys. Fluorescent frame (35c.) or two fluorescent bands (others). P 13.
962 15c. Type **432**............................... 10 10
963 17c. Hobby-horse......................... 10 10
964 35c. Rag-doll (*vert*)........................ 25 1·00
 a. Gold omitted........................... £800
962/964 Set of 3 .... 35 1·00

433 "Child watering Tree of Life" (painting by Marie-Annick Viatour) **434** Canadair CL-215

(Des J. Morin. Litho Ashton-Potter)
1979 (24 Oct). International Year of the Child. P 13.
965 **433** 17c. multicoloured......................... 15 30

(Des R. Bradford and J. Charette. Litho Ashton-Potter)
1979 (15 Nov). Canadian Aircraft (1st series). Flying Boats. T **434** and similar horiz designs. Multicoloured. P 12½.
966 17c. Type **434**............................... 25 20
 a. Pair. Nos. 966/7...................... 50 70
967 17c. Curtiss HS-2L......................... 25 20
968 35c. Vickers Vedette..................... 65 65
 a. Pair. Nos. 968/9...................... 1·25 1·25
969 35c. Consolidated PBY-5A Canso................ 65 65
966/969 Set of 4 .... 1·60 1·50
Nos. 966/7 and 968/9 were each printed together, *se-tenant*, in horizontal and vertical pairs throughout the sheet.
See also Nos. 996/9, 1026/9 and 1050/3.

435 Map of Arctic Islands  **436** Skiing

(Des Gottschalk and Ash Ltd. Litho Ashton-Potter)
1980 (23 Jan). Centenary of Arctic Islands Acquisition. P 13.
970 **435** 17c. multicoloured......................... 15 30

(Des C. Malenfant. Litho C.B.N.)
1980 (23 Jan). Winter Olympic Games, Lake Placid, U.S.A. P 13.
971 **436** 35c. multicoloured......................... 55 85

437 "A Meeting of the School Trustees" (painting by Robert Harris) **438** Canadian Whitefish (*Coregonus canadensis*)

(Des J. Morin. Litho Ashton-Potter)
1980 (6 Mar). Centenary of Royal Canadian Academy of Arts. T **437** and similar horiz designs. Multicoloured. P 13.
972 17c. Type **437**............................... 25 20
 a. Pair. Nos. 972/3...................... 50 75
973 17c. "Inspiration" (sculpture by Philippe Hébert).......................... 25 20
974 35c. "Sunrise on the Saguenay" (painting by Lucius O'Brien)............ 50 55
 a. Pair. Nos. 974/5...................... 1·00 1·75
975 35c. Sketch of design for original Parliament Buildings by Thomas Fuller........ 50 55
972/975 Set of 4 .... 1·40 1·40
Nos. 972/3 and 974/5 were each printed together, *se-tenant*, in horizontal and vertical pairs throughout the sheet.

(Des M. Dumas (No. 976), R. Bateman (No. 977). Litho Ashton-Potter)
1980 (6 May). Endangered Wildlife (4th series). T **438** and similar horiz design. Multicoloured. P 12½.
976 17c. Type **438**............................... 30 15
977 17c. Prairie Chicken (*Tympanuchus cupido pinnatus*)................. 30 15

439 Garden Flowers  **440** "Helping Hand"

(Des Heather Cooper. Litho Ashton-Potter)
1980 (29 May). International Flower Show, Montreal. P 13.
978 **439** 17c. multicoloured......................... 15 20

(Des R. Harder. Litho and embossed Ashton-Potter)
1980 (29 May). Rehabilitation. P 12½.
979 **440** 17c. gold and ultramarine.................... 15 20

441 Opening Bars of "O Canada" 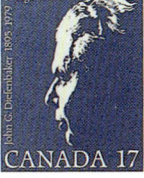 **442** John G. Diefenbaker

(Des F. Peter. Litho Ashton-Potter)
1980 (6 June). Centenary of "O Canada" (national song). T **441** and similar horiz design. Multicoloured. P 12½.
980 17c. Type **441**............................... 15 15
 a. Pair. Nos. 980/1...................... 30 30
981 17c. Calixa Lavallee (composer), Adolphe-Basile Routhier (original writer) and Robert Stanley Weir (writer of English version)................... 15 15
Nos. 980/1 were printed together, *se-tenant*, in horizontal and vertical pairs throughout the sheet.

CANADA

(Des B. Reilander. Eng Y. Baril. Recess C.B.N.)

1980 (20 June). John G. Diefenbaker (former Prime Minister) Commemoration. P 13½×13.

| 982 | **442** | 17c. deep ultramarine | 15 | 20 |

443 Emma Albani (singer)  **444** Alberta

(Des C. Webster (No. 985), H. Brown (others). Litho Ashton-Potter)

1980 (4 July). Famous Canadians. T **443** and similar multicoloured designs. P 13.

983	17c. Type **443**	15	25
	a. Pair. Nos. 983/4	30	1·25
984	17c. Healey Willan (composer)	15	25
985	17c. Ned Hanlan (oarsman) (*horiz*)	15	15
983/985 Set of 3		40	60

Nos. 983/4 were printed together, *se-tenant*, in horizontal and vertical pairs throughout the sheet.

(Des G. Hunter and C. Yaneff. Litho Ashton-Potter)

1980 (27 Aug). 75th Anniv of Alberta and Saskatchewan Provinces. T **444** and similar horiz design. Multicoloured. P 13.

| 986 | 17c. Type **444** | 15 | 15 |
| 987 | 17c. Saskatchewan | 15 | 15 |

445 Uraninite Molecular Structure  **446** "Christmas Morning" (J. S. Hallam)

(Des J. Charette. Litho C.B.N.)

1980 (3 Sept). Uranium Resources. P 13.

| 988 | **445** | 35c. multicoloured | 30 | 30 |
| | | a. Printed on the gummed side | £500 | |

(Des R. Derreth. Litho C.B.N.)

1980 (25 Sept). Canadian Eskimos ("Inuits") (4th series). Spirits. Horiz designs as T **413**. Multicoloured. P 13½.

989	17c. "Return of the Sun" (print by Kenojouak)	20	15
	a. Pair. Nos. 989/90	40	1·00
990	17c. "Sedna" (sculpture by Ashoona Kiawak)	20	15
991	35c. "Shaman" (print by Simon Tookoome)	35	55
	a. Pair. Nos. 991/2	70	1·60
992	35c. "Bird Spirit" (sculpture by Doris Hagiolok)	35	55
989/992 Set of 4		1·00	1·25

Nos. 989/90 and 991/2 were each printed together, *se-tenant*, in horizontal and vertical pairs throughout the sheet.

(Des Yvon Laroche. Litho Ashton-Potter)

1980 (22 Oct). Christmas. Paintings. T **446** and similar vert designs. Multicoloured. P 12½×12.

993	15c. Type **446**	10	10
994	17c. "Sleigh Ride" (Frank Hennessy)	15	10
995	35c. "McGill Cab Stand" (Kathleen Morris)	30	1·40
993/995 Set of 3		50	1·40

447 Avro (Canada) CF-100 Canuck Mk 5

(Des R. Bradford and J. Charette. Litho C.B.N.)

1980 (10 Nov). Canadian Aircraft (2nd series). T **447** and similar horiz designs. Multicoloured. P 13.

996	17c. Type **447**	40	20
	a. Pair. Nos. 996/7	80	60
997	17c. Avro Type 683 Lancaster	40	20
998	35c. Curtiss JN-4 Canuck	60	65
	a. Pair. Nos. 998/9	1·25	1·25
999	35c. Hawker Hurricane Mk 1	60	65
996/999 Set of 4		1·90	1·60

Nos. 996/7 and 998/9 were each printed together, *se-tenant*, in horizontal and vertical pairs throughout the sheet.

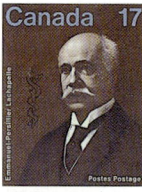

448 Emmanuel-Persillier Lachapelle  **449** Mandora Instrument (18th-century)

(Des J. Morin. Litho Ashton-Potter)

1980 (5 Dec). Dr. Emmanuel-Persillier Lachapelle (founder of Notre-Dame Hospital, Montreal) Commemoration. P 13½.

| 1000 | **448** | 17c. cobalt, chocolate and brown | 15 | 15 |

(Des C. Webster. Litho Ashton-Potter)

1981 (19 Jan). "The Look of Music" Exhibition, Vancouver. P 12½.

| 1001 | **449** | 17c. multicoloured | 15 | 15 |

450 Henrietta Edwards  **451** Vancouver Marmot (*Marmota vancouverensis*)

(Des Muriel Wood and D. Goddard. Litho C.B.N.)

1981 (4 Mar). Feminists. T **450** and similar horiz designs. Multicoloured. P 13.

1002	17c. Type **450**	30	30
	a. Block of 4. Nos. 1002/5	1·00	1·00
1003	17c. Louise McKinney	30	30
1004	17c. Idola Saint-Jean	30	30
1005	17c. Emily Stowe	30	30
1002/1005 Set of 4		1·00	1·00

Nos. 1002/5 were printed together, *se-tenant*, in different combinations throughout the sheet, giving ten blocks of 4 and ten single stamps.

(Des M. Dumas (17c.), R. Bateman (35c.). Litho C.B.N.)

1981 (6 Apr). Endangered Wildlife (5th series). T **451** and similar horiz design. Multicoloured. P 13.

| 1006 | 17c. Type **451** | 15 | 10 |
| 1007 | 35c. American Bison (*Bison bison athabascae*) | 35 | 30 |

452 Kateri Tekakwitha  **453** "Self Portrait" (Frederick H. Varley)

CANADA

(Des L. Marquart. Litho Ashton-Potter)

1981 (24 Apr). 17th-century Canadian Catholic Women. Statues by Emile Brunet. T **452** and similar vert design. P 12½.
1008	17c. red-brown and pale grey-olive		15	20
	a. Pair. Nos. 1008/9		30	40
1009	17c. steel blue and new blue		15	20

Designs:—No. 1008, Type **452**; No. 1009, Marie de l'Incarnation.
Nos. 1008/9 were printed together, *se-tenant*, in horizontal and vertical pairs throughout the sheet.

(Des P. Fontaine. Litho Ashton-Potter (17c. (both)), B.A.B.N. (35c.))

1981 (22 May). Canadian Paintings. T **453** and similar multicoloured designs. P 12½ (17c. (both)) or 13×13½ (35c.).
1010	17c. Type **453**		20	10
1011	17c. "At Baie Saint-Paul" (Marc-Aurele Fortin) (horiz)		20	10
1012	35c. "Untitled No. 6" (Paul-Emile Borduas)		40	45
1010/1012	Set of 3		70	60

454 Canada in 1867

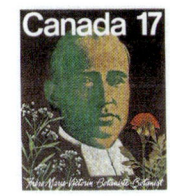

455 Frère Marie-Victorin

(Des R. Bellemare. Litho B.A.B.N.)

1981 (30 June). Canada Day. Maps showing evolution of Canada from Confederation to present day. T **454** and similar horiz designs. Multicoloured. P 13½.
1013	17c. Type **454**		15	20
	a. Horiz strip of 4. Nos. 1013/16		55	70
1014	17c. Canada in 1873		15	20
1015	17c. Canada in 1905		15	20
1016	17c. Canada since 1949		15	20
1013/1016	Set of 4		55	70

Nos. 1013/16 were printed together, *se-tenant*, in horizontal strips of 4 throughout the sheet.

(Des R. Hill. Litho and embossed Ashton-Potter)

1981 (22 July). Canadian Botanists. T **455** and similar vert design. Multicoloured. P 12½×12.
1017	17c. Type **455**		20	30
	a. Pair. Nos. 1017/18		40	1·40
1018	17c. John Macoun		20	30

Nos. 1017/18 were printed together, *se-tenant*, in horizontal and vertical pairs throughout the sheet.

456 The Montreal Rose

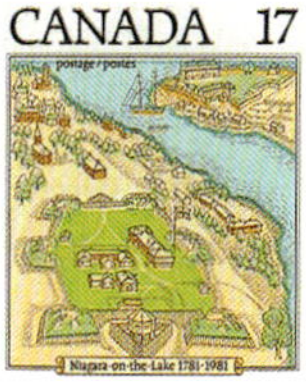

457 Drawing of Niagara-on-the-Lake

(Des J.-P. Beaudin, J. Morin and T. Yakobina. Litho C.B.N.)

1981 (22 July). Montreal Flower Show. P 13½.
1019	**456**	17c. multicoloured	15	20

(Des J. Mardon. Recess and litho B.A.B.N.)

1981 (31 July). Bicentenary of Niagara-on-the-Lake (town). P 13×13½.
1020	**457**	17c. multicoloured	15	20

458 Acadian Community

459 Aaron R. Mosher

(Des N. DeGrâce. Litho Ashton-Potter)

1981 (14 Aug). Centenary of first Acadia (community) Convention. P 13½.
1021	**458**	17c. multicoloured	15	20

(Des R. Hill. Litho Ashton-Potter)

1981 (8 Sept). Birth Centenary of Aaron R. Mosher (founder of Canadian Labour Congress). P 13½.
1022	**459**	17c. multicoloured	15	20

460 Christmas Tree, 1781

461 De Havilland D.H.82C Tiger Moth

(Des Anita Kunz and W. Tibbles. Litho Ashton-Potter)

1981 (16 Nov). Christmas. Bicentenary of First Illuminated Christmas Tree in Canada. T **460** and similar vert designs. Multicoloured. P 13½.
1023	15c. Type **460**	20	15
1024	15c. Christmas Tree, 1881	20	15
1025	15c. Christmas Tree, 1981	20	15
1023/1025	Set of 3	55	40

(Des R. Bradford and J. Charette. Litho Ashton-Potter)

1981 (24 Nov). Canadian Aircraft (3rd series). T **461** and similar horiz designs. Multicoloured. P 12½.
1026	17c. Type **461**	25	15
	a. Pair. Nos. 1026/7	50	40
1027	17c. Canadair CL-41 Tutor	25	15
1028	35c. Avro (Canada) CF-102 jet airliner	45	40
	a. Pair. Nos. 1028/9	90	80
1029	35c. De Havilland D.H.C.7 Dash Seven	45	40
1026/1029	Set of 4	1·25	1·00

The two designs of each value were printed together, *se-tenant*, in horizontal and vertical pairs throughout the sheet.

462 Canadian Maple Leaf Emblem

463 1851 3d. Stamp

(Des R. Bellemare. Recess B.A.B.N. No. 1030*a*), C.B.N. (others))

1981 (29 Dec). Ordinary paper.

(a) Sheet stamp. P 13×13½
1030	**462**	A (30c.) bright scarlet	20	45
		a. Carmine-red, chalk-surfaced paper	20	45
		b. Printed on the gummed side	£375	

(b) Coil stamp. Imperf×perf 10
1031	**462**	A (30c.) bright scarlet	40	1·00
		a. Imperf (pair)	£250	£150

Nos. 1030/1 were printed before a new first class domestic letter rate had been agreed, "A" representing the face value of the stamp later decided at 30c. Because of U.P.U. regulations these stamps were only intended for use within Canada.

(Recess, or recess and photo (Nos. 1032/*b*), B.A.B.N. (Nos. 1032/5*b*) or C.B.N. (Nos. 1036/*b*))

1982 (1 Mar)–**84**. Designs as Nos. 1030/1 but including face values.

(a) Sheet stamps (Nos. 1032, 1032b) or from booklets (Nos. 1032a, 1032ba). Chalk-surfaced paper. P 13×13½
1032	**462**	30c. vermilion, slate-blue and azure (11.5.82)	30	60
		a. Perf 12×12½ (from booklets) (30.6.82)	70	1·50
		ab. Booklet pane. No. 1032a×20 plus one printed label	15·00	

55

CANADA

1032b	32c. vermilion, orange-brown and stone (10.2.83)		45	45
	ba. Perf 12×12½ (from booklets) (8.4.83)		75	1·40
	bb. Booklet pane. No. 1032ba×25 plus two printed labels		18·00	
	bc. Ordinary paper (15.2.84)		90	1·25
	bd. Booklet pane. No. 1032bc×25 plus two printed labels		21·00	
	(b) Booklet stamps. Ordinary paper. P 12×12½			
1033	462	5c. maroon	10	20
	a. Booklet pane. Nos. 1033×2, 1034 and 1035 plus two printed labels in bottom row		2·50	
	ab. Ditto. Printed labels in top row (10.82)		2·75	
	b. Chalk-surfaced paper (8.82)		40	80
	ba. Booklet pane. Nos. 1033b×2, 1034a and 1035a plus two printed labels in bottom row		8·00	
	bb. Ditto. Printed labels in top row (10.82)		8·00	
	c. Booklet pane. Nos. 1033×2, 1033d and 1035b plus two printed labels (15.2.83)		3·00	
1033d	8c. indigo (15.2.83)		1·75	2·50
1034	10c. bottle green		1·50	2·25
	a. Chalk-surfaced paper		4·00	4·00
1035	30c. carmine-red		1·50	2·50
	a. Chalk-surfaced paper		4·00	4·00
1035b	32c. Indian red (15.2.83)		2·00	3·00
	(c) Coil stamps. Ordinary paper. Imperf×perf 10			
1036	462	30c. bright scarlet (20.5.82)†	35	40
	a. Imperf (pair)		£180	
1036b	32c. Indian red (10.2.83)		1·50	2·50
	ba. Imperf (pair)		90·00	

*The 30c. and 32c. values are perforated on two sides, the other values on three.

†The 30c. coil stamp was originally intended for release on 11 May, but, due to production difficulties, it was not placed on sale until 20 May; F.D.C.s, however, carry the 11 May postmark.

(Des Gottschalk and Ash Ltd. Litho C.B.N.)

1982 (11 Mar–20 May). "Canada. 82" International Philatelic Youth Exhibition, Toronto. Stamps on Stamps. T **463** and similar horiz designs. Multicoloured. P 13½.

1037	30c. Type **463**		30	30
1038	30c. 1908 Centenary of Quebec 15c. commemorative (20.5.82)		30	30
1039	35c. 1935 10c. R.C.M.P.		30	50
1040	35c. 1928 10c. (20.5.82)		30	50
1041	60c. 1929 50c. (20.5.82)		60	1·00
1037/1041	Set of 5		1·60	2·40
MS1042	159×108 mm. Nos. 1037/41 (20.5.82)		2·25	3·75

464 Jules Léger

465 Stylised Drawing of Terry Fox

(Des P. Fontaine from photograph by M. Bedford. Litho Ashton-Potter)

1982 (2 Apr). Jules Léger (politician) Commemoration. P 13½.
1043   **464**   30c. multicoloured 20   20

(Des F. Peter. Litho Ashton-Potter)

1982 (13 Apr). Cancer-victim Terry Fox's "Marathon of Hope" (Trans-Canada fund-raising run) Commemoration. Fluorescent frame. P 12½.
1044   **465**   30c. multicoloured 20   20

466 Stylised Open Book

(Des F. Peter. Litho Ashton-Potter)

1982 (16 Apr). Patriation of Constitution. P 12×12½.
1045   **466**   30c. multicoloured 20   20

467 1880's Male and Female Salvationists with Street Scene

468 "The Highway near Kluane Lake" (Yukon Territory) (Jackson)

(Des T. Dimson. Litho C.B.N.)

1982 (25 June). Centenary of the Salvation Army in Canada. P 13½.
1046   **467**   30c. multicoloured 20   20

(Des J. Morin and P. Sasseville. Litho Ashton-Potter)

1982 (30 June). Canada Day. Paintings of Canadian Landscapes. T **468** and similar horiz designs. Multicoloured. P 12½×12.

1047a.	30c. Type **468**		35	40
	ab. Sheetlet. Nos. 1047a/l		4·75	6·50
1047b.	30c. "Street Scene, Montreal" (Quebec) (Hébert)		35	40
1047c.	30c. "Breakwater" (Newfoundland) (Pratt)		35	40
1047d.	30c. "Along Great Slave Lake" (Northwest Territories) (Richard)		35	40
1047e.	30c. "Till Hill" (Prince Edward Island) (Lamb)		35	40
1047f.	30c. "Family and Rain-storm" (Nova Scotia) (Colville)		35	40
1047g.	30c. "Brown Shadows" (Saskatchewan) (Knowles)		35	40
1047h.	30c. "The Red Brick House" (Ontario) (Milne)		35	40
1047i.	30c. "Campus Gates" (New Brunswick) (Bobak)		35	40
1047j.	30c. "Prairie Town—Early Morning" (Alberta) (Kerr)		35	40
1047k.	30c. "Totems at Ninstints" (British Columbia) (Plaskett)		35	40
1047l.	30c. "Doc Snider's House" (Manitoba) (FitzGerald)		35	40
1047a/1047l	Set of 12		4·75	6·50

Nos. 1047a/l were printed together, *se-tenant*, in sheetlets of 12.

469 Regina Legislature Building   **470** Finish of Race

(Des Kim Martin and R. Russell. Litho Ashton-Potter)

1982 (3 Aug). Regina Centenary. P 13½×13.
1048   **469**   30c. multicoloured 20   20

(Des B. Reilander. Litho Ashton-Potter)

1982 (4 Aug). Centenary of Royal Canadian Henley Regatta. P 12½.
1049   **470**   30c. multicoloured 20   25

471 Fairchild FC-2W1   **472** Decoy

(Des R. Bradford. Litho Ashton-Potter)

1982 (5 Oct). Canadian Aircraft (4th series). Bush Aircraft. T **471** and similar horiz designs. Multicoloured. P 12½.

1050	30c. Type **471**		35	20
	a. Pair. Nos. 1050/1		70	95
1051	30c. De Havilland D.H.C.2 Beaver		35	20
1052	60c. Fokker Super Universal		65	85
	a. Pair. Nos. 1052/3		1·25	2·00
1053	60c. Noorduyn Norseman		65	85
1050/1053	Set of 4		1·90	1·90

Nos. 1050/1 and 1052/3 were each printed together, *se-tenant*, in horiz and vert pairs throughout the sheet.

(Des J.-P. Beaudin and J. Morin. Litho C.B.N. (Nos. 1054b/ba, 1055b/bc, 1056b, 1057b/ba, 1058b) or Ashton-Potter (others))

1982 (19 Oct)–**87**. Heritage Artifacts. T **472** and similar designs. No fluorescent bands (1c. to 5c.). Chalk-surfaced paper (25, 42, 50, 72c.). P 12×12½ (37c. to 72c.) or 14×13½ (others).

1054	1c. black, grey-brown and brown	10	10
	a. Chalk-surfaced paper (4.7.86)	20	10
	b. Perf 13×13½ (10.1.85)	40	30
	ba. Chalk-surfaced paper (6.8.85)	1·50	1·00
1055	2c. black, pale turquoise-blue and deep blue-green	10	10
	a. Chalk-surfaced paper (4.7.86)	30	65
	b. Perf 13×13½ (10.2.84)	30	50
	ba. Imperf (horiz pair)	£1100	
	bb. Printed on the gummed side	35·00	
	bc. Ordinary paper (23.1.86)	10	10
1056	3c. black, dull violet-blue and chalky blue	10	10
	a. Chalk-surfaced paper (4.7.86)	75	1·00
	b. Perf 13×13½ (10.1.85)	75	1·00
1057	5c. black, flesh and chestnut	10	10
	a. Chalk-surfaced paper (15.8.86)	30	10
	b. Perf 13×13½ (*chalk-surfaced paper*) (6.7.84)	20	20
	ba. Ordinary paper (1.3.85)	20	30
1058	10c. black, light blue and deep turquoise-blue	10	10
	a. Chalk-surfaced paper (22.8.86)	50	50
	b. Perf 13×13½ (15.3.85)	70	30
1059	20c. black, brownish grey and sepia	20	10
	a. Chalk-surfaced paper (4.7.86)	50	50
1060	25c. multicoloured (6.5.87)	1·25	10
1061	37c. grey-black, deep yellow-green and sage-green (8.4.83)	45	70
	a. Chalk-surfaced paper (18.5.84)	1·00	1·10
1062	39c. brownish black, violet-grey and slate-violet (1.8.85)	1·75	2·00
1063	42c. multicoloured (6.5.87)	2·25	1·00
1064	48c. blackish brown, red-brown and pale pink (8.4.83)	50	40
	a. Chalk-surfaced paper (19.12.83)	80	1·00
1065	50c. black, dull turquoise-blue & turquoise-blue (1.8.85)	1·75	20
1066	55c. multicoloured (6.5.87)	2·00	30
1067	64c. grey-black, black & pale grey (8.4.83)	60	35
	a. Chalk-surfaced paper (29.6.84)	1·50	1·40
1068	68c. black, pale brown and reddish brown (1.8.85)	1·75	50
1069	72c. multicoloured (6.5.87)	2·00	35
1054/1069	Set of 16	13·00	5·50

Designs: *Vert* (*as* T **472**)—2c. Fishing spear; 3c. Stable lantern; 5c. Bucket; 10c. Weathercock; 20c. Skates; 25c. Butter stamp. *Horiz (26×20 mm)*—37c. Plough; 39c. Settle-bed; 42c. Linen chest; 48c. Cradle; 50c. Sleigh; 55c. Iron kettle; 64c. Kitchen stove; 68c. Spinning wheel; 72c. Hand-drawn cart.

No. 1058b has a fluorescent frame instead of bands.

Nos. 1070/9 are vacant.

475 Mary, Joseph and Baby Jesus

476 Globes forming Symbolic Designs

(Des J. Eby. Litho C.B.N.)

1982 (3 Nov). Christmas. Nativity Scenes. T **475** and similar vert designs. Multicoloured. P 13.

1080	30c. Type **475**	20	10
1081	35c. The Shepherds	25	60
1082	60c. The Three Wise Men	45	1·50
1080/1082	Set of 3	80	2·00

(Des R. Bellemare. Litho Ashton-Potter)

1983 (10 Mar). World Communications Year. Fluorescent frame. P 12×12½.

1083	**476**	32c. multicoloured	30	30

477 Map of World showing Canada

(Des R. Harder. Litho Ashton-Potter)

1983 (14 Mar). Commonwealth Day. Without fluorescent bands. P 12½.

1084	**477**	$2 multicoloured	2·00	3·25

478 Scene from Novel "Angéline de Montbrun" by Laure Conan (Félicité Angers)

479 St. John Ambulance Badge and "100"

(Des R. Milot (No. 1085), Claire Pratt (No. 1086), adapted W. Tibbles. Litho C.B.N.)

1983 (22 Apr). Canadian Writers (4th series). T **478** and similar horiz design. Multicoloured. P 13.

1085	32c. Type **478**	40	90
	a. Pair. Nos. 1085/6	80	1·75
1086	32c. Woodcut illustrating "Sea-gulls" (poem by E. J. Pratt)	40	90

Nos. 1085/6 were printed together, *se-tenant*, in horizontal and vertical pairs throughout the sheet.

(Des L. Fishauf. Litho Ashton-Potter)

1983 (3 June). Centenary of St. John Ambulance in Canada. P 13.

1087	**479**	32c. bright rose-red, gold and deep chocolate	30	30

480 Victory Pictogram

481 Fort William, Ontario

(Des Krista Huebner, D. Kilvert and P.-Y. Pelletier. Litho C.B.N.)

1983 (28 June). "Universiade 83" World University Games, Edmonton. P 13.

1088	**480**	32c. multicoloured	25	15
		a. Printed on the gummed side	£550	
1089		64c. multicoloured	50	70

(Des R. Harder. Litho Ashton-Potter)

1983 (30 June). Canada Day. Forts (1st series). T **481** and similar horiz designs. Multicoloured. P 12½×13.

1090	32c. Fort Henry, Ontario (44×22 *mm*)	55	80
	a. Booklet pane. Nos. 1090/9	5·00	7·00
1091	32c. Type **481**	55	80
1092	32c. Fort Rodd Hill, British Columbia	55	80
1093	32c. Fort Wellington, Ontario (28×22 *mm*)	55	80
1094	32c. Fort Prince of Wales, Manitoba (28×22 *mm*)	55	80
1095	32c. Halifax Citadel, Nova Scotia (44×22 *mm*)	55	80
1096	32c. Fort Chambly, Quebec	55	80
1097	32c. Fort No. 1, Point Levis, Quebec	55	80
1098	32c. Coteau-du-Lac Fort, Quebec (28×22 *mm*)	55	80
1099	32c. Fort Beauséjour, New Brunswick (28×22 *mm*)	55	80
1090/1099	Set of 10	5·00	7·00

Nos. 1090/9 were only available from $3.20 stamp booklets, No. SB93, containing the *se-tenant* pane, No. 1090a.

See also Nos. 1163/72.

CANADA

482 Scouting Poster by Marc Fournier (aged 12)
483 Cross Symbol

(Des F. Dallaire. Litho Ashton-Potter)

1983 (6 July). 75th Anniv of Scouting in Canada and 15th World Scout Jamboree, Alberta. P 13.
1100   **482**   32c. multicoloured 30   30

(Des G. Tsetsekas. Recess and photo B.A.B.N.)

1983 (22 July). Sixth Assembly of the World Council of Churches, Vancouver. P 13.
1101   **483**   32c. blue-green and grey-lilac................. 30   20

484 Sir Humphrey Gilbert (founder)
485 "NICKEL" Deposits 

(Des R. Hill. Litho C.B.N.)

1983 (3 Aug). 400th Anniv of Newfoundland. P 13.
1102   **484**   32c. multicoloured 30   30

(Des J. Capon. Litho ("NICKEL" die-stamped) C.B.N.)

1983 (12 Aug). Centenary of Discovery of Sudbury Nickel Deposits. P 13.
1103   **485**   32c. multicoloured 30   30
          a. Silver ("NICKEL") omitted £650

486 Josiah Henson and Escaping Slaves
487 Robert Stephenson's Locomotive *Dorchester*, 1836 

(Des T. Kew and J. Hamel. Litho B.A.B.N.)

1983 (16 Sept). Nineteenth-century Social Reformers. T **486** and similar horiz design. Multicoloured. P 13×13½ (No. 1104) or 13 (No. 1105).
1104   32c. Type **486** 35   50
1105   32c. Father Antoine Labelle and rural village (32×26 mm) 35   50

(Des E. Roch. Litho Ashton-Potter)

1983 (3 Oct). Railway Locomotives (1st series). T **487** and similar horiz designs. Multicoloured. P 12½×13.
1106   32c. Type **487** .... 1·00   1·00
        a. Pair. Nos. 1106/7 .... 2·00   2·00
1107   32c. Locomotive *Toronto*, 1853 .... 1·00   1·00
1108   37c. Timothy Hackworth's locomotive *Samson*, 1838 .... 1·00   1·00
1109   64c. Western Canadian Railway locomotive *Adam Brown*, 1855 .... 1·60   2·50
1106/1109 *Set of 4* .... 4·25   5·00
Nos. 1106/7 were printed together, *se-tenant*, in horizontal and vertical pairs throughout the sheet.
See also Nos. 1132/6, 1185/8 and 1223/6.

488 School Coat of Arms
489 City Church 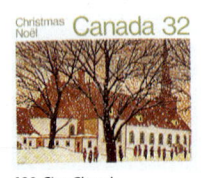

(Des Denise Saulnier. Litho C.B.N.)

1983 (28 Oct). Centenary of Dalhousie Law School. P 13.
1110   **488**   32c. multicoloured 30   40

(Des C. Simard. Litho Ashton-Potter)

1983 (3 Nov). Christmas. Churches. T **489** and similar horiz designs. Multicoloured. P 13.
1111   32c. Type **489** 30   10
1112   37c. Family walking to church 40   90
1113   64c. Country chapel .... 1·00   2·00
1111/1113 *Set of 3* .... 1·50   2·75

490 Royal Canadian Regiment and British Columbia Regiment

(Des W. Southern and R. Tibbles. Litho C.B.N.)

1983 (10 Nov). Canadian Army Regiments. T **490** and similar vert design. Multicoloured. Fluorescent frame. P 13.
1114   32c. Type **490** 75   1·25
        a. Pair. Nos. 1114/15 .... 1·50   2·50
1115   32c. Royal Winnipeg Rifles and Royal Canadian Dragoons 75   1·25
Nos. 1114/15 were printed together, *se-tenant*, in horizontal and vertical pairs throughout the sheet.

(*Illustration reduced; actual size 112×88 mm*)

"STICK 'N TICK" POSTAGE LABELS. Prepaid labels in the above design, printed in a combination of red, green and black, were tested by the Canadian Post Office in Winnipeg, Manitoba, between 21 November and 17 December 1983. These self-adhesive labels were sold to the public in kits of 12 or 25, at a saving of 35c. or $1.11 on the normal postage. They were primarily intended for use on Christmas cards and were only valid on mail posted to Canadian addresses.

The label was affixed to normally addressed envelopes, but the user was then required to mark the postal code on the three lines at the foot. It was hoped that this incentive would increase the use of the postal codes and so speed automatic mail sorting.

The system was extended to seven other cities in 1984. The second version had separate postage paid and Postal Code labels, being available from 5 November until 17 December 1984.

491 Gold Mine in Prospecting Pan
492 Montreal Symphony Orchestra 

58

CANADA

(Des K. Hughes. Litho Ashton-Potter)

1984 (15 Mar). 50th Anniv of Yellowknife. P 13½.
1116   **491**   32c. multicoloured 30   30

(Des J. Delisle and P. Kohler. Litho Ashton-Potter)

1984 (24 Mar). 50th Anniv of Montreal Symphony Orchestra. P 12½.
1117   **492**   32c. multicoloured 35   30

493 Jacques Cartier

494 *Eagle* (U.S. Coastguard cadet ship)

(Des Y. Paquin, Engraved C. Haley. Recess French Govt Ptg Wks, Perigueux)

1984 (20 Apr). 450th Anniv of Jacques Cartier's Voyage to Canada. P 13.
1118   **493**   32c. multicoloured 40   30

(Des O. Schenk. Litho Ashton-Potter)

1984 (18 May). Tall Ships Visit. Fluorescent frame. P 12×12½.
1119   **494**   32c. multicoloured 35   30

495 Service Medal

496 Oared Galleys

(Des W. Tibbles and C. Webster. Litho Ashton-Potter)

1984 (28 May). 75th Anniv of Canadian Red Cross Society. P 13½.
1120   **495**   32c. multicoloured 35   40

(Des P. Dorn. Photo and recess B.A.B.N.)

1984 (18 June). Bicentenary of New Brunswick. P 13½.
1121   **496**   32c. multicoloured 35   30

497 St. Lawrence Seaway

(Des E. Barenscher. Litho C.B.N.)

1984 (26 June). 25th Anniv of St. Lawrence Seaway. Fluorescent frame. P 13.
1122   **497**   32c. multicoloured 45   30

498 New Brunswick

499 Loyalists of 1784

(Des J. Morin and T. Yakobina. Litho C.B.N.)

1984 (29 June). Canada Day. Paintings by Jean Paul Lemieux. T **498** and similar multicoloured designs. P 13.
1123*a*   32c. Type **498** 50   60
        ab. Sheetlet. Nos. 1123*a*/*l*................ 5·50   6·50
1123*b*   32c. British Columbia 50   60
1123*c*   32c. Northwest Territories 50   60
1123*d*   32c. Quebec 50   60
1123*e*   32c. Manitoba 50   60
1123*f*   32c. Alberta 50   60
1123*g*   32c. Prince Edward Island 50   60
1123*h*   32c. Saskatchewan 50   60
1123*i*   32c. Nova Scotia (*vert*) 50   60
1123*j*   32c. Yukon Territory 50   60
1123*k*   32c. Newfoundland 50   60
1123*l*   32c. Ontario (*vert*) 50   60
1123*a*/1123*l* Set of 12 .... 5·50   6·50

Nos. 1123*a*/1123*l* were printed, *se-tenant*, in sheetlets of 12. The captions on the Northwest Territories and Yukon Territory paintings were transposed at the design stage.

(Des W. Davies. Litho B.A.B.N.)

1984 (3 July). Bicentenary of Arrival of United Empire Loyalists. P 13×13½.
1124   **499**   32c. multicoloured 30   30

500 St. John's Basilica

501 Coat of Arms of Pope John Paul II

(Des J. Morin and R. Ethier. Litho C.B.N.)

1984 (17 Aug). Bicentenary of Roman Catholic Church in Newfoundland. P 13½.
1125   **500**   32c. multicoloured 30   25

(Des L. Rivard. Litho Ashton-Potter)

1984 (31 Aug). Papal Visit. P 12½.
1126   **501**   32c. multicoloured 40   20
1127   64c. multicoloured 85   1·10

502 Louisbourg Lighthouse, 1734

(Des D. Noble and K. Rodmell. Litho Ashton-Potter)

1984 (21 Sept). Canadian Lighthouses (1st series). T **502** and similar horiz designs. Multicoloured. P 12½.
1128   32c. Type **502** .... 1·75   1·75
            a. Block of 4. Nos. 1128/31 .... 6·25   6·25
1129   32c. Fisgard Lighthouse, 1860 .... 1·75   1·75
1130   32c. Ile Verte Lighthouse, 1809 .... 1·75   1·75
1131   32c. Gibraltar Point Lighthouse, 1808 .. 1·75   1·75
1128/1131 Set of 4 .... 6·25   6·25

Nos. 1128/31 were printed together, *se-tenant*, in different combinations throughout the sheet, giving ten blocks of 4 and ten single stamps.
See also Nos. 1176/80.

503 Great Western Railway Locomotive, *Scotia*, 1860

(Des E. Roch. Litho Ashton-Potter)

1984 (25 Oct). Railway Locomotives (2nd series). T **503** and similar horiz designs. Multicoloured. P 12½×13.
1132   32c. Type **503** .... 1·40   1·40
            a. Pair. Nos. 1132/3 .... 2·75   2·75
1133   32c. Northern Pacific Railroad locomotive *Countess of Dufferin*, 1872 .... 1·40   1·40
1134   37c. Grand Trunk Railway Class E3 locomotive, 1886 .... 1·40   1·60
1135   64c. Canadian Pacific Class D10a steam locomotive .... 2·00   2·75
1132/1135 Set of 4 .... 5·50   7·00
MS1136 153×104 mm. As Nos. 1132/5, but with background colour changed from pale green to pale grey-blue .... 5·50   6·50

Nos. 1132/3 were issued together, *se-tenant*, in horizontal and vertical pairs throughout the sheet.
No. **MS**1136 commemorates "CANADA 84" National Stamp Exhibition, Montreal.
See also Nos. 1185/8 and 1223/6.

59

CANADA

504 "The Annunciation" (Jean Dallaire)

505 Pilots of 1914–18, 1939–45 and 1984

(Des J. Morin and T. Yakobina. Litho Ashton-Potter)

1984 (2 Nov). Christmas. Religious Paintings. T **504** and similar horiz designs. Multicoloured. P 13½.

1137	32c. Type **504**	40	10
1138	37c. "The Three Kings" (Simone Bouchard)	70	1·00
1139	64c. "Snow in Bethlehem" (David Milne)	90	1·75
1137/1139	Set of 3	1·75	2·50

(Des W. Southern and R. Tibbles. Litho Ashton-Potter)

1984 (9 Nov). 60th Anniv of Royal Canadian Air Force. Fluorescent frame. P 12×12½.

1140	**505**	32c. multicoloured	35	30

506 Trefflé Berthiaume (editor)

507 Heart and Arrow

(Des P-Y. Pelletier. Litho Ashton-Potter)

1984 (16 Nov). Centenary of *La Presse* (newspaper). Fluorescent frame. P 13×13½.

1141	**506**	32c. agate, vermilion & pale grey-brown	35	30

(Des F. Dallaire. Litho Ashton-Potter)

1985 (8 Feb). International Youth Year. P 12½.

1142	**507**	32c. multicoloured	30	30

508 Astronaut in Space, and Planet Earth

509 Emily Murphy

(Des L. Holloway. Litho Ashton-Potter)

1985 (15 Mar). Canadian Space Programme. P 13½.

1143	**508**	32c. multicoloured	40	30

(Des Muriel Wood and R. Tibbles. Litho Ashton-Potter)

1985 (17 Apr). Women's Rights Activists. T **509** and similar horiz design. Multicoloured. P 13½.

1144	32c. Type **509**	40	90
	a. Horiz pair. Nos. 1144/5	80	1·75
1145	32c. Therese Casgrain	40	90

Nos. 1144/5 were printed together, *se-tenant*, in horizontal pairs throughout the sheet.

510 Gabriel Dumont (Métis leader) and Battle of Batoche, 1885

(Des R. Derreth. Litho Ashton-Potter)

1985 (6 May). Centenary of the North-West Rebellion. P 14×13½.

1146	**510**	32c. blue, carmine and grey	30	30

511 Rear View, Parliament Building, Ottawa

512 Queen Elizabeth II

512a Queen Elizabeth II in 1984 (from photo by Karsh)

(Des R. Bellemare. Eng R. Couture (Nos. 1161/2). Des T. Yakobina and C. Candlish (Nos. 1162a/h), R. Harder (others))

1985 (21 June)–**2000**. No fluorescent bands (1c. to 6c.) or fluorescent frame (34, 36, 39, 40, 42, 43, 45, 46c., 47c.).

*(a) T **511** and similar horiz designs*

(i) Booklet stamps. Recess B.A.B.N. Chalk-surfaced paper (6c. (No. 1150b), 37c, 38c.) or ordinary paper (others). P 12½×12

1147	–	1c. grey-olive (30.3.87)	80	2·50
		a. Booklet pane. Nos. 1147×2, 1150×2, 1152 and label	7·00	
		b. Chalk-surfaced paper (1.10.87)	1·00	80
		ba. Booklet pane. Nos. 1147b×2, 1150a×2,1152a and label	6·00	
		bb. Booklet pane. Nos. 1147b, 1150a×2, 1153 and two labels (3.2.88)	3·25	
1148		2c. bottle green	25	1·50
		a. Booklet pane. Nos. 1148×3, 1149×2 and 1151	4·00	
		b. Chalk-surfaced paper (18.1.89)	30	40
		ba. Booklet pane. Nos. 1148b×3, 1150b, 1154 and label	5·50	
1149	–	5c. sepia	75	1·75
1150		6c. chestnut (30.3.87)	1·50	2·50
		a. Chalk-surfaced paper (1.10.87)	70	50
1150b		6c. blackish purple (18.1.89)	2·50	1·90
1151	**511**	34c. blue-black	2·25	2·75
1152		36c. reddish purple (30.3.87)	4·00	5·00
		a. Chalk-surfaced paper (1.10.87)	3·50	4·50
1153		37c. dull ultramarine (3.2.88)	1·75	30
1154		38c. deep blue (18.1.89)	2·75	1·25

(ii) Litho C.B.N. (Nos. 1155 (from sheets), 1156/7c), B.A.B.N. (No. 1155 (from booklets) or Ashton-Potter (Nos. 1155b, 1156a, 1157a/ba, 1157ca/cb). Chalk-surfaced paper (Nos. 1155b/ba, 1156, 1156b/bb and 1157c/cb). P 13×13½ (No. 1157c) or 13½×13 (others)

1155	**511**	34c. multicoloured	60	10
		a. Booklet pane. No. 1155×25 (1.8.85)	13·00	
		b. Perf 13½×14 (4.7.86)	1·25	1·75
		ba. Booklet pane. No. 1155b×25	26·00	
1156		36c. multicoloured (30.3.87)	1·25	30
		a. Ordinary paper	30	45
		b. Perf 13½×14	1·40	1·75
		ba. Booklet pane. No. 1156b×10	12·00	
		bb. Booklet pane. No. 1156b×25 (19.5.87)	27·00	
		c. Imperf (pair)	£375	
1157		37c. multicoloured (30.12.87)	85	10
		a. Perf 13½×14 (5.1.88)	1·00	1·00
		ab. Booklet pane. No. 1157a×10	13·00	
		ac. Booklet pane. No. 1157a×25 (2.5.88)	15·00	
		ad. Chalk-surfaced paper (5.1.88)	1·50	1·00
		ae. Booklet pane. No. 1157ad×25	27·00	
1157c		38c. multicoloured (29.12.88)	65	10
		ca. Booklet pane. No. 1157c×10 and two labels	6·00	
		cb. Booklet pane. No. 1157c×25 and two labels	15·00	
		cc. Printed on the gummed side	45·00	

(iii) Coil stamps. Recess C.B.N. P 10×imperf

1158	**511**	34c. purple-brown (1.8.85)	2·25	3·00
		a. Imperf (pair)	£100	
1159		36c. carmine-vermilion (19.5.87)	2·25	55
		a. Imperf (pair)	£150	
1160		37c. deep ultramarine (22.2.88)	1·00	40
		a. Imperf (pair)	£100	
1160b		38c. bottle green (1.2.89)	50	30
		ba. Imperf (pair)	£200	

(b) Recess and photo B.A.B.N. P 13×13½

1161	**512**	34c. black and cobalt (12.7.85)	1·40	30
1162		36c. reddish purple (1.10.87)	2·75	1·10

(c) Litho B.A.B.N. (Nos. 1162a/c), Ashton-Potter (Nos. 1162bc, 1162ca, 1162d/e, 1162fa), C.B.N. (Nos. 1162f/g, 1162i) or Ashton-Potter Canada (No. 1162h). Chalk-surfaced paper (40c. to 47c.). P 13½×13 (Nos. 1162a, 1162h/i), 13×12½ (No. 1162b) or 13×13½ (Nos. 1162c, 1162d/g)

1162a	**512a**	37c. multicoloured (30.12.87)	3·50	10
1162b		38c. multicoloured (29.12.88)	1·50	20
		ba. Imperf (horiz pair)	£275	
		bb. Imperf at top and sides (horiz pair)	£225	
		bc. Perf 13×13½. Chalk-surfaced paper	65	65
		bd. Booklet pane. No. 1162bc×10 and two labels	6·00	
		be. Imperf between (horiz pair) (from pane No. 1162bd)	£550	
1162c		39c. multicoloured (12.1.90)	1·00	20
		ca. Chalk-surfaced paper	2·00	80
		cb. Booklet pane. No. 1162ca×10 and two labels	18·00	
		cc. Perf 13×12½ (2.90)	7·50	1·00
1162d		40c. multicoloured (28.12.90)	1·00	20
		da. Booklet pane. No. 1162d×10 and two labels	13·00	
		db. Ordinary paper (24.5.91)	1·25	
1162e		42c. multicoloured (27.12.91)	1·00	40
		ea. Booklet pane. No. 1162e×10	15·00	
1162f		43c. multicoloured (30.12.92)	1·25	80
		fa. Booklet pane. No. 1162f×10	13·00	
1162g		45c. multicoloured (31.7.95)	2·50	80
		ga. Booklet pane. No. 1162g×10	22·00	
1162h		46c. multicoloured (28.12.98)	1·00	45
1162i		47c. multicoloured (28.12.00)	1·00	60

Designs:—1c., 5c., 6c. (No. 1150b) East Block, Parliament Building; 2c., 6c. (No. 1150) West Block, Parliament Building; 37c. (No. 1157) Front view, Parliament Building; 38c. (No. 1157c) Side view, Parliament Building.

Stamps from booklet panes Nos. 1147a, 1147ba/bb and 1148a/b have one or two adjacent sides imperforate. Stamps from the first and last vertical columns of booklet panes Nos. 1155a, 1155ba, 1156ba/bb, 1157ab/ac, 1157ae, 1157ca/cb, 1162bd, 1162cb, 1162da 1162ea, 1162fa and 1162ga are imperforate at left or right. Those from the bottom row of No. 1157ac are also imperforate at foot.

Nos. 1157c and 1162b/i have a slightly larger design image 21×17 mm.

Printings of booklet pane No. 1162fa from booklet No. SB164 were initially by Ashton-Potter. On 7 January 1994 the printer changed to C.B.N. and the booklet cover to Type B **37**. This booklet is listed as No. SB177. There were further printings by C.B.N. before production reverted to Ashton-Potter Canada for supplies released on 27 March 1995.

Nos. 1162g/ga were reissued on 6 October 1995 showing a change of printer to Ashton-Potter Canada. There are no listable differences between these stamps and the previous printings.

(Des R. Harder. Litho Ashton-Potter)

1985 (28 June). Canada Day. Forts (2nd series). Horiz designs as T **481**. Multicoloured. P 12½×13.

1163		34c. Lower Fort Garry, Manitoba (44×22 mm)	50	60
		a. Booklet pane. Nos. 1163/72	4·50	5·50
1164		34c. Fort Anne, Nova Scotia	50	60
1165		34c. Fort York, Ontario	50	60
1166		34c. Castle Hill, Newfoundland (28×22 mm)	50	60
1167		34c. Fort Whoop Up, Alberta (28×22 mm)	50	60
1168		34c. Fort Erie, Ontario (44×22 mm)	50	60
1169		34c. Fort Walsh, Saskatchewan	50	60
1170		34c. Fort Lennox, Quebec	50	60
1171		34c. York Redoubt, Nova Scotia (28×22 mm)	50	60
1172		34c. Fort Frederick, Ontario (28×22 mm)	50	60
1163/1172 Set of 10			4·50	5·50

Nos. 1163/72 were only available from $3.40 stamp booklets (No. SB96) containing the *se-tenant* pane, No. 1163a.

513 Louis Hébert (apothecary)

514 Parliament Buildings and Map of World

515 Guide and Brownie Saluting

(Des C. Malenfant. Litho Ashton-Potter)

1985 (30 Aug). 45th International Pharmaceutical Sciences Congress of Pharmaceutical Federation, Montreal. Fluorescent frame. P 12½.
1173 **513** 34c. multicoloured 45 45

(Des E. Barenscher. Litho Ashton-Potter)

1985 (3 Sept). 74th Conference of Inter-Parliamentary Union, Ottawa. P 13½.
1174 **514** 34c. multicoloured 45 45

(Des Barbara Griffin. Recess and photo B.A.B.N.)

1985 (12 Sept). 75th Anniv of Girl Guide Movement. Fluorescent frame. P 13½×13.
1175 **515** 34c. multicoloured 45 35

516 Sisters Islets Lighthouse

517 Santa Claus in Reindeer-drawn Sleigh

(Des B. Reilander (No. **MS**1180), L. Rivard (others). Litho Ashton-Potter)

1985 (3 Oct). Canadian Lighthouses (2nd series). T **516** and similar horiz designs. Multicoloured. P 13½.

1176		34c. Type **516**	2·00	2·00
		a. Block of 4. Nos. 1176/9	7·00	8·00
1177		34c. Pelee Passage Lighthouse	2·00	2·00
1178		34c. Haut-fond Prince Lighthouse	2·00	2·00
1179		34c. Rose Blanche Lighthouse, Cains Island	2·00	2·00
1176/1179 Set of 4			7·00	7·00
MS1180 109×90 mm. Nos. 1176/9			7·50	8·00

Nos. 1176/9 were printed together, *se-tenant*, in different combinations throughout the sheet, giving ten blocks of 4 and ten single stamps.

No. **MS**1180 publicises "Capex 87" International Stamp Exhibition, Toronto.

(Des Barbara Carroll and C. Yaneff. Litho Ashton-Potter)

1985 (23 Oct). Christmas. Santa Claus Parade. T **517** and similar horiz designs. Multicoloured. P 13½.

1181		32c. Canada Post's parade float	60	85
		a. Booklet pane. No. 1181×10	5·50	
1182		34c. Type **517**	70	20
1183		39c. Acrobats and horse-drawn carriage	1·00	1·25
1184		68c. Christmas tree, pudding and goose on float	1·90	2·50
1181/1184 Set of 4			3·75	4·25

No. 1181 was only available from $3.20 stamp booklets, No. SB98, which had the upper and lower edges of the pane imperforate. This value was intended for use on greeting cards posted on or before 31 January 1986, and represented a 2c. saving of postage. After this date these stamps could be used for any postal purpose in conjunction with other values.

(Des E. Roch. Litho Ashton-Potter)

1985 (7 Nov). Railway Locomotives (3rd series). Horiz designs as T **503**. Multicoloured. P 12½×13.

1185		34c. Grand Trunk Railway Class K2 steam locomotive	1·25	1·75
		a. Pair. Nos. 1185/6	2·50	3·50
1186		34c. Canadian Pacific Class P2a steam locomotive	1·25	1·75
1187		39c. Canadian Northern Class 010a steam locomotive	1·25	1·50
1188		68c. Canadian Govt Railway Class H4D steam locomotive	2·00	2·75
1185/1188 Set of 4			5·25	7·00

Nos. 1185/6 were printed together, *se-tenant*, in horizontal and vertical pairs throughout the sheet.

518 Naval Personnel of 1910, 1939–45 and 1985

519 "The Old Holton House, Montreal" (James Wilson Morrice)

CANADA

(Des W. Southern and R. Tibbles. Litho C.B.N.)

1985 (8 Nov). 75th Anniv of Royal Canadian Navy. Fluorescent frame. P 13½×13.

| 1189 | 518 | 34c. multicoloured | 65 | 65 |

(Des L. Parent and J. Morin. Litho C.B.N.)

1985 (15 Nov). 125th Anniv of Montreal Museum of Fine Arts. P 13½.

| 1190 | 519 | 34c. multicoloured | 40 | 50 |

520 Map of Alberta showing Olympic Sites

(Des P-Y. Pelletier. Litho Ashton-Potter)

1986 (13 Feb). Winter Olympic Games, Calgary (1988) (1st issue). Fluorescent frame. P 12½×13.

| 1191 | 520 | 34c. multicoloured | 40 | 50 |

See also Nos. 1216/17, 1236/7, 1258/9 and 1281/4.

521 Canada Pavilion

522 Molly Brant

(Des Debbie Adams. Recess and photo B.A.B.N.)

1986 (7 Mar). "Expo '86" World Fair Vancouver (1st issue). T **521** and similar horiz design. Multicoloured. Fluorescent frame. P 13×13½.

| 1192 | | 34c. Type **521** | 1·25 | 50 |
| 1193 | | 39c. Early telephone, dish aerial and satellite | 2·00 | 3·25 |

See also Nos. 1196/7.

(Des Sara Tyson. Litho Ashton-Potter)

1986 (14 Apr). 250th Birth Anniv of Molly Brant (Iroquois leader). P 13½.

| 1194 | 522 | 34c. multicoloured | 40 | 50 |

523 Philippe Aubert de Gaspé and Scene from *Les Anciens Canadiens*

524 Canadian Field Post Office and Cancellation, 1944

(Des P. Fontaine and Y. Paquin. Litho Ashton-Potter)

1986 (14 Apr). Birth Bicentenary of Philippe Aubert de Gaspé (author). Fluorescent frame. P 12½.

| 1195 | 523 | 34c. multicoloured | 40 | 50 |

(Des Debbie Adams. Recess and photo B.A.B.N.)

1986 (28 Apr). "Expo '86" World Fair, Vancouver (2nd issue). Multicoloured designs as T **521**. Fluorescent frame. P 13½×13 (34c.) or 13×13½ (68c.).

| 1196 | | 34c. Expo Centre, Vancouver (*vert*) | 70 | 50 |
| 1197 | | 68c. Early and modern trains | 1·40 | 3·25 |

(Des J. DesRosiers. Litho Ashton-Potter)

1986 (9 May). 75th Anniv of Canadian Forces Postal Service. P 13½.

| 1198 | 524 | 34c. multicoloured | 60 | 60 |

525 Great Blue Heron

526 Railway Rotary Snowplough

(Des P. Fontaine and J.-L. Grondin. Litho Ashton-Potter)

1986 (22 May). Birds of Canada. T **525** and similar horiz designs. Multicoloured. P 13½.

1199		34c. Type **525**	1·75	2·25
		a. Block of 4. Nos. 1199/1202	6·25	8·00
1200		34c. Snow Goose	1·75	2·25
1201		34c. Great Horned Owl	1·75	2·25
1202		34c. Spruce Grouse	1·75	2·25
1199/1202	Set of 4		6·25	8·00

Nos. 1199/1202 were printed together, *se-tenant*, in different combinations throughout the sheet, giving ten blocks of 4 and ten single stamps.

(Des R. Hill. Litho C.B.N.)

1986 (27 June). Canada Day. Science and Technology. Canadian Inventions (1st series). T **526** and similar vert designs. Multicoloured. P 13½.

1203		34c. Type **526**	1·75	2·25
		a. Block of 4. Nos. 1203/6	6·25	8·00
1204		34c. Space shuttle *Challenger* launching satellite with Canadarm	1·75	2·25
1205		34c. Pilot wearing anti-gravity flight suit and Supermarine Spitfire	1·75	2·25
1206		34c. Variable-pitch propellor and Avro 504 airplane	1·75	2·25
1203/1206	Set of 4		6·25	8·00

Nos. 1203/6 were printed together, *se-tenant*, in blocks of 4 throughout the sheet.

See also Nos. 1241/4 and 1292/5.

527 C.B.C. Logos over Map of Canada

528 Ice Age Artefacts, Tools and Settlement

(Des R. Mah and G. Tsetsekas. Litho Ashton-Potter)

1986 (23 July). 50th Anniv of Canadian Broadcasting Corporation. P 12½.

| 1207 | 527 | 34c. multicoloured | 40 | 50 |

(Des F. Hagan. Litho Ashton-Potter)

1986 (29 Aug–1 Oct). Exploration of Canada (1st series). Discoverers. T **528** and similar horiz designs. Multicoloured. P 12½×13.

1208		34c. Type **528**	1·50	2·00
		a. Block of 4. Nos. 1208/11	5·50	7·25
1209		34c. Viking ships	1·50	2·00
1210		34c. John Cabot's *Matthew*, 1497, compass and Arctic Char (fish)	1·50	2·00
1211		34c. Henry Hudson cast adrift, 1611	1·50	2·00
1208/1211	Set of 4		5·50	7·25
MS1212	119×84 mm. Nos. 1208/11 (1 Oct)		5·50	7·50

Nos. 1208/11 were printed together, *se-tenant*, in different combinations throughout the sheet, giving ten blocks of 4 and ten single stamps.

No. **MS**1212 publicises "Capex '87" International Stamp Exhibition, Toronto.

See also Nos. 1232/5, 1285/8 and 1319/22.

529 Crowfoot (Blackfoot Chief) and Indian Village

530 Peace Dove and Globe

62

CANADA

(Des Wanda Lewicka and J. Morin. Litho C.B.N.)

1986 (5 Sept). Founders of the Canadian West. T **529** and similar horiz design. Multicoloured. P 13×13½.
1213	34c. Type **529**...	80	1·00
	a. Pair. Nos. 1213/14................................	1·60	2·00
1214	34c. James Macleod of the North West Mounted Police and Fort Macleod............	80	1·00

Nos. 1213/14 were printed together, *se-tenant*, in horizontal and vertical pairs throughout the sheet.

(Des Carole Jeghers. Litho and embossed Ashton-Potter)

1986 (16 Sept). International Peace Year. P 13½.
1215	**530**	34c. multicoloured...............................	60	60

531 Ice Hockey

532 Angel with Crown

(Des P.-Y. Pelletier. Litho C.B.N.)

1986 (15 Oct). Winter Olympic Games, Calgary (1988) (2nd issue). T **531** and similar vert design. Multicoloured. P 13½×13.
1216	34c. Type **531**...	1·75	1·75
	a. Pair. Nos. 1216/17................................	3·50	3·50
1217	34c. Biathlon..	1·75	1·75

Nos. 1216/17 were printed together, *se-tenant*. in horizontal and vertical pairs throughout the sheet.
See also Nos. 1236/7, 1258/9 and 1281/4.

(Des T. Dimson. Litho Ashton-Potter)

1986 (29 Oct). Christmas. T **532** and similar multicoloured designs. Fluorescent frame (34 to 68c.). P 13½× imperf (29c.) or 12½ (others).
1218	29c. Angel singing carol (36×22 *mm*)..............	65	35
	a. Booklet pane. No. 1218×10.....................	6·00	
	b. Perf 12½× imperf.....................................	5·50	30
	ba. Booklet pane. No. 1218b×10	50·00	
1219	34c. Type **532**...	60	25
1220	39c. Angel playing lute..................................	1·00	1·60
1221	68c. Angel with ribbon..................................	1·75	3·00
1218/1221 *Set of 4*..		3·50	5·00

Nos. 1218/b were only available from $2.90 stamp booklets, Nos. SB99/a, which had the sides of the pane imperforate. In addition to the design each stamp in the pane included an integral horizontal label showing a bar code. This value was intended for use on greeting cards posted on or before 31 January 1987, and represented a 5c. saving when used in conjunction with special postcoded envelopes. These stamps were valid for normal postal purposes after 31 January when used with other values.

533 John Molson with Theatre Royal, Montreal, *Accommodation* (paddle-steamer) and Railway Train

534 Toronto's First Post Office

(Des C. Malenfant. Litho Ashton-Potter)

1986 (4 Nov). 150th Death Anniv of John Molson (businessman). P 12½.
1222	**533**	34c. multicoloured...............................	1·25	75

(Des E. Roch. Litho Ashton-Potter)

1986 (21 Nov). Railway Locomotives (4th series). Horiz designs as T **503**, but size 60×22 mm. Multicoloured. P 12½×13.
1223	34c. Canadian National Class V-1-a diesel locomotive No. 9000..................................	1·90	1·90
	a. Pair. Nos. 1223/4...................................	3·75	3·75
1224	34c. Canadian Pacific Class T1a steam locomotive No. 9000..................................	1·90	1·90
1225	39c. Canadian National Class U-2-a steam locomotive...	1·90	1·00
1226	68c. Canadian Pacific Class H1c steam locomotive No. 2850..................................	2·50	3·50
1223/1226 *Set of 4*..		7·50	7·50

Nos. 1223/4 were issued together, *se-tenant*, in horizontal and vertical pairs throughout the sheet.

(Des J. Mardon (stamps) and B. Reilander (sheet). Recess and litho B.A.B.N.)

1987 (16 Feb–12 June). "Capex '87" International Stamp Exhibition, Toronto. T **534** and similar horiz designs showing Post Offices. Fluorescent frame. P 13×13½.
1227	34c. Type **534**...	60	20
1228	36c. Nelson-Miramichi, New Brunswick (12.6)..	65	45
1229	42c. Saint-Ours, Quebec (12.6)	70	65
1230	72c. Battleford, Saskatchewan (12.6)	1·00	1·25
1227/1230 *Set of 4*..		2·75	2·25
MS1231 155×92 mm. 36c. As No. 1227 and Nos. 1228/30, but main inscr in bright green (12.6)......................		3·25	2·75

535 Étienne Brûlé exploring Lake Superior

(Des J. Britton and F. Hagan. Litho Ashton-Potter)

1987 (13 Mar). Exploration of Canada (2nd series). Pioneers of New France. T **535** and similar horiz designs. Multicoloured. P 12½×13.
1232	34c. Type **535**...	1·75	2·00
	a. Block of 4. Nos. 1232/5.........................	6·25	7·25
1233	34c. Radisson and des Groseilliers with British and French flags	1·75	2·00
1234	34c. Jolliet and Father Marquette on the Mississippi...	1·75	2·00
1235	34c. Jesuit missionary preaching to Indians..	1·75	2·00
1232/1235 *Set of 4*..		6·25	7·25

Nos. 1232/5 were printed together, *se-tenant*, in different combinations throughout the sheet, giving ten blocks of 4 and ten single stamps.

(Des P.-Y. Pelletier. Litho C.B.N.)

1987 (3 Apr). Winter Olympic Games, Calgary (1988) (3rd issue). Vert designs as T **531**. Multicoloured. P 13½×13.
1236	36c. Speed skating...	50	40
1237	42c. Bobsleighing...	75	60

536 Volunteer Activities

537 Canadian Coat of Arms

(Des W. Davies. Litho Ashton-Potter)

1987 (13 Apr). National Volunteer Week. P 12½×13.
1238	**536**	36c. multicoloured...............................	30	35

(Des R. Tibbles. Litho Ashton-Potter)

1987 (15 Apr). Fifth Anniv of Canadian Charter of Rights and Freedoms. Fluorescent frame. P 14×13½.
1239	**537**	36c. multicoloured...............................	75	35
		a. Imperf (pair)...................................	£1000	

538 Steel Girder, Gear Wheel and Microchip

539 R. A. Fessenden (AM Radio)

CANADA

(Des L. Holloway, R. Kerr and Nita Wallace. Litho Ashton-Potter)

1987 (19 May). Centenary of Engineering Institute of Canada. P 12½×13.
1240	**538**	36c. multicoloured	75	40

(Des R. Hill. Litho C.B.N.)

1987 (25 June). Canada Day. Science and Technology. Canadian Inventors (2nd series). T **539** and similar vert designs. Multicoloured. P 13½.
1241	36c. Type **539**		1·25	1·75
	a. Block of four. Nos. 1241/4		4·50	6·25
1242	36c. C. Fenerty (newsprint pulp)		1·25	1·75
1243	36c. G.-E. Desbarats and W. Leggo (half-tone engraving)		1·25	1·75
1244	36c. F. N. Gisborne (first North American undersea telegraph)		1·25	1·75
1241/1244	Set of 4		4·50	6·25

Nos. 1241/4 were printed together, *se-tenant*, in blocks of four throughout the sheet.

540 Segwun

541 Figurehead from *Hamilton*, 1813

(Des D. Champion. Litho C.B.N.)

1987 (20 July). Canadian Steamships. T **540** and similar multicoloured design. P 13.
1245	36c. Type **540**		1·75	2·50
	a. Horiz pair. Nos. 1245/6		3·50	5·00
1246	36c. *Princess Marguerite* (52×22 mm)		1·75	2·50

Nos. 1245/6 were printed together horizontally, *se-tenant*, throughout the sheet of 25, with No. 1245 occurring in columns 1, 3 and 5 and No. 1246 in columns 2 and 4.

(Des L.-A. Rivard. Litho Ashton-Potter)

1987 (7 Aug). Historic Shipwrecks. T **541** and similar horiz designs. Multicoloured. P 13½×13.
1247	36c. Type **541**		1·50	2·00
	a. Block of four. Nos. 1247/50		5·50	7·25
1248	36c. Hull of *San Juan*, 1565		1·50	2·00
1249	36c. Wheel from *Breadalbane*, 1853		1·50	2·00
1250	36c. Bell from *Ericsson*, 1892		1·50	2·00
1247/1250	Set of 4		5·50	7·25

Nos. 1247/50 were printed together, *se-tenant*, in different combinations throughout the sheet, giving ten blocks of 4 and ten single stamps.

542 Air Canada Boeing 767-200 and Globe

543 Summit Symbol

(Des Debbie Adams and D. Carter. Litho C.B.N.)

1987 (1 Sept). 50th Anniv of Air Canada. P 13½.
1251	**542**	36c. multicoloured	1·00	35

(Des C. Gaudreau. Litho Ashton-Potter)

1987 (2 Sept). Second International Francophone Summit, Quebec. Fluorescent frame. P 13×12½.
1252	**543**	36c. multicoloured	30	35

544 Commonwealth Symbol

545 Poinsettia

(Des G. Tsetsekas. Litho Ashton-Potter)

1987 (13 Oct). Commonwealth Heads of Government Meeting, Vancouver. Fluorescent frame. P 13×12½.
1253	**544**	36c. multicoloured	35	40

(Des C. Simard. Litho Ashton-Potter)

1987 (2 Nov). Christmas. Christmas Plants. T **545** and similar multicoloured designs. Fluorescent frame. P 12½×13 (31c) or 13½ (others).
1254	31c. Decorated Christmas tree and presents (36×20 mm)		90	50
	a. Booklet pane. No. 1254×10		8·00	
	b. Imperf between (horiz pair) (from booklet)		£1200	
1255	36c. Type **545**		40	20
1256	42c. Holly wreath		1·25	50
1257	72c. Mistletoe and decorated tree		1·75	80
1254/1257	Set of 4		3·75	1·75

On No. 1254 the left-hand third of the design area is taken up by a bar code which has fluorescent bands between the bars. This value was only available from $3.10 stamp booklets, No. SB103, which had the sides of the pane imperforate. This value was intended for use on greeting cards posted on or before 31 January 1988 and represented a 5c. saving when used in conjunction with special postcoded envelopes.

(Des P.-Y. Pelletier. Litho C.B.N.)

1987 (13 Nov). Winter Olympic Games, Calgary (1988) (4th issue). Vert designs as T **531**. Multicoloured. Fluorescent frame. P 13½×13.
1258	36c. Cross-country skiing		90	75
	a. Pair. Nos. 1258/9		1·75	1·50
1259	36c. Ski-jumping		90	75

Nos. 1258/9 were printed together, *se-tenant*, in horizontal and vertical pairs throughout the sheet.

546 Football, Grey Cup and Spectators

(Des L. Holloway. Litho Ashton-Potter)

1987 (20 Nov). 75th Grey Cup Final (Canadian football championship), Vancouver. Fluorescent frame. P 12½.
1260	**546**	36c. multicoloured	35	40

547 Flying Squirrel

548 Lynx

548a Runnymede Library, Toronto

(Des Gottschalk & Ash International (1c. to 25c.), B. Tsang (43c. to 80c.), R. Bellemare ($1, $2, $5). Litho Ashton-Potter (1c. to 80c.), Recess and litho B.A.B.N. to June 1992, thereafter C.B.N. ($1, $2, $5))

1988 (18 Jan)–**93**. Canadian Mammals and Architecture. Multicoloured. Fluorescent frame (10c. and 43c. to 80c.).

(a) Horiz designs as T **547**. Chalk-surfaced paper. P 13×13½
1261	1c. Type **547** (3.10.88)	10	10
	a. Perf 13×12½ (1.92)	3·00	2·00
1262	2c. Porcupine (3.10.88)	10	10
1263	3c. Muskrat (3.10.88)	10	10
1264	5c. Varying Hare (3.10.88)	10	10
1265	6c. Red Fox (3.10.88)	10	10
1266	10c. Striped Skunk (3.10.88)	10	10
	a. Perf 13×12½ (2.91)	3·75	1·50
	b. No fluorescent frame (25.10.91)	45	10
1267	25c. American Beaver (3.10.88)	30	15
	a. No fluorescent frame (22.4.92)	1·50	55

*(b) Horiz designs as T **548**. Chalk-surfaced paper (45, 46, 57, 61, 63, 78, 80c.) or ordinary paper (others). P 12×12½ (43, 57, 74c.) or 14½×14 (others)*

1268	43c. Type **548**...	1·40	1·25
1269	44c. Walrus (18.1.89).................................	1·40	20
	a. Perf 12½×13. Chalk-surfaced paper........	1·40	55
	ab. Booklet pane. No. 1269a×5 and label with margins all round.................................	6·00	
	b. Chalk-surfaced paper (9.6.89)................	4·00	1·50
	c. Perf 13½×13. Chalk-surfaced paper (1989)..	£180	16·00
1270	45c. Pronghorn (12.1.90).............................	50	40
	a. Perf 12½×13...	2·00	40
	ab. Booklet pane. No. 1270a×5 and label with margins all round.................................	9·00	
	b. Perf 13 (6.90).......................................	12·00	50
1270c	46c. Wolverine (28.12.90)..........................	1·50	1·50
	ca. Perf 13..	3·00	3·25
	cb. Perf 12½×13..	1·75	50
	cc. Booklet pane. No. 1270cb×5 and label with margins all round.................................	8·00	
1271	57c. Killer Whale...	2·00	55
	a. Ordinary paper (26.9.88)........................	3·75	1·75
1272	59c. Musk Ox (18.1.89)................................	3·50	2·75
	a. Chalk-surfaced paper (1.11.89)..............	7·50	3·75
	b. Perf 13. Chalk-surfaced paper (1.11.89)..	6·00	3·75
1273	61c. Wolf (12.1.90)......................................	70	1·25
	a. Perf 13 (7.90).......................................	27·00	2·00
1273b	63c. Harbour Porpoise (28.12.90)...............	2·00	2·50
	ba. Perf 13..	9·50	4·75
1274	74c. Wapiti..	1·60	50
	a. Chalk-surfaced paper.............................	£250	7·00
1275	76c. Brown Bear (18.1.89)...........................	2·50	50
	a. Perf 12½×13. Chalk-surfaced paper...	1·75	70
	ab. Booklet pane. No. 1275a×5 and label with margins all round.................................	8·50	
	b. Chalk-surfaced paper (25.8.89)..............	6·00	3·25
	c. Perf 13. Chalk-surfaced paper (1989)......	19·00	8·50
1276	78c. White Whale (12.1.90).........................	1·00	55
	a. Perf 12½×13...	2·25	70
	ab. Booklet pane. No. 1276a×5 and label with margins all round.................................	11·00	
	b. Perf 13 (4.90).......................................	30·00	5·50
1276c	80c. Peary Caribou (28.12.90)....................	1·00	60
	ca. Perf 13..	4·50	1·00
	cb. Perf 12½×13..	2·25	60
	cc. Booklet pane. No. 1276cb×5 and label with margins all round.................................	10·00	

*(c) Horiz designs as T **548a**. Chalk-surfaced paper ($5) or ordinary paper (others). P 13½*

1277	$1 Type **548a** (brown roof) (5.5.89)........	1·50	30
	a. Chalk-surfaced paper (28.8.92).............	4·75	1·10
	ab. Black (recess inscr) inverted................	£6500	
	ac. Imperf (pair)..	£800	
	ad. Black roof (1993).................................	10·00	1·25
1278	$2 McAdam Railway Station, New Brunswick (5.5.89).............................	2·25	50
	a. Chalk-surfaced paper (29.7.92)..............	11·00	2·40
	ab. Imperf (pair)..	£700	
1279	$5 Bonsecours Market, Montreal (28.5.90)....................................	4·75	4·00
1261/1279 Set of 22...		24·00	15·00

The later issues of the mammal series are slightly larger than the original three, measuring 27×21 mm.

Nos. 1269a, 1270a, 1270cb, 1275a, 1276a and 1276cb were only issued in stamp booklets, Nos. SB110, SB124, SB134, SB113, SB126 and SB136.

Nos. 1277a/ac and 1278a were printed by C.B.N. There was also a printing of the $5 by C.B.N. in September 1992, but this does not differ from the B.A.B.N. version. All C.B.N. printings are on thinner paper, less crisp than the initial printings.

No. 1277ad appears to be from new plates. In addition to the differences in the roof colour it shows a less solid blue background around the building.

For further designs as Type **548a**, but in a changed format, see Nos. 1479/81.

No. 1280 is vacant.

(Des P.-Y. Pelletier. Litho Ashton-Potter)

1988 (12 Feb). Winter Olympic Games, Calgary (1988) (5th issue). Vert designs as T **531**. Multicoloured. Fluorescent frame. P 12×12½ (37c.) or 12½ (others).

1281	37c. Slalom skiing......................................	85	50
	a. Pair. Nos. 1281/2..................................	1·60	1·00
1282	37c. Curling..	85	50
1283	43c. Figure skating....................................	85	45
1284	74c. Luge...	1·40	80
1281/1284 Set of 4...		3·50	2·00

Nos. 1281/2 were printed together, *se-tenant*, in horizontal and vertical pairs throughout the sheet.

549 Trade Goods, Blackfoot Encampment and Page from Anthony Henday's Journal

(Des F. Hagan. Litho Ashton-Potter)

1988 (17 Mar). Exploration of Canada (3rd series). Explorers of the West. T **549** and similar horiz designs. Multicoloured. Fluorescent frame. P 12½×13.

1285	37c. Type **549**..	1·00	70
	a. Block of 4. Nos. 1285/8........................	3·50	2·50
1286	37c. *Discovery* and map of George Vancouver's voyage...................................	1·00	70
1287	37c. Simon Fraser's expedition portaging canoes..	1·00	70
1288	37c. John Palliser's surveying equipment and view of prairie...................................	1·00	70
1285/1288 Set of 4...		3·50	2·50

Nos. 1285/8 were printed together, *se-tenant*, in different combinations throughout the sheet, giving ten blocks of 4 and ten single stamps.

550 "The Young Reader" (Ozias Leduc)

551 Mallard landing on Marsh

(Des P.-Y. Pelletier. Eng G. Prosser. Recess and photo B.A.B.N.)

1988 (20 May). Canadian Art (1st series). No fluorescent bands. P 13×13½.

1289	**550** 50c. multicoloured.............................	70	70

No. 1289 was issued in sheets of 16 with descriptive texts on the margins.

See also Nos. 1327, 1384, 1421, 1504, 1539, 1589, 1629, 1681, 1721, 1825, 1912, 2011, 2097 and 2133.

(Des J. Gault and T. Telmet. Litho C.B.N.)

1988 (1 June). Wildlife and Habitat Conservation. T **551** and similar horiz design. Multicoloured. Fluorescent frame. P 13×13½.

1290	37c. Type **551**..	1·00	50
	a. Pair. Nos. 1290/1..................................	2·00	1·00
1291	37c. Moose feeding in marsh.....................	1·00	50

Nos. 1290/1 were printed together, *se-tenant*, in horizontal and vertical pairs throughout the sheet.

552 Kerosene Lamp and Diagram of Distillation Plant

553 *Papilio brevicauda*

(Des R. Hill. Litho Ashton-Potter)

1988 (17 June). Canada Day. Science and Technology. Canadian Inventions (3rd series). T **552** and similar vert designs. Multicoloured. Fluorescent frame. P 12½×13.

1292	37c. Type **552**..	1·00	1·00
	a. Block of 4. Nos. 1292/5........................	3·50	3·50
1293	37c. Ears of Marquis wheat.......................	1·00	1·00

CANADA

1294	37c. Electron microscope and magnified image		1·00	1·00
1295	37c. Patient under "Cobalt 60" cancer therapy		1·00	1·00
1292/1295	Set of 4		3·50	3·50

Nos. 1292/5 were printed together, *se-tenant*, in blocks of 4 throughout the sheet.

(Des Heather Cooper. Litho Ashton-Potter)

1988 (4 July). Canadian Butterflies. T **553** and similar vert designs. Multicoloured. Fluorescent frame. P 12×12½.

1296	37c. Type **553**		80	1·00
	a. Block of four. Nos. 1296/9		2·75	3·50
1297	37c. *Lycaeides idas*		80	1·00
1298	37c. *Oeneis macounii*		80	1·00
1299	37c. *Papilio glaucus*		80	1·00
1296/1299	Set of 4		2·75	3·50

Nos. 1296/9 were printed together, *se-tenant*, in different combinations throughout the sheet, giving ten blocks of 4 and ten single stamps.

554 St. John's Harbour Entrance and Skyline

555 Club Members working on Forestry Project and Rural Scene

(Des L.-A. Rivard. Litho Ashton-Potter)

1988 (22 July). Centenary of Incorporation of St. John's, Newfoundland. Fluorescent frame. P 13½×13.

1300	**554**	37c. multicoloured	35	40

(Des Debbie Adams. Litho Ashton-Potter)

1988 (5 Aug). 75th Anniv of 4-H Clubs. Fluorescent frame. P 13½×13.

1301	**555**	37c. multicoloured	35	40

556 Saint-Maurice Ironworks

557 Tahltan Bear Dog

(Des Michèle Cayer and Hélène Racicot. Eng. Y. Baril. Recess and litho C.B.N.)

1988 (19 Aug). 250th Anniv of Saint-Maurice Ironworks, Québec. Fluorescent frame. P 13½.

1302	**556**	37c. black, pale orange and cinnamon	40	40

(Des Mia Lane and D. Nethercott. Litho Ashton-Potter)

1988 (26 Aug). Canadian Dogs. T **557** and similar horiz designs. Multicoloured. Fluorescent frame. P 12½×12.

1303	37c. Type **557**		1·25	1·40
	a. Block of 4. Nos. 1303/6		4·50	5·00
1304	37c. Nova Scotia Duck Tolling Retriever		1·25	1·40
1305	37c. Canadian Eskimo Dog		1·25	1·40
1306	37c. Newfoundland		1·25	1·40
1303/1306	Set of 4		4·50	5·00

Nos. 1303/6 were printed together, *se-tenant*, in different combinations throughout the sheet, giving ten blocks of 4 and ten single stamps.

558 Baseball, Glove and Pitch

559 Virgin with Inset of Holy Child

(Des L. Holloway. Litho C.B.N.)

1988 (14 Sept). 150th Anniv of Baseball in Canada. Fluorescent frame. P 13½×13.

1307	**558**	37c. multicoloured	35	40

(Des E. Roch and T. Yakobina. Litho Ashton-Potter)

1988 (27 Oct). Christmas. Icons. T **559** and similar multicoloured designs. Fluorescent frame. P 12½×13 (32c.) or 13½ (others).

1308	32c. Holy Family (36×21 *mm*)		45	55
	a. Booklet pane. No. 1308×10		4·00	
1309	37c. Type **559**		45	20
1310	43c. Virgin and Child		50	45
1311	74c. Virgin and Child (*different*)		90	75
1308/1311	Set of 4		2·00	1·75

On No. 1308 the left-hand third of the design area is taken up by a bar code which has fluorescent bands between the bars. This value was only available from $3.20 stamp booklets, No. SB109, which had the sides and bottom of the pane imperforate. It was intended for use on greeting cards posted on or before 31 January 1989.

No. 1309 also commemorates the Millennium of Ukrainian Christianity.

560 Bishop Inglis and Nova Scotia Church

561 Frances Ann Hopkins and "Canoe manned by Voyageurs"

(Des S. Slipp and K. Sollows. Litho Ashton-Potter)

1988 (1 Nov). Bicentenary of Consecration of Charles Inglis (first Canadian Anglican bishop) (1987). Fluorescent frame. P 12½×12.

1312	**560**	37c. multicoloured	35	40

(Des D. Nethercott. Litho Ashton-Potter)

1988 (18 Nov). 150th Birth Anniv of Frances Ann Hopkins (artist). Fluorescent frame. P 13½×13.

1313	**561**	37c. multicoloured	35	40

562 Angus Walters and *Bluenose* (yacht)

563 Chipewyan Canoe

(Des R. Hill. Litho Ashton-Potter)

1988 (18 Nov). 20th Death Anniv of Angus Walters (yachtsman). Fluorescent frame. P 13½.

1314	**562**	37c. multicoloured	40	40

(Des B. Leduc and L.-A. Rivard. Litho Ashton-Potter)

1989 (1 Feb). Small Craft of Canada (1st series). Native Canoes. T **563** and similar horiz designs. Multicoloured. Fluorescent frame. P 13½×13.

1315	38c. Type **563**		90	70
	a. Block of 4. Nos. 1315/18		3·25	2·50
1316	38c. Haida canoe		90	70
1317	38c. Inuit kayak		90	70
1318	38c. Micmac canoe		90	70
1315/1318	Set of 4		3·25	2·50

Nos. 1315/18 were printed together, *se-tenant*, throughout the sheet, giving ten blocks of 4 and ten single stamps.

See also Nos. 1377/80 and 1428/31.

564 Matonabbee and Hearne's Expedition

565 Construction of Victoria Bridge, Montreal and William Notman

CANADA

(Des F. Hagan. Litho Ashton-Potter)

1989 (22 Mar). Exploration of Canada (4th series). Explorers of the North. T **564** and similar horiz designs. Multicoloured. Fluorescent frame. P 12½×13.

1319	38c. Type **564**...	1·25	75
	a. Block of 4. Nos. 1319/22........................	4·50	2·75
1320	38c. Relics of Franklin's expedition and White Ensign...	1·25	75
1321	38c. Joseph Tyrrell's compass, hammer and fossil...	1·25	75
1322	38c. Vilhjalmur Stefansson, camera on tripod and sledge dog team........................	1·25	75
1319/1322 Set of 4...		4·50	2·75

Nos. 1319/22 were printed together, *se-tenant*, in different combinations throughout the sheet, giving ten blocks of 4 and ten single stamps.

(Des J. Morin and T. Yakobina. Litho Ashton-Potter)

1989 (23 June). Canada Day. "150 Years of Canadian Photography". T **565** and similar horiz designs, each showing early photograph and photographer. Multicoloured. P 12½×12.

1323	38c. Type **565**...	85	85
	a. Block of 4. Nos. 1323/6..........................	3·00	3·00
1324	38c. Plains Indian village and W. Hanson Boorne...	85	85
1325	38c. Horse-drawn sleigh and Alexander Henderson...	85	85
1326	38c. Quebec street scene and Jules-Ernest Livernois...	85	85
1323/1326 Set of 4...		3·00	3·00

Nos. 1323/6 were printed together, *se-tenant*, in blocks of 4 throughout the sheet.

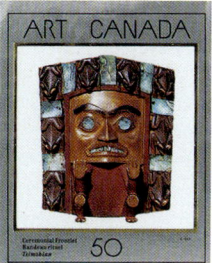

566 Tsimshian Ceremonial Frontlet, *c* 1900

567 Canadian Flag and Forest

(Des P-Y. Pelletier. Litho and die-stamped Ashton-Potter)

1989 (29 June). Canadian Art (2nd series). No fluorescent bands. P 12½×13.

1327	**566**	50c. multicoloured.......................................	1·00	60

No. 1327 was issued in a similar sheet format to No. 1289.

(Des Gottschalk & Ash International, Litho Ashton-Potter)

1989 (30 June)–93. T **567** and similar horiz designs. Multicoloured. Fluorescent frame. Self-adhesive. Die-cut.

1328	38c. Type **567**...	1·50	2·75
	aa. Blue omitted...	£650	
	ab. Yellow omitted.......................................	£325	
	a. Booklet pane. No. 1328×12....................	14·00	
1328*b*	39c. Canadian flag and prairie (8.2.90).........	1·50	2·75
	ba. Booklet pane. No. 1328*b*×12.................	14·00	
1328*c*	40c. Canadian flag and sea (11.1.91)..............	1·75	1·75
	ca. Booklet pane. No. 1328*c*×12.................	16·00	
1328*d*	42c. Canadian flag and mountains (28.1.92)..	2·00	3·00
	da. Booklet pane. No. 1328*d*×12.................	22·00	
1328*e*	43c. Canadian flag over lake (15.2.93)...........	1·75	2·50
	ea. Booklet pane. No. 1328*e*×12.................	16·00	
1328/1328*e* Set of 5..		7·75	11·00

Nos. 1328, 1328*b*, 1328*c*, 1328*d* and 1328*e* were only available from self-adhesive booklets, Nos. SB116, SB127, SB139, SB153 and SB168, in which the backing card forms the booklet cover.

568 Archibald Lampman

569 *Clavulinopsis fusiformis*

(Des R. Milot. Litho Ashton-Potter)

1989 (7 July). Canadian Poets. T **568** and similar horiz design. Multicoloured. Fluorescent frame. P 13½.

1329	38c. Type **568**...	1·25	1·40
	a. Pair. Nos. 1329/30....................................	2·50	2·75
1330	38c. Louis-Honoré Fréchette........................	1·25	1·40

Nos. 1329/30 were printed together, *se-tenant*, in horizontal and vertical pairs throughout the sheet.

(Des E. Roch. Litho Ashton-Potter)

1989 (4 Aug). Mushrooms. T **569** and similar vert designs. Multicoloured. Fluorescent frame. P 13½.

1331	38c. Type **569**...	70	1·00
	a. Block of 4. Nos. 1331/4...........................	2·50	3·50
1332	38c. *Boletus mirabilis*...................................	70	1·00
1333	38c. *Cantharellus cinnabarinus*....................	70	1·00
1334	38c. *Morchella esculenta*..............................	70	1·00
1331/1334 Set of 4...		2·50	3·50

Nos. 1331/4 were printed together, *se-tenant*, in different combinations throughout the sheet, giving ten blocks of 4 and ten single stamps.

570 Night Patrol, Korea

571 Globe in Box

(Des N. Fontaine, J. Gault and T. Telmet. Eng Y. Baril. Recess and litho C.B.N.)

1989 (8 Sept). 75th Anniv of Canadian Regiments. T **570** and similar horiz design. Multicoloured. Fluorescent frame. P 13.

1335	38c. Type **570** (Princess Patricia's Canadian Light Infantry)..	1·75	1·75
	a. Vert pair. Nos. 1335/6.............................	3·50	3·50
1336	38c. Trench raid, France, 1914–18 (Royal 22e Régiment)................................	1·75	1·75

Nos. 1335/6 were printed together, *se-tenant*, in vertical pairs throughout the sheet.

(Des L. Holloway and Nita Wallace. Litho Ashton-Potter)

1989 (2 Oct). Canada Export Trade Month. Fluorescent frame. P 13½×13.
1337	**571**	38c. multicoloured.......................................	40	45

572 Film Director

573 "Snow II" (Lawren S. Harris)

(Des W. Tibbles from paper sculptures by J. Milne. Litho Ashton-Potter)

1989 (14 Oct). Arts and Entertainment. T **572** and similar vert designs. Fluorescent frame. P 13×13½.

1338	38c. grey-brown, blackish brown and bright reddish violet..	1·00	1·25
	a. Block of 4. Nos. 1338/41........................	3·50	4·50
1339	38c. grey-brown, blackish brown and bright green..	1·00	1·25
1340	38c. grey-brown, blackish brown & bright magenta...	1·00	1·25
1341	38c. grey-brown, blackish brown and new blue..	1·00	1·25
1338/1341 Set of 4...		3·50	4·50

Designs:—No. 1339, Actors; No. 1340, Dancers; No. 1341, Musicians.
Nos. 1338/41 were printed together, *se-tenant*, in different combinations throughout the sheet, giving ten blocks of 4 and ten single stamps.

(Des D. Nethercott and Viviane Warburton. Litho Ashton-Potter)

1989 (26 Oct). Christmas. Paintings of Winter Landscapes. T **573** and similar multicoloured designs. Fluorescent frame. P 12½×13 (33c.), 13×13½ (38c.) or 13½ (others).

1342	33c. "Champ-de-Mars, Winter" (William Brymner) (35×21 *mm*)................	1·00	65
	a. Booklet pane. No. 1342*x*×10....................	9·00	
	b. Imperf between (horiz pair) (from booklet)..	£1200	

67

1343	38c. "Bend in the Gosselin River" (Marc-Aurèle Suzor-Coté) (21×35 mm)		40	25
	a. Perf 13×12½		3·50	1·25
	ab. Booklet pane. No. 1343a×10		32·00	
1344	44c. Type **573**		65	50
	a. Booklet pane. No. 1344×5 plus one printed label		13·00	
1345	76c. "Ste. Agnès" (A. H. Robinson)		1·40	85
	a. Booklet pane. No. 1345×5 plus one printed label		22·00	
1342/1345 Set of 4			3·00	2·00

On No. 1342 the left-hand third of the design area is taken up by a bar code which has fluorescent bands between the bars. This value was only available from $3.30 stamp booklets, No. SB118, which had the sides and bottom of the pane imperforate. It was intended for use on greeting cards posted on or before 31 January 1990.

No. 1343a was only issued in $3.80 stamp booklets, SB119.

Booklet pane No. 1343ab has the outer edges of the pane imperforate while Nos. 1344a and 1345a (from SB117 and SB120) have the vertical edges imperforate.

574 Canadians listening to Declaration of War, 1939

(Des J.-P. Armanville and P.-Y. Pelletier. Litho C.B.N.)

1989 (10 Nov). 50th Anniv of Second World War (1st issue). T **574** and similar horiz designs. Fluorescent frame. P 13½.

1346	38c. black, silver and slate-purple	1·10	1·25
	a. Block of 4. Nos. 1346/9	4·00	4·50
1347	38c. black, silver and olive-grey	1·10	1·25
1348	38c. black, silver and grey-green	1·10	1·25
1349	38c. black, silver and azure	1·10	1·25
1346/1349 Set of 4		4·00	4·50

Designs:—No. 1347, Army mobilization; No. 1348, British Commonwealth air crew training; No. 1349, North Atlantic convoy.

Nos. 1346/9 were printed together, *se-tenant*, in different combinations throughout the sheet, giving four blocks of 4.

See also Nos. 1409/12, 1456/9, 1521/4, 1576/9, 1621/4 and 1625/8.

575 Canadian Flag

576

1989 (28 Dec)–2005. No fluorescent bands (1, 5c.) or fluorescent frame (39, 40, 42, 43, 45, 46, 47, 48, 49, 50, 51c.).

(a) Booklet stamps. T **575** *and similar horiz designs, each showing Canadian flag. Litho Ashton-Potter. Chalk-surfaced paper. P 13½×14*

1350	**575**	1c. multicoloured (12.1.90)	20	1·00
		a. Booklet pane. Nos. 1350, 1351×2 and 1352	1·40	
		b. Perf 12½×13	15·00	17·00
		ba. Booklet pane. Nos. 1350b, 1351a×2 and 1352a	40·00	
		c. Booklet pane. Nos. 1350×2, 1351 and 1353 (28.12.90)	2·00	
1351	–	5c. multicoloured (12.1.90)	40	30
		a. Perf 12½×13	7·50	8·50
1352	–	39c. multicoloured (12.1.90)	1·40	2·25
		a. Perf 12½×13	15·00	17·00
1353	–	40c. multicoloured (28.12.90)	2·00	2·75

(b) Litho (for printers see below). Chalk-surfaced paper. P 14½ (45c.), 13×13½ (46c.) or 13½×13 (others)

1354	**576**	39c. multicoloured	70	10
		a. Booklet pane. No. 1354×10 and two labels	10·00	
		b. Booklet pane. No. 1354×25 and two labels	20·00	
		c. Perf 12½×13 (2.90)	4·00	4·25
1355		40c. multicoloured (28.12.90)	80	10
		a. Booklet pane. No. 1355×10 and two labels	12·00	
		b. Booklet pane. No. 1355×25 and two labels	26·00	
1356		42c. multicoloured (27.12.91)	1·00	15
		a. Booklet pane. No. 1356×10	15·00	
		b. Booklet pane. No. 1356×25 and two labels	27·00	
		c. Booklet pane. No. 1356×50 and two labels	60·00	
1357	–	43c. multicoloured (30.12.92)	1·00	1·50
		a. Booklet pane. No. 1357×10	12·00	
		b. Booklet pane. No. 1357×25 and two labels	27·00	
		c. Perf 14½ (18.1.94)	1·60	1·75
		ca. Booklet pane. No. 1357c×10	14·00	
		cb. Booklet pane. No. 1357c×25 and two labels	27·00	
		cc. Imperf between (vert pair)	£550	
1358	–	45c. mult (17×21 mm) (31.7.95)	80	1·50
		a. Booklet pane. No. 1358×10	8·00	
		b. Booklet pane. No. 1358×25 and two labels	16·00	
		c. Perf 13½×13 (6.10.95)	1·40	1·50
		ca. Booklet pane. No. 1358c×10	12·00	
		cb. Booklet pane. No. 1358c×25 and two labels	26·00	
		d. Perf 13×13½ (16×20 mm) (2.2.98)	1·00	1·00
		da. Booklet pane. No. 1358d×10	9·00	
		db. Booklet pane. No. 1358d×30 (two blocks of 15 (5×3) separated by vertical gutter)	22·00	
1359	–	46c. mult (16×20 mm) (28.12.98)	1·10	65
		a. Booklet pane. No. 1359×10	10·00	

*(c) Coil stamps. Designs as T **575**, but different folds in flag. Recess C.B.N. P 10×imperf*

1360	–	39c. deep purple (8.2.90)	60	75
		a. Imperf (pair)	55·00	
1361	–	40c. indigo (28.12.90)	40	60
		a. Imperf (pair)	£130	
1362	–	42c. scarlet-vermilion (27.12.91)	40	60
		a. Imperf (pair)	65·00	
1363	–	43c. deep olive (30.12.92)	1·50	2·25
		a. Imperf (pair)	55·00	
1364	–	45c. bluish green (31.7.95)	65	1·50
		a. Imperf (pair)	55·00	
1365	–	46c. carmine-red (28.12.98)	60	1·25

(d) Self-adhesive booklet stamps. Litho Ashton-Potter Canada (Nos. 1366/a, 1367b, 1368), C.B.N. (Nos. 1367a and 1370/4e), Ashton-Potter, C.B.N. or Lowe-Martin (Nos. 1369/a). Chalk-surfaced paper. Die-cut perf 9 (48c.) or die cut (others)

1366	–	46c. multicoloured (28.12.98)	80	75
		a. Booklet pane. No. 1366×30	22·00	
1367	–	47c. multicoloured (28.12.00)	1·00	75
		a. Booklet pane. No. 1367×10	9·00	
		b. Booklet pane. No. 1367×30	26·00	
1368	–	48c. multicoloured (2.1.02)	80	1·50
		a. Booklet pane. No. 1368×10	7·00	
1369	–	49c. multicoloured (19.12.03)	1·10	1·50
		a. Booklet pane. No. 1369×10	10·00	
1370		50c. multicoloured (20.12.04)	1·10	1·25
		a. Booklet pane. Nos. 1370/4, each×2	10·00	
1371		50c. multicoloured (20.12.04)	1·10	1·25
1372		50c. multicoloured (20.12.04)	1·10	1·25
1373		50c. multicoloured (20.12.04)	1·10	1·25
1374		50c. multicoloured (20.12.04)	1·10	1·25

(d) Self-adhesive booklet stamps. Litho CBN. Fluorescent frame. Die-cut

1374a	51c. multicoloured (19.12.05)	1·00	1·25
	ab. Booklet pane. Nos. 1374a/e, each×2	9·00	
1374b	51c. multicoloured (19.12.05)	1·00	1·25
1374c	51c. multicoloured (19.12.05)	1·00	1·25
1374d	51c. multicoloured (19.12.05)	1·00	1·25
1374e	51c. multicoloured (19.12.05)	1·00	1·25

Designs: *Vert*—40c. (No. 1355) Canadian flag over forest; 42c. (No. 1356) Flag over mountains; 43c. (No. 1357) Flag over prairie; 45c. (No. 1358) Flag and skyscraper; 46c. (Nos. 1359, 1366) Canadian flag and iceberg; 47c. Canadian flag and inukshuk (Inuit cairn). *Horiz*—48c. Flag in front of Canada Post Headquarters, Ottawa; 49c. Flag and Edmonton; 50c.: (No. 1370) Broadway Bridge, Saskatoon; (1371) Durrell, South Twillingate Island, (1372) Shannon Falls, Squamish; (1373) Church of Saint-Hilaire, Quebec; No. 1374 Cruise boat and skyline, Toronto; 51c.: (1374a) Winter scene near New Glasgow, Prince Edward Island; (1374) Bridge, Bouctouche, New Brunswick; (1374c) Wind turbines, Pincher Creek, Alberta; (1374d) Southwest bastion, Lower Fort Garry National Historic Site, Manitoba; (1374e) Dogsled, St. Elias Mountains, Yukon.

Booklet panes Nos. 1350a/b, 1356a/c, 1357ca/cb, 1358a/b, 1358ca/cb, 1358da/db and 1359a have the vertical edges of the panes imperforate and each shows a margin at foot. Booklet panes Nos. 1354a/b, 1355a/b and 1357a/b are imperforate at top and bottom.

Booklet pane No. 1368a was printed in two vertical strips of three and one of four with the stamps within each strip separated by the die-cut perforations and the surplus self-adhesive backing paper around the stamps removed.

Due to changes in the Canada Post contracts the printing history of Nos. 1354/9 is very complex. Details are provided below with Ashton-Potter Ltd. printings shown as AP, Canadian Bank Note Co as CBN, Leigh-Mardon Ltd as LM and Ashton-Potter Canada Ltd. as APC.

39c. (No. 1354) CBN (28.12.89), AP (14.2.90)
(No. 1354a/b) AP (28.12.89)
(No. 1354c) AP (2.90)
40c. (No. 1355) CBN (28.12.90)
(Nos. 1355a/b) AP (28.12.90)
42c. (No. 1356/c) AP (27.12.91)
43c. (Nos. 1357/b) AP (30.12.92), CBN (14.11.94)
(Nos. 1357c/cb) LM (18.1.94)
45c. Nos. 1358/b) LM (31.7.95)
(No. 1358c/cb) CBN (6.10.95)
(No. 1358d) CBN (2.2.98), APC (2.2.98)
(No. 1358da) CBN (2.2.98)
(No. 1358db) APC (2.2.96)
46c. (No. 1359) CBN (28.12.98)

The C.B.N. printings of the 45c. (No. 1358c) show the copyright date on flag changed from "1990" to "1995".

Postal forgeries of Nos. 1359 and 1362 exist showing heavier printing across the foot of the design.

577 Norman Bethune in 1937, and performing Operation, Montreal

578 Maple Leaf Mosaic

(Des Wanda Lewicka, J. Morin and Liu Xiang Ping. Eng Hu Zhenyuan and Yan Bingwu. Recess and litho C.B.N.)

1990 (2 Mar). Birth Centenary of Dr. Norman Bethune (surgeon). T **577** and similar horiz design. Multicoloured. Fluorescent frame. P 13×13½.

1375	39c. Type **577**	1·75	2·25
	a. Pair. Nos. 1375/6	3·50	4·50
1376	39c. Bethune in 1939, and treating wounded Chinese soldiers	1·75	2·25

Nos. 1375/6 were printed together, se-tenant, in horizontal and vertical pairs throughout the sheet.

(Des B. Leduc and L.-A. Rivard. Litho Ashton-Potter)

1990 (15 Mar). Small Craft of Canada (2nd series). Early Work Boats. Horiz designs as T **563**. Multicoloured. Fluorescent frame. P 13½×13.

1377	39c. Fishing dory	1·10	1·50
	a. Block of 4. Nos. 1377/80	4·00	5·50
1378	39c. Logging pointer	1·10	1·50
1379	39c. York boat	1·10	1·50
1380	39c. North canoe	1·10	1·50
1377/1380	Set of 4	4·00	5·50

Nos. 1377/80 were printed together, se-tenant, throughout the sheet, giving ten blocks of 4 and ten single stamps.

(Des F. Peter. Recess and litho C.B.N.)

1990 (5 Apr). Multiculturalism. P 13.

1381	**578**	39c. multicoloured	35	40
		a. Black omitted	£750	

579 Mail Van (facing left)

580 Amerindian and Inuit Dolls

(Des J. Morin and A. Rochon. Litho Ashton-Potter)

1990 (3 May). "Moving the Mail". T **579** and similar horiz design. Multicoloured. Fluorescent frame. P 13½.

1382	39c. Type **579**	75	75
	a. Booklet pane. Nos. 1382/3, each×4	6·00	
	b. Booklet pane. Nos. 1382×5, 1383×4 and 3 labels	17·00	
1383	39c. Mail van (facing right)	75	75

Nos. 1382/3 were only issued in $9.75 stamp booklets No. SB128.

(Des P.-Y. Pelletier. Litho and die-stamped Ashton-Potter)

1990 (3 May). Canadian Art (3rd series). Vert design as T **550**. Multicoloured. No fluorescent bands. P 12½×13.

1384	50c. "The West Wind" (Tom Thomson)	1·00	1·00

No. 1384 was issued in a similar sheet format to No. 1289.

(Des Nita Wallace. Litho Ashton-Potter)

1990 (8 June). Dolls. T **580** and similar horiz designs. Multicoloured. Fluorescent frame. P 12½×12.

1385	39c. Type **580**	1·25	1·50
	a. Block of 4. Nos. 1385/8	4·50	5·50
1386	39c. 19th-century settlers' dolls	1·25	1·50
1387	39c. Commercial dolls, 1917–36	1·25	1·50
1388	39c. Commercial dolls, 1940–60	1·25	1·50
1385/1388	Set of 4	4·50	5·50

Nos. 1385/8 were printed together, se-tenant, in different combinations throughout the sheet, giving ten blocks of 4 and ten single stamps.

581 Canadian Flag and Fireworks

582 Stromatolites (fossil algae)

(Des C. Malenfant. Litho Ashton-Potter)

1990 (1 July*). Canada Day. Fluorescent frame. P 13×12½.

1389	**581**	39c. multicoloured	50	50
		a. Silver (inscr and value) omitted	£2000	

No. 1389 was issued in sheets of 16 with descriptive texts on the coloured margins.

*First day covers of No. 1389 are postmarked 29 June 1990. The stamp was available from two temporary post offices in Ottawa on Sunday 1 July, but was not sold throughout Canada until 3 July.

(Des R. Harder. Eng Y. Baril. Recess and litho C.B.N.)

1990 (12 July). Prehistoric Canada (1st series). Primitive Life. T **582** and similar horiz designs. Multicoloured. Fluorescent frame. P 13×13½.

1390	39c. Type **582**	1·25	1·50
	a. Block of 4. Nos. 1390/3	4·50	5·50
1391	39c. Opabinia regalis (soft invertebrate)	1·25	1·50
1392	39c. Paradoxides davidis (trilobite)	1·25	1·50
1393	39e. Eurypterus remipes (sea scorpion)	1·25	1·50
1390/1393	Set of 4	4·50	5·50

Nos. 1390/3 were printed together, se-tenant, in different combinations throughout the sheet, giving four blocks of 4 and four single stamps.

See also Nos. 1417/20, 1568/71 and 1613/16.

583 Acadian Forest

584 Clouds and Rainbow

(Des M. and Jan Waddell. Litho Ashton-Potter)

1990 (7 Aug). Canadian Forests. T **583** and similar horiz designs. Multicoloured. Fluorescent frame. P 12½×13.

1394	39c. Type **583**	80	70
	a. Block of 4. Nos. 1394/7	2·75	2·50
1395	39c. Great Lakes–St. Lawrence forest	80	70
1396	39c. Pacific Coast forest	80	70
1397	39c. Boreal forest	80	70
1394/1397	Set of 4	2·75	2·50

Nos. 1394/7 were printed together, se-tenant, in different combinations throughout the sheet, giving four blocks of 4 and four single stamps.

Nos. 1394/7 also exist as blocks of four of the same design surrounded by margins. Such blocks were not available from post offices, but could be obtained for $1 each at Petro-Canada filling stations by using a previously-distributed voucher in conjunction with the purchase of 25 litres of petrol. They could also be obtained, at face value, from the Canadian Philatelic Service by post.

(Des D. L'Allier and Dominique Trudeau. Litho Ashton-Potter)

1990 (5 Sept). 150th Anniv of Weather Observing in Canada. Fluorescent frame. P 12½×13½.

1398	**584**	39c. multicoloured	60	50

No. 1398 has a break in the lower vertical sides of the fluorescent frame to allow the clouds to run on to the margins.

CANADA

69

CANADA

585 "Alphabet" Bird
586 Sasquatch 

(Des Debbie Adams. Recess and litho C.B.N.)

1990 (7 Sept). International Literacy Year. Fluorescent frame. P 13½×13.
| 1399 | 585 | 39c. multicoloured | 40 | 50 |

(Des A. Cormack, Deborah Drew-Brook and R. Tibbles. Litho Ashton-Potter)

1990 (1 Oct). Legendary Creatures. T **586** and similar horiz designs. Multicoloured. Fluorescent frame. P 12½×13½.
1400	39c. Type **586**	1·25	1·50
	a. Block of 4. Nos. 1400/3	4·50	5·50
	b. Perf 12½×12	6·50	6·50
	ba. Block of 4. Nos. 1400b/3b	24·00	24·00
1401	39c. Kraken	1·25	1·50
	b. Perf 12½×12	6·50	6·50
1402	39c. Werewolf	1·25	1·50
	b. Perf 12½×12	6·50	6·50
1403	39c. Ogopogo	1·25	1·50
	b. Perf 12½×12	6·50	6·50
1400/1403	Set of 4	4·50	5·50

Nos. 1400/3 were printed together, *se-tenant*, in different combinations throughout the sheet, giving ten blocks of four and ten single stamps.

Stamps perforated 12½×12 come from a small percentage of the "non-philatelic" stock without imprints. Examples have also been found on official First Day Covers included in Presentation Packs.

587 Agnes Macphail
588 "Virgin Mary with Christ Child and St. John the Baptist" (Norval Morrisseau) 

(Des M. and Jan Waddell. Litho Ashton-Potter)

1990 (9 Oct). Birth Centenary of Agnes Macphail (first woman elected to Parliament). Fluorescent frame. P 13×13½.
| 1404 | 587 | 39c. multicoloured | 40 | 50 |

(Des C. Malenfant. Litho Ashton-Potter)

1990 (25 Oct). Christmas. Native Art. T **588** and similar designs. Fluorescent frame. P 12½×13 (34c.) or 13½ (others).
1405	34c. multicoloured (35×21 *mm*)	65	55
	a. Booklet pane. No. 1405×10	6·00	
1406	39c. multicoloured	30	20
	a. Booklet pane. No. 1406×10	8·00	
1407	45c. multicoloured	35	45
	a. Booklet pane. No. 1407×5 plus one printed label	4·25	
1408	78c. black, bright scarlet and violet-grey	70	75
	a. Booklet pane. No. 1408×5 plus one printed label	9·00	
1405/1408	Set of 4	1·75	1·75

Designs:—34c. "Rebirth" (Jackson Beardy); 45c. "Mother and Child" (Inuit sculpture, Cape Dorset); 78c. "Children of the Raven" (Bill Reid).

On No. 1405 the left-hand third of the design area is taken up by a bar code which has fluorescent bands between the bars. This value was only available from $3.40 stamp booklets, No. SB130, which had the sides and bottom of the pane imperforate. It was intended for use on greeting cards posted on or before 31 January 1991.

Booklet panes Nos. 1406a, 1407a and 1408a (from Nos. SB129 and SB131/2)also have the side and bottom edges imperforate.

(Des J.-P. Armanville and P.-Y. Pelletier. Litho Ashton-Potter)

1990 (9 Nov). 50th Anniv of Second World War (2nd issue). Horiz designs as T **574**. Fluorescent frame. P 12½×12.
1409	39c. black, silver and grey-olive	2·00	2·00
	a. Block of 4. Nos. 1409/12	7·25	7·25
1410	39c. black, silver and red-brown	2·00	2·00
1411	39c. black, silver and bistre-brown	2·00	2·00
1412	39c. black, silver and dull mauve	2·00	2·00
1409/1412	Set of 4	7·25	7·25

Designs:—No. 1409, Canadian family at home, 1940; No. 1410, Packing parcels for the troops; No. 1411, Harvesting; No. 1412, Testing anti-gravity flying suit.

Nos. 1409/12 were printed together, *se-tenant*, in different combinations throughout the sheet, giving four blocks of 4.

589 Jennie Trout (first woman physician) and Women's Medical College, Kingston
590 Blue Poppies and Butchart Gardens, Victoria 

(Des R. Milot. Litho Ashton-Potter)

1991 (15 Mar). Medical Pioneers. T **589** and similar vert designs. Multicoloured. Fluorescent frame. P 13½.
1413	40c. Type **589**	1·10	90
	a. Block of 4. Nos. 1413/16	4·00	3·25
1414	40c. Wilder Penfield (neurosurgeon) and Montreal Neurological Institute	1·10	90
1415	40c. Frederick Banting (discoverer of insulin) and University of Toronto medical faculty	1·10	90
1416	40c. Harold Griffith (anesthesiologist) and Queen Elizabeth Hospital, Montreal	1·10	90
1413/1416	Set of 4	4·00	3·25

Nos. 1413/16 were printed together, *se-tenant*, in different combinations throughout the sheet, giving ten blocks of 4 and ten single stamps.

(Des R. Harder. Eng L. Bloss. Recess and litho Ashton-Potter)

1991 (5 Apr). Prehistoric Canada (2nd series). Primitive Vertebrates. Horiz designs as T **582**. Multicoloured. Fluorescent frame. P 12½×13½.
1417	40c. Foord's Crossopt (*Eusthenopteron foordi*) (fish fossil)	2·25	2·50
	a. Block of 4. Nos. 1417/20	8·00	9·00
1418	40c. *Hylonomus lyelli* (land reptile)	2·25	2·50
1419	40c. Fossil Conodonts (fossil teeth)	2·25	2·50
1420	40c. *Archaeopteris halliana* (early tree)	2·25	2·50
1417/1420	Set of 4	8·00	9·00

Nos. 1417/20 were printed together, *se-tenant*, in different combinations throughout the sheet, giving four blocks of 4 and four single stamps.

(Des P.-Y. Pelletier. Litho and die-stamped Ashton-Potter)

1991 (7 May). Canadian Art (4th series). Vert design as T **550**. Multicoloured. No fluorescent bands. P 12½×13.
| 1421 | 50c. "Forest, British Columbia" (Emily Carr) | 1·25 | 1·75 |

No. 1421 was issued in a similar sheet format to No. 1289.

(Des G. Gauci and D. Wyman. Litho Ashton-Potter)

1991 (22 May). Public Gardens. T **590** and similar vert designs. Multicoloured. Fluorescent frame. P 13×12½.
1422	40c. Type **590**	70	70
	a. Booklet pane. Nos. 1422/6, each×2	6·50	
1423	40c. Marigolds and International Peace Garden, Boissevain	70	70
1424	40c. Lilac and Royal Botanical Gardens, Hamilton	70	70
1425	40c. Roses and Montreal Botanical Gardens	70	70
1426	40c. Rhododendrons and Halifax Public Gardens	70	70
1422/1426	Set of 5	3·25	3·25

Nos. 1422/6 were only available from $4 stamp booklets (No. SB140) containing No. 1422a, which is imperforate at top and bottom.

CANADA

591 Maple Leaf   **592** South Nahanni River

(Des Lisa Miller, R. Séguin and J.-P. Veilleux. Litho C.B.N.)

1991 (28 June). Canada Day. Fluorescent frame. P 13½×13.
1427	**591**	40c. multicoloured	50	60

No. 1427 was issued in sheets of 20 with inscribed and decorated margins.

(Des B. Leduc and L.-A. Rivard. Litho Ashton-Potter)

1991 (18 July). Small Craft of Canada (3rd series). Horiz designs as T **563**. Multicoloured. Fluorescent frame. P 13½×13.
1428	40c. Verchère rowboat	1·40	1·40
	a. Block of 4. Nos. 1428/31	5·00	5·00
1429	40c. Touring kayak	1·40	1·40
1430	40c. Sailing dinghy	1·40	1·40
1431	40c. Cedar strip canoe	1·40	1·40
1428/1431	Set of 9	5·00	5·00

Nos. 1428/31 were printed together, *se-tenant*, throughout the sheet, giving ten blocks of 4 and ten single stamps.

(Des M. and Jan Waddell. Litho Ashton-Potter)

1991 (20 Aug). Canadian Rivers (1st series). T **592** and similar vert designs. Multicoloured. Fluorescent frame. P 13×12½.
1432	40c. Type **592**	1·00	1·40
	a. Booklet pane. Nos. 1432/6, each×2 with margins all round	8·00	
1433	40c. Athabasca River	1·00	1·40
1434	40c. Boundary Waters, Voyageur Waterway	1·00	1·40
1435	40c. Jacques-Cartier River	1·00	1·40
1436	40c. Main River	1·00	1·40
1432/1436	Set of 5	4·50	6·25

Nos. 1432/6 were only issued in $4 stamp booklets, No. SB141. See also Nos. 1492/6, 1558/62 and 1584/8.

593 "Leaving Europe"   **594** Ski Patrol rescuing Climber

(Des J. Gault and T. Telmet. Litho C.B.N.)

1991 (29 Aug). Centenary of Ukrainian Immigration. Panels from "The Ukrainian Pioneer" by William Kurelek. T **593** and similar vert designs. Multicoloured. Fluorescent frame. P 13½×13.
1437	40c. Type **593**	80	85
	a. Block of 4. Nos. 1437/40	2·75	3·00
1438	40c. "Canadian Winter"	80	85
1439	40c. "Clearing the Land"	80	85
1440	40c. "Harvest"	80	85
1437/1440	Set of 4	2·75	3·00

Nos. 1437/40 were printed together, *se-tenant*, in different combinations throughout the sheet, giving four blocks of 4 and four single stamps.

(Des Suzanne Duranceau. Litho C.B.N.)

1991 (23 Sept). Emergency Services. T **594** and similar vert designs. Multicoloured. Fluorescent frame. P 13½.
1441	40c. Type **594**	2·25	2·25
	a. Block of 4. Nos. 1441/4	8·00	8·00
1442	40c. Police at road traffic accident	2·25	2·25
1443	40c. Firemen on extending ladder	2·25	2·25
1444	40c. Boeing-Vertol CH-147 Chinook rescue helicopter and *Spindrift* (lifeboat)	2·25	2·25
1441/1444	Set of 4	8·00	8·00

Nos. 1441/4 were printed together, *se-tenant*, in different combinations throughout the sheet, giving ten blocks of 4 and ten single stamps.

595 "The Witched Canoe"   **596** Grant Hall Tower

(Des A. Cormack, Deborah Drew-Brook and R. Tibbles. Litho Ashton-Potter)

1991 (1 Oct). Canadian Folktales. T **595** and similar vert designs. Multicoloured. Fluorescent frame. P 13½×12½.
1445	40c. Type **595**	1·40	95
	a. Block of 4. Nos. 1445/8	5·00	3·50
1446	40c. "The Orphan Boy"	1·40	95
1447	40c. "Chinook"	1·40	95
1448	40c. "Buried Treasure"	1·40	95
1445/1448	Set of 4	5·00	3·50

Nos. 1445/8 were printed together, *se-tenant*, in different combinations throughout the sheet, giving ten blocks of 4 and ten single stamps.

(Des L. Holloway and R. Kerr. Litho Ashton-Potter)

1991 (16 Oct). 150th Anniv of Queen's University, Kingston. Fluorescent frame. P 13×12½.
1449	**596**	40c. multicoloured	1·10	1·00
		a. Booklet pane. No. 1449×10 plus two printed labels with margins all round	9·50	

No. 1449 was only issued in $4 stamp booklets, No. SB142.

597 North American Santa Claus   **598** Players jumping for Ball

(Des S. Slipp. Litho Ashton-Potter)

1991 (23 Oct). Christmas. T **597** and similar multicoloured designs. Fluorescent frame. P 12½×13 (35c.) or 13½ (others).
1450	35c. British Father Christmas (35×21 *mm*)	1·00	1·00
	a. Booklet pane. No. 1450×10	10·00	
1451	40c. Type **597**	1·00	20
	a. Booklet pane. No. 1451×10	10·00	
1452	46c. French Bonhomme Noel	1·25	1·60
	a. Booklet pane. No. 1452×5 plus one printed label	6·25	
1453	80c. Dutch Sinterklaas	2·00	3·75
	a. Booklet pane. No. 1453×5 plus one printed label	10·00	
1450/1453	Set of 4	4·75	6·00

On No. 1450 the left-hand third of the design area is taken up by a bar code which has fluorescent bands between the bars. This value was only available from $3.50 stamp booklets, No. SB144, which had the edges of the pane imperforate. It was intended for use on greeting cards posted on or before 31 January 1992.

Nos. 1451a, 1452a and 1453a (from Nos. SB143 and SB145/6) also have the vertical edges of the panes imperforate.

(Des J. Gault, C. Reynolds and T. Telmet. Litho Ashton-Potter)

1991 (25 Oct). Basketball Centenary. T **598** and similar vert designs. Multicoloured. Fluorescent frame. P 13×13½.
1454	40c. Type **598**	1·50	75
MS1455	155×90 mm. 40c. Type **598**, but with shorter inscr below face value; 46c. Player taking shot; 80c. Player challenging opponent	6·50	6·00

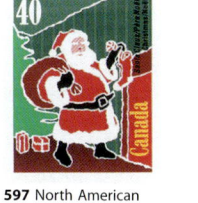

(Des J.-P. Armanville and P.-Y. Pelletier. Litho C.B.N.)

1991 (8 Nov). 50th Anniv of Second World War (3rd issue). Horiz designs as T **574**. Fluorescent frame. P 13½.
1456	40c. black silver and greenish blue	2·00	2·00
	a. Block of 4. Nos. 1456/9	7·25	7·25
1457	40c. black, silver and brown	2·00	2·00

71

STANLEY GIBBONS

Commonwealth Department

Newly listed Canada errors
recently offered from our ever changing stock

SG899a
1977 Inuit, grey omitted.
25 reported

SG883a
1977-86 50c "Ghost town",
brown omitted. 150 possible

SG1479a
1991-96 $1 Court House, perf 14½x14
dark blue omitted. 25 existed

SG1480a
1991-96 $2 Truro School, perf 14½x14 dark
turquoise-blue omitted. Circa 100 reported

SG884ba
1977-86 $1 Glacier, blue omitted

If you would like to receive our bi-monthly illustrated list, contact
Pauline MacBroom on 020 7557 4450 or by email at pmacbroom@stanleygibbons.com
or Brian Lucas on 020 7557 4418 or by email at blucas@stanleygibbons.com

Stanley Gibbons Limited, 399 Strand, London WC2R 0LX
Tel: 020 7836 8444   Fax: 020 7557 4499

To view all of our stock 24 hours a day visit **www.stanleygibbons.com**

1458	40c. black, silver and lilac		2·00	2·00
1459	40c. black, silver and ochre		2·00	2·00
1456/1459	Set of 4		7·25	7·25

Designs:—No. 1456, Women's services, 1941; No. 1457, Armament factory; No. 1458, Cadets and veterans; No. 1459, Defence of Hong Kong.

Nos. 1456/9 were printed together, *se-tenant*, in different combinations throughout the sheet, giving four blocks of 4.

599 Blueberry   **600** McIntosh Apple

600a Court House, Yorkton

(Des Tania Craan and D. Noble (1c. to 25c.), C. Malenfant (48c. to 90c.), R. Bellemare ($1, $2, $5))

1991 (27 Dec)–**96**. Multicoloured. Chalk-surfaced paper.

(a) Edible Berries. Litho (for printers see below). T **599** *and similar horiz designs. No fluorescent frame. P 13×13½ (5.8.92)*

1460	1c. Type **599**		10	10
1461	2c. Wild Strawberry		10	10
1462	3c. Black Crowberry		50	10
1463	5c. Rose Hip		10	10
1464	6c. Black Raspberry		10	10
1465	10c. Kinnikinnick		10	10
	a. Imperf (horiz pair)			
1466	25c. Saskatoon Berry		25	25

(b) Fruit and Nut Trees. Litho (for printers see below). T **600** *and similar horiz designs. Three fluorescent bands (90c.) or fluorescent frame (others). P 13*

1467	48c. Type **600**		50	35
	a. Perf 14½×14		1·60	1·00
	ab. Booklet pane. No. 1467a×5 and label		8·00	
1468	49c. Delicious Apple (30.12.92)		2·50	1·00
	a. Booklet pane. No. 1468×5 and label (7.1.94)		11·00	
	b. Perf 14½×14		2·00	1·75
	ba. Booklet pane. No. 1468b×5 and label		9·00	
1469	50c. Snow Apple (25.2.94)		1·50	1·00
	a. Booklet pane. No. 1469×5 and label		7·50	
	b. Perf 14½×14 (27.3.95)		3·25	2·00
	ba. Booklet pane. No. 1469b×5 and label		15·00	
1470	52c. Gravenstein Apple (31.7.95)		1·60	50
	a. Booklet pane. No. 1470×5 and label		7·00	
	b. Perf 14½×14 (6.10.95)		3·00	70
	ba. Booklet pane. No. 1470b×5 and label		13·00	
1471	65c. Black Walnut		1·75	50
1472	67c. Beaked Hazelnut (30.12.92)		1·75	1·25
1473	69c. Shagbark Hickory (25.2.94)		2·75	1·25
1474	71c. American Chestnut (31.7.95)		3·00	1·00
	a. Perf 14½×14 (6.10.95)		3·25	1·75
1475	84c. Stanley Plum		1·00	75
	a. Perf 14½×14		3·00	1·50
	ab. Booklet pane. No. 1475a×5 and label		13·00	
1476	86c. Bartlett Pear (30.12.92)		2·75	1·00
	a. Booklet pane. No. 1476×5 and label (7.1.94)		12·00	
	b. Perf 14½×14		3·50	4·25
	ba. Booklet pane. No. 1476b×5 and label		16·00	
1477	88c. Westcot Apricot (25.2.94)		1·75	1·60
	a. Booklet pane. No. 1477×5 and label		11·00	
	b. Three fluorescent bands (14.11.94)		3·25	3·75
	ba. Booklet pane. No. 1477b×5 and label		15·00	
	c. Perf 14½×14. Three fluorescent bands (27.3.95)		3·75	4·25
	ca. Booklet pane. No. 1477c×5 and label		17·00	
1478	90c. Elberta Peach (31.7.95)		1·60	1·00
	a. Booklet pane. No. 1478×5 and label		7·00	
	b. Perf 14½×14 (6.10.95)		3·00	2·50
	ba. Booklet pane. No. 1478b×5 and label		13·00	

(c) Architecture. Recess and litho Leigh-Mardon Ltd, Melbourne (Nos. 1479/80) or C.B.N. (Nos. 1479a, 1480a, 1481). T **600a** *and similar horiz designs. P 14½×14 ($1, $2) or 13½×13 ($5)*

1479	$1 Type **600a** (21.2.94)		2·25	1·00
	a. Deep turquoise-blue (recess inscr) omitted		£1200	
	b. Perf 13½×13 (20.2.95)		2·75	1·00
	ba. Deep turquoise-blue (recess inscr) omitted		£1100	
1480	$2 Provincial Normal School, Truro (21.2.94)		2·75	2·25
	a. Deep turquoise-blue (recess inscr) omitted		£700	
	b. Perf 13½×13 (20.2.95)		3·50	1·60
	ba. Deep turquoise blue (recess inscr) omitted		£1200	
	bb. Deep turquoise-blue (recess inscr) inverted		£4250	
1481	$5 Public Library, Victoria (29.2.96)		7·00	4·75
1460/1481	Set of 22		26·00	17·00

Nos. 1460/6 were so printed that each horizontal row formed a composite design.

Nos. 1467a, 1468b, 1469b, 1475a, 1476b and 1477c were only issued in stamp booklets.

Booklet panes Nos. 1467ab, 1468a, 1468ba, 1475a, 1476a, 1476ab, 1477a and 1477ba each have the vertical edges of the pane imperforate and margins at top and bottom.

Due to changes in the Canada Post contracts the printing history of Nos. 1460/80 is very complex. Details are provided below with Ashton-Potter Ltd printings shown as AP, Canadian Bank Note Co as CBN, Leigh-Mardon Ltd as LM and Ashton-Potter Canada Ltd as APC.

1c. No. 1460 AP (5.8.92), CBN (19.8.94), APC (3.4.95)
2c. No. 1461 AP (5.8.92), CBN (22.4.94), APC (1.8.95)
3c. No. 1462 AP (5.8.92), CBN (22.4.94), APC (2.5.97)
5c. No. 1463 AP (5.8.92), CBN (11.3.94), APC (20.9.95)
6c. No. 1464 AP (5.8.92), CBN (11.3.94)
10c. No. 1465 AP (5.8.92), CBN (11.3.94), APC (1.9.95)
25c. No. 1466 AP (5.8.92), CBN (22.4.94), APC (1.5.96)
48c. Nos. 1467/ab AP (27.12.91)
49c. No. 1468 AP (30.12.92), CBN (7.1.94)
  No. 1468a CBN (7.1.94)
  Nos. 1468b/ba AP (30.12.92)
50c. No. 1469 CBN (25.2.94), APC (10.4.95)
  No. 1469a CBN (25.2.94)
  Nos. 1469b/ba APC (27.3.95)
52c. No. 1470 CBN (31.7.95), APC (6.10.95)
  No. 1470a CBN (31.7.95), APC (1997)
  Nos. 1470b/ba APC (6.10.95)
65c. No. 1471 AP (27.12.91)
67c. No. 1472 AP (30.12.92)
69c. No. 1473 CBN (25.2.94), APC (10.4.95)
71c. No. 1474 CBN (31.7.95), APC (6.10.95)
  No. 1474a APC (6.10.95)
84c. Nos. 1475/ab AP (27.12.91)
86c. No. 1476 AP (30.12.92), CBN (7.1.94)
  No. 1476a CBN (7.1.94)
  Nos. 1476b/ba AP (30.12.92)
88c. Nos. 1477/a CBN (25.2.94)
  No. 1477b CBN (14.11.94), APC (10.4.95)
  No. 1477ba CBN (14.11.94)
  Nos. 1477c/ca APC (27.3.95)
90c. No. 1478 CBN (31.7.95), APC (6.10.95)
  No. 1478a CBN (31.7.95), APC (1997)
  Nos. 1478b/ba APC (6.10.95)
$1 No. 1479 LM (21.2.94)
  No. 1479a CBN (20.2.95)
$2 No. 1480 LM (21.2.94)
  No. 1480a CBN (20.2.95)
$5 No. 1481 CBN (29.2.96)

601 Ski Jumping

(Des Gottschalk & Ash International. Litho Ashton-Potter)

1992 (7 Feb). Winter Olympic Games, Albertville. T **601** and similar horiz designs. Multicoloured. Fluorescent frame. P 12½×13.

1482	42c. Type **601**		1·25	1·25
	a. Booklet pane. Nos. 1482/6, each×2 with margins all round		11·00	
1483	42c. Figure skating		1·25	1·25
1484	42c. Ice hockey		1·25	1·25
1485	42c. Bobsleighing		1·25	1·25
1486	42c. Alpine skiing		1·25	1·25
1482/1486	Set of 5		5·75	5·75

Nos. 1482/6 were only available from $4.20 stamp booklets, No. SB154.

CANADA

602 Ville-Marie in 17th Century

603 Road Bed Construction and Route Map

(Des Suzanne Duranceau and P.-Y. Pelletier. Litho C.B.N.)

1992 (25 Mar). "CANADA 92" International Youth Stamp Exhibition, Montreal. T **602** and similar horiz designs. Multicoloured. Fluorescent frame. P 13½.

1487	42c. Type **602**	1·50	1·50
	a. Pair. Nos. 1487/8	3·00	3·00
1488	42c. Modern Montreal	1·50	1·50
1489	48c. Compass rose, snow shoe and crow's nest of Cartier's ship *Grande Hermine*	2·25	1·25
1490	84c. Atlantic map, Aztec "calendar stone" and navigational instrument	3·50	4·50
1487/1490 Set of 4		8·00	8·00
MS1491 181×120 mm. Nos. 1487/90		8·00	8·00

Nos. 1487/8 were printed together, *se-tenant*, in horizontal and vertical pairs throughout the sheet.

No. **MS**1491 also exists showing the facsimile signature of Paul Chomedy de Maisonneuve printed at bottom right. These miniature sheets were prepared in connection with "CANADA '92", but were not sold by the Canadian Post Office.

(Des M. and Jan Waddell. Litho Ashton-Potter)

1992 (22 Apr). Canadian Rivers (2nd series). Multicoloured designs as T **592**, but horiz. Fluorescent frame. P 12½×13.

1492	42c. Margaree River	1·50	1·50
	a. Booklet pane. Nos. 1492/6, each×2	13·00	
1493	42c. West (Eliot) River	1·50	1·50
1494	42c. Ottawa River	1·50	1·50
1495	42c. Niagara River	1·50	1·50
1496	42c. South Saskatchewan River	1·50	1·50
1492/1496 Set of 5		6·75	6·75

Nos. 1492/6 were only issued in $4.20 stamp booklets, No. SB155.

Booklet pane No. 1492a has the horizontal edges of the pane imperforate.

(Des J. Charette and Vivian Lalibérté. Litho C.B.N.)

1992 (15 May). 50th Anniv of Alaska Highway. Fluorescent frame. P 13½.

1497	**603**	42c. multicoloured	1·50	70

(Des Gottschalk & Ash International. Litho Ashton-Potter)

1992 (15 June). Olympic Games, Barcelona. Horiz designs as T **601**. Multicoloured. Fluorescent frame. P 12½×13.

1498	42c. Gymnastics	1·10	1·25
	a. Booklet pane. Nos. 1498/1502 each×2 with margins all round	10·00	
1499	42c. Athletics	1·10	1·25
1500	42c. Diving	1·10	1·25
1501	42c. Cycling	1·10	1·25
1502	42c. Swimming	1·10	1·25
1498/1502 Set of 5		5·00	5·50

Nos. 1498/1502 were only available from $4.20 stamp booklets, No. SB156.

No. 1503 is vacant.

604 "Quebec, Patrimoine Mondial" (A. Dumas)

605 Jerry Potts (scout)

(Des P.-Y. Pelletier. Litho Ashton-Potter)

1992 (29 June). Canada Day. Paintings. T **604** and similar diamond-shaped designs. Multicoloured. Fluorescent frame. P 13×12½.

1503a	42c. Type **604**	1·50	1·75
	ab. Sheetlet. Nos. 1503a/l	16·00	19·00
1503b	42c. "Christie Passage, Hurst Island, British Columbia" (E. J. Hughes)	1·50	1·75
1503c	42c. "Torono Landmarks of Time" (Ontario) (V. McIndoe)	1·50	1·75
1503d	42c. "Near the Forks" (Manitoba) (S. Gouthro)	1·50	1·75
1503e	42c. "Off Cape St. Francis" (Newfoundland) (R. Shepherd)	1·50	1·75
1503f	42c. "Crowd at City Hall" (New Brunswick) (Molly Bobak)	1·50	1·75
1503g	42c. "Across the Tracks to Shop" (Alberta) (Janet Mitchell)	1·50	1·75
1503h	42c. "Cove Scene" (Nova Scotia) (J. Norris)	1·50	1·75
1503i	42c. "Untitled" (Saskatchewan) (D. Thauberger)	1·50	1·75
1503j	42c. "Town Life" (Yukon) (T. Harrison)	1·50	1·75
1503k	42c. "Country Scene" (Prince Edward Island) (Erica Rutherford)	1·50	1·75
1503l	42c. "Playing on an Igloo" (Northwest Territories) (Agnes Nanogak)	1·50	1·75
1503a/1503l Set of 12		16·00	19·00

(Des P.-Y. Pelletier. Litho and die-stamped Ashton-Potter)

1992 (29 June). Canadian Art (5th series). Vert design as T **550**. Multicoloured. No fluorescent bands. P 12½×13.

1504	50c. "Red Nasturtiums" (David Milne)	1·25	1·40

No. 1504 was issued in a similar sheet format to No. 1289.

(Des A. Cormack, Deborah Cormack and R. Tibbles. Litho Ashton-Potter)

1992 (8 Sept). Folk Heroes. T **605** and similar vert designs. Multicoloured. Fluorescent frame. P 12½.

1505	42c. Type **605**	1·25	1·50
	a. Block of 4. Nos. 1505/8	4·50	5·50
1506	42c. Capt. William Jackman and wreck of *Sea Clipper*, 1867	1·25	1·50
1507	42c. Laura Secord (messenger)	1·25	1·50
1508	42c. Jos Montferrand (lumberjack)	1·25	1·50
1505/1508 Set of 4		4·50	5·50

Nos. 1505/8 were printed together, *se-tenant*, in different combinations throughout the sheet, giving ten blocks of 4 and ten single stamps.

606 Copper

607 Satellite and Photographs from Space

(Des R. Bellemare. Litho Ashton-Potter)

1992 (21 Sept). 150th Anniv of Geological Survey of Canada. Minerals. T **606** and similar horiz designs. Multicoloured. Fluorescent frame. P 12½.

1509	42c. Type **606**	1·75	2·00
	a. Booklet pane. Nos. 1509/13, each×2 with margins all round	15·00	
1510	42c. Sodalite	1·75	2·00
1511	42c. Gold	1·75	2·00
1512	42c. Galena	1·75	2·00
1513	42c. Grossular	1·75	2·00
1509/1513 Set of 5		8·00	9·00

Nos. 1509/13 were only issued in $4.20 stamp booklets, No. SB157.

(Des Debbie Adams. Litho C.B.N.)

1992 (1 Oct). Canadian Space Programme. T **607** and similar horiz design. Multicoloured. Fluorescent frame. P 13.

1514	42c. Type **607**	1·25	1·75
	a. Horiz pair. Nos. 1514/15	2·50	3·50
	b. Silver omitted	£2250	
1515	42c. Space Shuttle over Canada (hologram) (32×26 *mm*)	1·25	1·75
	a. Hologram omitted	£1500	

Nos. 1514/15 were printed together, *se-tenant*, in horizontal pairs throughout the sheet of 20 with No. 1514 occurring on the first and fourth vertical rows and No. 1515 on the second and third.

608 Babe Siebert, Skates and Stick

609 Companion of the Order of Canada Insignia

(Des L. Holloway and R. Kerr. Litho Ashton-Potter)

1992 (9 Oct). 75th Anniv of National Ice Hockey League. T **608** and similar horiz designs. Multicoloured. Fluorescent frame. P 13×12½.
1516	42c. Type **608**...	1·60	1·75
	a. Booklet pane. No. 1516×8 plus one printed label with margins all round.......	11·50	
1517	42c. Claude Provost, Terry Sawchuck and team badges..	1·60	1·75
	a. Booklet pane. No. 1517×8 plus one printed label with margins all round.......	11·50	
1518	42c. Hockey mask, gloves and modern player .	1·60	1·75
	a. Booklet pane. No. 1518×9 with margins all round	13·00	
1516/1518 Set of 3		4·25	4·75

Nos. 1516/18 were only issued in $10.50 stamp booklets, No. SB158.
Booklet pane Nos. 1516a/18a only exist folded between the first and second vertical rows.

(Des Tania Craan. Litho Ashton-Potter)

1992 (21 Oct). 25th Anniv of the Order of Canada and Daniel Roland Michener (former Governor-General) Commemoration. T **609** and similar vert design. Multicoloured. Fluorescent frame. P 12½.
1519	42c. Type **609**...	1·40	1·75
	a. Pair. Nos. 1519/20...........................	2·75	3·50
1520	42c. Daniel Roland Michener..................	1·40	1·75

Nos. 1519/20 were printed together, *se-tenant*, within the sheet of 25 (5×5) with sixteen examples of No. 1519 (R. 1/1-5, 2/1, 2/5, 3/1, 3/5, 4/1, 4/5, 5/1-5) and nine of No. 1520 (R. 2/2-4, 3/2-4, 4/2-4).

(Des J.-P. Armanville and P.-Y. Pelletier. Litho C.B.N)

1992 (10 Nov). 50th Anniv of Second World War (4th issue). Horiz designs as T **574**. Fluorescent frame. P 13½.
1521	42c. black, silver and sepia....................	2·25	2·50
	a. Block of 4. Nos. 1521/4....................	8·00	9·00
1522	42c. black, silver and dull blue-green.........	2·25	2·50
1523	42c. black, silver and brown....................	2·25	2·50
1524	42c. black, silver and light blue................	2·25	2·50
1521/1524 Set of 4		8·00	9·00

Designs:—No. 1521, Reporters and soldiers, 1942; No. 1522, Consolidated Liberator bombers over Newfoundland; No. 1523, Dieppe raid; No. 1524, U-boat sinking merchant ship.
Nos. 1521/4 were printed together, *se-tenant*, in different combinations throughout the sheet, giving four blocks of 4.

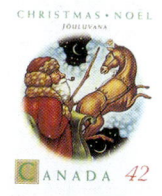

610 Estonian Jouluvana

611 Adelaide Hoodless (women's movement pioneer)

(Des R. MacDonald (37c.), Anita Kunz (42c.), J. Bennett (48c.), S. Ng (84c.), adapted L. Fishauf and Stephanie Power. Litho Ashton-Potter)

1992 (13 Nov). Christmas. T **610** and similar multicoloured designs. Fluorescent frame. P 12½×imperf (37c.), 12½ (42c.) or 13½ (others).
1525	37c. North American Santa Claus (35×21 *mm*).	1·10	80
	a. Booklet pane. No. 1525×10................	10·00	
1526	42c. Type **610**..	40	20
	a. Perf 13½..	1·25	75
	ab. Booklet pane. No. 1526a×10.............	11·00	
1527	48c. Italian La Befana.............................	1·50	2·25
	a. Booklet pane. No. 1527×5 plus one printed label..	9·00	
1528	84c. German Weihnachtsmann..................	2·25	3·25
	a. Booklet pane. No. 1528×5 plus one printed label..	11·00	
1525/1528 Set of 4		4·75	6·00

On No. 1525 the left-hand third of the design area is taken up by a bar code which has fluorescent bands between the bars. This value was only available from $3.70 stamp booklets (No. SB160) which had the vertical edges of the pane imperforate. It was intended for use on greeting cards posted on or before 31 January 1993.
No. 1526a was only issued in $4.20 stamp booklets, No. SB161.
Nos. 1526ab, 1527a and 1528a have the vertical edges of the panes imperforate.

(Des Heather Cooper. Litho Ashton-Potter)

1993 (8 Mar). Prominent Canadian Women. T **611** and similar vert designs. Multicoloured. Fluorescent frame. P 12½.
1529	43c. Type **611**..	1·10	1·50
	a. Block of 4. Nos. 1529/32...................	4·00	5·50
1530	43c. Marie-Josephine Gérin-Lajoie (social reformer).................................	1·10	1·50
1531	43c. Pitseolak Ashoona (Inuit artist)...........	1·10	1·50
1532	43c. Helen Kinnear (lawyer)....................	1·10	1·50
1529/1532 Set of 4		4·00	5·50

Nos. 1529/32 were printed together, *se-tenant*, in different combinations throughout the sheet, giving ten blocks of 4 and ten single stamps.

612 Ice Hockey Players with Cup

613 Coverlet, New Brunswick

(Des F. Dallaire and Lise Giguère. Litho C.B.N.)

1993 (16 Apr). Centenary of Stanley Cup. Fluorescent frame. P 13½.
1533	**612**	43c. multicoloured...........................	1·00	60

(Des P. Adam. Litho Ashton-Potter)

1993 (30 Apr). Hand-crafted Textiles. T **613** and similar square designs. Multicoloured. Fluorescent frame. P 13×12½.
1534	43c. Type **613**..	1·50	2·00
	a. Booklet pane. Nos. 1534/8, each×2........	13·00	
1535	43c. Pieced quilt, Ontario........................	1·50	2·00
1536	43c. Doukhobor bedcover, Saskatchewan.....	1·50	2·00
1537	43c. Ceremonial robe, Kwakwaka'wakw......	1·50	2·00
1538	43c. Boutonné coverlet, Quebec................	1·50	2·00
1534/1538 Set of 5		6·75	9·00

Nos. 1534/8 were only available from $4.30 stamp booklets, No. SB169.
Booklet pane No. 1534a has the horizontal edges of the pane imperforate and margins at both left and right.

(Des P.-Y. Pelletier. Litho and die-stamped Ashton-Potter)

1993 (17 May). Canadian Art (6th series). Vert design as T **550**. Multicoloured. Fluorescent frame. P 12½×13.
1539	86c. "The Owl" (Kenojuak Ashevak)..............	2·25	3·25

No. 1539 was issued in a similar sheet format to No. 1289.

614 Empress Hotel, Victoria

615 Algonquin Park, Ontario

(Des G. Tsetsekas. Litho Ashton-Potter)

1993 (14 June). Historic Hotels. T **614** and similar horiz designs. Multicoloured. Fluorescent frame. P 13½.
1540	43c. Type **614**..	60	1·10
	a. Booklet pane. Nos. 1540/4, each×2........	5·50	
1541	43c. Banff Springs Hotel..........................	60	1·10
1542	43c. Royal York Hotel, Toronto.................	60	1·10
1543	43c. Le Chateau Frontenac, Quebec............	60	1·10
1544	43c. Algonquin Hotel, St. Andrews.............	60	1·10
1540/1544 Set of 5		2·75	5·00

Nos. 1540/4 were only issued in $4.30 stamp booklets, No. SB170.
Booklet pane No. 1540a has the horizontal edges of the pane imperforate and margins at both left and right.

CANADA

1993 (30 June). Canada Day. Provincial and Territorial Parks. T **615** and similar horiz designs. Multicoloured. Fluorescent frame. P 13.
(Des M. and Jan Waddell. Litho C.B.N.)

1545	43c. Type **615**	70	80
	a. Sheetlet. Nos. 1545/56	7·50	8·80
1546	43c. De La Gaspésie Park, Québec	70	80
1547	43c. Cedar Dunes Park, Prince Edward Island	70	80
1548	43c. Cape St. Mary's Seabird Reserve, Newfoundland	70	80
1549	43c. Mount Robson Park, British Columbia	70	80
1550	43c. Writing-on-Stone Park, Alberta	70	80
1551	43c. Spruce Woods Park, Manitoba	70	80
1552	43c. Herschel Island Park, Yukon	70	80
1553	43c. Cypress Hills Park, Saskatchewan	70	80
1554	43c. The Rocks Park, New Brunswick	70	80
1555	43c. Blomidon Park, Nova Scotia	70	80
1556	43c. Katannilik Park, Northwest Territories	70	80
1545/1556 Set of 12		7·50	8·50

Nos. 1545/56 were printed together, *se-tenant*, in sheetlets of 12, which come with or without a large illustrated and inscribed margin at top.

616 Toronto Skyscrapers   **617** Taylor's Steam Buggy, 1867

1993 (6 Aug). Bicentenary of Toronto. Fluorescent frame. P 13½×13.
(Des R. Heeney and V. McIndoe. Litho C.B.N.)

1557	**616**	43c. multicoloured	1·00	70

1993 (10 Aug). Canadian Rivers (3rd series). Vert designs as T **592**. Multicoloured. Fluorescent frame. P 13×12½.
(Des M. and Jan Waddell. Litho Ashton-Potter.)

1558	43c. Fraser River	80	1·10
	a. Booklet pane. Nos. 1558/62, each×2	7·00	
1559	43c. Yukon River	80	1·10
1560	43c. Red River	80	1·10
1561	43c. St. Lawrence River	80	1·10
1562	43c. St. John River	80	1·10
1558/1562 Set of 5		3·50	5·00

Nos. 1558/62 were only issued in $4.30 stamp booklets, No. SB171.

1993 (23 Aug). Historic Automobiles (1st series). Sheet, 177×125 mm, containing T **617** and similar horiz designs. Multicoloured. Fluorescent frame. P 12½×13.
(Des J. Gault, T. Telmet and C. Wykes. Litho C.B.N.)

MS1563 43c. Type **617**; 43c. Russel "Model L" touring car, 1908; 49c. Ford "Model T" touring car, 1914 (43×22 mm); 49c. Studebaker "Champion Deluxe Starlight" coupe, 1950 (43×22 mm); 86c. McLaughlin-Buick "28-496 special", 1928 (43×22 mm); 86c. Gray-Dort "25 SM" luxury sedan, 1923 (43×22 mm) .... 7·50   8·00

See also Nos. **MS**1611, **MS**1636 and **MS**1683/4.

618 "The Alberta Homesteader"   **619** Polish Swiety Mikolaj

(Des Deborah Cormack, A. Cormack and R. Tibbles. Litho Ashton-Potter.)

1993 (7 Sept). Folk Songs. T **618** and similar horiz designs. Multicoloured. Fluorescent frame. P 12½.

1564	43c. Type **618**	70	1·00
	a. Block of 4. Nos. 1564/7	2·50	
1565	43c. "Les Raftmans" (Quebec)	70	1·00
1566	43c. "I'se the B'y that Builds the Boat" (Newfoundland)	70	1·00
1567	43c. "Onkwá:ri Tenhanónniahkwe" (Mohawk Indian)	70	1·00
1564/1567 Set of 4		2·50	3·50

Nos. 1564/7 were printed together, *se-tenant*, in different combinations throughout the sheet, giving ten blocks of 4 and ten single stamps.

(Des R. Harder. Litho Ashton-Potter.)

1993 (1 Oct). Prehistoric Canada (3rd series). Dinosaurs. Horiz designs as T **582**, but 40×28 mm. Multicoloured. Fluorescent frame. P 13½.

1568	43c. Massospondylus	80	80
	a. Block of 4. Nos. 1568/71	2·75	2·75
1569	43c. Stryacosaurus	80	80
1570	43c. Albertosaurus	80	80
1571	43c. Platecarpus	80	80
1568/1571 Set of 4		2·75	2·75

Nos. 1568/71 were printed together, *se-tenant*, in different combinations throughout the sheet, giving four blocks of 4 and four single stamps.

(Des J. Bennett (38c.), J. Jackson (43c.), B. Dawson (49c.), B. Blitt (86c.), adapted L. Fishauf and Stephanie Power. Litho C.B.N.)

1993 (4 Nov). Christmas. T **619** and similar multicoloured designs. Fluorescent frame. P 13×imperf (38c.) or 13½ (others).

1572	38c. North American Santa Claus (35×22 mm)	90	90
	a. Booklet pane. No. 1572×10	9·00	
1573	43c. Type **619**	55	20
	a. Booklet pane. No. 1573×10	9·50	
	b. Imperf between (horiz pair)	£750	
1574	49c. Russian Ded Moroz	1·10	1·40
	a. Booklet pane. No. 1574×5 plus one printed label	5·50	
1575	86c. Australian Father Christmas	1·90	2·75
	a. Booklet pane. No. 1575×5 plus one printed label	9·50	
1572/1575 Set of 4		4·00	4·75

On No. 1572 the left-hand third of the design area is taken up by a barcode which has fluorescent bands between the bars. This value was only available from $3.80 stamp booklets (No. SB173) which had the vertical edges of the pane imperforate. It was intended for use on greeting cards posted before 31 January 1994.

Nos. 1573a/5a are from Nos. SB172 and SB174/5 and have the vertical edges of the panes imperforate.

No. 1573b appears to originate from the incorrect use of the booklet pane perforation on ordinary sheet stock.

(Des J.-P. Armanville and P.-Y. Pelletier. Litho C.B.N.)

1993 (8 Nov). 50th Anniv of Second World War (5th issue). Horiz designs as T **574**. Fluorescent frame. P 13½.

1576	43c. black, silver and brown-olive	2·25	2·25
	a. Block of 4. Nos. 1576/9	8·00	8·00
1577	43c. black, silver and slate-blue	2·25	2·25
1578	43c. black, silver and dull-violet blue	2·25	2·25
1579	43c. black, silver and chestnut	2·25	2·25
1576/1579 Set of 4		8·00	8·00

Designs:—No. 1576, Loading munitions for Russia, 1943; No. 1577, Loading bombs on Avro Type 683 Lancaster; No. 1578, Escorts attacking U-boat; No. 1579 Infantry advancing, Italy.

Nos. 1576/9 were printed together, *se-tenant*, in different combinations throughout the sheet, giving four blocks of 4.

620 (face value at right)

(Des Tarzan Communication Graphique. Litho Leigh-Mardon Ltd, Melbourne)

1994 (28 Jan). Greetings stamps. T **620** and similar horiz design. Multicoloured. Inscriptions behind face value and *"CANADA"* show names of family events. Fluorescent outline. Self-adhesive. Die-cut.

1580	43c. Type **620**	1·00	1·00
	a. Booklet pane. Nos. 1580/1, each×5, and 35 circular greetings labels	9·00	
1581	43c. As Type **620**, but face value at left	1·00	1·00

Nos. 1580/1 were only available from $4.50 self-adhesive booklets, No. SB181, in which the backing card formed the cover. It was intended that the sender should insert the appropriate greetings label into the circular space on each stamp before use.

For 45c. values in this design see Nos. 1654/5.

76

621 Jeanne Sauvé

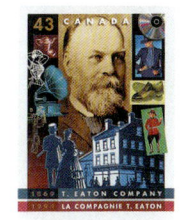

622 Timothy Eaton, Toronto Store of 1869 and Merchandise

(Des J. Morin and T. Yakobina. Litho C.B.N.)

1994 (8 Mar). Jeanne Sauvé (former Governor-General) Commemoration. Fluorescent frame. P 12½×13.
1582   **621**   43c. multicoloured 60   60

No. 1582 was printed in sheets of 20 (4×5), the horizontal rows containing four stamps, each with a differently-inscribed 6×22½ mm *se-tenant* label. These are at the right of the stamps on rows 1, 3 and 5 and at left on rows 2 and 4.

(Des L. Fishauf. Litho C.B.N.)

1994 (17 Mar). 125th Anniv of T. Eaton Company Ltd (department store group). Fluorescent frame. P 13½×13.
1583   **622**   43c. multicoloured 55   75
            a. Booklet pane. No. 1583×10 and 2
               labels with margins all round .... 5·50

No. 1583 was only available from $4.30 stamp booklets, No. SB184.

(Des M. and Jan Waddell. Litho C.B.N.)

1994 (22 Apr). Canadian Rivers (4th series). Horiz designs as T **592**. Multicoloured. Fluorescent frame. *P 13½×13*.
1584   43c. Saguenay River 80   90
               a. Booklet pane. Nos. 1584/8 each×2 ...... 7·00
1585   43c. French River 80   90
1586   43c. Mackenzie River 80   90
1587   43c. Churchill River 80   90
1588   43c. Columbia River 80   90
1584/1588 Set of 5 .... 3·50   4·00

Nos. 1584/8 were only issued in $4.30 stamp booklets, No. SB185.
Booklet pane No. 1584a has the vertical edges of the pane imperforate.

(Des P.-Y. Pelletier. Litho and die-stamped Leigh-Mardon Ltd, Melbourne)

1994 (6 May). Canadian Art (7th series). Vert design as T **550**. Multicoloured. Fluorescent frame. P 14×14½.
1589   88c. "Vera" (detail) (Frederick Varley) .... 1·50   2·00

No. 1589 was issued in a similar sheet format to No. 1289.

623 Lawn Bowls

624 Mother and Baby

(Des D. Coates and R. Roodenburg. Litho and die-stamped Leigh-Mardon Ltd, Melbourne)

1994 (20 May–5 Aug). 15th Commonwealth Games. Victoria. T **623** and similar horiz designs. Multicoloured. Fluorescent frame. P 14.
1590   43c. Type **623** 50   70
               a. Pair. Nos. 1590/1 .... 1·00   1·40
1591   43c. Lacrosse 50   70
1592   43c. Wheelchair race (5 Aug) 50   70
               a. Pair. Nos. 1592/3 .... 1·00   1·40
1593   43c. High jumping (5 Aug) 50   70
1594   50c. Diving (5 Aug) 50   55
               Gold omitted £800
1595   88c. Cycling (5 Aug) .... 2·25   2·00
               Gold omitted £1000
1590/1595 Set of 6 .... 4·25   4·75

Nos. 1590/1 and 1592/3 were printed together, *se-tenant*, in horizontal and vertical pairs throughout the sheets.

(Des Suzanne Duranceau. Litho Leigh-Mardon Ltd, Melbourne)

1994 (2 June). International Year of the Family. Sheet 178×134 mm, containing T **624** and similar vert designs. Multicoloured. Fluorescent paper. P 14×14½.
MS1596 43c. Type **624**; 43c. Family outing; 43c. Grandmother and granddaughter; 43c. Computer class; 43c. Play group, nurse with patient and female lawyer .... 3·00   3·50

625 Big Leaf Maple Tree

626 Billy Bishop (fighter ace) and Nieuport 17

(Des D. Noble. Litho C.B.N.)

1994 (30 June). Canada Day. Maple Trees. T **625** and similar horiz designs. Multicoloured. Fluorescent frame. P 13×13½.
1597   43c. Type **625** 80   90
               a. Sheetlet. Nos. 1597/1608 .... 8·50   9·75
1598   43c. Sugar Maple 80   90
1599   43c. Silver Maple 80   90
1600   43c. Striped Maple 80   90
1601   43c. Norway Maple 80   90
1602   43c. Manitoba Maple 80   90
1603   43c. Black Maple 80   90
1604   43c. Douglas Maple 80   90
1605   43c. Mountain Maple 80   90
1606   43c. Vine Maple 80   90
1607   43c. Hedge Maple 80   90
1608   43c. Red Maple 80   90
1597/1608 Set of 12 .... 8·50   9·75

Nos. 1597/1608 were printed together, *se-tenant*, in sheetlets of 12, which come with or without a large illustrated and inscribed margin at top.

(Des P. Fontaine and B. Leduc. Litho C.B.N.)

1994 (12 Aug). Birth Centenaries. T **626** and similar horiz design. Multicoloured. Fluorescent frame. P 13½.
1609   43c. Type **626** .... 1·00   1·25
               a. Pair. Nos. 1609/10 .... 2·00   2·50
1610   43c. Mary Travers ("La Bolduc") (singer) and musicians .... 1·00   1·25

Nos. 1609/10 were printed together, *se-tenant*, in horizontal and vertical pairs throughout the sheet.

(Des J. Gault, T. Telmet, and C. Wickes. Litho C.B.N.)

1994 (19 Aug). Historic Automobiles (2nd issue). Sheet 177×125 mm, containing horiz designs as T **617**. Multicoloured. Fluorescent frame. P 12½×13.
MS1611 43c. Ford "Model F60L-AMB" military ambulance, 1942–43; 43c. Winnipeg police wagon, 1925; 50c. Sicard snowblower, 1927 (43×22 *mm*); 50c. Bickle "Chieftain" fire engine, 1936 (43×22 *mm*); 88c. St. John Railway Company tramcar No. 40, 1894 (51×22 *mm*); 88c. Motor Coach Industries "Courier 50 Skyview" coach, 1950 (51×22 *mm*) .... 10·00   10·00

No. **MS1611** was sold in a protective pack.

627 Symbolic Aircraft, Radar Screen and Clouds

628 Carol Singing around Christmas Tree

(Des Gottschalk & Ash International, Katalin Kovats and S. Napoleone. Litho C.B.N.)

1994 (16 Sept). 50th Anniv of International Civil Aviation Organization. Fluorescent frame. P 13.
1612   **627**   43c. multicoloured .... 1·00   70

CANADA

77

CANADA

(Des R. Harder. Litho C.B.N.)

1994 (26 Sept). Prehistoric Canada (4th series). Mammals. Multicoloured designs as T **582**, but 40×28 mm. Fluorescent frame. P 13½.

1613	43c. Coryphodon	2·00	2·00
	a. Block of 4. Nos. 1613/16	7·25	7·25
1614	43c. Megacerops	2·00	2·00
1615	43c. Arctodus simus (bear)	2·00	2·00
1616	43c. Mammuthus primigenius (mammoth)	2·00	2·00
1613/1616	Set of 4	7·25	7·25

Nos. 1613/16 were printed together, se-tenant, in different combinations throughout the sheet, giving four blocks of 4 and four single stamps.

(Des Nina Berkson, Diti Katona and J. Pylypczak. Litho C.B.N.)

1994 (3 Nov). Christmas. T **628** and similar multicoloured designs. Fluorescent frame. P 13×imperf (No. 1617) or 13½ (others).

1617	(–) c. Carol singer (35×21 mm)	65	75
	a. Booklet pane. No. 1617×10	6·00	
1618	43c. Type **628**	50	20
	a. Booklet pane. No. 1618×10	7·00	
1619	50c. Choir (vert)	1·00	1·40
	a. Booklet pane. No. 1619×5 plus one printed label	4·75	
1620	88c. Couple carol singing in snow (vert)	2·25	3·25
	a. Booklet pane. No. 1620×5 plus one printed label	8·00	
1617/1620	Set of 4	4·00	5·00

No. 1617 was only available from $3.80 stamp booklets, No. SB187, with the vertical edges of the pane imperforate. The stamp is without face value, but was intended for use as a 38c. on internal greetings cards posted before 31 January 1995. The design shows a barcode at left with fluorescent bands between the bars.

Nos. 1617a/20a are from booklets, Nos. SB186/9, and have the vertical edges of the panes imperforate.

Stamps as Nos. 1618/20, but with face values of 45c., 52c. and 90c. were prepared, but not issued. Examples of the 52c. and 90c. are known.

(Des J.-P. Armanville and P.-Y. Pelletier. Litho C.B.N.)

1994 (7 Nov). 50th Anniv of Second World War (6th issue). Horiz designs as T **574**. Fluorescent frame. P 13½.

1621	43c. black, silver and dull green	2·25	2·25
	a. Block of 4. Nos. 1621/4	8·00	8·00
1622	43c. black, silver and Venetian red	2·25	2·25
1623	43c. black, silver and light blue	2·25	2·25
1624	43c. black, silver and violet-grey	2·25	2·25
1621/1624	Set of 4	8·00	8·00

Designs:—No. 1621, D-Day landings, Normandy; No. 1622, Canadian artillery, Normandy; No. 1623, Hawker Typhoons on patrol; No. 1624, Canadian infantry and disabled German self-propelled gun, Walcheren.

Nos. 1621/4 were printed together, se-tenant, in different combinations throughout the sheet, giving four blocks of 4.

(Des J.-P. Armanville and P.-Y. Pelletier. Litho C.B.N.)

1995 (20 Mar). 50th Anniv of Second World War (7th issue). Horiz designs as T **574**. Fluorescent frame. P 13½.

1625	43c. black, silver and reddish purple	2·25	2·25
	a. Block of 4. Nos. 1625/8	8·00	8·00
1626	43c. black, silver and yellow-brown	2·25	2·25
1627	43c. black, silver and dull yellowish green	2·25	2·25
1628	43c. black, silver and light greenish blue	2·25	2·25
1625/1628	Set of 4	8·00	8·00

Designs:—No. 1625, Returning troopship; No. 1626, Canadian P.O.W's celebrating freedom; No. 1627, Canadian tank liberating Dutch town; No. 1628, Parachute drop in support of Rhine Crossing.

Nos. 1625/8 were printed together, se-tenant, in different combinations throughout the sheet, giving four blocks of 4.

(Des P.-Y. Pelletier. Litho and die-stamped C.B.N.)

1995 (21 Apr). Canadian Art (8th series). Vert design as T **550**. Multicoloured. Fluorescent frame. P 13×13½.

1629	88c. "Floraison" (Alfred Pellan)	1·50	2·25
	a. Gold (frame) omitted	£1000	

No. 1629 was issued in a similar sheet format to No. 1289.

629 Flag and Lake

(Des Gottschalk & Ash International. Litho C.B.N.)

1995 (1 May). 30th Anniv of National Flag. Fluorescent frame. P 13½×13.

1630	**629** (43c.) multicoloured	1·00	50

No. 1630 is without any indication of face value, but was sold for 43c.

PRINTER. Following a change in ownership, and the awarding of a further Canada Post contract, the previous Ashton-Potter Ltd was known as Ashton Potter Canada Ltd from 1995. The imprint reverted to Ashton Potter at the beginning of 1998. From mid-2001 many Ashton Potter issues were printed in the U.S.A.

630 Louisbourg Harbour

(Des R. Harder. Litho Ashton-Potter Canada)

1995 (5 May). 275th Anniv of Fortress of Louisbourg. T **630** and similar horiz designs. Multicoloured. "All-over" fluorescent. P 12½×13.

1631	(43c.) Type **630**	70	80
	a. Booklet pane. Nos. 1631/5 each×2 with margins all round	6·00	
1632	(43c.) Barracks (32×29 mm)	70	80
1633	(43c.) King's Bastion (40×29 mm)	70	80
1634	(43c.) Site of King's Garden, convent and hospital (56×29 mm)	70	80
1635	(43c.) Site of coastal fortifications	70	80
1631/1635	Set of 5	3·00	3·50

Nos. 1631/5 are without any indication of face value, but were sold in booklets of 10 (No. SB190) for $4.30.

(Des J. Gault, T. Telmet and C. Wykes. Litho C.B.N.)

1995 (26 May). Historic Automobiles (3rd issue). Sheet 177×25 mm, containing horiz designs as T **617**. Multicoloured. Fluorescent frame. P 12½×13.

MS1636 43c. Cockshutt "30" farm tractor, 1950; 43c. Bombardier "Ski-Doo Olympique 335" snowmobile, 1970; 50c. Bombardier "B-12 CS" multi-passenger snowmobile, 1948 (43×22 mm); 50c. Gotfredson "Model 20" farm truck, 1924 (43×22 mm); 88c. Robin-Nodwell "RN 110" tracked carrier, 1962 (43×22 mm); 88c. Massey-Harris "No. 21" self-propelled combine harvester, 1942 (43×22 mm) .... 7·00 7·50

No. MS1636 was sold in a protective pack.

631 Banff Springs Golf Club, Alberta

(Des P. Adam. Litho Ashton-Potter Canada)

1995 (6 June). Centenaries of Canadian Amateur Golf Championship and of the Royal Canadian Golf Association. T **631** and similar horiz designs. Fluorescent frame. P 13½×13.

1637	43c. Type **631**	80	80
	a. Booklet pane. Nos. 1637/41 each×2	7·00	
1638	43c. Riverside Country Club, New Brunswick	80	80
1639	43c. Glen Abbey Golf Club, Ontario	80	80
1640	43c. Victoria Golf Club, British Columbia	80	80
1641	43c. Royal Montreal Golf Club, Quebec	80	80
1637/1641	Set of 5	3·50	3·50

Nos. 1637/41 were only issued in $4.30 stamp booklets, No. SB191. Booklet pane No. 1637a has the vertical edges of the pane imperforate.

632 "October Gold" (Franklin Carmichael)

633 Academy Building and Ship Plan

CANADA

(Des A. Leduc. Litho C.B.N.)

1995 (29 June). Canada Day. 75th Anniv of "Group of Seven" (artists). Miniature sheets, each 180×80 mm, containing T **632** and similar square designs. Multicoloured. Fluorescent paper. P 13.

MS1642a	43c. Type **632**; 43c. "From the North Shore, Lake Superior" (Lawren Harris); 43c. "Evening, Les Eboulements, Quebec" (A. Jackson)	3·00	3·50
MS1642b	43c. "Serenity, Lake of the Woods" (Frank Johnston); 43c. "A September Gale, Georgian Bay" (Arthur Lismer); 43c. "Falls, Montreal River" (J. E. H. MacDonald); 43c. "Open Window" (Frederick Varley)	3·00	3·50
MS1642c	43c. "Mill Houses" (Alfred Casson); 43c. "Pembina Valley" (Lionel FitzGerald); 43c. "The Lumberjack" (Edwin Holgate)	3·00	3·50

The three sheets were sold together in an envelope which also includes a small descriptive booklet.

(Des B. Mackay-Lyons and S. Slipp. Litho C.B.N.)

1995 (29 June). Centenary of Lunenburg Academy. Fluorescent frame. P 13.

1643	**633**	43c. multicoloured	50	45

634 Aspects of Manitoba

635 Monarch Butterfly

(Des T. Gallagher and S. Rosenberg. Litho Ashton-Potter Canada)

1995 (14 July). 125th Anniv of Manitoba as Canadian Province. Fluorescent frame. P 13½×13.

1644	**634**	43c. multicoloured	50	45

Two Types of Belted Kingfisher design:
Type I. Inscr "aune migratrice" in error.
Type II. Inscr corrected to "faune migratrice".

(Des Debbie Adams. Litho C.B.N.)

1995 (15 Aug–26 Sept). Migratory Wildlife. T **635** and similar vert designs. Fluorescent paper. P 13×12½.

1645	**635**	45c. Type **635**	1·10	1·40
		a. Block of 4. Nos. 1645/6 1648/9	4·25	5·00
		b. Block of 4. Nos. 1645, 1647/9 (26 Sept)..	4·25	5·00
1646		45c. Belted Kingfisher (I)	1·10	1·40
1647		45c. Belted Kingfisher (II) (26 Sept)	1·10	1·40
1648		45c. Pintail	1·10	1·40
1649		45c. Hoary Bat	1·10	1·40
1645/1649		Set of 5	5·00	6·25

The inscription error on No. 1646 was corrected in a new printing issued 26 September 1995.

The four different designs were printed together, *se-tenant*, throughout the sheet, giving four blocks of 4 and four single stamps, showing an overall background design of migration routes.

636 Quebec Railway Bridge

637 Mountain, Baffin Island, Polar Bear and Caribou

(Des J. Gault, T. Telmet and C. Wykes. Litho Ashton-Potter Canada)

1995 (1 Sept). 20th World Road Congress, Montreal. Bridges. T **636** and similar horiz designs. Multicoloured. Fluorescent paper. P 12½×13.

1650	**636**	45c. Type **636**	2·25	2·25
		a. Block of 4. Nos. 1650/3	8·00	8·00
1651		45c. 401-403-410 Interchange, Mississauga....	2·25	2·25
1652		45c. Hartland Bridge, New Brunswick	2·25	2·25
1653		45c. Alex Fraser Bridge, British Columbia....	2·25	2·25
1650/1653		Set of 4	8·00	8·00

Nos. 1650/3 were printed together, *se-tenant*, throughout the sheet, giving four blocks of 4 and four single stamps.

Two Types of Background to Nos. 1654/5:
Type I. Inscriptions behind face value and "CANADA" show names of Canadian Provinces.
Type II. Inscription behind face value and "CANADA" show names of family events.

(Des Tarzan Communication Graphique. Litho Ashton-Potter Canada (Nos. 1654/5) or Leigh-Mardon Ltd, Melbourne (Nos. 1654b/5b)).

1995 (1 Sept)–96. Greetings stamps. Horiz designs as T **620**. Multicoloured. Fluorescent outline. Self-adhesive. *Die-cut*.

1654		45c. Face value at right (I)	60	75
		a. Booklet pane. Nos. 1654/5, each×5	5·50	
		b. Type II (15.1.96)	80	80
		ba. Booklet pane. Nos. 1654b and 1655b each×5	7·50	
1655		45c. Face value at left (I)	60	75
		b. Type II (15.1.96)	80	80

Nos. 1654/5 were only available from $4.70 self-adhesive booklets, Nos. SB197 and SB205, in which the backing card formed the cover. Booklets containing Nos. 1654/5 also include a separate pane of 15 self-adhesive labels which it was intended the sender should insert in the circular space on each stamp before use. Booklets containing Nos. 1654b/5b included 35 circular greetings labels on the same pane as the stamps.

(Des Eskind Waddell. Litho C.B.N.)

1995 (15 Sept). 50th Anniv of Arctic Institute of North America. T **637** and similar horiz designs. Multicoloured. Fluorescent paper. P 13×12½.

1656		45c. Type **637**	1·00	1·25
		a. Booklet pane. Nos. 1656/60, each×2, with margins all round	9·00	
1657		45c. Arctic poppy, Auyuittuq National Park and cargo canoe	1·00	1·25
1658		45c. Inuk man and igloo	1·00	1·25
1659		45c. Ogilvie Mountains, dog team and ski-equipped airplane	1·00	1·25
1660		45c. Inuit children	1·00	1·25
1656/1660		Set of 5	4·50	5·50

Nos. 1656/60 were only issued in $4.50 stamp booklets, No. SB199.

638 Superman

639 Prime Minister MacKenzie King signing U.N. Charter, 1945

(Des L. Fishauf. Litho Ashton-Potter Canada)

1995 (2 Oct). Comic Book Superheroes. T **638** and similar vert designs. Multicoloured. Fluorescent frame. P 13×12½.

1661		45c. Type **638**	80	90
		a. Booklet pane. Nos. 1661/5, each×2, with margins all round	7·00	
1662		45c. Johnny Canuck	80	90
1663		45c. Nelvana	80	90
1664		45c. Captain Canuck	80	90
1665		45c. Fleur de Lys	80	90
1661/1665		Set of 5	3·50	4·00

Nos. 1661/5 were only issued in $4.50 stamp booklets, No. SB200.

(Des L. Holloway and R. Kerr. Litho and die-stamped C.B.N.)

1995 (24 Oct). 50th Anniv of United Nations. Fluorescent frame. P 13½.

1666	**639**	45c. multicoloured	75	50

No. 1666 was issued in sheets of 10 with a large illustrated and inscribed margin at top.

640 "The Nativity"

641 World Map and Emblem

CANADA

(Des F. Dallaire. Litho Ashton-Potter Canada (40c.) or C.B.N. (others))

1995 (2 Nov). Christmas. T **640** and similar multicoloured designs showing sculptured capitals from Ste.-Anne-de-Beaupré Basilica designed by Emilé Brunet (Nos. 1668/70). Fluorescent frames. P 12½×13 (40c.) or 13½ (others).

1667		40c. Sprig of holly (35×22 mm)	85	70
		a. Booklet pane. No. 1667×10	8·00	
1668		45c. Type **640**	50	20
		a. Booklet pane. No. 1668×10	10·00	
1669		52c. "The Annunciation"	1·60	1·60
		a. Booklet pane. No. 1669×5 plus one printed label	7·25	
1670		90c. "The Flight to Egypt"	2·25	2·75
		a. Booklet pane. No. 1670×5 plus one printed label	10·00	
1667/1670 Set of 4			4·75	4·75

On No. 1667 the left-hand third of the design area is taken up by a barcode which has fluorescent bands between the bars. This value was only available from $4 stamp booklets, No. SB202, which had the vertical edges of the pane imperforate. It was intended for use on greetings cards posted before 31 January 1996.

Nos. 1668a/70a (from Nos. SB201 and SB203/4) have the vertical edges of the panes imperforate.

(Des A. Leduc. Litho Ashton-Potter Canada)

1995 (6 Nov). 25th Anniv of La Francophonie and The Agency for Cultural and Technical Co-operation. Fluorescent frame. P 13×13½.

1671	**641**	45c. multicoloured	60	50

642 Concentration Camp Victims, Uniform and Identity Card

(Des Q30 Design. Litho Ashton-Potter Canada)

1995 (9 Nov). 50th Anniv of the End of The Holocaust. Fluorescent paper. P 12½×13.

1672	**642**	45c. multicoloured	70	50

Horizontal strips of No. 1672 form a continuous design which is carried over on to the vertical sheet margins.

643 American Kestrel

644 Louis R. Desmarais (tanker), Three-dimensional Map and Radar Screen

(Des R. Bellemare and P. Leduc. Litho C.B.N.)

1996 (9 Jan). Birds (1st issue). T **643** and similar horiz designs. Multicoloured. Fluorescent frame. P 13½.

1673		45c. Type **643**	1·90	1·75
		a. Horiz strip of 4. Nos. 1673/6	6·75	6·25
1674		45c. Atlantic Puffin	1·90	1·75
1675		45c. Pileated Woodpecker	1·90	1·75
1676		45c. Ruby-throated Hummingbird	1·90	1·75
1673/1676 Set of 4			6·75	6·25

Nos. 1673/6 were printed together, se-tenant, in panes of 12 (4×3) containing three examples of No. 1673a. Those panes intended for philatelic sale had inscribed margins so arranged as to produce a diamond-shaped format.

See also Nos. 1717/20, 1779/82, 1865/72, 1974/81 and 2058/65.

(Des Q30 Design Inc. Litho C.B.N.)

1996 (15 Feb). High Technology Industries. T **644** and similar horiz designs. Multicoloured. Fluorescent paper. P 13½.

1677		45c. Type **644**	65	1·00
		a. Booklet pane. Nos. 1677/80, each×3	6·75	
1678		45c. Canadair Challenger 601-3R, jet engine and navigational aid	65	1·00
1679		45c. Map of North America and eye	65	1·00
1680		45c. Genetic engineering experiment and Canola (plant)	65	1·00
1677/1680 Set of 4			2·40	3·50

Nos. 1677/80 were only available from $5.40 stamp booklets, No. SB206, which had the vertical edges of the pane imperforate.

(Des P.-Y. Pelletier. Litho and die-stamped Ashton-Potter Canada)

1996 (30 Apr). Canadian Art (9th series). Vert design as T **550**. Multicoloured. Fluorescent paper. P 12½×13.

1681		90c. "The Spirit of Haida Gwaii" (sculpture) (Bill Reid)	1·40	2·25

No. 1681 was issued in a similar sheet format to No. 1289.

645 "One World, One Hope" (Joe Average)

(Des G. Tsetsekas. Litho Ashton Potter Canada)

1996 (8 May). 11th International Conference on AIDS, Vancouver. Fluorescent frame. P 13½.

1682	**645**	45c. multicoloured	70	70

(Des J. Gault, T. Telmet and C. Wickes. Litho C.B.N.)

1998 (8 June). Historic Automobiles (4th issue). Sheet 177×125 mm, containing horiz designs as T **617**. Multicoloured. Fluorescent frame. P 12½×13.

MS1683 45c. Still Motor Co. electric van, 1899; 45c. Waterous Engine Works steam roller, 1914; 52c. International "D.35" delivery truck, 1938; 52c. Champion road grader, 1936; 90c. White "Model WA 122" articulated lorry, 1947 (51×22 mm); 90c. Hayes "HDX 45-115" logging truck, 1975 (51×22 mm) .... 7·50 8·00

No. **MS**1683 also includes the "CAPEX '96" International Stamp Exhibition logo on the sheet margin and was sold in a protective pack.

(Des J. Gault, T. Telmet and C. Wickes. Litho C.B.N.)

1996 (8 June). "CAPEX '96" International Stamp Exhibition, Toronto. Sheet, 368×182 mm, containing horiz designs as Nos. **MS**1563, **MS**1611, **MS**1636, **MS**1683, but with different face values and one new design (45c.). Fluorescent frame (45c.). P 12½×13.

MS1684 5c. Bombardier "Ski-Doo Olympique 335" snowmobile, 1970; 5c. Cockshutt "30" farm tractor, 1950; 5c. Type **617**; 5c. Ford "Model F160L-AMB" military ambulance, 1942; 5c. Still Motor Co electric van, 1895; 5c. International "D.35" delivery truck, 1936; 5c. Russel "Model L" touring car, 1908; 5c. Winnipeg police wagon, 1925; 5c. Waterous Engine Works steam roller, 1914; 5c. Champion road grader, 1936; 10c. White "Model WA 122" articulated lorry, 1947 (51×22 mm); 10c. St. John Railway Company tramcar, 1894 (51×22 mm); 10c. Hayes "HDX 45-115" logging truck, 1975 (51×22 mm); 10c. Motor Coach Industries "Courier 50 Skyview" coach, 1950 (51×22 mm); 20c. Ford "Model T" touring car, 1914 (43×22 mm); 20c. McLaughlin-Buick "28-496 special", 1928 (43×22 mm); 20c. Bombardier "B-12 CS" multi-passenger snowmobile, 1948 (43×22 mm); 20c. Robin-Nodwell "RN 110" tracked carrier, 1962 (43×22 mm); 20c. Studebaker "Champion Deluxe Starlight" coupe, 1950 (43×22 mm); 20c. Gray-Dort "25 SM" luxury sedan, 1923 (43×22 mm); 20c. Gotfredson "Model 20" farm truck, 1924 (43×22 mm); 20c. Massey-Harris "No. 21" self-propelled combine-harvester, 1942 (43×22 mm); 20c. Bickle "Chieftain" fire engine, 1936 (43×22 mm); 20c. Sicard snowblower, 1927 (43×22 mm); 45c. Bricklin "SV-1" sports car, 1975 (51×22 mm) .... 8·00 9·00

No. **MS**1684 was sold folded within a special pack at $3.75, a premium of 40c. over the face value. It was only possible to obtain an unfolded example by purchasing an uncut press sheet, containing three miniature sheets, of which only 25000 were made available. The price quoted for No. **MS**1684 is for a folded example.

646 Skookum Jim Mason and Bonanza Creek

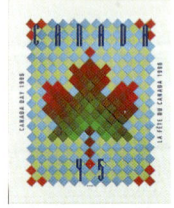

647 Patchwork Quilt Maple Leaf

80

CANADA

(Des S. Slipp. Litho and gold die-stamped Ashton-Potter Canada)

1996 (13 June). Centenary of Yukon Gold Rush. T **646** and similar horiz designs. Multicoloured. Fluorescent paper. P 13½.

1685	45c. Type **646**	80	1·00
	a. Horiz strip of 5. Nos. 1685/9	3·50	4·50
1686	45c. Prospector and boats on Lake Laberge..	80	1·00
1687	45c. Superintendent Sam Steele (N.W.M.P.) and U.S.A.–Canada border	80	1·00
1688	45c. Dawson saloon	80	1·00
1689	45c. Miner with rocker box and sluice	80	1·00
1685/1689	Set of 5	3·50	4·50

Nos. 1685/9 were printed together, *se-tenant*, in sheetlets of 10, containing two examples of No. 1685a.

(Des R. Bellemare. Litho Ashton-Potter Canada)

1996 (28 June). Canada Day. Self-adhesive. Fluorescent frame. *Die-cut.*

| 1690 | **647** | 45c. multicoloured | 1·00 | 60 |

No. 1690 was printed in sheets of 12 with each stamp separate on the backing paper.

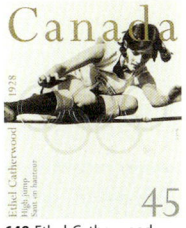

648 Ethel Catherwood (high jump), 1928

649 Indian Totems, City Skyline, Forest and Mountains

(Des M. Koudys. Litho and die-stamped Ashton-Potter Canada)

1996 (8 July). Canadian Olympic Gold Medal Winners. T **648** and similar vert designs. Multicoloured. Fluorescent paper. P 13×12½.

1691	45c. Type **648**	70	85
	a. Booklet pane. Nos. 1691/5, each×2 with margins all round	6·50	
1692	45c. Etienne Desmarteau (56lb weight throw), 1904	70	85
1693	45c. Fanny Rosenfeld (400 metres relay), 1928	70	85
1694	45c. Gerald Ouellette (small bore rifle, prone), 1956	70	85
1695	45c. Percy Williams (100 and 200 metres), 1928	70	85
1691/1695	Set of 5	3·25	3·75

Nos. 1691/5 were only issued in $4.50 stamp booklets, No. SB207.

(Des M. Warburton. Litho Ashton-Potter Canada)

1996 (19 July). 125th Anniv of British Columbia. Fluorescent paper. P 13×12½.

| 1696 | **649** | 45c. multicoloured | 50 | 50 |

650 Canadian Heraldic Symbols

651 *L'Arrivee d'un Train en Gare* (1896)

(Des D. Sarty and R. Gaynor. Litho Ashton-Potter Canada)

1996 (19 Aug). 22nd International Congress of Genealogical and Heraldic Sciences, Ottawa. Fluorescent paper. P 12½.

| 1697 | **650** | 45c. multicoloured | 50 | 50 |

(Des P.-Y. Pelletier. Litho C.B.N.)

1996 (22 Aug). Centenary of Cinema. Two sheets, each 180×100 mm containing T **651** and similar vert designs. Multicoloured. Self-adhesive. Fluorescent paper. *Die-cut.*

| **MS**1698a | 45c. Type **651**; 45c. *Back to God's Country* (1919); 45c. *Hen Hop!* (1942); 45c. *Pour la Suite du Monde* (1963); 45c. *Goin' Down the Road* (1970) | 4·25 | 4·75 |
| **MS**1698b | 45c. *Mon Oncle Antoine* (1971); 45c. *The Apprenticeship of Duddy Kravitz* (1974); 45c. *Les Ordres* (1974); 45c. *Les Bons Debarras* (1980); 45c. *The Grey Fox* (1982) | 4·25 | 4·75 |

The two sheets of No. **MS**1698 were sold together in an envelope with a descriptive booklet.

652 Interlocking Jigsaw Pieces and Hands

653 Edouard Montpetit and Montreal University

(Des Debbie Adam. Litho Ashton-Potter Canada)

1996 (9 Sept). Literacy Campaign. Fluorescent paper. P 13×12½.

| 1699 | **652** | 45c.+5c. multicoloured | 85 | 1·00 |
| | | a. Booklet pane. No. 1699×10 with margins all round | 8·00 | |

No. 1699 has one piece of the jigsaw removed by die-cutting and was only issued in $5 stamp booklet, No. SB208.

(Des J. Beauchesne. Litho Ashton-Potter Canada)

1996 (26 Sept). Edouard Montpetit (academic) Commemoration. Fluorescent frame. P 12×12½.

| 1700 | **653** | 45c. multicoloured | 50 | 50 |

654 Winnie and Lt. Colebourn, 1914

655 Margaret Laurence

(Des Wai Poon. Litho Ashton-Potter Canada)

1996 (1 Oct). Stamp Collecting Month. Winnie the Pooh. T **654** and similar horiz designs. Multicoloured. Fluorescent frame. P 12½×13.

1701	45c. Type **654**	1·75	1·50
	a. Double sheetlet of 16. Nos. 1701/4 each×4	25·00	
1702	45c. Christopher Robin Milne and teddy bear, 1925	1·75	1·50
1703	45c. Illustration from *Winnie the Pooh*, 1926..	1·75	1·50
1704	45c. Winnie the Pooh at Walt Disney World, 1996	1·75	1·50
1701/1704	Set of 4	6·25	6·25
MS1705	152×112 mm. Nos. 1701/4	6·25	6·50

Nos. 1701/4 were printed together, *se-tenant*, as blocks of 4 in double sheetlets, used as a cover to "The True Story of Winnie the Pooh" booklet.

(Des A. Leduc. Recess and litho C.B.N.)

1996 (10 Oct). Canadian Authors. T **655** and similar vert designs. Fluorescent paper. P 13½×13.

1706	45c. multicoloured	80	1·40
	a. Booklet pane. Nos. 1706/10 each×2	7·00	
1707	45c. black, greenish grey and scarlet-vermilion	80	1·40
1708	45c. multicoloured	80	1·40
1709	45c. multicoloured	80	1·40
1710	45c. multicoloured	80	1·40
1706/1710	Set of 5	3·50	6·25

Designs:—No. 1706 Type **655**; No. 1707 Donald G. Creighton; No. 1708, Gabrielle Roy; No. 1709, Felix-Antoine Savard; No. 1710, Thomas C. Haliburton.

Nos. 1706/10 were only issued in $4.50 stamp booklets, No. SB209, with the horizontal edges of the pane imperforate and margins at left and right.

656 Children tobogganing

657 Head of Ox

81

CANADA

(Des T. Harrison (45c.), Pauline Paquin (52c.), Joan Bacquie (90c.). Litho C.B.N. (45c.) or Ashton Potter Canada (others))

1996 (1 Nov). Christmas. 50th Anniv of U.N.I.C.E.F. T **656** and similar vert designs. Multicoloured. Fluorescent frame. P 13½ (45c.) or 12½×12 (others).

1711	45c. Type **656**..	50	20
	a. Booklet pane. No. 1711×10.....................	6·50	
1712	52c. Father Christmas skiing	70	1·00
	a. Perf 13½	90	1·00
	ab. Booklet pane. No. 1712a×5 plus one printed label..	4·00	
1713	90c. Couple ice-skating.................................	1·25	2·00
	a. Perf 13½	1·25	2·00
	ab. Booklet pane. No. 1713a×5 plus one printed label..	5·50	
1711/1713	Set of 3	2·25	2·75

Nos. 1712a and 1713a were only issued in stamp booklets.

Nos. 1711a, 1712ab and 1713ab come from booklets, Nos. SB210/12, and have the vertical edges of the panes imperforate and margins at top and bottom.

(Des Ivy Li and Liu Xiang-Ping. Litho Ashton-Potter Canada)

1997 (7 Jan). Chinese New Year ("Year of the Ox"). Fluorescent frame. P 13×12½.

1714	**657**	45c. multicoloured...	85	90
MS1715 155×75 mm*. No. 1714×2...................................			2·00	2·50

*No. **MS**1715 is an extended fan shape with overall measurements as quoted.

Two examples of No. 1714, taken from the miniature sheet, have been found with the gold ("Canada, 45", etc.) omitted.

1997 (7 Jan). "HONG KONG '97" International Stamp Exhibition. As No. **MS**1715, but with exhibition logo added to the sheet margin in gold. Fluorescent frame. P 13×12½.

MS1716 155×75 mm. No. 1714×2................................... 6·50 7·50

(Des R. Bellemare and P. Leduc. Litho Ashton-Potter Canada)

1997 (10 Jan). Birds (2nd series). Horiz designs as T **643**. Multicoloured. Fluorescent frame. P 12½×13.

1717	45c. Mountain Bluebird................................	1·25	1·40
	a. Block of 4. Nos. 1717/20	4·50	5·00
1718	45c. Western Grebe	1·25	1·40
1719	45c. Northern Gannet	1·25	1·40
1720	45c. Scarlet Tanager	1·25	1·40
1717/1720	Set of 4	4·50	5·00

Nos. 1717/20 were printed together, *se-tenant*, in different combinations throughout the sheet, giving four blocks of 4 and four single stamps.

(Des P.-Y. Pelletier. Litho and die-stamped Ashton-Potter Canada)

1997 (17 Feb). Canadian Art (10th series). Vert design as T **550**. Multicoloured. Fluorescent paper. P 12½×13½.

1721	90c. "York Boat on Lake Winnipeg, 1930" (Walter Phillips)..	1·50	2·25

No. 1721 was issued in a similar sheet format to No. 1289.

658 Man and Boy with Bike, and A. J. and J. W. Billes (company founders)

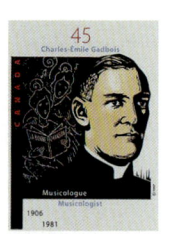

659 Abbé Charles-Emile Gadbois

(Des Fuel Design. Litho Ashton-Potter Canada)

1997 (3 Mar). 75th Anniv of Canadian Tire Corporation. Fluorescent frame. P 13×13½.

1722	**658**	45c. multicoloured...	80	70

No. 1722 was printed in sheets of 12 which were supplied in special envelopes each with a pamphlet on the history of the company.

(Des Marie Lessard. Litho C.B.N.)

1997 (20 Mar). Abbé Charles-Emile Gadbois (musicologist) Commemoration. Fluorescent frame. P 13½×13.

1723	**659**	45c. multicoloured...	60	50

For a full range of Stanley Gibbons catalogues, please visit **www.stanleygibbons.com**

---

660 Blue Poppy

661 Nurse attending Patient

(Des C. Simard. Litho Ashton-Potter Canada)

1997 (4 Apr). "Quebec in Bloom" International Floral Festival. Fluorescent frame. P 13×12½.

1724	**660**	45c. multicoloured...	75	55
		a. Booklet pane. No. 1724×12...............	8·00	

No. 1724 was only issued in $5.40 booklets, No. SB213. No. 1724a has the horizontal edges of the pane imperforate and margins at left and right.

(Des Margaret Issenman. Litho Ashton Potter Canada)

1997 (12 May). Centenary of Victorian Order of Nurses. Fluorescent frame. P 12½×13.

1725	**661**	45c. multicoloured...	1·25	50

662 Osgoode Hall and Seal of Law Society

663 Great White Shark

(Des L. Holloway. Litho C.B.N.)

1997 (23 May). Bicentenary of Law Society of Upper Canada. Fluorescent frame. P 13½×13.

1726	**662**	45c. multicoloured...	75	50

(Des Q30 Design. Litho Ashton-Potter Canada)

1997 (30 May). Ocean Fish. T **663** and similar horiz designs. Multicoloured. Fluorescent frame. P 12½×13.

1727	45c. Type **663**...	1·00	1·25
	a. Block of 4. Nos. 1727/30	3·50	4·50
1728	45c. Pacific Halibut.......................................	1·00	1·25
1729	45c. Common Sturgeon...............................	1·00	1·25
1730	45c. Blue-finned Tuna	1·00	1·25
1727/1730	Set of 4	3·50	4·50

Nos. 1727/30 were printed together, *se-tenant*, throughout the sheet giving four blocks of 4 and four single stamps.

664 Lighthouse and Confederation Bridge

(Des C. Burke and J. Hudson. Litho C.B.N.)

1997 (31 May). Opening of Confederation Bridge, Northumberland Strait. T **664** and similar horiz design. Multicoloured. Fluorescent frame. P 12½×13.

1731	45c. Type **664**...	1·40	1·00
	a. Horiz pair. Nos. 1731/2 and centre label..	2·75	2·00
1732	45c. Confederation Bridge and Great Blue Heron	1·40	1·00

Nos. 1731/2 were printed together, horizontally *se-tenant*, in sheets of 20 (4×5) with labels measuring 16×23½ mm between vertical rows 1 and 2 and 3 and 4 which link the two designs.

665 Gilles Villeneuve in Ferrari T-3

666 Globe and the *Matthew*

82

(Des J. Gault and N. Skinner. Litho C.B.N.)

1997 (12 June). 15th Death Anniv of Gilles Villeneuve (racing car driver). T **665** and similar horiz design. Multicoloured. Fluorescent frame. P 12½×13.

1733	45c. Type **665**	1·00	60
1734	90c. Villeneuve in Ferrari T-4	2·00	2·25
MS1735	203×115 mm. Nos. 1733/4 each×4	8·00	8·00

No. **MS**1735 was sold in an illustrated folder.

(Des Susan Warr. Litho Ashton-Potter Canada)

1997 (24 June). 500th Anniv of John Cabot's Discovery of North America. Fluorescent paper. P 12½×13.

| 1736 | **666** | 45c. multicoloured | 1·00 | 55 |

667 Sea to Sky Highway, British Columbia, and Skier

(Des L. Cable. Litho C.B.N.)

1997 (30 June). Scenic Highways (1st series). T **667** and similar horiz designs. Multicoloured. Fluorescent frame. P 12½×13.

1737	45c. Type **667**	1·25	1·40
	a. Block of 4. Nos. 1737/40	4·50	5·00
1738	45c. Cabot Trail, Nova Scotia, and rug-making	1·25	1·40
1739	45c. Wine route, Ontario, and glasses of wine	1·25	1·40
1740	45c. Highway 34, Saskatchewan, and cowboy	1·25	1·40
1737/1740 Set of 4		4·50	5·00

Nos. 1737/40 were printed together, *se-tenant*, in sheets of 20 containing four blocks of 4 and four single stamps.

See also Nos. 1810/13 and 1876/9.

668 Kettle, Ski-bike, Lounger and Plastic Cases

(Des F. Dallaire. Litho C.B.N.)

1997 (23 July). 20th Congress of International Council of Societies for Industrial Design. Fluorescent frame. P 12½×13.

| 1741 | **668** | 45c. multicoloured | 60 | 50 |

No. 1741 was printed in sheets of 24 (4×6), the horizontal rows containing four stamps each with a different 11½×24 mm *se-tenant* label showing examples of Canadian industrial design. These labels are on the right of the stamps in rows 1, 3 and 5 and to the left in rows 2, 4 and 6.

669 Caber Thrower, Bagpiper, Drummer and Highland Dancer

670 Knights of Columbus Emblem

(Des F. Ross. Litho C.B.N.)

1997 (1 Aug). 50th Anniv of Glengarry Highland Games, Ontario. Fluorescent frame. P 12½×13.

| 1742 | **669** | 45c. multicoloured | 1·00 | 50 |

(Des A. Leduc. Litho C.B.N.)

1997 (5 Aug). Centenary of Knights of Columbus (welfare charity) in Canada. Fluorescent frame. P 13.

| 1743 | **670** | 45c. multicoloured | 50 | 50 |

CANADA

671 Postal and Telephone Workers with P.T.T.I. Emblem

673 Paul Henderson celebrating Goal

672 C.Y.A.P. Logo

(Des Epicentre. Litho C.B.N.)

1997 (18 Aug). 28th World Congress of Postal, Telegraph and Telephone International Staff Federation, Montreal. Fluorescent frame. P 13.

| 1744 | **671** | 45c. multicoloured | 50 | 50 |

(Des K. Fung. Litho C.B.N.)

1997 (25 Aug). Canada's Year of Asia Pacific. Fluorescent frame. P 13½.

| 1745 | **672** | 45c. multicoloured | 1·00 | 50 |

(Des C. Vinh. Litho Ashton-Potter Canada)

1997 (20 Sept). 25th Anniv of Canada–U.S.S.R. Ice Hockey Series. T **673** and similar horiz design. Multicoloured. Fluorescent frame. P 12½×13.

1746	45c. Type **673**	1·25	1·25
	a. Booklet pane. Nos. 1746/7, each×5 with margins all round	11·00	
1747	45c. Canadian team celebrating	1·25	1·25

Nos. 1746/7 were only issued in $4.50 stamp booklets, No. SB214, with a partial fluorescent frame around each stamp.

Examples of the booklet pane, No. 1746a, exist overprinted "SERIES OF THE CENTURY 97-09-28 Anniversaire 25 Anniversary LA SERIE DU SIECLE" and player Paul Henderson's signature. These come from Collector Gift Sets which also included a sweatshirt, puck and print.

674 Martha Black

675 Vampire and Bat

(Des S. Hepburn. Litho C.B.N.)

1997 (26 Sept). Federal Politicians. T **674** and similar vert designs. Multicoloured. Fluorescent frame. P 13½×13.

1748	45c. Type **674**	70	1·00
	a. Block of 4. Nos. 1748/51	2·50	3·50
1749	45c. Lionel Chevrier	70	1·00
1750	45c. Judy LaMarsh	70	1·00
1751	45c. Réal Caouette	70	1·00
1748/1751 Set of 4		2·50	3·50

The four different designs were printed together, *se-tenant*, throughout the sheet, giving four blocks of 4 and four single stamps.

(Des L. Fishauf, J. Bennett, B. Drawson, T. Hunt, S. Ng. Litho Ashton-Potter Canada)

1997 (1 Oct). The Supernatural. Centenary of Publication of Bram Stoker's *Dracula*. T **675** and similar square designs. Multicoloured. Fluorescent paper. P 12½×13.

1752	45c. Type **675**	65	85
	a. Block of 4. Nos. 1752/5	2·40	3·00
1753	45c. Werewolf	65	85
1754	45c. Ghost	65	85
1755	45c. Goblin	65	85
1752/1755 Set of 4		2·40	3·00

Nos. 1752/5 were printed together, *se-tenant*, in blocks of 4 throughout the sheet.

CANADA

676 Grizzly Bear

679 Tiger

680 John Robarts (Ontario, 1961–71)

(Des R. Mah. Litho Ashton-Potter Canada)

1998 (8 Jan). Chinese New Year ("Year of the Tiger"). Fluorescent frame. P 13½×12½.

| 1767 | **679** | 45c. multicoloured | 60 | 50 |

MS1768 130×110 mm. As No. 1767×2. P 13×12½........ 1·25   1·50

No. **MS**1768 is diamond-shaped with overall measurements as quoted.

As originally issued the miniature sheet was surrounded by a plain gold margin. Examples from the "Lunar New Year" pack issued on 28 January were additionally inscribed with design and printing information on this gold margin at foot.

(Des R. Bellemare. Litho C.B.N.)

1998 (18 Feb). Canadian Provincial Premiers. T **680** and similar horiz designs. Multicoloured. Fluorescent frame. P 13½.

1769	45c. Type **680**	65	75
	a. Sheetlet. Nos. 1769/78	5·75	6·75
1770	45c. Jean Lesage (Quebec, 1960–66)	65	75
1771	45c. John McNair (New Brunswick, 1940–52)	65	75
1772	45c. Tommy Douglas (Saskatchewan, 1944–61)	65	75
1773	45c. Joseph Smallwood (Newfoundland, 1949–72)	65	75
1774	45c. Angus MacDonald (Nova Scotia, 1933–40, 1945–54)	65	75
1775	45c. W. A. C. Bennett (British Columbia, 1960–66)	65	75
1776	45c. Ernest Manning (Alberta, 1943–68)	65	75
1777	45c. John Bracken (Manitoba, 1922–43)	65	75
1778	45c. J. Walter Jones (Prince Edward Island, 1943–53)	65	75
1769/1778 Set of 10		5·75	6·75

Nos. 1769/78 were printed together, *se-tenant*, in sheetlets of 10 with illustrated margins.

(Des R. Bellemare and P. Leduc. Litho C.B.N.)

1998 (13 Mar). Birds (3rd series). Horiz designs as T **643**. Multicoloured. Fluorescent frame. P 13×13½.

1779	45c. Hairy Woodpecker	1·40	1·25
	a. Block of 4. Nos. 1779/82	5·00	4·50
1780	45c. Great Crested Flycatcher	1·40	1·25
1781	45c. Eastern Screech Owl	1·40	1·25
1782	45c. Gray-crowned Rosy-finch	1·40	1·25
1779/1782 Set of 4		5·00	4·50

Nos. 1779/82 were printed together se-tenant in different combinations throughout the sheet, giving four blocks of 4 and four single stamps.

676 Grizzly Bear

(Des R.-R. Carmichael and Steven Slipp (1756), Xerxes Irani (1757), Pierre Leduc (1758), Steven Slipp and B. Townsend (1759), Dwayne Harty (1760), David Preston-Smith and Steven Slipp (1762), A. Leduc (1762*b*), Suzanne Duranceau and Fugazi (1762*c*). Eng. M. Morck (1759), Jorge Peral (others). Recess and litho CBN)

1997 (15 Oct)–**2010**. Fauna. T **676** and similar horiz designs. Multicoloured. Fluorescent frames (1757/8, 1760/1, **MS**1762*d*). P 13½×13 (1756, 1759), 12½×13 (1757/8, 1760/1, **MS**1762*d*) or 12½×13 (1762*c*).

1756	$1 Loon (47×39 *mm*) (27.10.98)	1·00	90
	a. Chalk-surfaced paper (4.2.03)	1·00	90
1757	$1 White-tailed deer (47×39 *mm*) (20.10.05)	1·50	1·50
	a. Pair. Nos. 1757/8	3·00	3·00
1758	$1 Atlantic walrus (47×39 *mm*) (20.10.05)	1·50	1·50
1759	$2 Polar bear (47×39 *mm*) (27.10.98)	2·25	1·75
	a. Chalk-surfaced paper (4.2.03)	2·75	1·75
1760	$2 Peregrine falcon (47×39 *mm*) (19.12.05)	2·25	2·50
	a. Pair. Nos. 1760/1	4·50	5·00
1761	$2 Sable Island horses (mare and foal) (47×39 *mm*) (19.12.05)	2·25	2·50
1762	$5 Moose (19.12.03)	8·00	7·00
	a. Brown (Moose) ptd albino	£2750	
1762*b*	$8 Type **676**	9·00	9·00
1762*c*	$10 Blue whale (128×49 *mm*) (4.10.2010)	9·00	9·00
1756/1762 Set of 9		32·00	32·00

MS1762*d* Two sheets, each 155×130 *mm*. (a) Nos. 1757/8, each×2. (b) Nos. 1760/1, each×2 *Set of 2 sheets* .... 15·00   17·00

Nos. 1757/8 and 1760/1 were each printed together, *se-tenant*, in horizontal and vertical pairs in sheets of 16 stamps.

No. 1758 was printed in sheets of 4.

677 "Our Lady of the Rosary" (detail, Holy Rosary Cathedral, Vancouver)

678 Livestock and Produce

(Des G. Nincheri (45c.), Ellen Simon (52c.), C. Wallis (90c.). Litho Ashton-Potter Canada)

1997 (3 Nov). Christmas. Stained Glass Windows. T **677** and similar horiz designs. Multicoloured. Fluorescent frame. P 12½×13.

1763	45c. Type **677**	40	20
	a. Perf 12½×imperf	50	40
	ab. Booklet pane. No. 1763a×10	4·75	
1764	52c. "Nativity" (detail, Leith United Church, Ontario)	60	65
	a. Perf 12½×imperf	85	70
	ab. Booklet pane. No. 1764a×5	3·75	
1765	90c. "Life of the Blessed Virgin" (detail, St. Stephen's Ukrainian Catholic Church, Calgary)	1·00	1·40
	a. Perf 12½×imperf	1·00	1·25
	ab. Booklet pane. No. 1765a×5	4·75	
1763/1765 Set of 3		1·75	2·00

Nos. 1763a/5a were only issued in stamp booklets, Nos. SB215/17, with the vertical edges of the panes imperforate and margins at top and bottom.

(Des Heather Lafleur and Shelagh Armstrong. Litho C.B.N.)

1997 (6 Nov). 75th Anniv of Royal Agricultural Winter Fair, Toronto. Fluorescent frame. P 12½×13.

| 1766 | **678** | 45c. multicoloured | 1·50 | 55 |

681 Maple Leaf   **682** Coquihalla Orange Fly

(Des Gottschalk & Ash. Litho Avery Dennison, U.S.A.)

1998 (14 Apr). Self-adhesive. Automatic Cash Machine Stamp. Fluorescent paper. *Die-cut*.

| 1783 | **681** | 45c. multicoloured | 45 | 40 |

No. 1783 was issued, in sheets of 18 (3×6), from bank automatic cash machines and philatelic centres.

For stamps in this design, but without "POSTAGE POSTES" at top left see Nos. 1836/40.

(Des P. Brunelle. Litho Ashton Potter Canada)

1998 (16 Apr). Fishing Flies. T **682** and similar horiz designs. Multicoloured. Fluorescent frame. P 12½×13.

1784	45c. Type **682**	90	90
	a. Booklet pane. Nos. 1784/9, each×2	9·00	
1785	45c. Steelhead Bee	90	90
1786	45c. Dark Montréal	90	90

1787	45c. Lady Amherst		90	90
1788	45c. Coho Blue		90	90
1789	45c. Cosseboom Special		90	90
1784/1789 Set of 6			4·75	4·75

Nos. 1784/9 were only issued in stamp booklets, No. SB220, containing pane No. 1784a which incorporates an inscribed margin at left.

683 Mineral and Petroleum Excavation and Pickaxe

684 1898 2c. Imperial Penny Postage Stamp and Postmaster General Sir William Mulock

(Des Monique Dufour and Sophie Lafortune. Litho Ashton Potter Canada)

1998 (4 May). Centenary of Canadian Institute of Mining, Metallurgy and Petroleum. Fluorescent frame. P 12½.

1790	**683**	45c. multicoloured	70	50

(Des F. Dallaire. Litho C.B.N.)

1998 (29 May). Centenary of Imperial Penny Postage. Fluorescent frame. P 12½×13.

1791	**684**	45c. multicoloured	1·00	55

No. 1791 was printed in sheets of 14 stamps with a label showing the Imperial State Crown appearing in the centre of the sheet.

685 Two Sumo Wrestlers

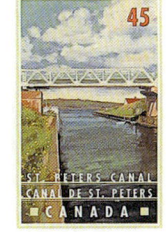

686 St. Peters Canal, Nova Scotia

(Des G. Takeuchi and S. Dittberner. Litho and embossed Ashton Potter Canada)

1998 (5 June). First Canadian Sumo Basho (tournament), Vancouver. T **685** and similar horiz design. Multicoloured. Fluorescent frame. P 12½×13.

1792		45c. Type **685**	65	75
		a. Pair. Nos. 1792/3	1·25	1·50
1793		45c. Sumo wrestler in ceremonial ritual	65	75
MS1794 84×152 mm. Nos. 1792/3			1·25	1·50

On Nos. 1792/4 the outlines of the wrestlers are embossed.

Nos. 1792/3 were printed together, *se-tenant*, both horizontally and vertically in sheets of 20 (4×5). The horizontal rows include labels 7×30 mm either side of each stamp with that on the left inscribed in English and that on the right in Japanese.

(Des V. McIndoe, G. George and D. Martin. Litho Ashton-Potter Canada)

1998 (17 June). Canadian Canals. T **686** and similar vert designs. Multicoloured. Fluorescent frame. P 12½.

1795		45c. Type **686**	1·10	1·25
		a. Booklet pane. Nos. 1795/1804 and ten stamp-size labels	10·00	
1796		45c. St. Ours Canal, Quebec	1·10	1·25
1797		45c. Port Carling Lock, Ontario	1·10	1·25
1798		45c. Lock on Rideau Canal, Ontario	1·10	1·25
1799		45c. Towers and platform of Peterborough Lift Lock, Trent–Severn Waterway, Ontario	1·10	1·25
1800		45c. Chambly Canal, Quebec	1·10	1·25
1801		45c. Lachine Canal, Quebec	1·10	1·25
1802		45c. Rideau Canal in winter, Ontario	1·10	1·25
1803		45c. Boat on Big Chute incline railway, Trent–Severn Waterway, Ontario	1·10	1·25
1804		45c. Sault Ste. Marie Canal, Ontario	1·10	1·25
1795/1804 Set of 10			10·00	11·00

Nos. 1795/1804 were only issued in $4.50 stamp booklets, No. SB221, with the ten labels in the pane providing a location map for the canals depicted.

687 Staff of Aesculapius and Cross

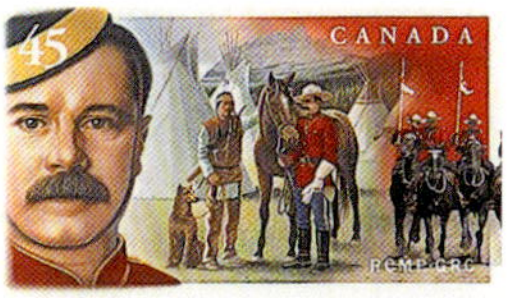

688 Policeman of 1873 and Visit to Indian Village

(Des P.-Y. Pelletier. Typo (embossed) and litho Ashton-Potter Canada)

1998 (25 June). Canadian Health Professionals. Fluorescent paper. P 12½.

1805	**687**	45c. multicoloured	1·00	55

(Des A. Valko and Circle Design. Litho (No. **MS**1808 also embossed) Ashton-Potter Canada)

1998 (3 July). 125th Anniv of Royal Canadian Mounted Police. T **688** and similar horiz design. Multicoloured. Fluorescent frame. P 12½×13.

1806		45c. Type **688**	90	75
		a. Horiz pair. Nos. 1806/7 with label	1·75	1·50
1807		45c. Policewoman of 1998 and aspects of modern law enforcement	90	75
MS1808 160×102 mm. Nos. 1806/7			1·75	1·90

Nos. 1806/7 were printed together, *se-tenant*, in pairs both horizontally and vertically, throughout the sheet of 20 (4×5). The horizontal rows include labels, 15×26 mm, on either side of each stamp. There are two label designs, one showing the R.C.M.P. crest and the other the Musical Ride which continues the design shown on the two stamps.

No. **MS**1808 also exists from a limited printing with the facsimile signature of Lieut-Col. G. A. French, the first commissioner, added to the bottom margin.

No. **MS**1808 was also issued overprinted with the logos of "Portugal 98" or "Italia 98" for sale at these International Stamp Exhibitions.

689 William J. Roue (designer) and *Bluenose* (schooner)

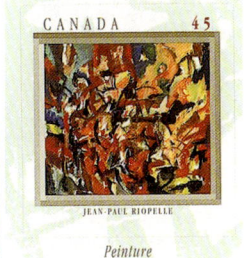

690 "Painting" (Jean-Paul Riopelle)

(Des L. Herbert. Recess and litho C.B.N.)

1998 (24 July). William James Roue (naval architect) Commemoration. Fluorescent frame. P 13.

1809	**689**	45c. multicoloured	70	50

(Des L. Cable. Litho Ashton-Potter Canada)

1998 (28 July). Scenic Highways (2nd series). Horiz designs as T **667**. Multicoloured. Fluorescent frame. P 12½×13.

1810		45c. Dempster Highway, Yukon, and caribou	65	75
		a. Block of 4. Nos. 1810/13	2·40	2·75
1811		45c. Dinosaur Trail, Alberta, and skeleton	65	75
1812		45c. River Valley Drive, New Brunswick, and fern	65	75
1813		45c. Blue Heron Route, Prince Edward Island, and lobster	65	75
1810/1813 Set of 4			2·40	2·75

Nos. 1810/13 were printed together, *se-tenant*, in sheets of 20 containing four blocks of 4 and four single stamps.

(Des R. Bellemare. Litho C.B.N.)

1998 (7 Aug). 50th Anniv of *Refus Global* (manifesto of The Automatistes group of artists). T **690** and similar multicoloured designs. Self-adhesive. Fluorescent frame. *Die-cut*.

1814		45c. Type **690**	1·10	1·10
		a. Booklet pane. Nos. 1814/20	7·00	
1815		45c. "La dernière campagne de Napoléon" (Fernand Leduc) (37×31½ *mm*)	1·10	1·10
1816		45c. "Jet fuligineux sur noir torture" (Jean-Paul Mousseau)	1·10	1·10
1817		45c. "Le fond du garde-robe" (Pierre Gauvreau) (29½×42 *mm*)	1·10	1·10

CANADA

1818	45c. "Joie lacustre" (Paul-Emile Borduas)		1·10	1·10
1819	45c. "Seafarers Union" (Marcelle Ferron) (36×34 mm)		1·10	1·10
1820	45c. "Le tumulte à la mâchoire crispée" (Marcel Barbeau) (36×34 mm)		1·10	1·10
1814/1820	Set of 7		7·00	7·00

Nos. 1814/20 were only available from $3.15 self-adhesive booklets, No. SB222, in which the backing card formed the cover.

691 Napoléon Alexandre Comeau (naturalist)

692 Indian Wigwam

(Des Catherine Bradbury and D. Bartsch. Litho C.B.N.)

1998 (15 Aug). Legendary Canadians. T **691** and similar vert designs. Multicoloured. Fluorescent frame. P 13½.

1821	45c. Type **691**		55	75
	a. Block of 4. Nos. 1821/4		2·00	2·75
1822	45c. Phyllis Munday (mountaineer)		55	75
1823	45c. Bill Mason (film-maker)		55	75
1824	45c. Harry Red Foster (sports commentator)		55	75
1821/1824	Set of 4		2·00	2·75

Nos. 1821/4 were printed together, *se-tenant*, in sheets of 20 containing four blocks of 4 and four single stamps.

(Des P.-Y. Pelletier. Litho and die-stamped Ashton Potter Canada)

1998 (8 Sept). Canadian Art (11th series). Vert design as T **550**. Multicoloured. Fluorescent frame. P 12½×13.

1825	90c. "The Farmer's Family" (Bruno Bobak)		1·00	1·60

No. 1825 was issued in a similar sheet format to No. 1289.

(Des C. Gibson and P. Scott. Litho Ashton Potter Canada)

1998 (23 Sept). Canadian Houses. T **692** and similar horiz designs. Multicoloured. Fluorescent frame. P 12½×13.

1826	45c. Type **692**		50	70
	a. Sheetlet. Nos. 1826/34		4·00	5·50
1827	45c. Settler sod hut		50	70
1828	45c. Maison Saint-Gabriel (17th-cent farmhouse), Quebec		50	70
1829	45c. Queen Anne style brick house, Ontario		50	70
1830	45c. Terrace of town houses		50	70
1831	45c. Prefabricated house		50	70
1832	45c. Veterans' houses		50	70
1833	45c. Modern bungalow		50	70
1834	45c. Healthy House, Toronto		50	70
1826/1834	Set of 9		4·00	5·50

Nos. 1826/34 were printed together, *se-tenant*, in sheetlets of 9 with additional side margins carrying design descriptions.

693 University of Ottawa

694 Performing Animals

(Des Harris Design Associates. Litho C.B.N.)

1998 (25 Sept). 150th Anniv of University of Ottawa. Fluorescent frame. P 13½.

1835	**693**	45c. multicoloured	50	50

1998 (30 Sept–28 Dec). As T **681**, but without "POSTAGE POSTES" at top left.

(a) Litho Ashton Potter Canada. Fluorescent frame. P 13×13½

1836	**681**	55c. multicoloured (28 Dec)	1·75	1·75
		a. Booklet pane. No. 1836×5 plus printed label	8·00	
1837		73c. multicoloured (28 Dec)	1·25	1·40
1838		95c. multicoloured (28 Dec)	2·25	2·25
		a. Booklet pane. No. 1838×5 plus printed label	10·00	

(b) Coil stamp. Litho and die-stamped (gold) Ashton Potter Canada. Fluorescent frame. P 13

1839	**681**	45c. multicoloured	1·25	1·25

(c) Self-adhesive automatic cash machine stamp. Litho Avery Dennison, U.S.A. Fluorescent paper. Die-cut

1840	**681**	46c. multicoloured (28 Dec)	1·00	1·25

Booklet panes Nos. 1836a and 1838a come from SB229/30 and have the vertical edges of the panes imperforate and margins at top and bottom.

No. 1839 was available in rolls of 100 on which the surplus self-adhesive paper around each stamp was removed.

No. 1840 was issued in sheets of 18 (3×6), from bank automatic cash machines and philatelic centres.

Nos. 1841/50 are vacant.

(Des Monique Dufour, Sophie Lafortune and Paule Thibault. Litho Ashton-Potter Canada)

1998 (1 Oct). Canadian Circus. T **694** and similar vert designs, each incorporating a different clown. Multicoloured. Fluorescent frame. P 13.

1851	45c. Type **694**		1·25	1·25
	a. Booklet pane. Nos. 1851/4, each×3		13·00	
1852	45c. Flying trapeze and acrobat on horseback		1·25	1·25
1853	45c. Lion tamer		1·25	1·25
1854	45c. Acrobats and trapeze artists		1·25	1·25
1851/1854	Set of 4		4·50	4·50
MS1855	133×133 mm. Nos. 1851/4		4·00	4·50

Nos. 1851/4 only exist from $5.40 booklets, No. SB223, in which the upper and lower edges of the pane are imperforate.

The fluorescent frames on Nos. 1851/4 are broken at various points where the designs encroach onto the margins.

695 John Peters Humphrey (author of original Declaration draft)

(Des J. Hudson. Litho C.B.N.)

1998 (7 Oct). 50th Anniv of Universal Declaration of Human Rights. Fluorescent frame. P 13×13½.

1856	**695**	45c. multicoloured	50	50

696 H.M.C.S. *Sackville* (corvette)

(Des T. Hawkins and D. Page. Litho C.B.N.)

1998 (4 Nov). 75th Anniv of Canadian Naval Reserve. T **696** and similar horiz design. Multicoloured. Fluorescent frame. P 12½×13.

1857	45c. Type **696**		80	90
	a. Pair. Nos. 1857/8		1·60	1·75
1858	45c. H.M.C.S. *Shawinigan* (coastal defence vessel)		80	90

Nos. 1857/8 were printed together, *se-tenant*, in horizontal and vertical pairs throughout the sheet.

697 Angel blowing Trumpet

698 Rabbit

CANADA

(Des Anita Zeppetelli. Litho Ashton Potter Canada)

1998 (6 Nov). Christmas. Statues of Angels. T **697** and similar vert designs. Multicoloured. Fluorescent frame. P 13 (45c.) or 13×13½ (others).

1859	45c. Type **697**	50	20
	a. Booklet pane. No. 1859×10	7·00	
	b. Perf 13×13½	1·40	1·40
	ba. Booklet pane. No. 1859b×10	16·00	
1860	52c. Adoring Angel	1·40	1·50
	a. Booklet pane. No. 1860×5 plus one printed label	7·50	
	b. Perf 13	85	75
	ba. Booklet pane. No. 1860b×5 plus one printed label	3·75	
1861	90c. Angel at prayer	3·25	3·50
	a. Booklet pane. No. 1861×5 plus one printed label	15·00	
	b. Perf 13	1·60	2·00
	ba. Booklet pane. No. 1861b×5 plus one printed label	7·50	
1859/1861b *Set of 3*		2·75	2·75

Nos. 1860b and 1861b only come from stamp booklets. Sheets of the 45c. are known in either perforation, but sheet stamps in the 13×13½ gauge are rare (*Price £50 mint for example with perforations on all four sides*).

The booklet panes come from Nos. SB224/6a and show vertical edges of the panes imperforate and margins at top and bottom.

(Des K. Koo and K. Fung. Litho Ashton-Potter Canada)

1999 (8 Jan). Chinese New Year ("Year of the Rabbit"). Fluorescent frame. P 13½.

1862	**698**	46c. multicoloured	50	50
		a. Red omitted	£500	
MS1863 Circular 100 mm diam. **698** 95c. mult (40×40 *mm*). P 12½×13			1·75	2·25
		a. Red omitted	£800	

No. **MS**1863 also exists with the "CHINA '99" World Stamp Exhibition, Beijing, logo overprinted in gold on the top of the margin.

The omission of the colour causes the background to appear yellow rather than orange.

699 Stylized Mask and Curtain

700 "The Raven and the First Men" (B. Reid) and The Great Hall

(Des Y. Paquin and Marie Rouleau. Litho C.B.N.)

1999 (16 Feb). 50th Anniv of Le Théâtre du Rideau. Fluorescent frame. P 13×12½.

1864	**699**	46c. multicoloured	50	50

(Des R. Bellemare and P. Leduc. Litho Ashton-Potter Canada)

1999 (24 Feb). Birds (4th series). Horiz designs as T **643**. Multicoloured. Fluorescent frame.

(a) P 12½×13

1865	46c. Northern Goshawk	85	85
	a. Block of 4. Nos. 1865/8	3·00	3·00
1866	46c. Red-winged Blackbird	85	85
1867	46c. American Goldfinch	85	85
1868	46c. Sandhill Crane	85	85
1865/1868 *Set of 4*		3·00	3·00

(b) Self-adhesive. P 11½

1869	46c. Northern Goshawk	85	85
	b. Booklet pane. Nos. 1869/72, each×3, with margins all round	10·00	
1870	46c. Red-winged Blackbird	85	85
1871	46c. American Goldfinch	85	85
1872	46c. Sandhill Crane	85	85
1869/1872 *Set of 4*		3·00	3·00

Nos. 1865/8 were printed together *se-tenant* in different combinations throughout the sheet, giving four blocks of 4 and four single stamps.

Nos. 1869/72 were only issued in $5.52 stamp booklets, No. SB231, on which the surplus self-adhesive paper was retained.

(Des Barbara Hodgson. Litho C.B.N.)

1999 (9 Mar). 50th Anniv of University of British Columbia Museum of Anthropology. Fluorescent frame. P 13½.

1873	**700**	46c. multicoloured	50	50

701 *Marco Polo* (full-rigged ship)

702 Inuit Children and Landscape

(Des J. Franklin Wright. Litho Ashton-Potter Canada)

1999 (19 Mar). Canada–Australia Joint Issue. *Marco Polo* (emigrant ship). Multicoloured. Fluorescent frame. P 13×12½.

1874	46c. Type **701**	50	50
MS1875 160×95 mm. 85c. As No. 1728 of Australia. P 13; 46c. Type **701**. P 13½ (No. **MS**1875 was sold at $1.25 in Canada)		1·75	2·00

No. **MS**1875 includes the "Australia '99" emblem on the sheet margin and was postally valid in Canada to the value of 46c.

The same miniature sheet was also available in Australia.

(Des L. Cable. Litho Ashton-Potter Canada)

1999 (31 Mar). Scenic Highways (3rd series). Horiz designs as T **667**. Multicoloured. Fluorescent frame. P 12½×13.

1876	46c. Route 132, Quebec, and hang-glider	75	85
	a. Block of 4. Nos. 1876/9	2·75	3·00
1877	46c. Yellowhead Highway, Manitoba, and Bison	75	85
1878	46c. Dempster Highway, Northwest Territories, and Indian village elder	75	85
1879	46c. The Discovery Trail, Newfoundland, and whale's tailfin	75	85
1876/1879 *Set of 4*		2·75	3·00

Nos. 1876/9 were printed together, *se-tenant*, in sheets of 20 comprising four blocks of 4 and four single stamps.

(Des Susan Point and Bonne Zabolotney. Litho Ashton-Potter Canada)

1999 (1 Apr). Creation of Nunavut Territory. Fluorescent frame. P 12½×13.

1880	**702**	46c. multicoloured	50	50

703 Elderly Couple on Country Path

704 Khanda (Sikh symbol)

(Des Sheila Armstrong-Hodgson, P. Hodgson and S. Peters. Litho C.B.N.)

1999 (12 Apr). International Year of Older Persons. Fluorescent frame. P 13½.

1881	**703**	46c. multicoloured	50	50

(Des S. Zabolotney. Litho C.B.N.)

1999 (19 Apr). Centenary of Sikhs in Canada. Interrupted fluorescent frame. P 13.

1882	**704**	46c. multicoloured	50	50

705 *Arethusa bulbosa* (orchid)

706 Bookbinding

CANADA

(Des Marlene Wou, Poon Kuen Chow and Y. Lai.
Litho Ashton-Potter Canada)

1999 (27 Apr). 16th World Orchid Conference, Vancouver. T **705** and similar vert designs. Multicoloured. Fluorescent frame. P 13×12½.
1883	46c. Type **705**...	75	75
	a. Booklet pane. Nos. 1883/6, each×3, with margins all round..........	8·00	
1884	46c. Amerorchis rotundifolia..................	75	75
1885	46c. Cypripedium pubescens..................	75	75
1886	46c. Platanthera psycodes.......................	75	75
1883/1886 Set of 4		2·75	2·75

Nos. 1883/6 were initially only issued in $5.52 stamp booklets, No. SB232, but later appeared in No. **MS**1917.

(Des Monique Dufour and Sophie Lafortune. Litho Ashton-Potter Canada or C.B.N (1c., 5c., 10c., 25c.) or Ashton-Potter Canada (others))

1999 (29 Apr)–**2002**. Traditional Trades. T **706** and similar vert designs. Multicoloured.

(a) No fluorescent frame. P 13×13½
1887	1c. Type **706**...	10	10
1888	2c. Decorative ironwork........................	10	10
1889	3c. Glass-blowing..................................	10	10
1890	4c. Oyster farming.................................	10	10
1891	5c. Weaving..	10	10
1892	9c. Quilting...	10	10
1893	10c. Wood carving.................................	10	15
1894	25c. Leatherworking..............................	20	25
1887/1894 Set of 8		60	70

(b) Self-adhesive. Chalk-surfaced paper. Fluorescent frame. Die-cut perf 9×imperf
1895	65c. Jewellery making (*horiz*) (2.1.02).....	50	55
	a. Pane of 6..	2·50	
1896	77c. Basket-weaving (*horiz*) (2.1.02)......	1·50	1·50
1897	$1.25 Wood-carving (*horiz*) (2.1.02).....	1·00	1·10
	a. Pane of 6..	5·50	
1895/1897 Set of 3		2·75	2·75

Nos. 1895/7 were issued in coils of 50, with the surplus self-adhesive paper between each stamp removed, or as panes of 6 (65c., $1.25 only) where the surplus paper was retained.

Nos. 1898/1902 are vacant.

707 "Northern Dancer" (racehorse)

708 Logo engraved on Limestone

(Des P.-Y. Pelletier. Litho Ashton-Potter Canada)

1999 (2 June). Canadian Horses. T **707** and similar horiz designs. Multicoloured. Fluorescent frame.

(a) P 13×13½
1903	46c. Type **707**...	80	80
	a. Block of 4. Nos. 1903/6....................	3·00	3·00
1904	46c. "Kingsway Skoal" (rodeo horse).....	80	80
1905	46c. "Big Ben" (show jumper)...............	80	80
1906	46c. "Armbro Flight" (trotter)...............	80	80
1903/1906 Set of 4		3·00	3·00

(b) Self-adhesive. P 11½×11
1907	46c. Type **707**...	70	75
	a. Booklet pane. Nos. 1907/10, each×3, with margins all round.............	7·50	
1908	46c. "Kingsway Skoal" (rodeo horse).....	70	75
1909	46c. "Big Ben" (show jumper)...............	70	75
1910	46c. "Armbro Flight" (trotter)...............	70	75
1907/1910 Set of 4		2·50	2·75

Nos. 1903/6 were printed together, *se-tenant*, in blocks of 4 throughout sheets of 16.

Nos. 1907/10 were only issued in $5.52 stamp booklets, No. SB233, on which the surplus self-adhesive paper was retained.

(Des P. Fontaine. Litho C.B.N.)

1999 (3 June). 150th Anniv of Barreau du Québec (Quebec lawyers' association). Fluorescent frame. P 13½.
1911	**708** 46c. multicoloured...........................	50	50

(Des P-Y. Pelletier. Litho and die-stamped Ashton-Potter Canada)

1999 (3 July). Canadian Art (12th series). Vert design as T *550*. Multicoloured. Fluorescent inner frame. P 12½×13.
1912	95c. "Coq licorne" (Jean Dallaire)...........	1·25	1·75
	a. Silver omitted....................................	£1300	

No. 1912 was issued in a similar sheet format to No. 1289.

709 Athletics

(Des Circle Design. Litho Ashton-Potter Canada)

1999 (12 July). 13th Pan-American Games, Winnipeg. T **709** and similar square designs. Multicoloured. Fluorescent frame. P 13½.
1913	46c. Type **709**...	85	90
	a. Block of 4. Nos. 1913/16..................	3·00	3·25
1914	46c. Cycling..	85	90
1915	46c. Swimming.......................................	85	90
1916	46c. Football...	85	90
1913/1916 Set of 4		3·00	3·25

Nos. 1913/16 were printed together, *se-tenant*, as blocks of 4 in sheets of 16.

(Des Chris Dahl Design, Poon Kuen Chow and Y. Lai. Litho Ashton-Potter Canada)

1999 (21 Aug). "China '99" International Stamp Exhibition, Beijing. Sheet 78×133 *mm*, containing Nos. 1883/6. Multicoloured. Fluorescent frame. P 13×12½.
MS1917 46c. Type **705**; 46c. Amerorchis rotundifolia; 46c. Cypripedium pubescens; 46c. Platanthera psycodes.......	2·25	2·75

710 Female Rower

(Des P. Haslip and A. Lum. Litho Ashton-Potter Canada)

1999 (22 Aug). 23rd World Rowing Championships, St. Catharines. Fluorescent frame. P 12½×13.
1918	**710** 46c. multicoloured...........................	50	50

711 U.P.U. Emblem and World Map

(Des P.-Y. Pelletier. Litho C.B.N.)

1999 (26 Aug). 125th Anniv of Universal Postal Union. Fluorescent frame. P 12½×13.
1919	**711** 46c. multicoloured...........................	75	50

712 De Havilland Mosquito F.B. VI

(Des T. Telmet, M. Barac and G. Lay. Litho C.B.N.)

1999 (4 Sept). 75th Anniv of Canadian Air Force. T **712** and similar horiz designs. Multicoloured. Fluorescent frame. P 12½×13.
1920	46c. Type **712**...	75	85
	a. Sheetlet. Nos. 1920/35.....................	11·00	12·00
1921	46c. Sopwith F.1 Camel.........................	75	85
1922	46c. De Havilland Canada DHC-3 Otter...........	75	85
1923	46c. De Havilland Canada CC-108 Caribou.....	75	85
1924	46c. Canadair CL-28 Argus Mk 2..........	75	85
1925	46c. Canadair (North American) F-86 Sabre 6...	75	85
1926	46c. McDonnell Douglas CF-18............	75	85
1927	46c. Sopwith 5.F.1 Dolphin...................	75	85
1928	46c. Armstrong Whitworth Siskin IIIA..............	75	85

CANADA

1929	46c. Canadian Vickers (Northrop)Delta II		75	85
1930	46c. Sikorsky CH-124A Sea King helicopter ...		75	85
1931	46c. Vickers-Armstrong Wellington Mk II		75	85
1932	46c. Avro Anson Mk I		75	85
1933	46c. Canadair (Lockheed) CF-104G Starfighter		75	85
1934	46c. Burgess-Dunne		75	85
1935	46c. Avro 504K		75	85
1920/1935	Set of 16		11·00	12·00

Nos. 1920/35 were printed together, *se-tenant*, in sheetlets of 16.

713 Fokker DR-1

(Des T. Telmet and M. Barac. Litho C.B.N.)

1999 (4 Sept). 50th Anniv of Canadian International Air Show. T **713** and similar horiz designs. Multicoloured. Fluorescent frame. P 12½×13.

1936	46c. Type **713**..	85	90
	a. Sheetlet. Nos. 1936/9.......................	3·00	3·25
1937	46c. H101 Salto glider................................	85	90
1938	46c. De Havilland DH100 Vampire Mk III....	85	90
1939	46c. Wing-walker on Stearman A-75.........	85	90
1936/1939	Set of 4	3·00	3·25

Nos. 1936/9 were printed together, *se-tenant*, in sheetlets of 4 forming a composite design which includes a nine-plane "snowbird" formation of Canadair CT114 Tutor in the background.

714 N.A.T.O. Emblem and National Flags

(Des Bonnie Ross and F. Ross. Litho Ashton Potter Canada)

1999 (21 Sept). 50th Anniv of North Atlantic Treaty Organization. Fluorescent frame. P 12½×13.

1940	**714**	46c. multicoloured	1·00	50

715 Man ploughing on Book    **716** Master Control Sports Kite

(Des Q30 Design. Litho C.B.N.)

1999 (24 Sept). Centenary of Frontier College (workers' education organization). Fluorescent frame. P 13×13½.

1941	**715**	46c. multicoloured	50	50

The fluorescent frame on No. 1941 is incomplete as there are breaks at top right and at the lower left-hand corner.

(Des Debbie Adams. Litho Ashton-Potter Canada)

1999 (1 Oct). Stamp Collecting Month. Kites. T **716** and similar multicoloured designs. *Die-cut perforations*.

1942	46c. Type **716**..	55	65
	a. Booklet pane. Nos. 1942/5×2	4·00	
1943	46c. Indian Garden Flying Carpet (*irregular rectangle, 35×32 mm*)................................	55	65
1944	46c. Gibson Girl box kite (*horiz, 38½×25 mm*)...	55	65
1945	46c. Dragon Centipede (*oval, 39×29 mm*)	55	65
1942/1945	Set of 4	2·00	2·40

Nos. 1942/5 were only issued in stamp booklets, No. SB234, containing pane No. 1942a.

717 Boy holding Dove    **718** Angel playing Drum

(Des P-Y. Pelletier (46c.), Monique Dufour and Sophie Lafortune (55c.), J. Peral (95c.))

1999 (12 Oct). New Millennium. Three sheets, each 108×108 *mm*, containing T **717** and similar square designs in blocks of 4.

(a) Litho Ashton-Potter Canada (hologram by Crown Canada). Self-adhesive. Die-cut

MS1946	46c.×4 multicoloured.....................................	2·00	2·50

(b) Litho Ashton-Potter Canada. P 13½

MS1947	55c.×4 multicoloured.....................................	4·50	4·75

(c) Recess C.B.N. P 13

MS1948	95c.×4 red-brown...	3·75	4·50

Designs:—46c. Holographic image of dove in flight; 95c. Dove with olive branch.

Designs as Nos. **MS**1946/8 also exist in similar-sized miniature sheets each containing one stamp. These were only available in the Canada Post "Official Millennium Keepsake" which presented them in a tin box, together with a certificate and a medallion, for $8.99.

(Des Tannis Hopkins, K. Tsetsekas and Bonne Zabolotney. Litho C.B.N.)

1999 (4 Nov). Christmas. Victorian Angels. T **718** and similar vert designs. Multicoloured. Fluorescent frame. P 13½.

1949	46c. Type **718**..	60	20
	a. Booklet pane. No. 1949×10.................	6·50	
1950	55c. Angel with toys	80	50
	a. Booklet pane. No. 1950×5 plus one printed label...	4·75	
1951	95c. Angel with star	1·40	2·25
	a. Booklet pane. No. 1951×5 plus one printed label...	6·50	
1949/1951	Set of 3	2·40	2·75

Nos. 1949a/51a come from booklet Nos. SB235/7 and show the vertical edges of the panes imperforate and have margins at top and bottom.

719 Portia White (singer)    **720** Millennium Partnership Programme Logo

(Des F. and B. Ross, A. Dunkelman, R. Willms and Y. Laroche (No. **MS**1952); J. Michaud, P. Haslip, Geneviève Caron and C. Malenfant (**MS**1953); T. Gregoraschuk, M. Serre, D. Fortin, G. Fok and Alexis Brothers, Sheri Hancock and Hélène L'Heureux (2) (**MS**1954); K. Tsetsekas and G. Kehrig, H. Chung, D. Corriveau, P. Scott and Glenda Rissman, B. Canning and M. Waddell (**MS**1955). Litho Ashton-Potter Canada)

1999 (17 Dec). Millennium Collection (1st series). Entertainment and Arts. Miniature sheets, each 108×112 mm, containing T **719** and similar vert designs. Multicoloured. Fluorescent frame. P 13½.

MS1952	46c. Type **719**; 46c. Glenn Gould (pianist); 46c. Guy Lombardo (conductor of "Royal Canadians"); 46c. Félix Leclerc (musician, playwright and actor)............	2·25	2·75
MS1953	46c. Artists looking at painting (Royal Canadian Academy of Arts); 46c. Cloud, stave and pencil marks (The Canada Council); 46c. Man with video camera (National Film Board of Canada); 46c. News-reader (Canadian Broadcasting Corporation)........................	2·25	2·75
MS1954	46c. Calgary Stampede; 46c. Circus performers; 46c. Ice hockey (Hockey Night); 46c. Goalkeeper (Ice hockey live from The Forum)...	2·25	2·75

CANADA

MS1955 46c. IMAX cinema; 46c. Computer image (Softimage); 46c. Ted Rogers Sr ("Plugging in the Radio"); 46c. Sir William Stephenson (inventor of radio facsimile system) .... 2·25 2·75
MS1952/1955 Set of 4 sheets .... 8·00 10·00

In addition to Nos. MS1952/5, these designs were also available in a presentation album showing two stamps per page.

On stamps from the presentation album the copyright date is 2 mm long, but only 1.75 mm long on those from miniature sheets.

See also Nos. MS1959/62, MS1969/73 and MS1982/5.

(Des karacters design group. Litho C.B.N.)

2000 (1 Jan). Canada Millennium Partnership Programme. Fluorescent frame. P 13×12½.
1956   720   46c. bright red, myrtle-green and light grey-blue 50   50

721 Chinese Dragon

(Des K. Fung and K. Woo. Litho and embossed Ashton-Potter Canada)

2000 (5 Jan). Chinese New Year ("Year of the Dragon"). Fluorescent frame. P 12½.
1957   721   46c. multicoloured 50   50
MS1958 150×85 mm. 721 95c. mult. P 13½ .... 1·25   1·50

(Des R. Tibbles, P.-Y. Pelletier, Koo Creative Group Inc, and L. Cable (No. MS1959); L. Fishauf, Louise Delisle and J.-C. Guénette, Stéphane Huot, and T. Yakobina (No. MS1960); R. Bellemare, Margaret Issenman and Bonnie Ross, Letterbox Design Group, and Circle Design Incorporated (No. MS1961); F. Blais, Orange, F. Dallaire and B. Leduc, and Gaynor and D. Sarty (No. MS1962). Litho Ashton-Potter Canada)

2000 (17 Jan). Millennium Collection (2nd series). Charities, Medical Pioneers, Peace-keepers and Social Reforms. Miniature sheets, each 108×112 mm, containing vert designs as T **719**. Multicoloured. Fluorescent frame. P 13½.
MS1959 46c. Providing equipment (Canadian International Development Agency); 46c. Dr. Lucille Teasdale (medical missionary); 46c. Terry Fox (Marathon of Hope); 46c. Delivering meal (Meals on Wheels) .... 2·25   2·50
MS1960 46c. Sir Frederick Banting (discovery of insulin); 46c. Armand Frappier (developer of BCG vaccine); 46c. Dr. Hans Selye (research into stress); 46c. "Dr. Maude Abbott" (pathologist) (M. Bell Eastlake) .... 2·25   2·50
MS1961 46c. Senator Raoul Dandurand (diplomat); 46c. Pauline Vanier and Elizabeth Smellie (nursing pioneers); 46c. Lester B. Pearson (diplomat); 46c. One-legged man (Ottawa Convention on Banning Landmines) .... 2·25   2·50
MS1962 46c. Nun and surgeon (medical care); 46c. "Women are Persons" (sculpture by Barbara Paterson) (Appointment of women senators); 46c. Alphonse and Dorimène Desjardins (People's bank movement); 46c. Father Moses Coady (Adult education pioneer) .... 2·25   2·50
MS1959/1962 Set of 4 sheets .... 8·00   9·00

In addition to Nos. MS1959/62, these designs were also available in a presentation album showing two stamps per page.

722 Wayne Gretzky (ice-hockey player)

723 Judges and Supreme Court Building

(Des D. Fell and V. McIndoe. Litho C.B.N.)

2000 (5 Feb). National Hockey League. All-Star Game Players (1st series). T **722** and similar square designs. Multicoloured. Fluorescent circular frame around central design. P 13.
1963   46c. Type **722** 80   80
       a. Sheetlet. Nos. 1963/8 .... 4·25   4·25
1964   46c. Gordie Howe (No. 9 in white jersey) 80   80
1965   46c. Maurice Richard (No. 9 in blue and red jersey) 80   80
1966   46c. Doug Harvey (No. 2) 80   80
1967   46c. Bobby Orr (No. 4) 80   80
1968   46c. Jacques Plante (No. 1) 80   80
1963/1968 Set of 6 .... 4·25   4·25

Nos. 1963/8 were printed together, se-tenant, in sheetlets of 6 with portraits of the players shown on the sheet margins alongside the individual stamps.

Nos. 1963/8 commemorate the 50th National Hockey League All-Stars Game.

See also Nos. 2052/7, 2118/23, 2178/83 and 2250/6f.

(Des R. Harder, S. Bhandari and G. Khayat, J. Skipp and J. Evans and S. Slipp (No. MS1969); I. Drolet, B. Tsang, P. Fontaine, and Zabolotney Graphic Design (MS1970); D. Bartsch, P. Fontaine, Lise Giguère and G. Ludwig (MS1971); D. Bartsch, P. Fontaine, Lise Giguère and G. Ludwig (MS1972); Debbie Adams, D. Page and T. Hawkins, T. Nokes and R. Harder (MS1973). Litho Ashton-Potter Canada)

2000 (17 Feb). Millennium Collection (3rd series). First Inhabitants, Great Thinkers, Culture and Literary Legends, and Charitable Foundations. Miniature sheets, each 108×112 mm, containing vert designs as T **719**. Multicoloured. Fluorescent frame. P 13½.
MS1969 46c. Pontiac (Ottawa chief); 46c. Tom Longboat (long-distance runner); 46c. "Inuit Shaman" (sculpture by Paul Toolooktook); 46c. Shaman and patient (Indian medicine) .... 2·25   2·50
MS1970 46c. Prof. Marshall McLuhan (media philosopher); 46c. Northrop Frye (literary critic); 46c. Roger Lemelin (novelist); 46c. Prof. Hilda Marion Neatby (educator) .... 2·25   2·50
MS1971 46c. Bow of Viking longship (L'Anse aux Meadows World Heritage Site); 46c. Immigrant family (Pier 21 monument); 46c. Neptune mask (Neptune Theatre, Halifax); 46c. Auditorium and actor (The Stratford Festival) .... 2·25   2·50
MS1972 46c. W. O. Mitchell (writer); 46c. Gratien Gélinas (actor, producer and play-wright); 46c. Text and fountain pen (Cercle du Livre de France); 46c. Harlequin and roses (Harlequin Books) .... 2·25   2·50
MS1973 46c. Hart Massey (Massey Foundation); 46c. Izaak Walton Killam and Dorothy Killam; 46c. Eric Lafferty Harvie (Glenbow Foundation); 46c. Macdonald Stewart Foundation .... 2·25   2·50
MS1969/1973 Set of 5 sheets .... 10·00   11·00

In addition to Nos. MS1969/73, these designs were also available in a presentation album showing two stamps per page.

(Des P. Leduc and R. Bellemare. Litho Ashton-Potter Canada)

2000 (1 Mar). Birds (5th series). Horiz designs as T **643**. Multicoloured. Fluorescent frame.

(a) P 12½×13
1974   46c. Canadian Warbler 85   90
       a. Block of 4. Nos. 1974/7 .... 3·00   3·25
1975   46c. Osprey 85   90
1976   46c. Pacific Loon 85   90
1977   46c. Blue Jay 85   90
1974/1977 Set of 4 .... 3·00   3·25

(b) Self-adhesive. P 11½
1978   46c. Canadian Warbler 70   80
       a. Booklet pane. Nos. 1978/81, each×3 .... 7·50
1979   46c. Osprey 70   80
1980   46c. Pacific Loon 70   80
1981   46c. Blue Jay 70   80
1978/1981 Set of 4 .... 2·50   3·00

Nos. 1974/7 were printed together se-tenant in different combinations throughout the sheet, giving four blocks of 4 and four single stamps.

Nos. 1978/81 were only available from $5.52 stamp booklets, No. SB238.

(Des Taylor/Sprules Corporation and P. Sayers, M. Koudis, D. Preston Smith and P.-M. Brunelle and J. Hudson (No. MS1982); Susan Scott, N. Smith, Monique Dufour and Sophie LaFortune and Doreen Colonello and S. Ash (MS1983); T. Telmet and M. Barac, S. Slipp and D. Preston Smith, J. LeBlanc and Bonnie Ross and Michèle Cayer and T. Kapas (MS1984); K. van der Leek and A. McKinley, E. Roch, T. Yakobina and N. Skinner, J. Gault and N.C.K. Engineering (MS1985). Litho Ashton-Potter Canada)

2000 (17 Mar). Millennium Collection (4th series). Canadian Agriculture, Commerce and Technology. Miniature sheets, each 108×112 mm, containing vert designs as T **719**. Multicoloured. Fluorescent frame. P 13½.
MS1982 46c. Sir Charles Saunders (developer of Marquis wheat); 46c. Baby (Pablum baby food); 46c. Dr. Archibald Gowanlock Huntsman (frozen fish pioneer); 46c. Oven chips and field of potatoes (McCain Frozen Foods) .... 2·25   2·50
MS1983 46c. Early trader and Indian (Hudson's Bay Company); 46c. Satellite over earth (Bell Canada Enterprises); 46c. Jos. Louis biscuits and Vachon family (Vachon Family Bakery); 46c. Bread and eggs (George Weston Limited) .... 2·25   2·50

MS1984 46c. George Klein and cog wheels (inventor of electric wheelchair and microsurgical staple gun); 46c. Abraham Gesner (developer of kerosene); 46c. Alexander Graham Bell (inventor of telephone); 46c. Joseph-Armand Bombardier (inventor of snowmobile) .... 2·25 2·50
MS1985 46c. Workers and steam locomotive (Rogers Pass rail tunnel); 46c. Manic 5 dam (Manicouagan River hydro-electric project); 46c. Mobile Servicing System for International Space Station (Canadian Space Program); 46c. CN Tower (World's tallest building) .... 2·25 2·50
MS1982/1985 *Set of* 4 sheets .... 8·00 9·00

In addition to Nos. **MS**1982/5, these designs were also available in a presentation album showing two stamps per page.

(Des C. Le Sauter. Litho C.B.N.)

2000 (10 Apr). 125th Anniv of Supreme Court of Canada. Fluorescent frame. P 12½×13.
1986   723   46c. multicoloured 50 50

724 Lethbridge Bridge, Synthetic Rubber Plant, X-ray of Heart Pacemaker and Microwave Radio System

725

(Des D. Freeman. Litho Ashton-Potter Canada)

2000 (25 Apr). 75th Anniv of Ceremony for Calling of an Engineer. Fluorescent frame. P 12½×13.
1987   724   46c. multicoloured 50 50
              a. *Tête-bêche* (vert pair).. 1·00 1·00

No. 1987 was printed in sheets of 16 (4×4), with a central horizontal gutter, showing rows 2 and 4 *tête-bêche*. Each vertical pair completes the engineer's ring as shown on Type **724**.

(Des S. Spazuk. Litho Ashton-Potter Canada)

2000 (28 Apr). "Picture Postage" Greetings Stamps. Self-adhesive. Fluorescent frame. P 11½.
1988   725   46c. multicoloured 50 50
              a. Booklet pane. No. 1988×5, and 5 rectangular greetings labels .... 2·50

No. 1988 was either available from $2.30 booklets, No. SB239, including appropriate greetings labels which could be inserted into the rectangular space on each stamp, or from sheets of 25 issued in connection with a mail order scheme which provided frames and personalised labels for $24.95 a sheet.

See also Nos. 2020 and 2045/9.

726 Coastal-style Mailboxes in Autumn

(Des R. Bellemare and M. Côté. Litho Ashton-Potter Canada)

2000 (28 Apr). Traditional Rural Mailboxes. T **726** and similar horiz designs. Multicoloured. Fluorescent frame. P 12½×13.
1989   46c. Type **726**.. 75 75
                a. Booklet pane. Nos. 1989/92, each×3....... 8·00
1990   46c. House and cow-shaped mailboxes in Spring 75 75
1991   46c. Tractor-shaped mailbox in Summer........ 75 75
1992   46c. Barn and duck-shaped mailboxes in Winter 75 75
1989/1992 *Set of* 4 .... 2·75 2·75

Nos. 1989/92 were only available from $5.52 stamp booklets (No. SB240) in a *se-tenant* pane of 12, containing three of each design, with margins at top and bottom and imperforate vertical edges.

727 Gorge and Fir Tree

(Des Mia Mattes and Maximage Design. Litho Ashton Potter Canada)

2000 (23 May). Canadian Rivers and Lakes. T **727** and similar horiz designs. Multicoloured. Fluorescent frame. Self-adhesive. *Die-cut serpentine roul.*
1993   55c. Type **727**.. 60 65
                a. Booklet pane. Nos. 1993/7.............................. 2·75
1994   55c. Lake and water lilies....................................... 60 65
1995   55c. Glacier and reflected mountains.................. 60 65
1996   55c. Estuary and aerial view.................................. 60 65
1997   55c. Waterfall and forest edge 60 65
1998   95c. Iceberg and mountain river .... 95 1·10
                a. Booklet pane. Nos. 1998/2002 .... 4·25
1999   95c. Rapids and waterfall...................................... 95 1·10
2000   95c. Moraine and river... 95 1·10
2001   95c. Shallows and waves on lake .... 95 1·10
2002   95c. Forest sloping to waters edge and tree . 95 1·10
1993/2002 *Set of* 10.. 7·00 7·75

Nos. 1993/7 and 1998/2002 were only available from $2.75 or $4.75 booklets, Nos. SB241/2, on which the self-adhesive paper formed the booklet covers.

728 Queen Elizabeth the Queen Mother with Roses

729 Teenager with Two Children

(Des Gottschalk and Ash. Litho C.B.N.)

2000 (23 May). Queen Elizabeth the Queen Mother's 100th Birthday. Fluorescent frame. P 13×12½.
2003   728   95c. multicoloured .... 1·40 1·40
              a. Sheetlet of 9.. 12·00

No. 2003 was printed in sheetlets of 9, with enlarged inscribed right margin, for which an illustrated presentation folder was provided.

(Des Gottschalk and Ash. Litho C.B.N.)

2000 (1 June). Centenary of Boys and Girls Clubs of Canada. Fluorescent frame. P 13.
2004   729   46c. multicoloured 50 50

730 Clouds over Rockies and Symbol

731 "Space Travellers and Canadian Flag" (Rosalie Anne Nardelli)

(Des Malcolm Waddell Associates. Litho Ashton-Potter Canada)

2000 (29 June). 57th General Conference Session of Seventh-day Adventist Church, Toronto. Fluorescent frame. P 13½×13.
2005   730   46c. multicoloured 50 50

(Litho C.B.N.)

2000 (1 July). "Stampin' the Future" (children's stamp design competition). T **731** and similar horiz designs. Multicoloured. Fluorescent frame. P 13½.
2006   46c. Type **731**.. 60 70
                a. Strip of 4. Nos. 2006/9................................... 2·25 2·50
2007   46c. "Travelling to the Moon" (Sarah Lutgen) 60 70
2008   46c. "Astronauts in shuttle" (Andrew Wright) 60 70
2009   46c. "Children completing Canada as jigsaw" (Christine Weera).. 60 70
2006/2009 *Set of* 4 .... 2·25 2·50
MS2010 114×90 mm. Nos. 2006/9 .... 2·40 3·00

Nos. 2006/9 were printed together, *se-tenant*, as horizontal or vertical strips of 4 in sheets of 16.

(Des P.-Y. Pelletier. Litho and die-stamped Ashton-Potter Canada)

2000 (7 July). Canadian Art (13th series). Vert design as T **550**. Multicoloured. Fluorescent inner frame. P 12½×13.
2011   95c. "The Artist at Niagara, 1858" (Cornelius Krieghoff)... 1·25 1·75

No. 2011 was issued in a similar sheet format to No. 1289.

CANADA

732 Tall Ships, Halifax Harbour

(Des F. Ross and Bonnie Ross. Litho Ashton-Potter Canada)

2000 (19 July). Tall Ships Race. T **732** and similar horiz design. Multicoloured. Self-adhesive. Fluorescent frame. *Die-cut serpentine roul.*
2012	46c. Type **732**		75	85
	a. Booklet pane. Nos. 2012/13, each×5		6·75	
2013	46c. Tall Ships, Halifax Harbour (face value top right)		75	85

Nos. 2012/13 were only issued in $4.60 stamp booklets, No. SB243, on which the surplus self-adhesive paper was retained. The stamps are arranged as five *se-tenant* pairs on a background photograph of Halifax Harbour.

733 Workers, Factory and Transport

734 Petro-Canada Sign, Oil Rig and Consumers

(Des P. Hodgson and Sandra Dionisi. Litho C.B.N.)

2000 (1 Sept). Centenary of Department of Labour. Fluorescent frame. P 12½×13.
2014	**733**	46c. multicoloured	50	50

(Des D. L'Allier and R. Gendron. Litho C.B.N.)

2000 (13 Sept–4 Oct). 25th Anniv of Petro-Canada (oil company). Self-adhesive. Fluorescent frame. *Die-cut with central zigzag showing two points at right and foot, one point at top and left.*
2015	**734**	46c. multicoloured	75	50
		a. Booklet pane. No. 2015×12	8·00	
		b. With two points at top and left, one point at right and foot (4 Oct.)	4·00	7·50

No. 2015 was only available in $5.52 stamp booklets, No. SB245, on which the surplus self-adhesive paper was retained. The die-cutting does not separate the backing paper.

No. 2015b comes from various packs issued by Canada Post at the end of 2000. The die-cutting device has reversed and used to cut through the backing paper to create single stamps.

735 Narwhal (*Monodon manoceros*)

(Des K. Martin. Litho Ashton Potter)

2000 (2 Oct). Whales. T **735** and similar horiz designs. Multicoloured. Fluorescent frame. P 12½×13.
2016	46c. Type **735**		1·40	1·40
	a. Block of 4. Nos. 2016/19		5·00	5·00
2017	46c. Blue Whale (*Balaenoptera musculus*)		1·40	1·40
2018	46c. Bowhead Whale (*Balaena mysticetus*)		1·40	1·40
2019	46c. White Whales (*Delphinapterus leucas*)		1·40	1·40
2016/2019	Set of 4		5·00	5·00

Nos. 2016/19 were printed together, as *se-tenant* blocks of 4, in sheets of 16 with the backgrounds forming an overall composite design.

736

737 "The Nativity" (Susie Matthias)

(Des S. Spazuk. Litho Ashton-Potter Canada)

2000 (5 Oct). "Picture Postage" Christmas Greetings. Self-adhesive. Fluorescent frame. P 11½.
2020	**736**	46c. multicoloured	50	50
		a. Booklet pane. No. 2020×5 plus 5 Christmas labels	2·50	

No. 2020, which could be used in either a horizontal or vertical format, was either available from $2.30 self-adhesive booklets, No. SB246, which included five Christmas labels so that the sender could complete the design, or in panes of 25 available by mail order as part of a personalised labels offer.

(Des L. and Kelly Burke. Litho Ashton-Potter Canada)

2000 (3 Nov). Christmas. Religious Paintings by Mouth and Foot Artists. T **737** and similar vert designs. Multicoloured. Fluorescent frame. P 13½.
2021	46c. Type **737**		50	20
	a. Booklet pane. No. 2021×10		5·50	
2022	55c. "The Nativity and Christmas Star" (Michael Guillemette)		65	60
	a. Booklet pane. No. 2022×6		4·00	
2023	95c. "Mary and Joseph journeying to Bethlehem" (David Allan Carter)		1·25	1·90
	a. Booklet pane. No. 2023×6		7·00	
2021/2023	Set of 3		2·10	2·40

Nos. 2021a/3a show the vertical edges of the panes imperforate and have margins at top and bottom.

738 Lieut.-Col. Sam Steele, Lord Strathcona's Horse

739 Red Fox

(Des P-Y. Pelletier. Litho C.B.N.)

2000 (11 Nov). Canadian Regiments. T **738** and similar vert design. Multicoloured. Fluorescent frame. P 13½×13.
2024	46c. Type **738**		75	75
	a. Pair. Nos. 2024/5		1·50	1·50
2025	46c. Drummer, Voltigeurs de Québec		75	75

Nos. 2024/5 were printed together, *se-tenant*, as horizontal or vertical pairs in sheets of 16.

(Des P-Y. Pelletier and R. Milot. Litho Ashton-Potter Canada)

2000 (28 Dec). Wildlife. T **739** and similar horiz designs. Multicoloured. Self-adhesive. Chalk-surfaced paper. Fluorescent frame. P 9×imperf.
2026	60c. Type **739**		65	75
	a. Pane of 6		3·50	
2027	75c. Grey Wolf		1·25	1·25
2028	$1.05 White-tailed Deer		1·10	1·25
	a. Pane of 6		6·00	
2026/2028	Set of 3		2·75	3·00

Nos. 2026/8 were only issued as coils (all three values) or as small panes of 6 (2×3) (60c., $1.05). On the coils the surplus self-adhesive paper between each stamp was removed, but this was retained on the two panes. The horizontal pairs on the panes are separated by die-cutting.

Postal forgeries of Nos. 2028/a are known.

740 Maple Leaves

740a Maple Leaves and Key

740b Red Maple Leaf and Stem

(Des P-Y. Pelletier (47c., 48c.), J. Gault (49c.), Monique Dufour and Sophie Lafortune (80c., $1.40). CBN (No. 2031a), Litho Ashton-Potter Canada or Lowe-Martin (80c., $1.40), Ashton-Potter Canada (others))

2000 (28 Dec)–03. Ordinary paper (Nos. 2031a, 2032a, 2033a) or Chalk-surfaced paper (others). Fluorescent frame.

(a) Self-adhesive coil stamps. P 9×imperf (47c., 48c.), 8×imperf (49c.) or imperf×8 (80c., $1.40)
2029	**740**	47c. multicoloured	1·00	1·00
		a. Blue (country name and value) omitted	£400	
2030	–	48c. multicoloured (2.1.02)	1·00	1·00
2031	**740a**	49c. multicoloured (19.12.03)	1·00	1·00
		a. Imperf (9.2004)		

92

CANADA

2032	**740b**	80c. multicoloured (19.12.03)	1·10	1·10
		a. Perf 8×imperf (9.2004)	1·10	1·10
2033	–	$1.40 multicoloured (19.12.03)	2·00	2·00
		a. Perf 8×imperf (9.2004)	2·00	2·00

(b) Self-adhesive booklet stamps. Die-cut

2035	**740b**	80c. multicoloured (19.12.03)	1·10	1·10
		a. Pane. No. 2035/×6	6·50	
2036	–	$1.40 multicoloured (19.12.03)	1·90	1·90
		a. Pane. No. 2036/×6	11·00	

Designs: 48c. As Type **740** but leaves in three shades of green; $1.40 As Type **740b** but green leaf.

On Nos. 2029/30 the surplus self-adhesive paper between each stamp was removed, but on Nos. 2031/6 it was retained.

No. 2034 has been left for additions to this series.

Nos. 2035/6 were only issued in $4.80 or $8.40 panes of six stamps. Originally printed by Ashton Potter Canada, they were reprinted by Lowe-Martin from 2 July 2004.

Postal forgeries of Nos. 2036/a are known.

Nos. 2037/44 are vacant.

(Des. S. Spazuk. Litho Ashton-Potter Canada)

2000 (28 Dec). "Picture Postage" Greetings Stamps. T **725**, **736** and similar horiz frames. Multicoloured. Self-adhesive. Fluorescent frame. P 11½.

2045		47c. Type **725**	55	60
		a. Booklet pane. Nos. 2045/9 plus 5 rectangular greetings labels	2·50	
2046		47c. Type **736**	55	60
2047		47c. Roses frame	55	60
2048		47c. Mahogany frame	55	60
2049		47c. Silver frame	55	60
2045/2049 Set of 5			2·50	2·75

Nos. 2045/9, which could be used in either a horizontal or vertical format, were either available from $2.35 self-adhesive booklets, SB252, which included five greetings labels so that the sender could complete the design, or in panes of twenty-five of one design which could only be obtained by mail order as part of a personalised labels offer.

For designs as Nos. 2045/7 and 2049, but inscr "Domestic Lettermail Postes-lettres du régime intérieur" see also Nos. 2099/103.

741 Green Jade Snake

742 Highjumping

(Des Marlene Wou. Litho and embossed Ashton-Potter Canada)

2001 (5 Jan). Chinese New Year. ("Year of the Snake"). T **741** and similar horiz design. Multicoloured. Two fluorescent bands. P 13½.

2050		47c. Type **741**	50	50
		a. Gold omitted	£950	
MS2051	112×75 mm. $1.05, Brown jade snake	1·25	1·60

(Des S. Huot and C. Vinh. Litho Ashton-Potter Canada)

2001 (18 Jan). National Hockey League. All-Star Game Players (2nd series). Square designs as T **722**. Multicoloured. Fluorescent circular frame around central design. P 12½×13.

2052		47c. Jean Bèliveau (wearing No. 4)	75	75
		a. Sheetlet. Nos. 2052/7	4·00	4·00
2053		47c. Terry Sawchuk (on one knee)	75	75
2054		47c. Eddie Shore (wearing No. 2)	75	75
2055		47c. Denis Potvin (wearing No. 5)	75	75
2056		47c. Bobby Hull (wearing No. 9)	75	75
2057		47c. Syl Apps (in Toronto jersey)	75	75
2052/2057 Set of 6			4·00	4·00

Nos. 2052/7 were printed together, *se-tenant*, in sheetlets of 6 containing two vertical strips of three separated by labels featuring further portraits of the players shown on the stamps. Nos. 2052, 2054 and 2056 are imperforate at left and the others imperforate at right.

(Des R. Bellemare and P. Leduc. Litho Ashton-Potter Canada)

2001 (1 Feb). Birds (6th series). Horiz design as T **643**. Multicoloured. Fluorescent frame.

(a) P 12½×13

2058		47c. Golden Eagle	75	75
		a. Block of 4. Nos. 2058/61	2·75	2·75
2059		47c. Arctic Tern	75	75
2060		47c. Rock Ptarmigan	75	75
2061		47c. Lapland Longspur	75	75
2058/2061 Set of 4			2·75	2·75

(b) Self-adhesive. P 11½

2062		47c. Golden Eagle	65	70
		a. Booklet pane. Nos. 2062/5, each×3	7·00	
2063		47c. Arctic Tern	65	70
2064		47c. Rock Ptarmigan	65	70
2065		47c. Lapland Longspur	65	70
2062/2065 Set of 4			2·40	2·50

Nos. 2058/61 were printed together *se-tenant* in different combinations throughout the sheet, giving four blocks of 4 and four single stamps.

Nos. 2062/5 were only issued in $5.64 stamp booklets, No. SB253, on which the surplus self-adhesive paper was retained.

(Des C. Malenfant. Litho C.B.N.)

2001 (28 Feb). Fourth Francophonie Games. T **742** and similar vert design. Multicoloured. Fluorescent frame. P 13½.

2066		47c. Type **742**	70	70
		a. Horiz pair. Nos. 2066/7	1·40	1·40
2067		47c. Folk dancing	70	70

Nos. 2066/7 were printed together, *se-tenant*, as horizontal pairs throughout the sheet.

743 Ice Dancing

744 Three Pence Beaver Stamp of 1851

(Des Barbara Hodgson. Litho C.B.N.)

2001 (19 Mar). World Figure Skating Championships, Vancouver. T **743** and similar horiz designs. Multicoloured. Fluorescent frame. P 13×12½.

2068		47c. Type **743**	80	80
		a. Block of 4. Nos. 2068/71	3·00	3·00
2069		47c. Pairs	80	80
2070		47c. Men's singles	80	80
2071		47c. Women's singles	80	80
2068/2071 Set of 4			3·00	3·00

Nos. 2068/71 were printed together, *se-tenant*, as blocks of 4 in sheets of 16 (two panes 4×2).

(Des T. Yakobina. Recess and litho C.B.N)

2001 (6 Apr). 150th Anniv of the Canadian Postal Service. Fluorescent frame around centre. P 12½.

2072	**744**	47c. multicoloured	1·00	1·00

No. 2072 was only available in sheets of 8 (2×4) in a special folder with a commemorative leaflet.

745 Toronto Blue Jay Emblem, Maple Leaf and Baseball

746 North and South America on Globe

(Des P. Haslip. Litho Ashton-Potter Canada)

2001 (9 Apr). 25th Season of the Toronto Blue Jays (baseball team). Fluorescent outline. Self-adhesive. Die-cut.

2073	**745**	47c. multicoloured	60	70
		a. Booklet pane of 8	4·25	

No. 2073 was only available from $3.76 stamp booklets No. SB254.

(Des D. L'Allier. Litho Ashton-Potter Canada)

2001 (20 Apr). Summit of the Americas, Quebec. Fluorescent frame. P 13.

2074	**746**	47c. multicoloured	1·00	50

CANADA

747 Butchart Gardens, British Columbia

748 Christ on Palm Sunday and Khachkar (stone cross)

(Des Bradbury Design. Litho C.B.N.)

2001 (11 May). Tourist Attractions (1st series). T **747** and similar horiz designs. Multicoloured. Fluorescent frame. Self-adhesive. P 11 (die-cut).

2075	60c. Type **747**	95	1·10
	a. Booklet pane of 5. Nos. 2075/9	4·25	
2076	60c. Apple Blossom Festival, Nova Scotia	95	1·10
2077	60c. White Pass and Yukon Route	95	1·10
2078	60c. Sugar Bushes, Quebec	95	1·10
2079	60c. Court House, Niagara-on-the-Lake, Ontario	95	1·10
2080	$1.05 The Forks, Winnipeg, Manitoba	1·40	1·60
	a. Booklet pane of 5. Nos. 2080/4	6·25	
2081	$1.05 Barkerville, British Columbia	1·40	1·60
2082	$1.05 Canadian Tulip Festival, Ontario	1·40	1·60
2083	$1.05 Auyuittuq National Park, Nunavut	1·40	1·60
2084	$1.05 Signal Hill, St. John's, Newfoundland	1·40	1·60
2075/2084	Set of 10	10·50	12·00

Nos. 2075/9 and 2080/4 were only available in $3 or $5.25 stamp booklets, Nos. SB255/6.

See also Nos. 2143/52, 2205/14 and 2257/61.

(Des Debbie Adams. Litho Ashton-Potter Canada)

2001 (16 May). 1700th Anniv of Armenian Church. Fluorescent frame. P 13×12½.

2085	**748**	47c. multicoloured	60	70

No. 2085 was printed in sheets of 16 containing 4 blocks of four separated by vertical and horizontal gutters showing an Armenian manuscript.

749 Cadets, Mackenzie Building and Military Equipment

(Des J. Hudson. Litho C.B.N.)

2001 (1 June). 125th Anniv of Royal Military College of Canada. Fluorescent frame. P 12½×13.

2086	**749**	47c. multicoloured	70	45

750 Pole-vaulting

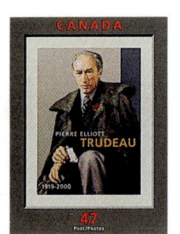

751 "Pierre Trudeau" (Myfanwy Pavelic)

(Des T. Nokes. Litho Ashton-Potter Canada)

2001 (25 June). Eighth International Amateur Athletic Federation World Championships, Edmonton. T **750** and similar vert design. Multicoloured. Fluorescent frame. P 12½.

2087		47c. Type **750**	80	1·00
		a. Pair. Nos. 2087/8	1·60	2·00
2088		47c. Sprinting	80	1·00

Nos. 2087/8 were printed together, *se-tenant*, both vertically and horizontally in sheets of 16.

(Des T. Yakobina. Litho Ashton-Potter Canada)

2001 (1 July). Pierre Trudeau (former Prime Minister) Commemoration. Fluorescent frame. P 13×12½.

2089	**751**	47c. multicoloured	60	45
MS2090	128×155 mm. No. 2089×4		2·00	2·25

No. **MS**2090 was sold in a commemorative folder.

752 "Morden Centennial" Rose

(Des G. Takeuchi. Litho Ashton-Potter Canada)

2001 (1 Aug). Canadian Roses. T **752** and similar horiz designs. Multicoloured. Fluorescent frame.

(a) Self-adhesive. Die-cut

2091		47c. Type **752**	1·00	1·10
		a. Booklet pane. Nos. 2091/4, each×3	11·00	
2092		47c. "Agnes"	1·00	1·10
2093		47c. "Champlain"	1·00	1·10
2094		47c. "Canadian White Star"	1·00	1·10
2091/2094	Set of 4		3·50	4·00

(b) PVA gum. P 12½×13

MS2095	145×90 mm. Nos. 2091/4	3·50	4·00

Nos. 2091/4 were only issued in $5.64 stamp booklets, No. SB257, on which the surplus self-adhesive paper was retained.

753 Ottawa Chief Hassaki addressing Peace Delegates

(Des N. Tessier and F. Back. Litho Ashton-Potter Canada)

2001 (3 Aug). 300th Anniv of Great Peace Treaty of Montréal between Indians and New France. Fluorescent frame. P 12½×13.

2096	**753**	47c. multicoloured	60	70

No. 2096 was printed in sheets of 16 containing a block of 8 (2×4) with a vertical strip of 4 on either side separated by a narrow vertical gutter showing pictographs.

(Des P-Y Pelletier. Litho and die-stamped C.B.N.)

2001 (24 Aug). Canadian Art (14th series). Vert design as T **550**. Multicoloured. Fluorescent inner frame. P 13×13½.

2097		$1.05 "The Space Between Columns 21 (Italian)" (Jack Shadbolt)	1·40	1·75

No. 2097 was issued in a similar sheet format to No. 1289.

754 Clown juggling with Crutches and Handicapped Boy

755 Toys and Flowers

(Des Monique Dufour and Sophie Lafortune. Litho C.B.N.)

2001 (19 Sept). The Shriners (charitable organisation) Commemoration. Fluorescent frame. P 13½×13.

2098	**754**	47c. multicoloured	60	45

(Des S. Spazuk. Litho Ashton-Potter Canada)

2001 (21 Sept). "Picture Postage" Greetings Stamps. T **755** and horiz frames as Nos. 2045/7 and 2049, but each inscr *"Domestic Lettermail Postes-lettres du régime intérieur"*. Multicoloured. Self-adhesive. Fluorescent frame. P 11½.

2099		(–) As Type **725**	60	60
		a. Booklet pane. Nos. 2099/103 plus 5 rectangular greetings labels	2·75	
2100		(–) As Type **736**	60	60

94

2101	(–) As Type **755**		60	60
2102	(–) Roses frame		60	60
2103	(–) Silver frame		60	60
2099/2103 Set of 5			2·75	2·75

Nos. 2099/103, which could be used in either a horizontal or a vertical format, and were either available from stamp booklets (No. SB258), initially sold at $2.35, which included five greetings labels so that the sender could complete the design, or in panes of twenty-five of one design which could only be obtained by mail order as part of a personalised labels offer.

756 Jean Gascon and Jean-Louis Roux (founders of Théâtre du Nouveau Monde, Montreal)

(Des Graphème of Montreal. Litho Ashton-Potter Canada)

2001 (28 Sept). Theatre Anniversaries. T **756** and similar horiz design. Multicoloured. Fluorescent frame. P 12½.

2104	47c. Type **756** (50th anniv)		65	80
	a. Horiz pair. Nos. 2104/5		1·25	1·60
2105	47c. Ambrose Small (founder of Grand Theatre, London, Ontario) (centenary)		65	80

Nos. 2104/5 were printed together, *se-tenant*, in horizontal pairs throughout the sheets of 16.

757 Hot Air Balloons

(Des Lise Giguère and D. Fell. Litho C.B.N.)

2001 (1 Oct). Stamp Collecting Month. Hot Air Balloons. T **757** and similar triangular designs. Multicoloured, background colours different below. Self-adhesive. Fluorescent frame. Die-cut.

2106	47c. Type **757** (green background)		80	90
	a. Booklet pane. Nos. 2106/9, each×2		5·75	
2107	47c. Balloons with lavender background		80	90
2108	47c. Balloons with mauve background		80	90
2109	47c. Balloons with bistre background		80	90
2106/2109 Set of 4			3·00	3·25

Nos. 2106/9 were only available in $3.76 stamp booklets, No. SB259.

758 Horse-drawn Sleigh and Christmas Lights

759 Pattern of Ys Logo

(Des Circle Design Incorporated. Litho C.B.N.)

2001 (1 Nov). Christmas. Festive Lights. T **758** and similar horiz designs. Multicoloured. Fluorescent frame. P 12½×13.

2110	47c. Type **758**		70	20
	a. Booklet pane. No. 2110×10 with margins all round		8·00	
2111	60c. Ice skaters and Christmas lights		1·00	1·00
	a. Booklet pane. No. 2111×6 with margins all round		7·00	
2112	$1.05 Children with snowman and Christmas lights		1·40	1·90
	a. Booklet pane. No. 2112×6 with margins all round		10·00	
2110/2112 Set of 3			2·75	2·75

(Des Hélène L'Heureux. Litho C.B.N.)

2001 (8 Nov). 150th Anniv of Y.M.C.A. in Canada. Fluorescent frame. P 13½.

2113	**759** 47c. multicoloured		70	45

760 Statues from Canadian War Memorial, Ottawa, and Badge

(Des N. Smith. Litho C.B.N.)

2001 (11 Nov). 75th Anniv of Royal Canadian Legion. Fluorescent frame. P 12½×13.

2114	**760** 47c. multicoloured		70	45

761 Queen Elizabeth II and Maple Leaf

762 Horse and Bamboo Leaves

(Des Gottschalk and Ash. Litho Ashton-Potter Canada)

2002 (2 Jan). Golden Jubilee. Chalk-surfaced paper. Fluorescent frame. P 13×12½.

2115	**761** 48c. multicoloured		70	45
	a. Imperf (pair)			

See also No. 2203.

(Des Up Inc. Litho and embossed Ashton-Potter Canada)

2002 (3 Jan). Chinese New Year ("Year of the Horse"). T **762** and similar vert design. Multicoloured. Fluorescent frame. P 13½ (with one diamond-shaped hole on each vertical side).

2116	48c. Type **762**		60	45
MS2117	102×102 mm. (octagonal). $1.25, Horse and peach blossom		1·40	1·75

No. 2116, which is an octagonal design, was printed in sheets of 25, with small red diamond-shaped labels at each corner surrounded by perforations and bisected horizontally and vertically by roulettes. The design within No. **MS**2117 is in normal vertical format.

(Des S. Huot, C. Vinn and P. Rousseau. Litho C.B.N.)

2002 (12 Jan). National Hockey League. All-Star Game Players (3rd series). Square designs as T **722**. Multicoloured. Fluorescent circular frame around central design. P 12½×13.

2118	48c. Tim Horton (wearing Maple Leaf No. 7 jersey)		1·00	1·00
	a. Sheetlet. Nos. 2118/23		5·50	5·50
2119	48c. Guy Lafleur (wearing Canadiens No. 10 jersey)		1·00	1·00
2120	48c. Howie Morenz (wearing Canadiens jersey and brown gloves)		1·00	1·00
2121	48c. Glenn Hall (wearing Chicago Blackhawks jersey)		1·00	1·00
2122	48c. Red Kelly (wearing Maple Leaf No. 4 jersey)		1·00	1·00
2123	48c. Phil Esposito (wearing Boston Bruins No. 7 jersey)		1·00	1·00
2118/2123 Set of 6			5·50	5·50

Nos. 2118/23 were printed together, *se-tenant*, in sheetlets of 6 containing two vertical strips of three separated by labels featuring further portraits of the players shown on the stamps. Nos. 2118, 2120 and 2121 are imperforate at left, and the others at right.

763 Speed Skating

764 Lion Symbol of Governor-General and Rideau Hall, Ottawa

CANADA

(Des Bahandari and Plater. Litho Ashton-Potter Canada)

2002 (25 Jan). Winter Olympic Games, Salt Lake City. T **763** and similar vert designs. Multicoloured. Fluorescent frame. P 13.

2124	48c. Type **763**	75	85
	a. Block of 4. Nos. 2124/7	2·75	3·00
2125	48c. Curling	75	85
2126	48c. Aerial ski-ing	75	85
2127	48c. Women's ice hockey	75	85
2124/2127 *Set of 4*		2·75	3·00

Nos. 2124/7 were printed together, *se-tenant*, as blocks and strips of 4 in sheets of 16. The Olympic symbol appears in varnish on each stamp and the yellow ink is fluorescent.

(Des N. Smith. Litho Ashton-Potter Canada)

2002 (1 Feb). 50th Anniv of First Canadian Governor-General. Fluorescent frame. P 13×12½.

2128	**764**	48c. multicoloured	60	45

765 University of Manitoba (125th Anniv)

766 "City of Vancouver" Tulip and Vancouver Skyline

(Des S. Slipp. Litho Ashton-Potter Canada)

2002 (28 Feb–27 May). Canadian Universities' Anniversaries (1st issue). T **765** and similar horiz designs. Multicoloured. Fluorescent frame. P 13½.

2129	48c. Type **765**	85	85
	a. Booklet pane. No. 2129×8 with margins all round	6·50	
2130	48c. Université Laval, Quebec (150th anniv of charter) (4 Apr)	85	85
	a. Booklet pane. No. 2130×8 with margins all round	6·50	
2131	48c. Trinity College, Toronto (150th anniv of foundation) (30 Apr)	85	85
	a. Booklet pane. No. 2131×8 with margins all round	6·50	
2132	48c. Saint Mary's University, Halifax (bicent) (27 May)	85	85
	a. Booklet pane. No. 2132×8 with margins all round	6·50	
2129/2132 *Set of 4*		3·00	3·00

Nos. 2129/32 were only available in four separate $3.84 stamp booklets, Nos. SB264/7.

See also Nos. 2190/4 and 2271/2.

(Des P-Y Pelletier. Litho and die-stamped Ashton-Potter Canada)

2002 (22 Mar). Canadian Art (15th series). Vert design as T **550**. Multicoloured. Fluorescent inner frame. P 12½×13.

2133	$1.25 "Church and Horse" (Alex Colville)	1·40	1·60

No. 2133 was issued in a similar sheet format to No. 1289.

(Des Monique Dufour and Sophie Lafortune. Litho Lowe-Martin)

2002 (3 May). 50th Canadian Tulip Festival, Ottawa. Tulips. T **766** and similar vert designs. Multicoloured. Self-adhesive. Fluorescent frame. Die-cut.

2134	48c. Type **766**	70	85
	a. Booklet pane. Nos. 2134/7, each×2	5·00	
2135	48c. "Monte Carlo" and Dows Lake tulip beds	70	85
2136	48c. "Ottawa" and National War Memorial	70	85
2137	48c. "The Bishop" and Ottawa Hospital	70	85
2134/2137 *Set of 4*		2·50	3·00

Nos. 2134/7 were only available in $3.84 stamp booklets, No. SB268. For Nos. 2134/7 in miniature sheet see No. **MS**2157.

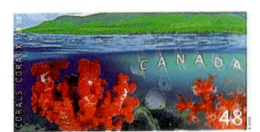

767 *Dendronepthea gigantea* and *Dendronepthea* (corals)

(Des B. Kwan (Nos. 2138/9), Signals Design Group (others). Litho Lowe-Martin)

2002 (19 May). Canada–Hong Kong Joint Issue. Corals. T **767** and similar horiz designs. Multicoloured. Fluorescent frame. P 12½×13.

2138	48c. Type **767**	70	85
	a. Block of 4. Nos. 2138/41	2·50	3·00
2139	48c. *Tubastrea*, *Echinogorgia* and island	70	85
2140	48c. North Atlantic Pink Tree coral, Pacific Orange Cup and North Pacific Horn coral	70	85
2141	48c. North Atlantic Giant Orange Tree coral and Black coral	70	85
2138/2141 *Set of 4*		2·50	3·00
MS2142	161×87 mm. Nos. 2138/41. P 13½×13	2·25	3·00

Nos. 2138/41 were printed together, *se-tenant*, as blocks of 4 throughout the sheets.

(Des Bradbury Design. Litho C.B.N.)

2002 (1 June). Tourist Attractions (2nd series). Horiz designs as T **747**. Multicoloured. Self-adhesive. Fluorescent frame. P 11.

2143	65c. Yukon Quest Sled Dog Race	1·00	1·10
	a. Booklet pane. Nos. 2143/7	4·50	
2144	65c. Icefields Parkway, Alberta	1·00	1·10
2145	65c. Train in Agawa Canyon, Northern Ontario	1·00	1·10
2146	65c. Old Port, Montreal	1·00	1·10
2147	65c. Saw mill, Kings Landing, New Brunswick	1·00	1·10
2148	$1.25 Northern Lights, Northwest Territories	1·75	2·00
	a. Booklet pane. Nos. 2148/52	8·00	
2149	$1.25 Stanley Park, British Columbia	1·75	2·00
2150	$1.25 Head-Smashed-In Buffalo Jump, Alberta	1·75	2·00
2151	$1.25 Saguenay Fjord, Quebec	1·75	2·00
2152	$1.25 Lighthouse, Peggy's Cove, Nova Scotia	1·75	2·00
2143/2152 *Set of 10*		12·00	14·00

Nos. 2143/7 and 2148/52 were only available in $3.25 or $6.25 stamp booklets, Nos. SB269/70.

768 "Embâcle" (Charles Daudelin)

(Des Suzanne Morin. Litho C.B.N.)

2002 (10 June). Sculptures. T **768** and similar horiz design. Multicoloured. Fluorescent frame. P 13½.

2153	48c. Type **768**	60	70
	a. Pair. Nos. 2153/4	1·10	1·40
2154	48c. "Lumberjacks" (Leo Mol)	60	70

Nos. 2153/4 were printed together, *se-tenant*, as horizontal and vertical pairs throughout the sheet.

769 1899 Queen Victoria 2 c. Stamp, Stonewall Post Office and Postmark

770 World Youth Day Logo

(Des C. Candlish. Litho C.B.N.)

2002 (5 July). Centenary of Canadian Postmasters and Assistants Association. Fluorescent frame. P 13×12½.

2155	**769**	48c. multicoloured	60	70

No. 2155 was printed in sheets of 16 with the horizontal rows separated by 8 mm gutters into which the 2c. stamp and the postmark intrude. The fluorescent frame around each stamp is broken where these features cross the perforations.

(Des Lise Giguère. Litho Ashton-Potter Canada)

2002 (23 July). 17th World Youth Day, Toronto. Self-adhesive. Fluorescent frame. Die-cut.

2156	**770**	48c. multicoloured	60	70
		a. Booklet pane. Nos. 2156×8	4·25	

The die-cutting on No. 2156 forms the shape of a cross which is followed by the fluorescent frame.

No. 2156 was only available in $3.84 stamp booklets, No. SB271.

CANADA

(Des Monique Dufour and Sophie Lafortune. Litho Lowe-Martin)

2002 (30 Aug). "Amphilex 2002" International Stamp Exhibition, Amsterdam. Phosphor frame. P 13×12½.
MS2157 160×97 mm. As Nos. 2134/7, but PVA gum...... 2·25 2·75

771 Hands gripping Rope and P.S.I. Logo

(Des D. L'Allier. Litho Lowe-Martin)

2002 (4 Sept). Public Services International World Congress, Ottawa. Fluorescent frame. P 12½×13.
2158 **771** 48c. multicoloured.. 60 45
The fluorescent frame around each stamp is broken by the PSI logo.

772 Tree in Four Seasons

(Des Debbie Adams. Litho C.B.N.)

2002 (10 Sept). 75th Anniv of Public Pensions. Fluorescent frame. P 13½.
2159 **772** 48c. multicoloured.. 60 45

773 Mount Elbrus, Russia   **774** Teacher writing on Board

(Des Q30 Design. Litho Lowe-Martin)

2002 (1 Oct). International Year of Mountains. T **773** and similar mountain-shaped designs. Multicoloured. Self-adhesive. Fluorescent frame. Die-cut.
2160   48c. Type **773**.. 70 85
             a. Sheetlet. Nos. 2160/7.................................. 5·00 6·00
2161   48c. Puncak Jaya, Indonesia........................ 70 85
2162   48c. Mount Everest, Nepal............................ 70 85
2163   48c. Mount Kilimanjaro, Tanzania................. 70 85
2164   48c. Vinson Massif, Antarctica..................... 70 85
2165   48c. Mount Aconcagua, Argentina................ 70 85
2166   48c. Mount McKinley, U.S.A.......................... 70 85
2167   48c. Mount Logan, Canada.......................... 70 85
2160/2167 Set of 8 .... 5·00 6·00
Nos. 2160/7 were only available in circular sheetlets of 8 with the stamps arranged individually around the circumference. Each design forms a rectangle with a *se-tenant* inscribed label which includes a separate small circular illustration showing wildlife. Philatelic stocks were sold in a card folder.

(Des M. Koudis. Litho C.B.N.)

2002 (4 Oct). World Teachers' Day. Fluorescent frame. P 12½×13.
2168 **774** 48c. multicoloured.. 60 45

775 Frieze from Toronto Stock Exchange and Globe

(Des I. Novotny, J. Taylor and P. Sayers. Litho C.B.N.)

2002 (24 Oct). 150th Anniv of Toronto Stock Exchange. Fluorescent frame. P 12½×13.
2169 **775** 48c. multicoloured.. 60 45

776 Sir Sandford Fleming, Map of Canada and *Iris* (cable ship)   **777** "Genesis" (painting by Daphne Odjig)

(Des Susan Warr. Litho Lowe-Martin)

2002 (31 Oct). Communications Centenaries. T **776** and similar vert design. Multicoloured. Fluorescent frame. P 13×12½.
2170   48c. Type **776** (opening of Pacific Cable)........ 65 75
             a. Horiz pair. Nos. 2170/1 .... 1·25 1·50
2171   48c. Guglielmo Marconi, Map of Canada and wireless equipment (first Transatlantic radio message).. 65 75
Nos. 2170/1 were printed together, *se-tenant*, as horizontal pairs in sheets of 16 (8×2).

(Des Signals Design Group. Litho Lowe-Martin)

2002 (4 Nov). Christmas. Aboriginal Art. T **777** and similar vert designs. Multicoloured. Fluorescent frame. P 12½×13.
2172   48c. Type **777**... 55 20
             a. Booklet pane of 10 with margins all round.. 5·50
2173   65c. "Winter Travel" (painting by Cecil Youngfox).. 70 70
             a. Booklet pane of 6 with margins all round.. 4·25
2174 $1.25 "Mary and Child" (sculpture by Irene Katak Angutitaq)... 1·25 1·75
             a. Booklet pane of 6 with margins all round.. 6·75
2172/2174 Set of 3 .... 2·25 2·40

778 Conductor's Hands and Original Orchestra

(Des Monique Dufour and Sophie Lafortune. Litho Lowe-Martin)

2002 (17 Nov). Centenary of Quebec Symphony Orchestra. Fluorescent frame. P 12½×13.
2175 **778** 48c. multicoloured.. 1·00 45

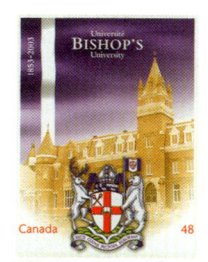

779 Sculpture of Ram's Head   **779a** Bishop's University, Quebec (150th anniv of university status)

97

CANADA

(Des Rosina Li from sculptures by C. Reid. Litho Lowe-Martin (foil embossing and die-cutting by Gravure Choquet)

2003 (3 Jan). Chinese New Year ("Year of the Ram") . T **779** and similar vert design. Multicoloured. Fluorescent frame. P 14*.
2176	48c. Type 779..	60	45
	a. Gold omitted.......................................	£300	
MS2177	125×103 mm. $1.25 Sculpture of goat's head (33×57 mm)..	1·25	1·50

*The horizontal perforations of Nos. 2176/7 are arranged as a wavy line. On the vertical perforations there are 10 mm gaps at the top left and bottom right of each stamp where the separation is by straight die-cutting. The top of No. **MS**2177 is die-cut in the shape of a ram's horn with a small barcode label attached to the bottom right hand corner.

(Des S. Huot, C. Vinh and P. Rousseau. Litho C.B.N.)

2003 (18 Jan). National Hockey League. All-Star Game Players (4th series). Square designs as T **722**. Multicoloured. Fluorescent frame.

(a) PVA gum. P 12½×13
2178	48c. Frank Mahovlich (wearing Maple Leaf No. 27 jersey)..	80	90
	a. Sheetlet. Nos. 2178/83	4·25	4·75
2179	48c. Raymond Bourque (wearing Boston Bruins No. 77 jersey)..................................	80	90
2180	48c. Serge Savard (wearing Canadiens No. 18 jersey)..	80	90
2181	48c. Stan Mikita (wearing Chicago Blackhawks No. 21 jersey)..........................	80	90
2182	48c. Mike Bossy (wearing New York Islanders No. 22 jersey)..............................	80	90
2183	48c. Bill Durnan (wearing Canadiens jersey and brown gloves)......................................	80	90
2178/2183	Set of 6	4·25	4·75

(b) Self-adhesive. Die-cut
2184	48c. Frank Mahovlich (wearing Maple Leaf No. 27 jersey)..	75	90
	a. Pane. Nos. 2184/9................................	4·00	4·75
2185	48c. Raymond Bourque (wearing Boston Bruins No. 77 jersey)..................................	75	90
2186	48c. Serge Savard (wearing Canadiens No. 18 jersey)..	75	90
2187	48c. Stan Mikita (wearing Chicago Blackhawks No. 21 jersey)..........................	75	90
2188	48c. Mike Bossy (wearing New York Islanders No. 22 jersey)..............................	75	90
2189	48c. Bill Durnan (wearing Canadiens jersey and brown gloves)......................................	75	90
2184/2189	Set of 6	4·00	4·75

Nos. 2178/83 were printed together, *se-tenant*, in sheetlets of 6 containing two vertical strips of three separated by labels featuring further portraits of the players shown on the stamps. Nos. 2178, 2180 and 2182 are imperforate at left, and the others at right.

Nos. 2184/9 were only available as $2.88 panes on which the surplus self-adhesive paper around each stamp was retained. The additional photographs, shown on the central labels of Nos. 2178/83, appear on the reverse of the backing paper of the self-adhesive versions.

(Des Denis L'Allier. Litho C.B.N.)

2003 (28 Jan). Canadian Universities' Anniversaries (2nd issue). T **779a** and similar vert designs. Multicoloured. Fluorescent frame. P 13½.
2190	48c. Type **779a** (150th anniv of university status)...	70	75
	a. Booklet pane. No. 2190×8 with margins all round...................................	5·00	
2191	48c. University of Western Ontario, London (150th anniv) (19 Mar)..............................	70	75
	a. Booklet pane. No. 2191×8 with margins all round...................................	5·00	
2192	48c. St. Francis Xavier University, Nova Scotia (150th anniv) (4 Apr)............	70	75
	a. Booklet pane. No. 2192×8 with margins all round...................................	5·00	
2193	48c. Macdonald Institute, University of Guelph, Ontario (centenary) (20 June) ...	70	75
	a. Booklet pane. No. 2193×8 with margins all round...................................	5·00	
2194	48c. University of Montréal (125th anniv) (4 Sept)..	70	75
	a. Booklet pane. No. 2194×8 with margins all around.................................	5·00	
2190/2194	Set of 5	3·25	3·25

Nos. 2190/4 were only available in $3.84 stamp booklets, Nos. SB275/9.

780 Leach's Storm Petrel

(Des R. Harder. Litho Lowe-Martin)

2003 (21 Feb). Bird Paintings by John J. Audubon (1st series). T **780** and similar multicoloured designs. Fluorescent frame.

(a) PVA gum. P 13×12½
2195	48c. Type **780**...	85	85
	a. Block of 4. Nos. 2195/8......................	3·00	3·00
2196	48c. Brent Goose ("Brant")............................	85	85
2197	48c. Great Cormorant.....................................	85	85
2198	48c. Common Murre.......................................	85	85
2195/2198	Set of 4	3·00	3·00

(b) Self-adhesive. Die-cut
2199	65c. Gyrfalcon (*vert*)......................................	2·00	2·50
	a. Booklet pane. No. 2199×6	11·00	

Nos. 2195/8 were printed together, *se-tenant*, as blocks of 4 throughout the sheet.

No. 2199 was only available in $3.90 stamp booklets, No. SB280, on which the surplus self-adhesive paper around each stamp was retained. See also Nos. 2274/8.

781 Ranger looking through Binoculars

782 Greek Figure with Dove

(Des O. Hill and D. Page. Litho Lowe-Martin)

2003 (3 Mar). 60th Anniv of Canadian Rangers. Fluorescent frame. P 12½×13.
2200	**781**	48c. multicoloured..........................	70	45

(Des K. Tsetsekas and J. Belisle. Litho C.B.N.)

2003 (25 Mar). 75th Anniv of American Hellenic Educational Progressive Association in Canada. Fluorescent frame. P 12½×13.
2201	**782**	48c. multicoloured..........................	70	45

783 Firefighter carrying Boy and Burning Buildings

784 Queen Elizabeth II and Maple Leaf

(Des F. Dallaire. Litho C.B.N.)

2003 (30 May). Volunteer Firefighters. Fluorescent frame. P 13½.
2202	**783**	48c. multicoloured..........................	1·25	65

(Des Saskia van Kampen. Litho Lowe-Martin)

2003 (2 June). 50th Anniv of Coronation. Fluorescent frame. P 13×12½.
2203	**784**	48c. multicoloured..........................	1·00	55

785 Québec City (*c*. 1703) Seal and Excerpt from Letter

Vancouver 2010 (**786**)

(Des C. Malenfant. Litho C.B.N.)

2003 (6 June). Pedro da Silva (first official courier of New France). Fluorescent frame. P 13.
2204	**785**	48c. multicoloured..........................	70	55

(Des Bradbury Design. Litho Ashton-Potter)

2003 (12 June). Tourist Attractions (3rd series). Horiz designs as T **747**. Multicoloured. Self-adhesive. Fluorescent frame. P 11½.
2205	65c. Wilberforce Falls, Nunavut....................	1·10	1·40
	a. Booklet pane. Nos. 2205/9.................	5·00	
2206	65c. Inside Passage, British Columbia.........	1·10	1·40

2207	65c. Royal Canadian Mounted Police Depot Division, Regina, Saskatchewan		1·10	1·40
2208	65c. Casa Loma, Toronto		1·10	1·40
2209	65c. Gatineau Park, Québec		1·10	1·40
2210	$1.25 Dragon boat race, Vancouver		1·75	1·90
	a. Booklet pane. Nos. 2210/14		8·00	
2211	$1.25 Polar bear, Churchill, Manitoba		1·75	1·90
2212	$1.25 Niagara Falls, Ontario		1·75	1·90
2213	$1.25 Magdalen Islands, Québec		1·75	1·90
2214	$1.25 Province House, Charlottetown, Prince Edward Island		1·75	1·90
2205/2214 Set of 10			13·00	15·00

Nos. 2205/9 and 2210/14 were only available in $3.25 or $6.25 stamp booklets, Nos. SB281/2.

2003 (11 July). Vancouver's Successful Bid for Winter Olympic Games, 2010. No. 1368 optd with T **786** in red.

2215	48c. multicoloured		80	80
	a. Booklet pane. No. 2215×10		7·25	

787 Mountains and Sea

2003 (19 July). Canada–Alaska Cruise "Picture Postage". T **787** and similar horiz design. Multicoloured. Litho. Self-adhesive. Die-cut.

2216	(-) Type **787**		3·75	4·50
2217	(-) Tail fin of whale, mountains and sea		3·75	4·50

Nos. 2216/17 were issued in sheets of ten containing five of each of the two designs and three stamp-size Picture Post labels. The stamps were inscribed "POSTAGE PAID PORT PAYÉ" and could be used as postage from Canada to anywhere in the world. The sheets of 10 were sold at $12.50 and could only be purchased by cruise guests or through the National Philatelic Centre.

788 Assembly Logo

790 Anne Hébert

789 Canadian F-86 Sabre Fighter Plane, Sailors and Infantrymen

(Des P. Fontaine. Litho Lowe-Martin)

2003 (21 July). 10th Lutheran World Federation Assembly, Winnipeg. Fluorescent frame. P 12½×13.

2218	**788**	48c. multicoloured	70	55

(Des S. Slipp. Litho C.B.N.)

2003 (25 July). 50th Anniv of Signing of Korea Armistice. Fluorescent frame. P 13.

2219	**789**	48c. multicoloured	70	55

(Des Katalin Kovats. Litho C.B.N.)

2003 (8 Sept). 50th Anniv of National Library of Canada. Booklet stamps. T **790** and similar horiz designs showing authors and portions of their handwritten text. Multicoloured. Fluorescent frame. P 13×12½.

2220	48c. Type **790**		80	85
	a. Booklet pane. Nos. 2220/3×2		5·75	
2221	48c. Hector de Saint-Denys Garneau		80	85
2222	48c. Morley Callaghan		80	85
2223	48c. Susanna Moodie and Catharine Parr Traill		80	85
2220/2223 Set of 4			3·00	3·00

Nos. 2220/3 were only issued in $3.84 booklets, No. SB284.

791 Cyclists in Road Race

(Des Doreen Colonello. Litho C.B.N.)

2003 (10 Sept). World Road Cycling Championships, Hamilton, Ontario. Booklet stamp. Fluorescent frame. P 12½×13.

2224	**791**	48c. multicoloured	1·10	70
	a. Booklet pane. No. 2224×8		8·00	

No. 2224 was only issued in $3.84 booklets, No. SB285.

792 Marc Garneau

793 Maple Leaves, Canada

(Des P.-Y. Pelletier. Litho Lowe-Martin)

2003 (1 Oct). Stamp Collecting Month. Canadian Astronauts. T **792** and similar circular designs. Multicoloured. Self-adhesive. Fluorescent frame. Die-cut.

2225	48c. Type **792**	85	1·00
	a. Pane. Nos. 2225/32	6·00	7·00
2226	48c. Roberta Bondar	85	1·00
2227	48c. Steve MacLean	85	1·00
2228	48c. Chris Hadfield	85	1·00
2229	48c. Robert Thirsk	85	1·00
2230	48c. Bjarni Tryggvason	85	1·00
2231	48c. Dave Williams	85	1·00
2232	48c. Julie Payette	85	1·00
2225/2232 Set of 8		6·00	7·00

Nos. 2225/32 were only available as $3.84 panes on which the surplus self-adhesive paper around each stamp was retained.

(Des R. Bellemare (No. 2231) or Veena Chantanatat (No. 2232). Litho Ashton-Potter)

2003 (4 Oct). National Emblems. T **793** and similar vert design. Multicoloured. Fluorescent frame. P 12½.

2233	48c. Type **793**	1·00	1·00
	a. Pair. Nos. 2233/4	2·00	2·00
2234	48c. *Cassis fistula* flowers, Thailand	1·00	1·00
MS2235 120×96 mm. Nos. 2233/4		2·00	2·25

Nos. 2233/4 were printed together, *se-tenant*, in horizontal and vertical pairs in sheets of 16.

No. **MS**2235 commemorates Bangkok 2003 International Stamp Exhibition, Thailand.

Stamps of the same designs were issued by Thailand.

794 White Birds

CANADA

(Des S. Spazuk. Litho Lowe-Martin)

2003 (7 Oct). 80th Birth Anniv of Jean-Paul Riopelle (painter and sculptor). T **794** and similar horiz designs showing details from fresco "L'Hommage à Rosa Luxemburg". Multicoloured. Fluorescent frame. P 12½×13.

| MS2236 | 178×244 mm. 48c. Type **794**; 48c. Two white herons and white birds; 48c. Flying bird, flower and three white birds in cameo; 48c. Grouse on moor, white bird and sun; 48c. Two flying white birds in cameo and silhouette of falcon; 48c. Two white birds and cameo of flying duck | 4·00 | 5·00 |
| MS2237 | 159×95 mm. $1.25 Eggs and bird silhouette. P 13 | 2·00 | 2·50 |

795 Ice Skates and Wrapped Presents

796 Queen Elizabeth II, 2002

(Des P. David. Litho Lowe-Martin)

2003 (4 Nov). Christmas. Self-adhesive booklet stamps. T **795** and similar square designs. Multicoloured. Fluorescent frame. Die-cut.

2238	48c. Type **795**	70	55
	a. Booklet pane. No. 2238×12	7·50	
2239	65c. Teddy bear and wrapped presents	1·25	1·50
	a. Booklet pane. No. 2239×6	6·75	
2240	$1.25 Toy duck on wheels and wrapped presents	1·90	2·50
	a. Booklet pane. No. 2240×6	10·00	
2238/2240	Set of 3	3·50	4·00

Nos. 2238/40 were only available in separate $3.90, $5.76 or $7.50 booklets, Nos. SB286/8.

(Des Saskia van Kampen (49c.) or Gottschalk and Ash International (50c.). Litho C.B.N.)

2003 (19 Dec)–**04**. Self-adhesive booklet stamps. Fluorescent frame. Die-cut.

2241	**796**	49c. black, dull mauve and scarlet	1·10	80
		a. Booklet pane. No. 2241×10	10·00	
2242		50c. multicoloured (20.12.04)	70	80
		a. Booklet pane. No. 2241×10	7·00	

Nos. 2241/2 were only issued in separate booklets, Nos. SB292 and SB313. Numbers have been left for additions.

Postal forgeries of Nos. 2241/a are known.

Nos. 2243/6 are vacant.

797 Monkey King on Cloud

798 Bonhomme (Snowman), Québec Winter Carnival

(Des Anita Kunz and Louis Fishauf. Litho and embossed C.B.N.)

2004 (8 Jan). Chinese New Year ("Year of the Monkey"). T **797** and similar vert design showing scenes from "Journey to the West" by Wu Ch'eng-en. Multicoloured. Fluorescent frame. P 13×12½.

| 2247 | | 49c. Type **797** | 1·00 | 70 |
| MS2248 | 115×82 mm. $1.40 Monkey on road to India | 1·90 | 2·25 |

No. **MS**2248 has a barcode tab attached at right.

2004 (8 Jan). Hong Kong 2004 International Stamp Exhibition. No. **MS**2248 optd "Hong Kong Stamp Expo 2004" and exhibition emblem in gold on sheet margin.

| MS2249 | 115×82 mm. $1.40 Monkey on road to India | 1·90 | 2·25 |

(Des Stéphane Huot, Charles Vinh and Pierre Rousseau. Litho Lowe-Martin)

2004 (24 Jan). National Hockey League. All-Star Game Players (5th series). Square designs as T **722**. Multicoloured. Fluorescent frame.

(a) PVA gum. P 12½×13

2250	49c. Larry Robinson (wearing Canadiens jersey)	1·40	1·40
	a. Sheetlet. Nos. 2250/5	7·50	7·50
2251	49c. Marcel Dionne (wearing Los Angeles Kings jersey)	1·40	1·40
2252	49c. Ted Lindsay (wearing Detroit Red Wings jersey)	1·40	1·40
2253	49c. Johnny Bower (wearing Toronto Maple Leafs goal keeper kit)	1·40	1·40
2254	49c. Brad Park (wearing New York Rangers jersey)	1·40	1·40
2255	49c. Milt Schmidt (wearing Boston Bruins jersey)	1·40	1·40
2250/2255	Set of 6	7·50	7·50

(b) Self-adhesive. Die-cut

2256	49c. Larry Robinson (wearing Canadiens jersey)	1·00	1·25
	a. Pane. Nos. 2256/f	5·50	6·75
2256b	49c. Marcel Dionne (wearing Los Angeles Kings jersey)	1·00	1·25
2256c	49c. Ted Lindsay (wearing Detroit Red Wings jersey)	1·00	1·25
2256d	49c. Johnny Bower (wearing Toronto Maple Leafs goal keeper kit)	1·00	1·25
2256e	49c. Brad Park (wearing New York Rangers jersey)	1·00	1·25
2256f	49c. Milt Schmidt (wearing Boston Bruins jersey)	1·00	1·25
2256/2256f	Set of 6	5·50	6·75

Nos. 2250/5 were printed together, *se-tenant*, in sheetlets of 6 containing two vertical strips of three separated by labels featuring further portraits of the players shown on the stamps. Nos. 2250, 2252 and 2254 are imperforate at left, and the others at right.

Nos. 2256/f were only available as $2.94 panes on which the surplus self-adhesive paper around each stamp was retained. The additional photographs, shown on the central labels of Nos. 2250/5, appear on the reverse of the backing paper of the self-adhesive versions.

(Des Bradbury Branding and Design. Litho Lowe-Martin)

2004 (29 Jan–19 July). Tourist Attractions (4th series). T **798** and similar horiz designs. Multicoloured. Fluorescent frame. Self-adhesive. Die-cut.

2257	49c. Type **798**	1·25	1·40
	a. Booklet pane. No. 2257×6	6·75	
2258	49c. St. Joseph's Oratory (2 Apr)	1·25	1·40
	a. Booklet pane. No. 2258×6	6·75	
2259	49c. Audience at International Jazz Festival, Montréal (1 June)	1·25	1·40
	a. Booklet pane. No. 2259×6	6·75	
2260	49c. People watching Traversée Internationale du Lac St-Jean (18 June)	1·25	1·40
	a. Booklet pane. No. 2260×6	6·75	
2261	49c. People at Canadian National Exhibition and Prince's Gate (19 July)	1·25	1·40
	a. Booklet pane. No. 2261×6	6·75	
2257/2261	Set of 5	5·75	6·25

Nos. 2257/61 were only available in five separate $2.94 stamp booklets, Nos. SB293/7.

799 Governor General Ramon Hnatyshyn

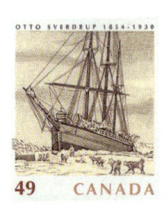

800 *Fram* (polar research ship)

(Des Susan Mavor. Litho Lowe-Martin)

2004 (16 Mar). 70th Birth Anniv of Governor General Ramon Hnatyshyn. Fluorescent frame. P 12½×13.

| 2262 | **799** | 49c. multicoloured | 70 | 70 |

(Des and Eng Martin Mörck. Recess and litho Posts and Telegraph Office, Copenhagen, Denmark)

2004 (26 Mar). 150th Birth Anniv of Otto Sverdrup (polar explorer). T **800** and similar vert design. Each blackish purple and buff. P 13.

| 2263 | 49c. Type **800** | 1·50 | 70 |
| MS2264 | 166×60 mm. $1.40 As No. 2263 plus two labels | 2·25 | 2·50 |

No. **MS**2264 was issued with two stamp-size labels showing stamp designs of Greenland and Norway.

Stamps of similar designs were issued by Greenland and Norway.

801 Silhouettes of Cadets

(Des André Perro. Litho C.B.N.)

2004 (26 Mar). 125th Anniv of Royal Canadian Army Cadets. Fluorescent frame. Self-adhesive. Imperf.
2265	**801**	49c. multicoloured	1·25	1·00
		a. Booklet pane. No. 2265×8	9·00	

No. 2265 was only available in $3.92 self-adhesive stamp booklets, No. SB298.

802 Subway Train, Toronto

(Des Debbie Adams. Litho C.B.N.)

2004 (30 Mar). Light Rail Urban Transit. T **802** and similar horiz designs. Multicoloured. Fluorescent frame. P 12½×13.
2266		49c. Type **802**	1·50	1·50
		a. Vert strip of 4. Nos. 2266/9	5·50	5·50
2267		49c. TransLink SkyTrain, Vancouver	1·50	1·50
2268		49c. Métro train, Montréal	1·50	1·50
2269		49c. CTrain, Calgary	1·50	1·50
2266/2269 Set of 4			5·50	5·50

Nos. 2266/9 were printed together, *se-tenant*, in vertical strips of four stamps in sheets of 16. The designs of the stamps provide a horizontal illusion of motion throughout the strips.

803 Canadian Map and Employee

(Des Ron Mugford. Litho Lowe-Martin)

2004 (19 Apr). 40th Anniv of Home Hardware (co-operative business). Fluorescent frame. Self-adhesive. P 11.
2270	**803**	49c. multicoloured	90	90
		a. Booklet pane. No. 2270×10 plus central label	8·00	

No. 2270 was only available in $4.90 stamp booklets, No. SB299.

(Des Dennis L'Allier. Litho C.B.N.)

2004–8 May). Canadian Universities Anniversaries (3rd issue). Vert designs as T **779***a*. Multicoloured. Fluorescent frame. P 13½.
2271		49c. University of Sherbrooke (50th anniv)	90	90
		a. Booklet pane. No. 2271×8	6·50	
2272		49c. University of Prince Edward Island (bicent) (8 May)	90	90
		a. Booklet pane. No. 2272×8	6·50	

Nos. 2271/2 were only available in two separate $3.92 stamp booklets, Nos. SB300/1.

804 Teddy Bears

805 Ruby-crowned Kinglet

(Des Monique Dufour and Sophie Lafortune. Litho Lowe-Martin)

2004 (6 May). Centenary of Montreal Children's Hospital. Fluorescent frame. Self-adhesive. P 9½×10½.
2273	**804**	49c. multicoloured	90	90
		a. Booklet pane. No. 2273×8	6·50	

No. 2273 was only available in $3.92 stamp booklets, No. SB302.

(Des Rolf Harder. Litho Lowe-Martin)

2004 (14 May). Bird Paintings by John J. Audubon (2nd series). T **805** and similar vert designs. Multicoloured. Fluorescent frame.

(a) PVA Gum. P 12½×13
2274		49c. Type **805**	85	85
		a. Block of 4. Nos. 2274/7	3·00	3·00
2275		49c. White-winged Crossbill	85	85
2276		49c. Bohemian Waxwing	85	85
2277		49c. Boreal Chickadee	85	85
2274/2277 Set of 4			3·00	3·00

(b) Self-adhesive. Imperf
2278		80c. Lincoln's Sparrow	2·00	2·25
		a. Booklet pane. No. 2278×6	11·00	

Nos. 2274/7 were printed together, *se-tenant*, as blocks of 4 stamps in sheets of 16.

No. 2278 was only available in $4.80 stamp booklets (No. SB303) in which the surplus self-adhesive paper around each stamp was retained.

806 Sir Samuel Cunard

806*a* Butterfly on Flower

(Des Oliver Hill and Dennis Page. Litho Lowe-Martin)

2004 (28 May). Sir Samuel Cunard and Sir Hugh Allan (founders of transatlantic mail service) Commemorations. T **806** and similar horiz design. Multicoloured. Fluorescent frame. Self-adhesive. P 13×12½.
2279		49c. Type **806**	80	1·00
		a. Horiz pair. Nos. 2279/80	1·60	2·00
2280		49c. Sir Hugh Allan	80	1·00

Nos. 2279/80 were printed together, *se-tenant*, as horiz pairs in sheets of 16, each pair forming a composite design and also breaking up the fluorescent frame.

2004 (31 May). "Write me…Ring me" Greetings Stamps. T **806***a* and similar horiz designs. Multicoloured. Fluorescent frame. Self-adhesive. P 11½×12.
2280*a*		(49c.) Type **806***a*	2·00	2·00
2280*b*		(49c.) Two young children at beach	2·00	2·00
2280*c*		(49c.) Red rose	2·00	2·00
2280*d*		(49c.) Pug (dog)	2·00	2·00
2280*a*/2280*d* Set of 4			7·25	7·25

Nos. 2280*a*/*d* are inscribed "Domestic Lettermail" (initial value was 49c.), and were each issued in panes of two. Each pane was sold in a $5.99 greeting card which also contained a phone card.

807 Soldiers storming Juno Beach, Normandy

808 Pierre Dugua de Mons

(Des Derwyn Goodall. Litho Lowe-Martin)

2004 (6 June). 60th Anniv of D-Day Landings. Fluorescent frame. P 13×12½.
2281	**807**	49c. multicoloured	1·25	80

(Des Rejearz Myette and Suzanne Duranceau. Eng André Lavergne. Recess and litho C.B.N.)

2004 (26 June). 400th Anniv of First French Settlement in Acadia, St. Croix Island. Fluorescent frame. P 13×12½.
2282	**808**	49c. ochre, royal blue and orange	80	70

CANADA

809 Spyros Louis (Greek athlete) and Marathon Runner

(Des Pierre-Yves Pelletier. Litho C.B.N.)

2004 (28 July). Olympic Games, Athens, Greece. T **809** and similar horiz design. Multicoloured. Fluorescent frame. P 12½×13.

2283	49c. Type **809**	1·50	1·50
	a. Horiz pair. Nos. 2283/4	3·00	3·00
2284	49c. Girls playing football	1·50	1·50

Nos. 2283/4 were printed together, *se-tenant*, in horizontal pairs throughout sheets of 16.

810 Golfer and Trophy from Early Tournament

811 Segmented Heart

(Des Q30 Design Inc. Litho and embossed Lowe-Martin and Choquet Engraving Inc)

2004 (12 Aug). Canadian Open Golf Championship. T **810** and similar circular design. Multicoloured. Self-adhesive. Fluorescent frame. Die-cut.

2285	49c. Type **810**	1·00	1·25
	a. Pane. Nos. 2285/6, each ×4	7·25	9·00
2286	49c. Golfer and trophy from modern tournament	1·00	1·25

Nos. 2285/6 were only available as $3.92 panes of 8 stamps presented in illustrated portfolios. The surplus self-adhesive paper around each stamp is retained.

(Des Guénette and Delisle Design. Litho Lowe-Martin)

2004 (15 Sept). 50th Anniv of Montréal Heart Institute. Self-adhesive. Fluorescent frame. P 13½.

2287	**811**	49c. multicoloured	80	1·00
		a. Booklet pane. No. 2287 ×8	5·75	

No. 2287 was only available from $3.92 stamp booklets (No. SB306) on which the surplus self-adhesive backing paper was retained.

812 Goldfish in Bowl

(Des Isabelle Toussaint. Litho Lowe-Martin)

2004 (1 Oct). Pets. T **812** and similar horiz designs. Multicoloured. Fluorescent frame. Self-adhesive. Imperf.

2288	49c. Type **812**	1·10	1·25
	a. Booklet pane. Nos. 2288/91 each×2	8·00	
2289	49c. Two cats on chair	1·10	1·25
2290	49c. Child with rabbit	1·10	1·25
2291	49c. Child with dog	1·10	1·25
2288/2291	Set of 4	4·00	4·50

Nos. 2288/91 were only available in $3.92 stamp booklets, No. SB307.

813 Gerhard Herzberg (Chemistry, 1971)

(Des HM&E Design and Communications. Litho Lowe-Martin)

2004 (4 Oct). Nobel Prize Winners. T **813** and similar horiz design. Multicoloured. Fluorescent frame and imprint date. P 12½×13.

2292	49c. Type **813**	90	1·00
	a. Pair. Nos. 2292/3	1·75	2·00
2293	49c. Michael Smith (Chemistry, 1993)	90	1·00

Nos. 2292/3 were printed together, *se-tenant*, in horizontal and vertical pairs in sheets of 16. The designs in the silhouettes are overprinted with blue fluorescent ink.

Nos. 2292/3 also have a hidden imprint date visible only under U.V. light.

814 Maple Leaf in Photo Album Frame

815 Victoria Cross (embossed)

(Des Steven Spazuk and Jean-Francois Renaud. Litho C.B.N.)

2004 (8 Oct). Picture Postage. T **814** and similar horiz design. Multicoloured. Fluorescent frame. Self-adhesive. P 12½×13.

2294	49c. Type **814**	90	1·00
	a. Pane. No. 2294×20	16·00	
2295	49c. Maple leaf in silver frame	90	1·00
	a. Pane. No. 2295×20	16·00	

Nos. 2294/5 were both inscribed "Domestic Postage Paid" and sold for 49c.

Nos. 2294/5 were both only available of panes of 20 stamps including a "keepsake" stamp and enlarged image, or panes of 40 stamps.

(Des Pierre-Yves Pelletier. Litho and embossed C.B.N. and Choquet Engraving Inc)

2004 (21 Oct). 150th Anniv of First Canadian Recipient of the Victoria Cross. T **815** and similar vert design. Multicoloured. Fluorescent frame. P 13×12½.

2296	49c. Type **815**	1·10	1·25
	a. Sheetlet. Nos. 2296/7 both×8	16·00	
2297	49c. Victoria Cross and signature of Queen Elizabeth II	1·10	1·25

Nos. 2296/7 were printed together *se-tenant* in sheetlets of 16 around a central illustration and listing of 94 Canadians who have received the Victoria Cross.

Nos. 2296/7 also have a hidden imprint date visible only under U.V. light.

816 "Self-portrait", 1974

817 Santa in his Sleigh and Reindeer

(Des Gottschalk & Ash International. Litho Lowe-Martin)

2004 (22 Oct). "Art Canada". Birth Centenary of Jean Paul Lemieux. T **816** and similar multicoloured designs. Fluorescent frame. P 13.

2298	49c. Type **816**	1·00	85
MS2299	150×86 mm. 49c. Type **816**; 80c. "A June Wedding", 1972 (53×34 mm); $1.40 "Summer", 1959 (64×31 mm)	4·50	5·00

CANADA

(Des Saskia van Kampen and Tim Zeltner. Litho C.B.N.)

2004 (2 Nov). Christmas. Self-adhesive booklet stamps. T **817** and similar horiz designs. Multicoloured. Fluorescent frame. P 7×imperf.

2300	49c. Type **817**	1·00	45
	a. Booklet pane. No. 2300×12	11·00	
2301	80c. Santa driving a Cadillac and towing a house	1·60	2·00
	a. Pane. No. 2301×6	8·75	
2302	$1.40 Santa driving a train	2·50	3·00
	a. Pane. No. 2302×6	13·50	
2300/2302 *Set of 3*		4·75	5·00

Nos. 2300/2 were only available in No. SB309, $4.80 or $8.40 panes of six, all with the surplus self-adhesive paper around each stamp retained.

818 Red Calla Lily

819 Rooster facing East (right)

(Des Monique Dufour and Sophie LaFortune (51, 89c., $1.05, $1.49 from illustrations by Sigmond Pifco). Litho Lowe-Martin)

2004 (20 Dec)–05. Flowers. T **818** and similar vert designs. Multicoloured. Fluorescent frame. Self-adhesive.

(a) Coil stamps. P 8½×imperf (50, 85c., $1.45) or 7½×imperf (others)

2303	50c. Type **818**	70	80
2304	51c. Red bergamot (19.12.05)	70	55
2305	85c. Yellow calla lily	1·00	1·25
2306	89c. Lady's slipper orchids (19.12.05)	1·25	1·25
2307	$1.05 Pink fairy slipper orchids (19.12.05)	1·50	1·60
2308	$1.45 Purple Dutch Iris	1·90	2·00
2309	$1.49 Himalayan blue poppies (19.12.05)	1·90	2·00
2303/2309 *Set of 7*		8·00	8·50

(b) Booklet stamps. Imperf

2310	85c. Yellow calla lily	70	75
	a. Pane. No. 2310×6	4·00	
2311	89c. Lady's slipper orchids (19.12.05)	75	80
	a. Pane. No. 2311×6	4·50	
2312	$1.05 Pink fairy slipper orchids (19.12.05)	1·30	1·40
	a. Pane. No. 2312×6	7·50	
2313	$1.45 Purple Dutch Iris	1·40	1·50
	a. Pane. No. 2313×6	7·50	
2313b	$1.49 Himalayan blue poppies (19.12.05)	1·40	1·50
	ba. Pane. No. 2313b×6	8·25	
2310/2313b *Set of 5*		5·00	5·50

Nos. 2310/13b were issued in separate $5.10, $5.34, $6.30, $8.70 or $8.94 panes of six.

(Des Hélène L'Heureux. Litho and embossed CBN)

2005 (7 Jan). Chinese New Year ("Year of the Rooster"). 35th Anniv of Diplomatic Relations with China (**MS**2315b). T **819** and similar multicoloured designs. Fluorescent frame. P 13½ (50c.) or 12½×13 ($1.45).

2314	50c. Type **819**	1·00	60
	a. Red omitted	£1300	

MS2315 Two sheets, each 105×82 mm. (a) $1.45 Rooster facing west (left) (40×41 mm). (b) $1.45 As No **MS**2315a *Set of 2 sheets* ... 2·50 3·00

Nos. **MS**2315a/b both have a barcode tab attached at foot.
No. **MS**2315b is optd with the flags of Canada and China and the dates "1970" and "2005" in gold foil on the margin.

(Des Stéphane Huot, François Escalmel and Pierre Rousseau. Litho CBN)

2005 (24 Jan). National Hockey League. All-Star Game Players (6th series). Square designs as T **722**. Multicoloured. Fluorescent frame.

(a) PVA gum. P 12½×13

2316	50c. Henri Richard (wearing Habs jersey)	1·40	1·40
	a. Sheetlet. Nos. 2316/21	7·50	7·50
2317	50c. Grant Fuhr (wearing Oilers goal keeper kit)	1·40	1·40
2318	50c. Allan Stanley (wearing Toronto Maple Leafs jersey)	1·40	1·40
2319	50c. Pierre Pilote (wearing Chicago Black Hawks jersey)	1·40	1·40
2320	50c. Bryan Trottier (wearing New York Islanders jersey)	1·40	1·40
2321	50c. John Bucyk (wearing Boston Bruins jersey)	1·40	1·40
2316/2321 *Set of 6*		7·50	7·50

(b) Self-adhesive. Die-cut

2322	50c. Henri Richard (wearing Habs jersey)	1·00	1·40
	a. Pane. Nos. 2322//7	5·50	7·50
2323	50c. Grant Fuhr (wearing Oilers goal keeper kit)	1·00	1·40
2324	50c. Allan Stanley (wearing Toronto Maple Leafs jersey)	1·00	1·40
2325	50c. Pierre Pilote (wearing Chicago Black Hawks jersey)	1·00	1·40
2326	50c. Bryan Trottier (wearing New York Islanders jersey)	1·00	1·40
2327	50c. John Bucyk (wearing Boston Bruins jersey)	1·00	1·40
2322/2327 *Set of 6*		5·50	7·50

Nos. 2316/21 were printed together, *se-tenant*, in sheetlets of 6 containing two vertical strips of three separated by labels featuring further portraits of the players shown on the stamps. Nos. 2316, 2318 and 2320 are imperforate at left, and the others at right.

Nos. 2322/7 were only available as $3 panes on which the surplus self-adhesive paper around each stamp was retained. The additional photographs, shown on the central labels of Nos. 2316/21, appear on the reverse of the backing paper of the self-adhesive versions.

820 Alevin Fishing Fly

(Des Circle Design and Alain Massicotte. Litho CBN)

2005 (4 Feb). Fishing Flies. T **820** and similar horiz designs. Multicoloured. Fluorescent frame.

(a) PVA gum. P 12½×13

MS2328 190×112 mm. 50c.×4 Type **820**; Jock Scott; P.E.I. Fly; Mickey Finn ... 3·00 3·25

(b) Self-adhesive. Straight-edge and P 10

2329	50c. Type **820**	1·25	1·25
	a. Booklet pane. Nos. 2329/32, each×2	9·00	
2330	50c. Jock Scott	1·25	1·25
2331	50c. Mickey Finn	1·25	1·25
2332	50c. P.E.I. Fly	1·25	1·25
2329/2332 *Set of 4*		4·50	4·50

Nos. 2329/32 were only issued in $4 stamp booklets (SB316) which contained two panes of No. 2329a and an additional pane inscribed with information about the flies and photographs of the tiers.

(Des Denis L'Allier. Litho Lowe-Martin)

2005 (14 Feb). Canadian Universities Anniversaries (4th series). Vert design as T **779a** (No. 2190). Multicoloured. Fluorescent frame. P 13.

2333	50c. Nova Scotia Agricultural College	80	75
	a. Booklet pane. No. 2333 ×8	5·75	

No. 2333 was only available in $4 stamp booklets (SB317).

No. 2334 is vacant.

821 Inukshuk of Five Rocks

822 Yellow Daffodils

(Des Paul Haslip. Litho CBN)

2005 (4 Mar). Expo 2005 International Exhibition, Aichi, Japan. Fluorescent frame. P 13½.

2335	**821**	50c. multicoloured	70	50

(Des Isabelle Toussaint. Litho Lowe-Martin)

2005 (10 Mar). Daffodils. T **822** and similar horiz design. Multicoloured. Fluorescent frame.

(a) Self-adhesive. P 10

2336	50c. Type **822**	90	90
	a. Booklet pane. Nos. 2336/7, each ×5	8·00	
2337	50c. White daffodils with yellow trumpets	90	90

(b) PVA gum. P 13½

MS2338 120×80 mm. No. 2336/7 ... 1·25 1·60

Nos. 2336/7 were only available in $5 booklets, No. SB319, in which the surplus self-adhesive paper around each stamp was retained.
No. **MS**2338 also commemorates Pacific Explorer 2005 World Stamp Expo Exhibition, Sydney, Australia.

CANADA

823 TD Bank Building of c.1900, Cashier and TD Tower, Toronto

824 Horned Lark

(Des q30 design inc. Litho Lowe-Martin)
2005 (18 Mar). 150th Anniv of TD Bank Financial Group. Fluorescent frame. Self-adhesive. P 11½.
2339	**823**	50c. multicoloured	80	80
		a. Booklet pane. No. 2339×10	7·00	

No. 2339 was only issued in $5 booklets, No. SB320.

(Des Rolf Harder. Litho Lowe-Martin)
2005 (23 Mar). Bird Paintings by John Audubon (3rd series). T **824** and similar horiz designs. Multicoloured. Fluorescent frame.

(a) PVA gum. P 12½×13½
2340	50c. Type **824**	1·25	1·25
	a. Block of 4. Nos. 2340/3	4·50	4·50
2341	50c. Piping Plover	1·25	1·25
2342	50c. Stilt Sandpiper	1·25	1·25
2343	50c. Willow Ptarmigan	1·25	1·25
2340/2343 Set of 4		4·50	4·50

(b) Size 45×35 mm. Self-adhesive. Imperf
2344	85c. Double-crested Cormorant	1·90	2·25
	a. Booklet pane. No. 2344×6	10·00	

Nos. 2340/3 were printed together, *se-tenant*, as blocks of 4 in sheets of 16.
No. 2344 was only available in $5.10 booklets, No. SB321, in which the surplus self-adhesive paper around each stamp was retained.

825 Jacques Cartier Bridge, Montreal, Quebec

(Des Smith-Boake Designwerke Inc. Litho CBN)
2005 (2 Apr). Bridges. T **825** and similar horiz designs. Multicoloured. Fluorescent frame. Self-adhesive. P 12½×13½.
2345	50c. Type **825**	75	1·00
	a. Block of 4. Nos. 2345/8	2·75	3·50
2346	50c. Souris Swinging Bridge, Manitoba	75	1·00
2347	50c. Angus L. Macdonald Bridge, Halifax, Nova Scotia	75	1·00
2348	50c. Canso Causeway, Nova Scotia	75	1·00
2345/2348 Set of 4		2·75	3·50

Nos. 2345/8 were printed together, *se-tenant*, in different combinations in sheets of 16, giving four blocks of 4 or four horizontal and vertical strips of 4.
The backing paper shows further illustrations of these bridges.

826 Magazine Covers of 1911, 1954, 1962 and 1917

827 Saskatoon Berries and Osprey, Waterton Lakes National Park, Alberta, Canada

(Des 52 Pick-up Inc. Litho Lowe-Martin)
2005 (12 Apr). Centenary of Maclean's Magazine. Fluorescent frame. P 12½×13½.
2349	**826**	50c. multicoloured	60	50

(Des Xerxes Irani and Jeff Spokes (No. 2350) or Finbarr O'Connor (No. 2351). Litho Lowe-Martin)
2005 (22 Apr). Biosphere Reserves. T **827** and similar horiz design. Multicoloured. Fluorescent frame. P 12½×13½.
2350	50c. Type **827**	1·10	1·10
	a. Pair. Nos. 2350/1	2·10	2·10
2351	50c. Red Deer stags, Killarney National Park, Ireland	1·10	1·10
MS2352 120×70 mm. Nos. 2350/1		2·10	2·40

Nos. 2350/1 were printed together, *se-tenant*, in horizontal and vertical pairs in sheets of 16.
Stamps in similar designs were issued by Ireland.

828 Sailor Lookout, Canadian Navy Corvette and Survivors in Lifeboat

(Des Derek Sarty. Litho Lowe-Martin)
2005 (29 Apr). 60th Anniv of Battle of the Atlantic. Fluorescent frame. P 12½×13½.
2353	**828**	50c. multicoloured	1·00	60

829 Candle, Silhouettes, Memorial Cross GRV and New Museum Building

(Des Tiit Telmet and Marko Barac. Litho Lowe-Martin)
2005 (6 May). Opening of New Canadian War Museum Building, Ottawa. Fluorescent frame. Self-adhesive. P 8.
2354	**829**	50c. multicoloured	70	70
		a. Booklet pane. No. 2354×8	5·00	

No. 2354 was only issued in $4 booklets, No. SB322.

830 "Down in the Laurentides"

(Des Hélène L'Heureux. Litho Lowe-Martin)
2005 (27 May). "Art Canada". 150th Birth Anniv of Homer Watson (artist). T **830** and similar horiz design showing his paintings. Multicoloured. Fluorescent frame. P 13½.
2355	50c. Type **830**	70	50
MS2356 150×87 mm. 50c. Type **830** (p 13½); 85c. "The Flood Gate" (53×39 mm) (p 13½×13)		1·10	1·40

No. **MS**2356 also commemorates the 125th anniversary of the National Gallery of Canada.

831 Volunteer with Search Dog, Crashed Aircraft and Satellite

832 Ellen Fairclough and Parliament Buildings, Ottawa

104

CANADA

(Des François Dallaire. Litho Lowe-Martin)

2005 (13 June). Search and Rescue. Sheet 260×170 mm containing T **831** and similar vert designs. Multicoloured. Fluorescent frame. P 13×13½.

MS2357 50c.×2 Type **831**; 50c.×2 Rescuers, crew in life raft and sinking ship; 50c.×2 Seaman winched into helicopter and float plane; 50c.×2 Mountain rescue team with stretcher and satellite .... 6·50 6·50

No. **MS**2357 contains two strips of the four designs with the strips arranged tête-bêche.

(Des Katalin Kovats. Litho CBN)

2005 (21 June). Birth Centenary of Ellen Fairclough (first woman federal cabinet minister). Fluorescent frame. P 13½×12½.
2358 **832** 50c. multicoloured 70 50

833 Diver spinning in Mid-Air

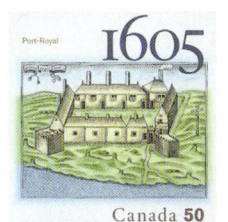

834 Port-Royal, 1605 (from drawing by Samuel de Champlain)

(Des Fugazi. Litho Lowe-Martin)

2005 (5 July). 11th FINA (Fédération Internationale de Natation) World Championships, Montreal. T **833** and similar multicoloured design. Fluorescent frame. P 13½.
2359   50c. Type **833**................................... 75 90
        a. Pair. Nos. 2359/60........................... 1·50 1·75
2360   50c. Swimmer in butterfly stroke 75 90

Nos. 2359/60 were printed together, se-tenant, in pairs in sheetlets of eight. Both stamps can be oriented either vertically or horizontally.

(Des Fugazi and Eng Martin Côté. Recess and litho CBN)

2005 (16 July). French Settlement in North America (2nd issue). 400th Anniv of Founding of Port-Royal, Nova Scotia. Fluorescent frame. P 13×12½.
2361 **834** 50c. multicoloured 70 55

835 Chemicals Plant, Calgary Skyline, Mount Grassi and Railway Line

837 1930 50c. Acadian Memorial Church Stamp and Acadian Flag

836 Woman with Arms outstretched, Sunflowers and Legislature Building, Regina

(Des Matthias Reinicke. Litho Lowe-Martin)

2005 (21 July). Centenary of Alberta Province. Fluorescent frame. Self-adhesive. P 12½×13½.
2362 **835** 50c. multicoloured 70 55

The backing paper is illustrated with four different scenes, each running across two stamps: Calgary Stampede; Jasper Avenue, Edmonton, 1963; Lake Minnewanka, Banff; and oil refinery of c. 1912.

(Des Bradbury. Litho CBN)

2005 (2 Aug). Centenary of Saskatchewan. Fluorescent frame. P 13×12½.
2363 **836** 50c. multicoloured 70 55

(Des Pierre-Yves Pellietier. Litho CBN)

2005 (15 Aug). 250th Anniv of Deportation of French Settlers from Acadia (Nova Scotia) to British Colonies of North America. Fluorescent frame. P 13×12½.
2364 **837** 50c. multicoloured 80 60

838 Oscar Peterson

839 Children playing and discarded Leg Braces

(Des Tiit Telmet. Litho CBN)

2005 (15 Aug). 80th Birthday of Oscar Peterson (jazz composer and musician). Fluorescent frame. P 13½×12½.
2365 **838** 50c. multicoloured .... 1·00 50
MS2366 112×116 mm. No. 2365×4 .... 3·50 4·25

(Des Debbie Adams. Litho CBN)

2005 (2 Sept). 50th Anniv of Mass Polio Vaccination in Canada. Fluorescent frame. P 12½×13.
2367 **839** 50c. multicoloured 70 50

840 Wall climbing

841 Puma concolor (cougar)

(Des Circle Design. Litho Lowe-Martin)

2005 (1 Oct). Youth Sports. T **840** and similar multicoloured designs. Fluorescent frames. Self-adhesive. Imperf×p 10.
2368   50c. Type **840**................................... 60 70
        a. Booklet pane. Nos. 2368/71, each×2 .... 4·25
2369   50c. Skateboarding............................ 60 70
2370   50c. Mountain biking......................... 60 70
2371   50c. Snowboarding............................ 60 70
2368/2371 Set of 4 .... 2·25 2·50

Nos. 2368/71 were only issued in $4 booklets, SB322.
Nos. 2368/71 can be oriented either horizontally or vertically. The outer edges of the stamps are die-cut in irregular shapes around the design. The two inner edges each have one set of nine teeth.

(Des Keith Martin and Liu Jibiao. Litho Lowe-Martin)

2005 (13 Oct). 35th Anniv of Canada—China Diplomatic Relations. Carnivores. T **841** and similar horiz design. Multicoloured. Fluorescent frame. P 13½.
2372   50c. Type **841**................................... 60 70
        a. Horiz pair. Nos. 2372/3 .... 1·10 1·40
2373   50c. Panthera pardus orientalis (Amur leopard) 60 70
MS2374 108×58 mm. Nos. 2372/3 .... 1·25 1·60

Nos. 2372/3 were printed together, se-tenant, in horizontal pairs in sheets of 16 stamps, each se-tenant pair having one "maple-leaf" perforation.
Stamps of the same design were issued by China (People's Republic).

842 Snowman

843 Crèche by Michel Forest

105

CANADA

(Des Hélène L'Heureux. Litho with holographic stamping Lowe-Martin)

2005 (2 Nov). Christmas (1st issue). Self-adhesive booklet stamps. Fluorescent frame. P 8½×imperf.
2375	**842**	50c. multicoloured	70	50
		a. Booklet pane. No. 2375×12	7·50	

No. 2375 was only available from $6 stamp booklets, No. SB323.

(Des Israël Charney. Litho Lowe-Martin)

2005 (2 Nov). Christmas (2nd issue). T **843** and similar vert designs showing Christmas crèches. Self-adhesive booklet stamps. Fluorescent frame. P 7×imperf.
2376		50c. Type **843**	70	50
		a. Booklet pane. No. 2376×12	7·50	
2377		85c. Crèche with aboriginal figures by Keena (31×39 mm)	1·40	2·00
		a. Pane. No. 2377×6	6·00	
2378		$1.45 Crèche by Sylvia Daoust (27×40 mm)	2·25	3·00
		a. Pane. No. 2378×6	9·75	
2376/2378	*Set of 3*		4·00	5·00

No. 2376 was only available from $6 stamp booklets, No. SB325.
No. 2377/8 were issued in separate panes of six.

844 Chow
845 Queen Elizabeth II, Ottawa, 2002 

(Des Joseph Gault and Suzanne Duranceau. Litho and embossed Lowe-Martin)

2006 (6 Jan). Chinese New Year ("Year of the Dog"). T **844** and similar vert design. Multicoloured. Fluorescent frame. P 13½.
2379		51c. Type **844**	60	60
MS2380 129×106 mm. $1.49 Chow with puppy			2·50	3·00

No. 2379 has a slightly arched top representing a temple gate. It was printed in sheets of 25 stamps with narrow horizontal labels with elliptical perforation holes at each vertical side above each stamp.

The stamp within **MS**2380 also has a slightly arched top and a single elliptical perforation hole above each vertical side, representing a temple gate.

The foot of No. **MS**2380 is cut in an arch with a barcode tab attached in the centre.

(Des q30 design inc. Litho CBN)

2006 (12 Jan). 80th Birthday of Queen Elizabeth II (1st issue). Fluorescent frame. Self-adhesive. P 10.
2381	**845**	51c. multicoloured	70	70
		a. Booklet pane. No. 2381×10 and 10 stickers	6·25	

No. 2381 was only issued in $5.10 booklets, No. SB331, in which the surplus self-adhesive paper was retained.
Booklet pane No. 2381a also included ten floral stickers in two different designs.

846 Team Pursuit Speed Skating

(Des Metaform Communication Design. Litho Lowe-Martin)

2006 (3 Feb). Winter Olympic Games, Turin, Italy. T **846** and similar horiz design. Multicoloured. Fluorescent frame. P 12½×13½.
2382		51c. Type **846**	75	75
		a. Horiz pair. Nos. 2382/3	1·50	1·50
2383		51c. Skeleton (sled)	75	75

Nos. 2382/3 were printed together, *se-tenant*, in horizontal pairs in sheets of 16 stamps.

847 Trilliums and Black-throated Blue Warbler (Shade Garden)
848 Balloons 

(Des Debbie Adams and Jeffrey Domm. Litho Lowe-Martin)

2006 (8 Mar). Gardens. T **847** and similar vert designs. Multicoloured. Fluorescent frame. Self-adhesive. P 10 (interrupted at corners).
2384		51c. Type **847**	1·25	1·25
		a. Booklet pane. Nos. 2384/7, each×2	9·00	
2385		51c. Purple coneflowers and American painted lady butterfly (flower garden)	1·25	1·25
2386		51c. Water lilies and green darner dragonfly	1·25	1·25
2387		51c. Rock garden and blue-spotted salamander	1·25	1·25
2384/2387	*Set of 4*		4·50	4·50

Nos. 2384/2387 were only issued in $4.08 booklets, No. SB332.

(Des Designwerke Inc. Litho Lowe-Martin)

2006 (3 Apr). Greetings Stamp. Fluorescent frame. Self-adhesive. P 7×imperf.
2388	**848**	51c. multicoloured	75	75
		a. Pane. No. 2388×6	4·25	

No. 2388 was issued in panes of six.

849 "The Field of Rapeseed"
850 Hands enclosing Globe 

(Des Hélène L'Heureux. Litho Lowe-Martin)

2006 (7 Apr). "Art Canada". Paintings by Dorothy Knowles. T **849** and similar multicoloured design. Fluorescent frame. P 13×12½.
2389		51c. Type **849**	75	50
MS2390 150×87 mm. 51c. Type **849** (p 13×12½); 89c. "North Saskatchewan River" (42×51 mm) (p 13)			2·25	2·75

(Des Steven Spazuk. Litho CBN)

2006 (20 Apr). 50th Anniv of Canadian Labour Congress. Fluorescent frame. P 13½.
| 2391 | **850** | 51c. multicoloured | 70 | 50 |

(Des q30 design inc. Litho CBN)

2006 (21 Apr). 80th Birthday of Queen Elizabeth II (2nd issue). Sheet 125×75 mm. Multicoloured. Fluorescent frame. PVA gum. P 12½×13.
| **MS**2392 $1.49×2 As Type **845** but 39×31 mm | 4·75 | 5·50 |

851 Colophon emerging from Book
852 Mid 19th-Century Transformation Mask and Other Exhibits

CANADA

(Des James Roberts. Litho Lowe-Martin)

2006 (26 Apr). Centenary of McClelland & Stewart (publishing house). Fluorescent frame. Self-adhesive. P 11½×11.

2393	851	51c. slate-blue and silver	1·40	1·25
		a. Booklet pane. No. 2393×8 and 8 labels	10·00	

No. 2393 was only issued in $4.10 booklets, No. SB334. Booklet pane No. 2393a also included eight small stickers showing the McClelland & Stewart colophon and "100".

(Des Neville Smith. Litho Lowe-Martin)

2006 (11 May). 150th Anniv of Canadian Museum of Civilization, Gatineau, Quebec. Fluorescent frame. Self-adhesive. P 8 (interrupted)×straight edge.

2394	852	89c. multicoloured	1·75	2·25
		a. Booklet pane. No. 2394×8	12·00	

No. 2394 was only issued in $7.12 booklets, No. SB335.
The two horizontal edges each have a set of seven perforations.

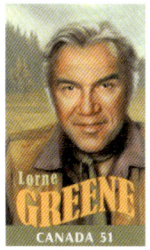

853 Lorne Greene

854 Champlain's Ship

(Des Neal Armstrong, John Belisle and Kosta Tsetsekas. Litho Lowe-Martin)

2006 (26 May). Canadians in Hollywood. T **853** and similar vert designs. Multicoloured. Fluorescent frame.

(a) Self-adhesive. P 10

2395	51c. Type **853**	75	85
	a. Booklet pane. Nos. 2395/8, each×2	5·50	
2396	51c. Fay Wray	75	85
2397	51c. Mary Pickford	75	85
2398	51c. John Candy	75	85
2395/2398	Set of 4	2·75	3·00

(b) PVA gum. P 13×12½

MS2399	180×63 mm. As Nos. 2395/8	3·25	3·75

Nos. 2395/8 were only issued in $4.08 booklets, Nos. SB336/c, in which the surplus self-adhesive paper around each stamp was retained. Booklet pane No. 2395a also included eight small stickers. It exists in four versions which differ in the order of the stamps within the two blocks of four which form the booklet pane.

(Des Francis Back, Martin Côté and Fugazi. Recess and litho CBN (No. 2400) or Ashton-Potter (**MS**2401))

2006 (28 May). French Settlement in North America (3rd issue). 400th Anniv of Samuel de Champlain's Survey of East Coast of North America. Fluorescent frame (Canada stamps). P 13×12½.

2400	51c. Type **854**	70	50
MS2401	204×146 mm. 51c. Type **854**; 39c.×2 As Type **2879** of USA. P 11	1·00	1·25

No. **MS**2401 also commemorates Washington 2006 International Stamp Exhibition. A self-adhesive stamp in the same design and an identical miniature sheet were also issued by the United States.

855 Girl watching Beluga Whale

(Des Kevin van der Leek. Litho Lowe-Martin)

2006 (15 June). 50th Anniv of Vancouver Aquarium. Fluorescent frame. Self-adhesive. P 10.

2402	855	51c. multicoloured	70	60
		a. Booklet pane. No. 2402×10	6·25	

No. 2402 was only issued in $5.10 booklets, No. SB337.

856 Pilot and Snowbirds

(Des Wade Stewart and Tiit Telmet. Litho CBN)

2006 (28 June). 35th Anniv of Snowbirds Demonstration Team (431 Squadron). T **856** and similar horiz design. Multicoloured. Fluorescent frame. P 12½×13.

2403	51c. Type **856**	1·25	1·25
	a. Horiz pair. Nos. 2403/4	2·50	2·50
2404	51c. Snowbirds and emblem	1·25	1·25
MS2405	130×65 mm. Nos. 2403/4	2·50	2·50

Nos. 2403/4 were printed together, *se-tenant*, in horizontal pairs in sheets of 16 stamps.

857 James White (Chief Geographer), Proportional Dividers and Modern Map

(Des Ivan Murphy and Karen Smith. Litho Lowe-Martin)

2006 (30 June). Centenary of "The Atlas of Canada". Fluorescent frame. P 13½×12½.

2406	857	51c. multicoloured	1·25	1·00

No. 2406 was printed in sheets of 16 containing 2×2 rows of four stamps separated by an illustrated gutter.

858 Player and Event Tickets

859 Early and Modern Climbers

(Des Yvan Meunier and Tom Yakobina. Litho Lowe-Martin)

2006 (6 July). World Lacrosse Championships, London, Ontario. Fluorescent frame. Self-adhesive. P 12×imperf.

2407	858	51c. multicoloured	70	70
		a. Pane. No. 2407×8	5·00	

No. 2407 was issued in $4.08 panes of eight.

(Des Xerxes Irani. Litho Lowe-Martin)

2006 (19 July). Centenary of the Alpine Club of Canada. Fluorescent frame. Self-adhesive. P 12½×13.

2408	859	51c. multicoloured	1·00	85
		a. Booklet pane. No. 2408×8	7·00	

No. 2408 was only issued in $4.08 booklets, No. SB339.

860 Barrow's Goldeneye

861 "g" as Beaver enclosing "50"

(Des Oliver Hill, Dennis Page and Pierre Leduc. Litho CBN)

2006 (3 Aug). Duck Decoys. T **860** and similar vert designs. Multicoloured. Fluorescent frame. P 13×12½.

2409	51c. Type **860**	1·10	1·10
	a. Block of 4. Nos. 2409/12	4·00	4·00
2410	51c. Mallard (decoy with white ring around neck)	1·10	1·10

107

CANADA

2411	51c. Black duck (plain brown decoy)	1·10	1·10
2412	51c. Red-breasted merganser (black and white decoy with red bill)	1·10	1·10
2409/2412 Set of 4		4·00	4·00
MS2413 130×145 mm. Nos. 2409/12		4·00	4·25

Nos. 2409/12 were printed together, *se-tenant*, as blocks of 4 in sheets of 16.

(Des Ion Design Inc. Litho Lowe-Martin)

2006 (16 Aug). 50th Anniv of the Society of Graphic Designers of Canada. Fluorescent frame. P 12½×13½.

| 2414 | 861 | 51c. multicoloured | 70 | 50 |

862 Glasses of Wine

(Des Derwyn Goodall. Litho Lowe-Martin)

2006 (23 Aug). Canadian Wine and Cheese. T **862** and similar multicoloured designs. Fluorescent frame. Self-adhesive. Die-cut.

2415	51c. Type **862**	80	90
	a. Booklet pane. Nos. 2415/18, each×2	5·50	
2416	51c. Wine taster (horiz as Type **862**)	80	90
2417	51c. Canadian cheeses (wedge-shaped, 36×38 mm)	80	90
2418	51c. Serving cheese platter at fromagerie (wedge-shaped, 36×38 mm)	80	90
2415/2418 Set of 4		2·75	3·25

Nos. 2415/18 were only issued in $4.08 booklets, No. SB340.

(Des Denis L'Allier. Litho Lowe-Martin)

2006 (26 Sept). Canadian Universities Anniversaries (5th series). Vert design as T **779a** (No. 2190). Multicoloured. Fluorescent frame. Self-adhesive. P 13×13½.

| 2419 | 51c. Macdonald College, Sainte-Anne-de-Bellevue, Quebec (centenary) | 1·00 | 85 |
| | a. Booklet pane. No. 2419×8 | 7·00 | |

No. 2419 was only available in $4.08 stamp booklets, No. SB341.

863 Newfoundland Marten

(Des Doug Martin, David Sacha and Karen Satok. Litho Lowe-Martin)

2006 (29 Sept). Endangered Species (1st series). T **863** and similar horiz designs. Multicoloured. Fluorescent frame.

(a) Self-adhesive. Die-cut

2420	51c. Type **863**	1·10	1·10
	a. Pane. Nos. 2420/3, each×2	8·00	8·00
2421	51c. Blotched tiger salamander	1·10	1·10
2422	51c. Blue racer	1·10	1·10
2423	51c. Swift fox	1·10	1·10
2420/2423 Set of 4		4·00	4·00

(b) PVA gum. Size 48×24 mm. P 13½

| MS2424 160×74 mm. Nos. 2420/3 | 4·00 | 4·50 |

Nos. 2420/3 were issued in panes of eight, containing two of each design.

864 Maureen Forrester and Place des Arts, Montréal

(Des Alanna Cavanagh, Paul Haslip and Judith Lacerte. Litho CBN)

2006 (17 Oct). Canadian Opera Singers. T **864** and similar horiz designs. Multicoloured. Fluorescent frame. P 12½×13½.

2425	51c. Type **864**	1·10	1·10
	a. Vert strip of 5. Nos. 2425/9	5·00	5·00
2426	51c. Raoul Jobin and Palais Garnier, Paris	1·10	1·10
2427	51c. Léopold Simoneau, Pierrette Alarie and Opéra-Comique, France	1·10	1·10
2428	51c. Jon Vickers and La Scala, Milan	1·10	1·10
2429	51c. Edward Johnson and Metropolitan Opera Company, New York	1·10	1·10
2425/2429 Set of 5		5·00	5·00

Nos. 2425/9 were printed together, *se-tenant*, as vertical strips of five in sheetlets of ten.

865 "Madonna and Child" (detail) (Antoine-Sébastien Falardeau)

866 "Snowman" (Yvonne McKague Housser)

(Des Pierre Fontaine. Litho Lowe-Martin)

2006 (1 Nov). Christmas (1st issue). Self-adhesive booklet stamps. Fluorescent frame. Die-cut.

| 2430 | **865** | 51c. multicoloured | 85 | 55 |
| | | a. Booklet pane. No. 2430×12 | 9·50 | |

No. 2430 was only available from $6.12 stamp booklets, No. SB343.

(Des Peter Steiner. Litho CBN)

2006 (1 Nov). Christmas (2nd issue). T **866** and similar vert designs showing Christmas cards from 1931 "Painters of Canada" series. Self-adhesive booklet stamps. Fluorescent frame. P 13½×imperf.

2431	51c. Type **866**	85	55
	a. Booklet pane. No. 2431×12	9·50	
2432	89c. "Winter Joys" (J. E. Sampson)	1·75	2·25
	a. Pane. No. 2432×6	8·25	
2433	$1.49 "Contemplation" (Edwin Holgate)	2·25	3·25
	a. Pane. No. 2433×6	12·50	
2431/2433 Set of 3		4·25	5·50

Nos. 2431 was only available from $5.34, booklets, No. SB344.
Nos. 2432/3 were issued in separate panes of six.

867 Ice Fields and Fjord, Sirmilik National Park, Nunavut

868 Queen Elizabeth II, 2005

869 Spotted coralroot

(Des Gottschalk+Ash International. Litho CBN)

2006 (16 Nov)–**10**. T **867** and similar vert designs inscr "P" instead of face value, each showing Canadian flag. Multicoloured. Fluorescent frame.

(a) Self-adhesive booklet stamps. Die-cut (Nos. 2434/8) or die-cut perf 13½ (Nos. 2439/49)

2434	(51c.) Type **867**	1·10	1·25
	a. Booklet pane. Nos. 2434/8, each×2	10·00	
	b. Booklet pane. Nos. 2434/8, each×6	27·00	
2435	(51c.) Coast and ancient trees, Chemainus, British Columbia	1·10	1·25
2436	(51c.) Polar bears, Churchill, Manitoba	1·10	1·25
2437	(51c.) Lighthouse at Bras d'Or lake, Nova Scotia	1·10	1·25
2438	(51c.) Tuktut Nogait National Park, Northwest Territories	1·10	1·25
2439	(52c.) Sambro Island lighthouse, Nova Scotia (27.12.07)	1·40	1·40
	a. Pane. Nos. 2439/43, each×2	12·00	
	b. Booklet pane. Nos. 2439/42 and 2444, each×6 (1.5.08)	35·00	
	c. Pane. Nos. 2439/42 and 2444, each×2 (2.7.08)	12·00	

2440	(52c.)	Point Clark lighthouse, Ontario (27.12.07)	1·40	1·40
2441	(52c.)	Cap-des-Rosiers lighthouse, Quebec (27.12.07)	1·40	1·40
2442	(52c.)	Warren Landing lighthouse, Manitoba (27.12.07)	1·40	1·40
2443	(52c.)	Pachena Point lighthouse, British Columbia (27.12.07)	1·40	1·40
2444	(52c.)	Pachena Point lighthouse and part of Keeper's house (at right) (1.5.08)	1·40	1·40
2445	(57c.)	Watson's Mill (three storey stone building), Manotick, Ontario (11.1.2010)	1·40	1·40
		a. Pane. Nos. 2445/9, each×2	12·50	
		b. Booklet pane. Nos. 2445/9, each×6	38·00	
2446	(57c.)	Keremeos Grist Mill (wooden building with waterwheel at left), British Columbia (11.1.2010)	1·40	1·40
2447	(57c.)	Old Stone Mill National Historic Site (four storey stone building with red doors), Delta, Ontario (11.1.2010)	1·40	1·40
2448	(57c.)	Riordon Grist Mill (two storey stone building), Caraquet, New Brunswick (11.1.2010)	1·40	1·40
2449	(57c.)	Cornell Mill (weir at right), Stanbridge East, Quebec (11.1.2010)	1·40	1·40
2434/2449 Set of 16			19·00	20·00

(b) Ordinary gum. Fluorescent frame. P 13×13½

MS2450 130×70 mm. As Nos. 2445/9 (11.1.2010)......... 6·25 7·00

Nos. 2434/8 were only available in $5.10 (SB347) or $15.30 (SB348) booklets. They were all inscribed "P" and initially sold for 51c. each. Nos. 2439/44 were all inscr "P" and initially sold for 52c. Nos. 2439/43 were first issued in panes of ten stamps. Subsequently Nos. 2439/42 together with No. 2444 were issued in panes of ten and booklets of 30, No. SB378, which was originally priced at $15.60. Nos. 2445/9 were all inscribed "P" and initially sold for 57c. They were available in panes of ten sold for $5.70 and booklets of 30 (SB405) sold for $17.10.

Nos. 2451/63 are left for possible additions to these definitive stamps.

(Des q30 design inc (No. 2464) or Gottschalk+Ash International (2465/7). Litho CBN)

2006 (16 Nov)–**10**. Self-adhesive booklet stamp. Fluorescent frame. Die-cut (No. 2464) or die-cut perf 13½ (Nos. 2465/7).

2464	**868**	(51c.) multicoloured	90	90
		a. Booklet pane. No. 2464×10	8·00	
2465		(52c.) Queen Elizabeth II, Saskatoon, 2005 (27.12.07)	1·00	1·00
		a. Pane. No. 2465×10	9·00	
2466		(54c.) Queen Elizabeth II in Canada, 19 May 2005 (ruby red background) (12.1.2009)	1·25	1·25
		a. Pane. No. 2466×10	11·00	
2467		(57c.) Queen Elizabeth II (wearing deep blue jacket and hat) (11.1.2010)	1·40	1·40
		a. Pane. No. 2467×10	12·50	
2464/2467 Set of 4			4·25	4·25

No. 2464 was only issued in $5.10 booklets, No. SB349. It was inscribed "P" and initially sold for 51c. each.

No. 2465 was issued in panes of ten stamps. It was inscribed "P" and initially sold for 52c. each.

No. 2466 was issued in panes of ten stamps. It was inscribed "P" and initially sold for 54c. each.

No. 2467 was issued in panes of ten stamps. It was inscribed "P" and initially sold for 57c. each.

Nos. 2468/9 are left for possible additions to these definitive stamps.

(Des Sigmond Pifco, Monique Dufour and Sophie Lafortune. Litho Lowe-Martin)

2006 (16 Nov). Flowers (2nd series). Multicoloured. Fluorescent frame.

(a) Self-adhesive coil stamps. P 9½×imperf (No. 2470) or 8½×imperf (others)

2470	**869**	(51c.) Spotted coralroot	60	35
2471		93c. Flat-leaved bladderwort (19.12.06)	1·10	1·25
2472		$1.10 Marsh skullcap (19.12.06)	1·25	1·50
2473		$1.55 Little larkspur (19.12.06)	1·75	2·25
2470/2473 Set of 4			4·25	4·75

(b) Self-adhesive booklet stamps. Die-cut

2474		93c. Flat-leaved bladderwort (19.12.06)	1·10	1·25
		a. Pane. No. 2474×6	6·50	
2475		$1.10 Marsh skullcap (19.12.06)	1·25	1·50
		a. Pane. No. 2475×6	7·50	
2476		$1.55 Little larkspur (19.12.06)	1·75	2·25
		a. Pane. No. 2476×6	10·50	

(c) PVA gum. P 13½×13

MS2477 120×72 mm. As Nos. 2470/3 (19.12.06) .... 6·00 7·00
No. 2470 was inscribed "P" and initially sold for 51c. each.
Nos. 2474/6 were issued in separate panes of six.

> **POSTAL FORGERIES.** During 2010 postal forgeries of three different panes were detected. In all cases the print quality is poorer than the genuine panes and forgeries do not have fluorescent bands. The panes concerned are Nos. 2439/b, 2466a and 2584a.

870 Pig

(Des John Belisle and Kosta Tsetsekas. Litho and embossed Lowe-Martin)

2007 (5 Jan). Chinese New Year ("Year of the Pig"). T **870** and similar horiz design. Multicoloured. Fluorescent frame. P 13½.

2478		52c. Type **870**	1·25	60
		a. Gold (flowers) omitted	£100	
MS2479 98×97 mm. $1.55 Pig (running to right)			2·25	2·75

No. 2479 is cut in a lantern shape.

871 Ribbons and Confetti

872 King Eider (*Somateria spectabilis*)

(Des Karen Smith. Litho Lowe-Martin)

2007 (15 Jan). Greetings Stamp. Fluorescent frame. Self-adhesive. P 7½×imperf.

2480	**871**	52c. multicoloured	85	1·00
		a. Pane. No. 2480×6	4·50	

No. 2480 was only issued in $3.12 panes of six stamps.

(Des q30 design inc. Litho Lowe-Martin)

2007 (12 Feb). International Polar Year. T **872** and similar horiz design. Multicoloured. Fluorescent frame*. P 13½.

2481		52c. Type **872**	1·50	1·50
		a. Horiz pair. Nos. 2481/2	3·00	3·00
2482		52c. *Crossota millsaeare* (deep-sea jellyfish)	1·50	1·50
MS2483 105×70 mm. As No. 2481/2			3·00	3·00

Nos. 2481/2 were printed together, *se-tenant*, as horizontal pairs in sheetlets of 16, containing two blocks of eight stamps separated by a narrow vertical gutter. Each *se-tenant* pair (including the stamps within **MS**2483) has one "maple-leaf" perforation.

*Nos. 2481/2 and the stamps within **MS**2483 have a fluorescent frame around the horizontal pair, giving No. 2481 a fluorescent frame at top, left and bottom and No. 2482 a fluorescent frame at top, right and bottom.

873 *Syringa vulgaris* "Princess Alexandra"

874 "Jelly Shelf"

(Des Isabelle Toussaint. Litho CBN)

2007 (1 Mar). Lilacs. T **873** and similar horiz design. Multicoloured. Fluorescent frame.

(a) Self-adhesive. Die-cut

2484		52c. Type **873**	90	90
		a. Booklet pane. Nos. 2484/5, each×5	8·00	
2485		52c. *Syringa×prestoniae* "Isabella"	90	90

(b) PVA gum. P 13

MS2486 128×80 mm. As Nos. 2484/5 .... 1·75 2·00
Nos. 2484/5 were only issued in $5.20 booklets, No. SB354, in which the surplus self-adhesive paper around each stamp was retained. Booklet pane No. 2484a also included ten small stickers.

(Des Denis L'Allier. Litho Lowe-Martin)

2007 (12 Mar). Canadian Universities' Anniversaries (6th issue). Vert design as T **779a** (No. 2190). Multicoloured. Fluorescent frame. Self-adhesive. P 13×13½.

2487		52c. HEC (École des hautes études commerciales), Montréal (centenary)	85	85
		a. Booklet pane. No. 2487×8	6·25	
2488		52c. University of Saskatchewan (3 Apr)	85	85
		a. Booklet pane. No. 2488×8	6·25	

Nos. 2487/8 were only issued in separate $4.16 stamp booklets, Nos. SB355/6.

CANADA

(Des Hélène L'Heureux. Litho CBN)

2007 (15 Mar). "Art Canada". Paintings by Mary Pratt. T **874** and similar horiz design. Multicoloured. Fluorescent frame. P 13×12½.
2489   52c. Type **874** 75   50
MS2490 150×87 mm. 52c. Type **874**; $1.55 "Iceberg in the North Atlantic" (62×40 mm) .... 3·00   3·50

875 Parliament Buildings, Ottawa, 2007 and Lumberers Regatta, 1860

(Litho (with embossing on $1.55) Lowe-Martin)

2007 (3 May). 150th Anniv of Ottawa as Capital of Canada. Fluorescent frame.

(a) Self-adhesive. P 7½×imperf
2491   **875**   52c. multicoloured .... 1·00   85
           a. Booklet pane. No. 2491×8 .... 7·25

(b) PVA gum. P 13
MS2492 102×102 mm. 52c. As No. 2491; $1.55 As No. 2491 .... 3·50   3·75

876 University of Lethbridge (Arthur Erickson), 1971

(Des Ivan Novotny. Litho Lowe-Martin)

2007 (9 May). Centenary of Royal Architectural Institute of Canada. T **876** and similar horiz designs. Multicoloured. Fluorescent frame. P 13.
2493   52c. Type **876** .... 1·00   1·00
           a. Vert strip of 4. Nos. 2493/6 .... 3·50   3·50
2494   52c. St. Mary's Church (Douglas Cardinal), 1969 .... 1·00   1·00
2495   52c. Ontario Science Centre (Raymond Moriyama), 1969 .... 1·00   1·00
2496   52c. National Gallery of Canada (Moshe Safdie), 1988 .... 1·00   1·00
2493/2496 *Set of 4* .... 3·50   3·50

Nos. 2493/6 were printed together, *se-tenant*, as vertical strips of four in sheetlets of eight stamps. The sheetlets also contain eight *se-tenant* half stamp-size labels which form composite designs with the stamps. The four labels at left show the original sketches for the buildings and those at right the architects.

877 Capt. George Vancouver

878 Official U-20 World Cup Football and Canadian Team in Action

(Des Niko Potton. Litho and embossed Lowe-Martin)

2007 (22 June). 250th Birth Anniv of Captain George Vancouver (explorer of west coast of North America). Fluorescent frame. P 13×12½.
2497   **877** $1.55 multicoloured .... 2·50   2·50
MS2498 70×120 mm. **877** $1.55 multicoloured. P 13 .... 2·50   3·00

(Des Debbie Adams. Litho CBN)

2007 (26 June). FIFA U-20 World Cup, Canada. Partial fluorescent frame. P 12½×13.
2499   **878**   52c. multicoloured .... 1·00   85

The fluorescent frame on No. 2499 is broken at lower left and right sides of the stamp.

879 Gordon Lightfoot

880 Sunrise over Alexander Bay, Terra Nova National Park, Newfoundland

(Des Circle Design Inc. Litho Lowe-Martin)

2007 (29 June). Canadian Recording Artists (1st series). T **879** and similar square designs. Multicoloured. Fluorescent frame.

(a) Self-adhesive. P 13½
2500   52c. Type **879** .... 1·00   1·10
           a. Booklet pane. Nos. 2500/3, each×2 .... 7·25
2501   52c. Joni Mitchell .... 1·00   1·10
2502   52c. Anne Murray .... 1·00   1·10
2503   52c. Paul Anka .... 1·00   1·10
2500/2503 *Set of 4* .... 3·50   4·00

(b) PVA gum. P 12½×13
MS2504 Circular 105×105 mm. As Nos. 2500/3 .... 3·25   4·00

Nos. 2500/3 were only issued in $4.16 stamp booklets, No. SB358/c, in which the surplus self-adhesive paper around each stamp was retained. Booklet pane 2500a also included eight small stickers. It exists in four versions which differ in the order of the stamps within the two blocks of four which form the booklet pane.

See also Nos. 2618/21 and 2798/**MS**2806.

(Des Saskia van Kampen. Litho Lowe-Martin)

2007 (6 July). 50th Anniv of Terra Nova National Park, Newfoundland. Fluorescent frame. Self-adhesive. P 13½.
2505   **880**   52c. multicoloured .... 1·00   1·00
           a. Booklet pane. No. 2505×10 .... 9·00

The fluorescent frame on No. 2505 is broken at lower left. It was only issued in $5.20 stamp booklets, No. SB359.

881 Jasper National Park

882 Scouts forming Emblem

(Des Saskia van Kampen. Litho Lowe-Martin)

2007 (20 July). Centenary of Jasper National Park, Alberta. Fluorescent frame. Self-adhesive. Fluorescent frame. P 13½.
2506   **881**   52c. multicoloured .... 1·00   1·00
           a. Booklet pane. No. 2506×10 .... 9·00

The fluorescent frame on No. 2506 is broken at lower left. It was only issued in $5.20 stamp booklets, No. SB360.

(Des Matthias Reinicke. Litho Lowe-Martin)

2007 (25 July). Centenary of Scouting. Fluorescent frame. Self-adhesive. P 13½.
2507   **882**   52c. multicoloured .... 1·25   1·00
           a. Booklet pane. No. 2507×8 .... 9·00

No. 2507 was only issued in $4.16 stamp booklets, No. SB361.

883 Membertou (Grand Chief of the Mi'kmaq) and French Settlement, Port Royal

884 Founding Members and Registry Roll

(Des Suzanne Duranceau and Fugazi. Eng Jorge Peral. Litho and recess CBN)

2007 (26 July). French Settlement in North America (4th issue). Chief Membertou. Fluorescent frame. P 13×12½.
2508   **883**   52c. multicoloured .... 1·00   85

CANADA

(Des Bradbury Branding Design Inc. Litho CBN)

2007 (13 Sept). Centenary of the Law Society of Saskatchewan. Fluorescent frame. P 13.
2509	**884**	52c. multicoloured	1·00	1·00

No. 2509 was printed in sheets containing eight stamps and eight stamp-size labels.

885 Books, Photograph of James Muir (first President) and Gavel

886 *Hippodamia convergens* (convergent lady beetle)

(Des Xerxes Irani. Litho Lowe-Martin)

2007 (13 Sept). Centenary of the Law Society of Alberta. Fluorescent frame. P 12½×13.
2510	**885**	52c. multicoloured	1·00	85

(Des Doug Martin, David Sacha and Karen Satok. Litho Lowe-Martin)

2007 (1 Oct). Endangered Species (2nd series). Horiz designs as T **863**. Multicoloured. Fluorescent frame.

(a) Self-adhesive. Die-cut
2511		52c. North Atlantic right whale	1·40	1·40
		a. Pane. Nos. 2511/14, each×2	10·00	10·00
2512		52c. Northern cricket frog	1·40	1·40
2513		52c. White sturgeon	1·40	1·40
2514		52c. Leatherback turtle	1·40	1·40
2511/2514	*Set of 4*		5·00	5·00

(b) PVA gum. Size 48×24 mm. P 13½
MS2515	160×75 mm. As Nos. 2511/14	5·00	5·00

Nos. 2511/14 were issued in $4.16 panes of eight stamps containing two of each design.

(Des Keith Martin. Litho CBN)

2007 (12 Oct)–**10**. Beneficial Insects. T **886** and similar vert designs. Multicoloured. P 13×13½.
2516		1c. Type **886**	10	10
2517		2c. *Danaus plexippus* (monarch caterpillar) (22.4.09)	10	10
2518		3c. *Chrysopa oculata* (golden-eyed lacewing)	10	10
2518*a*		4c. *Polistes fuscatus* (paper wasp) (19.10.10)	10	10
2519		5c. *Bombus polaris* (northern bumblebee)	10	10
2519*a*		6c. *Zelus luridus* (assassin bug) (19.10.10)	15	10
2519*b*		7c. *Oncopeltus fasciatus* (large milkweed bug) (19.10.10)	20	15
2519*c*		8c. *Chauliognathus marginatus* (margined leatherwing) (19.10.10)	25	20
2519*d*		9c. *Chrysochus auratus* (dogbane beetle) (19.10.10)	25	20
2520		10c. *Aeshna canadensis* (Canada darner dragonfly)	25	20
2521		25c. *Hyalophora cecropia* (cecropia moth)	50	40
2516/2521	*Set of 11*		2·50	1·60
MS2522	133×58 mm. Nos. 2516 and 2518/2521	1·00	1·25
MS2523	133×58 mm. Nos. 2518*a* and 2519*a*/*d* (19.10.10)	1·00	1·25

Nos. 2524/5 are left in case of additions to this definitive set.

887 Reindeer

888 Nativity ('HOPE')

(Des Hélène L'Heureux. Litho Lowe-Martin)

2007 (1 Nov). Christmas (1st issue). Self-adhesive booklet stamps. Fluorescent frame. P 9×imperf.
2526	**887**	(52c.) multicoloured	1·00	85
		a. Booklet pane. No. 2526×12	11·00	

No. 2526 was inscribed 'P' and initially sold for 52c. It was only available from $6.24 stamp booklets, No. SB363.

(Des Stephanie Carter, Steve Hepburn, Jonathon Milne and Tandem Design. Litho Lowe-Martin)

2007 (1 Nov). Christmas (2nd issue). T **888** and similar square designs. Multicoloured. Self-adhesive booklet stamps. Fluorescent frame. P 13½.
2527		(52c.) Type **888**	1·00	85
		a. Booklet pane. No. 2527×12	11·00	
2528		93c. Angel playing trumpet ('JOY')	2·00	2·50
		a. Pane. No. 2528×6	10·50	
2529		$1.55 Dove ('PEACE')	2·75	3·25
		a. Pane. No. 2529×6	14·50	
2527/2529	*Set of 3*		5·25	6·00

No. 2527 was inscribed 'P' and initially sold for 52c. It was only available from booklets of 12, No. SB365, originally sold for $6.24.

Nos. 2528/9 were issued in separate $5.58 or $9.30 panes of six stamps.

889 *Odontioda* Island Red

890 Rat Bride

(Des Sigmond Pifco, Monique Dufour and Sophie Lafortune. Litho Lowe-Martin)

2007 (27 Dec). Flowers (3rd series). Canadian Hybrid Orchids. T **889** and similar horiz designs. Multicoloured. Fluorescent frame and security markings.

(a) Coil stamps. P 9×imperf
2530		(52c.) Type **889**	1·00	85
		a. Perf 9½×imperf	1·00	85
2531		96c. *Potinara* Janet Elizabeth "Fire Dancer"	1·75	1·75
2532		$1.15 *Laeliocattleya* Memoria Evelyn Light	1·90	1·90
2533		$1.60 *Masdevallia* Kaleidoscope "Conni"	2·75	3·00
2530/2533	*Set of 4*		6·50	6·75

(b) Stamps from self-adhesive panes. Imperf
2534		96c. As No. 2531	1·75	2·00
		a. Pane. No. 2534×6	9·75	
2535		$1.15 As No. 2532	2·25	2·75
		a. Pane. No. 2535×6	12·00	
2536		$1.60 As No. 2533	2·75	3·25
		a. Pane. No. 2536×6	15·00	
2534/2536	*Set of 3*		6·00	7·25

(c) PVA gum. P 13½×13
MS2537	120×72 mm. As Nos. 2530/3	7·50	8·50

No. 2530 was inscribed 'P' and initially sold for 52c. It was issued in vertical coils with the perforated top and bottom edges of the stamps meeting each other.

No. 2530*a* was issued in horizontal coils with the backing paper around each stamp removed, the stamps being spaced along the backing paper.

Nos. 2534/6 were issued in separate $5.76, $6.90 or $9.60 panes of six stamps.

(Des Harvey Chan and Tandem Design Associates Ltd. Litho and embossed Lowe-Martin)

2008 (8 Jan). Chinese New Year ('Year of the Rat'). T **890** and similar vert design. Multicoloured. Fluorescent frame. P 13½.
2538		52c. Type **890**	1·25	1·00
MS2539	130×100 mm. $1.60 Rat groom		2·75	3·25

No. 2538 was printed in sheets of 25 stamps with narrow vertical labels at the side of each stamp.

891 Fireworks

892 *Paeonia lactiflora* 'Elgin'

(Des Michael Zavacky. Litho Lowe-Martin)

2008 (15 Jan). Greetings Stamp. Fluorescent frame. Self-adhesive. P 13½×imperf.
2540	**891**	(52c.) multicoloured	1·25	1·25
		a. Pane. No. 2540×6	6·75	

No. 2540 was inscribed 'P' and initially sold for 52c. It was issued in panes of six stamps sold for $3.12.

CANADA

(Des Isabelle Toussaint. Litho Lowe-Martin, Canada)

2008 (3 Mar). Peonies. T **892** and similar horiz design. Multicoloured.

(a) Self-adhesive. P 13½

2541	52c. Type **892**	1·00	1·00
	a. Booklet pane. Nos. 2541/2, each×5	9·00	
2542	52c. *Paeonia lactiflora* 'Coral 'n Gold'	1·00	1·00

(b) PVA gum. P 13×13½

MS2543 120×84 mm. As Nos. 2541/2 .... 2·00 2·25

Nos. 2541/2 were only issued in $5.20 stamp booklets, No. SB373, in which the surplus self-adhesive paper around each stamp was retained. Booklet pane No. 2541a also included ten small stickers.

893 Dentistry Building, University of Alberta (centenary)

894 Ice Hockey Players

(Des Metaform Communication Design. Litho Lowe-Martin)

2008 (7 Mar). Canadian Universities' Anniversaries (7th issue). T **893** and similar horiz design. Multicoloured. Fluorescent frame. Self-adhesive. P 13½.

2544	52c. Type **893**	1·00	1·00
	a. Pane. No. 2544×8	7·00	
2545	52c. Walter C. Koerner Library, University of British Columbia (centenary)	1·00	1·00
	a. Pane. No. 2545×8	7·00	

No. 2544/5 were issued in separate $4.16 panes of eight stamps.

Nos. 2544/8 were also issued cut so as to give strips of four each of Nos. 2544/5 separated by a vertical gutter.

These were only available from Canada Post Natural Philatelic Centre.

(Des Ho Che Anderson, Lionel Gadoury and Dave Hurds. Litho Lowe-Martin)

2008 (3 Apr). International Ice Hockey Federation World Championship, Halifax and Québec. Fluorescent frame. Self-adhesive. P 13½.

2546	**894**	52c. multicoloured	1·00	1·00
		a. Booklet pane. No. 2546×10	9·00	

No. 2546 was only issued in $5.20 stamp booklets, No. SB376/a.

895 Guide Dog at Work

896 Welder working on Pipeline

(Des Designwerke Inc. Litho Lowe-Martin)

2008 (21 Apr). Guide Dogs. Fluorescent frame. Self-adhesive. P 13½×13.

2547	**895**	52c. multicoloured	1·40	1·40
		a. Booklet pane. No. 2547×10	12·00	

No. 2547 was only issued in $5.20 stamp booklets, No. SB377. It has the face value in Braille.

(Des Tim Nokes. Litho Lowe-Martin)

2008 (2 May). Oil and Gas Industry. T **896** and similar horiz design. Multicoloured. Fluorescent frame. Self-adhesive. P 13½.

2548	52c. Type **896**	1·10	1·10
	a. Booklet pane. Nos. 2548/9, each×5	10·00	
2549	52c. James Miller Williams (drilled first Canadian oil well, 1858) and Charles Tripp (developed bitumen deposits of southwest Ontario, 1850s)	1·10	1·10

Nos. 2548/9 were only issued in $5.20 stamp booklets, No. SB379.

897 Samuel de Champlain's Ship, Native Canoe and New Settlement of Québec, 1608

898 Self-portrait

(Des Francis Back and Fugazi. Eng Jorge Peral. Recess and litho CBN)

2008 (16 May). French Settlement in North America (5th issue). 400th Anniv of City of Québec. Fluorescent frame. P 13×12½.

2550	**897**	52c. multicoloured	1·00	90

A stamp in a similar design was issued by France.

(Des Hélène L'Heureux. Litho Lowe-Martin)

2008 (21 May). Art Canada. Birth Centenary of Yousuf Karsh (portrait photographer). T **898** and similar vert designs. Multicoloured. Fluorescent frame.

(a) PVA gum. P 13×12½

2551	52c. Type **898**	1·00	90

MS2552 150×87 mm. 52c. Type **898**; 96c. Audrey Hepburn; $1.60 Winston Churchill .... 5·25 6·00

(b) Self-adhesive. Die-cut

2553	96c. Audrey Hepburn	2·00	2·50
	a. Booklet pane. No. 2553×8	14·00	
2554	$1.60 Winston Churchill	3·50	4·00
	a. Booklet pane. No. 2554×8	25·00	

Nos. 2553/4 were only available in stamp booklets, Nos. SB380/1.

899 50 Cent Coin, 1908

900 Nurse

(Des Stéphane Huot. Litho and embossed Lowe-Martin)

2008 (4 June). Centenary of the Royal Canadian Mint. Fluorescent frame. P 13×13½.

2555	**899**	52c. multicoloured	1·00	90

(Des Gottschalk+Ash International. Litho CBN)

2008 (16 June). Centenary of Canadian Nurses Association. Fluorescent frame. Self-adhesive. P 13½.

2556	**900**	52c. multicoloured	1·10	1·10
		a. Booklet pane. No. 2556×10	10·00	

No. 2556 was only issued in $5.20 stamp booklets, No. SB382.

901 Anne

902 Athlete and Canadian Flag

(Des Dennis Page and Oliver Hill, illustrations Ben Stahl (2557) and Christopher Kovacs (2558). Litho Lowe-Martin)

2008 (20 June). Centenary of Publication of *Anne of Green Gables* by Lucy Maud Montgomery. T **901** and similar horiz design. Multicoloured. Fluorescent frame*.

(a) Self-adhesive. P 13½×13

2557	52c. Type **901**	1·00	1·00
	a. Booklet pane. Nos. 2557/8, each×5	9·00	
2558	52c. Green Gables (house), Cavendish, Prince Edward Island	1·00	1·00

(b) PVA gum. P 13½

MS2559 124×72 mm. As Nos. 2557/8 .... 1·75 2·00

Nos. 2557/8 were only issued in $5.20 booklets, No. SB383. Booklet pane No. 2557a also included ten small flower design stickers.

Nos. 2557/8 and the stamps within **MS**2559 have a fluorescent frame around the horizontal pair, giving No. 2557 a fluorescent frame at top, left and bottom, and No. 2558 a fluorescent frame at top, right and bottom.

The pair of stamps within **MS**2559 have one "maple leaf" perforation.

(Des Neal Armstrong, John Belisle and Kosta Tsetsekas. Litho Lowe-Martin)

2008 (30 June). Canadians in Hollywood (2nd series). Vert designs as T **853**. Multicoloured. Fluorescent frame.

(a) Self-adhesive. P 13½

2560	52c. Norma Shearer	1·25	1·25
	a. Booklet pane. Nos. 2560/3, each×2	9·00	
2561	52c. Chief Dan George	1·25	1·25
2562	52c. Marie Dressler	1·25	1·25
2563	52c. Raymond Burr	1·25	1·25
2560/2563 Set of 4		4·50	4·50

(b) PVA gum. P 13×12½

MS2564 136×77 mm. As Nos. 2560/3 .... 4·00   4·50

Nos. 2560/3 were only issued in $4.16 booklets, Nos. SB384/c. Booklet pane No. 2560a also included eight small stickers. It exists in four versions which differ in the order of the stamps within the two blocks of four which form the booklet pane.

(Des Laurie Lafrance and q30 design inc. Litho Lowe-Martin)

2008 (18 July). Olympic Games, Beijing. Fluorescent frame. Self-adhesive. P 13½.

2565	**902**	52c. multicoloured	1·40	1·40
		a. Booklet pane. No. 2565×10	12·00	

No. 2565 was only issued in $5.20 booklets, No. SB385.

903 Lifeguard and Water Rescue

(Des Derwyn Goodall. Litho Lowe-Martin)

2008 (25 July). Centenary of Lifesaving Society. Fluorescent frame. Self-adhesive. P 13½×13.

2566	**903**	52c. multicoloured	1·00	1·00
		a. Booklet pane. No. 2566×10	9·00	

No. 2566 was only issued in $5.20 booklets, No. SB386.

904 Panning for Gold

(Des Adam Rogers and Subplot Design Inc. Litho Lowe-Martin)

2008 (1 Aug). 150th Anniv of British Columbia. Fluorescent frame. P 12½×13.

| 2567 | **904** | 52c. multicoloured | 1·40 | 1·00 |

No. 2567 is perforated through the backing paper, which is illustrated with eight historic photographs, each running across several stamps.

905 McLaughlin Buick, c. 1912 and Sam McLaughlin

906 Woman with Megaphone

(Litho Lowe-Martin)

2008 (8 Sept). Sam McLaughlin (founder of McLaughlin Motor Car Company and philanthropist) Commemoration. Fluorescent frame. P 12½×13.

| 2568 | **905** | 52c. multicoloured | 1·00 | 85 |

The fluorescent frame on No. 2568 is broken along the lower left side.

(Des David Sacha and Karen Satok. Litho Lowe-Martin)

2008 (1 Oct). Endangered Species (3rd series). Horiz designs as T **863**. Multicoloured. Fluorescent frame.

(a) Self-adhesive. Die-cut

2569	52c. Prothonotary warbler	1·40	1·40
	a. Pane. Nos. 2569/72, each×2	10·00	
2570	52c. Taylor's checkerspot (butterfly)	1·40	1·40
2571	52c. Roseate tern	1·40	1·40
2572	52c. Burrowing owl	1·40	1·40

(b) PVA gum. Size 48×24 mm. P 13½

2569/2572 Set of 4		5·00	5·00
MS2573 160×75 mm. As Nos. 2569/72		5·00	5·50

Nos. 2569/72 were issued in $4.18 panes of eight stamps, containing two of each design.

(Des Paul Haslip. Litho Lowe-Martin)

2008 (6 Oct). Mental Health. Fluorescent frame. Self-adhesive. P 13½.

2574	**906**	(52c.)+10c. multicoloured	1·25	1·40
		a. Booklet pane. No. 2574×10	11·00	

No. 2574 was inscribed 'P+10' and initially sold for 52c. plus a 10c. surcharge for the Canada Post Foundation for Mental Health.

No. 2574 was only issued in booklets, No. SB388, sold for $6.20.

907 Québec City Skyline

908 Infant Jesus (crèche figure by Antonio Caruso)

(Des Ian Drolet. Litho CBN)

2008 (15 Oct). 12th Francophone Summit, Québec. Fluorescent frame. P 12½×13.

| 2575 | **907** | 52c. multicoloured | 1·00 | 85 |

(Des Joseph Gault. Litho Lowe-Martin)

2008 (3 Nov). Christmas (1st issue). Self-adhesive booklet stamps. Fluorescent frame. P 13½.

2576	**908**	(52c.) multicoloured	1·10	85
		a. Booklet pane. No. 2576×12	12·00	

No. 2576 was inscribed 'P' and was initially valid for 52c. It was only available from stamp booklets, No. SB389.

909 Child making Snow Angels

910 Ox

(Des Susan Scott. Litho Lowe-Martin)

2008 (3 Nov). Christmas (2nd issue). Winter Fun. T **909** and similar vert designs showing children. Fluorescent frame. P 13½.

(a) Self-adhesive

2577	(52c.) Type **909**	1·10	85
	a. Booklet pane. No. 2577×12	12·00	
2578	96c. Child skiing	1·90	2·25
	a. Pane. No. 2578×6	10·00	
2579	$1.60 Child tobogganing	3·00	3·50
	a. Pane. No. 2579×6	16·00	
2577/2579 Set of 3		5·50	6·00

(b) PVA gum

MS2580 102×72 mm. As Nos. 2577/9 .... 5·50   6·50

No. 2577 was inscribed 'P' and was initially valid for 52c.

No. 2577 was only available from $6.24 stamp booklets, No. SB391.

Nos. 2578/9 were issued in separate $5.76 and $9.60 panes of six.

(Des Ivan Novotny. Litho and embossed Lowe-Martin)

2009 (8 Jan). Chinese New Year. Year of the Ox. T **910** and similar square design. Multicoloured. Fluorescent frame. P 12½.

| 2581 | (54c.) Type **910** | 1·40 | 1·00 |

MS2582 40×140 mm. $1.65 Earthenware cooking pot by Shu-Hwei Kao .... 3·25   3·75

No. 2581 was inscribed 'P' and initially sold for 54c. It has a background flower pattern which extends over the stamps and sheet margins.

The stamp within MS2582 has a partial fluorescent frame, which is absent from the upper left and top of the stamp.

CANADA

113

CANADA

2009 (8 Jan). China 2009 World Stamp Exhibition. No. **MS**2582 optd with CHINA 2009 logo in gold on the sheet margin.
MS2583 40×140 mm. $1.65 Earthenware cooking pot by Shu-Hwei Kao .... 3·25   3·75

911 Freestyle Skiing

912 Vancouver 2010 Winter Olympic Games Emblem

(Des John Belisle and Kosta Tsetsekas. Litho CBN)

2009 (12 Jan). Winter Olympic Games, Vancouver, 2010 (1st issue). Olympic Sports. T **911** and similar horiz designs. Multicoloured. Fluorescent frame. P 13.

(a) Self-adhesive
2584	(54c.) Type **911**	1·40	1·40
	a. Pane. Nos. 2584/8, each×2	12·00	
	b. Booklet pane. Nos. 2584/8, each×6	35·00	
2585	(54c.) Snowboarding	1·40	1·40
2586	(54c.) Ice sledge hockey	1·40	1·40
2587	(54c.) Bobsleigh	1·40	1·40
2588	(54c.) Curling	1·40	1·40
2584/2588 Set of 5		6·25	6·25

(b) Ordinary gum
MS2589 140×82 mm. As Nos. 2584/8 .... 5·75   6·25

Nos. 2584/8 and stamps from **MS**2589 were all inscribed 'P' and initially sold for 54c. each.
Nos. 2584/8 were issued in panes of ten and booklets of 30, No. SB393.
Postal forgeries: see note below **MS**2477.

(Des Meomi and VANOC/COVAN (emblems) Naomi Broudo and Violet Finvers (mascots). Litho Lowe-Martin)

2009 (12 Jan)–**09** (12 Feb). Winter Olympic Games, Vancouver, 2010 (2nd issue). Mascots and Emblems. T **912** and similar horiz designs. Multicoloured. Fluorescent frame with security markings.

(a) Self-adhesive coil stamps. Die-cut perf 9½×imperf (No. 2590) or 8×imperf (others)
2590	(54c.) Type **912**	1·00	1·25
	a. Vert pair. Nos. 2590/1	2·00	2·50
2591	(54c.) Vancouver 2010 Paralympic Games emblem	1·00	1·25
2592	98c. Miga skiing	2·00	2·25
2593	$1.18 Sumi curling (12 Feb)	2·25	2·75
2594	$1.65 Quatchi playing ice hockey	3·25	3·75
2590/2594 Set of 5		8·50	10·00

(b) Self-adhesive stamps from panes of six. Die-cut perf 9×imperf
2595	98c. As No. 2592	2·25	2·50
	a. Pane. No. 2595×6	12·00	
2596	$1.18 As No. 2593 (12 Feb)	2·50	3·00
	a. Pane. No. 2596×6	13·00	
2597	$1.65 As No. 2594	3·50	4·00
	a. Pane. No. 2597×6	19·00	

(c) Ordinary gum. P 13
MS2598 140×82 mm. As Nos. 2590/4 (12 Feb) .... 9·00   10·00

Nos. 2590/1 were initially sold for 54c. each. They were printed together, *se-tenant*, as vertical pairs in rolls of 100.
Nos. 2592/4 were printed in separate rolls of 50.
Nos. 2595/7 were issued in separate panes of six, sold for $5.88, $7.08 and $9.90.

913 Stylised Ribbons, Fireworks and Confetti bursting from Envelope

914 Rosemary Brown (civil rights campaigner) and BC Legislative Building

(Des Debbie Adams.)

2009 (2 Feb). Greetings Stamp. 'Celebrate'. Fluorescent frame. Self-adhesive. Die-cut perf 13×imperf.
2599	**913** (54c.) multicoloured	1·10	1·00
	a. Pane. No. 2599×6	6·00	

No. 2599, inscribed 'P', was initially sold for 54c. It was issued in panes of six.

(Des Suzanne Duranceau and Lara Minja. Litho CBN)

2009 (2 Feb). Black History Month. T **914** and similar square design. Multicoloured. Fluorescent frame. P 13×12½.
2600	54c. Type **914**	1·00	1·25
	a. Pair. Nos. 2600/1	2·00	2·50
2601	54c. Abraham Doras Shadd holding lantern and runaway slaves	1·00	1·25

Nos. 2600/1 were printed together, *se-tenant*, as horizontal and vertical pairs in sheets of 16.

915 Flight of *Silver Dart*, Bras d'Or Lake, Nova Scotia, 23 February 1909

(Des Michael Little, Crystal Oicle and Dennis Page. Litho Lowe-Martin)

2009 (23 Feb). Centenary of First Powered Flight in Canada. Fluorescent frame. Self-adhesive. P 12½×13.
2602	**915** (54c.) multicoloured	1·50	1·00

The backing paper is illustrated with five different scenes.

916 White Rhododendron with Pink Buds

917 *Striped Column* (Jack Bush), 1964

(Des Isabelle Toussaint. Litho Lowe-Martin)

2009 (13 Mar). Rhododendrons. T **916** and similar horiz design. Multicoloured. Fluorescent frame.

(a) Self-adhesive. P 13½×12½
2603	54c. Type **916**	1·10	1·25
	a. Booklet pane. Nos. 2603/4, each×5	10·00	
2604	54c. Deep pink rhododendron	1·10	1·25

(b) Ordinary gum. P 13
MS2605 120×74 mm. As Nos. 2603/4 .... 2·00   2·50

Nos. 2603/4 were only issued in $5.40 booklets, No. SB394, in which the surplus self-adhesive paper around each stamp was retained. Booklet pane No. 2603a also includes ten small stickers.
The top edge of No. **MS**2605 is cut around the shapes of the rhododendron flowers and foliage.

(Des Hélène L'Heureux. Litho Lowe-Martin)

2009 (20 Mar). Art Canada. Birth Centenary of Jack Bush (artist). T **917** and similar multicoloured design showing paintings. Fluorescent frame. P 13 (2606) or 12½×13 (**MS**2607).
2606	54c. Type **917**	1·00	85
MS2607 150×87 mm. 54c. Type **917**; $1.65 *Chopsticks*, 1977 (57×23 mm)		4·00	4·50

918 Horsehead Nebula and Dominion Astrophysical Observatory, Saanich, BC

919 Polar Bear

(Des Keith Martin. Litho Lowe-Martin)

2009 (2 Apr). International Year of Astronomy. T **918** and similar vert design. Multicoloured. Fluorescent frame. P 13.

(a) Self-adhesive

2608	54c. Type **918**...	1·10	1·25
	a. Booklet pane. Nos. 2608/9, each×5	10·00	
2609	54c. Eagle Nebula and Canada-France-Hawaii Telescope, Mauna Kea, Hawaii......	1·10	1·25

(b) Ordinary gum

MS2610	101×90 mm. As Nos. 2608/9 but 30×40 mm ...	2·00	2·50
	a. With fluorescent overprint............................		

Nos. 2608/9 were only issued in $5.40 booklets, No. SB395, in which the surplus self-adhesive paper around each stamp was retained. Booklet pane No. 2608a also included ten small stickers.

The fluorescent overprint on No. **MS**2610a appears above the left-hand stamp, depicts an adult and child, and appears red under UV light.

(Des Tiit Telmet and Wade Stewart . Litho Lowe-Martin)

2009 (9 Apr). Preserve the Polar Regions and Glaciers. T **919** and similar horiz design. Multicoloured. Fluorescent frame. P 13.

2611	54c. Type **919**...	1·25	1·25
	a. Pair. Nos. 2611/12...................................	2·50	2·50
2612	54c. Arctic tern	1·25	1·25
MS2613	120×80 mm. Nos. 2611/12.............................	2·50	2·50

Nos. 2611/12 were printed together, *se-tenant*, as horizontal and vertical pairs in sheetlets of 16 stamps.

920 Canadian Horse

921 Canadian Flag and Globe

(Des Wilco Design. Litho Lowe-Martin)

2009 (15 May). Canadian Horse and Newfoundland Pony. T **920** and similar horiz design. Multicoloured. Fluorescent frame. Self-adhesive. Die-cut perf 13.

2614	54c. Type **920**...	1·40	1·40
	a. Booklet pane. Nos. 2614/15, each×5	12·00	
2615	54c. Newfoundland Pony	1·40	1·40

Nos. 2614/15 were only issued in $5.40 stamp booklets, No. SB396. Nos. 2614/15 form a composite background design.

(Des Parable Communications and Cartesia. Litho Lowe-Martin)

2009 (1 June). Centenary of Department of Foreign Affairs and International Trade. Fluorescent frame. P 13.

2616	**921**	54c. multicoloured	1·25	1·00

922 Niagara Falls in 1909 and 2009

923 Robert Charlebois

(Des Paul Haslip. Litho Lowe-Martin)

2009 (12 June). Centenary of the Boundary Waters Treaty. Fluorescent frame. P 13.

2617	**922**	54c. multicoloured	1·00	85

(Des CIRCLE. Litho Lowe-Martin)

2009 (2 July). Canadian Recording Artists (2nd series). T **923** and similar square designs. Multicoloured. Fluorescent frame.

(a) Self-adhesive. Die-cut perf 13½

2618	54c. Type **923**...	80	90
	a. Booklet pane. Nos. 2618/21, each×2	6·00	
2619	54c. Edith Butler...	80	90
2620	54c. Stompin' Tom Connors	80	90
2621	54c. Bryan Adams..	80	90
2618/2621	Set of 4	3·00	3·25

(b) Ordinary gum. P 12½×13

MS2622	Circular 105×105 mm. As Nos. 2618/21	4·00	4·50

Nos. 2618/21 were only issued in $4.32 booklets, Nos. SB397/c. The circular booklet pane No. 2618a also included eight small stickers. It exists in four versions which differ in the order of the stamps within the two blocks of four which form the booklet pane.

924 Mr. PG, Prince George, British Columbia

925 Captain Bartlett with Sextant and *Roosevelt* in the Canadian Arctic

(Bonnie Ross and Fraser Ross. Litho Lowe-Martin)

2009 (6 July). Roadside Attractions (1st series). T **924** and similar multicoloured designs. Fluorescent frame.

(a) Self-adhesive. Die-cut perf 13½ (3 sides)

2623	54c. Type **924**...	1·40	1·50
	a. Booklet pane. Nos. 2623/6, each×2	10·00	
2624	54c. Sign Post Forest, Watson Lake, Yukon	1·40	1·50
2625	54c. Inukshuk (stone giant), Hay River, Northwest Territories	1·40	1·50
2626	54c. Pysanka (giant Easter egg), Vegreville, Alberta..	1·40	1·50
2623/2626	Set of 4	5·00	5·50

(b) Ordinary gum. P 13

MS2627	98×109 mm. As Nos. 2623/6............................	4·00	5·00

Nos. 2623/6 have irregularly shaped tops to the stamps. They are perforated on three sides and imperforate at top.

Nos. 2623/6 were only issued in $4.32 stamp booklets, No. SB398, in which the surplus self-adhesive paper around each stamp was retained. Booklet pane No. 2623a also included eight small stickers.

See also Nos. 2688/92 and 2807/11.

(Des Karen Smith Design. Litho Lowe-Martin)

2009 (10 July). Captain Robert Abram 'Bob' Bartlett (Arctic explorer, ice captain and scientist) Commemoration. P 13.

2628	**925**	54c. multicoloured	1·25	85

No. 2628 commemorates the centenary of Capt. Bartlett's attempt to reach the North Pole.

926 Five-pin Bowling

927 Tree and River inside Human Head and Sun breaking through Clouds

(Des q30design inc. Litho Lowe-Martin)

2009 (10 Aug). Canadian Inventions. Sports. T **926** and similar vert designs. Multicoloured. Fluorescent frame. Self-adhesive. Die-cut perf 13½.

2629	54c. Type **926**...	1·25	1·40
	a. Booklet pane. Nos. 2629/32, each×2	9·00	
2630	54c. Ringette	1·25	1·40
2631	54c. Lacrosse	1·25	1·40
2632	54c. Basketball	1·25	1·40
2629/2632	Set of 4	4·50	5·00

Nos. 2629/32 were only issued in $4.32 stamp booklets, No. SB399. Booklet pane No. 2629a also included eight small stickers showing sports shoes.

(Des Signals Design Group. Litho Lowe-Martin)

2009 (14 Sept). Mental Health. Fluorescent frame. Self-adhesive. Die-cut perf 13.

2633	**927**	(54c.)+10c. multicoloured	1·25	1·40
		a. Booklet pane. No. 2633×10....	11·00	

No. 2633 was inscr 'P+10' and was initially valid for 54c. plus a 10c. surcharge for the Canada Post Foundation for Mental Health.

No. 2633 was only issued in booklets of ten, No. SB400, initially sold for $6.40.

CANADA

115

CANADA

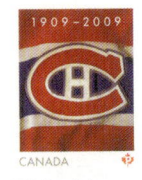

928 Detail from Maurice Richard's Hockey Sweater
929 Maurice Richard, 19 October 1957

(Des Stéphane Huot. Litho and lenticular (**MS**2635) Lowe-Martin)

2009 (17 Oct). Centenary of Montreal Canadiens (ice hockey team). Multicoloured. Self-adhesive.

(a) Fluorescent frame. Die-cut perf 13

2634	**928**	(54c.) multicoloured	1·25	1·25
		a. Booklet pane. No. 2634×10	11·00	

(b) T **929** and similar horiz designs showing 500th goals of famous players. P 13

MS2635 $3 Type **929**; Jean Béliveau, 11 February 1971; Guy Lafleur, 20 December 1983 .... 18·00 20·00

No. 2634 was inscribed 'P' and originally valid for 54c. It was only issued in booklets of ten, No. SB401, initially sold for $5.40.

The stamps within No. **MS**2635 are based on digital clips and use Motionstamp technology to show action replays of goals.

930 Two Soldiers (detail from National War Memorial, Ottawa)
931 Madonna and Infant Jesus

(Des Lionel Gadoury and Michael Wandelmaier. Litho Lowe-Martin)

2009 (19 Oct). 'Lest We Forget'. Fluorescent frame.

(a) Self-adhesive. Die-cut perf 13

2636	**930**	(54c.) multicoloured	1·10	1·10
		a. Booklet pane. No. 2636×10	10·00	

(b) Ordinary gum. P 12½

MS2637 108×60 mm. As Type **930**×2 .... 2·50 3·00

No. 2636 and the stamps within **MS**2637 were all inscr 'P' and were originally valid for 54c.

No. 2636 was only issued in booklets of ten, No. SB402, initially sold for $5.40.

MS2637 was originally sold for $1.08.

(Des Joseph Gault. Litho Lowe-Martin)

2009 (2 Nov). Christmas (1st issue). T **931** and similar vert designs showing crèche figures by Antonio Caruso. Multicoloured. Fluorescent frame.

(a) Self-adhesive. Die-cut perf 13½

2638		(54c.) Type **931**	1·25	95
		a. Booklet pane. No. 2638×12	13·00	
2639		98c. Magi with gift	2·00	2·50
		a. Pane. No. 2639×6	11·00	
2640		$1.65 Shepherd carrying lamb	3·25	4·00
		a. Pane. No. 2640×6	18·00	
2638/2640	Set of 3		6·00	6·75

(b) Ordinary gum. P 13×12½

MS2641 150×100 mm. As Nos. 2576 and 2638/40 .... 7·00 8·00

No. 2638 was inscr 'P' and was originally valid for 54c. It was issued in booklets of 12 stamps, No. SB403, initially sold for $6.48.

Nos. 2639/40 were issued in separate panes of six.

They were also available in $15.78 panes containing six of each design separated by a gutter.

932 Christmas Tree
933 Tiger Seal

(Des Hélène L'Heureux. Litho and holographic foil Lowe-Martin)

2009 (2 Nov). Christmas (2nd issue). Self-adhesive booklet stamps. Fluorescent frame. Die-cut p 9×imperf.

2642	**932**	(54c.) multicoloured	1·10	85
		a. Booklet pane. No. 2642×12	12·00	

No. 2642 was inscribed 'P' and was initially valid for 54c. It was only available from booklets of 12, No. SB404, originally sold for $6.48.

(Des Wilco Design. Litho and embossed Lowe-Martin)

2010 (8 Jan). Chinese New Year. Year of the Tiger. Fluorescent frame. P 12½.

2643		(57c.) Type **933**	1·25	1·00
MS2644	40×140 mm. 170c. Tiger's head seal		3·50	4·00

The fluorescent frame on **MS**2644 is on three sides, at the left, right and bottom of the stamp.

No. 2643 was inscr 'P' and initially sold for 57c.

934 Striped Coralroot (*Corallorhiza striata*)
935 Whistler, British Columbia

(Monique Dufour and Sophie Lafortune. Litho Lowe-Martin)

2010 (11 Jan). Flowers (4th series). Wild Orchids. T **934** and similar horiz designs. Multicoloured. Fluorescent frame.

(a) Self-adhesive stamps from vert coils. P 8×imperf

2645	(57c.) Type **934**	1·10	95
2646	$1 Giant helleborine (*Epipactis gigantea*)	2·25	2·00
2647	$1.22 Rose pogonia (*Pogonia ophioglossoides*)	2·40	2·75
2648	$1.70 Grass pink (*Calopogon tuberosus*)	3·50	3·75
2645/2648	Set of 4	8·25	8·50

(b) Self-adhesive stamps from horiz coils. P 9×imperf

| 2648a | (57c.) Type **934** | 1·10 | 95 |

(c) Self-adhesive stamps from panes of six. P 9½×imperf

2649	$1 As No. 2646	2·50	2·75
	a. Pane. No. 2649×6	13·00	
2650	$1.22 As No. 2647	2·75	3·25
	a. Pane. No. 2650×6	15·00	
2651	$1.70 As No. 2648	4·00	4·50
	a. Pane. No. 2651×6	22·00	
2649/2651	Set of 3	8·25	9·50

(d) Ordinary gum. P 13

MS2652 120×72 mm. As Nos. 2645/8 .... 9·25 9·75

No. 2645 was inscribed 'P' and originally sold for 57c.

Perforations are variable on Nos. 2645/8 but consistently 9·25 on No. 2648a. The latter may be identified by its rounded "perf" tips whereas those on No. 2645 are pointed ("saw tooth").

Nos. 2649/51 were only available in separate panes of ten stamps.

(Des Tandem Design Associates Ltd. Litho Lowe-Martin)

2010 (12 Jan). Olympic Winter Games, Vancouver (3rd issue). T **935** and similar horiz design. Multicoloured. Fluorescent frame.

(a) Self-adhesive. Die-cut perf 13½

2653	57c. Type **935**	1·40	1·40
	a. Booklet pane. Nos. 2653/4, each×5	12·50	
2654	57c. Vancouver	1·40	1·40

(b) Ordinary gum. P 13½

MS2655 141×83 mm. As Nos. 2653/4 .... 2·75 3·25

Nos. 2653/4 were only issued in $5.70 booklets, No. SB406.

936 William Hall, V.C. in 1900 and HMS *Shannon*
937 Roméo LeBlanc (Christan Nicholson)

(Des Suzanne Duranceau and Lara Minja. Litho Lowe-Martin)

2010 (1 Feb). Black History Month. Fluorescent frame. P 12½.

| 2656 | **936** | 57c. multicoloured | 1·50 | 1·10 |

116

CANADA

(Des Dennis Page and Oliver Hill. Litho Lowe-Martin)

2010 (8 Feb). Roméo LeBlanc (former Minister of Fisheries and Governor General of Canada 1995–9) Commemoration. Fluorescent frame. P 12½.

| 2657 | **937** | 57c. multicoloured | 1·25 | 1·10 |

938 Vancouver 2010 Olympic Gold Medal

939 Child with Painted Face, Bobsleigh and Speed Skaters

(Des Tandem Design Associates Ltd. Litho Lowe-Martin)

2010 (14 Feb). Olympic Winter Games, Vancouver (4th issue). Canada's First Olympic Gold on Canadian Soil. Fluorescent frame.

(a) Self-adhesive. Die-cut perf 13½

| 2658 | **938** | 57c. multicoloured | 1·40 | 1·25 |
| | | a. Booklet pane. No. 2658×10 | 12·50 | |

(b) Ordinary gum. P 12½

MS2659 150×60 mm. As Type **938**×2................ 2·50 2·75
No. 2658 was only issued in $5.70 booklets, No. SB407.

(Des Signals Design Group. Litho Lowe-Martin)

2010 (22 Feb). Olympic Winter Games, Vancouver (5th issue). T **939** and similar horiz design. Multicoloured. Partial fluorescent frame.

(a) Self-adhesive. Die-cut perf 13½

2660	57c. Type **939**	1·40	1·40
	a. Booklet pane. Nos. 2660/1, each×5	12·50	
2661	57c. Child with painted face, Chandra Crawford with gold medal (Turin 2006) and skiers	1·40	1·40

(b) Ordinary gum. P 13

MS2662 134×60 mm. As Nos. 2660/1................ 2·50 2·75
Nos. 2660/1 were only issued in $5.70 booklets, No. SB408.
The fluorescent frames were on three sides, being at top, right and foot of the stamp on Type **939**, and at top, left and foot of the stamp on No. 2661. The stamps within the miniature sheet have fluorescent frames as Nos. 2660/1.

940 African Violet 'Decelles' Avalanche'

941 Figures forming Maple Leaf and Star of David

(Des Isabelle Toussaint. Litho Lowe-Martin)

2010 (3 Mar). African Violets. T **940** and similar vert design. Multicoloured. Fluorescent frame.

(a) Self-adhesive. Die-cut perf 13½

2663	(57c.) Type **940**	1·40	1·40
	a. Booklet pane. Nos. 2663/4, each×5	12·50	
2664	(57c.) African violet 'Picasso' (violet and white flowers)	1·40	1·40

(b) Ordinary gum. P 13

MS2665 120×82 mm. As Nos. 2663/4................ 2·50 2·75
Nos. 2663/4 and the stamps within **MS**2665 were all inscr 'P' and were originally valid for 57c.
Nos. 2663/4 were only issued in booklets of ten, No. SB409, originally sold for $5.70. Booklet pane 2663a also contains ten small stickers.
MS2665 was originally sold for $1.14.
The top left portion of **MS**2665 is cut around the flowers.

(Des Yarek Waszul and q30design inc. Litho Lowe-Martin)

2010 (14 Apr). Canada–Israel, 60 Years of Friendship. Fluorescent frame. Self-adhesive. Die-cut perf 13.

| 2666 | **941** | $1.70 rosine, new blue and brownish grey | 4·25 | 4·50 |
| | | a. Booklet pane. No. 2666×6 | 23·00 | |

No. 2666 was only issued in $10.20 booklets, No. SB410.

942 Tee Yee Neen Ho Ga Row

943 HMCS *Niobe* and Sailor, c. 1910

(Des Sputnik Design Partners Inc. Litho Lowe-Martin)

2010 (19 Apr). *Four Indian Kings* paintings by John Verelst. T **942** and similar vert designs. Multicoloured. Fluorescent frame. P 12½.

2667	57c. Type **942**	1·60	1·60
	a. Strip of 4. Nos. 2667/70	5·75	5·75
2668	57c. Sa Ga Yeath Qua Pieth Tow	1·60	1·60
2669	57c. Ho Nee Yeath Taw No Row	1·60	1·60
2670	57c. Etow Oh Koam	1·60	1·60
2667/2670	Set of 4	5·75	5·75
MS2671	168×75 mm. Nos. 2667/70	5·75	5·75

Nos. 2667/70 were printed together, *se-tenant*, as horizontal and vertical strips of four in sheetlets of 16.
The portraits show representatives of the Iroquois and Algonquin nations who travelled to London in 1710 for an audience with Queen Anne.

2010 (19 Apr). London 2010 Festival of Stamps. No. **MS**2671 optd with 'LONDON 2010 FESTIVAL OF STAMPS' logo on the sheet margin.

MS2672 168×75 mm. Nos. 2667/70................ 5·00 5·50

(Des Designwerke Inc. Litho Lowe-Martin)

2010 (4 May). Centenary of the Canadian Navy. T **943** and similar horiz design. Multicoloured. Fluorescent frame.

(a) Self-adhesive. Die-cut perf 13×13½

2673	57c. Type **943**	1·40	1·40
	a. Booklet pane. Nos. 2673/4, each×5	12·50	
2674	57c. HMCS *Halifax* (modern frigate) and Wren	1·40	1·40

(b) Ordinary gum. P 12½

MS2675 108×64 mm. As Nos. 2673/4................ 2·75 3·00
Nos. 2673/4 were only issued in $5.70 booklets, No. SB411.

944 Harbour Porpoise (*Phocoena phocoena*)

945 *Selasphorus rufus* (hummingbird) (Wing Yan Tam)

(Des Martin Mörck. Eng Lars Sjööblom. Recess and litho Sweden Post)

2010 (13 May). Marine Life: Sea Otter and Harbour Porpoise. T **944** and similar horiz design, each black, dull ultramarine and turquoise-blue. Fluorescent frame. P 13×12½ (with one double elliptical perforation at right (2676) or left (2677), or 'maple leaf' perforation (**MS**2678).

2676	57c. Type **944**	1·40	1·40
	a. Booklet pane. Nos. 2676/7, each×4	10·00	
2677	57c. Sea otter (*Enhydra lutris*)	1·40	1·40
MS2678	105×69 mm. As Nos. 2676/7	2·50	2·75

Stamps of a similar design were issued by Sweden.
Nos. 2676/7 were only issued in $4.56 stamp booklets, No. SB412.

(Des Susan Scott. Litho CBN)

2010 (22 May). Canadian Geographic's Wildlife Photography of the Year. T **945** and similar multicoloured designs showing winning entries. Fluorescent frame.

(a) Self-adhesive. Die-cut perf 13

2679	57c. Type **945**	1·40	1·40
	a. Booklet pane. Nos. 2679/83, each×2	12·50	
2680	57c. *Tachycineta bicolor* (tree swallows) (Mark Bradley)	1·40	1·40
2681	57c. *Tettigoniidae* (katydid) (Julie Bazinet) (vert)	1·40	1·40
2682	57c. *Ardea herodias* (great blue heron) (Martin Cooper) (vert)	1·40	1·40
2683	57c. *Vulpes vulpes* (red fox) (Ben Boulter) (vert)	1·40	1·40
2679/2683	Set of 5	6·25	6·25

(b) Ordinary gum. P 12½×13

MS2684 150×100 mm. As Nos. 2679/83................ 6·25 6·75
Nos. 2679/83 were only issued in $5.70 booklets, No. SB413.

117

CANADA

946 Man wearing Rotary Vest    **947** *Rollande*, 1929

(Des Xerxes Irani. Litho Lowe-Martin)

2010 (18 June). Centenary of Rotary International. Fluorescent frame. Self-adhesive. Die-cut perf 13½×13.

2685	**946**	57c. multicoloured	1·40	1·40
		a. Booklet pane. No. 2685×8	10·00	

No. 2685 was only issued in $4.56 booklets, No. SB414.

(Des Hélène L'Heureux. Litho Lowe-Martin)

2010 (2 July). Art Canada. Paintings by Prudence Heward. T **947** and similar multicoloured design. Fluorescent frame. P 13.

2686		57c. Type **947**	1·25	1·10
MS2687	150×87 mm. 57c. Type **947**; $1.70 *At the Theatre*, 1928 (42×40 mm)		5·50	6·00

(Des Bonnie Ross and Fraser Ross. Litho Lowe-Martin)

2010 (5 July). Roadside Attractions (2nd series). Multicoloured designs as T **924**. Fluorescent frame.

(a) Self-adhesive. Die-cut perf 13½ (3 sides)

2688	(57c.) The Coffee Pot, Davidson, SK	1·40	1·40
	a. Booklet pane. Nos. 2688/91, each×2	10·00	
2689	(57c.) Happy Rock, Gladstone, Manitoba	1·40	1·40
2690	(57c.) Goose, Wawa, Ontario	1·40	1·40
2691	(57c.) Puffin, Longue-Pointe-de-Mingan, Quebec	1·40	1·40
2688/2691	Set of 4	5·00	5·00

(b) Ordinary gum. P 13

MS2692	99×109 mm. As Nos. 2688/91	5·00	5·00

Nos. 2688/91 have irregularly shaped tops to the stamps. They are perforated on three sides and imperforate at top.

Nos. 2688/91 and the stamps within **MS**2692 were all inscr 'P' and were originally valid for 57c.

Nos. 2688/91 were only issued in booklets of eight, No. SB415, originally sold for $4.56. Booklet pane No. 2688a included eight small stickers.

948 Guides    **949** Coins, Glass and Amber Trading Beads and 17th-century Map of Avalon Peninsula, Newfoundland

(Des Derwyn Goodall. Litho Lowe-Martin)

2010 (8 July). Centenary of Girl Guides of Canada. Fluorescent frame. Self-adhesive. Die-cut perf 13½

2693	**948**	(57c.) multicoloured	1·40	1·40
		a. Booklet pane. No. 2693×10	12·50	

No. 2693 was inscr 'P' and was originally valid for 57c. It was only issued in booklets of ten, No. SB416, originally sold for $5.70. Booklet pane No. 2693a also included ten small stickers.

(Des Steven Slipp. Litho Lowe-Martin)

2010 (17 Aug). 400th Anniv of Cupids, Newfoundland (first English settlement in Canada). Fluorescent frame. P 12½.

2694	**949**	57c. multicoloured	1·25	1·10

950 Immigrant Boy, Boy ploughing and SS *Sardinian*    **951** Mental Health Patient on Road to Recovery

(Des Debbie Adams. Litho Lowe-Martin)

2010 (1 Sept). 'Home Children' (British orphaned and abandoned children sent to Canada). Fluorescent frame. P 12½.

2695	**950**	57c. multicoloured	1·25	1·10

(Des Paprika. Litho Lowe-Martin)

2010 (7 Sept). Mental Health. Fluorescent frame. Die-cut perf 13.

2696	**951**	(57c.)+10c. multicoloured	1·40	1·40
		a. Booklet pane. No. 2696×10	12·50	

No. 2696 was inscr 'P+10' and was initially valid for 57c. plus a 10c. surcharge for the Canada Post Foundation for Mental Health.

No. 2696 was only issued in booklets of ten, No. SB417, initially sold for $6.70.

952 *Our Lady of the Night* (sculpture by Antonio Caruso)   **953** Red Baubles

(Des Joseph Gault. Litho Lowe-Martin)

2010 (1 Nov). Christmas (1st issue). Self-adhesive booklet stamp. Fluorescent frame. Die-cut perf 13½

2697	**952**	(57c.) multicoloured	1·25	1·10
		a. Booklet pane. No. 2697×12	15·00	

No. 2697 was inscribed 'P' and was initially valid for 57c. It was only available from booklets of 12, No. SB418, originally sold for $6.84.

(Des Michael Zavacky. Litho Lowe-Martin)

2010 (1 Nov). Christmas (2nd issue). Baubles. T **953** and similar square designs. Multicoloured. Fluorescent frame.

(a) Self-adhesive. Die-cut perf 13½

2698	(57c.) Type **953**	1·25	1·10
	a. Booklet pane. No. 2698×12	15·00	
2699	$1 Blue baubles	2·40	2·25
	a. Pane. No. 2699×6	14·00	
2700	$1.70 Pink baubles	3·75	3·50
	a. Pane. No. 2700×6	22·00	

(b) Ordinary gum. P 12½

MS2701	116×60 mm. As Nos. 2698/700	7·50	7·75

No. 2698 was inscr 'P' and was originally valid for 57c. It was issued in booklets of 12 stamps, No. SB419, initially sold for $6.84.

Nos. 2699/700 were each issued in separate panes of six.

They were also available together in $16.20 panes containing six of each design separated by a gutter.

954 Rabbit    **955** Arctic Hares

(Des Tracy Walker, Tan Chao Chang, Paul Haslip and Lauren Rand. Litho and embossed Lowe-Martin and Gravure Choquet)

2011 (7 Jan). Chinese New Year. Year of the Rabbit. T **954** and similar square design. Multicoloured. Fluorescent frame. P 12½.

2702	(59c.) Type **954**	1·25	1·10
MS2703	140×40 mm. $1.75 Two rabbits (on medallion)	3·75	3·50

No. 2702 was inscribed 'P' and initially sold for 59c.

The stamp within **MS**2703 has a fluorescent frame on three sides, at top, left and foot of the stamp.

(Des Monique Dufour and Sophie Lafortune. Litho Lowe-Martin)

2011 (17 Jan). Young Wildlife. T **955** and similar horiz designs. Multicoloured. Fluorescent frame.

(a) Self-adhesive coil stamps. Die-cut perf 8½×imperf

2704	(59c.) Type **955**	1·25	1·10
2705	$1.03 Red fox cub	2·25	2·10
2706	$1.25 Two Canada geese goslings	2·75	2·50
2707	$1.75 Polar bear cub	3·75	3·50
2704/2707	Set of 4	9·00	8·25

CANADA

(b) Self-adhesive stamps from panes of six.
Die-cut perf 9½×imperf

2708	$1.03 As No. 2705		2·25	2·10
	a. Pane. No. 2708×6		12·00	
2709	$1.25 As No. 2706		2·75	2·50
	a. Pane. No. 2709×6		15·00	
2710	$1.75 As No. 2707		3·75	3·50
	a. Pane. No. 2710×6		20·00	
2708/2710 Set of 3			8·00	7·25

(c) Ordinary gum. P 13

MS2711 120×72 mm. As Nos. 2704/7 .... 10·00 9·50
No. 2704 was inscribed 'P' and originally sold for 59c.
Nos. 2712/27 are left for additions to this definitive series.

956 Canadian Flag on Soldier's Uniform and Helicopter lifting Supplies

957 Carrie Best (journalist and civil rights campaigner)

(Des Lionel Gadoury and Terry Popik. Litho CBN)

2011 (17 Jan). 'Canadian Pride'. T **956** and similar vert designs showing Canadian flag. Multicoloured. Fluorescent bars.

(a) Self-adhesive booklet stamps. Die-cut perf 13½

2728	(59c.) Type **956**		1·25	1·10
	a. Pane. No. 2728/32, each×2		11·00	
	b. Booklet pane. No. 2728/32, each×6		34·00	
2729	(59c.) Canadian flag on hot air balloon		1·25	1·10
2730	(59c.) Canadian flag on search and rescue uniform and ship		1·25	1·10
2731	(59c.) Canadian flag on Canadarm		1·25	1·10
2732	(59c.) Canadian flag on backpack and Colosseum, Rome		1·25	1·10
2728/2732 Set of 5			5·75	5·00

(b) Ordinary gum. P 13

MS2749 148×70 mm. As Nos. 2728/32 .... 6·25 6·00
Nos. 2728/32 and the stamps within MS2733 were all inscr 'P' and originally valid for 59c. each.
Nos. 2728/32 and the stamps within MS2733 all have fluorescent bars at left and right, fluorescent maple leaf markings on the white circles which appear red under UV light and fluorescent printing at top and foot of the stamp: 'THE TRUE NORTH STRONG AND FREE!' and 'TON HISTOIRE EST UNE ÉPOPÉE DES PLUS BRILLIANTS EXPLOITS'.
Nos. 2728/32 were issued in panes of ten, originally sold for $5.90, and booklets of 30, No. SB420, originally sold for $17.70.
Nos. 2733/48 are left for additions to this definitive series.

(Des Lara Minja. Litho Lowe-Martin)

2011 (1 Feb). Black History Month. T **957** and similar horiz design. Multicoloured. Fluorescent frame. Self-adhesive. Die-cut perf 13½.

2750	59c. Type **957**		1·25	1·10
	a. Booklet pane. No. 2750×10		11·00	
2751	59c. Fergie (Ferguson) Jenkins (baseball pitcher)		1·25	1·10
	a. Booklet pane. No. 2751×10		11·00	

Nos. 2750/1 were issued in separate booklets of ten, Nos. SB421/2.

958 Wrapped Gift

959 Pow-wow Dancer, 1978

(Des Debbie Adams. Litho CBN)

2011 (7 Feb). Greetings Stamp. 'Celebration'. Fluorescent frame. Self-adhesive. Die-cut perf 13×imperf.

2752	**958** (59c.) multicoloured		1·25	1·10
	a. Pane. No. 2752×6		6·75	

No. 2752, inscribed 'P', was initially valid for 59c. It was issued in panes of six, originally sold for $3.54.

(Des Hélène L'Heureux. Litho Lowe-Martin)

2011 (21 Feb). Art Canada. Paintings by Daphne Odjig. T **959** and similar multicoloured designs. Fluorescent frame.

(a) Ordinary gum. P 12½

2753	59c. Type **959**		1·25	1·10

MS2754 150×87 mm. 59c. Type **959**; $1.03 Pow-wow, 1969 (32×39 mm); $1.75 Spiritual Renewal, 1984 (55×39 mm) .... 7·50 7·25

(b) Self-adhesive. Die-cut perf 13½×13

2755	$1.03 Pow-wow, 1969 (32×39 mm)		2·25	2·10
	a. Booklet pane. No. 2755×6		12·00	
2756	$1.75 Spiritual Renewal, 1984 (55×39 mm)		3·75	3·50
	a. Booklet pane. No. 2756×6		20·00	

Nos. 2755/6 were only available in $6.18 or $10.50 stamp booklets, Nos. SB423/4.

960 Sunflower 'Prado Red'

961 Sunflower 'Sunbright'

Des Isabelle Toussaint. Litho Lowe-Martin)

2011 (3 Mar). Sunflowers (*Helianthus annuus*). Multicoloured designs as T **960**/**961**. Fluorescent frame.

*(a) Coil stamps. Horiz designs as T **960**.*
Self-adhesive. Die-cut perf 8½×imperf

2757	(59c.) Type **960**		1·40	1·25
	a. Vert pair. Nos. 2757/8		2·75	2·50
2758	(59c.) Sunflower 'Sunbright'		1·40	1·25

*(b) Booklet stamps. Vert designs as T **961**.*
Self-adhesive. Die-cut perf 13½

2759	(59c.) Sunflower 'Prado Red'		1·40	1·25
	a. Booklet pane. Nos. 2759/60, each×5		12·50	
2760	(59c.) Type **961**		1·40	1·25

*(c) Ordinary gum. Sheet 120×84 mm containing T **961** and similar vert design*

MS2761 (59c.) Sunflower 'Prado Red'; (59c.) As Type **961** 2·50 2·25
Nos. 2757/60 and the stamps within MS2761 were all inscr 'P' and were originally valid for 59c.
Nos. 2757/8 come from rolls of 50 with the two designs alternating throughout.
Nos. 2759/60 were only issued in booklets of ten, No. SB425, originally sold for $5.90.
The top left portion of MS2761 is cut around in the shape of a sunflower.

962 Ram's Head

963 Tree

(Des Paprika. Litho Lowe-Martin)

2011 (21 Mar–22 June). Signs of the Zodiac. Multicoloured.

(a) Self-adhesive. Die-cut perf 13½

2762	(59c.) Type **962** (Aries)		1·40	1·25
	a. Booklet pane. No. 2762×10		10·00	
2763	(59c.) Taurus (21.4.11)		1·40	1·25
	a. Booklet pane. No. 2763×10		13·00	
2764	(59c.) Gemini (20.5.11)		1·40	1·25
	a. Booklet pane. No. 2764×10		13·00	
2765	(59c.) Cancer (22.6.11)		1·40	1·25
	a. Booklet pane. No. 2765×10		13·00	
2762/2765 Set of 4			5·50	5·00

(b) Ordinary gum. P 12½

MS2774 128x128mm. As Nos. 2762/5 (21.4.11) .... 5·50 5·00
Nos. 2762/5 and the stamps within MS2774 were all inscr 'P' and were originally valid for 59c.
Nos. 2762/5 were each issued in separate booklets of ten, Nos. SB426/9, all originally sold for $5.90.
Nos. 2766/73 and MS2775/6 are left for future additions to this set.

119

CANADA

(Des S. Gibson, M. Clark and Subplot Design Inc. Litho Lowe-Martin)

2011 (21 Apr). International Year of Forests. T **963** and similar vert design. Multicoloured. Fluorescent frame.

(a) Self-adhesive. Die-cut perf 13

2777	(59c.) Type **963**...		1·25	1·10
	a. Booklet pane. Nos. 2777/8, each×4.........		10·00	
2778	(59c.) Forest floor with fungi.............................		1·25	1·10

(b) Ordinary gum. P 13½×13

MS2779 70×125 mm. As Nos. 2777/8...........................		2·50	2·25

964 Prince William and Miss Catherine Middleton, November 2010

965 Mail Barrel rigged with Sail and Rudder, Magdalen Islands, 1910

(Des Isabelle Toussaint. Litho Lowe-Martin)

2011 (29 Apr). Royal Wedding. T **964** and similar vert design. Multicoloured. Fluorescent frame.

(a) Ordinary paper. P 12½×13½

2780	(59c.) Type **964**...		1·25	1·10
	a. Horiz pair. Nos. 2780/1.............................		5·00	4·50
2781	$1.75 Prince William and Miss Catherine Middleton embracing, November 2010.		3·75	3·50
MS2782 120×83 mm. No. 2780/1...................................			5·00	4·75
MS2783 As No. MS2782 but with gold crown on upper left sheet margin...................................			5·00	4·75

(b) Self-adhesive. Die-cut perf 13×13½

2784	(59c.) As Type **964**...		1·40	1·25
	a. Booklet pane. No. 2784×10......................		13·00	
2785	$1.75 As No. 2781...		4·00	3·75
	a. Booklet pane. No. 2785×10......................		38·00	

(Des Janice Kun and Karen Smith Design. Litho Lowe-Martin)

2011 (13 May). Methods of Mail Delivery. T **965** and similar horiz design. Multicoloured. Fluorescent frame. P 12½.

2786	59c. Type **965**...		1·25	1·10
	a. Horiz pair. Nos. 2786/7.............................		2·50	2·25
2787	59c. Dog sled carrying mail in winter, northern Canada..		1·25	1·10

Nos. 2786/7 were printed together, *se-tenant*, as horizontal pairs in sheetlets of 16, each pair forming a composite design.

Nos. 2786/7 had a fluorescent frame around the horizontal pair, giving No. 2786a fluorescent frame at top, left and foot, and No. 2787a fluorescent frame at top, right and foot.

966 Hiker, Moose and Eagle in Mountain Landscape

967 Concrete Tower of Burrard Bridge, Vancouver

(Des Tim Nokes. Litho CBN)

2011 (19 May). Centenary of Parks Canada. Self-adhesive. Fluorescent frame. Die-cut perf 13.

2788	**966**	59c. multicoloured...	1·40	1·25
		a. Booklet pane. No. 2788×10......................	13·00	

No. 2788 was issued in $5.90 booklets, No. SB433.

(Des Ivan Novotny. Litho Lowe-Martin)

2011 (9 June). Art Déco. T **967** and similar vert designs. Multicoloured. Self-adhesive. Fluorescent frame (at top, right and foot).

(a) Self-adhesive. Die-cut perf 13½

2789	(59c.) Type **967**...		1·40	1·25
	a. Booklet pane. Nos. 2789/93, each×2.......		13·00	
2790	(59c.) Wall of Cormier House with stone carving, Montreal..		1·40	1·25
2791	(59c.) R. C. Harris Water Treatment Plant, Toronto..		1·40	1·25
2792	(59c.) Detail from Supreme Court of Canada, Ottawa..		1·40	1·25
2793	(59c.) Dominion Building, Regina		1·40	1·25
2789/2793 Set of 5			7·00	6·25

(b) Ordinary gum. P 13×12½

MS2794 127×84 mm. As Nos. 2789/93	6·50	6·25

No. 2789/93 and the stamps within MS2794 were all inscr "P" and were originally valid for 59c.

No. 2789/93 were issued in booklets of ten, No. SB434, originally sold for $5.90.

968 Duke and Duchess of Cambridge in State Landau

969 Ginette Reno

(Des Isabelle Toussaint Design graphique. Litho Lowe-Martin)

2011 (22 June). Royal Wedding (2nd issue). Fluorescent frame.

(a) Self-adhesive. Die-cut perf 13

2795	**968**	(59c.) multicoloured...	1·40	1·25
		a. Booklet pane. No. 2795×10......................	13·00	

(b) Ordinary gum. P 12½×13

MS2796 120×84 mm. As Type **968**×2 (sheet margin showing Westminster Abbey)		3·00	2·75
MS2797 120×84 mm. As Type **968**×2 (sheet margin showing Parliament Buildings, Canada and optd with gold maple leaf and 'Royal Tour 2011 From June 30 to July 8' in English and French)..................................		3·00	2·75

No. 2795 and the stamps within MS2796/7 were inscr 'P' and were originally valid for 59c.

No. 2795 was issued in booklets of ten, No. SB435, originally sold for $5.90.

(Des CIRCLE. Litho Lowe-Martin)

2011 (30 June). Canadian Recording Artists (3rd series). T **969** and similar square designs. Multicoloured. Fluorescent frame.

(a) Self-adhesive. Die-cut perf 13½

2798	(59c.) Type **969**...		1·40	1·25
	a. Booklet pane. Nos. 2798/801, each×2		13·00	
2799	(59c.) Bruce Cockburn...		1·40	1·25
2800	(59c.) Robbie Robertson.....................................		1·40	1·25
2801	(59c.) Kate and Anna McGarrigle.........................		1·40	1·25

(b) Ordinary gum. P 12½×13 (MS2806) or 12½ (others)

2802	(59c.) As Type **969**...		1·40	1·25
2803	(59c.) As No. 2799...		1·40	1·25
2804	(59c.) As No. 2800...		1·40	1·25
2805	(59c.) As No. 2801...		1·40	1·25
2798/2805 Set of 8			11·00	10·50
MS2806 Circular 105×105 mm. As Nos. 2798/801............		10·00	9·50

Nos. 2798/5 and the stamps within MS2806 were all inscr 'P' and were originally valid for 59c.

Nos. 2798/801 were issued in booklets of eight, No. SB436/c, originally sold for $4.72. The circular booklet pane No. 2798a also included eight small stickers. It exists in four versions which differ in the order of the stamps within the two blocks of four which form the booklet pane.

Nos. 2802/5 were each issued in separate sheetlets of 16 with enlarged illustrated margins.

(Des Bonnie Ross and Fraser Ross. Litho Lowe-Martin)

2011 (7 July). Roadside Attractions (3rd series). Multicoloured designs as T **924**. Fluorescent frame.

(a) Self-adhesive. Die-cut perf 13½ (3 sides)

2807	(59c.) The World's Largest Lobster, Shediac, New Brunswick...		1·40	1·25
	a. Booklet pane. Nos. 2807/10, each×2.......		13·00	
2808	(59c.) The Wild Blueberry, Oxford, Nova Scotia		1·40	1·25
2809	(59c.) The Big Potato, O'Leary, Prince Edward Island..		1·40	1·25
2810	(59c.) The Giant Squid, Glover's Harbour, Newfoundland..		1·40	1·25
2807/2710 Set of 4			5·50	5·00

(b) Ordinary gum. P 12½

MS2811 98×109 mm. As Nos. 2807/10.........................		6·50	6·25

Nos. 2807/10 have irregularly shpaed tops to the stamps. They are perforated on three sides and imperforate at top.

Nos. 2807/10 and the stamps within MS2811 were all inscr 'P' and were originally valid for 59c.

Nos. 2807/10 were only issued in booklets of eight, No. SB437, originally sold for $4.72. Booklet pane No. 2807a included eight small stickers.

CANADA Design Index

DESIGN INDEX

The following index is intended to facilitate the identification of Canadian issues from 1942. Portrait stamps are usually listed under surnames only, views under the name of the town or city and other issues under the main subject or a prominent word and date chosen from the inscription. Simple abbreviations have occasionally been resorted to and when the same design or subject appears on more than one stamp, only the first of each series is indicated.

Abbott, J. 444
Abbott, M. **MS**1960
Academy of Arts 972
Acadia 1021, 2364
Aconcagua 2165
Adam Brown (loco) 1109
Aerospace Technology 1678
African Violets 2663, **MS**2665
Agawa Canyon 2145
"Agricultural Education" 782
AIDS 1682
Air Canada 1251
Art Deco 2789
Air Force 1140, 1623, 1920
Air Training camp 399
Aircraft 399, 438, 509, 540, 556, 636, 966, 996, 1026, 1050, 1251, 1623, 1678, 1920, 1936, 2219, **MS**2357
Alaska Highway 1497
Albani 983
Alberta 1511, 2362
Alberta and Saskatchewan 481
Alex Fraser Bridge 1653
Algonkians 723
Algonquin Park 1545
All-Star Games 1963, 2052, 2316
Allan 2285
Alouette 570
Alpine Club of Canada 2408
American Hellenic Education Progressive Association 2201
"Amphilex 2002" **MS**2157
Angels 1218, 1859, 1949, 2528
Anka 2503
Anne 2557
Anne of Green Gables 2557
Antique instruments 1001
Apple Blossom Festival, Nova Scotia 2076
Archer 845
Architecture 1275
Arctic 1656
Arctic hare 2704
Arctic Islands 970
"Armbro Flight" (horse) 1906
Armenian Church 2085
Arms and flowers 543
"Art Canada" 1289, 1327, 1384, 1421, 1504, 1539, 1589, 1629, 1681, 1721, 1825, 1912, 2011, 2097, 2133, 2355, 2389, 2489, 2551, 2606, **MS**2607, 2686, **MS**2687, 2753
Art Deco 2789
Artifacts 1054
Ashevak 1539
Ashoona 1531
Astronauts 2225
Athabasca (ship) 854
Athabasca River 1433
Athletics World Championships, Edmonton 2087
Audubon 2195, 2279, 2340
Automobiles **MS**1563, **MS**1611, **MS**1636, **MS**1683, **MS**1684
Autumn 679
Auyuittup National Park, Nunavut 2083
Avro 540K (aircraft) 1206
Avro Lancaster (aircraft) 997, 1577
Avro-Canada (aircraft) 996, 1028

Back to God's Country (film) **MS**1698
Balloons 2388
Banff 885c, 1541
Banff Springs Golf Club 1637
Banting 1415, **MS**1960
Barbeau 1820
Barkerville, British Columbia 2081
Barreau de Québec 1911

Baseball 1307, 2073
Basketball 829, 1454
Basket-weaving 1896
Bat 1649
Batoche 1146
Battle of the Atlantic 2353
Battleford Post Office 1230
Baubles 2698
"Be Prepared" 515
Beardy 1405
Beaver 473, 1267
Beaver (ship) 820
Bed 1061
Bed-clothes 1534
Bell, A. 408, **MS**1984
Bell Canada **MS**1983
Belted Kingfisher 1646
Beneficial Insects 2516, 2517
Bennett, R. B. 483, 697
Bennett, W. A. C. 1775
Bernier 893
Berries 1460, 2350
Berthiaume 1141
Bethune 1375
"Big Ben" (horse) 1905
Billes, A. J. & J. W. 1772
Binoculars 2200
Biological programme 649
Biotechnology 1680
Bird decoration 765
Birds 407, 443, 474, 479, 495, 539, 620, 638, 906, 1199, 1646, 1673, 1717, 1779, 1865, 1974, 2058, 2195, **MS**2236, 2279, 2340, 2350, 2384
Bishop 1609
Bison 1007
Black 1748
Black History Month 2600, 2601, 2656, 2750
Blomidon Park 1555
Blue Heron Route 1813
Blue Jays (baseball team) 2073
Blue Poppy 1724
Blue Racer 2422
Boats 1315, 1377, 1428
Bobak, B. **MS**1047, 1825
Bobak, M. **MS**1503
Bobsleigh 1237, 1485
Bohemian Waxwing 2281
Bombardier **MS**1984
Bondar 2226
Bonsecours Market, Montreal 1279
Bookbinding 1887
Books 2510
Borden 434, 695
Borduas 1012, 1818
Boreal Chickadee 2282
Bouchard 1137
Boundery Waters Treaty 2617
Bourassa 627
Bourgeoys 805
Bowell 476
Bowls 921
Boxing 815
Boys and Girls Clubs 2004
Bracken 1777
Brant 1194
Breadalbane (Ship) 1249
Brent Goose 2196
Bridges 2345
British Columbia 503, 685, 1696, 1737, 2567
Brock 643
Brown 626
Brown Bear 1275
Brûlé 1232
Brunet 1667
Brymner 1342
Bumblebee 2518
Buried Treasure 1448
Burr 2563
Butchart Gardens 1422, 2075
Butterflies 1296, 1645, 2385
By 943

Cabot 412, 1210, 1736
Cabot Trail 1738
Cadets 2270
Cains Island 1179
Calgary 812, 2362
Calgary Stampede **MS**1954
Callaghan 2222
Calling of an Engineer 1987
"CANADA 92" 1487
Canada—China Diplomatic Relations 2372
Canada Council **MS**1953

Canada Day **MS**944, 1013, **MS**1047, 1090, **MS**1123, 1163, 1203, 1241, 1292, 1323, 1389, 1427, **MS**1503, 1545, 1597, **MS**1642, 1690
Canada Export Month 1337
Canada Games 641
Canada Geese 407, 443, 539
Canada–Israel 60 Years of Friendship 2666
Canadair (aircraft) 966, 1027, 1678
Canadian Amateur Golf Championship 1637
Canadian Broadcasting Corporation 1207, **MS**1953
Canadian Flag 1630, 2434, 2728
Canadian Forces Postal Service 1198
Canadian Geographic's Wildlife 2679, **MS**2684
Canadian Horse and Newfoundland Pony 2614, 2615
Canadians in Hollywood 2395, 2560
Canadian Indians 721
Canadian International Air Show 1936
Canadian Inventions Spot 2629, 2632
Canadian Labour Congress 2391
Canadian National Exhibition 2266
Canadian Navy 2673, **MS**2675
Canadian Nurses Association 2556
Canadian Post, 150 Years 2072
Canadian Postmasters and Assistants Association 2155
Canadian Press 615
Canadian Rangers 2200
Canadian Recording Artists 2500, 2618, **MS**2622
Canadian Tire 1722
Canadian Tulip Festival, Ottawa 2082
Canadian War Museum 2354
Canadian Wine and Cheese 2415
Canals 1795
Candles 745, 2354
Candy 2398
Canoe 1315, 1380
Caouette 1751
Capae St. Mary's Seabird Reserve 1548
"Capex '78" 907, 914
"Capex '87" **MS**1212, 1227
"Capex '96" **MS**1684
Captain Canuck 1664
Captain Robert Abram 'Bob' Bartlett 2628
Cardinal 2494
Caribou 488, 1276c
Carmichael **MS**1642
Carol singing 1617
Carr 674, 1421
Cars **MS**1563, **MS**1611, **MS**1684
Cartier 1118
Cartography 742
Casa Loma, Toronto 2208
Casgrain 1145
Casson **MS**1642
Castle Hill 1166
Catherwood 1691
Cedar Dunes Park 1547
Census 683
Chair and Mace 508
Challenger (space shuttle) 1204
Chambly Canal 1800
Champlain 2400, 2550
Charlottetown 642
Charlottetown Conference 557
Charter of Rights and Freedoms 1239
Chemical Industry 489, 2362
Cherry blossom 650
Chevrier 1749
Chicora (ship) 853
Chief Justice Robinson (ship) 931
Child 824
Children playing 2367
Children's paintings 661, 882, 2006
"China '99" **MS**1917
China 2009 World Stamp Exhibition **MS**2583
Chinese New Year 1714, 1767, 1862, 1957, 2050, 2116, 2176, 2247, 2314, 2379, 2478, 2538, 2581, **MS**2582, 2643, **MS**2644
Chinese New Year 2702
Chinook 1447
Chown 807
Christ in manger 667
Christmas 560, 568, 570, 618, 630, 644, 661, 687, 745, 764, 792, 822, 848, 895, 928, 962, 993, 1023, 1080, 1111, 1137, 1181, 1218, 1254, 1308, 1342, 1405, 1450, 1525, 1572, 1617, 1667, 1711, 1763, 1859,

121

CANADA *Design Index*

1949, 2021, 2110, 2172, 2238, 2375, 2376, 2430, 2431, 2526, 2527, 2576, 2579, **MS**2580, 2638, **MS**2641, 2643, 2697, 2698
Christmas plants 1254
Christmas tree 669, 1023
Church 670, 1111
Churchill 565, 2554
Churchill River 1587
CIDA **MS**1959
Cinema **MS**1698
Circus 1851
Cirque du Soleil **MS**1954
Citizenship 409
City streets 880
City view 708
Civil aviation 480
Climbers 2408
Clown 2098
CN Tower **MS**1985
Coady **MS**1962
Coast and ancient trees 2435
Coat of arms and flowers 543
"Cobalt 60" 1295
Coin 2555
Colombo Plan 520
Colophon emerging from Book 2393
Columbia River 1588
Colville **MS**1047, 2133
Combine harvester 404, **MS**1636
Comeau 1821
Comic Superheroes 1661
Common Murre 2198
Commonwealth Day 1084
Commonwealth Games 908, 918, 1590
Commonwealth Heads of Government Meeting 1253
Commonwealth Parliamentary Association 575
Commonwealth Parliamentary Conference 894
Conan 1085
Confederation Bridge 1731
Congresses 741
Consolidated "Canso" (aircraft) 969
Constitution 1045
Cook, Dr. J. 808
Cook, James 910
Corals 2138
Coteau-du-Lac 1098
Cougar 886, 2372
Countess of Dufferin (loco) 1133
Country women 511
CP Class D10a (loco) 1135
Crab 2765
Cradle 1062
Crate 536
Crèche 2376, 2377
Creighton 1707
Cross 2354
Crowfoot 1213
Cunard 2284
Cupids, Newfoundland 2694
Curling 632, 789, 1282, 2125
Curtiss (aircraft) 967, 998
Cycling 770, 1595, 2224
Cypress Hills Park 1553

D-Day 2286
Da Silva 2204
Dalhousie Law School 1110
Dallaire 1137, 1912
Dan George 2561
Dance 1340
Dandurand **MS**1961
Daoust 2378
Daudelin 2153
Dawson 1688
De Champlain 2361
De Gaspé 1195
De Havilland (aircraft) 1026, 1051
De La Gaspésie Park 1546
De Mons 2287
De Saint-Denys Garneau 2221
Deer 2028
Dempster Highway 1810, 1878
Dentistry Building 2544
Department of Foreign Affairs and International Trade 2616
Desbarats 1243
Desjardins 806, **MS**1962
Desmarteau 1692
Destroyer 388
Diefenbaker 982
Dieppe 1523
Dinosaur Trail 1811
Dinosaurs 1568
Discovery Trail 1879
Diving 768, 1594, 2359
Dogs 1303, **MS**2357, 2379, 2547
Dollard des Ormeaux 516
Dolls 1385
Dorchester (loco) 1106
Dory 1377
Douglas 1772
Dove **MS**1946, 2201, 2529
Dragon boat race 2210
Dragonfly 2386, 2519
Dressler 2562
Drying furs 432
Duck 495, 1290, 2409
Duck Decoys 2409
Duke and Duchess of Cambridge 2795
Dumas **MS**1503
Dumont 1146

Eaton 1583
Education 522
Edwards 1002
Elbrus 2160
Electron microscope 1294
Elizabeth II 410, 450, 463, 512, 527, 559, 579, 613, 700, 759, 855, 867, 1161
Elizabeth II and Duke of Edinburgh 440, 500
Emergency Services 1441
Endangered Species 2420, 2511, 2569, **MS**2573
Energy 1790
Engineering Institute 1240
Erickson 2493
Ericsson (ship) 1250
Eskimo hunter 477
Excavators 913
Exploration 1208, 1232, 1285, 1319
Expo '67 611
Expo '86 1192, 1196
Expo 2005, Aichi, Japan 2335

Fairchild (aircraft) 1050
Fairclough 2358
Falardeau 2430
Family group 785, 825
Farm scene 382, 401
Fencing 814
Fenerty 1242
Ferron 1819
Ferry 587
Fessenden 1241
FIFA U-20 World Cup 2499
Films 1338
FINA World Championships, Montreal 2359
Fire Service 1443, 2202
Fireworks 2540
"First Land Route" 538
First Non-stop Flight 636
First Powered Flight in Canada 2602
Fisgard 1129
Fish 976, 1727, 1784
Fisherman 433
Fishing 491
Fishing Flies 1784, **MS**2328
FitzGerald **MS**1047, **MS**1642
Flag **MS**944, 1328, 1350, 1389, 1630, 2364
Flag and Canada 578
Fleming 893, 2170
Fleur de Lys 1665
Flower and buildings 838
Flowers 543, 650, 856, 978, 1019, 1422, 1680, 2234, 2303, 2336, 2384, 2470 2530, 2541, 2645, **MS**2652
Flying Squirrel 1261
Fokker (aircraft) 1052
Folk Songs 1564
Folktales 1445
Football 831, 2289
Forest 702, 1328, 1394
Forest, M. 2376
Forrester 2425
Forestry 441
Fort Anne 1164
Fort Beauséjour 1099
Fort Chambly 1096
Fort Erie 1168
Fort Frederick 1172
Fort Henry 1090
Fort Lennox 1170
Fort No. 1, Point Levis 1097
Fort Prince of Wales 1094
Fort Rodd Hill 1092
Fort Walsh 1169
Fort Wellington 1093
Fort Whoop Up 1167
Fort William 1091
Fort York 1175
Fortin 1011
Fossils 1390, 1417
Foster 1824
Founding members and Registry Roll 2509
Four Indians Kings (painting) 2667, **MS**2671
Fox 1265, 2026, 2423
Fox, T. 1044, **MS**1959
Fram (polar research ship) 2268
Francophone Summit 2575
Francophonie Games 2066
Franklin, Benjamin 839
Franklin, Sir John 1320
Frappier **MS**1960
Fraser 1287
Fraser River 1558
Frechette 1330
Free Press 501
Freestyle aerials (skiing) 2126
French 751
French River 1585
French Settlement in North America 2282, 2361, 2400, 2508, 2550
Frobisher 537
Frog 2512
Frontenac 720
Frontier College 1941
Frye **MS**1970
Fuller 975
Fundy 884

"g" as Beaver enclosing "50" 2414
Gadbois 1723
Gagnon 795
Games, flags 641
Gannet 474
Gardens 1422, 2384
Garneau 2225
Gateway 922
Gatineau Park, Quebéc 2209
Gauvreau 1817
Gélinas **MS**1972
Gemini 2774
Geography 744
Geological Survey 1509
Geology 743
George VI 375, 389, 414
Gérin-Lajoie 1530
Gesner **MS**1984
Gibraltar Point 1131
Gifts 2238
Gilbert 1102
Girl Guides 515, 1175, 2693
Girl watching Beluga Whale 2402
Gisborne 1244
Glacier 884
Glass-blowing 1889
Glasses of Wine 2415
Glen Abbey Golf Club 1639
Globe 510
Goin' Down the Road (film) **MS**1698
Gold Rush 1685, 2081
Golf 1637
Gould **MS**1952
Gouthro **MS**1503
Governor-General 2128, 2267
Grain elevator 379, 589
Grand Chief of the Mi'kmaq 2508
Great Bear Lake 402
Great Blue Heron 1199
Great Cormorant 2197
Great Horned Owl 1201
"Great Peace of Montreal" 2096
Greek figure 2201, 2288
Greene 2395
Greetings stamps 1580, 1654, 1988, 2020, 2045, 2099, 2388, 2480, 2540, 2599, 2752
Grenfell 563
Grey Cup 1260
Grey Jay 620
Griffith 1416
Grizzly Bear 1758
Group of Seven 660, **MS**1642
Grove 940
GT Class E3 (loco) 1134
Guevremont 847
Guide Dogs 2547
Gymnastics 830
Gyrfalcon 2199
Gzowski 535

CANADA *Design Index*

4-H Clubs 1301
Hadfield 2228
Haliburton 1710
Halifax 413, 1095
Halifax Public Gardens 1426
Hamilton (ship) 1247
Hands enclosing Globe 2391
Hanlan 985
Hanson Boorne 1324
Harlequin **MS**1972
Harris, Lawren 1344, **MS**1642
Harris, Robert 972
Harrison **MS**1503
Hartland Bridge 1652
Harvie **MS**1973
Haut-fond Prince 1178
Hawker Hurricane (aircraft) 999
Head-Smashed-In Buffalo Jump 2150
"Healing from Within" **MS**1969
Health Professionals 1805
Hearne 682, 1319
Hébert, A. 2220
Hébert, L. 1173
Hébert, P. 973, **MS**1047
Hémon 804
Hen Hop! (film) **MS**1698
Henday 1285
Henderson 1325
Hens 977
Henson 1104
Hepburn 2553
Heraldry 1697
Heritage 1054
Herschel Island Park 1552
High Jumping 1593
Highland Games 1742
Highway 584, 1737, 1876
Highway safety 572
Hiking 771, 2788
Hnatyshyn 2267
Hoary Bat 1649
Hockey 957, 2316
Hockey Night **MS**1954
Holgate **MS**1642, 2433
Holocaust 1672
"Home Children" 2695
Home hardware 2275
Hong Kong 1459
HONG KONG Stamp Exhibitions **MS**1716, **MS**2249
Hoodless 1529
Hopkins 1313
Horse-drawn sleigh 661
Horses 1903
Hot air balloons 2106
Hotels 1540
Houses 1826
Houses of Parliament 870
Housser 2431
Howe 755
Hudson 1211
Hudson's Bay Company **MS**1983
Hughes **MS**1503
Humphrey 1856
Hunting 898
Huntsman **MS**1982
Hurdling 811
Hydrological Decade 623

"I remember" 656
Ice Age artifacts 1208
Ice Fields and Fjord 2434
Ice Hockey 485, 1216, 1484, 1516, 1533, 1746, **MS**1954, 1963, 2052, 2118, 2127, 2178, 2546
Ice-skate 764, 2238
Iceberg **MS**2490
Iceberg and boatman 477
Icefields Parkway 2144
Icons 1308
Ile Verte 1130
IMAX **MS**1955
Imperial Penny Postage 1791
Indians of the Pacific Coast 725
Indians of the Plains 721
Industrial Design 1741
Infantrymen 2219
Information Technology 1679
Inglis 1312
Inside Passage, British Columbia 2206
Insulin 675
International Civil Aviation Organization 1612
International Co-operation Year 562
International Francophone Summit 1252
International Jazz Festival, Montréal 2264
International Labour Organization 635
International Literacy Year 1399
International Peace Year 1215
International Polar Year 2481
International Women's Year 813
International Year of Astonomy 2608, **MS**2610
International Year of Older Persons 1881
International Year of the Family **MS**1596
International Year of the Forest 2767
International Youth Year 1142
Interparliamentary Union 566, 1174
Inuits 898, 924, 958, 989, 1047, **MS**1969
Inukshuk of Five Rocks 2335
Ironwork 1888
Iroquoians 729, 739

Jackman 1506
Jackson **MS**1047, **MS**1642
Jacques-Cartier River 1435
Jamboree 482
Jasper National Park 2506
"Jelly Shelf" 2489
Jellyfish 2482
"Jesous Ahatonhia" 895
Jesuits 1235
Jet airliner 540, 556, 1028
Jewellery-making 1895
Jigsaw 1699
Jobin 2426
Jogging 769
John Verelst (painter) 2667, **MS**2671
Johnny Canuck 1662
Johnson, E. 2429
Johnson, E. P. 518
Johnston **MS**1642
Jones 1778
Judo 816

Kane 686
Katannilik Park 1556
Kayak 956, 1317, 1429
Karsh 2551
Keena 2377
Kelsey 654
Kerosene 1292
Kerr **MS**1047
Kilimanjaro 2163
Killam Legacy **MS**1973
Killer Whale 1271
King 435, 696, 1666
King Eider 2481
Kings Landing 2147
"Kingsway Skoal" (horse) 1904
Kinnear 1532
Kites 1942
Klein **MS**1984
Klondike Gold Strike 1685
Kluane 885
Knights of Columbus 1743
Knowles **MS**1047, 2389
Kraken 1401
Kreighoff 749, 2011
Kurelek 1437

L'Anse aux Meadows **MS**1971
L'Arrive d'un Train en Gare (film) **MS**1698
La Francophone 1671
La Mauricie 855*e*
"La Presse" 1141
La Salle 571
La Soiree du Hockey **MS**1954
La Verendyre 504
Labelle 1105
Labour 2014
Labrador (ship) 934
Lacewing 2517
Lachapelle 1000
Lachine Canal 1801
Lacrosse 625, 1591, 2407
Lady Beetle 2516
Lake Placid 971
Lakes 402, 1993
LaMarsh 1750
Lamb **MS**1047
Lampman 1329
Land Mines **MS**1961
Landscapes 584, 704, **MS**1047
Laporte 691
Launching 386
Laurence 1706
Laurier 694
Law Society of Alberta 2510
Law Society of Saskatchewan 2509
Law Society of Upper Canada 1726
Lawn Bowls 1590
Leach's Storm Petrel 2195
Leacock 646
Leatherworking 1894
Leaves 875
Leclerc **MS**1952
Leduc, F. 1815
Leduc, O. 1289
Leg braces 2367
Legendary Creatures 1400
Leger 1043
Leggo 1243
Lemelin **MS**1970
Lemieux 792, **MS**1123
Leopard 2373
Les Bons Debarras (film) **MS**1698
Les Hospitalieres de Quebec **MS**1962
Les Ordres (film) **MS**1698
Lesage 1770
"Lest We Forget" 2636, **MS**2637
Liberation 1627
Lifesaving Society 2566
Lightfoot 2500
Lighthouses 1128, 1176, 2152, 2437
Lilacs 2484
Lincoln's Sparrow 2283
Lion (symbol of Governor-General) 2128
Lismer **MS**1642
Literacy 1699
Livernois 1326
Lombardo **MS**1952
London 2010 Festival of Stamps **MS**2672
London Conference 573
Longboat **MS**1969
Loon 1756
Lord Strathcona's House 2024
Louis R. Desmarais (ship) 1677
Louis, S. 2288
Louisbourg 1128, 1631
Lower Fort Garry 1163
Loyalists 1124
Lumberers Regatta 2491
Lumbering 405
Lunenburg Academy 1643
Lutheran World Federation Assembly 2215
Lynx 1268

MacDonald, A. 1774
MacDonald, J. A. 693
MacDonald, J. E. H. 756, **MS**1642
MacDonald Stewart Foundation **MS**1973
MacKenzie, A. 445, 658
MacKenzie River 1586
Maclean 2227, 2349
Macleod 1214
Macoun 1018
Macphail 1404
"Madonna and Child" 2430
Magazine covers 2349
Magdalen Islands, Québec 2213
Mail coach 438
Mail delivery 2786
Mail trains 436
Mail van 1382
Mailboxes 1989
Main River 1436
Mammals 1261
Mammals (prehistoric) 1613
Mance 754
Manic Dams **MS**1985
Manitoba 647, 1644, 1877
Manning 1776
Maple leaf quilt 1690
Maple leaves and trees 542, 555, 558, 677, 684, 1030, 1427, 1597, 1783, 1836, 2029, 2233
Maps 536, 970, 1013, 1679, 2275, 2406
"Marathon of Hope" 1044, **MS**1959
Marco Polo (ship) 1874
Marconi 796, 2171
Margaree River 1492
Marie 1009
Marine Life 2676, **MS**2678
Marie-Victorin 1017
Marmot 1006
Marquette 1234
Mask 2394
Mason 1823
Massey Foundation **MS**1973
Massey, V. 633, 889
Masson 793
Matonabbee 1319
Matthew (ship) 412
McAdam Railway Station 1278

CANADA *Design Index*

McCain Foods **MS**1982
McClelland & Stewart 2393
McClung 761
McCrae 628
McIndoe **MS**1503
McKenzie, R. T. 801
McKinney 1003
McLaughlin Sam 2568
McLuhan **MS**1970
McNair 1771
Meals and Friends on Wheels **MS**1959
Medical Pioneers 1413
Meighen 519
Membertou 2508
Mental Health 2574, 2633, 2696
Merritt 797
"Merry Christmas" 993, 1023
Meteorology 621
Michener 1520
Microscope 502
Migratory Wildlife 1645
Millennium **MS**1946, **MS**1952, 1956, **MS**1959
Milne **MS**1047, 1139, 1504
Miner 499, 912
Minerals 1509, 1790
Mississauga Interchange 1651
Mitchell, Janet **MS**1503
Mitchell, Joni 2501
Mitchell, W. **MS**1972
Mol 2154
Molson 1022
Mon Oncle Antoine (film) **MS**1698
Monarch Butterfly 1645
Montferrand 1508
Montgomery 803, 2557
Montmorency-Laval 750
Montpetit 1700
Montreal 1487, 2146
Montreal Botanical Gardens 1425
Montreal Canadiens
(Ice hockey team) 2364, **MS**2635
Montreal Children's Hospital 2278
Montreal Museum of Fine Arts 1180
Montreal Symphony Orchestra 1117
Moodie 2223
Moose 448, 1291
Moriyama 2495
Morrice 1180
Morrisseau 1406
Mosher 1022
Moth 2520
Mount Everest 2162
Mount Logan 2167
Mount McKinley 2166
Mount Robson Park 1549
Mountain biking 2370
Mountain Goat 487
Mounted Police 751, 1687, 1806, 2207
Mousseau 1816
Mowat 659
Multiculturalism 1381
Munday 1822
Munitions factory 387
Murphy 1144
Murray 2502
Museum of Anthropology, BC 1873
Museum of Civilisation 2394
Mushrooms 1331
Music 1341
Musical Instrument 1001
Musk Ox 478, 1272
Muskrat 1263

Nanogak **MS**1503
Narwhal 622
National Film Board **MS**1953
National flag 564, 578, 1328, 1630
National Gallery of Canada 2496
National Hockey League 2316
National Parks 2350, 2434
Nativity 848, 1080, 2527
NATO 510, 1940
Neatby **MS**1970
Nelligan 941
Nelson-Miramichi Post Office 1228
Nelvana 1663
Neptune (ship) 819
Neptune Story **MS**1971
New Brunswick 1121, 1812
Newfoundland 1102, 1125, 1522, 1879
Newfoundland Marten 2420
Niagara Falls, Ontario 2212
Niagara River 1495
Niagara-on-the-Lake 1020, 2079
Nickel 1103

Nonsuch (ship) 624
Noorduyn "Norseman" (aircraft) 1053
Normandy 1621
Norris **MS**1503
Northcote (ship) 851
"Northern Dancer" (horse) 1903
Northern development 517
Northern Light (ship) 933
Northern lights 2148
Northwest Territories 648, 1878
Notman 1323
Nova Scotia 508, 1738
Nunavut Territory 1880, 2083
Nurse 506, 1725, 2556

"O Canada" 980
O'Brien 974
Ocean Technology 1677
Ogopogo 1403
Oil and Gas Industry 2548
Oil wells 431, 590
Olympic Games, Athens 2288
Olympic Games, Barcelona 1498
Olympic Games, Bejing 2565
Olympic Games, Montreal 762, 768, 786, 798, 809, 814, 829, 833, 842
Olympic Medal Winners 1691
Ontario 1739
Ontario Science Centre 2495
Opera Singers 2425
Orchestre Symphonique de Québec 2175
Orchids 1883, **MS**1917, 2306, 2530
Order of Canada 890, 1519
Orphan Boy 1446
Osler 637
"OSM 50 MSO" 1117
Ottawa as Capital 2491
Ottawa River 1494
Ottawa University 1835
Ouellette 1694
Oyster Farming 1890

Pablum **MS**1982
"Pacem in Terris" 541
Pacific Cable 2170
Paintings **MS**1123, 1137, 1289, 1421, **MS**1503, 1504, 1539, 1629, 2340, 2389, 2431
Palliser 1288
Pan-American Games (5th) 614
Pan-American Games (13th) 1913
Papal Visit 1126
Papineau 681
Parks 2788
Parliament Buildings 383, 567, 870, 1147, 1174, 2358, 2491
Passport (ship) 852
Payette 2232
Peace Bridge 891
Peace Dove **MS**1946
Peace Garden 1423
"Peaceful Uses" 574
Pearson 698, **MS**1961
Peggy's Cove 2152
Pelee Passage 1177
Pellan 1629
Penfield 1414
Peonies 2541
Peregrine Falcon 906
Peterson 2365
Petro-Canada 2015
Petroleum 507
Pharmaceutical Sciences Congress 1173
Philatelic Exhibition 1037
Phillips 1721
Photogrammetry 741
Photography 1323
Pickford 2397
"Picture Postage" .. 1988, 2020, 2045, 2099, 2217
Pier 21 .... **MS**1971
Pilot 2403
Pine tree 585
Pinky (boat) 902
Pintail 1648
Plains of Abraham 514
Plaskett **MS**1047
Plough 1060
Poets 1329
Point Pelée 855*d*
Pointer 1378
Polar Bear 447, 705, 1757, 2211, 2436
Pole-vaulting 809, 2087
Police 1442
Polio Vaccination 2367

Pontiac **MS**1969
Porcupine 1262
Porpoise 1273
Port Carling Canal 1797
Port-Royal 2361
Post Office 776
Postal Code 938
Postman 777
Postmark 2284
Potts 1505
Pour la Suite du Monde (film) **MS**1698
Power station 403
POW's 1626
Prairie 1328
Pratt, C. **MS**1047
Pratt, E. 1086
Pratt, M. 2489
Praying hands 576
Prehistoric Canada 1390, 1417, 1568, 1613
Preserve the Polar Regions
and Glaciers 2611, **MS**2613
"Prevent Fires" 490
Prince Edward Island 757, 1813
Prince's Gate 2266
Princess Marguerite (ship) 1246
Pronghorn 1270
Province House, Charlottetown 2214
Provincial and Territorial Parks 1545
PTTI Congress 1744
Public Pensions 2159
Public Services International
World Congress 2158
Pulp and Paper 488
Puncak Jaya 2161

Quadra (ship) 821
Quebec 505, 1543, 1876
Quebec Bridge 1650
Quebec Carnival 935
Quebec City 2204
"Quebec in Bloom" 1724
Queen Elizabeth II 2241, 2464, 2466
Queen Elizabeth II Coronation 2203
Queen Elizabeth II's Golden Jubilee 2115
Queen Elizabeth II's
80th Birthday 2381, **MS**2392
Queen Elizabeth the Queen Mother 2003
Queen's University, Kingston 1449
Quilting 1892

Rabbit 2702
Radio Canada 684
Radisson 1233
Railway line 2362
Railway locomotives 1106, 1132, 1185, 1223
Ram's head 2762
Rat Bride 2538
Recording Artists 2500, **MS**2504, 2618, **MS**2622, 2798, **MS**2806
Red Cross 442, 1120
Red Deer 2351
Red Fox 1265
Red River 1560
Red River Settlement 523
Regatta 1049
Regiments 1114, 1335, 2024
Regina 1048
Rehabilitation 979
Reid 1408, 1681
Reindeer 2526
Rescue Service 1444
Reservoir 403
"Resources for Tomorrow" 521
Responsible Government 411
Rhine Crossing 1628
Rhododendron 2603, **MS**2605
Ribbons and Confetti 2480
Richard **MS**1047
Rideau Canal 1798
Riel 657
Riopelle 1814, **MS**2236
River Scene 588
River Valley Drive 1812
Rivers 1432, 1492, 1558, 1584, 1993
Riverside Country Club 1638
Roadside Attractions 2623, **MS**2627, 2688, **MS**2692, 2807, **MS**2811
Robarts 1769
Robinson 1345
Rogers Pass **MS**1985
Rogers, T. **MS**1955
Roman Catholic Church (Newfoundland) . 1125
Roméo LeBlanc 2657
Rose 1019, 2091
Rosenfeld 1693

CANADA *Design Index*

Roue ... 1809
Rotary International ... 2685
Rowing ... 799
Roy ... 1708
Royal Agricultural Winter Fair ... 1766
Royal Architectural Institute ... 2493
Royal Botanical Gardens ... 1424
Royal Canadian Academy of Arts ... 973, **MS**1953
Royal Canadian Army Cadets ... 2270
Royal Canadian Golf Association ... 1637
Royal Canadian Legion ... 828, 2114
Royal Canadian Mint ... 2555
Royal Canadian Navy ... 1189
Royal Military College ... 840, 2086
Royal Montreal Golf Club ... 1641
Royal Visit ... 440, 512
Royal Wedding ... 2780, 2795
Ruby-crowned Kinglet ... 2279
Running ... 810, 919, 2088
Runnymede Library, Toronto ... 1277
Rutherford, E. ... **MS**1503
Rutherford, Lord ... 676

Sackville (ship) ... 1857
Safdie ... 2496
Saguenay Fjord ... 2151
Saguenay River ... 1584
Sailing ... 800
Sailors ... 2219, 2353
St. Andrews ... 1544
St. John Ambulance ... 1087
St. John River ... 1562
St. John's ... 1125, 1300
St. Joseph's Oratory ... 2263
St. Laurent ... 699
St. Lawrence Seaway ... 513, 1122, 1561
St. Mary's Church ... 2494
St. Ours Canal ... 1796
St. Ours Post Office ... 1229
St. Peters Canal ... 1795
St. Roch (ship) ... 932
Saint Maurice Ironworks ... 1302
Saint-Jean ... 1004
Salaberry ... 942
Salamander ... 2387, 2421
Salvation Army ... 1046
Sampson ... 2432
Samson (loco) ... 1108
San Juan (ship) ... 1248
Santa Claus ... 665, 766, 822, 1450
Santa Claus Parade ... 1181
Sapling ... 2215
Saskatchewan ... 987, 1740, 2363
Sasquatch ... 1400
Satellite ... 570, **MS**2357
Sault Ste. Marie Canal ... 1804
Saunders ... **MS**1982
Sauvé ... 1582
Savard ... 1709
Scotia (loco) ... 1132
Scottish settlers ... 758
Scouting ... 1100, 2507
Sculpture ... 1681, 2153
Search and Rescue ... **MS**2357
Second World War ... 1346, 1409, 1456, 1521, 1576, 1621, 1625, 2286
Secord ... 1507
Segwun (ship) ... 1245
Selye ... **MS**1960
Series of the Century ... 1746
"SERVICE" ... 1120
Service, R. ... 846
Seventh-day Adventist Church ... 2005
Shadbolt ... 2097
Shaman ... **MS**1969
Shawinigan (ship) ... 1858
Shearer ... 2560
Sheep ... 449, 703
Shelter ... 958
Shepherd ... 767
Shepherd, R. ... **MS**1503
Ships ... 386, 406, 412, 437, 818, 851, 902, 931, 1119, 1245, 1677, 1857, 1874, 2268, 2284, 2353, 2400, 2550
Shipwrecks ... 1247
Shooting ... 493
Shriners (charitable organization) ... 2098
Signal Hill, St. John's, Newfoundland ... 2084
Signs of the Zodiac ... 2762
Sikhs ... 1882
"Silver Dart" (aircraft) ... 509
Simoneau ... 2427
Sisters Islets ... 1176
Skateboarding ... 2369
Skating ... 692, 788, 823, 1483, 2068
Ski Patrol ... 1441
Ski-jumping ... 1259, 1482
Skiing ... 494, 664, 787, 1217, 1258, 1281, 1486, 2126
Skyscrapers ... 707
Sled ... 2383
Sleigh ... 1063
Smallwood ... 1773
Smellie ... **MS**1961
Smith ... 673
Snow Goose ... 1200
Snowbirds Demonstration Team ... 2403
Snowboarding ... 2371
Snowflake ... 687
Snowmen ... 663, 2262, 2375, 2431
Snowplough ... 1203
Society of Graphic Designers ... 2414
Softimage ... **MS**1955
South Nahanni River ... 1432
South Saskatchewan River ... 1496
Space Programme ... 1143, 1514, **MS**1985
Speed skating ... 1236, 2124, 2382
Spinning wheel ... 1063
Spirits ... 989
"Spitfire" (aircraft) ... 1205
Spring ... 677
Spruce Grouse ... 1202
Spruce Woods Park ... 1551
Stable and star ... 662
Stadium ... 918
Stained glass windows ... 848, 1763
"Stampin the Future" ... 2006
Stamps ... 439, 525, 907, 914, 1037, 2364
Stanley Cup ... 1533
Stanley Park ... 2149
Steamships ... 437, 1245
Stefansson ... 1322
Stephenson ... **MS**1955
Stove ... 1064
Stowe ... 1005
Stratford Festival ... **MS**1971
Striped Skunk ... 1266
Sturgeon ... 2513
Sub-Arctic Indians ... 727
Sugar Bushes, Quebec ... 2078
Summer ... 678
Summit of the Americas, Quebec ... 2074
Sumo wrestling ... 1792
Sunflowers ... 2757
Superman ... 1661
Supernatural ... 1752
Supreme Court ... 817, 1986
Suzor Côté ... 634, 1343
Swimming ... 492, 798, 2360

Tall Ships' visit ... 1119, 2012
Talon ... 524
Tank ... 384
Taurus ... 2763
TD Bank Building ... 2339
"Teaching = enseignment" ... 2168
Teasdale ... **MS**1959
Technology ... 1677
Tekatwitha ... 1008
Telephone ... 783, 1193
Terra Nova National Park ... 2505
Textile Industry ... 462
Textiles (hand-crafted) ... 1534
Thauberger ... **MS**1503
The Apprenticeship of Duddy Kravitz (film) ... **MS**1698
"The Atlas of Canada" ... 2406
The Forks, Winnipeg ... 2080
"The Globe" ... 626
The Grand Theatre ... 2105
The Grey Fox (film) ... **MS**1698
The Holocaust ... 1672
The Rocks Park ... 1554
"The World's in Edmonton 2001" ... 2087
Theatre ... 1339
Théâtre du Nouveau Monde ... 2104
Théâtre du Rideau Vert ... 1864
Thirsk ... 2229
Thompson, D. ... 496
Thompson, J. ... 475
Thomson ... 887, 1384
Tickets ... 2407
Tisseyre ... **MS**1972
Todd ... 794
Toronto ... 617, 1542, 1557
Toronto (loco) ... 1107
Toronto Post Office ... 1227
Toronto Stock Exchange ... 2169
Totem Pole ... 446
Tourist Attractions ... 2075, 2143, 2262
"Towards the Summits" ... 2160
Toys ... 962, 2239, 2278
Toyshop ... 668
Trades ... 1887
Traill ... 2223
Train ferry ... 406
Trains ... 436, 1197, 2271
Transatlantic Flight ... 636
Trans-Canada Highway ... 526
Travel ... 924
Travers ... 1610
Traversée Internationale du Lac St.-Jean ... 2265
Trees ... 827, 1467, 2777
Trees and sledge ... 672
Trent-Severn Waterway ... 1799
Tripp ... 2549
Troopship ... 1625
Trout, J. ... 1413
Trudeau ... 2089
Truro ... 1477
Tryggvason ... 2230
Tsimshian Frontlet ... 1327
Tulip Festival, Ottawa ... 2082, 2134
Tulips ... **MS**2157
Tupper ... 484
Turtle ... 936, 2514
Tyrell ... 1321

Ukrainian Immigration ... 1437
UNICEF ... 1711
United Empire Loyalists ... 1124
United Nations ... 655, 1666
Universal Declaration of Human Rights ... 1856
"Universiade 83" ... 1088
Universities ... 2129, 2190, 2276, 2333, 2419, 2487, 2493, 2544
UPU ... 497, 790, 1919
Uranium ... 988

Vachon ... **MS**1983
Vancouver Aquarium ... 2402
Vancouver, G. ... 2497
Vancouver, George ... 1286
Vanier, G. ... 616
Vanier, P. ... **MS**1961
Varley ... 1010, 1589, **MS**1642
Varying Hare ... 1264
Vickers, J. ... 2428
Vickers "Vedette" (aircraft) ... 968
Victoria, BC ... 525, 1481, 1540
Victoria Golf Club ... 1640
Victorian Order of Nurses ... 1725
Viking ships ... 1209
Villeneuve ... 1733
Vimy Monument ... 629
Vinson Massif ... 2164
Virgin and Child ... 928
Voltigeurs de Québec ... 2025
Volunteers ... 1238
"Votes for Women" ... 612
Voyageur Waterway ... 1434

Walcheren ... 1624
Wall climbing ... 2368
Walrus ... 472, 1269
Walters ... 1314
Wapiti ... 1274
Waterton Lakes ... 884*c*, 2350
Watson ... 2355
Weather observation ... 1398
Weaving ... 1891
Welder ... 2548
Werewolf ... 1402
West (Eliot) River ... 1493
Weston ... **MS**1983
Whales ... 622, 937, 1276, 2016, 2402, 2511
Wheat ... 1293
Wheelchair race ... 1592
White, J. ... 2406
White, P. ... **MS**1952
White Pass and Yukon Route ... 2077
White-winged Crossbill ... 2280
Whooping Cranes ... 479
Wigwam and furs ... 432
Wilberforce Falls, Nunavut ... 2205
Wildlife ... 2704
Wildlife Conservation ... 1290
Willan ... 984
William D. Lawrence (ship) ... 818
Williams, D. ... 2231
Williams, J. ... 2549
Williams, P. ... 1695
Wine Route ... 1739
Winnie the Pooh ... 1701

Winnipeg 775, 2080
Winter 680
Winter landscape... 586
Winter Olympic Games, Albertville............... 1482
Winter Olympic Games,
    Calgary........................... 1191, 1216, 1236,
                                       1258, 1281
Winter Olympic Games, Innsbruck.................. 832
Winter Olympic Games, Salt Lake City......... 2124
Winter Olympic Games, Turin 2382
Winter Olympic Games,
    Vancouver............................ 2584, **MS**2589,
              2590, **MS**2598, 2653, **MS**2655,
              2658, **MS**2659, 2660, **MS**2662
Wireless Telegraphy 2171
Witched Canoe.. 1445
Wolf 1273, 2027
Wolverine 1270c
Woman with Arms outstretched 2363
"Women are Persons" (sculpture) **MS**1962
Women's ice hockey 2127
Woodworking.. 1893
World Communications Year......................... 1083
World Council of Churches 1101
World Cycling Championships 784
World Figure Skating
    Championships 692, 2068
World Health Day 719
World Lacrosse Championships................... 2407
World Road Congress..................................... 1650
World Rowing Championships..................... 1918
World Youth Day 2156
Wrapped present.. 2752
Wray 2396
Writing-on-Stone Park.................................... 1550

Year of Asia Pacific... 1745
Year of the Child.. 965
Year of the Dog.. 2379
Year of the Dragon 1957
Year of the Horse 2116
Year of the Ox.. 1714
Year of the Pig... 2478
Year of the Rabbit... 1862
Year of the Rat.. 2538
Year of the Rooster... 2314
Year of the Snake.. 2050
Year of the Tiger.. 1767
Yellowhead Highway...................................... 1877
Yellowknife... 1116
YMCA 2113
York Boat.. 1379
York Redoubt 1171
Yorkton... 1476
Youth Sports.. 2368
Youville... 923
Yukon 1810
Yukon Gold Rush 1685
Yukon Quest (race)... 2143
Yukon River 1559

Zodiac 2762

STAMP BOOKLETS

Booklet Nos. SB1/48 are stapled.

All booklets up to and including No. SB41 contain panes consisting of two rows of three (3×2).

B 1

1900 (11 June). Red on pink cover. Two panes of six 2c. (No. 155ba).
SB1   25c. booklet. Cover as Type B **1** with English text......   £2000

1903 (1 July). Red on pink cover. Two panes of six 2c. (No. 176a).
SB2   25c. booklet. Cover as Type B **1** with English text......   £2500

1912 (Jan)–**16**. Red on pink cover. Two panes of six 2c. (No. 201a).
SB3   25c. booklet. Cover as Type B **1** with English text......   65·00
    a. Cover handstamped "NOTICE Change in Postal Rates For New Rates See Postmaster"...............   65·00
    b. French text (4.16)..............   £160
    ba. Cover handstamped "AVIS Changement des tarifs Postaux Pour les nouveaux tarifs consulter le maitre de poste"..............   £120

1913 (1 May)–**16**. Green on pale green cover. Four panes of six 1c. (No. 197a).
SB4   25c. booklet. Cover as Type B **1** with English text......   £450
    a. Containing pane No. 199a............   90·00
    ab. Cover handstamped "NOTICE Change in Postal Rates For New Rates See Postmaster"...............   90·00
    b. French text (28.4.16)..............   £700
    ba. Containing pane No. 199a............   £225
    bb. Cover handstamped "AVIS Changement des tarifs Postaux Pour les nouveaux tarifs consulter le maitre de poste"..............   £750

1922 (Mar). Black on brown cover. Two panes of four 3c. and 2 labels (No. 205a).
SB5   25c. booklet. Cover as Type B **1** with English text......   £350
    a. French text..............   £700

1922 (July–Dec). Black on blue cover. Panes of four 1c., 2c. and 3c. (Nos. 246aa, 247aa, 205a) and 2 labels.
SB6   25c. booklet. Cover as Type B **1** with English text......   £350
    a. French text (Dec)..............   £650

1922 (Dec). Black on orange cover. Four panes of six 1c. (No. 246ab).
SB7   25c. booklet. Cover as Type B **1** with English text......   £140
    a. French text..............   £170

1922 (Dec). Black on green cover. Two panes of six 2c. (No. 247ab).
SB8   25c. booklet. Cover as Type B **1** with English text......   £600
    a. French text..............   £700

1923 (Dec). Black on blue cover. Panes of four 1c., 2c. and 3c. (Nos. 246aa, 247aa, 248aa) and 2 labels.
SB9   25c. booklet. Cover as Type B **1** with English text......   £250
    a. French text..............   £650

1923 (Dec)–**24**. Black on brown cover. Two panes of four 3c. (No. 248aa) and 2 labels.
SB10   25c. booklet. Cover as Type B **1** with English text......   £200
    a. French text (5.24)..............   £375

B 2

1928 (16 Oct). Black on green cover. Two panes of six 2c. (No. 276a).
SB11   25c. booklet. Cover as Type B **2** with English text......   65·00
    a. French text..............   £110

1928 (25 Oct). Black on orange cover. Four panes of six 1c. (No. 275a).
SB12   25c. booklet. Cover as Type B **2** with English text......   £120
    a. French text..............   £225

1929 (6 Jan). Plain manilla cover. Three panes of six 1c., two panes of six 2c. and one pane of six 5c. (Nos. 275a, 276a, 279a).
SB13   72c. booklet. Plain cover..............   £400
    a. With "Philatelic Div., Fin. Br. P.O. Dept., Ottawa" circular cachet on front cover..............   £1400
    b. With "1928" in the centre of the circular cachet   £1500

1930 (17 June). Black on green cover. Two panes of six 2c. (No. 290a).
SB14   25c. booklet. Cover as Type B **2** with English text......   £110
    a. French text..............   £200

1930 (17 Nov). Black on red cover. Two panes of six 2c. (No. 291a).
SB15   25c. booklet. Cover as Type B **2** with English text......   65·00
    a. French text..............   £160

1931 (13 July). Black on red cover. Two panes of four 3c. (No. 293a) and 2 labels.
SB16   25c. booklet. Cover as Type B **2** with English text......   85·00
    a. French text..............   £130

1931 (21 July). Black on green cover. Four panes of six 1c. (No. 289b).
SB17   25c. booklet. Cover as Type B **2** with English text......   £130
    a. French text..............   £200

1931 (23 July). Black on brown cover. Two panes of six 2c. (No. 292a).
SB18   25c. booklet. Cover as Type B **2** with English text......   £140
    a. French text..............   £450

1931 (13 Nov). Black on blue cover. Panes of four 1c., 2c. and 3c. (Nos. 289db, 292ba, 293a) and 2 labels.
SB19   25c. booklet. Cover as Type B **2** with English text......   £300
    a. French text..............   £425

1933 (22 Aug–13 Nov). Black on red cover. Two panes of four 3c. (No. 321a) and 2 labels.
SB20   25c. booklet. Cover as Type B **2** with English text (13 Nov)..............   90·00
    a. French text (22 Aug)..............   £170

1933 (7 Sept). Black on brown cover. Two panes of six 2c. (No. 320a).
SB21   25c. booklet. Cover as Type B **2** with English text......   £225
    a. French text..............   £450

1933 (19 Sept–5 Dec). Black on blue cover. Panes of four 1c., 2c. and 3c. (Nos. 319b, 320b, 321ba) and 2 labels.
SB22   25c. booklet. Cover as Type B **2** with English text......   £200
    a. French text (5 Dec)..............   £300

1933 (28 Dec)–**34**. Black on green cover. Four panes of six 1c. (No. 319a).
SB23   25c. booklet. Cover as Type B **2** with English text......   £150
    a. French text (26.3.34)..............   £225

B 3

1935 (1 June–8 Aug). Red on white cover. Two panes of four 3c. (No. 343a) and 2 labels.
SB24   25c. booklet. Cover as Type B **3** with English text (8 Aug)..............   65·00
    a. French text (1 June)..............   £110

1935 (22 July–1 Sept). Blue on white cover. Panes of four 1c., 2c. and 3c. (Nos. 341b, 342b, 343a) and 2 labels.
SB25   25c. booklet. Cover as Type B **3** with English text......   £150
    a. French text (1 Sept)..............   £190

1935 (19 Aug–18 Oct). Green on white cover. Four panes of six 1c. (No. 341a).
SB26   25c. booklet. Cover as Type B **3** with English text......   90·00
    a. French text (18 Oct)..............   £130

1935 (16–18 Mar). Brown on white cover. Two panes of six 2c. (No. 342a).
SB27   25c. booklet. Cover as Type B **3** with English text......   70·00
    a. French text (18 Mar)..............   £120

CANADA / Stamp Booklets

B 4

1937 (14 Apr)–**38**. Blue and white cover. Panes of four 1c., 2c. and 3c. (Nos. 357a, 358a, 359a) and 2 labels.
SB28 25c. booklet. Cover as Type B **3** with English text...... 85·00
   a. French text (4.1.38) £150
SB29 25c. booklet. Cover as Type B **4** with English text
       57 mm wide... 70·00
   a. English text 63 mm wide £120
   b. French text 57 mm wide (4.1.38) .... 95·00
   ba. French text 63 mm wide £190

1937 (23–27 Apr). Red and white cover. Two panes of four 3c. (No. 359a) and 2 labels.
SB30 25c. booklet. Cover as Type B **3** with English
       text (27 Apr) .... 32·00
   a. French text (23 Apr) .... 60·00
SB31 25c. booklet. Cover as Type B **4** with English text
       57 mm wide (27 Apr).. 10·00
   a. English text 63 mm wide .... 60·00
   b. French text 57 mm wide (23 Apr) .... 13·00
   ba. French text 63 mm wide £180

1937 (18 May)–**38**. Green and white cover. Four panes of six 1c. (No. 357b).
SB32 25c. booklet. Cover as Type B **3** with English text...... 50·00
   a. French text (14.10.38) .... 65·00
SB33 25c. booklet. Cover as Type B **4** with English text
       57 mm wide... 29·00
   a. English text 63 mm wide .... 70·00
   b. French text 57 mm wide (14.10.38) .... 18·00
   ba. French text 63 mm wide £170

1938 (3 May)–**39**. Brown and white cover. Two panes of six 2c. (No. 358b).
SB34 25c. booklet. Cover as Type B **3** with English text...... 55·00
   a. French text (3.3.39) .... 80·00
SB35 25c. booklet. Cover as Type B **4** with English text
       57 mm wide... 23·00
   a. English text 63 mm wide .... 80·00
   b. French text 57 mm wide .... 35·00
   ba. French text 63 mm wide £120

1942 (20–29 Aug). Red and white cover. Two panes of four 3c. (No. 377a) and 2 labels.
SB36 25c. booklet. Cover as Type B **4** with English text...... 8·50
   a. French text (29 Aug) .... 12·00

1942 (12–14 Sept). Violet and white cover. Panes of four 1c., 2c. and 3c. (Nos. 375a, 376a, 377a), each with 2 labels.
SB37 25c. booklet. Cover as Type B **4** with English
       text (14 Sept) .... 48·00
   a. French text (12 Sept) .... 90·00

1942 (6 Oct)–**43**. Brown and white cover. Two panes of six 2c. (No. 376b).
SB38 25c. booklet. Cover as Type B **4** with English text...... 55·00
   a. French text (6.4.43) .... 70·00

1942 (24 Nov)–**46**. Green and white cover. Four panes of six 1c. (No. 375b).
SB39 25c. booklet. Cover as Type B **4** with English text...... 11·00
   a. French text (16.2.43) .... 17·00
   b. Bilingual text (8.1.46) .... 30·00

1943 (3 May)–**46**. Orange and white cover. One pane of six 4c. (No. 380a).
SB40 25c. booklet. Cover as Type B **4** with English text...... 4·00
   a. French text (12.5.43) .... 15·00
   b. Bilingual text (8.1.46) .... 18·00

1943 (28 Aug)–**46**. Purple and white cover. Two panes of four 3c. (No. 378a) and 2 labels.
SB41 25c. booklet. Cover as Type B **4** with English text...... 10·00
   a. French text (7.9.43) .... 28·00
   b. Bilingual text (8.1.46) .... 22·00

B 5

1943 (1 Sept)–**46**. Black and white cover. Panes of three 1c., 3c. and 4c. (Nos. 394a, 395a, 396a) (3×1).
SB42 25c. booklet. Cover as Type B **5** with English text...... 35·00
   a. French text (18.9.43) .... 48·00
   c. Bilingual text (23.1.46) .... 45·00

B 6

1947 (24 Nov). Brown on orange cover. Panes of six 3c. and 4c. (3×2) and two panes of four 7c. (2×2) (Nos. 378a, 380a, 407a).
SB43 $1 booklet. Cover as Type B **6** with English text......... 25·00
   a. French text .... 40·00

1950 (12 Apr–18 May). Purple and white cover. Two panes of four 3c. (No. 416a) and 2 labels (3×2).
SB44 25c. booklet. Cover as Type B **4** with English text...... 5·00
   a. Bilingual text (18 May) .... 5·00

1950 (5–10 May). Orange and white cover. One pane of six 4c. (No. 417a) (3×2).
SB45 25c. booklet. Cover as Type B **4** with English text...... 32·00
   a. Stitched .... 60·00
   b. Bilingual text (10 May) .... 48·00

1950 (18 May). Black and white cover. Panes of three 1c., 3c. and 4c. (Nos. 422ba, 423a, 423ba) (3×1).
SB46 25c. booklet. Cover as Type B **5** with English text...... 55·00
   a. Bilingual text .... 65·00

1951 (2 June). Orange and white cover. One pane of six 4c. (No. 417ba) (3×2).
SB47 25c. booklet. Cover as Type B **4** with English text...... 6·00
   a. Stitched .... 12·00
   b. Bilingual text .... 12·00

1951 (25 Oct)–**52**. Black and white cover. Panes of three 1c., 3c. and 4c. (Nos. 422ba, 423a, 423ca) (3×1).
SB48 25c. booklet. Cover as Type B **5** with English text...... 42·00
   a. Bilingual text (9.7.52) .... 48·00

1953 (6 July–19 Aug). Orange cover. One pane of six 4c. (No. 453a) (3×2).
SB49 25c. booklet. Cover as Type B **4** with English text...... 4·50
   a. Bilingual text (19 Aug) .... 7·50

1953 (17 July–20 Oct). Purple cover. Two panes of four 3c. (No. 452a) and 2 labels (3×2).
SB50 25c. booklet. Cover as Type B **4** with English text...... 4·00
   a. Bilingual text (20 Oct) .... 13·00

1953 (12 Aug). Grey cover. Panes of three 1c., 3c. and 4c. (Nos. 458a, 459a, 460a) (3×1).
SB51 25c. booklet. Cover as Type B **5** with English text...... 16·00
   a. Bilingual text .... 28·00

All the following booklets are bilingual

1954 (1 Apr–Nov). Blue cover as Type B **4**.
SB52 25c. booklet containing pane of five 5c. and 1 label
       (No. 473a) (3×2) .... 2·25
   a. Stitched (Nov) .... 3·25

1954 (14 July–Nov). Blue cover as Type B **4**.
SB53 25c. booklet containing pane of five 5c. and 1 label
       (No. 467a) (3×2) .... 2·00
   a. Stitched (Nov) .... 4·25

1955 (7 July). Violet cover as Type B **4**.
SB54 25c. booklet containing pane of six 4c.
       (No. 466a) (3×2) .... 4·75

B 7

1956 (1 June). Red and white cover as Type B **7**.
SB55   25c. booklet containing two panes of five 1c. and
       five 4c., each with 1 label
       (Nos. 463a, 466b) (3×2) .... 3·00

1956 (July). Blue and white cover as Type B **7**.
SB56   25c. booklet containing pane of five 5c. and 1 label
       (No. 467a) (3×2) .... 2·75

B **8**

1963 (May)–**67**. Blue and white cover as Type B **7**.
SB57   25c. booklet containing pane of five 5c. and 1 label
       (No. 531a) (2×3) .... 4·25
       a. Cover Type B 8 (1.67) .... 35·00

1963 (15 May). Red and white cover as Type B **7**.
SB58   25c. booklet containing two panes of five 1c.
       and five 4c., each with 1 label
       (Nos. 527a, 530a) (2×3) .... 8·00

1967 (Feb). Red cover as Type B **8**.
SB59   25c. booklet containing two panes of five 1c. and
       five 4c., each with 1 label
       (Nos. 579a, 582a) (2×3) .... 2·75

1967 (Mar). Blue cover as Type B **8**.
SB60   25c. booklet containing pane of five 5c. and 1 label
       (No. 583a) (2×3) .... 5·50

B **9**

1968 (Sept). Brown and cream cover, 70×48 mm, as Type B **9**.
SB61   25c. booklet containing se-tenant pane of five 1c.
       and five 4c. (No. 598a) (2×5) .... 1·75

1968 (Sept). Red and cream cover as Type B **9**.
SB62 $1 booklet containing pane of twenty-five 4c. and
       2 labels (No. 599a) (3×9) .... 6·50

1968 (Sept). Blue and cream cover, 82×48 mm, as Type B **9**.
SB63 $1 booklet containing pane of twenty 5c.
       (No. 600a) (2×10) .... 4·50

1968 (Oct). Orange and cream cover, 70×48 mm, as Type B **9**, but
without border.
SB64   25c. booklet containing se-tenant pane of one 1c.,
       four 6c. and 1 label (No. 598b) (2×3) .... 2·00

B **10** (Illustration reduced. Actual size 128×60 mm)

1968 (15 Nov). Christmas. Red and green cover as Type B **10**.
SB65 $1 booklet containing two panes of ten 5c.
       (No. 630a) (5×2) .... 4·50
       p. Phosphor (No. 630pa) .... 6·00
Nos. SB65/p exist with left or right opening (i.e. with selvedge at left or right of pane).

1969 (Jan). Orange-red on cream cover as Type B **9**, but without
border.
SB66 $1.50 booklet containing pane of twenty-five 6c. and
       2 labels (No. 601a) (3×9) .... 9·00

1969 (8 Oct). Christmas. Red cover size as Type B **10**.
SB67 $1 booklet containing two panes of ten 5c.
       (No. 644a) (5×2) .... 3·00
       p. Phosphor (No. 644pa) .... 5·00

1970 (Jan). Black on cream cover as Type B **9**, but without border.
SB68 $1.50 booklet containing pane of twenty-five 6c. and
       2 labels (No. 602a) (3×9) .... 14·00

1970 (Aug). Black on cream cover, 70×48 mm, as Type B **9**, but
without border.
SB69   25c. booklet containing pane of four 6c.
       (No. 603a) (2×2) .... 11·00

1970 (Aug). Black on cream cover as Type B **9**, but without border.
SB70 $1.50 booklet containing pane of twenty-five 6c. and
       2 labels (No. 607a) (3×9) .... 16·00

1970 (26 Oct). Indigo on cream cover, 70×50 mm. Inscr
"CANADIAN POSTAGE STAMPS ... MADE EXPRESSLY FOR OPAL
MANUFACTURING CO. LIMITED".
SB71   25c. booklet containing four 2c. and four 3c.
       (No. 580a) (2×2) with gutter margin between..... 1·75
No. SB71 was produced by the Canadian Bank Note Co for use in the private stamp-vending machines owned by the Opal Manufacturing Co Ltd, Toronto. To cover the cost of manufacture and installation these booklets were sold at 25c. each. They were not available from the Canadian Post Office.

1970 (Nov). Black on cream cover, 70×48 mm, as Type B **9**, but
without border.
SB72   25c. booklet containing pane of four 6c.
       (No. 608a) (2×2) .... 4·00

1971 (30 June). Green on cream cover, 70×48 mm, as Type B **9**, but
without border.
SB73   25c. booklet containing se-tenant pane of one 1c.,
       one 3c., three 7c. and 1 label (No. 604b) (2×3) .. 4·00
This exists with or without a black sealing strip inside the cover.

1971 (30 June). Green and buff cover, 82×47 mm, as Type B **9**, but
without border.
SB74 $1 booklet containing se-tenant pane of four 1c.,
       four 3c. and twelve 7c. (No. 604a) (2×10) .... 16·00

1971 (Aug). Booklet No. SB73 with label affixed giving the new
contents. Sold as an experiment in Toronto for 50c.
SB75   50c. booklet. Contents as No. SB73, but containing
       two panes .... 9·00
The experiment was later continued by the use of machines which issued two 25c. booklets for 50c.

1971 (30 Dec). Grey on cream cover, 70×48 mm, as Type B **9**, but
without border.
SB76   25c. booklet containing se-tenant pane of three 1c.,
       one 6c. and two 8c. (No. 604c) (2×3) .... 1·50
       f. White fluorescent paper (No. 604fa) .... 1·75
       q. With fluorescent bands (No. 604qc) .... 5·00
       r. With fluorescent bands on white fluorescent
          paper (No. 604qfa) .... 2·25

1971 (30 Dec). Grey on cream cover, 77×48 mm, as Type B **9**, but
without border.
SB77 $1 booklet containing se-tenant pane of six 1c.,
       one 6c. and eleven 8c. (No. 604d) (2×9)............... 7·00
       q. With fluorescent bands (No. 604qd)........................... 5·50

B **11**

CANADA / Stamp Booklets

129

1972 (Mar). As No. SB76, but with brown on cream illustrated covers as Type B **11**. Ten different designs showing Mail Transport: (a) Post Office, 1816; (b) Stage Coach, c 1820; (c) Paddle Steamer, 1855; (d) Rural postman, c 1900; (e) Motor car, 1910; (f) Ford Model "T", 1914; (g) Curtis "JN4", 1918; (h) Mail truck, 1921; (i) Motorcycle, 1923; (j) Horse-drawn mail wagon, 1926.

SB78	25c. booklet. Contents as No. SB76 (any cover)	1·50
	f. White fluorescent paper	1·75
	q. With fluorescent bands	2·00
	r. With fluorescent bands on white fluorescent paper	2·25
Set of 10 different cover designs (No. SB78)		13·00
Set of 10 different cover designs (No. SB78q)		18·00

1972 (Aug). Ten cover designs as No. SB78, but in blue on cream.

SB79	50c. booklet (any cover) containing se-tenant pane of one 6c., four 1c. and five 8c. (No. 604e) (2×5)	4·50
	q. With fluorescent bands (No. 604qe)	4·50
Set of 10 different cover designs (No. SB79)		42·00
Set of 10 different cover designs (No. SB79q)		42·00

This exists with black or white sealing strip inside the cover.

1974 (10 Apr). Red on cream covers as Type B **11**. Ten different designs showing aircraft: (a) Gibson "Twin-plane"; (b) Burgess Dunne seaplane; (c) Nieuport "Scout"; (d) Curtiss "HS-2L"; (e) Junkers "W-34"; (f) Fokker "Super Universal"; (g) "Mosquito"; (h) "Stranraer" flying-boat; (i) "CF-100 Canuck"; (j) "Argus".

SB80	25c. booklet (any cover) containing se-tenant pane of three 1c., one 6c. and two 8c. (No. 693a) (3×2)	75
Set of 10 different cover designs		6·50

B 12

1975 (17 Jan). Violet on cream cover as Type B **12**.

SB81	$1 booklet containing se-tenant pane of six 1c., one 6c. and eleven 8c. (No. 693b) (9×2)	2·25

1976 (1 Sept). Violet on cream cover. Designs as No. SB80.

SB82	50c. booklet (any cover) containing se-tenant pane of two 1c., four 2c. and four 10c. (No. 693c) (5×2)	1·50
Set of 10 different cover designs		14·00

1977 (1 Nov). Brown on cream covers, similar to Type B **11**, but vert. Ten different designs showing flowers or trees: (a) Bottle Gentian; (b) Western Columbine; (c) Canada Lily; (d) Hepatica; (e) Shooting Star; (f) Lady's Slipper; (g) Trembling Aspen; (h) Douglas Fir; (i) Sugar Maple; (j) Rose, Thistle, Shamrock, Lily and Maple leaf.

SB83	50c. booklet (any cover) containing se-tenant pane of two 1c. and four 12c. (No. 862a) (3×2)	3·00
Set of 10 different cover designs		27·00

1978 (1 Apr). Green on cream covers. Designs as No. SB83.

SB84	50c. booklet (any cover) containing se-tenant pane of four 2c., three 14c. and 1 label (No. 863a) (4×2)	2·75
Set of 10 different cover designs		25·00

B 13

1978 (13 Nov). Black on cream covers as Type B **13**. Five different designs showing postcode publicity cartoons: (a) Talking post box; (b) Woman throwing letter to man; (c) Running letters; (d) Letter running to post box; (e) Woman with letter and laughing post box.

SB85	$3.50 booklet (any cover) containing pane of twenty-five 14c. and 2 labels (No. 868ba) (9×3)	7·50
Set of 5 different cover designs		32·00

1979 (28 Mar). Blue on cream covers. Designs as No. SB83.

SB86	50c. booklet (any cover) containing se-tenant pane of one 1c., three 5c. and two 17c. (No. 870a) (3×2)	2·50
Set of 10 different cover designs		23·00

1979 (3 July)–**81**. Violet on cream covers. Designs as No. SB85.

SB87	$4.25 booklet (any cover) containing pane of twenty-five 17c. and 2 labels (No. 869ab) (9×3) (cover without wavy lines)	8·00
SB88	$4.25 booklet (any cover) containing No. 869ab (horizontal wavy lines across cover) (4.2.81)	11·00
Set of 5 different cover designs (No. SB87)		35·00
Set of 5 different cover designs (No. SB88)		48·00

B 14

1982 (1 Mar). Black on cream covers as Type B **14**. Ten different designs showing provincial legislature buildings: (a) Victoria, British Columbia; (b) Fredericton, New Brunswick; (c) Halifax, Nova Scotia; (d) Charlottetown, Prince Edward Island; (e) Quebec; (f) Edmonton, Alberta; (g) Toronto, Ontario; (h) Regina, Saskatchewan; (i) Winnipeg, Manitoba; (j) St. John's, Newfoundland.

SB89	50c. booklet (any cover) containing se-tenant pane of two 5c., one 10c., one 30c. and 2 labels (No. 1033a) (3×2)	2·50
	a. Containing pane No. 1033ab	2·75
	b. Containing pane No. 1033ba	8·00
	c. Containing pane No. 1033bb	8·00
Set of 10 different cover designs (No. SB89)		22·00

B **15** Parliament Buildings, Ottawa

1982 (30 June). Black on cream cover as Type B **15**.

SB90	$6 booklet containing pane of twenty 30c. and 1 label (No. 1032ab) (7×3)	15·00

1983 (15 Feb)–**85**. Indian red on cream covers as Type B **14**. Designs as No. SB89.

SB91	50c. booklet (any cover) containing se-tenant pane of two 5c., one 8c., one 32c. and 2 labels (No. 1033c) (3×2)	3·00
	a. Indian red on surfaced yellow cover (3.4.85)	3·00
Set of 10 different cover designs (No. SB91)		27·00
Set of 10 different cover designs (No. SB91a)		27·00

1983 (8 Apr). Indian red on cream cover as Type B **15**.

SB92	$8 booklet containing pane of twenty-five 32c. and 2 labels (No. 1032bb) (9×3)	18·00

1983 (30 June). Canada Day. Multicoloured cover, 100×78 mm, showing location map of various forts.

SB93	$3.20 booklet containing se-tenant pane of ten 32c. (No. 1090a) (5×2)	5·00

1984 (15 Feb). Cover as Type B **15**, but additionally inscribed "1984" below "POSTES".

SB94	$8 booklet containing pane of twenty-five 32c. and 2 labels (No. 1032bd) (9×3)	21·00

CANADA / Stamp Booklets

1985 (21 June). Reddish brown on grey-brown covers similar to Type B **14**. Ten different designs showing architectural or ornamental details from Parliament Buildings, Ottawa: (a) Clock from Peace Tower; (b) Library entrance; (c) Gargoyle from Peace Tower; (d) Indian mask sculpture; (e) Stone carving at Memorial Chamber entrance; (f) Door to House of Commons; (g) Stone ornament at House of Commons main entrance; (h) Carved head, Senate Chamber; (i) Windows, Centre Block; (j) Window and war memorial, Peace Tower.

SB95	50c. booklet (*any cover*) containing *se-tenant* pane of three 2c., two 5c. and one 34c. (No. 1148a) (2×3)	4·00
	a. "R" on bottom left-hand corner of back cover	4·00
Set of 10 *different cover designs* (No. SB95)		35·00
Set of 10 *different cover designs* (No. SB95a)		35·00

1985 (28 June). Canada Day. Black, pale brown and pale grey-brown cover, 100×78 mm, showing location map of various forts.

SB96	$3.40 booklet containing *se-tenant* pane of ten 34c. (No. 1163a) (5×2)	4·50

B **16** Parliament Buildings, Ottawa
(*Illustration reduced. Actual size 120×70 mm*)

1985 (1 Aug)–**86**. White on agate cover as Type B **16**.

SB97	$8.50 booklet containing pane of twenty-five 34c. (No. 1155a) (5×5)	13·00
	a. Containing pane No. 1155ba (4.7.86)	26·00

B **17** (*Illustration reduced. Actual size 121×61 mm*)

1985 (23 Oct). Christmas. Rosine and emerald cover as Type B **17**.

SB98	$3.20 booklet containing pane of ten 32c. (No. 1181a) (5×2)	5·50

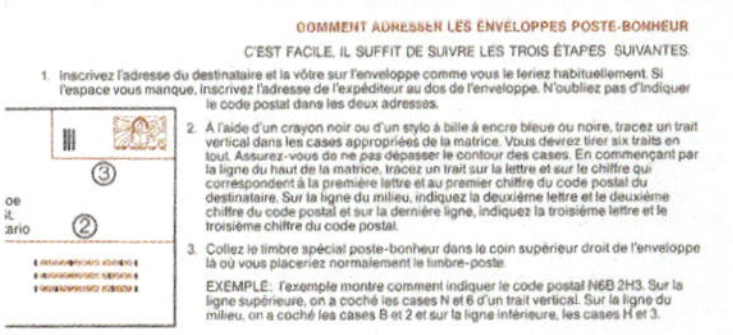

B **18** (*Illustration reduced. Actual size 150×72 mm*)

1986 (29 Oct). Christmas. Black and brown-red cover as Type B **18**.

SB99	$2.90 booklet containing pane of ten 29c. (No. 1218a) (1×10)	6·00
	a. Containing pane No. 1218ba	50·00

1987 (30 Mar). Ten cover designs as No. SB95 but in blackish olive on grey-brown.

SB100	50c. booklet (*any cover*) containing *se-tenant* pane of two 1c., two 6c., one 36c. and 1 label (No. 1147a) (2×3)	7·00
	a. Containing pane No. 1147ba (1.10.87)	6·00
Set of 10 *different cover designs* (No. SB100)		60·00
Set of 10 *different cover designs* (No. SB100a)		55·00

1987 (30 Mar). Yellow-orange on agate cover similar to Type B **16**, but 48×74 mm.

SB101	$3.60 booklet containing pane of ten 36c. (No. 1156ba) (2×5)	12·00

1987 (19 May). Yellow-orange on agate cover as Type B **16**.

SB102	$9 booklet containing pane of twenty-five 36c. (No. 1156bb) (5×5)	27·00

1987 (2 Nov). Christmas. Christmas Plants. Black and magenta cover as Type B **18**, but 148×80 mm.

SB103	$3.10 booklet containing pane of ten 31c. (No. 1254a) (2×5)	8·00

B **19**

1988 (5 Jan). White and black on bright green cover as Type B **19**.

SB104	$3.70 booklet (49×73 mm) containing pane of ten 37c. (No. 1157ab) (2×5)	13·00
SB105	$9.25 booklet (120×73 mm) containing pane of twenty-five 37c. (No. 1157ae) (5×5)	27·00

1988 (15 Jan). Covers as Type B **19**, but inscribed *"LUNCH SAVER"*.

SB106	$3.70 booklet (49×73 mm) containing pane of ten 37c. (No. 1157ab) (2×5)	13·00
SB107	$9.25 booklet (120×73 mm) containing pane of twenty-five 37c. (No. 1157ae) (5×5)	27·00

1988 (3 Feb). Deep blue on grey-brown covers as Type B **14**. Ten different designs as No. SB95.

SB108	50c. booklet (*any cover*) containing *se-tenant* pane of one 1c., two 6c., one 37c. and 2 labels (No. 1147bb) (2×3)	3·25
Set of 10 *different cover designs*		27·00

1988 (27 Oct). Christmas. Icons. Multicoloured cover as Type B **18**, but 150×80 mm, showing stamp illustration on the front.

SB109	$3.20 booklet containing pane of ten 32c. (No. 1308a) (2×5)	4·00

B **20** (*Illustration reduced. Actual size 79×152 mm*)

B **21** (*Illustration reduced. Actual size 79×152 mm*)

1988 (29 Dec)–**89**. Multicoloured stamps on bright scarlet and violet-blue covers (Type B **20**) or on scarlet with white inscr (Type B **21**).

SB110	$2.20 booklet containing pane of five 44c. and 1 label (No. 1269ab) (2×3) (18.1.89)	6·00
	a. Cover Type B **21** (17.3.89)	6·00
SB111	$3.80 booklet containing pane of ten 38c. and 2 labels (No. 1157ca) (3×4)	6·00
	a. Cover Type B **21** (17.3.89)	6·00
SB112	$3.80 booklet containing pane of ten 38c. and 2 labels (No. 1162bd) (3×4)	6·00
	a. Cover Type B **21** (17.3.89)	6·00
SB113	$3.80 booklet containing pane of five 76c. and 1 label (No. 1275ab) (2×3) (18.1.89)	8·50
	a. Cover Type B **21** (17.3.89)	8·50
SB114	$9.50 booklet containing pane of twenty-five 38c. and 2 labels (No. 1157cb) (3×9)	15·00
	a. Cover Type B **21** (17.3.89)	15·00

Booklet Nos. SB110/14 each exist with either "Lunch Savers" or "Would it be more convenient" advertisement on the reverse.

Booklet Nos. SB110a/14a also exist with "Your 'Rush' Connection" advertisement on the reverse.

CANADA / Stamp Booklets

1989 (18 Jan). Brown-purple on grey-brown covers as Type B **14**. Ten different designs as No. SB95.
SB115   50c. booklet (*any cover*) containing *se-tenant* pane of three 2c., one 6c., one 38c. and 1 label (No. 1148ba) (2×3) .... 5·50
Set of 10 different cover designs .... 50·00

B **22** (*Illustration reduced. Actual size 85×155 mm*).

B **23** Park Corner, Prince Edward Island

1989 (30 June). Multicoloured cover as Type B **22**.
SB116 $5 booklet containing pane of twelve self-adhesive 38c. (No. 1328a) (6×2)................. 14·00
Two types of cover exist for No. SB116 with one being the mirror image of the other.

1989 (26 Oct). Christmas. Paintings of Winter Landscapes. Multicoloured covers as Type B **21**.
SB117 $2.20 booklet containing pane of five 44c. and 1 label (No. 1344a) (2×3) (*cover 60×155 mm*).... 13·00
SB118 $3.30 4 booklet containing pane of ten 33c. (No. 1342a) (2×5) (*80×155 mm*) .... 9·00
SB119 $3.80 booklet containing pane of ten 38c. (No. 1343ab) (5×2) (*80×155 mm*) .... 32·00
SB120 $3.80 booklet containing pane of five 76c. and 1 label (No. 1345a) (2×3) (*60×155 mm*) .... 22·00

1989 (28 Dec). Multicoloured covers as Type B **21**.
SB121 $3.90 booklet containing pane of ten 39c. and 2 labels (No. 1354a) (4×3) .... 10·00
SB122 $9.75 booklet containing pane of twenty-five 39c. and 2 labels (No. 1354b) (9×3) .... 20·00

1990 (12 Jan). Multicoloured cover as Type B **23**.
SB123   50c. booklet containing *se-tenant* pane of one 1c., two 5c. and one 39c. (No. 1350a) (2×2) (p 13½×14) .... 1·40
     a. Containing pane No. 1350ba (p 12½×13)............. 40·00

1990 (12 Jan). Multicoloured covers as Type B **21**.
SB124 $2.25 booklet containing pane of five 45c. and 1 label (No. 1270ab) (2×3) .... 9·00
SB125 $3.90 booklet containing pane of ten 39c. and 2 labels (No. 1162cb) (3×4) .... 18·00
SB126 $3.90 booklet containing pane of five 78c. and 1 label (No. 1276ab) (2×3) .... 11·00

1990 (8 Feb). Multicoloured cover as Type B **22**, showing wheatfield.
SB127 $5 booklet containing pane of twelve self-adhesive 39c. (No. 1328ba) (2×6)................. 14·00
Two types of cover exist for No. SB127 with one being the mirror image of the other.

B **24** (*Illustration reduced. Actual size 170×100 mm*)

1990 (3 May). "Moving the Mail". Multicoloured cover as Type B **24**. Booklet contains text and illustrations on labels attached to the panes and on interleaving pages. Stitched.
SB128 $9.75 booklet containing two panes of eight 39c. (No. 1382a) (2×4) and one pane of nine 39c. (No. 1382b) (3×4)... 23·00

1990 (25 Oct). Christmas. Native Art. Multicoloured covers as Type B **21**.
SB129 $2.25 booklet containing pane of five 45c. (No. 1407a) (2×3) (*cover 60×155 mm*) .... 4·25
SB130 $3.40 booklet containing pane of ten 34c. (No. 1405a) (2×5) (*80×155 mm*) .... 6·00
SB131 $3.90 booklet containing pane of ten 39c. (No. 1406a) (2×5) (*60×155 mm*) .... 8·00
SB132 $3.90 booklet containing pane of five 78c. (No. 1408a) (2×3) (*60×155 mm*) .... 9·00

1990 (28 Dec). Multicoloured cover as Type B **23**, but showing Point Atkinson, British Columbia.
SB133   50c. booklet containing *se-tenant* pane of two 1c., one 5c. and one 40c. (No. 1350c) (2×2)......... 2·00
The face value of No. SB133 included 3c. Goods and Service Tax.

1990 (28 Dec). Covers as Type B **21** showing multicoloured stamps on scarlet background with white inscriptions.
SB134 $2.30 booklet containing pane of five 46c. and 1 label (No. 1270cc) (2×3) .... 8·00
SB135 $4 booklet containing pane of ten 40c. and 2 labels (No. 1162da) (3×4) .... 13·00
SB136 $4 booklet containing pane of five 80c. and 1 label (No. 1276cc) (2×3) .... 10·00
SB137 $4 booklet containing pane of ten 40c. and 2 labels (No. 1355a) (4×3)......................... 12·00
SB138 $10 booklet containing pane of twenty-five 40c. and 2 labels (No. 1355b) (9×3) .... 26·00

1991 (11 Jan). Multicoloured cover as Type B **22**, but showing coastal scene.
SB139 $5.25 booklet containing pane of twelve self-adhesive 40c. (No. 1328ca) (2×6)................ 16·00
Two types of cover exist for No. SB139 with one being the mirror image of the other.

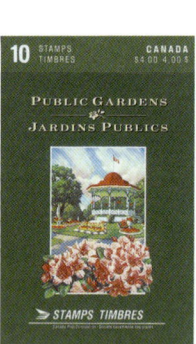

B **25** (*Illustration reduced. Actual size 80×125 mm*)

B **26** (*Illustration reduced. Actual size 64×156 mm*)

1991 (22 May). Public Gardens. Multicoloured cover as Type B **25**.
SB140 $4 booklet containing *se-tenant* pane of ten 40c. (No. 1422a) (5×2) .... 6·50

1991 (20 Aug). Canadian Rivers (1st series). Multicoloured cover as Type B **26**.
SB141 $4 booklet containing *se-tenant* pane of ten 40c. (No. 1432a) (10×1)............................ 8·00

B **27** (*Illustration reduced. Actual size 150×81 mm*)

1991 (16 Oct). 150th Anniv of Queen's University. Multicoloured cover as Type B **27**. Booklet contains text and illustrations on labels attached to the pane and on interleaving pages. Stitched.
SB142 $4 booklet containing pane of ten 40c. and
2 labels (No. 1449a) (4×3)... 9·50

1992 (7 Feb). Winter Olympic Games, Albertville. Multicoloured cover as Type B **30**.
SB154 $4.20 booklet containing *se-tenant* pane of ten 42c.
(No. 1482a) (5×2).. 11·00
Two types of cover exist for No. SB154 with one being the mirror image of the other.

1992 (22 Apr). Canadian Rivers (2nd series). Multicoloured vert cover as Type B **26**.
SB155 $4.20 booklet containing *se-tenant* pane of ten 42c.
(No. 1492a) (5×2).. 13·00

1992 (15 June). Olympic Games, Barcelona. Multicoloured cover as Type B **30**, but showing Olympic flag.
SB156 $4.20 booklet containing *se-tenant* pane of ten 42c.
(No. 1498a) (5×2).. 10·00
Two types of cover exist for No. SB156 with one being the mirror image of the other.

1992 (21 Sept). 150th Anniv of Geological Survey of Canada. Multicoloured cover as Type B **31**.
SB157 $4.20 booklet containing *se-tenant* pane of ten 42c.
(No. 1509a) (5×2).. 15·00

B **28** Christmas Tree    B **29**

1991 (23 Oct). Christmas. Multicoloured covers as Type B **28**.
SB143 $2.30 booklet containing pane of five 46c. and
1 label (No. 1452a) (2×3)............................. 6·25
SB144 $3.50 booklet containing pane of ten 35c.
(No. 1450a) (2×5) (punch bowl and candles
cover design, 80×155 mm)....................... 10·00
SB145 $4 booklet containing pane of ten 40c. (No. 1451a)
(2×5) (Christmas stocking cover design)........ 10·00
SB146 $4 booklet containing pane of five 80c. and 1 label
(No. 1453a) (2×3) (Christmas presents cover design) 10·00

1991 (27 Dec). Covers as Type B **29** showing multicoloured stamps on scarlet background with Olympic logo in black.
SB147 $2.40 booklet containing pane of five 48c. and
1 label (No. 1467ab) (2×3)......................... 8·00
SB148 $4.20 booklet containing pane of five 84c. and
1 label (No. 1475ab) (2×3)......................... 13·00
SB149 $4.20 booklet containing pane of ten 42c.
(No. 1162ea) (2×5).................................... 15·00
SB150 $4.20 booklet containing pane of ten 42c.
(No. 1356a) (2×5)....................................... 15·00
SB151 $10.50 booklet containing pane of twenty-five 42c.
and 2 labels (No. 1356b) (3×9)................. 27·00
SB152 $21 booklet containing pane of fifty 42c.
(No. 1356c) (4×13).................................... 60·00
The cover of booklet No. SB152 is made up of two $10.50 covers rouletted down the centre. It was issued in connection with a Canada Post special offer of a $1 coupon towards the cost of its purchase.

1992 (28 Jan). Multicoloured cover as Type B **22**, but showing mountain peaks.
SB153 $5.25 booklet containing pane of twelve
self-adhesive 42c. stamps (No. 1328da) (2×6)..... 22·00
Two types of cover exist for No. SB153 with one being the mirror image of the other.

B **32** Hockey Players (*Illustration reduced. Actual size* 171×105 *mm*)

1992 (9 Oct). 75th Anniv of National Ice Hockey League. Multicoloured cover as Type B **32**. Booklet contains text and illustrations on labels attached to the pane and on interleaving pages. Stitched.
SB158 $10.50 booklet containing twenty-five 42c. stamps in
two panes of 8 and 1 label and one pane of
9 (Nos. 1516a, 1517a, 1518a) (each 3×3)............ 32·00

B **33** Hand Bell    B **34** Hand-crafting Techniques (*Illustration reduced. Actual size* 81×156 *mm*)

B **30** Olympic Flame (*Illustration reduced. Actual size* 83×151 *mm*)   B **31** Prospecting Equipment (*Illustration reduced. Actual size* 90×151 *mm*)

1992 (13 Nov). Christmas. Multicoloured covers as Type B **33**.
SB159 $2.40 booklet containing pane of five 48c. and 1
label (No. 1527a) (2×3)............................. 9·00
SB160 $3.70 booklet containing pane of ten 37c.
(No. 1525a) (2×5) (candle and cookies cover
design, 80×156 mm).................................. 10·00
SB161 $4.20 booklet containing pane of ten 42c.
(No. 1526ab) (2×5) (hobby horse cover design). 11·00
SB162 $4.20 booklet containing pane of five 84c. and
1 label (No. 1528a) (2×3) (Christmas tree cover
design).. 11·00

CANADA / Stamp Booklets

1992 (30 Dec). Multicoloured covers as Type B **29**, but without Olympic symbol at top right.

SB163	$2.45 booklet containing pane of five 49c. and 1 label (No. 1468ba) (2×3)	9·00
SB164	$4.30 booklet containing pane of ten 43c. (No. 1162fa) (2×5)	13·00
SB165	$4.30 booklet containing pane of ten 43c. (No. 1357a) (2×5)	12·00
SB166	$4.30 booklet containing pane of five 86c. and 1 label (No. 1476ba) (2×3)	16·00
SB167	$10.75 booklet containing pane of twenty-five 43c. and 2 labels (No. 1357b) (3×9)	27·00

1993 (15 Feb). Multicoloured cover as Type B **22**, but showing lake.

SB168	$5.25 booklet containing pane of twelve self-adhesive 43c. stamps (2×6) (No. 1328ea)	16·00

Two types of cover exist for No. SB168 with one being the mirror image of the other.

1993 (30 Apr). Hand-crafted Textiles. Multicoloured cover as Type B **34**.

SB169	$4.30 booklet containing se-tenant pane of ten 43c. (5×2) (No. 1534a)	13·00

B **35** Postcards and Stamps (*Illustration reduced. Actual size 60×155 mm*)

B **36** Rabbit and Present

1993 (14 June). Historic Hotels. Multicoloured cover as Type B **35**.

SB170	$4.30 booklet containing se-tenant pane of ten 43c. (5×2) (No. 1540a)	5·50

1993 (10 Aug). Canadian Rivers (3rd series). Multicoloured vert cover as Type B **26**.

SB171	$4.30 booklet containing se-tenant pane of ten 43c. (10×1) (No. 1558a)	7·00

1993 (4 Nov). Christmas. Multicoloured covers as Type B **36**.

SB172	$2.45 booklet containing pane of five 49c. and 1 label (2×3) (No. 1574a)	5·50
SB173	$3.80 booklet containing pane of ten 38c. (2×5) (No. 1572a) (wooden puppet cover design, 80×156 mm)	9·00
SB174	$4.30 booklet containing pane of ten 43c. (2×5) (No. 1573a) (angel cover design)	9·50
SB175	$4.30 booklet containing pane of five 86c. and 1 label (2×3) (No. 1575a) (kangaroo cover design)	9·50

B **37**

B **38** (*Illustration reduced. Actual size 106×157 mm*)

1994 (7 Jan–14 Nov). Covers as Type B **37**, each showing multicoloured stamps in a continuous pattern on scarlet background.

SB176	$2.45 booklet containing pane of five 49c. and 1 label (No. 1468a) (2×3)	11·00
SB177	$4.30 booklet containing pane of ten 43c. (No. 1162fa) (2×5)	13·00
SB178	$4.30 booklet containing pane of ten 43c. (No. 1357ca) (p 14½) (2×5) (18 Jan)	14·00
	a. Containing pane No. 1357a (p 13½×13) (14 Nov)	12·00
SB179	$4.30 booklet containing pane of five 86c. (No. 1476a) and 1 label (2×3)	12·00
SB180	$10.75 booklet containing pane of twenty-five 43c. and 2 labels (No. 1357cb) (p 14½) (3×9) (18 Jan)	27·00
	a. Containing pane No. 1357b (p 13½×13) (14 Nov)	27·00

1994 (28 Jan). Greetings. Multicoloured cover as Type B **38**.

SB181	$4.50 booklet containing pane of ten self-adhesive 43c. (No. 1580a) and 35 circular greetings labels	9·00

1994 (25 Feb)–**95**. Covers as Type B **37** showing multicoloured stamps in a continuous pattern on scarlet backgrounds.

SB182	$2.50 booklet containing pane of five 50c. and 1 label (No. 1469a) (p 13) (2×3)	7·50
	a. Containing pane No. 1469ba (p 14½×14) (27.3.95)	15·00
SB183	$4.40 booklet containing pane of five 88c. and 1 label (No. 1477a) (fluorescent frame) (p 13) (2×3)	11·00
	a. Containing pane No. 1477ba (three fluorescent bands) (p 13) (14.11.94)	15·00
	b. Containing pane No. 1477ca (three fluorescent bands) (p 14½×14) (27.3.95)	17·00

B **39** Images of T. Eaton Company Ltd (*Illustration reduced. Actual size 151×101 mm*)

1994 (17 Mar). 125th Anniv of T. Eaton Company Ltd. Multicoloured cover as Type B **39**. Booklet containing text and illustrations on label attached to the pane and on interleaving pages. Stitched.

SB184	$4.30 booklet containing ten 43c. stamps and 2 labels (No. 1583a) (6×2)	5·50

134

CANADA / Stamp Booklets

1994 (22 Apr). Canadian Rivers (4th series). Multicoloured vert cover as Type B **26**.
SB185 $4.30 booklet containing *se-tenant* pane of ten 43c. (No. 1584a) (2×5)........................ 7·00

B **40** Carol Singer

B **41** Fortress Gateway (*Illustration reduced. Actual size 96×157 mm*)

1994 (3 Nov). Christmas. Multicoloured covers as Type B **40**.
SB186 $2.50 booklet containing pane of five 50c. and 1 label (2×3) (No. 1619a)............... 4·75
SB187 $3.80 booklet containing pane of ten (38c.) (2×5) (No. 1617a) (chorister wearing ruff cover design, 80×156 mm)........................ 6·00
SB188 $4.30 booklet containing pane of ten 43c. (2×5) (No. 1618a) (pair of singers cover design).......... 7·00
SB189 $4.40 booklet containing pane of five 88c. and 1 label (2×3) (No. 1620a) (singer in hat and scarf cover design)........................ 8·00

1995 (5 May). 275th Anniv of Fortress of Louisbourg. Multicoloured cover as Type B **41**.
SB190 $4.30 booklet containing pane of ten (43c.) (5×2) (No. 1631a)........................ 6·00

B **42** Player and Bunker (*Illustration reduced. Actual size 52×156 mm*)

B **43** Fountain Pen (*Illustration reduced. Actual size 78×156 mm*)

1995 (6 June). Centenaries of Canadian Amateur Golf Championship and of the Royal Canadian Golf Association. Multicoloured cover as Type B **42**.
SB191 $4.30 booklet containing *se-tenant* pane of ten 43c. (5×2) (No. 1637a)........................ 7·00

1995 (31 July–6 Oct). Covers as Type B **37**, each showing multicoloured stamps in a continuous pattern on scarlet background.
SB192 $2.60 booklet containing pane of five 52c. and 1 label (No. 1470a) (p 13) (2×3)............... 7·00
    a. Containing pane No. 1470ba (p 14½×14) (6 Oct).......... 13·00
SB193 $4.50 booklet containing pane of ten 45c. (No. 1162ga) (2×5)........................ 22·00
SB194 $4.50 booklet containing pane of ten 45c. (No. 1358a) (p 14½) (2×5)........................ 8·00
    a. Containing pane No. 1358ca (p 13½×13) (6 Oct).......... 12·00

SB195 $4.50 booklet containing pane of five 90c. and 1 label (No. 1478a) (p 13) (2×3)............... 7·00
    a. Containing pane No. 1478ba (p 14½×14) (6 Oct).......... 13·00
SB196 $11.25 booklet containing pane of twenty-five 45c. and 2 labels (No. 1358b) (p 14½) (3×9)............ 16·00
    a. Containing pane No. 1358cb (p 13½×13) (6 Oct).......... 26·00

Nos. SB192a, SB194a, SB195a and SB196a, together with a new printing of No. SB193 issued on the same date, show a revised back cover layout including a customer service phone number.

1995 (1 Sept). Greetings. Multicoloured cover as Type B **43**.
SB197 $4.70 booklet containing pane of ten self-adhesive 45c. (No. 1654a) and 15 circular greetings labels........................ 5·50

B **44** Aspects of Chiropractic Healing (*Illustration reduced. Actual size 78×156 mm*)

B **45** Superman (*Illustration reduced. Actual size 105×169 mm*)

1995 (15 Sept). Centenary of Chiropractic Healing in Canada. Multicoloured cover as Type B **44**.
SB198 $4.70 booklet containing pane of ten self-adhesive 45c. (No. 1654a) and 15 circular commemorative labels........................ 5·50

1995 (15 Sept). 50th Anniv of Arctic Institute of North America. Multicoloured cover as Type B **26**, but showing Inuk woman and Arctic scene.
SB199 $4.50 booklet containing *se-tenant* pane of ten 45c. (No. 1656a) (5×2)........................ 9·00

1995 (2 Oct). Comic Book Superheroes. Multicoloured cover as Type B **45**.
SB200 $4.50 booklet containing *se-tenant* pane of ten 45c. (No. 1661a) (5×2)........................ 7·00

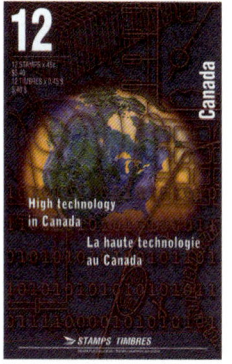

B **46** "The Annunciation"

B **47** Binary Codes and Globe (*Illustration reduced. Actual size 90×155 mm*)

135

CANADA / Stamp Booklets

1995 (2 Nov). Christmas. Multicoloured covers as Type B **46**.
SB201 $2.60 booklet containing pane of five 52c. and 1 label (2×3) (No. 1669a) .... 7·25
SB202 $4 booklet containing pane of ten 40c. (2×5) (No. 1667a) (Sprig of holly cover design, 80×156 mm) .... 8·00
SB203 $4.50 booklet containing pane of ten 45c. (2×5) (No. 1668a) ("The Nativity" cover design) .... 10·00
SB204 $4.50 booklet containing pane of five 90c. and 1 label (2×3) (No. 1670a) ("The Flight to Egypt" cover design) .... 10·00

1996 (15 Jan). Greetings. Multicoloured cover as Type B **38**.
SB205 $4.70 booklet containing pane of ten self-adhesive 45c. (No. 1654ba) and 35 circular greetings labels .... 7·50

1996 (15 Feb). High Technology Industries. Multicoloured cover as Type B **47**.
SB206 $5.40 booklet containing pane of twelve 45c. (No. 1677a) (2×6) .... 6·75

B **48** Ethel Catherwood
(Illustration reduced. Actual size 95×155 mm)

B **49** Father reading to Children
(Illustration reduced. Actual size 95×155 mm)

1996 (8 July). Canadian Olympic Gold Medal Winners. Multicoloured cover as Type B **48**.
SB207 $4.50 booklet containing pane of ten 45c. (No. 1691a) (5×2) .... 6·50

1996 (9 Sept). Literacy Campaign. Multicoloured cover as Type B **49**.
SB208 $5 booklet containing pane of ten 45+5c. (5×2) (No. 1699a) .... 8·00

B **50** Canadian Authors
(Illustration reduced. Actual size 80×155 mm)

B **51** Father Christmas

1996 (10 Oct). Canadian Authors. Multicoloured cover as Type B **50**.
SB209 $4.50 booklet containing pane of ten 45c. (5×2) (No. 1706a) .... 7·00

1996 (1 Nov). Christmas. 50th Anniv of U.N.I.C.E.F. Multicoloured covers as Type B **51**.
SB210 $2.60 booklet containing pane of five 52c. and 1 label (2×3) (No. 1712ab) .... 4·00
SB211 $4.50 booklet containing pane of ten 45c. (2×5) (No. 1711a) (Child tobogganing design) .... 6·50
SB212 $4.50 booklet containing pane of five 90c. and 1 label (2×3) (No. 1713ab) (Couple ice-skating design) .... 5·50

B **52** Blue Poppy

1997 (4 Apr). "Quebec in Bloom" International Floral Festival. Multicoloured cover as Type B **52**.
SB213 $5.40 booklet containing pane of twelve 45c. (6×2) (No. 1724a) .... 8·00

B **53** Paul Henderson celebrating

1997 (20 Sept). 25th Anniv of the Canada–U.S.S.R Ice Hockey Series. Multicoloured cover as Type B **53**.
SB214 $4.50 booklet containing pane of ten 45c. (2×5) (No. 1746a) .... 11·00

136

CANADA / Stamp Booklets

B **54** "The Holy Family"

B **54a** Flags and Skyscrapers

1997 (3 Nov). Christmas. Stained Glass Windows. Multicoloured covers as Type B **54**.
SB215	$2.60 booklet containing pane of five 52c. (No. 1764ab)	3·75
SB216	$4.50 booklet containing pane of ten 45c. (No. 1763ab) (cover showing "Regina SSi Rosarii")	4·75
SB217	$4.50 booklet containing pane of five 90c. (No. 1765ab) (cover showing "Madonna and Child")	4·75

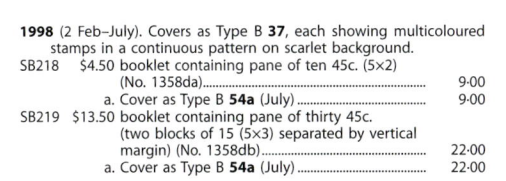

1998 (2 Feb–July). Covers as Type B **37**, each showing multicoloured stamps in a continuous pattern on scarlet background.
SB218	$4.50 booklet containing pane of ten 45c. (5×2) (No. 1358da)	9·00
	a. Cover as Type B **54a** (July)	9·00
SB219	$13.50 booklet containing pane of thirty 45c. (two blocks of 15 (5×3) separated by vertical margin) (No. 1358db)	22·00
	a. Cover as Type B **54a** (July)	22·00

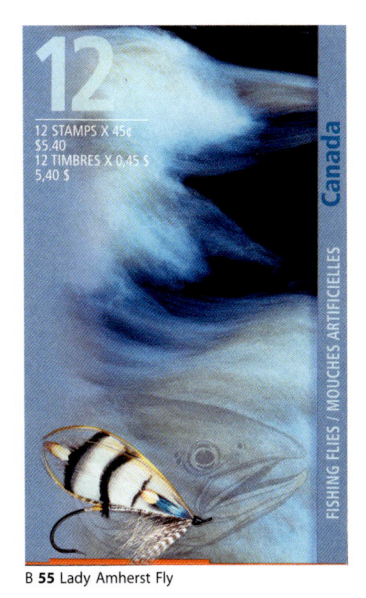

B **55** Lady Amherst Fly

1998 (16 Apr). Fishing Flies. Multicoloured cover as Type B **55**.
SB220	$5.40 booklet containing pane of twelve 45c. (1×12) (No. 1784a)	9·00

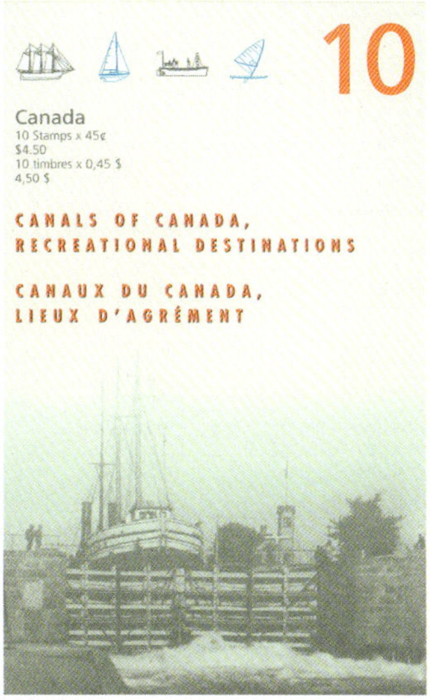

B **56** Ship in Canal Lock

1998 (17 June). Canadian Canals. Multicoloured cover as Type B **56**.
SB221	$4.50 booklet containing pane of ten 45c. and ten labels (No. 1795a) (10×2)	10·00

B **57** "Joie Lacustre" (Paul-Emile Borduas) (*Illustration reduced. Actual size* 130×115 *mm*)

1998 (7 Aug). 50th Anniv of *Refus Global* (manifesto of The Automatistes group of artists). Multicoloured cover as Type B **57**.
SB222	$3.15 booklet containing pane of seven self-adhesive 45c. (No. 1814a)	7·00

B **58** Circus Scenes and VIA Rail Train (*Illustration reduced. Actual size* 182×80 *mm*)

1998 (1 Oct). Canadian Circus. Multicoloured cover as Type B **58**.
SB223	$5.40 booklet containing *se-tenant* pane of twelve 45c. (No. 1851a) (6×2)	13·00

137

CANADA / Stamp Booklets

B **59** Adoring Angel

B **60**

1998 (6 Nov). Christmas. Statues of Angels. Multicoloured covers as Type B **59**.

SB224	$2.60 booklet containing pane of five 52c. and 1 label (2×3) (No. 1860a) (p 13×13½)	7·50
	a. Containing pane No. 1860ba (p 13)	3·75
SB225	$4.50 booklet containing pane of ten 45c. (2×5) (No. 1859a) (p 13) (cover showing Angel blowing trumpet)	7·00
	a. Containing pane No. 1859ba (p 13×13½)	16·00
SB226	$4.50 booklet containing pane of five 90c. and 1 label (2×3) (No. 1861a)(p 13×13½) (cover showing Angel at prayer)	15·00
	a. Containing pane No. 1861ba (p 13)	7·50

1998 (28 Dec)–**2000**. Multicoloured covers as Type B **60**.

SB227	$4.60 booklet containing pane of ten 46c. (2×5) (No. 1359a)	10·00
SB228	$13.80 booklet containing pane of thirty self-adhesive 46c. (3×10) (No. 1366a) (72×102 mm)	22·00
	a. Additional red on yellow "Pressure Sensitive Autocollants" inscription on front cover (2000)	22·00

B **61**

B **62** Birds' Heads (*Illustration reduced. Actual size* 110×157 *mm*)

1998 (28 Dec). Multicoloured covers as Type B **61**.

SB229	$2.75 booklet containing pane of five 55c. and 1 label (2×3) (No. 1836a)	8·00
SB230	$4.75 booklet containing pane of five 95c. and 1 label (2×3) (No. 1838a)	10·00

1999 (24 Feb). Birds (4th series). Multicoloured cover as Type B **62**. Self-adhesive.

SB231	$5.52 booklet containing pane of twelve 46c. (No. 1869b)	10·00

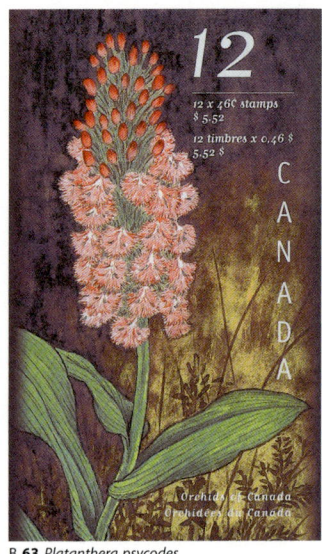

B **63** *Platanthera psycodes*

1999 (27 Apr). Orchids. Multicoloured cover as Type B **63**.

SB232	$5.52 booklet containing *se-tenant* pane of twelve 46c. (No. 1883a) (3×4)	8·00

B **64** "Big Ben" (show jumper)

1999 (2 June). Canadian Horses. Multicoloured cover as Type B **64**.

SB233	$5.52 booklet containing pane of twelve self-adhesive 46c. (No. 1907a)	7·50

B **65** Kites

138

1999 (1 Oct). Stamp Collecting Month. Kites. Multicoloured cover as Type B **65**. Self-adhesive.

| SB234 | $3.68 booklet containing *se-tenant* pane of eight 46c. (No. 1942a) | 4·00 |

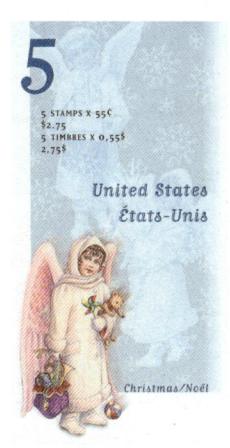

1999 (4 Nov). Christmas. Victorian Angels. Multicoloured covers as Type B **66**.

SB235	$2.75 booklet containing pane of five 55c. and 1 label (2×3) (No. 1950a)	4·75
SB236	$4.60 booklet containing pane of ten 46c. (2×5) (No. 1949a) (cover showing Angel playing drum)	6·50
SB237	$4.75 booklet containing pane of five 95c. and 1 label (2×3) (No. 1951a) (cover showing Angel with star)	6·50

2000 (1 Mar). Birds (5th series). Multicoloured cover as Type B **62**. Self-adhesive.

| SB238 | $5.52 booklet containing pane of twelve 46c. (No. 1978a) | 7·50 |

B **67**

2000 (28 Apr). "Picture Postage" Greetings Stamps. Multicoloured cover as Type B **67**. Self-adhesive.

| SB239 | $2.30 booklet containing pane of five 46c. and five greetings labels (No. 1988a) | 2·50 |

B **68**

2000 (28 Apr). Traditional Rural Mailboxes. Multicoloured cover as Type B **68**.

| SB240 | $5.52 booklet containing pane of twelve 46c. (2×6) (No. 1989a) | 8·00 |

B **69**

2000 (23 May). Canadian Rivers and Lakes. Multicoloured covers as Type B **69**. Self-adhesive.

| SB241 | $2.75 booklet containing pane of five 55c. (1×5) (No. 1993a) | 2·75 |
| SB242 | $4.75 booklet containing pane of five 95c. (1×5) (No. 1998a) | 4·25 |

NEW INFORMATION

The editor is always interested to correspond with people who have new information that will improve or correct this catalogue

CANADA / Stamp Booklets

B 70

2000 (19 July). Tall Ships Race. Multicoloured cover as Type B **70**. Self-adhesive.
SB243 $4.60 booklet containing *se-tenant* pane of ten 46c. (2×2+2×3) (No. 2012a)......................... 6·75

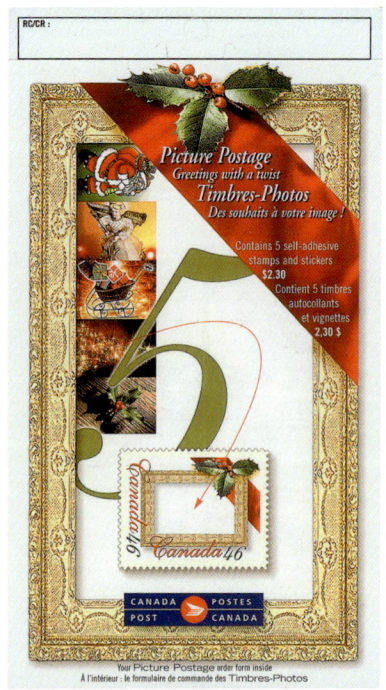

B 72

2000 (5 Oct). "Picture Postage" Christmas Greetings. Multicoloured cover as Type B **72**. Self-adhesive.
SB246 $2.30 booklet containing pane of five 46c. and five Christmas labels (No. 2020a)......................... 2·50

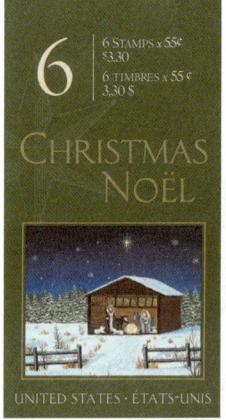

B 71

2000 (1 Sept). "Scratch & WIN Instantly!" Game. Multicoloured cover as Type B **71**, incorporating a scratch card as an additional panel. Self-adhesive.
SB244 $13.80 booklet containing pane of thirty 46c. (3×10) (No. 1366a) .... 22·00

B 73   B 74

2000 (3 Nov). Christmas. Religious Paintings by Mouth and Foot Artists. Multicoloured covers as Type B **73**.
SB247 $3.30 booklet containing pane of six 55c. (2×3) (No. 2022a)......................... 4·00
SB248 $4.60 booklet containing pane of ten 46c. (2×5) (No. 2021a) (cover design as 46c. stamp) .... 5·50
SB249 $5.70 booklet containing pane of six 95c. (2×3) (No. 2023a) (cover design as 95c. stamp) .... 7·00

2000 (28 Dec). Multicoloured covers as Type B **74**.
SB250 $4.70 booklet containing pane of ten self-adhesive 47c. (2×5) (No. 1367a) .... 9·00
SB251 $14.10 booklet containing pane of thirty self-adhesive 47c. (3×10) (No. 1367b) (72×102 *mm*) .... 26·00

No. SB251 comes with two different back covers, one concerning mail redirection and the other "Collection Canada 2000".

2000 (13 Sept). 25th Anniv of Petro-Canada (oil company). Multicoloured cover, 216×105 mm, showing design as No. 2015. Self-adhesive.
SB245 $5.52 booklet containing pane of twelve 46c. (4×3) (No. 2015a) and six pages of text......................... 8·00

LOOKING FOR THAT ELUSIVE STAMP?

Send your wants lists to our specialist stamp departments at:

399 Strand, London, WC2R 0LX, UK

CANADA / Stamp Booklets

2000 (28 Dec). "Picture Postage" Greetings Stamps. Multicoloured cover similar to Type B **72**. Self-adhesive.
SB252 $2.35 booklet containing pane of five different 47c. and five greetings labels (No. 2045a) ....   2·50

2001 (1 Feb). Birds (6th series). Multicoloured cover similar to Type B **62**. Self-adhesive.
SB253 $5.64 booklet containing pane of twelve 47c. (2×6) (No. 2062a) ....   7·00

B **75** Toronto Blue Jays Emblem, Maple Leaf and Baseball

2001 (9 Apr). 25th Season of the Toronto Blue Jays (baseball team). Multicoloured cover as Type B **75**. Self-adhesive.
SB254 $3.76 booklet containing pane of eight 47c. stamps (No. 2073a) ....   4·25

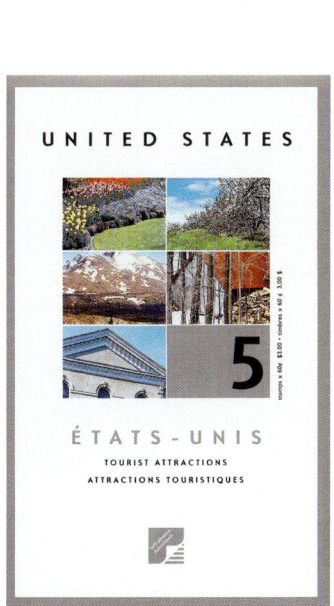

B **76** Details from Stamp Designs

2001 (11 May). Tourist Attractions (1st series). Multicoloured covers as Type B **76**. Self-adhesive.
SB255 $3 booklet containing pane of five 60c. stamps (No. 2075a) ....   4·25
SB256 $5.25 booklet containing five $1.05 stamps (No. 2080a) ....   6·25

B **77** Spray of Roses

2001 (1 Aug). Canadian Roses. Multicoloured cover as Type B **77**.
SB257 $5.64 booklet containing pane of twelve self-adhesive 47c. (3×4) (No. 2091a) ....   11·00

2001 (21 Sept). "Picture Postage" Greetings Stamps. Multicoloured cover similar to Type B **72**. Self-adhesive.
SB258   (–) booklet containing pane of five different domestic mail stamps and five greetings labels (No. 2099a) ....   2·75
No. SB258 was initially sold at $2.35.

B **78** Hot Air Balloons

2001 (1 Oct). Stamp Collecting Month. Hot Air Balloons. Multicoloured cover as Type B **78**. Self-adhesive.
SB259 $3.76 booklet containing pane of eight 47c. (No. 2106a) ....   5·75

Do you require a new album, stockbook or accessory?
Contact us on **0800 611 622** *(UK) or*
+44 (0)1425 472 363 *for a free product guide*

141

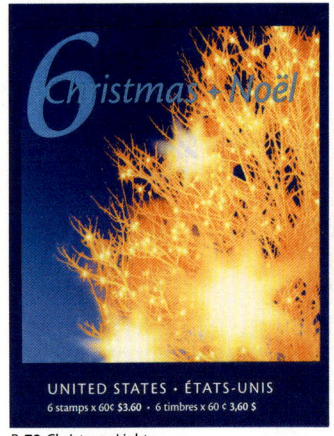

CANADA / Stamp Booklets

B **79** Christmas Lights    B **80**

2001 (1 Nov). Christmas Lights. Multicoloured covers as Type B **79**, each showing a different light pattern.
SB260 $3.60 booklet containing pane of six 60c. (2×3)
         (No. 2111a) .... 7·00
SB261 $4.70 booklet containing pane of ten 47c. (2×5)
         (No. 2110a) .... 8·00
SB262 $6.30 booklet containing pane of six $1.05 (2×3)
         (No. 2112a) .... 10·00

2002 (2 Jan). Multicoloured covers as Type B **80**.
SB263 $4.80 booklet containing pane of ten self-adhesive
         48c. (No. 1368a) (any cover)........................ 7·00
         a. Strip of three booklets showing complete
            cover design .... 20·00
         b. Slogan and websites added to back cover .... 7·00
         ba. Strip of three booklets showing complete
            cover design .... 20·00
   No. SB263b included the slogan "From anywhere to anyone" and the Canada Post website address.
   No. SB263/b were issued in horizontal strips of three booklets, separated by roulettes, each strip illustrating a complete cover design as No. 1368.

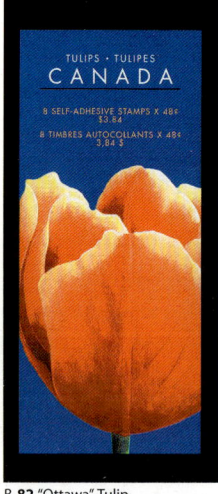

B **82** "Ottawa" Tulip

2002 (3 May). 50th Canadian Tulip Festival, Ottawa. Tulips. Multicoloured cover as Type B **82**.
SB268 $3.84 booklet containing eight self-adhesive
         48c. (No. 2134a) on which the self-adhesive
         paper around the stamps was retained............... 5·00

2002 (1 June). Tourist Attractions (2nd series). Multicoloured covers as Type B **76**. Self-adhesive.
SB269 $3.25 booklet containing pane of five 65c.
         (No. 2143a) .... 4·50
SB270 $6.25 booklet containing pane of five $1.25
         (No. 2148a) .... 8·00

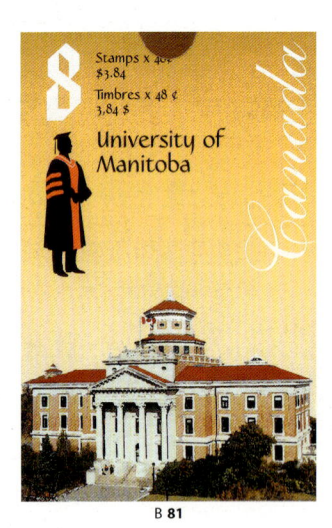

B **81**

B **83** Young People

2002 (28 Feb–27 May). Canadian Universities' Anniversaries. Multicoloured covers as Type B **81**.
SB264 $3.84 booklet containing pane of eight 48c. (4×2)
         (No. 2129a) .... 6·50
SB265 $3.84 booklet containing pane of eight 48c. (4×2)
         (No. 2130a) (Université Laval, Quebec) (4 Apr) ... 6·50
SB266 $3.84 booklet containing pane of eight 48c. (4×2)
         (No. 2131a) (Trinity College, Toronto) (30 Apr) ... 6·50
SB267 $3.84 booklet containing pane of eight 48c. (4×2)
         (No. 2132a) (Saint Mary's University, Halifax)
         (27 May)... 6·50

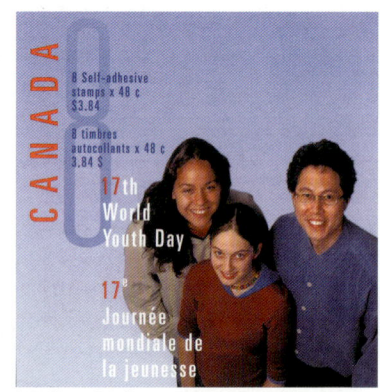

2002 (23 July). 17th World Youth Day, Toronto. Multicoloured cover as Type B **83**. Self-adhesive.
SB271 $3.84 booklet containing pane of eight 48c.
         (No. 2156a) .... 4·25

ARE YOU LOOKING TO SELL ALL OR PART OF YOUR COLLECTION?

Contact Stanley Gibbons Auctions on
020 7836 8444 for more information

CANADA / Stamp Booklets

B **84** "Winter Travel" (Cecil Youngfox)

2002 (4 Nov). Christmas. Aboriginal Art. Multicoloured covers as Type B **84**.
SB272 $3.90 booklet containing pane of six 65c. (2×5)
(No. 2173a) .... 4·25
SB273 $4.80 booklet containing pane of ten 48c. (2×3)
(No. 2172a) (cover showing "Genesis" (Daphne Odjig)) .... 5·50
SB274 $7.50 booklet containing pane of six $1.25 (2×3)
(No. 2174a) (cover showing "Mary and Child" (Irene Katak Angutitaq)) .... 6·75

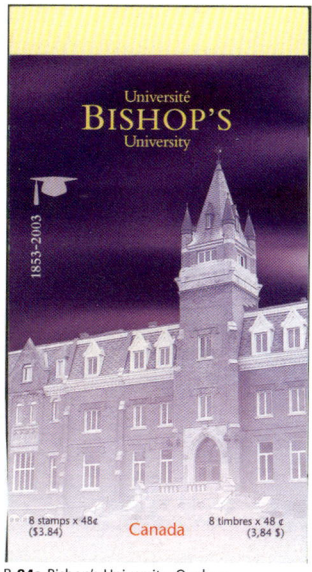

B **84a** Bishop's University, Quebec

2003 (28 Jan). Canadian Universities' Anniversaries (2nd issue). Multicoloured cover as Type B **84a**.
SB275 $3.84 booklet containing pane of eight 48c. (2×4)
(No. 2190a) (Bishop's University, Quebec) .... 5·00
SB276 $3.84 booklet containing pane of eight 48c. (2×4)
(No. 2191a) (University of Western Ontario, London) (19 Mar) .... 5·00

SB277 $3.84 booklet containing pane of eight 48c. (2×4)
(No. 2192a) (St. Francis Xavier University, Nova Scotia) (4 Apr) .... 5·00
SB278 $3.84 booklet containing pane of eight 48c. (2×4)
(No. 2193a) (Macdonald Institute, University of Guelph, Ontario) (20 June) .... 5·00
SB279 $3.84 booklet containing pane of eight 48c. (2×4)
(No. 2194a) (Université De Montréal) (4 Sept) .... 5·00

B **85** John Audubon

2003 (21 Feb). Bird Paintings by John Audubon. Multicoloured cover as Type B **85** Self-adhesive.
SB280 $3.90 booklet containing pane of six 65c. (3×2)
(No. 2199a) .... 11·00

2003 (12 June). Tourist Attractions (3rd series). Multicoloured covers as Type B **76**. Self-adhesive.
SB281 $3.25 booklet containing pane of five 65c.
(No. 2205a) .... 5·00
SB282 $6.25 booklet containing pane of five $1.25
(No. 2210a) .... 8·00

2003 (11 July). Vancouver's Successful Bid for Winter Olympic Games, 2010. No. SB263 with cover optd Vancouver 2010 in red.
SB283 $4.80 booklet containing pane of ten self-adhesive 48c. (No. 2215a) (any cover) .... 7·25
a. Strip of three booklets showing complete cover design .... 20·00

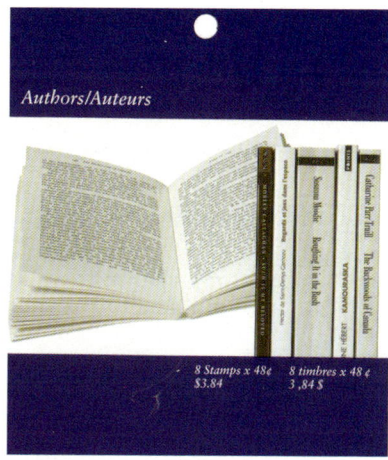

B **86** Books

2003 (8 Sept). 50th Anniv of National Library of Canada. Multicoloured cover as Type B **86**.
SB284 $3.84 booklet containing pane of eight 48c.
(No. 2220a) .... 5·75

143

CANADA / Stamp Booklets

B 87 Cyclists in Race

2003 (10 Sept). World Road Cycling Championships, Hamilton, Ontario. Multicoloured cover as Type B **87**.
SB285 $3.84 booklet containing pane of eight 48c.
(No. 2224a) .... 8·00

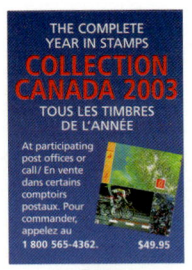

B 89

2003 (19 Dec). Multicoloured cover as Type B **89**. Self-adhesive.
SB289 $4.90 booklet containing pane of ten 49c.
(No. 1369a) .... 10·00

Nos. SB290/1 are vacant.

> Folded booklets and flat panes designed to be folded are listed in this catalogue as booklets. Flat panes not designed to be folded have been deleted from this booklet section. These panes are still listed after the stamps they contain.

2003 (19 Dec). Multicoloured cover as Type B **89**. Self-adhesive.
SB292 $4.90 booklet containing pane of ten 49c.
(No. 2241a) .... 10·00
Postal forgeries of SB292 are known.

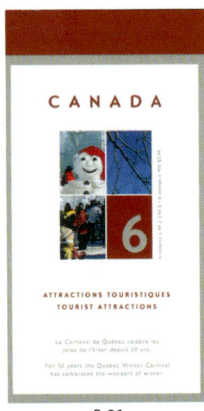

B 91

2004 (29 Jan–19 July). Tourist Attractions (4th series). Multicoloured covers as Type B **91**. Self-adhesive.
SB293 $2.94 booklet containing pane of six 49c. (No. 2257a)   6·75
SB294 $2.94 booklet containing pane of six 49c. (No. 2258a)   6·75
SB295 $2.94 booklet containing pane of six 49c. (No. 2259a)   6·75
SB296 $2.94 booklet containing pane of six 49c. (No. 2260a)   6·75
SB297 $2.94 booklet containing pane of six 49c. (No. 2261a)   6·75

B 88 Ice Hockey Player

2003 (4 Nov). Christmas. Multicoloured covers as Type B **88**. Self-adhesive.
SB286 $3.90 booklet containing pane of six 65c. (2×3)
(No. 2239a) .... 6·75
SB287 $5.76 booklet containing pane of twelve 48c. (2×6) (No. 2238a) (cover showing skater) .... 7·50
SB288 $7.50 booklet containing pane of six $1.25 (2×3)
(No. 2240a) (cover showing skier) .... 10·00

B 92

144

CANADA / Stamp Booklets

2004 (26 Mar). 125th Anniv of Royal Canadian Army Cadets. Multicoloured cover as Type B **92**. Self-adhesive.
SB298 $3.92 booklet containing pane of eight 49c. (No. 2265a) .... 9·00

2004 (27 July). Multicoloured cover as Type B **95**. Self-adhesive.
SB305 $4.90 booklet containing pane of ten 49c. (No. 2241a) .... 10·00

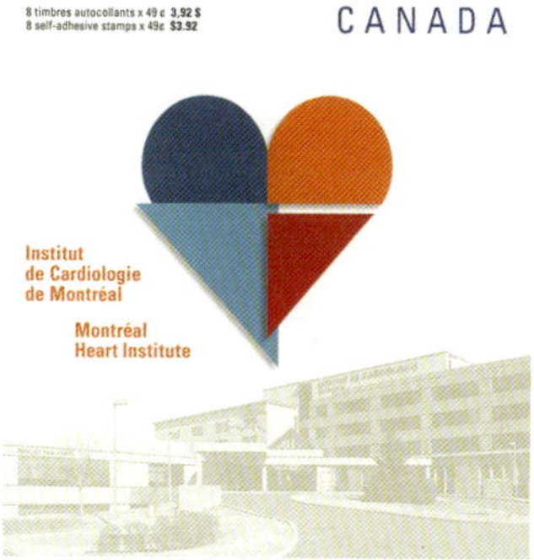

B **93**

2004 (19 Apr). 40th Anniv of Home Hardware (co-operative business). Multicoloured cover as Type B **93**. Self-adhesive.
SB299 $4.90 booklet containing pane of ten 49c. (4×3) plus a central label (No. 2270a), eight pages of text and illustrations and a pane of 15 self-adhesive labels .... 8·00

2004 (4 May–8 May). 8 May Canadian Universities Anniversaries (3rd issue). Multicoloured covers as Type B **84a**.
SB300 $3.92 booklet containing pane of eight 49c. (2×4) (No. 2271a) .... 6·50
SB301 $3.92 booklet containing pane of eight 49c. (2×4) (No. 2272a) .... 6·50

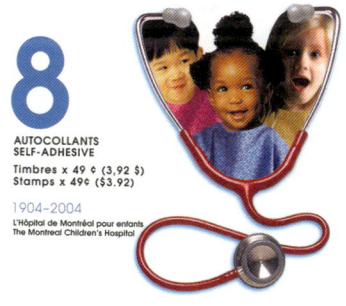

B **96**

2004 (15 Sept). 50th Anniv of Montréal Heart Institute. Multicoloured cover as Type B **96**. Self-adhesive.
SB306 $3.92 booklet containing pane of eight 49c. (No. 2287a) .... 5·75

B **94**

2004 (6 May). Centenary of Montreal Children's Hospital. Multicoloured as Type B **94**. Self-adhesive.
SB302 $3.92 booklet containing pane of eight 49c. (No. 2273a) .... 6·50

2004 (14 May). Bird Paintings by John Audubon (2nd series). Multicoloured cover as Type B **85** showing face of John Audubon. Self-adhesive.
SB303 $4.80 booklet containing pane of six 80c. (No. 2278a) .... 11·00

B **97**

2004 (1 Oct). Pets. Multicoloured cover as Type B **97**. Self-adhesive.
SB307 $3.92 booklet containing pane of eight 49c. (No. 2288a) .... 8·00

B **95**

2004 (2 July). Multicoloured cover as Type B **95**. Self-adhesive.
SB304 $4.90 booklet pane of ten 49c. (No. 1369a) .... 10·00

B **98**

145

2004 (2 Nov). Christmas. Multicoloured cover as Type B **98**. Self-adhesive.
SB309 $5.88 booklet containing pane of twelve 49c.
            (No. 2300a) .... 11·00

Nos. SB308 and SB310 are vacant.

B **100**

2004 (20 Dec). Multicoloured covers as Type B **100**. Five different cover designs showing the following advertisements in English and French: (a) "Picture yourself on a postage stamp!"; (b) "Looking for a hero?"; (c) "They'll take you places."; (d) "Collect famous masterpieces!"; (e) "You'll go wild over our stamps!". Self-adhesive.
SB311 $5 booklet (any cover) containing pane of ten
            50c. (No. 1370a) .... 10·00
   In addition to the five different front cover designs No. SB311 comes with five different back covers which reproduce parts of the designs on the stamps, giving twenty-five booklet cover variations.

B **101**

2004 (20 Dec). Multicoloured covers as Type B **101**. Five different cover designs showing advertisements as No. SB311 but with blue background. Self-adhesive.
SB312 $5 booklet (any cover) containing pane of ten
            50c. (No. 2242a) .... 7·00

Nos. SB313/4 are vacant.

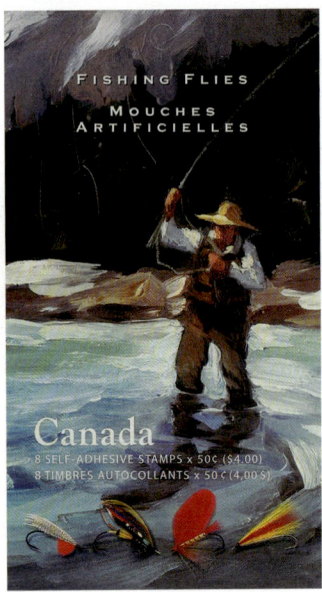

B **103**

2005 (4 Feb). Fishing Flies. Multicoloured cover as Type B **103**. Self-adhesive.
SB315 $4 booklet containing two panes of 50c.
            (No. 2329a) .... 9·00

2005 (14 Feb). Canadian Universities Anniversaries (4th series). Multicoloured cover as Type B **84a** (No. SB275) but 90×130 mm. Self-adhesive.
SB316 $4 booklet containing pane of eight 50c.
            (No. 2333a) .... 5·75

No. SB317 is vacant.

B **104** White Daffodil with Yellow Trumpet

2005 (10 Mar). Daffodils. Multicoloured cover as Type B **104**. Self-adhesive.
SB318 $5 booklet containing pane of ten 50c.
            (No. 2336a) .... 8·00

B **105** TD Bank Building in Early 20th Century and Cashier

2005 (18 Mar). 150th Anniv of TD Bank Financial Group. Multicoloured cover as Type B **105**. Self-adhesive.
SB319 $5 booklet containing pane of ten 49c. (5×2)
            (No. 2339a), eight pages of text and
            illustrations and a pane of 15 self-adhesive
            labels .... 7·00

CANADA / Stamp Booklets

B **106** John Audubon

2005 (23 Mar). Bird Paintings by John Audubon (3rd series). Multicoloured cover as Type B **106**. Self-adhesive.
SB320 $5.10 booklet containing pane of six 85c.
(No. 2344a) .... 10·00

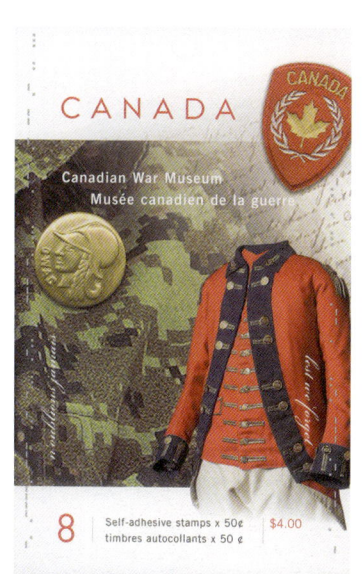

B **107** 18th-century Uniform and Modern Camouflage Material

2005 (6 May). Opening of New Canadian War Museum Building, Ottawa. Multicoloured cover as Type B **107**. Self-adhesive.
SB321 $4 booklet containing pane of eight 50c.
(No. 2354a) .... 5·00

B **108** Mountain Biker, Skateboarder, City and Forest

2005 (1 Oct). Youth Sports. Multicoloured cover as Type B **108**. Self-adhesive.
SB322 $4 booklet containing pane of eight 50c.
(No. 2368a) .... 4·25

B **109** Snowman

2005 (2 Nov). Christmas (1st issue). Multicoloured cover as Type B **109**. Self-adhesive.
SB323 $6 booklet containing pane of twelve 50c.
(No. 2375a) .... 7·50

No. SB324 is vacant.

B **110** Christmas Star    B **111** Balloons

2005 (2 Nov). Christmas (2nd issue). Multicoloured cover as Type B **110**. Self-adhesive.
SB325 $6 booklet containing pane of twelve 50c.
(No. 2376a) (cover 54×138 mm, unfolded).......... 7·50

No. SB326 is vacant.

2005 (19 Dec). Multicoloured cover as Type B **111**. Self-adhesive.
SB327 $5.10 booklet containing pane of ten 51c.
(No. 1374ab) .... 9·00

No. SB328/30 are vacant.

147

CANADA / Stamp Booklets

B 112 Queen Elizabeth II

2006 (12 Jan). 80th Birthday of Queen Elizabeth II. Multicoloured cover as Type B **112**. Self-adhesive.
SB331 $5.10 booklet containing pane of ten 51c. and 10 labels (No. 2381a) .... 6·25

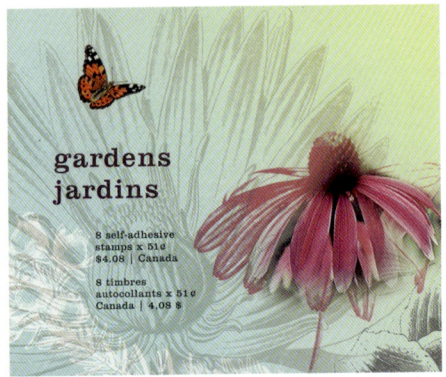

B 113 Purple Coneflower, other Flowers and American Painted Lady Butterfly

2006 (8 Mar). Gardens. Multicoloured cover as Type B **113**. Self-adhesive.
SB332 $4.08 booklet containing pane of eight 51c. (No. 2384a)   9·00

No. SB333 is vacant.

B 115 McClelland & Stewart's Colophon

2006 (26 Apr). Centenary of McClelland & Stewart (publishing house). Slate-blue and grey cover as Type B **115**. Self-adhesive.
SB334 $4.08 booklet containing pane of eight 51c. and 8 labels (No. 2393a) .... 10·00

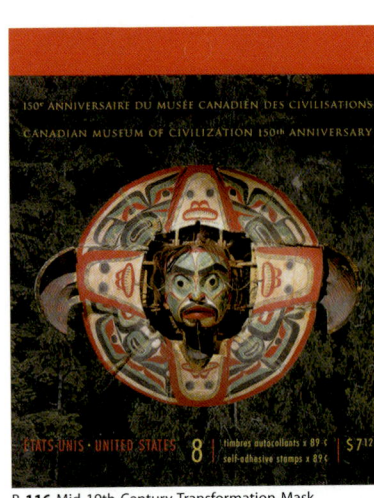

B 116 Mid 19th-Century Transformation Mask

2006 (11 May). 150th Anniv of Canadian Museum of Civilization, Gatineau, Quebec. Multicoloured cover as Type B **116**. Self-adhesive.
SB335 $7.12 booklet containing pane of eight 89c. (No. 2394a) .... 12·00

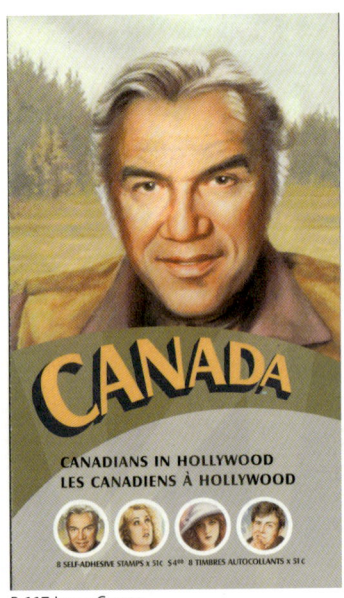

B 117 Lorne Greene

2006 (26 May). Canadians in Hollywood. Multicoloured covers in four different designs as Type B **117**. Self-adhesive.
SB336 $4.08 booklet containing pane of eight 51c. and 8 labels (No. 2395a) (Type B **117**) .... 5·50
  a. Cover showing Fay Wray .... 5·50
  b. Cover showing Mary Pickford .... 5·50
  c. Cover showing John Candy .... 5·50

The booklet panes in Nos. SB336/c differ in the order of the stamps within the two blocks of four which form the booklet pane.

148

CANADA / Stamp Booklets

B 118 Beluga Whale

2006 (15 June). 50th Anniv of Vancouver Aquarium. Multicoloured cover as Type B **118**. Self-adhesive.
SB337 $5.10 booklet containing pane of ten 51c.
(No. 2402a) .... 6·25

No. SB338 is vacant.

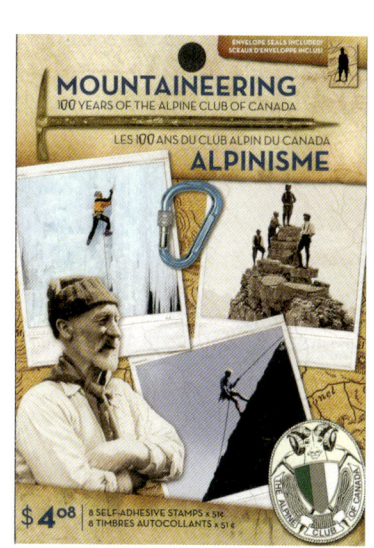

B **120** Arthur Wheeler (founder) and Early and Modern Climbers

2006 (19 July). Centenary of the Alpine Club of Canada. Multicoloured cover as Type B **120**. Self-adhesive.
SB339 $4.08 booklet containing pane of eight 51c.
(No. 2408a) .... 7·00

Stay up to date with all things philatelic.
Subscribe to **Gibbons Stamp Monthly** –
The UK's number one stamp magazine

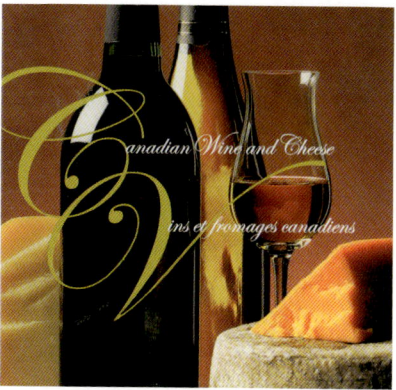

B **121**

2006 (23 Aug). Canadian Wine and Cheese. Multicoloured cover as Type B **121**. Self-adhesive.
SB340 $4.08 booklet containing pane of eight 51c.
(No. 2415a) .... 5·50

2006 (26 Sept). Canadian Universities Anniversaries (5th series). Multicoloured cover as Type B **84a** (No. SB275) but 90×130 mm. Self-adhesive.
SB341 $4.08 booklet containing pane of eight 51c.
(No. 2419a) .... 7·00

No. SB342 is vacant.

B **123** "Madonna and Child" (detail) (Antoine-Sébastien Falardeau)

2006 (1 Nov). Christmas (1st issue). Multicoloured cover as Type B **123**. Self-adhesive.
SB343 $6.12 booklet containing pane of twelve 51c.
(No. 2430a) .... 9·50

No. SB344 is vacant.

B **124** "Snowman" (Yvonne McKague Housser)

149

CANADA / Stamp Booklets

2006 (1 Nov). Christmas (2nd issue). Multicoloured covers as Type B **124**. Self-adhesive.
SB345 $6.12 booklet containing pane of twelve 51c.
(No. 2431a) .... 9·50

No. SB346 is vacant.

2007 (12 Mar). Canadian Universities' Anniversaries (6th issue). Multicoloured cover as Type B **84a** but 89×130 mm. Self-adhesive.
SB355 $4.16 booklet containing pane of eight 52c.
(No. 2487a) .... 6·25
SB356 $4.16 booklet containing pane of eight 52c.
(No. 2488a) (3.4.07) .... 6·25

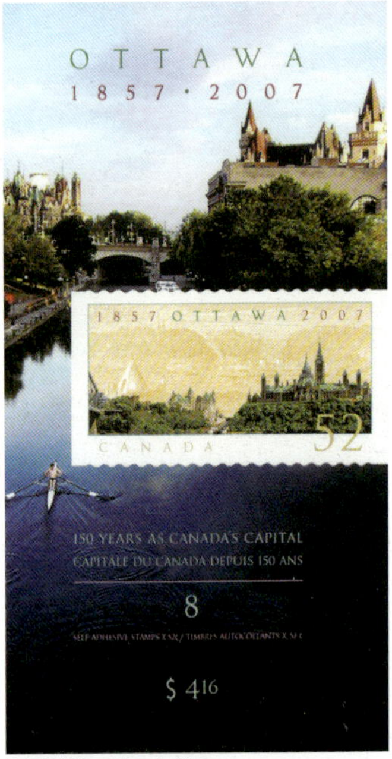

B **125** River and Forest    B **126**

2006 (16 Nov)–07. Multicoloured cover as Type B **125**. Self-adhesive.
SB347 $5.10 booklet containing pane of ten (51c.) stamps
(No. 2434a) (cover Type B **126**) .... 10·00
SB348 $15.30 booklet containing pane of thirty (51c.)
stamps (No. 2434b) (cover Type B **125**) .... 27·00
a. With barcode on booklet pane (2007) .... 27·00
No. 348 has the barcode on the back of the pane.

2006 (16 Nov). Multicoloured cover as Type B **126**. Self-adhesive.
SB349 $5.10 booklet containing pane of ten (51c.) stamps
(No. 2464a) .... 8·00

Nos. SB350/3 are vacant.

B **130** Rideau Canal, Ottawa
(Actual size 89×171 mm)

2007 (3 May). 150th Anniv of Ottawa as Capital of Canada. Multicoloured cover as Type B **130**. Self-adhesive.
SB357 $4.16 booklet containing pane of eight 52c.
(No. 2491a) .... 7·25

B **129** Syringa×prestoniae "Isabella"

2007 (1 Mar). Lilacs. Multicoloured cover as Type B **129**. Self-adhesive.
SB354 $5.20 booklet containing pane of ten 52c. and ten
labels (No. 2484a) .... 8·00

B **131** Gordon Lightfoot

2007 (29 June). Canadian Recording Artists (1st series). Multicoloured covers in four different designs as Type B **131**. Self-adhesive.
SB358 $4.16 booklet containing pane of eight 52c. and 8
labels (No. 2500a) (Type B **131**) .... 7·25
a. Cover showing Joni Mitchell .... 7·25
b. Cover showing Anne Murray .... 7·25
c. Cover showing Paul Anka .... 7·25
The booklet panes in Nos. SB358/c differ in the order of the stamps within the two blocks of four which form the booklet pane.

CANADA / Stamp Booklets

B **132** Seashore, Terra Nova National Park

B **133** Elk, Jasper National Park

2007 (6 July). 50th Anniv of Terra Nova National Park, Newfoundland. Multicoloured cover as Type B **132**. Self-adhesive.
SB359 $5.20 booklet containing pane of ten 52c.
(No. 2505a) .... 9·00

2007 (20 July). Centenary of Jasper National Park, Alberta. Multicoloured cover as Type B **133**. Self-adhesive.
SB360 $5.20 booklet containing pane of ten 52c.
(No. 2506a) .... 9·00

B **134** Scouts of 2007 and 1907

2007 (25 July). Centenary of Scouting. Multicoloured cover as Type B **134**. Self-adhesive.
SB361 $4.16 booklet containing pane of eight 52c.
(No. 2507a) .... 9·00

No. SB362 is vacant.

B **135** Reindeer

2007 (1 Nov). Christmas (1st issue). Multicoloured cover as Type B **135**. Self-adhesive.
SB363 $6.24 booklet containing pane of twelve (52c.) stamps (No. 2526a) .... 11·00

No. SB364 is vacant.

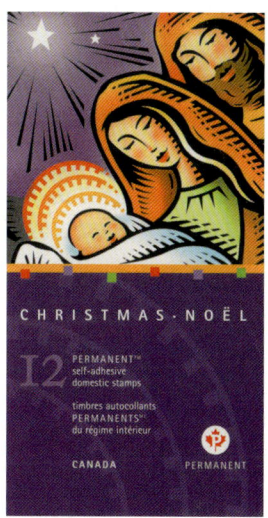

B **136** Angel playing Trumpet

2007 (1 Nov). Christmas (2nd issue). Multicoloured cover as Type B **136**. Self-adhesive.
SB365 $6.24 booklet containing pane of twelve (52c.) stamps (No. 2527a) (cover showing Nativity)...... 11·00

No. SB366/72 are vacant.

151

CANADA / Stamp Booklets

B **139** Peonies 'Elgin' and 'Coral 'n Gold'

2008 (3 Mar). Peonies. Multicoloured cover as Type B **139**. Self-adhesive.
SB373 $5.20 booklet containing pane of ten 52c. and ten labels (No. 2541a) .... 9·00

Nos. SB374/5 are vacant.

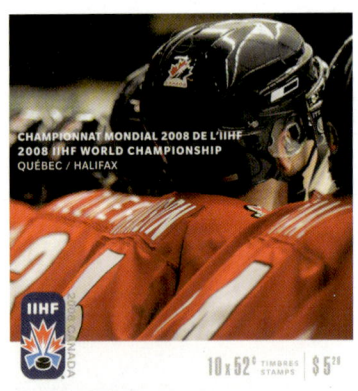

B **141** Team Canada Players

2008 (3 Apr). International Ice Hockey Federation World Championship, Halifax and Québec. Multicoloured covers as Type B **141**. Self-adhesive.
SB376 $5.20 booklet containing pane of ten 52c.
         (No. 2546a) .... 9·00
         a. Cover showing ice hockey players and stadium   9·00
No. SB376 also commemorates the Centenary of the International Ice Hockey Federation.

B **142** Guide Dog "Luke"

2008 (21 Apr). Guide Dogs. Multicoloured cover as Type B **142**. Self-adhesive.
SB377 $5.20 booklet containing pane of ten 52c.
         (No. 2547a) .... 12·00
No. SB377 also commemorates the Centenary of the Montreal Association for the Blind.

B **143** Sambro Island Lighthouse, Nova Scotia   B **144** Welder working on Pipeline

2008. Lighthouses. Multicoloured cover as Type B **143**. Self-adhesive.
SB378 $15.60 booklet containing pane of thirty (52c.) stamps (No. 2439b) .... 23·00

2008 (2 May). Oil and Gas Industry. Multicoloured cover as Type B **144**. Self-adhesive.
SB379 $5.20 booklet containing pane of ten 52c.
         (No. 2548a) .... 10·00

B **145** Audrey Hepburn

CANADA / Stamp Booklets

2008 (21 May). Art Canada. Birth Centenary of Yousuf Karsh (portrait photographer). Multicoloured covers as Type B **145**. Self-adhesive.

SB380	$7.68 booklet containing pane of eight 96c. (No. 2553a) (Type B **145**)	14·00
SB381	$12.80 booklet containing pane of eight $1.60 (No. 2554a) (cover showing Winston Churchill)	25·00

B **146** Nurse with Patient

2008 (16 June). Centenary of Canadian Nurses Association. Multicoloured cover as Type B **146**. Self-adhesive.

SB382	$5.20 booklet containing pane of ten 52c. (No. 2556a)	10·00

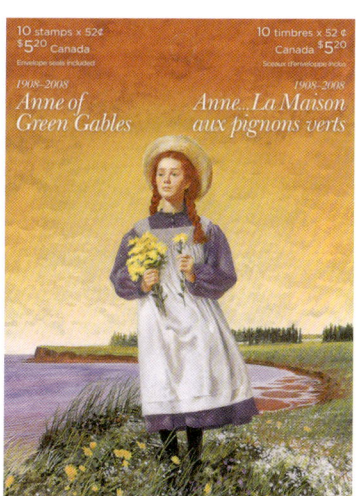

B **147** Anne

2008 (20 June). Centenary of Publication of *Anne of Green Gables* by Lucy Maud Montgomery. Multicoloured cover as Type B **147**. Self-adhesive.

SB383	$5.20 booklet containing pane of ten 52c. (No. 2557a)	9·00

When you buy an album look for the name **STANLEY GIBBONS**, it means quality combined with value for money

2008 (30 June). Canadians in Hollywood (2nd series). Multicoloured cover as Type B **117**. Self-adhesive.

SB384	$4.16 booklet containing pane of eight 52c. and 8 labels (No. 2560a) (cover showing Norma Shearer)	9·00
	a. Cover showing Chief Dan George	9·00
	b. Cover showing Marie Dressler	9·00
	c. Cover showing Raymond Burr	9·00

The booklet panes in Nos. SB383/c differ in the order of the stamps within the two blocks of four which form the booklet pane.

B **148** Athletes parading with Canadian Flag

2008 (18 July). Olympic Games, Beijing. Multicoloured cover as Type B **148**. Self-adhesive.

SB385	$5.20 booklet containing pane of ten 52c. (No. 2565a)	12·00

B **149** Lifeguards

2008 (25 July). Centenary of Lifesaving Society. Multicoloured cover as Type B **149**. Self-adhesive.

SB386	$5.20 booklet containing pane of ten 52c. (No. 2566a)	9·00

2008 (1 Oct). Endangered Species (3rd series). Multicoloured cover, 120×155 mm, as Type B **122**. Self-adhesive.

SB387	$4.18 booklet containing pane of eight 52c. (No. 2569a)	10·00

153

CANADA / Stamp Booklets

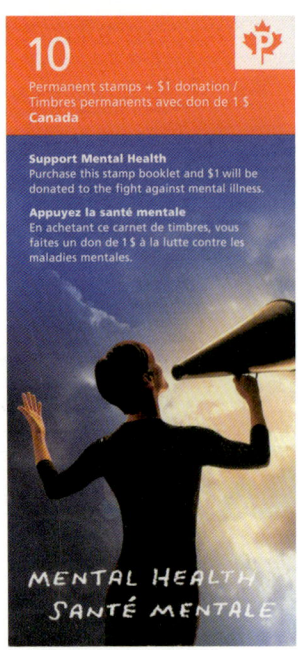

B **150** Woman with Megaphone
(*Illustration reduced. Actual size 60×127 mm*)

2008 (6 Oct). Mental Health. Multicoloured cover as Type B **150**. Self-adhesive.
SB388 $6.20 booklet containing pane of ten 52+10c.
        (No. 2574a) .... 11·00

B **151** Infant Jesus (crèche figure by Antonio Caruso) (*Illustration reduced. Actual size 70×125 mm*)

2008 (3 Nov). Christmas (1st issue). Multicoloured cover as Type B **151**. Self-adhesive.
SB389 ($6.24) booklet containing pane of twelve (52c.) stamps (No. 2576a) .... 12·00

For a full range of Stanley Gibbons catalogues, please visit www.stanleygibbons.com

No. SB390 is vacant.

B **152** Child Skiing   B **153** Bobsleigh
(*Illustration reduced. Actual size 75×135 mm*)

2008 (3 Nov). Christmas (2nd issue). Winter Fun. Multicoloured covers as Type B **152**. Self-adhesive.
SB391 ($6.24) booklet containing pane of twelve (52c.) stamps (No. 2577a) .... 12·00

No. SB392 is vacant.

2009 (12 Jan). Winter Olympic Games, Vancouver, 2010. Olympic Sports. Multicoloured covers as Type B **153**. Self-adhesive.
SB393 ($16.20) booklet containing pane of thirty (54c.) stamps (No. 2584b) .... 35·00

B **154** Rhododendron Flowers
(*Illustration reduced. Actual size 80×120 mm*)

CANADA / Stamp Booklets

2009 (13 Mar). Rhododendrons. Multicoloured cover as Type B **154**. Self-adhesive.
SB394 $5.40 booklet containing pane of ten 54c. and ten labels (No. 2603a) .... 10·00

B **155** Nebula (*Illustration reduced. Actual size 89×169 mm*)

2009 (2 Apr). International Year of Astronomy. Multicoloured cover as Type B **155**. Self-adhesive.
SB395 $5.40 booklet containing pane of ten 54c. and ten labels (No. 2608a) .... 10·00

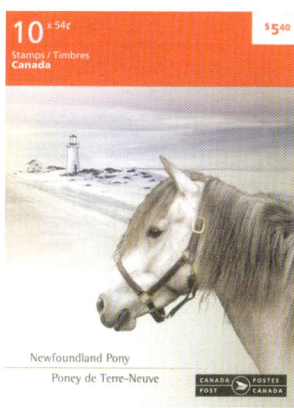

B **156** Newfoundland Pony

2009 (15 May). Canadian Horse and Newfoundland Pony. Multicoloured cover as Type B **156**. Self-adhesive.
SB396 $5.40 booklet containing pane of ten 54c. (No. 2614a) .... 12·00

HAVE YOU READ THE NOTES AT THE BEGINNING OF THIS CATALOGUE?
These often provide answers to the enquiries we receive

B **157** Robert Charlebois (*Illustration reduced. Actual size 105×100 mm*)

2009 (2 July). Canadian Recording Artists (2nd series). Multicoloured cover as Type B **157**. Self-adhesive.
SB397 $4.32 booklet containing pane of eight 54c. stamps and 8 labels (No. 2618a) (Type B **157**)... 6·00
  a. Cover showing Edith Butler .... 6·00
  b. Cover showing Stompin' Tom Connors .... 6·00
  c. Cover showing Bryan Adams .... 6·00
The booklet panes in Nos. SB397/c differ in the order of the stamps within the two blocks of four which form the booklet panes.

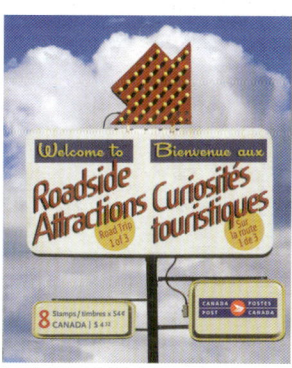

B **158** Signpost (*Illustration reduced. Actual size 102×120 mm*)

2009 (6 July). Roadside Attractions. Multicoloured cover as Type B **158**. Self-adhesive.
SB398 $4.32 booklet containing pane of eight 54c. stamps and 8 labels (No. 2623a) .... 10·00

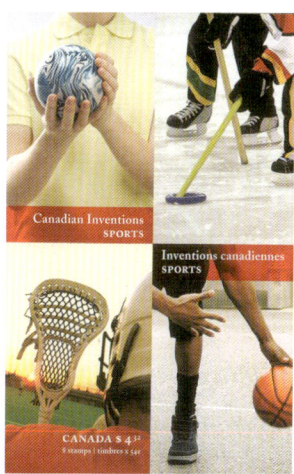

B **159** Ten-pin Bowling, Ringette, Lacrosse and Basketball

155

CANADA / Stamp Booklets

2009 (10 Aug). Canadian Inventions. Sports. Multicoloured cover as Type B **159**. Self-adhesive.
SB399 $4.32 booklet containing pane of eight 54c. stamps and eight labels (No. 2629a) .... 9·00

B **160** Tree and River inside Human Head and Sun breaking through Clouds

2009 (14 Sept). Mental Health. Multicoloured cover as Type B **160**. Self-adhesive.
SB400   ($6.64) booklet containing pane of ten (54c.)+10c. (No. 2633a) .... 11·00

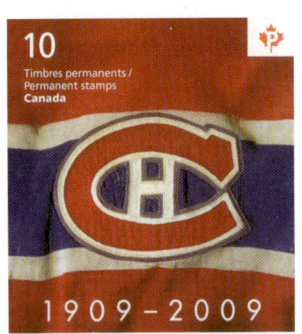

B **161** Detail from Maurice Richard's Hockey Sweater

2009 (17 Oct). Centenary of Montreal Canadiens (ice hockey team). Multicoloured cover as Type B **161**. Self-adhesive.
SB401   ($5.40) booklet containing pane of ten stamps (No. 2634a) .... 11·00

Stay up to date with all things philatelic.
Subscribe to **Gibbons Stamp Monthly** –
The UK's number one stamp magazine

B **162** Soldiers and Horses (detail from National War Memorial)

2009 (19 Oct). 'Lest We Forget'. Multicoloured cover as Type B **162**. Self-adhesive.
SB402   ($5.40) booklet containing pane of ten stamps (No. 2636a) .... 10·00

B **163** Madonna and Infant Jesus (*Illustration reduced. Actual size 70×125 mm*)

2009 (2 Nov). Christmas (1st issue). Multicoloured cover as Type B **163**. Self-adhesive.
SB403   ($6.48) booklet containing pane of twelve (54c.) stamps (No. 2638a) .... 13·00

B **164** Christmas Tree (*Illustration reduced. Actual size 72×80 mm*)

CANADA / Stamp Booklets

2009 (2 Nov). Christmas (2nd issue). Multicoloured cover as Type B **164**. Self-adhesive.
SB404 ($6.48) booklet containing pane of twelve (54c.) stamps (No. 2642a).. 12·00

B **165** Watson's Mill, Manotick, Ontario
(*Illustration reduced.*
Actual size 61×134 mm)

2010 (11 Jan). Mills. Multicoloured cover as Type B **165**. Self-adhesive.
SB405 ($17.10) booklet containing pane of thirty (57c.) stamps (No. 2445b).. 38·00

B **166** Inukshuk, Whistler Mountain

2010 (12 Jan). Winter Olympic Games, Vancouver. Multicoloured cover as Type B **166**. Self-adhesive.
SB406 $5.70 booklet containing pane of ten 57c. and ten small stickers (No. 2653a)... 12·50

B **167** Gold Medal

B **168** Chandra Crawford, Speed Skaters, Bobsleigh and Skiers

2010 (14 Feb). Olympic Winter Games, Vancouver. Canada's First Olympic Gold on Canadian Soil. Multicoloured cover as Type B **167**. Self-adhesive.
SB407 $5.70 booklet containing pane of ten 57c. (No. 2658a)... 12·50

2010 (22 Feb). Olympic Winter Games, Vancouver. Multicoloured cover as Type B **168**. Self-adhesive.
SB408 $5.70 booklet containing pane of ten 57c. (No. 2660a)... 12·50

B **169** African Violet 'Picasso'

2010 (3 Mar). African Violets. Multicoloured cover as Type B **169**. Self-adhesive.
SB409 ($5.70) booklet containing pane of ten (57c.) stamps and ten labels (No. 2663a)......................... 12·50

Do you require a new album, stockbook or accessory?
Contact us on **0800 611 622** (UK) or
+44 (0)1425 472 363 for a free product guide

157

CANADA / Stamp Booklets

B **170** Figures forming Maple Leaf and Star of David

2010 (14 Apr). Canada–Israel, 60 Years of Friendship. Multicoloured cover as Type B **170**. Self-adhesive.
SB410 $10.20 booklet containing pane of six $1.70 stamps
(No. 2666a) .... 23·00

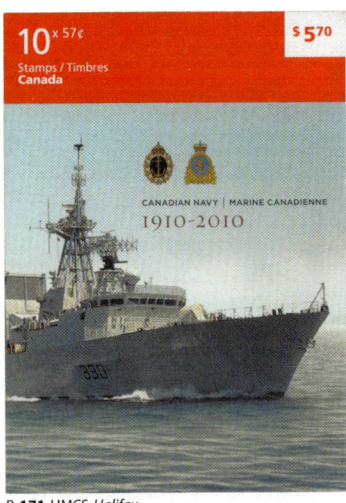

B **171** HMCS *Halifax*

2010 (4 May). Centenary of the Canadian Navy. Multicoloured cover as Type B **171**. Self-adhesive.
SB411 $5.70 booklet containing pane of ten 57c. stamps
(No. 2673a) .... 12·50

B **172** Sea Otter

2010 (13 May). Marine Life: Sea Otter and Harbour Porpoise. Black, dull ultramarine and new blue cover as Type B **172**. Pane attached by selvedge.
SB412 $4.56 booklet containing pane of eight 57c.
(No. 2676a) .... 10·00

B **173** Wildlife

2010 (22 May). Canadian Geographic's Wildlife Photography of the Year. Multicoloured cover as Type B **173**. Self-adhesive.
SB413 $5.70 booklet containing pane of ten 57c.
(No. 2679a) .... 12·50

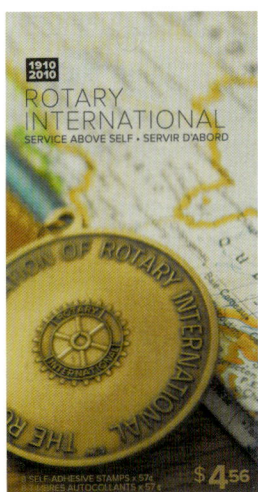

B **174** Rotary Badge

LOOKING FOR THAT ELUSIVE STAMP?

Send your wants lists to our specialist stamp departments at:

399 Strand, London, WC2R 0LX, UK

CANADA / Stamp Booklets

(Des Xerxes Irani. Litho Lowe-Martin)

2010 (18 June). Centenary of Rotary International. Multicoloured cover as Type B **174**. Self-adhesive.
SB414 $4.56 booklet containing pane of eight 57c. (No. 2685a) .... 10·00

2010 (5 July). Roadside Attractions (2nd series). Multicoloured cover as Type B **158**, but showing signpost with star and arrow. Self-adhesive.
SB415 ($4.56) booklet containing pane of eight (57c.) stamps and eight small stickers (No. 2688a) ..... 10·00

B **175** Guide

2010 (8 July). Centenary of Girl Guides of Canada. Multicoloured cover as Type B **175**. Self-adhesive.
SB416 ($5.70) booklet containing pane of ten (57c.) stamps and ten small stickers (No. 2693a) .... 12·50

B **176** Sun and Tree growing on Mountain Summit

2010 (7 Sept). Mental Health. Multicoloured cover as Type B **176**. Self-adhesive.
SB417 ($6.70) booklet containing pane of ten (57c.)+10c. (No. 2696a) .... 12·50

B **177** *Our Lady of the Night* (sculpture by Antonio Caruso)

2010 (1 Nov). Christmas (1st issue). Multicoloured cover as Type B **177**. Self-adhesive.
SB418 ($6.84) booklet containing pane of twelve (57c.) stamps (No. 2697a) .... 15·00

B **178** Red Baubles (*Illustration reduced. Actual size 70×130 mm*)

B **179** Canadian Flag on Hot-air Balloon (*Illustration reduced. Actual size 60×130 mm*)

2010 (1 Nov). Christmas (2nd issue). Baubles. Multicoloured cover as Type B **178**. Self-adhesive.
SB419 ($6.84) booklet containing pane of twelve (57c.) stamps (No. 2698a) .... 15·00

2011 (17 Jan). 'Canadian Pride'. Multicoloured cover, 60×135 mm, as Type B **179**. Self-adhesive.
SB420 ($17.70) booklet containing pane of thirty (59c.) (No. 2728b) .... 34·00

> **HAVE YOU READ THE NOTES AT THE BEGINNING OF THIS CATALOGUE?**
> These often provide answers to the enquiries we receive

159

CANADA / Stamp Booklets

B **180** Carrie Best (founder) reading *The Clarion* Newspaper

2011 (1 Feb). Black History Month. Carrie Best. Multicoloured cover, 76×100 mm, as Type B **180**. Self-adhesive.
SB421 $5.90 booklet containing pane of ten 59c.
          (No. 2750a) .... 11·00

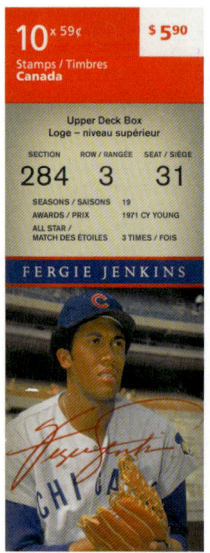

B **183** Sunflower 'Sunbright'

2011 (3 Mar). Sunflowers. Multicoloured cover, 80×120 mm, as Type B **183**. Self-adhesive.
SB425   ($5.90) booklet containing pane of ten (59c.)
          (No. 2759a) .... 12·50

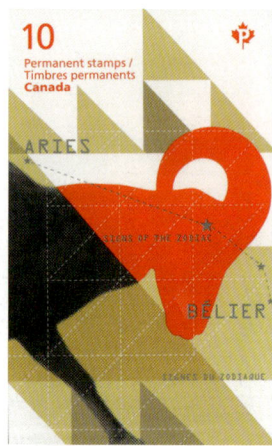

B **181** Fergie Jenkins    B **182** *Pow-wow*, 1969

2011 (1 Feb). Black History Month. Fergie Jenkins. Multicoloured cover, 55×145 mm, as Type B **181**. Self-adhesive.
SB422 $5.90 booklet containing pane of ten 59c.
          (No. 2951a) .... 11·00

B **184** Ram

2011 (21 Mar). Signs of the Zodiac. Multicoloured cover, 73×117 mm, as Type B **184**. Self-adhesive.
SB426   ($5.90) booklet containing pane of ten (59c.)
          (No. 2762a) .... 12·50
SB427   ($5.90) booklet containing pane of ten (59c.)
          (No. 2763a) (21.4) .... 13·00
SB428   ($5.90) booklet containing pane of ten (59c.)
          (No. 2764a) (20.5) .... 13·00
SB429   ($5.90) booklet containing pane of ten (59c.)
          (No. 2765a) (22.6) .... 13·00

2011 (21 Feb). Art Canada. Paintings by Daphne Odjig. Multicoloured covers as Type B **182**. Self-adhesive.
SB423 $6.18 booklet containing pane of six $1.03
          (No. 2755a) (cover Type B **182**, 50×118 mm) ....   12·00
SB424 $10.50 booklet containing pane of six $1.75
          (No. 2756a) (cover 66×142 mm showing detail
          from *Spiritual Renewal*) ....   20·00

160

CANADA / Stamp Booklets

B **185** Forest and Silhouettes of Wildlife

2011 (21 Apr). International Year of Forests. Multicoloured cover, 75×110 mm, as Type B **185**. Self-adhesive.
SB430 ($4.72) booklet containing pane of eight (59c.) stamps (No. 2777a) .... 10·00

B **186** Prince William and Miss Catherine Middleton, November 2010

2011 (29 Apr). Royal Wedding (1st issue). Multicoloured covers, 60×127 mm, as Type B **186**. Self-adhesive.
SB431 ($5.90) booklet containing ten (59c.) stamps (No. 2784a) 13·00
SB432 $17.50 booklet containing ten $1.75 stamps (No. 2785a) 38·00

B **187** Hiker, Eagle, Grizzly Bear and Waterfall in Mountain Landscape

2011 (19 May). Centenary of Parks Canada. Multicoloured cover, 75×140 mm, as Type B **187**. Self-adhesive.
SB433 $5.90 booklet containing pane of ten 59c. (No. 2788a) 13·00

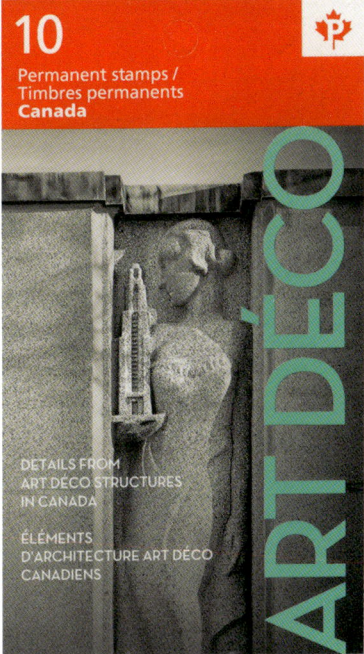

B **188** Wall of Cormier House with Stone Carving, Montreal

161

CANADA / Stamp Booklets / Registration Stamps / Special Delivery Stamps

2011 (9 June). Art Déco. Multicoloured cover, 67×117 mm, as Type B **188**. Self-adhesive.
SB434 ($5.90) booklet containing pane of (59c.) (No. 2789a) .. 13·00

B **189** Duke and Duchess of Cambridge in State Landau

2011 (22 June). Royal Wedding (2nd issue). Multicoloured cover, 60×127 mm, as Type B **189**. Self-adhesive.
SB435 ($5.90) booklet containing pane of ten (59c.) stamps (No. 2795a) .... 13·00

B **190** Ginette Russo

2011 (30 June). Canadian Recording Artists (3rd series). Multicoloured covers, 103×98 mm, as Type B **190**. Self-adhesive.
SB436 ($4.72) booklet containing pane of eight (59c.) stamps and eight labels (No. 2798a) (Type B **190**) .... 13·00

The booklet panes in Nos. SB436/c differ in the order of the stamps within the two blocks of four which form the booklet panes.

2011 (7 July). Roadside Attractions (3rd series). Multicoloured cover as Type B **158**, but showing red signpost with circular arrow. Self-adhesive.
SB437 ($4.72) booklet containing pane of eight (59c.) stamps and eight small stickers (No. 2807a) .... 13·00

REGISTRATION STAMPS

R **1**

(Eng and recess-printed British-American Bank Note Co, Montreal and Ottawa)

1875 (15 Nov)–**92**. White wove paper.

(a) P 12 (or slightly under)

R1	R **1**	2c. orange	60·00	1·00
R2		2c. orange-red (1889)	70·00	6·00
R3		2c. vermilion	75·00	8·50
		a. Imperf (pair)	†	£4500
R4		2c. rose-carmine (1888)	£150	55·00
R5		5c. yellow-green (1878)	£110	1·50
R6		5c. deep green	85·00	1·25
		a. Imperf (pair)	£900	
R7		5c. blue-green (1888)	90·00	1·50
R7*a*		5c. dull sea-green (1892)	£150	3·50
R8		8c. bright blue	£400	£300
R9		8c. dull blue	£375	£275

(b) P 12×11½ or 12×11¾

R10	R **1**	2c. orange	£325	60·00
R11		5c. green (*shades*)	£900	£150

SPECIAL DELIVERY STAMPS

PRINTERS. The following Special Delivery and Postage Due Stamps were recess-printed by the American Bank Note Co (to 1928), the British American Bank Note Co (to 1934), and the Canadian Bank Note Co (1935 onwards).

S **1**

1898–**1920**. P 12.

S1	S **1**	10c. blue-green (28.6.98)	85·00	12·00
S2		10c. deep green (12.13)	60·00	12·00
S3		10c. yellowish green (8.20)	70·00	12·00

The differences between Types I and II (figures "10" with and without shading) formerly illustrated were due to wear of the plate. There was only one die.

S **2**

S **3** Mail-carrying, 1867 and 1927

1922 (21 Aug). P 12.
S4   S **2**   20c. carmine-red .... 35·00   6·50
No. S4 exists in two slightly different sizes due to the use of "wet" or "dry" printing processes. See note below No. 195.

1927 (29 June). 60th Anniversary of Confederation. P 12.
S5   S **3**   20c. orange .... 11·00   13·00
No. S5 exists imperforate, imperf×perf or perf×imperf (*Price, in each instance, £170 per pair, un*).

S **4**

1930 (2 Sept). P 11.
S6   S **4**   20c. brown-red .... 42·00   7·00

1932 (24 Dec). Type as S **4**, but inscr "CENTS" in place of "TWENTY CENTS". P 11.
S7   20c. brown-red .... 45·00   18·00
No. S7 exists imperforate (*Price per pair £600, un*).

CANADA / Special Delivery Stamps / POSTAGE DUE Stamps / Official Stamps

S **5** Allegory of Progress

(Des A. Foringer)

1935 (1 June). P 12.
| S8 | S **5** | 20c. scarlet | 4·75 | 5·00 |

No. S8 exists imperforate (*Price per pair £650, un*).

S **6** Canadian Coat of Arms

1938–**39**. P 12.
| S9 | S **6** | 10c. green (1.4.39) | 21·00 | 4·00 |
| S10 | | 20c. scarlet (15.6.38) | 40·00 | 28·00 |

Nos. S9/10 exist imperforate (*Price £650, un, for each pair*).

(S **7**)

1939 (1 Mar). Surch with Type S **7**.
| S11 | S **6** | 10c. on 20c. scarlet | 10·00 | 17·00 |

S **8** Coat of Arms and Flags

S **9** Lockheed L.18 Lodestar

1942 (1 July)–**43**. War Effort. P 12.
(a) Postage
| S12 | S **8** | 10c. green | 9·50 | 30 |

(b) Air
| S13 | S **9** | 16c. ultramarine | 6·00 | 45 |
| S14 | | 17c. ultramarine (1.4.43) | 4·50 | 55 |

Nos. S12/14 exist imperforate (*Prices per un pair*) 10c. £650, 16c. £750, 17c. £750).

S **10** Arms of Canada and Peace Symbols

S **11** Canadair DC-4M North Star

1946 (16 Sept–5 Dec). P 12.
(a) Postage
| S15 | S **10** | 10c. green | 8·50 | 60 |

(b) Air
(i) Circumflex accent in "EXPRÊS"
| S16 | S **11** | 17c. ultramarine | 4·50 | 8·00 |

(ii) Grave accent in "EXPRÈS"
| S17 | S **11** | 17c. ultramarine (5.12.46) | 9·00 | 5·50 |

POSTAGE DUE STAMPS

PRINTERS. See note under "Special Delivery Stamps".

D **1**  D **2**

1906 (1 July)–**28**. P 12.
D1	D **1**	1c. dull violet	10·00	2·75
D2		1c. red-violet (1916)	15·00	4·25
		a. Thin paper (10.24)	15·00	20·00
D3		2c. dull violet	28·00	1·00
D4		2c. red-violet (1917)	30·00	2·25
		a. Thin paper (10.24)	32·00	20·00
D5		4c. violet (3.7.28)	45·00	55·00
D6		5c. dull violet	38·00	4·25
D7		5c. red-violet (1917)	40·00	4·25
		a. Thin paper (10.24)	20·00	35·00
D8		10c. violet (3.7.28)	32·00	23·00
D1/8	*Set of 5*		£120	75·00

The 1c., 2c. and 5c. values exist imperforate, without gum (*Price £375 for each un pair*).

Printings up to October 1924 used the "wet" method, those from mid 1925 onwards the "dry". For details of the differences between these two methods, see above No. 196.

1930–**32**. P 11.
D9	D **2**	1c. bright violet (14.7.30)	8·50	11·00
D10		2c. bright violet (21.8.30)	7·50	1·90
D11		4c. bright violet (14.10.30)	15·00	6·50
D12		5c. bright violet (12.12.31)	16·00	38·00
D13		10c. bright violet (24.8.32)	65·00	38·00
D9/13	*Set of 5*		£100	85·00

Nos. D9/11 and D13 exist imperforate, No. D13 also exists imperf×perf (*Price for vertical pair £1200, un*).

D **3**  D **4**  D **5**

1933–**34**. P 11.
D14	D **3**	1c. violet (5.5.34)	11·00	17·00
D15		2c. violet (20.12.33)	8·50	5·00
D16		4c. violet (12.12.33)	14·00	15·00
D17		10c. violet (20.12.33)	26·00	45·00
D14/17	*Set of 4*		55·00	75·00

No. D14 exists imperforate (*Price per pair £375, un*).

1935–**65**. P 12.
D18	D **4**	1c. violet (14.10.35)	80	10
D19		2c. violet (9.9.35)	3·75	10
D20		3c. violet (4.65)	6·00	5·00
D21		4c. violet (2.7.35)	1·50	10
D22		5c. violet (12.48)	6·00	4·75
D23		6c. violet (1957)	2·00	3·00
D24		10c. violet (16.9.35)	70	10
D18/24	*Set of 7*		19·00	11·50

The 1c., 2c., 4c. and 10c. exist imperforate (*Price £225 for each un pair*).

163

CANADA / Official Stamps

1967–78. Litho. P 12½×12 (20c., 24c., 50c.) or 12 (others).

(a) Size 20×17½ mm

D25	D **5**	1c. scarlet (3.67)	1·75	4·50
D26		2c. scarlet (3.67)	1·00	1·00
D27		3c. scarlet (3.67)	1·75	5·00
D28		4c. scarlet (2.67)	2·75	1·25
D29		5c. scarlet (3.67)	4·25	5·50
D30		6c. scarlet (2.67)	1·60	3·75
D31		10c. scarlet (1.67)	2·00	2·50
D25/31	Set of 7		13·50	21·00

(b) Size 19½×16 mm

D32	D **5**	1c. scarlet (12.70)	75	30
		a. White paper	75	30
		b. Perf 12½×12 (*white paper*) (11.77)	15	2·00
D33		2c. scarlet (*white paper*) (1972)	1·00	3·00
D34		3c. scarlet (*white paper*) (1.74)	2·75	4·00
D35		4c. scarlet (4.69)	60	60
		a. Printed on the gummed side	£750	
		b. White paper	60	60
		c. Perf 12½×12 (*white paper*) (11.77)	30	1·00
D36		5c. scarlet (2.69)	23·00	35·00
		a. Perf 12½×12 (*white paper*) (11.77)	30	2·00
D37		6c. scarlet (*white paper*) (1972)	2·75	3·75
D38		8c. scarlet (1.69)	30	45
		a. White paper	30	45
		b. Perf 12½×12 (*white paper*) (28.6.78)	75	1·40
D39		10c. scarlet (4.69)	40	45
		a. White paper	40	45
		b. Perf 12½×12 (*white paper*) (9.77)	40	60
D40		12c. scarlet (1.69)	30	50
		a. White paper	30	50
		b. Perf 12½×12 (*white paper*) (9.77)	80	1·50
D41		16c. scarlet (*white paper*) (1.74)	4·00	4·75
D42		20c. scarlet (*white paper*) (10.77)	30	1·25
D43		24c. scarlet (*white paper*) (10.77)	30	1·50
D44		50c. scarlet (*white paper*) (10.77)	40	2·00
D32/44	Set of 13		12·00	22·00

There are no records of dates of issue of the above but supplies were distributed to depots in the months indicated.

Both white and ordinary papers have been used for Nos. D32/41.

OFFICIAL STAMPS

Stamps perforated "O H M S" were introduced in May 1923 for use by the Receiver General's department in Ottawa and by the Assistant Receiver Generals' offices in provincial cities. From 1 July 1939 this use was extended to all departments of the federal government and such stamps continued to be produced until replaced by the "O.H.M.S." overprinted issue of 1949.

The perforated initials can appear either upright, inverted or sideways on individual stamps. The prices quoted are for the cheapest version. Stamps perforated with Type O **1** are only priced used. Only isolated examples are known mint and these are very rare.

A number of forged examples of the perforated "O.H.M.S." are known, in particular of Type O **1**. Many of these forged perforated initials were applied to stamps which had already been used and this can aid their detection. Genuine examples, postmarked after the perforated initials were applied, often show the cancellation ink bleeding into the holes.

(O **1**) (Five holes in vertical bars of "H")

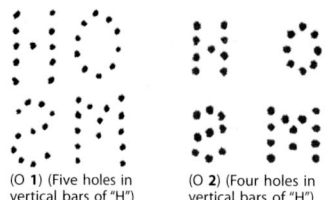

(O **2**) (Four holes in vertical bars of "H")

1923 (May). Nos. 196/215 punctured as Type O **1**.

O1	44	1c. yellow-green	—	24·00
O2		2c. carmine	—	22·00
O3		3c. deep brown	—	20·00
O4		5c. deep blue	—	24·00
O5		7c. yellow-ochre	—	38·00
O6		10c. reddish purple	—	38·00
O7		20c. olive	—	24·00
O8		50c. sepia	—	40·00
O1/8	Set of 8			£200

1923 (May). 50th Anniv of Confederation. No. 244 punctured as Type O **1**.

O9	48	3c. bistre-brown	—	£150

1923 (May)–**31**. Nos. 246/55 and 263 punctured as Type O **1**.

(a) P 12

O10	44	1c. chrome-yellow (Die I)	—	22·00
		a. Die II (1925)	—	22·00
O11		2c. deep green	—	16·00
O12		3c. carmine (Die I) (12.23)	—	16·00
		a. Die II (1924)	—	19·00
O13		4c. olive-yellow	—	22·00
O14		5c. violet	—	22·00
		a. Thin paper (1924)	—	24·00
O15		7c. red-brown (1924)	—	30·00
O16		8c. blue (1925)	—	35·00
O17		10c. blue	—	24·00
O18		10c. bistre-brown (1925)	—	17·00
O19		$1 brown-orange (7.23)	—	60·00
O10/19	Set of 10			£225

(b) P 12×8

O20	44	3c. carmine (Die II) (1931)	—	48·00

1927 (29 June). 60th Anniv of Confederation. Nos. 266/73 punctured as Type O **1**.

(a) Commemorative issue

O21	51	1c. orange	—	22·00
O22	52	2c. green	—	30·00
O23	53	3c. carmine	—	38·00
O24	54	5c. violet	—	26·00
O25	55	12c. blue	—	£160
O21/25	Set of 5			£250

(b) Historical issue

O26	56	5c. violet	—	22·00
O27	57	12c. green	—	£130
O28	58	20c. carmine	—	75·00
O26/28	Set of 3			£200

1928 (21 Sept). Air. No. 274 punctured as Type O **1**.

O29	59	5c. olive-brown	—	£110

1928–29. Nos. 275/85 punctured as Type O **1**.

O30	60	1c. orange	—	27·00
O31		2c. green	—	19·00
O32		3c. lake	—	42·00
O33		4c. olive-bistre	—	55·00
O34		5c. violet	—	19·00
O35		8c. blue	—	50·00
O36	61	10c. green	—	16·00
O37	62	12c. grey-black	—	£160
O38	63	20c. lake	—	48·00
O39	64	50c. blue	—	£250
O40	65	$1 olive-green	—	£190
O30/40	Set of 11			£800

1930–31. Nos. 288/97 and 300/5 punctured as Type O **1**.

O41	66	1c. orange (Die I)	—	27·00
O42		1c. green (Die I)	—	16·00
		a. Die II	—	14·00
O43		2c. green (Die I)	—	70·00
O44		2c. scarlet (Die I)	—	22·00
		a. Die II	—	19·00
O45		2c. deep brown (Die I)	—	23·00
		a. Die II	—	21·00
O46		3c. scarlet	—	16·00
O47		4c. yellow-bistre	—	48·00
O48		5c. violet	—	32·00
O49		5c. deep slate-blue	—	27·00
O50		8c. blue	—	55·00
O51		8c. red-orange	—	42·00
O52	67	10c. olive-green	—	22·00
O53	68	12c. grey-black	—	90·00
O54	69	20c. red	—	45·00
O55	70	50c. blue	—	65·00
O56	71	$1 olive-green	—	£170
O41/56	Set of 15			£700

1930 (4 Dec). Air. No. 310 punctured as Type O **1**.

O57	72	5c. deep brown	—	£170

1931 (30 Sept). No. 312 punctured as Type O **1**.

O58	73	10c. olive-green	—	23·00

1932 (22 Feb). Air. No. 313 punctured as Type O **1**.

O59	59	6c. on 5c. olive-brown	—	£120

1932 (21 June). Nos. 314/a punctured as Type O **1**.

O60	66	3c. on 2c. scarlet (Die I)	—	32·00
		a. Die II	—	27·00

1932 (12 July). Ottawa Conference. Nos. 315/18 punctured as Type O **1**.

(a) Postage

O61	76	3c. scarlet	—	19·00
O62	77	5c. blue	—	30·00
O63	78	13c. green	—	£180

(b) Air

O64	72	6c. on 5c. deep brown	—	£140
O61/64	Set of 4			£325

CANADA / Official Stamps

1932–33. Nos. 319/25 punctured as Type O **1**.

O65	80	1c. green	—	16·00
O66		2c. sepia	—	16·00
O67		3c. scarlet	—	16·00
O68		4c. yellow-brown	—	48·00
O69		5c. blue	—	24·00
O70		8c. red-orange	—	48·00
O71	68	13c. bright violet	—	48·00
O65/71 Set of 7			—	£200

1933 (18 May). U.P.U. Congress Preliminary Meeting. No. 329 punctured as Type O **1**.

O72	81	5c. blue	—	55·00

1933 (24 July). World's Grain Exhibition and Conference, Regina. No. 330 punctured as Type O **1**.

O73	69	20c. red	—	65·00

1933 (17 Aug). Centenary of First Trans-Atlantic Steamboat Crossing. No. 331 punctured as Type O **1**.

O74	83	5c. blue	—	55·00

1934 (1 July). Fourth Centenary of Discovery of Canada. No. 332 punctured as Type O **1**.

O75	84	3c. blue	—	65·00

1934 (1 July). 150th Anniv of Arrival of United Empire Loyalists. No. 333 punctured as Type O **1**.

O76	85	10c. olive-green	—	65·00

1934 (16 Aug). 150th Anniv of Province of New Brunswick. No. 334 punctured as Type O **1**.

O77	86	2c. red-brown	—	65·00

1935 (4 May). Silver Jubilee. Nos. 335/40 punctured as Type O **1**.

O78	87	1c. green	—	38·00
O79	88	2c. brown	—	42·00
O80	89	3c. carmine-red	—	55·00
O81	90	5c. blue	—	50·00
O82	91	10c. purple	—	£140
O83	92	13c. blue	—	£140
O78/83 Set of 6			—	£425

1935. Nos. 341/51 and 355 punctured as Type O **1**.

(a) Postage

O84	93	1c. green	—	18·00
O85		2c. brown	—	32·00
O86		3c. scarlet	—	29·00
O87		4c. yellow	—	50·00
O88		5c. blue	—	29·00
O89		8c. orange	—	50·00
O90	94	10c. carmine	—	40·00
O91	95	13c. purple	—	50·00
O92	96	20c. olive-green	—	55·00
O93	97	50c. deep violet	—	38·00
O94	98	$1 bright blue	—	£110

(b) Air

O95	99	6c. red-brown	—	95·00
O84/95 Set of 12			—	£550

1937 (10 May). Coronation. No. 356 punctured as Type O **1**.

O96	100	3c. carmine	—	50·00

1937–38. Nos. 357/67, 370 and 371 punctured as Type O **1**.

(a) Postage

O97	101	1c. green	—	3·75
O98		2c. brown	—	4·00
O99		3c. scarlet	—	3·75
O100		4c. yellow	—	12·00
O101		5c. blue	—	8·50
O102		8c. orange	—	21·00
O103	102	10c. rose-carmine	—	27·00
		a. Red	—	30·00
O104	103	13c. blue	—	38·00
O105	104	20c. red-brown	—	40·00
O106	105	50c. green	—	80·00
O107	106	$1 violet	—	£120
O97/107 Set of 11			—	£325

(b) Coil stamp

O108	101	3c. scarlet	—	70·00

(c) Air

O109	107	6c. blue	—	40·00

1939 (15 May). Royal Visit. Nos. 372/4 punctured as Type O **1**.

O110	108	1c. black and green	—	55·00
O111	109	2c. black and brown	—	60·00
O112	110	3c. black and carmine	—	55·00
O110/112 Set of 3			—	£150

1939 (1 July). Air. No. 274 punctured as Type O **2**.

O113	59	5c. olive-brown	29·00	19·00

1939 (1 July). Nos. 347/50 and 355 punctured as Type O **2**.

(a) Postage

O114	94	10c. carmine	£110	45·00
O115	95	13c. purple	£120	45·00
O116	96	20c. olive-green	£130	55·00
O117	97	50c. deep violet	£120	45·00

(b) Air

O118	99	6c. red-brown	80·00	60·00
O114/118 Set of 5			£500	£225

1939 (1 July). Coronation. No. 356 punctured as Type O **2**.

O119	100	3c. carmine	£100	55·00

1939 (1 July). Nos. 357/67, 369/70 and 371 punctured as Type O **2**.

(a) Postage

O120	101	1c. green	2·50	75
O121		2c. brown	3·25	75
O122		3c. scarlet	3·50	75
O123		4c. yellow	7·00	4·00
O124		5c. blue	4·50	1·25
O125		8c. orange	18·00	6·00
O126	102	10c. rose-carmine	70·00	3·50
		a. Red	15·00	75
O127	103	13c. blue	25·00	2·75
O128	104	20c. red-brown	45·00	3·75
O129	105	50c. green	70·00	10·00
O130	106	$1 violet	£140	38·00
O120/130 Set of 11			£300	60·00

(b) Coil stamps

O131	101	2c. brown	90·00	55·00
O132		3c. scarlet	90·00	55·00

(c) Air

O133	107	6c. blue	4·25	1·75

1939 (1 July). Royal Visit. Nos. 372/4 punctured as Type O **2**.

O134	108	1c. black and green	£120	48·00
O135	109	2c. black and brown	£120	48·00
O136	110	3c. black and carmine	£120	48·00
O134/136 Set of 3			£325	£130

1942–43. War Effort. Nos. 375/88 and 399/400 punctured as Type O **2**.

(a) Postage

O137	111	1c. green	1·50	50
O138	112	2c. brown	1·50	20
O139	113	2c. carmine-lake	3·50	1·50
O140		3c. purple	2·50	30
O141	114	4c. slate	9·00	2·50
O142	112	4c. carmine-lake	1·50	30
O143	111	5c. blue	2·50	1·25
O144	–	8c. red-brown	12·00	3·00
O145	116	10c. brown	7·00	30
O146	117	13c. dull green	12·00	10·00
O147		14c. dull green	13·00	2·00
O148	118	20c. chocolate	21·00	1·75
O149	119	50c. violet	48·00	7·50
O150	120	$1 blue	95·00	30·00

(b) Air

O151	121	6c. blue	5·00	5·50
O152		7c. blue	5·00	1·75
O137/152 Set of 16			£225	60·00

1946. Peace Re-conversion. Nos. 401/7 punctured as Type O **2**.

(a) Postage

O153	122	8c. brown	32·00	5·50
O154	123	10c. olive-green	4·00	15
O155	124	14c. sepia	11·00	2·25
O156	125	20c. slate	11·00	75
O157	126	50c. green	40·00	12·00
O158	127	$1 purple	75·00	19·00

(b) Air

O159	128	7c. blue	4·25	2·50
O153/159 Set of 7			£160	38·00

1949. Nos. 415 and 416 punctured as Type O **2**.

O160	136	2c. sepia	3·00	4·00
O161	137	3c. purple	3·00	4·00

O.H.M.S.
(O **3**)

1949. Nos. 375/6, 378, 380 and 402/7 optd as Type O **3** by typography.

(a) Postage

O162	111	1c. green	4·25	5·00
		a. Missing stop after "S"	£225	£100
O163	112	2c. brown	12·00	12·00
		a. Missing stop after "S"	£200	£120
O164	113	3c. purple	3·25	3·50
O165	112	4c. carmine-lake	4·25	4·50
O166	123	10c. olive-green	6·00	15
		a. Missing stop after "S"	£150	60·00

CANADA / Official Stamps / Official Special Delivery Stamps

O167	**124**	14c. sepia		11·00	5·50
		a. Missing stop after "S"		£170	85·00
O168	**125**	20c. slate		12·00	60
		a. Missing stop after "S"		£200	75·00
O169	**126**	50c. green		£170	£130
		a. Missing stop after "S"		£1300	£750
O170	**127**	$1 purple		45·00	60·00
		a. Missing stop after "S"		£5000	

(b) Air

O171	**128**	7c. blue		24·00	10·00
		a. Missing stop after "S"		£170	80·00
O162/171 Set of 10				£250	£200

Forgeries exist of this overprint. Genuine examples are 2.3×15 mm and show the tops of all letters aligned, as are the stops.

Only a few sheets of the $1 showed the variety, No. O170a.

MISSING STOP VARIETIES. These occur on R. 6/2 of the lower left pane (Nos. O162a, O163a, O175a and O176a) or R. 10/2 of the lower left pane (O166a, O167a, O168a, O169a, O170a and O171a). No. O176a also occurs on R. 8/8 of the upper left pane in addition to R. 6/2 of the lower left pane.

1949–50. Nos. 414/15, 416/17, 418 and 431 optd as Type O **3** by typography.

O172	**135**	1c. green		4·00	2·50
O173	**136**	2c. sepia		3·50	3·00
O174	**137**	3c. purple		2·75	2·50
O175	**138**	4c. carmine-lake		2·75	35
		a. Missing stop after "S"		£120	55·00
O176	**139**	5c. blue (1949)		7·50	2·25
		a. Missing stop after "S"		£110	50·00
O177	**141**	50c. green (1950)		38·00	40·00
O172/177 Set of 6				55·00	45·00

G (O **4**) **G** (O **5**) **G** (O **6**)

Variations in thickness are known in Type O **4** these are due to wear and subsequent cleaning of the plate. All are produced by typography. Examples showing the "G" applied by lithography are forgeries.

1950 (2 Oct)–**52.** Nos. 402/4, 406/7, 414/18 and 431 optd with Type O **4** (1 to 5c.) or O **5** (7c. to $1).

(a) Postage

O178	**135**	1c. green		1·50	10
O179	**136**	2c. sepia		4·00	4·75
O180		2c. olive-green (11.51)		1·75	10
O181	**137**	3c. purple		2·25	10
O182	**138**	4c. carmine-lake		4·75	2·00
O183		4c. vermilion (1.5.52)		3·00	60
O184	**139**	5c. blue		5·50	2·00
O185	**123**	10c. olive-green		3·00	10
O186	**124**	14c. sepia		23·00	11·00
O187	**125**	20c. slate		45·00	30
O188	**141**	50c. green		17·00	21·00
O189	**127**	$1 purple		75·00	75·00

(b) Air

O190	–	7c. blue		24·00	15·00
O178/190 Set of 13				£190	£120

1950–51. Nos. 432/3 optd with Type O **5**.

O191	**142**	10c. brown-purple		4·00	1·00
		a. Opt omitted in pair with normal		£900	£550
O192	**143**	$1 ultramarine (1.2.51)		75·00	80·00

On a small number of sheets of 10c. the opt was omitted from R7/1.

1952–53. Nos. 441, 443 and 446 optd with Type O **5**.

O193	**153**	7c. blue (3.11.52)		2·00	3·25
O194	**151**	20c. grey (1.4.52)		2·00	20
O195	**154**	$1 black (2.2.53)		10·00	15·00
O193/195 Set of 3				12·50	16·00

1953 (1 Sept)–**61.** Nos. 450/4 and 462 optd with Type O **4** (1 to 5c.) or O **5** (50c.).

O196	**158**	1c. purple-brown		15	10
O197		2c. green		20	10
O198		3c. carmine		20	10
O199		4c. violet		30	10
O200		5c. ultramarine		30	10
O201	**160**	50c. deep bluish green (2.11.53)		3·25	4·00
		a. Opt Type O **6** (24.4.61*)		2·50	4·75
O196/201 Set of 6				3·25	4·00

*Earliest recorded date.

1955–56. Nos. 463/4 and 466/7 optd with Type O **4**.

O202	**161**	1c. purple-brown (12.11.56)		65	20
O203		2c. green (19.1.56)		15	20
O204		4c. violet (23.7.56)		40	1·00
O205		5c. bright blue (11.1.55)		15	10
O202/205 Set of 4				1·25	1·25

1955–62. Nos. 477 and 488 optd with Type O **5**.

O206	**165**	10c. purple-brown (21.2.55)		70	60
		a. Opt Type O **6** (28.3.62*)		40	2·25
O207	**176**	20c. green (4.12.56)		3·25	30
		a. Opt Type O **6** (10.4.62*)		5·50	1·75

*Earliest recorded date.

1963 (15 May). Nos. 527/8 and 530/1 optd as O **4**.

O208		1c. chocolate		50	5·00
O209		2c. green		60	5·00
		a. Type O **4** omitted (vert pair with normal)		£850	
O210		4c. carmine-red		60	2·25
O211		5c. ultramarine		50	2·50
O208/211 Set of 4				2·00	13·00

No. O209a comes from the top row of an upper pane on which the overprint was misplaced downwards by one row. Owing to the margin between the panes the top row of the bottom pane had the overprint at the top of the stamp.

OFFICIAL SPECIAL DELIVERY STAMPS

1923 (May). Nos. S3/4 punctured as Type O **1**.

OS1	S **1**	10c. yellowish green		—	£160
OS2	S **2**	20c. carmine-red		—	£130

1927 (29 June). 60th Anniv of Confederation. No. S5 punctured as Type O **1**.

OS3	S **3**	20c. orange		—	£130

1930 (2 Sept). Inscr "TWENTY CENTS" at foot. No. S6 punctured as Type O **1**.

OS4	S **4**	20c. brown-red		—	£120

1932 (24 Dec). Inscr "CENTS" at foot. No. S7 punctured as Type O **1**.

OS5	S **4**	20c. brown-red		—	£110

1935 (1 June). No. S8 punctured as Type O **1**.

OS6	S **5**	20c. scarlet		—	£110

1938–39. Nos. S9/10 punctured as Type O **1**.

OS7	S **6**	10c. green		—	55·00
OS8		20c. scarlet		—	80·00

1939 (1 Mar). No. S11 punctured as Type O **1**.

OS9	S **6**	10c. on 20c. scarlet		—	80·00

1939 (1 July). Inscr "CENTS" at foot. No. S7 punctured as Type O **2**.

OS10	S **4**	20c. brown-red		£225	£100

1939 (1 July). No. S8 punctured as Type O **2**.

OS11	S **5**	20c. scarlet		£120	60·00

1939 (1 July). No. S9 punctured as Type O **2**.

OS12	S **6**	10c. green		9·00	9·00

1939 (1 July). No. S11 punctured as Type O **2**.

OS13	S **6**	10c. on 20c. scarlet		£150	70·00

1942–43. Nos. S12/14 punctured as Type O **2**.

(a) Postage

OS14	S **8**	10c. green		12·00	10·00

(b) Air

OS15	S **9**	16c. ultramarine		20·00	22·00
OS16		17c. ultramarine		15·00	12·00

1946–47. Nos. S15/17 punctured as Type O **2**.

(a) Postage

OS17	S **10**	10c. green		11·00	8·00

(b) Air

OS18	S **11**	17c. ultramarine (circumflex accent)		55·00	35·00
OS19		17c. ultramarine (grave accent)		90·00	80·00

1950. No. S15 optd as Type O **3**, but larger.

OS20	S **10**	10c. green		17·00	30·00

1950 (2 Oct). No. S15 optd as Type O **4**, but larger.

OS21	S **10**	10c. green		26·00	30·00

The use of official stamps was discontinued on 31 December 1963.

Index

Amherst 18
Amherst (Crowned-Circle Handstamps) 18

British Columbia 1
British Columbia & Vancouver Island 1

Canada 1
Canada (Design Index) 121
Canada (Official Special Delivery Stamps) 166
Canada (Official Stamps) 164
Canada (Postage Due Stamps) 163
Canada (Registration Stamps) 162
Canada (Special Delivery Stamps) 162
Canada (Stamp Booklets) 127
Colony of Canada 1
Colony of Canada (Crowned-Circle Handstamps) 1
Crowned-Circle Handstamps (Amherst) 18
Crowned-Circle Handstamps (Colony of Canada) 1
Crowned-Circle Handstamps (Newfoundland) 5
Crowned-Circle Handstamps (Nova Scotia) 18
Crowned-Circle Handstamps (Quebec) 1
Crowned-Circle Handstamps (St. John's) 5
Crowned-Circle Handstamps (St. Margarets Bay) 18

Design Index (Canada) 121
Dominion of Canada 20

New Brunswick 5
Newfoundland 5
Newfoundland (Crowned-Circle Handstamps) 5
Newfoundland (Postage Due Stamps) 18
Newfoundland (Stamp Booklets) 17
Nova Scotia 18
Nova Scotia (Crowned-Circle Handstamps) 18

Official Special Delivery Stamps (Canada) 166
Official Stamps (Canada) 164

Postage Due Stamps (Canada) 163
Postage Due Stamps (Newfoundland) 18
Prince Edward Island 19

Quebec 1
Quebec (Crowned-Circle Handstamps) 1

Registration Stamps (Canada) 162

Special Delivery Stamps (Canada) 162
St. John's 5
St. John's (Crowned-Circle Handstamps) 5
St. Margarets Bay 18
St. Margarets Bay (Crowned-Circle Handstamps) 18
Stamp Booklets (Canada) 127
Stamp Booklets (Newfoundland) 17

Vancouver Island 1

167

STANLEY GIBBONS
Est 1856

Dear Catalogue User,

As a collector and Stanley Gibbons catalogue user for many years myself, I am only too aware of the need to provide you with the information you seek in an accurate, timely and easily accessible manner. Naturally, I have my own views on where changes could be made, but one thing I learned long ago is that we all have different opinions and requirements.

I would therefore be most grateful if you would complete the form overleaf and return it to me. Please contact Lorraine Holcombe (lholcombe@stanleygibbons.co.uk) if you would like to be emailed the questionnaire.

Very many thanks for your help.

Yours sincerely,

Hugh Jefferies,
Editor.

Hugh Jefferies (Catalogue Editor)
Catalogue Questionnaire Responses
Stanley Gibbons Limited
7 Parkside, Ringwood
Hampshire BH24 3SH
United Kingdom

Questionnaire

2011 Canada Catalogue

1. Level of detail
   Do you feel that the level of detail in this catalogue is:
   a. too specialised ○
   b. about right ○
   c. inadequate ○

2. Frequency of issue
   How often would you purchase a new edition of this catalogue?
   a. Annually ○
   b. Every two years ○
   c. Every three to five years ○
   d. Less frequently ○

3. Design and Quality
   How would you describe the layout and appearance of this catalogue?
   a. Excellent ○
   b. Good ○
   c. Adequate ○
   d. Poor ○

4. How important to you are the prices given in the catalogue:
   a. Important ○
   b. Quite important ○
   c. Of little interest ○
   d. Of no interest ○

5. Would you be interested in an online version of this catalogue?
   a. Yes ○
   b. No ○

6. Do you like the new format?
   a. Yes ○
   b. No ○

7. What changes would you suggest to improve the catalogue? E.g. Which other indices would you like to see included?
   ....
   ....
   ....
   ....

8. Which of the SG Great Britain Specialised catalogues do you buy?
   ....
   ....
   ....
   ....

9. Would you like us to let you know when the next edition of this catalogue is due to be published?
   a. Yes ○
   b. No ○
   If so please give your contact details below.
   Name: ....
   Address:..
   ....
   ....
   ....
   Email: ....
   Telephone:...

10. Which other Stanley Gibbons Catalogues are you interested in?
    a. ....
    b. ....
    c. ....

Many thanks for your comments.

Please complete and return it to: Hugh Jefferies (Catalogue Editor)
Stanley Gibbons Limited, 7 Parkside, Ringwood, Hampshire BH24 3SH, United Kingdom
or email: lholcombe@stanleygibbons.co.uk to request a soft copy

Canada

From Stanley Gibbons, THE WORLD'S LARGEST STAMP STOCK

Priority order form – Four easy ways to order

Phone: 020 7836 8444   Overseas: +44 (0)20 7836 8444
Fax: 020 7557 4499   Overseas: +44 (0)20 7557 4499
Email: lmourne@stanleygibbons.co.uk
Post: Lesley Mourne, Stamp Mail Order Department, Stanley Gibbons Ltd, 399 Strand, London, WC2R 0LX, England

Customer Details

Account Number ....
Name ....
Address ....
....
Postcode .... Country ....
Email ....
Tel No. .... Fax No. ....

Payment details

Registered Postage & Packing £3.60

○ Please find my cheque/postal order enclosed for £ ....
Please make cheques payable to Stanley Gibbons Ltd.
Cheques must be in £ sterling and drawn on a UK bank

○ Please debit my credit card for £ .... in full payment.
○ Mastercard   ○ VISA   ○ Diners   ○ AMEX   ○ Switch

Card Number

CVC Number ☐   Issue No (Switch) ☐

Start Date (Switch & Amex) ☐ / ☐   Expiry Date ☐ / ☐

Signature .... Date ....

Canada

From Stanley Gibbons, THE WORLD'S LARGEST STAMP STOCK

Condition (mint/UM/used)	Country	SG No.	Description	Price	Office use only
			POSTAGE & PACKING	£3.60	
			GRAND TOTAL		

Minimum price. The minimum catalogue price quoted in 10p. For individual stamps, prices between 10p and 95p are provided as a guide for catalogue users. The lowest price charged for individual stamps or sets purchased from Stanley Gibbons Ltd is £1.

Please complete payment, name and address details overleaf

The Archive has everything from the first edition of the Monthly Journal in 1890 to the December 2009 issue of Gibbons Stamp Monthly.

Covering all of the articles, illustrations, notes and more. If it was in the magazine, then it's on the digital archive.

Just think of all of those great articles you can rediscover or read for the first time. You will have access to over 40,000 pages.

Gibbons Stamp Monthly exactly how *you* want it...

NEW and EXCLUSIVE

You can have every issue of GSM since 1890 at your fingertips to search, browse, print and store as you choose, when you choose, with the **Gibbons Stamp Monthly Digital Archive**

If you're passionate about collecting, you really don't want to be without it – the **GSM DIGITAL ARCHIVE**. It is the perfect complement to the hobby of kings.

You'll have private access to **a complete library of information on almost anything you can think of from the world of stamp collecting**. The Archive is an absolute treasure trove of facts, articles, images and commentary on everything from specific topics like Machins to High Value Keyplates to more general fields such as King George VI – and it spans 120 years of these riches.

In short, it is **GSM exactly how you want it** – without it taking up vast amounts of space, getting dog-eared or in the wrong order. At your leisure and at the touch of a button or click of a mouse, you'll be able to view front covers, contents lists, articles, correspondence, book reviews, illustrations, notes and jottings from 120 years of Gibbons Stamp Monthly, with **full search and full browse capabilities built in**.

You can be the editor of the world's most important stamp magazine. You will have access to over **40,000 pages worth of the most useful and interesting philatelic material available**, delivered to you in a convenient, easy to use, searchable, digital format.

This is the exclusive GSM Archive, covering all articles, features, editorial and other content right from the first issue of the Monthly Journal, Gibbons Stamp Weekly & Gibbons Stamp Monthly – from 1890 up to 2009.

Build your own library of information on any topic you can think of by saving articles to your own archive or **print them off and store them physically** if you choose.

With full unlimited printing capabilities available, you are not confined to reading the articles on your computer screen.

The NEW & EXCLUSIVE Gibbons Stamp Monthly Archive is available now.
The full 5 DVDs (+ bonus disc) are available to you for just £199.95 or, looking at it another way, just 20p per magazine! You can even pay in 3 equal instalments if that makes it easier for you.
Get *your* copy today – **JUST £199.95**

Prices correct as of November 2010 and subject to change.

Est 1856
STANLEY GIBBONS

Call us today on FREEPHONE 0800 611 622 *(UK)*
or +44 1425 472 363 *(International)* to secure your copy
www.stanleygibbons.com | Email: orders@stanleygibbons.co.uk

Give your collection the home it deserves

Frank Godden albums are a labour of love, with each individual album beautifully handmade to an unmistakable and unmatchable quality.

All leaves are now made to the internationally recognised standard for archival paper, the type that is used and recommended by all major museums.

Revered throughout the philatelic world for their supreme quality and craftsmanship, Frank Godden albums are built to last a lifetime and to offer you a lifetime of enjoyment.

If you are passionate about your collection, then Frank Godden provides the home it deserves.

Whether you are looking for the best quality albums, exhibition cases, protectors, leaves or interleaving, you can find whatever you are looking for at Stanley Gibbons, the new home of Frank Godden.

For more information, visit www.stanleygibbons.com/frankgodden

Stanley Gibbons Publications
7 Parkside, Christchurch Road, Ringwood, Hampshire, BH24 3SH
Tel: +44 (0)1425 472 363 | Fax: +44 (0)1425 470 247
Email: orders@stanleygibbons.co.uk
www.stanleygibbons.com

STANLEY GIBBONS Est 1856

How can Stanley Gibbons help you?

Our History

Stanley Gibbons started trading in 1856 and we have been at the forefront of stamp collecting for more than 150 years, making us the world's oldest philatelic company. We can help you build your collection in a wide variety of ways – all with the backing of our unrivalled expertise.

399 Strand, London, UK - Recently Refurbished!

'...I only wish I could visit more often...' JB, December 09

Our world famous stamp shop is a collector's paradise. As well as stamps, the shop stocks albums, accessories and specialist philatelic books. Plan a visit now!

Specialist Stamp Departments

When purchasing high value items you should definitely contact our specialist departments for advice and guarantees on the items purchased. Consult the experts to ensure you make the right purchase. For example, when buying early Victorian stamps our specialists will guide you through the prices – a penny red SG 43 has many plate numbers which vary in value. We can explain what to look for and where, and help you plan your future collection.

Stanley Gibbons Publications

Our catalogues are trusted worldwide as the industry standard, see the facing page for details on our current range. Keep up to date with new issues in our magazine, Gibbons Stamp Monthly, a must-read for all collectors and dealers. It contains news, views and insights into all things philatelic, from beginner to specialist.

Completing the set

When is it cheaper to complete your collection by buying a whole set rather than item by item? Use the prices in your catalogue, which lists single item values and a complete set value, to check if it is better to buy the odd missing item, or a complete set.

Auctions and Valuations

Buying at auction can be great fun. You can buy collections and merge them with your own - not forgetting to check your catalogue for gaps. But do make sure the condition of the collection you are buying is comparable to your own.

Stanley Gibbons Auctions have been running since the 1900's. They offer a range of auctions to suit both novice and advanced collectors and dealers. You can of course also sell your collection or individual rare items through our public auctions and regular postal auctions. Contact the auction department directly to find out more - email auctions@stanleygibbons.co.uk or telephone 020 7836 8444.

Condition

Condition can make a big difference on the price you pay for an item. When building your collection you must keep condition in mind and always buy the best condition you can find and afford. For example, ensure the condition of the gum is the same as issued from the Post Office. If the gum is disturbed or has had an adhesion it can be classed as mounted. When buying issues prior to 1936 you should always look for the least amount of disturbance and adhesion. You do have to keep in mind the age of the issue when looking at the condition.

The prices quoted in our catalogues are for a complete item in good condition so make sure you check this.

Ask the Experts

If you need help or guidance, you are welcome to come along to Stanley Gibbons in the Strand and ask for assistance. If you would like to have your collection appraised, you can arrange for a verbal evaluation Monday to Friday 9.00am – 4.30pm. We also provide insurance valuations should you require. Of course an up-to-date catalogue listing can also assist with the valuation and may be presented to an insurance agent or company.

Stanley Gibbons Publications

7 Parkside, Christchurch Road, Ringwood, Hants. BH24 3SH Tel: +44 (0)1425 472363 Fax: +44 (0)1425 470247
Email: orders@stanleygibbons.co.uk